CUBA

Jamaica

Mosquito Coast

Panama
1519

NEW G
1718/39

Bogota
1539

Quito
1534

1638

Lima
1535
PERU
1531/34
1542 Viceroyalty

Cuzco

16

1630·54
Neth.

oyalty

Bahia
1549

14 Days

1609

1630

Río de Janeiro, 1565

São Paulo, 1532

Paraná

Santa Fe
1573

Santiago
1541

Sacramento
1680 (Port.)

Buenos Aires
1536/80

CHILE

Acquisitions
Spain

Portugal

Great Britain

Netherlands

France

Denmark

Jesuit mission

THE
RED, WHITE,
AND BLACK CONTINENT

RED,

HERBERT WENDT

Translated by Richard and Clara Winston

Latin America today, as Herbert Wendt acutely reveals, is a battlefield of the Cold War and may well become the decisive battlefield. The reasons are clearly set forth here in a brilliant weaving of historical narrative with personal observation and incisive analysis of every part of Latin America —the Caribbean islands, Mexico, Central America, and South America. As a result, what has so often seemed a welter of comic-opera coups (Bolivia, for instance, has had 80 in 140 years) and confusing Spanish names now emerges as an immediate and crucial drama of heroes and traitors, of tycoons and martyrs, of tragic misunderstandings and mistakes.

Here, in dispassionate perspective and in candid close-ups are the forces and the individual personalities behind those recurring coups. Here is the unvarnished background for the anti-U.S. demonstrations and the rising influence not only of Castro but also of Red China. The developments in Cuba and in the Dominican Republic, the Panama crisis, the ramifications of the

(Continued on back flap)

BOOKS BY HERBERT WENDT
(PUBLISHED IN THE U.S.A.):

The Red, White, and Black Continent

The Road to Man

Out of Noah's Ark

In Search of Adam

The
Red, White, and Black
Continent

LATIN AMERICA—LAND OF
REFORMERS AND REBELS

Herbert Wendt

TRANSLATED FROM THE GERMAN BY
RICHARD AND CLARA WINSTON

Garden City, New York
DOUBLEDAY & COMPANY, INC.
1966

This book was published in Germany under the title *Der Schwarz Weiss Rote Kontinent,* Gerhard Stalling Verlag, 1964

TO MY WIFE, INGEBORG, WHO HAS SHARED ALL MY TRAVELS. WITHOUT HER
KEEN INSIGHT, HER EMPATHY, HER KINDNESS, AND HER GREAT LOVE FOR
THE CONTINENT OF LATIN AMERICA, THIS BOOK COULD NOT HAVE BEEN
WRITTEN.

CONTENTS

Preface

Latin America is a giant in chains, fettered by dead traditions, kept in perpetual adolescence by its own upper classes, made anemic by endless economic and political bloodletting. To be sure, it is a giant suffering acutely from neuralgia and of late straining powerfully against its bonds. Latin America is virgin and prostitute at one and the same time. A maltreated virgin and a chaste prostitute, a great continent repeatedly raped by conquistadors and by captains of commerce, utterly loose in its willing submission to strong men and countries that can pay a price, and nevertheless still chaste and virginal in its hopes and dreams of the future.

Latin America, twice as large as Europe, but only half so thickly populated, is the most idiosyncratic of all the developing regions and the most difficult to analyze. With colonialism dying, Africa today is attempting to leap from the Stone Age into the modern world; and the people who must make this leap are native Africans. Asia has reinvoked ancient but still vigorous historical traditions, and has tried to use them to solve the problems of the Atomic Age; and the people who must effect a union of their living history with the intrusive present are native Asiatics. But Latin America is a lopped tree with barren shoots grafted onto it.

The Ibero-American countries freed themselves from colonial rule more than one hundred fifty years ago. But it was not the Latin American people who cast off their previous masters. Rather, the masters themselves broke free from the European motherland only in order more firmly to establish their own dominion. The events that followed are set forth in Latin American history books as the national history of each country; but the people themselves took scarcely any part in them. With only a few exceptions, the people were not the active shapers of their history, as Europeans had been for half a millennium, and as the Africans and Asiatics wish to be today. They were the passive sufferers of constantly changing conditions which, for them, involved scarcely any changes at all and resulted in no national evolution. Moreover, these people who thus endured, rather than made, history were only to a very small extent native Americans. The majority of them were invading Europeans, immigrant Asiatics, slave Africans, and mestizos.

Aside from a few white countries, Latin America today (whether its inhabitants admit this or not) is a continent of people of mixed blood: mestizos, mulattoes, zambos, European-Indian, European-African, or Indian-African mixtures. A continent of white, black, and red. All these people, no matter what their blood, have adopted the civilization or pseudo-civilization of Europe; they have become Latins.

Latin America's greatest vitality lies in the racial mixture of its population, but this great racial mixture is one of the principal reasons that Latin America cannot be compared with the Latin countries of the Mediterranean area. Its problems are entirely different and must be viewed in entirely different terms from those of two of the mother countries, or perhaps one should say, father countries: Spain and Portugal.

Many other factors account for the differences: the climate, tropical or high plateau; the unfortunate historical vicissitudes of the last century and a half; the torero spirit of temperamental southerners which causes them to applaud the strong man—but also the habit of many Europeans, North Americans, and Asiatics of regarding the Latin American countries as economic colonies and of treating them as such.

STRUGGLE FOR THE GOLDEN THRONE

When Brazil declared its independence in 1822, the head of a German commercial concern exclaimed joyously: "This means we have acquired colonies!" The great importers, exporters, banks, shipping companies, and the industrial firms of Europe and North America which were engaged in overseas trade, reacted similarly, though perhaps somewhat less frankly, to the emancipation of the other Latin American countries. The rule of the Spanish and Portuguese colonial masters was replaced by the no less harsh and considerably more tenacious dominion of the coffee, sugar, banana, tin, saltpeter, copper, and petroleum interests of the world.

Like all forms of colonialism, this economic colonialism also brought money and employment into the colonized countries. And, like all forms of colonialism, economic colonialism depended upon "strong men" who could maintain the peace and good order which invested capital required. But strong men (or those who aspire to be such) are always in large supply in unstable countries. Latin American politics gradually became a matter of business; the struggle for the presidential seat became a struggle for the golden throne.

The former Venezuelan director Marcos Pérez Jiménez is now charged by his democratic successor with having spirited several hundred million dollars of public money out of the country for his personal use, besides leaving behind him the vast sum of $1,400,000,000 in debts. Such figures sound utterly fantastic, but a great many heads of states or dictators in Latin America have enriched themselves in the grand business of politics before they vanished into obscurity. Their successors were often no better. Latin American rebellions and revolutions are therefore, in the majority of cases, not genuine popular uprisings, but struggles among rival politicians for the pork barrel.

This is why Latin American history is a maze in which the *gringo*, European or American, can scarcely find his way. It is a commonplace to call the Latin Americans anarchistic individuals, gamblers, with a mania for *coups d'état* whose stakes often resemble a dangerous *vabanque*. Colonels and generals are raised on the shield, admired, hailed, idolized, and soon afterward mercilessly dropped. Reformers are cheered as heroes of the people, and before too long driven into exile as deceivers of the people. Since the Wars of Independence, Latin America has been ablaze with the fireworks of innumerable uprisings, military revolts, operatic coups, dictators' victories, and dictators' falls. And since for successful coups soldiers and arms are needed (arms which foreign business have only too willingly supplied to the innumerable factions), politicians in the Latin American countries to this day sit uncomfortably on the points of bayonets. Until recently, at least, political life has scarcely ever rested upon the broad shoulders of the people.

Amid the historical fireworks the people, at best, have played the part of an applauding or hissing audience. The people have admired the various Potemkin villages set up by the rulers, whether these were highways, workers' housing, palaces of industry, ambitious supermodern cities, or employment plans. The people, for the most part illiterate and ineligible to vote, have cheered their dictators' cardboard stage sets in much the same way that the German people cheered Hitler's *Autobahnen*. In Latin America, too, the people realized what was behind it all only when it was once more too late. But then, another strong man would be on the spot at once, backed by well-heeled foreign interests, who once more played upon the keyboard of mass psychology. And if at one time or another the people did not react quite in the manner that the ruler or aspirant-to-rule desired, the bayonet could always be employed.

CANCEROUS GROWTHS

In the course of several extended journeys, I have visited fifteen Central and South American countries, have witnessed two military coups, the overthrow of one dictator, and the afterpains of Castro's revolution in Cuba. But the continent I discovered had scarcely any resemblance to the Latin America of our stereotyped notions. To us, Latin America is still an unknown, mysterious quarter of the globe— full of contradictions which still remain to be resolved. What we have so far seen through our European and American spectacles has only been the epidermis, the outer layer of skin, the peeling veneer left over from the colonial past. We have identified Latin America with its oligarchy, with the upper class to whom politics has been a business, and business a branch of politics. We have worked together with this oligarchy, have respected its frozen traditions, and have at best gently reproved it because it has contributed scarcely anything to the solution of a continent's most important social, political, and economic questions. A great many of the problems of Latin America are of the kind that have long since been overcome in most civilized countries of the world, thanks to a long, continuous development.

In Latin America, however, we accept these problems as inescapable evils: political instability, corruption, palace revolutions, lame experiments in democracy, the cult of strong men, the constant threat of economic and financial catastrophes, the prevalence of illiteracy, the terrible gulf between poor and rich. Nationalistic Latin Americans take it amiss when we photograph a wretched hovel alongside a millionaire's palace; we know, of course, that such pictures are profoundly symbolic of the condition of Latin America, but we do not want to offend, do not want to make enemies. Yet what we regard as picturesque subjects for snapshots are, in reality, terrible miseries. Latin America offers inexhaustible material to journalists and travel writers, but as a rule the only moral drawn from the material is the casual: "Well, that's what the Latin American is like."

Today we are experiencing the consequences of four hundred years of fettering and bleeding the Latin American giant, the consequences of four hundred years of abuse. We see that alongside the oligarchy which hitherto has represented Latin America to us, and alongside the magnificent scenery and fabulous people which have formed our conception of Latin America, there are also the Latin American masses. Latin America is stirring beneath the surface, beneath the peeling epidermis; and what is happening no longer accords with our previous clichés. Radicals, extremists and Communists, social reformers, Castroites, Peronistas, People's Front, People's Action, and peasant movements are shaking the Latin American world from the Caribbean Sea all the way down to Tierra del Fuego. These movements refuse to conform to our patterns of thinking. We cannot say whether they are right or left, nationalistic, fascistic, socialistic, or communistic. In part, they run to all these shades. They are typical Latin American movements directed against existing conditions.

POVERTY AND IGNORANCE

These masses of people who have now begun to move between the Caribbean and Tierra del Fuego have, basically, only one thing in common: the majority of them are shockingly poor, alarmingly ignorant, and consequently deeply discontented. According to the latest UNESCO studies, there are still approximately seventy million illiterates in Latin America. Nineteen million children of school age receive no schooling. More than a half million teachers would be needed to fill this lack.

The percentage of illiterates in any given Latin American country is a clear index of the stage of political, economic, and social development it has attained. In the social-welfare state of Uruguay illiteracy is very low, as it is also in the model democracy of Costa Rica. The republics of Argentina and Chile, which have been heavily influenced by European liberalism, compare very favorably—with between 13 per cent and 20 per cent illiteracy—with their neighbors to the north. In Mexico and Venezuela, social-reformist governments have launched impressive campaigns to lift the level of education for both children and adults. Within six years Venezuela reduced illiteracy from 47 per cent to 16 per cent—at least according to official statistics. Mexico has had similar success, as has Cuba under the Castro regime.

One of the slogans of the Castro government claims—no doubt with some exaggeration: "Cuba—the only country in both Americas without illiterates!" Before the revolution, a quarter of the Cuban population could not read and write, and more than 45 per cent of the children of school age did not attend school. The slogans in which Castro proclaims improvement of the Cuban level of education and culture strike a far more appealing note than his usual rhetorical attacks on the Western world.

In all the other countries of Ibero-America, however, the general educational picture is dismal indeed. Huge Brazil has 50 per cent illiteracy. Before the military coup of March 1964, when there were still free elections in Brazil, only 12,000,000 of 63,000,000 Brazilians were permitted to vote. Turbulent Bolivia was able to reduce the number of her illiterates from 80 to 68 per cent between 1952 and 1964, during the comparatively peaceful era of the social-reformist MNR regime. The permanent unrest since the 1964 *coup d'état* put an end to this cheering development. Other estimates of illiteracy are appalling: Colombia, 49 per cent; Peru, 58 per cent; Guatemala, 70 per cent; Haiti, more than 80 per cent. The countries controlled by the military, by economic dictators, or by foreign companies have the highest percentages.

Equally depressing is the lack of vocational schools for technicians, craftsmen, and agricultural specialists. There is insufficient training of teachers; two-thirds of Latin American teachers have only been through elementary school. The instructors at the higher schools consist of only 30 per cent trained teachers; in many cases lawyers, journalists, and other intellectuals do some teaching on the side. The miserable salaries of teachers—which, moreover, in those countries threatened by inflation are often paid weeks or months late—have led to teachers' strikes throughout the continent, and to political radicalization of the professional and nonprofessional pedagogues.

The universities are attended by only a very small stratum of intellectuals. While in the United States approximately one-third of all youths between the ages of twenty and twenty-four go to college, in Latin America there are no more than 3 per cent—almost exclusively children of the upper class and of the numerically small middle class. Even in democratic Chile only 2 per cent of those studying at the state universities are the children of workers. There are virtually no students of peasant background.

Moreover, public education in Latin America is simply not in the same category as European or North American public education. Of lower-class pupils, only a fifth complete elementary school. This does not mean that the children of the poor are either stupid or lazy, but it is a direct reflection of the fact that they must work at home or in the fields, look after their smaller brothers and sisters, and often earn a little additional money for the family. They are overtired, undernourished, and frequently sick; they lack decent clothing, shoes, and many other things that European and North American children take for granted. And their parents are often too ignorant and apathetic to appreciate the value of schooling; for they themselves at best have learned the multiplication table and perhaps are just sufficiently literate to write their names.

In the universities, the struggle for social prestige, for a life of comfort, and for swift social advancement is of far more concern to many young members of the upper class than the actual choice of profession. Law, political economy, perhaps philosophy or medicine are studied; but there is a terrible shortage of young people studying to be technicians, scientists, veterinarians, agronomists, and teachers, all of whom are urgently needed everywhere in Latin America. Only Uruguay is a praiseworthy exception in this respect. In most Ibero-American countries the educated are so much in demand for all sorts of subsidiary occupations that only 20 per cent of the students in the European-type gymnasiums complete the course, and only 10 per cent obtain their final certification.

This cultural and educational chaos is compounded by the fact that the qualified specialists among educated Latin Americans frequently find neither suitable jobs nor adequate research facilities in their own countries. The result is that the best minds from Latin America often go to Western Europe or the United States in order to work at scholarly and scientific projects. Hermann P. Gebhardt, a German journalist familiar with South America, has described this curious situation in incisive language:

"Absurd as it is that Latin American countries ask for loans from the United States while their capitalists send their money to the United States, it seems grotesque that they request specialists for development aid from Western Europe or North America while their own first-class men must emigrate to North America or Western Europe."

ARE THE UNIVERSITIES GOING RED?

Although most students come from the upper or middle class, it seems as if the state universities are more and more rife with leftist liberal, leftist Catholic, and socialist tendencies—and what is more, with students subscribing to anti-Americanism, class struggle, and more or less open communist sympathies. Student strikes, student riots, nationalistic revolutionary demonstrations, manifestations in favor of Castro and against North American policies toward Cuba—all these things convey the impression that Latin American students are more interested in throwing tomatoes, hailing Castro, ogling Red China, and physically attacking those who disagree with them than in attending lectures and preparing themselves for their professions.

What is the cause of this student radicalism? In a number of countries it has clearly ascertainable and understandable causes. The students, and in part the professors as well, are discontented with the prevailing military dictatorship. Their protest against political and intellectual despotism is in such cases directed, not only against the dictatorship, but also against those powers whom they blame for giving moral and financial support to it. In practice, that means hostility toward the "gringos" and in general toward capitalism and the "ugly American."

The dictatorship in Brazil after the 1964 coup deprived many professors and student leaders of their political rights. Large numbers of academics emigrated, chiefly to France. It is understandable that the overwhelming majority of those who have remained behind are not particularly well disposed toward the regime of General Castelo Branco. The situation in Bolivia since the *coup d'état* of General Barrientos is similar: students in Cochabamba, La Paz, and Oruro reacted to the repression of freedom by staging violent riots.

The Ecuadorian students have become even more active since the military coup of 1963. Independents, liberals, socialists, and communists have joined in a united front. Students have been going in for silent marches, hunger strikes, and throwing stones at the palace of government—illustrating what this "university resistance movement" thinks of the ruling junta. In other dictatorships, like that in Guatemala, pro-Western student groups can barely hold their own in discussions and votes from anti-Western opponents.

Latin American universities form virtually a state within a state. As early as the beginning of this century they were citadels of liberalism; professors and students of these institutions, supported by public funds, struggled long, hard, and successfully to win a large measure of independence from government, clergy, and the other ruling powers. Today in all Ibero-American countries they represent virtually extraterritorial areas which may not be entered by police or the military without the consent of the university authorities and the student self-government. The state universities fervently defend this autonomy of theirs. And on a continent whose rulers customarily treat the principles of democracy, liberty, and justice with extreme laxity, there necessarily result a great many conflicts between the state power and the universities with their claims to autonomy.

The universities are in addition largely independent of the major economic powers that influence politics in Latin America—independent, that is, of the dollar, of mining, of petroleum, of coffee and bananas; independent of the steel, copper, oil, sugar, and fruit companies which even the most social-minded and reformist parties or governments obey with more or less readiness. Consequently, the students—even in democratic or semidemocratic countries—are always a few degrees further to the left, more radical, more anticapitalist, than any of the existing parties and government leaders.

Even in the welfare state of Uruguay, whose social problems are well in hand, the overwhelming majority of the students are radical leftists. They attack the Organization of American States (OAS) as "imperialistic" and declare themselves committed to the "revolutionary class struggle." Students who do not go along with these sentiments often cannot obtain tutors and have difficulties at their examinations. In socially progressive Venezuela, a majority of the young academics also sympathize with the radical, oppositionist Left Revolutionary Movement, which is regarded as pro-Castro. In Ar-

gentina, student groups of every political hue from Peronist and
ultranationalistic to left-reformist and communist, have taken part in
all kinds of demonstrations, bombings, and assassination attempts for
the past fifteen years, so that the country has been constantly in
turmoil since the fall of Perón. In Peru, in the university elections of
1965, the adherents of the radical leftist Revolutionary Students Front
consistently won victories over the followers of the two liberal reform
parties, APRA and Acción Popular. In Colombia, the students have
openly taken the side of rebellious guerrillas.

This situation in the universities is symptomatic of the movement
taking place in Latin America—far more symptomatic than all the
slogans on walls, the oratory, rebellions, and upheavals. For the young
men who are today protesting and demonstrating in the universities
do not belong to the amorphous masses. They are the intelligentsia;
they are the governing class of tomorrow and the day after tomorrow.
And what will happen then?

ALLIANCE FOR PROGRESS

The United States, Latin America's immediate neighbor, has long
sensed that the Latin American continent has become an active
volcano. After having displayed a benign tolerance for dictators for
all too long, the United States is now endeavoring to teach democracy
to the Latin American peoples in the North American manner and
with North American methods. The late President Kennedy proclaimed that "representative, democratic regimes" were the only acceptable form of government in both Americas. He hammered away
at the theme that only a voluntary change in their economic and
social structure could preserve the Latin American peoples both from
exploitation and revolutionary chaos. His Alliance for Progress was
a large-scale program for ten years of development aid. It demanded
great sacrifices from the American taxpayer; money from the pockets
of the fraternal neighbor to the north was, by decision of the American
government, to help solve the most pressing educational and social
problems of Latin America.

But the Alliance, inaugurated with so much fanfare, has yielded
only meager fruit. The program has so far chalked up rather scant
results. The development loans that the Latin American countries had
been receiving for years to build schools, housing projects, hospitals,

roads, power plants, and so on were simply booked to the credit of the Alliance—and for a while that was the extent of the progress. Then a number of countries, such as Brazil and Chile, were given hundreds of millions of dollars from the funds intended for the Alliance in order to overcome their balance-of-payments difficulties. Such gifts did not raise the standard of living of the masses of the people.

Above all, there was failure to carry out the plans of the Alliance because the oligarchy was determined to defend its old privileges at all costs. The Latin American upper classes, often assisted by the officer corps of the military services, saw to it—by skillful, often mysterious maneuvers—that the Alliance disturbed as little as possible the feudalistic agrarian structure and the early-capitalist industrial structure of Ibero-America. Although the Alliance program provided for a thoroughgoing modernization of agriculture, a division of the vast latifundia, and an expansion of the tiny class of small farmers, no genuine agrarian reform has yet been carried out under the auspices of the Alliance. Only Chile has made some small start in that direction since the presidency of Eduardo Frei.

North American lenders of capital, moreover, cannot shake off a sense of insecurity about Latin America. In most of the countries of the continent, galloping inflation undermines that self-financing aspect of the Alliance which was essential to Kennedy's plans. A thoroughly paradoxical situation has arisen: the Latin American countries expect financial aid, loans, extensive commitment of foreign capital; in other words, they assume that North America and the rest of the world will trust the stability of Latin American countries. But their own wealthy upper classes are without any such confidence. They invest more money abroad than pours into their countries in economic aid. The amount of Latin American refugee capital in Swiss and North American banks is estimated to be at least ten billion dollars.

Thus the Alliance for Progress has come in for sharp criticism, particularly in Latin America itself. It has been pointed out that the sum total of the development funds flowing from North to South America is scarcely larger than the financial aid the Soviet Union has granted to Cuba alone. Peruvian President Belaúnde declared with much bitterness in 1963 that as far as he was concerned the Alliance for Progress might just as well be abolished, that since its inception it had had no effect to speak of. And two years later Chilean President Frei made the ironical remark that it was an "alliance without progress."

DEMOCRATIZATION—BUT HOW?

North Americans cannot find it pleasant that such harsh words should be pronounced by two heads of state who have reached their position by the legal, democratic path of which the United States approves. Indeed, in the democratization of Latin America, the United States has bungled things as badly as in her program of economic development. Although the democratization of the continent is one of the prime goals of the Alliance, since its inception there have been military coups in ten of the eighteen participating Latin American states. Nine of these states were governed by dictators in 1963; three more were semidictatorships at this time; only five could be considered democracies.

According to the principle of nonintervention—the "Johnson Doctrine," as it is called in Latin America—OAS countries are forbidden to interfere in the internal affairs of other countries. This principle can be abrogated if a communist seizure of power is feared, but not when fascists or other despots of the right seize power. Thus the United States intervened against the democratic rebels in the Dominican Republic because the (unproved) rumor arose that there were communists among them. And thus the United States could support the undemocratic, unpopular junta whose tenor ran counter to the principles of the Alliance.

Now it must be granted that democratic heads of state in Latin America frequently offer no unmitigated good cheer to American capitalists and investors. A good many of the Latin American presidents who have taken over the helms of state in a democratic manner have forthwith nationalized the holdings of their North American patrons. No wonder many foreign capitalists long to see strong men back in the saddle. Yet presidents elected by the will of the people must be responsive to that will.

At present, the peoples of Latin America are trying to satisfy a century-old hunger for nationalism and socialism. They are doing so with an impetuosity that frequently alarms foreign investors. The West still fails to understand this inevitable historical process. Often simplifying dreadfully, the West blames it on communist propaganda. Even such mild social reformers as Betancourt and Leoni in Venezuela, or Belaúnde in Peru, who even by European and American standards must be considered democrats, are all too frequently denounced as socialistic radicals by the business world. If this continues, the East will soon effortlessly harvest the ripe fruit from the Latin American tree. Cuba has already fallen without effort on the part of the East.

The forces that have begun to stir in Latin America are particularly evident in three very different countries. These three countries attempted to set out on a path of their own, a hard, dubious path, to be sure, in the view of those who continue to look upon Latin America through the old, by now almost opaque, Euro-American spectacles. These three are the only Latin American countries which have passed through a genuine revolution in recent times, not just an operatic coup, a palace revolution, but a real uprising of the people. In the following pages I have tried to tell what the change has meant to these countries.

March, 1966

THE
RED, WHITE, AND BLACK
CONTINENT

Political Structure of Latin America

Dictatorship

Semi-dictatorship or military rule

Unstable democracy

Democracy or social democracy

Colonial dependencies

Under Communist influence

MEXICO

CUBA

BAHAMAS (Brit.)

BRIT. HONDURAS
HONDURAS

HAITI

DOM. REPUBLIC

GUATEMALA
EL SALVADOR

JAMAICA

PUERTO RICO (U.S.A.)

NICARAGUA

COSTA RICA

WEST IND. FED.

PANAMA

TRINIDAD

VENEZUELA

COLOMBIA

BRIT. GUIANA
SURINAM
FRENCH GUIANA

ECUADOR

PERU

BRAZIL

Pacific
Ocean

BOLIVIA

PARAGUAY

CHILE

URUGUAY

Atlantic
Ocean

ARGENTINA

FALKLAND ISLANDS (British)

CHAPTER 1

Three Revolutions

A LAMPPOST IN LA PAZ

On the Plaza Murillo, in the heart of the Bolivian metropolis of La Paz, there could be seen until the end of 1964 a remarkable lamppost that had become the symbol of an equally remarkable revolution. The lamppost shed its light on six buildings which, in the common view, are the centers of power of any Latin American country: the Government Office Building (usually called the Government Palace), the cathedral, the House of Parliament, the residence of the bishop, the Military Club, and the headquarters of the police. In La Paz, however, at the time of the revolution we wish to describe, these edifices were not especially impressive. La Paz is the seat of the Bolivian Government, but it is not, properly speaking, the capital of the country; the now unimportant provincial town of Sucre is still the official capital, as it has always been.

The walls of these six buildings were overlaid with posters: proclamations, announcements by parties, unions, and the government. In the whole city, there was scarcely a wall not inscribed with three large letters painted in black: MNR. But nothing was ever scrawled or posted on the lamppost. Two uniformed sentinels guarded it. Every so often it was decorated with flowers.

In July 1946 the then president of Bolivia, Major Gualberto Villaroel, was hanged by an enraged mob. Villaroel was co-founder of the reformist anticapitalist and pro-Indian MNR, the *Movimiento Nacional Revolucionario*, whose program called for expropriation of the powerful tin companies for the benefit of the Indian miners. By Western standards, then, Villaroel would be considered a left extremist. Nevertheless, the mob that killed him consisted of discontented left extremists. These leftists, however—and that is the real oddity of the matter—were acting in alliance with their bitterest enemies, the tin-mine owners. They had hanged their own man and thereby helped the tin kings to regain power. This is the confusing and typically Latin American story which leaves the visitor from abroad altogether perplexed, at least at first. The background of the story is equally complicated. Major Villaroel was no offspring of the exploited working classes, but belonged to the most illustrious family in Bolivia. His ancestor was no other than the conquistador Juan de Villaroel, who had discovered the tremendous silver riches of Potosí in 1545 and had thus become one of the richest men of his time. Within three decades, the silver city of Potosí developed into the largest city in South America and, after Venice, the second largest city of the Latin world. It attracted adventurers and treasure hunters from all quarters of the globe. Legend has it that these not only ate from silver plates but even used silver chamber pots. Bolivia, then called Upper Peru, became the treasure chest of the Spanish Empire.

Mining, however, requires a large labor force. With merciless cruelty the Spaniards drove the Indians of the Bolivian plateau into the silver mines; at the time of the silver boom it is said that many thousands of Indians died there under the harsh conditions of forced labor. However, the natives took an inadvertent vengeance upon their exploiters. From Potosí the Spaniards carried syphilis to Europe. Moreover, the flood of silver produced the greatest depreciation of currency that Europe had ever experienced. Historians believe that the resulting financial crash ushered in the decline of the great Spanish Empire.

TIN POLITICS—AND A HANGED MAN

For more than three centuries Upper Peru remained a sleeping beauty on the fringes of history. Once-brilliant Potosí was reduced to the rank of a minor provincial town. But in 1905, almost a century after Bolivia's liberation from Spanish rule, another lucky discovery was made there, one which was to determine the future fate of the country. This time the finder of hidden treasure was not a high-born Spaniard, but an Indian named Simón Patiño. Patiño, an employee of a German trading firm, had played rather fast and loose with the company's money in order to aid a friend of his, the owner of a small tin mine. The German firm discharged him, but in order to make it possible for him to repay the embezzled funds, the court gave Patiño possession of his friend's tin mine.

It had been known since the middle of the preceding century that there was tin as well as silver in Bolivia. But only a few petty mineowners had bothered about the exploitation of Bolivian tin. Patiño, however, quickly learned that a whim of fate had literally tossed into his lap one of the largest caches of tin ore on the face of the earth. He raised money, bought up the neighboring tin-rich mountains, and within ten years became one of the richest men in the world. He was not the only tin king. Along with the Simón Patiño Tin Company, the concerns of Aramayo and Hochschild also became immensely rich. These three tin kings soon had in their hands the entire Bolivian production of tin, the second largest in the world. When it turned out that Bolivia was also rich in wolfram, antimony, zinc, and iron, the roof of South America once again became the El Dorado of great mining interests.

But tin mining also requires a large labor reservoir. Once again the plateau Indians were the logical victims. They were lured into the mines with whiskey and coca. There they died in countless numbers from undernourishment, exhaustion, alcoholism, and silicosis. The leaves of the coca plant had, of course, been used in pre-Columbian America by the Indians of the Andes region as a stimulant; but it was the labor slavery under the silver and tin kings that made the Indians so dependent upon coca they could no longer live without their *acullico,* their quid made of coca leaves, pulped potato, and ashes. Silver and tin had made drug addicts of an entire people.

In 1930 another economic factor came to the fore in Bolivia: oil. Sizable reserves of oil were discovered in the Chaco, the disputed region between Bolivia and Paraguay. The international oil companies began a struggle to obtain possession of this newly discovered wealth. They fought out their rivalries by warlike means as they had previously done in the Near East, in Mexico, and in other lands where black gold lay beneath the surface of the ground. Shell Oil lined up behind Paraguay, Standard Oil behind Bolivia. The two countries carried on a senseless war in which both nearly bled to death. The war ended indecisively. Paraguay, to be sure, obtained the greater part of the Chaco, but the oil lands fell to Bolivia.

Those were times of uneasiness and suffering for the population of Bolivia. The common man fell heir to none of the great new wealth of the country. Only the oligarchy of Spanish descent and the few Indians who had followed in Patiño's footsteps were able to obtain some crumbs. The metal kings of the country sent their money abroad and built themselves princely residences on the Rivieras of our planet. But the highland Indians who worked in the mines lived in holes in the ground, debilitated by their cocaine addiction, unable to read and write, unable to vote, and seeing no prospect of ever escaping from their misery.

As a result of these conditions, all sorts of radical parties and movements sprang up. Bolivia went through fascistic experiments such as that headed by the dictator Germán Busch. Busch was of German descent and one of his advisers was Hitler's crony, Ernst Röhm. Gradually however—and secretly at first—there grew up a political force based upon the Indian majority of the population. This was the MNR. The first MNR government, under Major Villaroel, failed because the expropriated tin kings skillfully contrived to depress the price of tin on the world market and so undermined the new government's budget. Villaroel was unable to keep his promises and was lynched by the disappointed mineworkers.

The story goes on, however. Barely six years after Major Villaroel's martyr's death, the masses who had hanged their reformist president, and thus restored the tin kings to their thrones, once again revolted in the streets of La Paz. This time their wrath was directed against Dictator Ballivián, who represented the interests of the tin kings; they now expressed their sympathy with the members of Villaroel's party. The Bolivians had realized at last that they had killed the wrong man. The Easter revolution of 1952 cost three thousand deaths in La Paz alone. It brought the MNR back to the helm. For the next twelve years the party of the hanged martyr ruled Bolivia, and the lamppost which served as Villaroel's gallows was lovingly regarded as a national monument.

THE GREATEST NUMBER OF COUPS IN THE WORLD

From the foregoing, it is apparent that the heartland of South America, the Andean republic of Bolivia, with its predominantly Indian population, is characterized by a most explosive political climate. Bolivia has always been unusually favorable terrain for coups of every imaginable type. Before the MNR appeared on the scene, these coups were almost entirely palace revolutions, taking place within the circles of the upper class. The Indians, like the masses of the people in other Latin American countries, scarcely participated. With its one hundred eighty revolutions in one hundred forty years, Bolivia holds the absolute record in *coups d'état*. More than half of these revolts have been successful. Every sixth Bolivian head of state has been lynched, shot, or dispatched to the hereafter in some other speedy manner. From 1825 to 1952 only six presidents completed their terms of office. It is evident, then, that the sudden ups and downs in the fortunes of the anticapitalist MNR are perfectly compatible with the anarchistic climate of the country.

The gallows on which Major Villaroel was hanged was a favorite photographic subject for foreign tourists. They admired the cunning of the tin-mine owners in allying themselves with the radical left in order to get rid of an inconvenient social reformer. They wanted also to express admiration for the MNR which succeeded in turning the tables once again by exploiting latent popular wrath. And most such foreign tourists, if they had any opinion at all, would have said that the next coup would no doubt bring the other side to power again, and the martyr's monument would be degraded to an ordinary lamppost once more.

That is exactly what happened. In December 1964, Air Force General René Barrientos staged an uprising; he deposed the MNR government, destroyed the apparatus in which its power was concentrated, and above all the miners' unions, made himself dictator, and drove the MNR leaders into exile. What had happened, seemingly, was the usual trivial end of a social-revolutionary experiment; one of those only too common Latin American military revolts which at most elicit a shrug from us.

But this first impression is deceptive. If the complex MNR revolution had been merely one more coup among so many, and if General Barrientos' rebellion had been no more than the traditional reprisal of the propertied class, it would not be necessary to give these two events in Bolivia any more than a mention in an analysis of Latin America. Coups are a dime a dozen on this continent. But the case of Bolivia is in reality a prime example of the political transformation which can be felt more or less distinctly almost everywhere in Latin America. And it is perhaps the most interesting example of all.

As a rule, when a social-reformist government is overthrown by a military dictator in Latin America, the dictator excludes the revolutionary left from politics as a matter of course. But as a rule he will also revoke the reforms and nationalizations—for the benefit of the oligarchy, which applauds him, and to the detriment of the common people, who have to be kept down by bayonets. Bolivia's new ruler, however, has himself come from the ranks of the MNR. He has been careful not to return the nationalized mines to private hands. He attacks the former tin kings just as sharply as did the revolutionary leaders. He is able to hold power only if he talks about "social progress" in much the same terms as the MNR, and only if his slogans and program sound no less anticapitalist than those of the revolutionaries.

Bolivia today demonstrates that the old-fashioned rebellious general has given way to a new type. Such generals can no longer afford to come forth as representatives of the upper crust, who claim to be the legitimate heirs of the Spanish conquistadors. Barrientos still relies on the army, which is to say, on force; but he must make concessions to the masses of the people—concessions that formerly would have been denounced as "socialistic" and "products of class struggle," and that would have been unthinkable before Castro's time.

The MNR revolution, in spite of its present eclipse, has awakened a slumbering force in Bolivia: the masses of the people. The West today must reckon with these masses if it wishes to preserve the good will of Latin Americans. The age of oligarchies, the age of feudal dictators, military men, and puppet presidents, of wealthy clans and omnipotent companies, is coming to an end. The common man in Ibero-America is coming of age.

Europeans and North Americans have been observing this process with some concern. They have watched the events in Cuba; they have witnessed the popular rage which has swept away dictators such as Ballivián, Pérez Jiménez, Batista, and Trujillo. They hear about anti-American excesses and antiforeign slogans, and they fear that the awakening of the people will bring still greater turbulence and instability to this restless continent.

The decade which followed the MNR revolution in La Paz seemed to have confirmed many of these fears. In practice, there were two governments in Bolivia thereafter, or at least two rival power blocs: on the one hand the president with his cabinet; on the other hand the unions with their tight organization. The leader of the revolution and the president of the country, Victor Paz Estenssoro, was considered a moderate whose revolutionary fervor had cooled, and who now aimed at long-range reforms and collaboration with the United States, and at close contact with the International Monetary Fund. His long-time deputy, however, the union leader Juan Lechín, who had the well-armed masses of the Indian tin miners behind him, was considered a man of the radical left, and some Western businessmen even decried him as a friend of the Communists. The fierce and sometimes bloody struggles for power between the government bloc and the trade union bloc were constantly cited by the world press as evidence that the Bolivian MNR government was after all extremely unstable and would soon fall prey to the radical leftists in its own ranks.

Some of the allegations were undoubtedly true. Exhausted Bolivia had been unable to carry out needed economic and social reforms to the extent that the tin miners and the Indian masses demanded. Wildcat strikes were common, as were violent attacks by trade union leaders upon their own government. The tin workers regarded the COMIBOL, the government mining company, with much the same suspicion that they felt for their former exploiters. Miners once kept the president of the COMIBOL in a mine by force and made him share the wretched food served to the workers. Most of the strikes broke out when the government managers of the mine, for economy reasons, tried to dismiss superfluous workers who had hitherto been kept on the job for reasons of solidarity alone. And most of the outbreaks of shooting between union militia and the government troops arose from the government's habit of sending workers to jail for petty misdemeanors. Bolivian unionists remembered only too well the days when the tin kings and their political henchmen exercised a savage and wholly arbitrary dominion over the workers. Now that their own men were in the seats of government, they wanted to warn them against summoning up even the slightest reminder of those days.

Toward the end of 1963 a harsh struggle for power typical of present conditions in Bolivia developed between the government and the unions. The government had arrested the leftist radical union leaders Pimentel and Escobar, who were rumored to have engaged in political blackmail and attempted uprising. The Catavi miners thereupon took fifteen prominent foreigners as hostages, declaring that they would not release them until Pimentel and Escobar were set free.

Government troops set out for Catavi; in reply, the miners' union mobilized its own militia. Foreign newspapers spoke of an imminent civil war. The crisis was, however, settled, though with difficulty. The hostages—who had suffered no harm—were released. The arrested trade union leaders were assured a fair trial. But the question remained: would not such radical union groups sooner or later win power by the vote in the land of tin? Would the people's movement of the MNR lead to a further people's uprising capable of transforming a reformist Indian-socialist government into a communist people's democracy? Would Bolivia, then, become a second Cuba?

Undoubtedly it was this danger that prompted Victor Paz Estenssoro, the liberal MNR president, once again to concede more power to the military, in the hope of creating a counterpoise to the unions and their workers' militia. The Bolivian Government formed an alliance with the right in order to contain the left. In doing so, it sealed its fate. It could not exorcise the spirits it had summoned.

What kind of movement had it been—the MNR, which for twelve years dominated Bolivia and then overnight was liquidated by a general and vanished seemingly without a trace? What was so special about this Bolivian revolution? What did it accomplish? What did it mean for Latin America? Why did it fail in spite of its bold, imaginative reform programs? And what does the future probably hold for the restive land of Bolivia?

The story of the MNR is the story of a Latin American people's movement that tried to find a third road midway between capitalism and socialism, between rigid tradition and revolutionary upheaval, between military dictatorship and anarchy. The MNR experiment was a test that involved the fundamental, fateful question of Latin America: whether the continent can avoid, by courageous, sincere reforms, a violent, cataclysmic overthrow of its petrified hierarchical social order. Today there are a number of such tests going on, a number of "third roads" being tried in the Ibero-American area. We shall speak of them later. For the present, let us turn to the facts of the situation in Bolivia.

INDIOS UNDER ARMS

History has taught us to regard popular movements of all types with considerable distrust. We know how easily these may end in fascistic mass intoxication, communistic totalitarianism, or anarchistic chaos. But must these precedents necessarily apply to Latin America? We have taken Bolivia as an example because developments in that country are highly typical of conditions in Latin America. The rapid rises and falls of the MNR movement can stand as representative of the hopes, as well as the dangers, that can spring from such experiments with a "third road."

The MNR could with more justice be called a genuine popular movement than most of the other reformist, popular frontist, and revolutionary movements in neighboring countries. It set up no dictatorship; it did not ban a single opposition party. It governed by votes and not by bayonets. The MNR leaders were therefore not far wrong when they maintained that the people stood behind the MNR.

Before the Easter revolution of 1952 the Bolivian people, four fifths of them unable to read and write, took only a passive part in political events. In keeping with Latin American custom, the majority of them, as illiterates, were barred from voting and therefore were unable to elect and depose presidents. The MNR reform put an end to such second-class citizenship. Every adult Bolivian, male or female, Indio or white, illiterate or not, was entitled to vote. Logically enough, the people then elected MNR candidates, in spite of (or perhaps just because of) the various internal antagonisms within the party. The widened franchise condemned all the other parties to insignificance.

In the time at its disposal, the MNR government also built another safety feature into the system to insure its own survival. It created an armed workers' militia to neutralize the power of the army. Its staff of union leaders functioned as a counterpoise to the general staff. And since the Bolivian miners are overwhelmingly of Indian blood, the armed Indios played a key part in the national revolutionary government.

The Indian rural population was won over by a large-scale agrarian reform on the Mexican pattern. The MNR undertook an interesting and promising experiment in opening up new land, not (as has been usual) with the aid of foreign colonists, but with the aid of native Indians. Extensive regions in the tropical and subtropical valleys and lowlands, for the most part almost virgin wilderness, were expropriated. Large numbers of Indians from the overpopulated highlands were settled in this territory. They were to form the core of a new peasant middle class.

Although this measure helped to place Bolivia on a self-subsistent basis, it encountered violent criticism—from the left as well as the right. For among the resettled people were dismissed tin miners whose jobs had become superfluous. The MNR could no longer employ them profitably, and therefore tried to provide them with a new basis for livelihood in the countryside. The union functionaries, however, bitterly protested this "forced deportation into exile," as they put it. Thus, even land reform served to sharpen the antagonisms between the government and its union supporters.

This criticism of Bolivian agrarian reform was entirely unjustified. Every visitor to the yungas, the subtropical valleys on the eastern slope of the Andes, cannot but be impressed by the new settlements. Hardly anywhere else in Latin America have I encountered such cheerful, capable, hard-working people as those Indian settlers of MNR days. Granted, the highland Indians did not find it easy to adjust to the subtropical climate. In their new jungle villages many of them continued to wear the warm, multicolored woolens that had protected them against wind and cold in the High Andes. But they cleared and tilled land, planted and harvested with a passion quite uncommon in Latin America. A new self-assurance and sense of responsibility grew up in these newly cleared lands. There Indian pariahs developed into full citizens, owners of property, and creators of new values.

Excellent though the results of such experiments and reforms seem to be, the European inclines to be skeptical when he hears about them. He remembers the unpleasant experiences of his own continent. By Western standards, a party that has the "people" behind it is usually a totalitarian party. Moreover, anyone who traveled through Bolivia with his eyes open quickly realized that only the politically most active section of the population, the miners, played a significant part in the MNR. Even the present dictatorship has to reckon with them. But the events of the recent past seem to have passed over the highland Indians and the inhabitants of remote districts without leaving a trace. As in the old days, they continue to obey their local caciques.

When in addition we hear that the MNR leaders have studied the works of Marx, Lenin, Hitler, and Mussolini, our forebodings increase. We may even be inclined to thank Providence that General Barrientos was able to liquidate the MNR regime. Was not the military coup perhaps the lesser evil? There are many observers of Latin American conditions who think so.

Moreover, the question arises: what is meant by the concept of "the people" within Latin America? Here and there in the Ibero-American area there are countries where popular education comes up to European standards—Uruguay and Costa Rica, for example. But these model countries remain praiseworthy exceptions. When popular education and development have been almost completely neglected for centuries, these sins of omission sooner or later exact a bitter toll. Again Bolivia is a prime example of what form the payment takes.

Bolivia's population consists of 60 per cent pure-blooded Indians and 30 per cent people of mixed blood, the so-called cholos, many of whom have grown up among the Indians. In twelve years the MNR almost doubled the number of elementary schools; nevertheless, even today most of the population still cannot read or write. Do these amorphous masses, living in an economy of bare subsistence in the mining regions in the Indio villages of the Andes plateau and the remote settlements of the jungle valley, have any political will of their own? Are they capable of making political decisions? Can they become a political factor that will ultimately change the face of this continent?

If we have said that the common man in Latin America is beginning to come of age, that statement does not imply that he has all at once become capable of taking the wheel and guiding his own destiny. Illiterate or semiliterate masses whose educational level is often appallingly low, and whose political aspirations are often identical with the satisfaction of their animal needs, are all too easy prey to every clever demagogue who comes along. If the demagoguery of a single man sufficed to turn an intelligent and highly cultivated German nation into a herd of sheep, such a danger is all the more acute in a continent in which illiteracy has actually been promoted by the ruling classes. The doctrine that the people must be kept stupid is, to this day, frequently voiced by members of the Ibero-American oligarchy.

The stupefied common people must be educated to self-consciousness, self-confidence, and responsibility before they can be permitted to participate in political events. A hundred years ago it was denied that the European worker had the capacity to educate himself and learn to share political responsibility. Today the worker is a basic factor in the political life of most civilized countries. In Latin America, however, such social evolution has been ignored or artificially checked, up to very recent times. The question now is, how can this age-long neglect be overcome? How effective are methods of the sort undertaken by the MNR?

FROM EXPERIMENT TO COMPROMISE

From the start the MNR was a highly heterogeneous structure. On the left wing stood Juan Lechín and the other union leaders, who intermittently allowed their miners to strike against their own government. On the right wing stood the liberal political economist Hernán Siles Zuazo, who during his presidency once emulated Gandhi and went on a hunger strike when Lechín's workers threatened to scuttle his political plans. The balance between radicalism and nonviolence was held by the founder of the party and leader of the revolution, Victor Paz Estenssoro, who was periodically criticized by extremists of his own party for "servility to America."

Similar tensions prevailed between the rural and the urban population and above all, as already mentioned, between the state mining company, COMIBOL, and the unions. An additional source of trouble was the egotism of professional functionaries. The tin workers, of course, wanted to enjoy the blessings of the social reforms and give as little as possible in return. Proletarian masses who have hitherto known only exploitation, humiliation, and an ugly pariah existence do not develop overnight the sense of responsibility of European and American industrial workers. The terrible toll that the tin kings had for so long taken of the *mineros* had to be paid for by the MNR.

Reforms, social benefits, improved working conditions, and wage increases made the nationalized mines unprofitable. The unions, however, prevented layoffs even in mines that had become uneconomic and had been idled. In the crisis year of 1964 there were twice as many miners in the tin mines as before 1932, but they produced only half as much tin as in the days of the independent tin companies. COMIBOL, as a result, was losing from one half to one million dollars a month. The MNR leaders, and in particular sensible President Paz Estenssoro, fully realized that these symptoms of crisis were only diseases of infancy, typical of every country that tries to compress the great leap from economically exploited colony to modern social-welfare state into a few years. Such initial setbacks have occurred in other social-reformist or social-revolutionary countries—in Mexico, for example. They can be overcome if the country can count on aid from abroad.

Paz Estenssoro availed himself of such aid to a greater extent than the anticapitalistic, increasingly radical unions liked. The credits, loans, and gifts of the United States to a Bolivia that was busily nationalizing its basic industries amounted to a larger sum per capita than was accorded to any other Latin American country. American money helped the Bolivians build bold "miracle highways" into the interior of the country, and thus begin the land reform in the yungas. The United States, West Germany, and the Inter-American Development Bank devised a three-cornered plan to bail out the tin mines; they jointly invested some twenty-seven million dollars in Bolivia.

Despite the fact that the MNR had also expropriated Standard Oil, American oil companies once again began operating in Bolivia. Together with the Bolivians, they expanded the oil refineries of Cochabamba, built new pipelines, and opened up new oil fields—with the result that Bolivia in the MNR period was able to supply not only its own requirements for oil, but also to export increasing amounts to the oil-rich countries of Brazil and Argentina.

All in all, revolutionary Bolivia seemed on its way to becoming a model of peaceful coexistence, a splendid example of how successful the Alliance for Progress could be in promoting nonviolent development of the peoples and economies of Latin America, just as Kennedy had hoped. The MNR-governed state behaved like a model pupil of its American patrons and re-educators. But Paz Estenssoro knew all the while that he could keep the good will of his capitalist friends and financiers only if he quelled radicalism in his own ranks. Striking, rioting, and rebellious miners, attacks on foreign advisers, exorbitant wage demands, and fanatical demonstrations for Castro and against the Yankees impeded peaceful collaboration and deepened the suspicions, widely held in the West, of Bolivian socialistic experiments. A good many Europeans and Americans were already beginning to sense that Lechín, the powerful union leader, might become a second Castro.

In order to save the cause of peaceful evolution in his country, Paz Estenssoro adopted a perilous stratagem. He tried to play the army off against the unions. In the 1964 elections Lechín lost his post as vice-president and was replaced by Air Force General Barrientos. The army regained its prerevolutionary positions of power. With the aid of its troops, Paz Estenssoro hoped to block the demands of the extremists, defend internal peace, and so save his regime.

That was a miscalculation. In this respect, too, Bolivia became a classic example. Latin American countries which attempt to curb the danger from the left with bayonets frequently find that they have invited a greater danger. For their generals are not noted for circumspection.

René Barrientos was not, it is true, a conservative military leader. He was not a representative of the oligarchy. As we have said, he belonged to the MNR and was considered one of the president's closest confidants—in fact, his pampered, courted friend and favorite associate. Paz Estenssoro, therefore, could scarcely have foreseen that this man would betray and overthrow him.

Barrientos justified his coup with the time-honored excuse of Latin American dictators: his sole purpose was to restore order. The measures he employed to this end were quite as summary as those of other military dictators: he smashed the MNR and exiled the entire top leadership of the movement. Some three hundred politicians and union leaders were deported across the frontier, most of them to Argentina. He also sent soldiers to occupy the mining regions and proclaimed martial law. The three most prominent men of the MNR fled—Paz Estenssoro to Lima, Siles Zuazo to Montevideo, and Lechín to Asunción.

It may be assumed that Barrientos was driven by increasing pressure from the right to deal so harshly with the revolutionary movement to which he himself belonged and to which he had devoted the best years of his life. The oligarchy forced him soon after the coup to accept as co-president the ultrarightist army commander Alfredo Ovando. And it is probably due primarily to Ovando—or rather to the groups backing Ovando—that the previously dominant party and the unions were so completely stripped of rights and eliminated from public life.

Henceforth, the unions were regarded as a "hostile political force." Strikes were outlawed. The junta decreed civilian labor service for all Bolivians between eighteen and fifty years of age—and the whole civilian labor service was placed under martial law. In the future, only "actively employed workers" could be elected as representatives of the workers, and the only acceptable candidates were those who "had not previously held a political office." In other words, such representatives must be politically untutored and willing tools of the new regime. Every election would be valid only for a year, and in addition every candidate had to be approved by the minister of labor.

The Indian tin miners reacted to these measures with predictable anger. Bloody battles that brought Bolivia to the verge of civil war were fought in the mines, and are still going on with uncertain outcome. Repeatedly, miners attempted to assassinate the dictator; several times Barrientos barely escaped with his life. Bolivia has become less, not more, peaceful as a result of the military coup. The country may well be facing a new revolution even more radical and bloody than the Easter uprising of 1952.

Barrientos is as well aware of that possibility as those foreign observers who are watching political events in Bolivia with great concern. Barrientos represents an entirely new type of rebellious general, a type that is becoming more and more common in Latin America. He is not absolutely bent on subjugating the people; he would like to cajole them. He is quite in earnest when he talks about "social progress." He treats the expropriated mineowners and the other feudal lords as harshly as the deposed union functionaries. His army is employed not only to repress rebellious miners, but also to force the feudalistic propertied class to accept a "social compromise"—in other words, to surrender many of their positions of power. He is sincere in his statements that his regime wants to carry the revolution further.

In other words, the coup has not entirely turned back the clock of history in Bolivia. Barrientos is a child of the revolution, and he cannot deny his past in spite of his antirevolutionary, antiunion, and antidemocratic measures. With remarkable courage, he ventures among the miners wearing their peculiar dress; he visits them in the mine shafts and tries to talk them around. He has revoked pay raises and instituted a wage freeze; but on the other hand he has assured the miners a 50-per-cent share in the profits of the mines. He wants to push the agrarian reforms ahead by force, in order to obtain better and cheaper food supplies for the entire population. He believes firmly that a strong hand will be better able to promote a new social and economic order in Bolivia than the previous bureaucratic democracy with its heterogeneous, mutually hostile camps and its restive people's militia.

But the determined and perhaps somewhat artificial pro-labor attitudes of the new President seem so far to have failed to convince the miners and peasants, the Indios and cholos. The twelve MNR years gave the people too great a taste of freedom for them now to regard even the most pro-labor dictatorship as a progressive regime. They see it as a dictatorship like any other. Many Bolivians fear, moreover, that Barrientos may soon be outmaneuvered by his archconservative Co-president Ovando, or by other counterrevolutionaries.

What does the future hold for Bolivia? Perhaps we can answer this question if we turn our attention to the country that obviously served as the model for the Bolivian experiment. The Bolivian revolutionaries may have studied Lenin and Hitler thoroughly; but they have not concocted a communistic-fascistic mixture as the result of their reading. Their guiding ideal has not been a European, but a Latin American country—a country that today irresistibly attracts and inspires countless Ibero-Americans.

In this country, too, the masses of the people erupted with the violence of a natural force from their previous lethargy; there, too, the leaders of the people were periodically replaced by generals whose intentions were obscure, so that there was no saying whether they wished to choke off the revolution or urge it onward. And in this country, too, Marx and Lenin (though not Hitler and Mussolini) were read avidly; but its leaders did not thereby become party-line Marxists or Leninists. They found a way of their own, a genuine Latin American way. And the outcome of the upheavals there was the one genuinely successful revolution in Latin America since the wars of liberation from the mother countries—the only revolution that deserves the name.

That country is Mexico.

A PERMANENT REVOLUTION

Mexico, too, has passed through a genuine popular revolution in which the common man has at last been recognized as a functioning member of the body politic. This revolution now belongs to the past; it took place between 1910 and 1912, with some violence continuing to break out in the years following. The books of B. Traven, the writer who has kept his identity shrouded in mystery, present a vivid account of that eruptive upheaval: the struggle against the tyranny of "the wicked old man" Porfirio Díaz, the rivalries of the oil companies, the uprising of the expropriated masses of Indians and agricultural workers, the unfortunate intervention of the United States, and the ultimate victory of the people in the "revolution of the hanged."

A different story is presented by the companies which had previously been doing business in Mexico, or in the books of writers sympathetic to the ruling circles. There we may read of ruthless expropriations, of massacre and slaughter committed by the revolutionaries, of anticlerical excesses, of the most brutal assaults upon private property ever attempted by proletarian mobs—this was before the Bolshevik revolution in Russia. Verdicts on the Mexican revolution remain contradictory to this day. What to one historian was an outbreak of the ugliest and lowest human passions is to others the birth pangs of a new age.

What took place during the following decade and a half in Mexico likewise remains arcane to the majority of people outside Latin America. One disturbance succeeded another; revolutions and counter-revolutions followed in rapid succession before the new government was finally able to stabilize. During these upsets, three presidents were killed. Several times the churches were closed, then thrown open again. Periodically, the revolutionary leader in power purged the government party of his predecessor's followers—in many cases that predecessor having been his closest associate and fellow fighter. Rigorous political purges in the ranks of revolutionary parties were not invented in the Soviet Union or in Hitler Germany, but in Mexico. The old Aztec land of Mexico remained a tumultuous country for years after its revolution.

RETURN TO INDIAN WAYS

Today conditions in Mexico are relatively tranquil. The government party, which under various names has controlled the administrative apparatus for three decades (today it is called the *Partido Revolucionario Institucional*), has long since overcome its early weaknesses and is today the strongest party in power in Latin America. And this Mexican PRI, which turned to the trade unions for support, as did the Bolivian MNR, has nationalized mineral resources and sources of energy, has divided up the latifundia, and has introduced a universal franchise which includes illiterates. Only the Mexican PRI has decades of experience in all these matters, whereas the Bolivian MNR was only beginning when its career was cut short.

Both the Mexican and the Bolivian parties tended to break with the Spanish traditions in their countries' past and to profess proud allegiance to the Indian tradition. Both countries do not regard their history as beginning with the discovery of America, but go back many centuries to the rise of the pre-Columbian Indian empires—the Maya and Aztec empires in Mexico, and the Tiahuanaco and Inca empires in Bolivia. This positive attitude toward the Indian past can be plainly felt in Mexico, whereas it was felt less plainly in Bolivia. Probably the reason for this is only that Bolivia has not yet produced any great Indian leaders like the Mexicans Juárez, Calles, and Cárdenas. Recently Mexican legislators have even debated whether they should not establish the Aztec Nahuatl language as the national language in place of Spanish. To a large percentage of the Mexican population the Nahuatl dialect is still their mother tongue, whereas for more than half the Mexicans Spanish has remained a foreign language which they must learn in school. The Mexicans finally decided to abide by the language of their conquerors only in order not to lose their linguistic ties with the other Ibero-American countries.

When we examine the structure of the two government parties, we are even more forcibly impressed by the parallels between Mexico and Bolivia. The PRI is by no means a homogeneous, politically consistent, strictly organized body with a specific party program. The moderate wing would be called, in Europe, mildly liberal, the radical wings distinctly left socialist. To the PRI belong such different personalities as the Socialist and Stalin prize-winner General Lázaro Cárdenas (who in 1938 expropriated the Anglo-American oil companies), and the moderate but corrupt president Alemán Valdés (who from 1948 to 1952 steered to the right again and attracted new foreign investment into Mexico). Since then, men of the center like López Mateos have held office, who on the one hand have practiced a mild policy of expropriation, on the other hand have maintained good-neighborly relations with the United States.

Since the consolidation of the revolution in Mexico, however, this multicolored political palette has by no means resulted in chaos within the government party. On the contrary, thanks to it the Mexican government party has been able to tack skillfully back and forth between the extremes. To the outsider this maneuver frequently looks like very abrupt swings of the pendulum. The extreme wings are occasionally as far apart as a pair of fighting cocks. The opponent within the party is feared, denounced, and fought as in other countries the opposing party. But for years it has been apparent that this very internal tension gets things moving in Mexico. Radical presidents advance socialization; their moderate successors repair errors by cautious correction or strategic retreat. Political life does not stagnate and policy does not run the country into blind alleys because the party is blessedly free of the doctrinaire elements of Marxism and the totalitarianism of fascism. Mexico, in a phrase very popular there, is in a state of "permanent revolution." This goes so far that the president himself does not wear evening clothes when he attends the theater; he appears in an ordinary business suit—for after all he is a revolutionary. But the revolution comes from above. Its leaders are not rebels, and its arena is not the streets. The permanent revolution takes place within the government party and is directed by the party group dominant at any given time.

The consequence has been a political stability uncommon in Latin American countries. Mexico is a democracy, not only in name but in fact. In addition to the government party a wide variety of other parties put up candidates. There are no banned parties and restrictions on political activity. Nevertheless, basically this democracy comes down to a one-party system and hence (if we wish to use an unfriendly term) to a party dictatorship. For the other parties have not the slightest prospect of defeating the all-powerful government party, not even the Communist Party of Mexico, which, with its eighty thousand members, is the strongest Communist Party in Latin America—much stronger than the party in the "People's Democracy" of Cuba.

If we study the history and structure of the Mexican PRI, the question posed for us by Bolivian events proves less difficult to answer. That was the question of whether in the foreseeable future a depressed people long excluded from any participation in the state can be converted into citizens of a democracy without inviting political chaos. The Mexican example seems to indicate that people are not only represented by their government but also educated by it. Even the lowest section of the population can be trained and guided gently along an upward path in a manner which does not infringe on individual liberties. A revolution by evolution—in Mexico that is what has taken place.

AGRARIAN REFORMS

As those who know Mexico will constantly assure us with eloquence and passion, it is a scintillating, exotic country, difficult to fathom. A land in which childlike gaiety and cruel obsessiveness exist side by side. A land of wild contrasts which has still to deal with multitudinous problems: with Indian and Spanish traditions, with the wealth of the luxury resorts and the poverty in the Indio villages, with the anti-clericalism of the ruling group and the naïve faith of the masses of the people, with great resources of oil, projects for industrialization, an agrarian program, and a latent, almost traumatic hatred for the Yankees. A land that after many bloody revolutions has embarked on a succession of bloodless revolutions whose daring experiments often resemble perilous peregrinations on the brink of an abyss. A land of many faces, some of which seem as mysterious as the masks of the ancient Aztecs.

For a balanced picture of the country, however, we must supplement the exotic vignettes of tourist literature with a sober evaluation of social achievements of the past several decades. After her expropriation fever cooled, Mexico faced the task of tapping and refining her oil, of exploiting her silver mines, her mica, and her other mineral resources, of modernizing her transportation system and harnessing the water power of her rivers. She had to do all this with her own as yet inadequate equipment and know-how. In spite of prolonged disputes with the angered capitalistic powers, the Mexicans ultimately mastered all these tasks. Mexico has lifted herself by her own bootstraps out of the mire of the past. She has conquered the resources of her own soil and liberated herself from economic colonialism.

Like Bolivia, Mexico comes under severe blame by European and American economic experts. They point out that the profitability of mines, oil stocks, and industrial enterprises declined considerably after nationalization. Bolivia was more exposed to this criticism than Mexico, for as we have mentioned Bolivian tin production dropped by 50 per cent in the first decade after the revolution. But the critics forget all too easily that a fundamental change in economic structure is bound to bring such setbacks in its train. The foreign geologists, engineers, and other specialists left with their masters after the revolution. The training of new native specialists took time. Moreover a great variety of social problems such as housing had to be solved. The foreign companies had scarcely concerned themselves with such matters, the cost of which would naturally eat deep into the profit of the nationalized companies. A new government, moreover, lacking international financial relations and economic ties, does not find it easy to compete on the world market with the big established European or American firms. If, in addition, there is an open or concealed boycott against the new government, as was true in the cases of both Mexico and Bolivia, economic setbacks are inevitable.

Nevertheless, Mexico has done so well that she can no longer be counted among the underdeveloped countries in the strict sense of the word. The Mexicans are even in a position to offer assistance to other Latin American countries. At the same time as the industrial revolution took place, however, a slower, less noticed, but far more vital revolution was taking place in Mexican agriculture.

The land is the touchstone of social change in every Latin American country. In Mexico 80 per cent of the population lives by agriculture. Agricultural proletarians and plantation workers, small farmers and tenant farmers form so large a class numerically in the other Latin American countries, as well, that political decisions could be made on the land. Throughout most of Latin America, however, agriculture is to a large extent organized in a feudal way. Hence the cry for agrarian reform which is heard throughout the continent. Castro won in Cuba largely because he appealed to the land hunger of the people. In Latin America the masses on the land are not conservatives but revolutionaries, just as they were in Europe during the peasant wars of the sixteenth century (although the issue then was more a matter of restitution of rights that had been lost). Today Latin American landowners face much the same situation that the great landowners of Europe faced four centuries ago. An economy of latifundia is a colonial economy. That truth remains, however the economists sing praises for the achievements of big landowners and of coffee, sugar, and fruit companies in opening up new soil, pioneering new methods, and investing large amounts of capital.

In prerevolutionary Mexico only 5 per cent of the agricultural population owned their own land. It was poor land which scarcely provided a livelihood for the small farmer. Porfirio Díaz, the dictator, continued the confiscation of the property of communes begun earlier. This forced the great mass of the country people into a condition of dependence upon the large landowners which was equivalent to serfdom. The greatest landowner of all was still the Catholic Church. It owned approximately a third of Mexico's tillable land. The Church's resistance to all agrarian reform was one of the principal reasons for the struggle against the Church during the revolution and for the anticlerical tendencies of the PRI which are apparent to this day.

By a succession of agrarian reforms, the revolutionary government has taken over a large part of the arable land, including church property, and returned it to the village communities. These reforms gradually created a class of small and middling farmers who had at first to lean heavily upon government support to keep going. Irrigation projects were carried out. The government saw to improvement of livestock feed and to fertilization of arable land that had been badly neglected during the era of latifundia. As a result agricultural production in Mexico has more than doubled during the past twenty years. Mexico has dramatically refuted the common claim that agrarian reform necessarily results in a decline in production.

THE NEW AZTECS

All these successes, however, which have made Mexico so dear to Ibero-American social reformers, have been surpassed by a psychological victory which was likewise won on the land. Mexicans have succeeded in freeing themselves from the paralyzing burden of conservative colonial tradition. To be sure, a four-hundred-year period of history cannot be extirpated from the body politic of a nation without damage. To this day Mexico's social, cultural, and religious life is largely rooted in the Spanish past. But the Mexican has rediscovered the *Indian* in himself. Perhaps this is the real source of the energies that are stirring in Mexico today.

The Mexican nation, like the Bolivian, is composed largely of persons of Indian blood. About 55 per cent of the Mexicans are mestizos, part white and part Indian; about 30 per cent are pure Indians, and only about 15 per cent are white. The mestizos of all shadings, moreover, are vigorously engaged in re-Indianization. This process must be held among the most amazing developments taking place in Mexico today. For after the discovery of the New World, the Indians as a cultural group suffered enormous losses in human dignity and inner substance. To be sure, the light-skinned upper classes of Central and South America today like to point out that Spanish laws affecting the native population were more tolerant and humane than those of the English and other conquerors. But law is one thing, practice another. Civilized Indian nations whose artistic, architectural, and political achievements have been admired by the whole world, since archaeology first called attention to them, were reduced by the prophets of colonization to a horde of despised, impoverished, exploited pariahs. That is the fact, nor is it altered by the current literary fashion which—after a century of excessive respect for Mayas and Incas—takes a more reserved view of these ancient societies. The Incas and Aztecs may have been harsh masters, but the sacrifices they demanded of their people cannot be compared with the brutality of the Spaniards who killed off entire peoples.

The greatest damage to the Indian psyche, however, was done not by the Spanish colonial masters but by their successors, the white and half-white Creoles who took possession of the Latin American countries after independence was won. The complete disintegration of Indian culture and the total degradation of the Indians began under conditions of newly acquired freedom. In many of the countries, members of the white-skinned upper class to this day contemptuously refer to the Indian as an "animal," a subhuman, a useless if not harmful marginal member of the human race. The massacres of Indians in Paraguay and Argentina, the murders of Indians at the time of the rubber boom on the Amazon, the ordeals of chained Indian slaves in the silver mines in Mexico, and the impressment of highland Indians for work in the Bolivian mines must be counted among the darkest chapters in Latin American history. Since the days of Alexander von Humboldt, the wretchedness of the proletarianized Indians and mestizos of Central and South America has been described in countless travel books, examined in countless sociological publications. Yet all without effect. Conditions remained the same.

Have they changed in Mexico? Have the twenty-four million brown-skinned Mexicans become so mature politically, so firmly established humanly, that they can be regarded as active citizens of the state? Or are they merely being used as a reservoir of votes?

A glance at the Mexican leadership of the last several decades provides a clear answer to these questions. Most of the presidents, most of the party leaders and parliamentary deputies came and come from the common people. Many pure-blooded Indians are among them. When ex-President Cárdenas, a part Tarasco Indian, rides horseback from his native village to the capital (in spite of his advanced age he disdains to this day to use an automobile), he is greeted on his way with more applause than his successors. The applause is meant not just for his political record, or for his radicalism; it is a tribute to Cárdenas the *Indian.* And when the Mexicans gaze at the colossal frescoes of Diego Rivera in the National Palace or other government buildings of the capital—avant-garde paintings in which the revolution is represented as a victory of the Indians over the Spaniards—the little man identifies himself with those revolutionary Indians.

Tourists and travel writers all too often describe Rivera and his pupils, Orozco and Siqueiros, as political fanatics who see no good at all in the Spanish period. The Mexicans, however, take a different view. To them the message of those paintings is utterly self-evident. Those historical paintings that adorn the walls of Mexico City are, to be sure, scarcely done in a spirit of meekness and mildness—but the Spaniards, too, did not write history with a gentle hand.

The revival of Indian participation in political life has also produced a renaissance of Indian art. Mexican architects use elements of Aztec style; Mexican sculptors produce abstract versions of ancient Indian sculpture. The vast University of Mexico City with its pyramidal and cubic buildings might be some palace complex of the Aztec Empire. With its forty thousand students incidentally, it is one of the largest universities in the world. Nor are these neo-Mexican architects, sculptors, and painters imitators laboriously trying to resurrect a time long past. They have developed something wholly new out of the elements of Indian culture in their past. And it can be said without exaggeration that in so doing they have greatly enriched modern art in the rest of the world.

The traveler in Mexico has the feeling that a people who have lain asleep for four hundred years have suddenly awakened and realized their full strength. Mexico needs a great deal of strength, for it is still a land of vast misery and vast ignorance. The education of the Indians, however, is progressing faster there than in any other Latin American country. Illiteracy has been enormously reduced. The self-assurance of the meanest rustic has greatly increased. In Mexico the Indians have proved that they are by no means condemned by nature to the role of inferiors, as the light-skinned upper class in other Indian countries continues to assert. Given equal opportunities, their performance is equal to that of their white fellow citizens. Awareness of this fact has fundamentally changed the attitude toward life of Mexicans of Indian blood. The Indio inferiority complex, from which every non-white-skinned Latin American has consciously or unconsciously suffered, has been overcome in Mexico.

Yet this opportunity would never have been offered to the Mexican Indians but for the revolution from above. By himself the Indio would scarcely have been able to work his way up to the level of the whites. The long history of oppression had done too much psychological damage, had left too many qualities buried, shattered, choked off. Freedom accompanied by ignorance would have resulted in inconceivable disaster. There are examples enough of that in Latin American history—as there were in the initial stages of the Mexican Revolution. The Indian, ignorant of the rules of the democratic game, needed skillful, understanding leadership in order to make up for all that he had missed intellectually, culturally, and politically for four hundred years. His ignorance was the fault of his white masters, but the ignorance was there. For that reason the Mexican Revolution had to devolve into a one-party state; and for that reason Diego Rivera had to glorify the Aztecs and vilify Cortez in his frescoes.

The elimination of the Indian inferiority complex was the greatest act of the Mexican Revolution. Undoubtedly "permanent revolution" has much more than that to its credit. We have already spoken of its economic policy, an interesting, often turbulent, but on the whole successful economic policy. The economic upsurge in Mexico in the past twenty years stands in happy contrast to the economic calamities of other Latin American countries. Critics of the new Mexico like to attribute these successes to Mexico's having profited by the Second World War. But that should also be true for other Central and South American countries which likewise did a thriving business as suppliers of raw materials to the United States. Mexico, however, invested her profits in the country itself, whereas elsewhere small groups of profiteers merely pocketed the gains.

The economic skill that the Mexicans have demonstrated in times of crisis is amazing enough in itself. But what most commends the mild party dictatorship in Mexico is the human dignity it has restored to the Indians.

THE STANDARDS ARE DIFFERENT

In these introductory pages I have so far spoken little of parliamentary democracy, of protection of property, of free economy, of intellectual tolerance, and other ideals to which most of the Western world is deeply attached. Instead, I have been using words and phrases that must necessarily disturb the ordinary citizen of America or Europe. I have spoken of uprisings, expropriations, division of the land, nationalization of mines and sources of energy, workers' militias, struggle against foreign influence. Many such matters remain to be discussed, for Latin America cannot be measured by our standards. The selfsame principles that guarantee political, economic, and personal freedom to Europeans and North Americans may, if applied in Latin America, lead only to the consolidation of serfdom. Colonialism is far from dead in the Ibero-American region. It merely bears another name.

Of what value is the principle of protection of property to the Latin American if he himself has no property? Why should he prize a free economy if it barely guarantees him the minimum he needs to survive? What good is democracy to him if he is not allowed to vote? And of what use to him are our ideals if they apply only to the oligarchy and not to the common people? It is not surprising that popular movements in Latin America have had to follow other paths than are being pursued in the rest of the Western world. Some of these directions are without doubt deplorable, for those groups who have hitherto regarded the South American Continent as a convenient source of easy profits. But the direction taken by the popular movements can be a threat to the Western world only if the attempt is made, for selfish reasons, to check them. In other words, only if these countries are treated as Cuba was.

Our mention of Cuba raises a serious question that has been asked repeatedly in recent years whenever Latin American reform movements come under discussion. The question is: are the measures which are being taken in Mexico and were being tried in Bolivia not exactly the same as those on which Fidel Castro's revolutionary program is based?

The answer is yes! They are basically the same. But while Cuba, boycotted by the United States and outlawed by the Western world, has been driven into the arms of the Soviet Union, Mexico and Bolivia have, after some vacillation, long since been accepted by the Western camp. Although Mexico continues to expropriate whenever she feels the need, although she maintains unclouded relations with the Soviet Union and consistently votes against American Cuban policy, she receives sizable credit and gifts from the United States. North American money has enabled Mexico, among other things, to make exemplary improvements in her road network. This has been happening in spite of the fact that the left wing of the government party is periodically denounced for communistic leanings.

Here we have still another riddle, so it seems. In order to solve it, we must examine what really happened in Cuba. In Cuba, too, the leaders have read Marx, but they have also read the writings of Abraham Lincoln; they have read the history of the Mexican Revolution; they have read books of all shades describing national struggles for liberation. The intellectual platform for the Cuban Revolution was not one of reformed socialism as in Mexico or Bolivia, but one of emphatic nationalism. The overthrow of the Batista regime in Cuba was a far cry from a Marxist revolution, and still more remote from the revolutionary program in Mexico.

Nevertheless, Khrushchev embraced Fidel Castro. Nevertheless, today Cuba calls herself a People's Democracy. Who or what is to blame for this situation?

A MAN FROM THE BUSH

Eleven months after the victory of Fidel Castro's revolution, I took a cab in the small east Cuban town of Holguín and rode into the mountainous forests in which the bearded guerrillas had fought. When I hired the cab, the driver was delighted as a child: it was near Christmas and as a result of the decline in tourism he no longer had a peso in his pocket. In fact, he first had to borrow money from

another driver in order to fill his tank with gasoline. To express his
joy, as we started off he sang at the top of his voice the song of
the Castro revolutionaries: "*Adelante, Cubanos! Viva la revolución!*"

It turned out to be a strange ride. Again and again the driver
stopped. Cubans, some of them wearing the beards that identified
them as fighters in the revolution, came up and asked whether they
could ride along part of the way, and when I nodded to them they
crowded into the cab or stood on the running board, grinning at me,
patting the driver on the back, and also singing: "*Adelante, Cubanos! . . .*" When they got out, others got in and again the singing
went on: "*Viva la revolución!*" Night fell. The road went through
wooded valleys cut by deep gorges. Here and there a solitary bonfire
glowed in the dark landscape and the rattle of the ancient vehicle,
the laboring of its senile motor, was drowned out by the loud and
enthusiastic "*Viva la revolución! Viva Fidel!*" It was so infectious
that in the end I sang along with them, for these people were
sincerely rejoicing.

Among others who sincerely rejoiced were the dark-skinned little
enthusiastic "*Viva la revolución! Viva Fidel!*" It was so infectious
the portrait of the bearded Fidel in the dust of the streets, all the
while chanting in cha-cha-cha rhythm the song of the *barbudos*, the
victorious revolutionaries. And the colored folk of Havana also rejoiced. Before the revolution they had stayed inside their slums on the
fringes of the luxury quarter; now they sauntered cheerfully through
the best streets. For Castro had transformed the formerly white
metropolis of La Habana into a rich medley of races—not without a
side glance at the wicked Southerners of the United States, as if to
say: In our country the colored people enjoy full civil rights. The
petty clerks of Havana's business firms also rejoiced. As they explained, in the past they had not in the least been interested in
politics, but now they were going back to school in order to fit
themselves for government service "for now we are free and are no
longer working for foreign interests."

During the months of November and December 1959 I rode through
a laughing, singing country, a country exuberant with relief, a country
whose population was working as never before—on innumerable building sites, in the co-operatives of the INRA, the Cuban land reform
organization, in the newly built schools, in the fashionable seaside
resorts, which were to be made into beaches for the people, in the

villages and the big cities. The stores were full, prices were low. I saw no signs of the famine which was direly predicted by the world press. I saw discontented and anxious faces only when I visited fine villas, business houses, or air-conditioned clubs. From these, people were already preparing to fly to Miami, but at the end of 1959 these opponents of Castro represented only a minute proportion of the Cuban people.

Beforehand, I had imagined that the sights behind Cuba's Sugar Curtain would resemble what one saw behind Europe's Iron Curtain. And during the first few hours I spent in Cuba I did, in fact, notice a few superficial parallels between the Red dictatorships of the East and the Cuban revolutionary dictatorship. Again and again I came across bearded men with submachine guns standing in front of buildings, ardently guarding something. But with the worst will in the world these *barbudos* could not be compared with the people's militia or the people's police of Eastern European countries. It was easy to get into conversation with them and the talk was always friendly and frequently cordial. And then, when they learned that I was not an American, they put their weapons in a corner, told tales about the fighting in the mountains, and complained about those malicious newspapermen who called them communists when they were merely Cuban patriots. After smoking two or three cigarettes with them, I was usually permitted, with their benevolent tolerance, to enter the sacrosanct area they were guarding. I was allowed to take photographs where signs read that cameras were strictly forbidden. I doubt that there is any country of the Eastern bloc where such laxness would ever have been possible.

During that first year after the revolution, Cuba was anything but a police state. The island was only prey to a mass intoxication like nothing it had ever known before. It seemed as if the revolution had turned the entire nation inside out, as though it had exposed the most hidden depths of Cuban souls. Singing songs and chanting slogans, the sugar workers marched into the cities to hail Castro, who would at last be giving land to them, the eternally landless. Waving little flags, children poured through the streets. Everywhere groups gathered; everywhere the speeches of the revolutionary heroes, which poured in a steady stream from the loudspeakers, were loudly applauded. It must be added, however, that this interminable speechifying aroused disturbing memories, as did the endless signs and posters, streamers and scribbled slogans.

What was going on in Cuba? An orgiastic discharge of the repressions of the mass psyche? A blind leader cult, something only too familiar to us Europeans? Inevitably, in view of all the parades and the bellowing of the loudspeakers, every Western visitor to Cuba finds such comparisons forced upon him. For Castro is a skilled propagandist and has learned from every predecessor who had anything to teach him. The shouting, singing reactions to his demagogic tricks were suspiciously reminiscent of brown and red party demonstrations. Nevertheless the Cubans were genuinely rejoicing.

DICTATORSHIP BY CASTRATION

The Cubans were genuinely rejoicing, for Castro had liberated them from a bloody tyranny which belonged among the darkest periods in their history. It is probable that in 1959 most Cubans applauded their bearded Fidel not from ideological reasons but only because they hoped to be able to breathe freely at last, after an era of cruel oppression. In those days there were Castro followers in every stratum of the population. Conservatives and liberals, nationalists and Marxists, syndicalists and anarchists had joined together because they had had enough of the dictatorship of Fulgencio Batista. But the majority of his admirers consisted of the ordinary people, the unpolitical people for whom things had gone anything but well in the sixty-year history of the Cuban republic and who now fixed their hopes upon this new man—who wore the nimbus of victory.

The dictatorship of Fulgencio Batista, which gave rise to the Castro revolution, had nearly perfected the techniques of the police state in a manner hitherto achieved by very few Latin American rulers. Kidnaping, torture, mutilation, mass hanging, and mass shooting of political opponents had become commonplace in Fulgencio Batista's Cuba. If there was trouble in any city or village, Batista's police hanged any convenient victim from the nearest lamppost. It did not matter whether the victim was guilty or innocent; the point was to terrify the populace.

It was "dictatorship by castration," as a North American newspaper once described the character of the Batista regime. Under Batista's rule the Cuban unions were transformed into gangster syndicates that controlled the workers by terror and extortion. Under Batista, Havana, Cuba's capital, became a gigantic gambling hell, America's brothel, where North American tourists could engage in all the vices forbidden in their own country. Batista himself took a share of the profits of the amusement industry, which yielded him a royal income.

But Cuban history resembles a merry-go-round. For this same ruthless scoundrel Fulgencio Batista had once—twenty-five years before his fall—denounced a similar butcher, trumpeting anticapitalist and social reform slogans just like Castro's. He could call himself (with far more justification than Castro) a man of the people, for he had started out as a banana picker and bartender, had then entered the army, risen to the rank of sergeant, and organized that famous revolution of the "noncoms," which put an end to the bloody era of his predecessor, the dictator Gerardo Machado. Possibly Batista had studied Machado's life too thoroughly, for Machado too had begun his career as a social reformer and ended as a mass murderer. As I have said, Cuba's history is a merry-go-round.

The portrait I have sketched of Fulgencio Batista is a fairly ugly one. There exist friendlier pictures of the former Cuban dictator, just as there were more favorable pictures of Hitler, representing the German tyrant as a smiling benefactor of his people who put an end to unemployment and set up a host of new industries. The ruler who wields unlimited power and has unlimited means at his disposal can create housing, factories, and highways out of nothing if such projects suit his schemes. Hitler did, Batista did, the majority of dictators do. The fact that the people pay for these things with blood, sweat and tears is omitted from the reckoning, or is discovered only when the final score is drawn up. Only afterward did the United States realize the guilt it had incurred by its support of Batista. Despite their passion for freedom and democracy, the North Americans for a long time had an unfortunate weakness for Latin American dictators. While the United States went to war against fascism in Europe, in Ibero-America she zealously supplied Latin "fascism" with dollars. The reason was simple: she needed political tools to secure her economic interests in Latin America.

For six decades the real masters of Cuba, though they remained very much in the shadows, were the American sugar companies. They were exceedingly tolerant as far as dictators were concerned. They allowed Machado to carry on his murderous activities. They were not perturbed when other Cuban presidents indulged in the corruption which was customary, or even made off to Miami with the national treasury. They permitted Batista to carry out tortures and murders on a mass scale. All they asked was that peace and good order should prevail on the island of sugar. By peace and good order the companies meant the preservation of existing conditions, as far as that was possible.

Yet there were those in the United States who found these conditions shocking. "They scarcely differ from the conditions in the old colonial era," as one New York newspaper put it. As Bolivia depended on its tin, Venezuela on its oil, Brazil on its coffee, and Central America on its bananas, Cuba depended on its sugar—a one-crop culture which blocked all healthy economic development. The economy could be kept going only by guaranteed purchases from the United States. Moreover, sugar work is seasonal work; the landless and propertyless day laborers worked only for a few months a year on the sugar plantations. The rest of the time they idled about the streets.

Cuba is rich in resources. Her iron ore reserves are estimated at three and one half billion tons. Ninety per cent of these reserves were owned by North American steel companies and were not exploited because the companies did not want to compete with themselves. Hence, the Cubans did not benefit from their wealth of ore. Among the few who did well in Fulgencio Batista's Cuba were those who worked in the ports and in the tourist industry. As a result of the influx of tourists, attracted to the island by the bathing resorts, the gambling casinos, and the dens of vice, the government's income had risen sharply in the last years before the revolution. Cuba was thereby provided with a garish, glittering façade which furthered the illusion that things were really not bad under the dictatorship of Batista and the sugar monopolies.

Tourists are easily taken in by such façades. In Cuba, they did not see the political system with its accompaniments of military domination, parasitism, corruption, and outright murder. Industry and agriculture were unstable and were kept going only by grace of subsidies. Freedom of speech was unknown. Social conditions were such as to arouse widespread discontent among the agricultural workers, the intellectuals, and the middle class. Such conditions provide ideal soil for political radicalism, strikes, uprisings, and attempted coups. In Cuba there had never been any lack of these, ever since the island achieved its independence from Spain in 1898.

Yet such disturbances were precisely what the sugar companies wished to avert. They had already had a good deal of trouble in Cuba and had suffered many a financial loss. To put the matter bluntly, undisturbed continuance of their profitable business was more important to them than the liberalization and democratization of the Cuban Government. For North American finance had invested about one billion dollars in Cuba.

Therefore the sugar companies almost invariably supported the strong men whose names have studded Cuban history. As far as they were concerned, a harsh dictator was a good dictator. They ignored the revelations of Batista's torture and terror as reported by American newspapers. They did not mind even if Cuban rulers dropped bombs and used artillery against rebellious villages. The American government, too, in the pre-Kennedy era, influenced by the lobbyists of these same companies, closed its eyes to what was going on under the Batista dictatorship (just as it did in the cases of Trujillo, Pérez Jiménez, and Somoza). In the era of John Foster Dulles, Washington even helped Batista on several occasions in his brutal suppression of strikes and supplied the weapons he needed to put down rebellions. And when half the Cuban people had already gone over to Castro, one of the leading American businessmen in Havana voiced the significant remark: "Every day we pray that nothing will happen to Batista."

ADVENTURER OR POPULAR HERO?

The inevitable result of this situation was that the Cuban Revolution acquired a distinctly anti-American tone. In the eyes of the bearded revolutionaries, Batista was the *Yanquis'* man, in the direct employ of the rich neighbor to the north. A further source of antagonism between Cuba and America arose out of Castro's social program.

Castro had already drafted this program before the beginning of the revolution, during his exile in Mexico. He had obviously learned a good deal from the Mexicans. The program was no redder, no more radical than that of ex-President Cárdenas or of the MNR in Bolivia. Castro demanded what the Mexican revolutionaries had once demanded and obtained: nationalization of the means of distribution, breakup of the large plantations, socialization of a part of industry, development of the mineral reserves, resettlement of landless plantation workers, and finally confiscation of all fortunes that had been acquired with the aid of the corrupt dictatorship. But since the greater part of the plantations, business enterprises, and property values were in North American hands, Castro was regarded from the first day of the revolution as a potentially dangerous adventurer.

To many North Americans, Cárdenas in Mexico had similarly been a potentially dangerous adventurer whom they combated with all means at their disposal. Nevertheless the United States had long since made it up with Mexico. Would it not be possible to come to an agreement with Castro also? Batista had run amok so ferociously in the last months of the revolution that at first the sympathies of the American press (and of the American public also) spontaneously turned toward the bearded rebel. We may suppose that the sugar companies also began slowly revising their opinions. With his mass persecutions and mass shootings, Batista had gone too far. It was recalled that after all Batista was nothing but a megalomaniac sergeant, of mulatto extraction, moreover, with whom it was really no longer possible to collaborate. Castro, however, was of a fine old Spanish family, the son of a wealthy sugar plantation owner, and had early distinguished himself as a brilliant lawyer.

Perhaps it was hoped that this rebellious member of the upper class would come to his senses again once the intoxication of revolution had worn off. Batista, too, had quickly become reasonable after the success of his revolution, after all. Castro seemed to be just another strong man—"an overwhelming personality, with ideals, with courage and with remarkable qualities of leadership," as one American newspaper report put it. Possibly he would develop into a superior Batista, more cultivated, less cruel, less bloodthirsty, and less corrupt—a popular dictator with whom it would be easy to come to an understanding.

That conclusion was a fateful error. The American intelligence agencies and the State Department informers had overlooked the fact that the Castro rebellion was not an ordinary *coup d'état* but a popular revolution, the third genuine popular revolution in Latin America after the Mexican and the Bolivian revolutions.

Batista possessed the most formidable army in the Ibero-American area. His forty thousand soldiers were opposed at the outset by only a few hundred rebels—toward the end of the revolution by at most three thousand. Without the support of the majority of the people this tiny, ill-equipped band could never have had a chance. But the people were obviously on the side of Castro. And once the waves of a mass delirium had carried the bearded rebels into Havana, it should have been clear that a historic event had taken place and that the clock could no longer be turned back. Castro *had to* carry out his program.

The structure of the Cuban population differs significantly from that of the Mexican and Bolivian populations. The Indian element is lacking in Cuba, aside from a few persons of mixed blood whose pitch-black hair and prominent cheekbones indicate that they have still preserved some of the physical characteristics of the aboriginal inhabitants. About 70 per cent of the Cubans are whites of Spanish origin; 28 per cent are Negroes and mulattoes. There are, in addition, a great many Chinese living in the cities and villages who intermarry freely with other Cubans. For many years Havana was the springboard for illegal Chinese immigration into North America, and those Chinese who did not make it remained on the island.

No significant color barriers exist. The fact that Batista had a little Negro blood bothered no one in Cuba and was remembered at all only by racially conscious North Americans after the dictator's star had begun to decline. Before the revolution the number of illiterates amounted to about 20 per cent—that is, far less than in most Central American countries. In the countryside, however, in Batista's day, about half the children of school age received no education because Batista preferred building barracks to new schools. Nevertheless, Cuba was a far more favorable area for political reforms than Mexico, let alone Bolivia.

The average Cuban is a friendly, openhearted person who has grown up with Western traditions and who is accustomed to the good things of Western civilization. I can compare the cordiality and hospitality of Cubans only with the cordiality and hospitality of Brazilians and Chileans. In these three countries people seem to carry their hearts in their hands. By contrast, the masklike faces of Mexican and Bolivian Indians seem to belong to another world; they are alien, aloof, unapproachable, and impenetrable.

AMERICA PLAYS WITH FIRE

Yet in spite of these positive factors, relations with Cuba were disastrously mismanaged. Today Castro is the bugbear of both Americas, the chief troublemaker of the hemisphere. Even objective and sober-minded politicians have nothing good to say for him. Only the realistic French are apparent exceptions, for in spite of the boycott the West has imposed upon Cuba, De Gaulle has sent his experts to look into possibilities for investments in Cuba. Since the Cuban revolutionary leader has taken his country into the Eastern camp and dotted the island with Soviet rocket bases, no Western observer, aside from the French, has been able to look at Cuban developments with the impartiality of the historian. Anyone who has proposed the unconventional, not to say, heretical proposition that the dangerous trends in Cuba are due not to the wickedness or fanaticism of Fidel Castro, but to a great many errors of omission or commission by the United States, has been immediately suspected of being himself either a Castroite or a Communist.

Yet it is this very attitude that prevents a solution of the Cuban problem. If the West refuses to recognize what has really happened in Cuba and what could have been done to prevent the Cuban Revolution from veering to the left, it is liable to misinterpret other (and no less inevitable) historical developments in Latin America, to damn them as heresies, and drive them toward the East. Cuba can serve as a lesson—unfortunately a negative lesson—to us in the Western world.

The United States made many mistakes in Cuba and is to blame for a great deal. It is not only that America supported Batista as she supported in Asia a Syngman Rhee, a Chiang Kai-shek, and a Ngo Dinh Diem. Grave as it was, this political blunder would not have sufficed to make Castro a partisan of the East and to transform Cuba into a satellite of Moscow. America has supported and financed many a dictator—in Venezuela, in the Dominican Republic, in Peru, in Mexico. But in every case in which the United States, after the overthrow of the dictators, aligned herself on the side of the reformers in good time, the new government quickly forgot the offenses of the past.

If at least after the end of the revolution Washington had seriously looked into the mood of the Cuban people, American business would probably have realized that it had no choice but to accept the revolution and adjust to it as a historical fact. In 1959 the United States was faced with the problem of finding a *modus vivendi* with the new regime. That problem was perfectly soluble. I realized that clearly as I drove through the Cuban countryside. It was forcibly impressed upon me in every conversation I had with Cubans. There was no other way to keep Cuba aligned with the West.

The solution would have been bought at a price, but a smaller one than is being paid now. The Cuban reform program would undoubtedly have injured the interests of the sugar companies, the steel firms, and the financial institutions with investments in Cuba. But those interests are not necessarily identical with the interests of the Western world. The freedom and security of the West were not shaken when Mexico and Iran nationalized their oil resources, when Indonesia carried out her program of nationalization, and when Bolivia took over her tin mines. Historical forces which have led to the political withdrawal from colonies would also necessitate a withdrawal from economic colonies. If Washington had smiled upon the program for Cuban agrarian and social reform and had given vigorous aid to the much-tried island, Cuba would in all probability have vanished from the headlines of the world's newspapers years ago.

But was an arrangement with the rebels possible at all? The tendency nowadays is to deny that; Castro is made out to have been a "wild man," with whom no one could speak a reasonable word. Nevertheless, arrangements have proved possible with Nasser, Sukarno, and Kwame Nkrumah, exotic politicians who were also at one time denounced as wild men. Arrangements will have to be arrived at with the revolutionary governments in Algeria, in Guinea, and in Yemen. I am convinced that a Castroism tolerated by the United States would, after casting its skin a few times, have followed the pattern of the revolutions in Mexico and Bolivia. Russia is on the other side of the globe; Cuba is a Latin American country and the broad masses of its people have no concrete notion of communist ideology. What the Cubans needed, after their revolution, was help and understanding. In their situation they would not have rejected any hand offered to them. Not even the hand of their big neighbor to the north. For, as Nietzsche said, people have to love one another if they cannot escape one another.

Initially, Castro by no means put on the guise of an especially ferocious expropriator. He was prepared to pay compensation for the factories and land he intended to nationalize, on the usual repayment schedule of twenty to twenty-five years, which the British and Americans had worked out with Mexico. To be sure, Castro hit on the cunning idea of assigning to the properties in question the values their owners had given in their tax declarations. Thus he pricked one of the nastiest boils in the body politic of Latin America: the dishonesty of big capitalists in regard to taxation. That the companies responded to this proposal with shrieks of indignation is understandable enough from their point of view. But it is incomprehensible that the State Department should have joined in the outcry.

The great error of United States policy was to place the interest of certain moneyed groups above the interest of her own security and that of her allies. In 1959 America had already missed the one chance out of the Cuba dilemma. Instead of meeting Castro halfway, she had turned her back on him. What had Washington imagined would happen after that? Did anyone intend to bring Batista back to Havana by force? Did they have any thought of establishing a new dictator? Did Washington imagine that Castro could be forced to his knees, so that he would give up his projects? If any such ideas were held, none were realistic. It was clear even then that an American boycott would impel the Cubans to look around for other allies, whose presence in Cuba would be far more costly for the United States than the most generous concessions to the Castro regime.

Certainly no world power likes to capitulate before threats and demands from a petty island revolutionary. It was bitter for France to withdraw from Algeria. England did not enjoy giving up her colonial empire. It was certainly not pleasant for the Dutch to yield to American pressure and surrender their excellently governed colony of New Guinea to the Indonesians. And the United States was not amused when Lázaro Cárdenas, in 1938, expropriated the Anglo-American oil companies. Nevertheless, the French, British, Dutch, and Americans ultimately swallowed such unpleasant morsels. The Americans yielded in Mexico because they had to consider the world situation, particularly the dangers that might arise in a Second World War, which was already in the offing. Enmity with Mexico might easily have brought war to America's door.

In 1959 the world situation was just as tense. America should have given the same consideration to the Soviet danger as she had twenty years before given to the danger of Hitler. Circumspection was as necessary in 1959 as it had been in 1938, and the island of Cuba cried out for economic and social reform as urgently as Mexico had in the time of Cárdenas.

But the United States in Roosevelt's day apparently had greater sensitivity for political tacking than the United States in the days of John Foster Dulles. Although the powerful Soviet Union lurked in the wings, Cuba was boycotted by America, outlawed, and expelled from the community of the Western world.

The fact that Castro himself, by his arrogant behavior, contributed to this outcome is no excuse. The leaders of other young nations have often behaved with offensive arrogance. Nasser had no reason to be friendly to England. Sukarno had no reason to love Holland. Ben Bella had no reason to feel grateful to France. Similarly, Castro had no reason to embrace America. But if neighbors wish to live side by side in peace, they must try to understand one another and come to an agreement even though there is much cause for animosity. Washington never really sought a basis for accord with Cuba. On the contrary, the sharp American warning to Castro, that serious consequences would result if he put his program of agrarian reform into effect, was a slap in the face that inevitably heightened the fanaticism of an already fanatic revolutionary. And the American decision to stop buying sugar from Cuba was anything but a clever stroke of diplomacy. Castro was then forced to look around for other buyers, and he found them in the Eastern camp.

Washington's Cuba policy, then, was the greatest mistake the United States had made since the unfortunate decision which led to the partition of Germany. Had the State Department really given no thought to the fact that another power was standing by, ready to reap what it had not sowed, as always in such cases? Had it been forgotten how much ground this power had gained in Asia as a result of antiquated policies of economic colonialism? Did Washington imagine that after the first threats of boycott Castro would hastily throw his reform plans into the fire and follow the example of Batista in smashing the revolutionary *esprit* he had awakened in his people? Was the American intelligence service so ill-informed as to believe the liberal wing of the revolution would be able to overthrow the hero of the people? And did America have another attractive system

to offer to the Cubans? One that would guide the Cuban mass intoxication into moderate channels? Nothing of the kind. One can only
wonder what the State Department was thinking of when it conceived its measures against Castro.

WHAT HAPPENED BEHIND THE SUGAR CURTAIN?

The dénouement was inevitable. Castro, still entirely inexperienced
at governing a country, plunged into the gratifying role of the popular
hero who was being driven too far by events, and primarily by
American reprisals.

Under normal circumstances this ambitious, somewhat unstable, but
extremely talented man would scarcely have become a thorn in the
side of the whole world. His predecessors in Cuba, in their brutality,
their lack of ideas, their defects of character, and their utter corruption, had almost all been far more unpleasant personalities. It is
impossible to say how Castro would have developed had he been
given time and breathing space to grow into the role of a head of state.
Unquestionably he had been, from the very outset of his struggle,
passionately committed to his ideals and to his people. And those
ideals were no worse than the dreams and illusions of other rebels and
popular leaders who have won places for themselves in the history of
Latin America. Castro was faced with the decision either of surrender-
ing his aims or accomplishing them with Communist aid. That is a
decision that even more seasoned statesmen find hard indeed, as
recent history shows. It became the reef on which the Cuban Revolution foundered.

The die was cast in Cuba by the summer of 1959, although there
were still no clear signals of the stormy weather ahead. As in Mexico
and Bolivia, the revolutionary movement in Cuba also had two wings.
The liberal wing was farsighted enough to recognize the dangers of
contact with the East; but in view of the American attitude it had no
practical alternative to offer to the Cubans. Consequently the left
wing won out. Castro forced the resignation of President Manuel
Urrutia and five liberal ministers of the revolutionary government who
did not want to collaborate on an anti-American course. With the
elimination of these anti-Communists from the government, there
was no one to oppose the policy of closer ties with the East. And now
Fidel Castro went off the deep end. The revolutionary hero suddenly

discovered the Marxist inside himself. He sold his sugar to the East and thereby sold himself and his revolution to the East.

To undernourished Latin Americans, living in misery and scarcely acquainted with freedom, communism is in any case no such specter as it is to members of Western countries. A man whose greatest concern is to feed himself and his children is usually more interested in wages and bread than in political ideology.

Thus the Cuban Sugar Curtain gradually became an Iron Curtain. Although ships from Western ports continued to dock in the islands and tourists were not yet kept out, the power shifts in the hierarchy which took place during the next few years remained obscure and can now only be guessed at. Groups of Soviet and Czech experts established themselves in Cuba. Ernesto Guevara, an old Communist from Argentina, took over a central key position in the new government and for a time seemed to wield more power than Castro himself. Economically Cuba became merely a recipient of alms from the Soviet Union. Politically and militarily it became a strong point of the East in the Western Hemisphere.

Step by step, the great drama of Cuban liberty became a tragedy. The elation of the Cubans leaked away in the grayness of everyday life in a pseudo-communist state. Prices rose, shops were emptied, food supplies dwindled. Once again the people saw themselves betrayed. Once again a popular hero became an oppressor. Once again the pattern so familiar in Cuban history began: terror, arrests, and shooting. Blind and helpless, a football in world politics, Cuba reeled from the tyranny of the Batista regime to the tyranny of communism. At first, however, in the grip of rising hatred for the *Yanquis*, this may not have been so clear to many Cubans—perhaps not even to Fidel Castro himself.

Meanwhile the United States continued to intervene clumsily in the Cuban tragedy. A single thread runs from the kindly welcome given the Batista followers who had fled to Miami to the disastrous attempted invasion at the Bay of Pigs, and that dangerous threat in 1962 which could have set the world in flames. Although John Kennedy originally had taken a very different and far friendlier attitude toward Castro than John Foster Dulles, he too seemed unable to extricate himself from the toils of ill-advised policy. Among the many thousands of exiled Cubans who have transformed Miami virtually into a Latin American city, there are undoubtedly a good many idealists. Among them are disillusioned followers of Fidel Castro who are genuinely concerned for the liberty of their country. But these are in a minority; the majority consists of members of the former Batista Gestapo, or members of the Cuban oligarchy who are not particularly interested in the fate of the people as a whole. Nevertheless, it was years before the American State Department decided to keep such elements at arm's length. Only since 1964 has the United States come to accept the thought that there is only one course open to it: preservation of the *status quo* in Cuba.

KARL MARX AND THE BARBUDOS

But what is this *status quo* like? Castro and the other revolutionary leaders in Cuba may be demagogues, perhaps unpleasant demagogues, to our minds; they may be inciters of the masses; they may behave with the utmost arrogance; they may have other unengaging personal characteristics. But aside from men like Guevara and Franqui, most of them were not Communists well into the first year of the new regime. In the West we are by now so used to dividing humanity into Communists and anti-Communists that we have become quite blind to other shadings. Among the followers of Castro are nationalists, liberals, anarchists, agrarian and industrial socialists, as well as a number of well-trained Communists. The Castro revolution was initially supported by conservatives, by a part of the clergy, by the intelligentsia, by students, young army officers, and a great part of the common people. The Communist Party, which in the beginning comprised some thirty thousand members, took part, as it usually does in all upheavals.

At the end of the revolution the direction that Cuba would take was still unpredictable. Her future course depended not on the East, but in large part on skillful maneuvering by the West. An objective and benevolent attitude toward the Cuban reform program would certainly have reconciled a majority of the revolutionaries to the United States. Cuba had fixed her hopes upon the United States. Nor does it matter very much whether Castro's Marxism was genuine or not. At first Castro vigorously denied Marxist leanings; later he proclaimed them just as vigorously. And a real Marxist, the Soviet statesman Mikoyan, was so puzzled by the Fidelist variety of Marxism that in 1962 after visiting Cuba he declared, shaking his head: "Castro is simply a madman!"

To any party-line Marxist, a man like Castro must really seem insane, for Latin American reform movements do not have party lines —not in Mexico, not in Bolivia, and not in Cuba. A violent jump to the left may be succeeded by an equally violent jump to the right. Good relations with the Church may be followed by strong anti-clericalism, hatred of *Yanquis* by trade agreements with the United States, collaboration with the Communists with a ban on the Communist Party. The Latin American improvises; he adjusts to circumstances; the end justifies the means, the paths he chooses, and the collaborators he elects. Castroism might have taken any number of turns.

The Cubans probably were rather pleased when the Soviets set up their rocket bases on the island. Not that they wanted to turn their island over to the Russians—rather, they regarded the Russian rockets as excellent insurance against new attempts at American invasion. And when the Soviets yielded to American pressure and began dismantling the rocket bases, they lost a good deal of their popularity with the Cubans. If the Soviet Union should someday completely evacuate its advanced Cuban bridgehead for practical reasons, the Cuban regime would in all probability make another about-face—at best in the direction of Mexico, at worst, in the direction of Red China.

Lately, as a matter of fact, the Russians have seemed more interested in a neutralist Cuba than in a Soviet satellite which costs them a million dollars a day. Since 1964 the Kremlin has repeatedly indicated that it would be pleased by restoration of normal relations between the United States and Cuba. The consequence of this Russian compromise policy, however, is that the Cubans behaved more radically than ever. A number of pro-Soviet Communists have been expelled from Castro's revolutionary party. Red China has carried on vigorous propaganda in Cuba, accusing not only the Americans but also the Soviets of sinister, imperialistic machinations. And Cuba's former minister of economics, the Communist Guevara, in his radio talks from time to time voiced arguments which were not too remote from those of the Red Chinese. If the United States and the Soviet Union began a policy of rapprochement at the expense of Cuba, the Red Chinese might very soon prove to be the real victors of the Cuban Revolution. For the present, however, it looks as if Cuba is choosing closer ties to Moscow out of necessity; she seems to prefer peaceful coexistence to Peking's militant revolutionary thesis. In 1965 Guevara resigned his posts and left the island; the full background of this step has not yet been clarified, but it may mean a highly significant shift in Cuban power-relationships. It is also astonishing that Castro—contrary to the inhuman practices that are customary in most countries of the Eastern bloc, which have reached their peak in the Berlin Wall—permits discontented citizens to emigrate freely.

Cuba also illustrates the fact that Ibero-American social revolutions are far from doctrinaire; indeed, that they are extremely flexible. This should contravene the obsession that the many radical parties and groups now mobilizing the peoples of Central and South America are dominated by communist ideology. To this day, European and American businessmen continue to lump even moderate social reformers like Haya de la Torre, in Peru, or democratic Socialists like the left wing of the Brazilian workers' party together with Communists.

To the moneyed aristocracy of Latin America, the word *socialist* has much the same sound as the word *communist* to Europeans and Americans. In Venezuela even the anticommunist President Betancourt, a stout opponent of Castro, is so dubbed because he stands for a measure of social reform. The Venezuelan currency has, since the beginning of his presidency, been contemptuously called the "socialist dollar" by Latin American businessmen. This sort of obduracy naturally does not endear the moneyed aristocracy to the reform-minded factions of Latin America.

The reform movement in Central and South America has certain ideals, certain intentions, certain aims which are dictated by the conditions of each country. In each case there are good reasons for such reforms on a continent which has lagged far behind Europe and North America in its social, political, cultural, and economic development. If these ideals, intentions and aims cannot be accomplished with the aid of the West, there is always the danger that the reformers will try to accomplish them with the aid of the East. The formula is very simple.

In Cuba even toward the end of 1959 I kept noticing one recurrent slogan among the many revolutionary posters, inscriptions on walls, and government announcements. When I asked Cubans their attitude toward communism, they would always point to this slogan. It read: "*Comunismo no, INRA sí!*"—communism no, land reform yes. Had the United States behaved more wisely, and had this slogan become the leitmotif of the postrevolutionary period in Cuba, we would have no Cuban problem. We would have been spared the harrowing days of the Cuban blockade as well as the psychological victory the Soviet Union won by yielding. Cuba would not be a glowing fuse which might at any moment set the world aflame, but at most a half-socialist country on good terms with the West—much like Mexico and Bolivia.

And most people would not frown at the name of Fidel Castro.

A FEW SLOGANS

Today other slogans are current, and not only in Cuba. I have seen pro-Cuban and anti-American inscriptions chalked on walls all the way from the Caribbean Sea to southern Chile: *"Cuba sí, Yanquis no!"* or *"Viva Fidel,"* but also *"Cuba sí, Yanquis no! Comunismo no!,"* and finally as a timid answer on the part of the opponents of Castro: *"Cuba sí, Castro no!"*

Such slogans are absent only in those dictatorships where free political activity is banned. But even in those countries you will no more find a *Yanquis sí* than a *Cuba no*. The Cuban Revolution has grown popular in Latin America. Even more popular than the by now established revolution in Mexico.

In 1961 President Kennedy created the Alliance for Progress with the avowed purpose of democratizing Latin America by providing generous economic and cultural aid. But so far all hopes of thus defusing the Latin American time bomb have proved vain. New sources of crises have arisen. The democracies maintained by grace of U.S. subsidies stand on feet of clay. Meanwhile Cuba has become a propaganda center fomenting anti-American agitation from Guatemala down to Argentina.

Latin Americans are extremely touchy about political intervention from outside. This touchiness stems from a certain inferiority complex and a powerful latent nationalism. The bearded Cuban leader is not unconditionally loved in the Latin American world, but on the whole Latin Americans wish that the United States would let him alone. They flare up immediately when the great neighbor to the north attempts to influence a fellow Latin American nation. The man in the street considers the policies of Cuba solely the business of the Cuban people.

Consequently, slogans on the walls proliferate; and consequently the Cubans play on the latent anti-American feeling throughout the Latin American continent.

THE MAN AND THE POWER

Bolivia, Mexico, Cuba—three cases in which Latin American nations have attempted to take the leap into political maturity. Three significant cases. I have discussed them first in order to make my bias plain.

Anyone who loves Latin America must love her in anger. Otherwise he loves only the glories of the landscape, the tourist attractions, and the grace and polish of the social life. But not the Latin American people with all their potentialities and all their inadequacies. For anyone who loves the Latin American people must be prepared to take a position—against all that violates their human dignity; against the military and economic dictatorship so common on the South American Continent; against the antiquated, hidebound outlook of the higher clergy; even against those Latin traditions that hamper the free development of human beings.

At one time I traveled for a few days in a bus with some thirty North American tourists who, in the usual way, were "doing" all of South America in forty-five days. The tour moved so fast that the tourists could not always say exactly what country they were in. But all of them had the most definite opinion on one point: the countries themselves were entrancingly beautiful, but the people in them exceedingly miserable. Only too frequently in the clubs and luxury hotels of the capitals I heard someone say: "Think of what could be done with Latin America if only different people lived here." In more or less veiled fashion, this criticism of the Latin American can be detected running through most of the literature on the subject.

No doubt the Latin American has his seamy side. He has a great deal of catching up to do and it is essential that he catch up as quickly as possible. In such circumstances, tensions and explosions are inevitable. The social gradient is alarmingly precipitous. The Latin Americans are no more unstable, no lazier, no more unreliable, of no worse character than the members of other civilized lands. They are only less well established politically and socially than Europeans and North Americans. Then, too, they are not yet as well molded into mass society; they wage their struggle for existence and their political struggles with means that strike us as archaic. They can shift rapidly from charm and cordiality to cruelty and ruthlessness. But that is hardly their fault. It is the fault of those who have kept them in a state of political and social immaturity for hundreds of years.

RETHINKING OR RE-EDUCATION?

Of the twenty-one Latin American countries, only seven can be regarded as democracies, even by a lenient definition. And even these are not democracies in the Western sense. The rest are open dictatorships, semidictatorships, limping economic colonies, or sham democracies resting on the army. Big Brother in the north has decreed that the governments and parliaments must represent the people. So far, except for Mexico, only Chile, Uruguay, and Costa Rica have obeyed this decree. Since in most Latin American countries a majority of the people do not have the franchise, the governments that emerge from elections can scarcely be genuinely democratic governments.

But the people, whether or not they can vote, are impatiently pushing their way toward the top in all Latin American countries. Latin America can easily become a powder keg. As we have seen, the Cuban fuse has already been placed in the hands of the East. The fact that it has not been used is testimony to the Kremlin's cautious, restrained, and therefore probably skillful tactics with regard to Latin America.

What will become of Latin America after the dissolution of the dictatorships depends, however, not upon the tactics of the Kremlin, but upon the tactics of the West and in particular, of the business world of the West. Businessmen will have to swallow a good deal. Henceforth they will have to think more of the Latin American people than of Latin American resources and trade balances. Henceforth the West will not be able to back Batistas, Trujillos, and military juntas. Limits will have to be set to the old flirtations with the moneyed Latin American aristocracy. Many lessons must be drawn from the three revolutions—in Mexico, in Bolivia, and in Cuba.

The Mexican way might very well be followed without any severe penalty to the interests of the West. There are other feasible ways I shall take up later. All of them involve sacrifices for the Europeans and Americans who have invested capital and managerial talent in the continent. But the cost would be far greater if the Cuban fuse should ignite. For the West must realize one thing above all: Latin America today has become a battlefield of the cold war. It may even be the decisive battlefield.

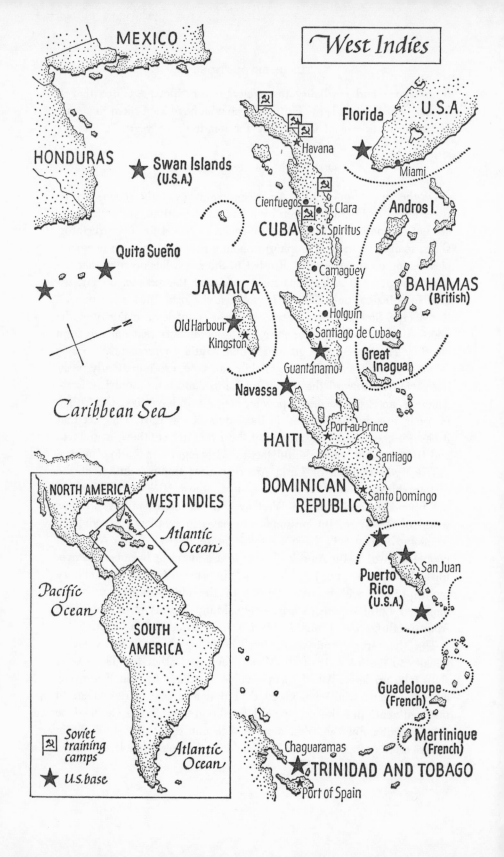

CHAPTER 2

Hurricane Over the Caribbean

PARADE OF THE DICTATORS

Their names are: Trujillo, Batista, Pérez Jiménez, Somoza, Duvalier. In addition to these, many another strong man of similar complexion has held reign in the Caribbean region for a while. All set up gigantic monuments to themselves and wrote their names with steel and blood in the histories of their countries. A listing of their deeds and misdeeds would be monotonous, for they followed a similar pattern. Granted, they did not liquidate as many of their subjects as European dictators have done, but then, their countries have smaller populations, and their opponents were (or are) of fewer number.

Of course, the dictators differed from one another in more or less subtle ways. Pérez Jiménez in Venezuela was probably the greediest, Batista in Cuba the cruelest, Trujillo in the Dominican Republic the most blasphemous.

Duvalier in Haiti found support in the superstition of his subjects; the Somoza clan in Nicaragua depends more upon its own cleverness. But they all feel themselves to be great men, the *caudillos* of the Caribbean.

Just as the German people were once taught to regard the parvenu Hitler as "the greatest general of all time," so the Caribbean dictators have taught their people to adorn their names with ceremonial flourishes. The Dominican dictator, Rafael Leonidas Trujillo, was officially called *El Benefactor*. The grand old man of Nicaragua, Anastasio Somoza, insisted on the title *Máximo Propulsor del Progreso*—"Greatest Motive Force of Progress." The ruler of the petroleum paradise of Venezuela, Marcos Pérez Jiménez, extolled himself as "Improver of the Physical, Moral, and Essential Capacities of All Venezuelans." Somewhat more modestly, the voodooist patron Dr.

Duvalier titles himself merely "socialist." Even after one of these semi-divine rulers is assassinated or driven from the country, the grandiose titles live on like pious legends. Dominican workers to this day, years after the death of Trujillo, cannot get out of the habit of calling the greatest plunderer of their country The Benefactor.

BENEFACTION YIELDS PROFIT

Caribbean dictators seldom spend peaceful retirement years in their homeland. The business of converting a whole country into a private estate for a single family entails certain risks. Anastasio Somoza was murdered by rebels in 1956. In May 1961, Rafael Leonidas Trujillo expired under a hail of machine-gun bullets. Batista fled from Fidel Castro's revolution first to his fellow dictator Trujillo, then to Portuguese Madeira, and finally to Franco's Spain. Pérez Jiménez, too, after expulsion, planned to live comfortably on the millions of dollars he had transferred to the United States, but after some indecision the Americans finally turned him over to his Venezuelan judges.

Somoza's sons, Tacho and Luis, took the place of their assassinated father and to this day dominate the Nicaraguan puppet government. Duvalier is holding on with equal stubbornness in Haiti. He, to be sure, has an easier time of it than his lighter-skinned colleagues, for if need be he can always appeal to the fetishistic superstitions of the Haitian populace.

For the Caribbean dictators, the rewards are commensurate with the risks. Batista and Pérez Jiménez sent astronomical sums to safety abroad. Whether the Venezuelans will ever be able to block Pérez Jiménez's American bank accounts is questionable. The United States extradited the oil dictator only on condition that he be tried not for his political crimes but solely for his illegal financial dealings.

Nevertheless, in this respect Pérez Jiménez has come off far worse than his colleagues in the Antilles and in Central America. For Castro is scarcely likely ever to be able to lay his hands on the person of Batista or his ill-gotten fortune. The two hundred and fifty million dollars the Trujillo clan transferred to Europe is tucked away in Swiss banks. Nicaragua still belongs to a single family—the Somoza clan. The Somozas draw profits from the chief cotton and coffee plantations, from cattle ranches, factories, shipping and airlines; and René Schick, the country's present president, is a good friend of the "sons of progress."

The foreigner who first hears of the financial manipulations of Caribbean dictators can only shake his head and ask how it could be that North American and European financiers and businessmen tolerated, or continue to tolerate, such conditions for such a long time. And when, in addition, he is told how the Caribbean dictators usually treated their political opponents, he remembers the disclosures in the trials of nazis, and similar atrocities which have always horrified Americans.

BEGGING FORBIDDEN!

In countries still in the grip of dictatorship, foreign business is on the whole quite content with the situation. In those countries where the dictatorships have been replaced by a democratic regime, foreign businessmen wax nostalgic for the good old days. I have talked with many such businessmen, who often seemed quite sensible and possessed of a good knowledge of the country. It was all the more amazing, then, to hear them express the view that the dictatorship, in spite of its excesses, had had a better record than the subsequent democratic regime. The dictator had kept order. He had got things done. He had fostered building, established industries, built roads, cleaned up the ports and the cities, regulated wages, provided welfare legislation, and this had given common people what the common people needed. Freedom and the franchise, after all, were fictions, and hardly relevant to conditions in Latin America. Latin Americans had to be forced to work by gentle means or tough, or everything would go to hell and gone.

When the United States was preparing to extradite Pérez Jiménez to Venezuela, many foreign businessmen active in Venezuela protested vigorously. They pointed to the accomplishments of the oil dictator. He had made his country one of the richest in the world, they said; he had lured a stream of investments and industrial projects to Venezuela. On the other hand, the argument continued, after five years of democracy the economy was stagnant, unemployment was increasing, and a steady flight of capital was eroding the currency. Venezuelan democracy was an illusion, they argued, because the people lacked the necessary maturity. If things went on as they were going, the law of the jungle would soon prevail.

Tourists and writers who visited the Dominican Republic during its all too brief democratic intermezzo in 1963 came to hold similar views. Under Trujillo, they said, the republic had paid off its debts. The Benefactor had begun to exploit the natural resources; he had developed native industry and increased fivefold the area of land under cultivation. He had taught the school children how to wash and brush their teeth; he banished beggars and street peddlers from the main streets of his cities. To be sure, Trujillo's claim to be "God's steward" was perhaps a little conceited, but after all, a vain dictator might be preferable to a weak democrat. For the democracy, under intellectual President Juan Bosch, was letting the country go to rack and ruin again. Moreover, it was virtually a sure bet that Caribbean democrats would sympathize with Castro.

Some of these points were quite accurate. It is true that during the Trujillo era no beggars ever molested a foreign tourist—The Benefactor had forbidden begging under threat of severe punishment. Nor were Dominicans seen going barefoot in the street, at least not in the capital—The Benefactor had also forbidden that. People worked hard in the Dominican Republic under Trujillo—The Benefactor took Draconian measures against shirkers. On the other hand, one statistic which can be found even in quite serious books should arouse distrust. It is alleged that under Trujillo the percentage of illiterates dropped from seventy-five to twenty-five. Under the succeeding democratic government it once again amounted to seventy-five per cent. It is hard to believe that the Dominicans forgot how to read or write quite so rapidly, within the space of a few months. In other words, the partisans of El Benefactor fell for a statistical swindle such as every dictator practices.

The posthumous praise of the dictator and the scorn heaped upon the young and still weak democracy had bitter consequences for the Dominican Republic. The Trujillo propaganda machine accused the honorable university president Juan Bosch, a pro-Western democrat promoted by John Kennedy, of crypto-Castroism. Foreign supporters of El Benefactor joined in this refrain. Anyone in the Caribbean area who attempts democratic reforms runs the risk of being lumped together with Castro. In September 1963 a military coup choked out the life of the democratic experiment in the Dominican Republic. The dictatorship that followed terminated in 1965 in one of the most chaotic civil wars in Caribbean history. We shall have more to say about that later.

The Somozas in Nicaragua are not as loved by the business world as were the Trujillos or Pérez Jiménez. They were thought rather too pinko for a while. Luis Somoza had introduced a number of rather radical social welfare measures and minimum wage ordinances. But in the meantime the Somoza clan has been forgiven such slips to the left. The Nicaraguan dictators are now being credited with the usual accomplishments of benefactors: the establishment of order, improvement of hygiene, industrialization, the building of houses and roads, the protection of foreign business, and the suppression of all opposition.

Only in Haiti does the picture seem somewhat different. Here, ever since the afterpains of the French Revolution, there has no longer been a white-skinned oligarchy. The upper class is composed of barely three hundred mulatto families, who for decades considered themselves Frenchmen, had their children educated in France, and owned virtually everything in Haiti that was worth owning. The present dictator, however, is a Negro and presumably represents the interests of the black majority of the population. Although "Papa Doc," as the Haitians call him, makes use of those methods of forced labor and oppression shared by his Latin colleagues in the Caribbean, he seems to be too black for European and American tastes. For a long time Duvalier has not enjoyed anything like so good a press as the mass murderer Batista, the benefactor Trujillo, and the Motive Force of Progress, Somoza.

STRONG MEN—IMPOVERISHED PEOPLES

Hitler, too, saw to order after his fashion. Hitler, too, launched vast building programs, constructed superhighways, created new industries, broke new soil to the plow, dispensed social welfare, suppressed the opposition, persecuted the socialists, and gave the average German exactly what, to his mind, the average German needed. And, like the Caribbean dictatorships, Hitlerism was regarded as a kind of bulwark against the East. The consequence is that communism today is established on the Elbe.

The consequences of the parade of Caribbean dictators are: Castro-

ism in Cuba, growing leftist extremism on the part of the intellectuals, instability of democracy in those countries where despotism
has been toppled. For of course all totalitarian regimes can do things
that at first glance may impress the foreign visitor. All they need is
force. By force streets can be kept clean, beggars banished, school
children taught to brush their teeth, the masses driven to work, and
even economic successes achieved. But everywhere the reverse side
of the coin is the same: a police state, terror, slavery, judicial murder
—strangulation of the natural evolution that every people on earth
must pass through.

From the time President Kennedy took office, Washington declared
repeatedly and energetically that the age of dictators must come to
an end in the Caribbean area, that the United States wished to see
democratic elections. But at the same time (and herein lies the
dilemma of American policy in the Caribbean area), the State Department feels distinctly uneasy when it thinks of the possible results of
such elections. After the overthrow of the dictator in Venezuela, the
democratic Betancourt and Leoni governments managed to stay in
the saddle. Foreign capital, however, has ever since been fearful of
political earthquakes and has been trying as far as possible to withdraw its investments from that oil-rich country. In the Dominican
Republic the unfortunate legacy of the Trujillo era still hangs like
a menacing shadow over the struggles for power between ultrarightist
military men and rebellious democrats. In Cuba the overthrow of the
dictator led to a political cataclysm. In Nicaragua a majority of the
population is engaged in passive resistance against the government.
The United States fears that many of the leftist liberal politicians
who would like to replace the Caribbean dictatorial system by a
democratic system will eventually take a wild political risk similar
to that of Fidel Castro.

The regret of the business groups at the twilight of the Caribbean
dictatorship is understandable. Under the strong men, their earnings
in Latin America were very good indeed. Where strikes are outlawed,
there is no need to worry about wage demands. Where the troops
and the police clear the streets, labor peace is assured. Even if the
dictators put 50 per cent of the profits into their own pockets, as
was the case in Nicaragua in the time of the Somozas, it was worth
the toll to be assured a steady business climate. Hardly any of the
businessmen who collaborated so long and so closely with the Carib-

bean dictators ever observed that the people under such systems were reduced to emaciated pariahs. Profitable countries—poor people: that is the sum that must be drawn up on any balance sheet on the Caribbean dictators.

But then, what kind of people live in the Caribbean region? Why do dictatorships seem to flourish here? And how is it that a small state like Costa Rica, in spite of similar climatic and economic conditions, has been able to remain relatively free of the "strong men"?

The Caribbean area has a turbulent, excessive, and often bloody history behind it. Ever since the discovery of America this region has been a playground for treasure hunters of all kinds—from the gold-hungry Spaniards to the banana-planting United Fruit Company.

THE WEST INDIAN PATCHWORK QUILT

Latin America begins at the southern border of Texas and ends, at least in the dreams of Chileans and Argentines, at the South Pole. Right off Latin America lies perhaps the most colorful archipelago on our globe, the island world of the Antilles, where Columbus and the Spanish conquistadors first set foot to claim what they believed was India for their king. Other powers, too, quickly realized that the Antilles would serve as an ideal springboard to the New World. The consequences of these historical conflicts have left ineradicable traces upon the Caribbean area. They have transformed the picturesque Antilles into a seething medley of peoples, races, languages, and passions.

Half a dozen other nations established themselves in the Antilles: Great Britain, France, the Netherlands, the United States, temporarily Denmark and Sweden also. Five tongues are spoken on the islands of the Caribbean Sea. People from four continents have settled there: Africans, Europeans, North Americans, South Americans, East Indians, Chinese, Indonesians, Syrians, and Lebanese. The aboriginal Indians have vanished everywhere, except for two islands.

Thus the sociological landscape of the Caribbean region is checkered. The historical development of the separate islands and nations is equally checkered, and so the future offers little but riddles. The parade of Caribbean dictators can only be explained and interpreted if we can expose the historical roots of Caribbean politics.

It is due to Columbus' erroneous geography that this region of the world was first called the West Indies. The misleading name has remained to this day. Three independent nations stand out in the galaxy of islands and islets: Cuba, the Republic of Haiti, and the Dominican Republic. Two others have recently gained independence: Jamaica and Trinidad; while the West Indian Federation is on its way and the Dutch Antilles have an equal status with the Netherlands under the Dutch crown. Still governed by mother countries are: the American Commonwealth of Puerto Rico, the American Virgin Islands, the French Lesser Antilles, and the British Bahamas. The mother countries have tended to put their continental colonies and their island possessions under a single administration. British Honduras and the three Guianas will therefore be considered along with the islands in this section, since historically and politically they belong to the Caribbean patchwork quilt.

Thus, in the Caribbean region the colonial system left behind an irrational mosaic. This is basically why to this day no sound, orderly, economically stable government exists in the Antilles. The borders of the present nations were often decided by flagrant chance. Linguistic, racial, and governmental barriers bisect the island of Hispaniola, separating the black Republic of Haiti in the west from the brown Dominican Republic in the east. The arc of islands comprising the British West Indies runs suddenly smack into groups of islands colonized by the French or the Dutch. Half of the small island of St. Martin is dependent upon Dutch Curaçao, the other half on French Guadeloupe. Islands and groups of islands have changed owners more than once. No wonder the link with the one-time European motherland is only very loose on some of the islands. Cuba and Puerto Rico alone belong in the strictest sense of the word to the Ibero-American cultural region. The Dominican Republic could also be considered as belonging in that category. Nevertheless, Puerto Rico, in spite of periodic eruptions of hectic nationalism, is firmly in the hands of the United States.

MARKETS FOR THE SLAVE TRADE

The islands in the Caribbean Sea differ from the Central American mainland chiefly in their aboriginal population having been destroyed before the era of colonialism reached full bloom. They have one thing in common with the equally variegated islands of the Pacific Ocean: they are as lovely as the legendary Islands of the Blessed. For that reason they have become favorite tourist spots, vacation resorts, and millionaire refuges. All the same, not very much bliss has prevailed on these islands since their discovery. Columbus called the region "a country full of precious things and unheard-of wonders." What he meant by that is clear from his diaries: "There is much gold and it will be possible to make many slaves." The conquerors followed this prescription to the letter. Colonial masters in those days were in the habit of saying exactly what they really meant. To be sure, the supplies of gold on Haiti and Jamaica were swiftly exhausted; and the Carib and Arawak Indians proved stubbornly disinclined to slave labor. But soon afterward the mainland of Central and South America was discovered. Columbus' hope was fulfilled that "God would show us where was the source of gold."

Thenceforth the Caribbean region was assigned the role it was to play for centuries, to the point of utter exhaustion. It became the gateway to the New World, the point of rendezvous for the gold, silver, and pirate ships. As the refractory Indians on the islands were gradually exterminated and replaced by "black ivory" from Africa, the region also became a vast mart for the trade in human beings. Some of the old slave markets have been preserved to this day. They have become tourist attractions; and the guides who explain their one-time purpose to overseas visitors are usually dark-skinned. The white tourists cannot help wondering what such a grandson of slaves must feel when, for a tip, he shows the whites the calvaries of his ancestors.

In 1748 the French writer Montesquieu defended Negro slavery in the West Indies with one incisive argument: "There must be slaves, or else the sugar would be too expensive." Therein Montesquieu summed up the two arch-evils of the region, the consequences of which it suffers from to this day: the unrestricted import of human beings and the equally unrestricted monoculture. With the lucidity of a modern economist, he recognized that a plantation economy is profitable only if there is a sufficient supply of cheap labor. Montesquieu regarded this combination of feudalism and slavery not as an evil, but as one of the major pillars of colonialism and mercantilism. To this day there are plenty of members of the Central and South

American oligarchy and of overseas coffee, sugar, and fruit companies who not too secretly hold the same opinion.

Not only the sugar would have been too dear without slave work, but also the cotton, the tobacco, the cocoa, the coffee, the rice, and the fruit. For after treasure hunting and piracy ceased to be profitable activities, most of the Caribbean islands were transformed into enormous plantations based on the labor of Negro slaves imported from Africa.

Writers on Latin America like to lay stress on the foresighted entrepreneur's spirit of Europe and North America which created such empires out of the wilderness. What they forget is that the hands of slaves built and tended the sugar farms in Cuba, Haiti, Jamaica, and Brazil, the tobacco and cotton fields in the American southland, the coffee plantations in Central and South America, and the fruit plantations in the tropics. The hands of slaves cleared the forests, built houses, cities, ports, and streets. Thanks to slaves, the Creole upper classes could lead a life of luxury for centuries. Without slaves, the conquerors would scarcely have been able to tap the wealth of the Americas, and since American wealth also made Europe rich, the slave system remained down into the nineteenth century one of the pillars of the world economy. Planters and merchantmen, shipowners and ship captains, industrialists, bankers, stockholders, whole social classes, whole branches of the economy and whole areas of countries lived directly or indirectly on the labor of slaves.

A member of the Brazilian oligarchy once said to me that there were two persons in Brazilian history who had ruined the country: the Emperor Pedro II, who freed the slaves in 1888 (actually, it was his daughter who issued the proclamation), and President Getulio Vargas, who issued the first labor and social welfare laws thirty years ago.

Even today Latin American employers are so used to commanding an almost inexhaustible reservoir of agricultural workers that they attribute to communist influences any desire on the part of these workers for improvement in their lives. Any honest effort to reform conditions on the land is regarded as a dire economic threat, just as in the past century all efforts to free the slaves were equated with a deadly assault upon plantation economy.

The slaves, however, have long since been freed; and the majority of their descendants well understand that most of what has been accomplished in those countries is based upon the work of their forcibly imported ancestors. It is understandable, therefore, that the grandchildren of the dark-skinned slaves want at last to have the fruit of what their people sowed. They are now in a position to exert the necessary pressure. For in the Caribbean area the objects of the slave trade avenged themselves upon their masters not only by periodic uprisings but also by their fertility, by increasing and multiplying very rapidly indeed. In most parts of this region the black men outnumber all other groups of the population.

FEAR OF THE BLACK MAN

Aside from Cuba and Puerto Rico, the Antilles have become black islands. In Jamaica the population is composed of 96 per cent Negroes and mulattoes as against 3 per cent immigrant Asiatics and 1 per cent whites. On the other islands which belonged to the British, French, or Dutch colonial empires, the proportion is similar. Haiti became a Negro republic, Santo Domingo a mulatto republic. Everywhere in the Antilles today, dark-skinned West Indians represent the people as chiefs of state, cabinet ministers, senators, or deputies.

The second largest population group in the British West Indies consists of the descendants of another mass influx. In 1833–34 Great Britain abolished slavery and paid the plantation owners varying compensations for the release of the Negro slaves. With some of this money, the British planters hastily brought new labor power from the East Indies. Legally the imported Indian coolies were not regarded as slaves, but to all intents and purposes they were serfs. A British historian has called the five-year contract on which they were imported "a contract on a slave-like basis." It was not until 1916 that England, at India's insistence, abolished the coolie system. Many Indians, however, remained in the West Indies and in the British mainland colonies. They rose socially, became craftsmen, dealers, and big businessmen; they entered the academic professions and went into politics. On Trinidad their descendants form one third of the population; in British Guiana almost one half. These Indians, too, have called their debtors to account.

If we disregard the special cases of Cuba and Puerto Rico, we find in the West Indies a small white minority and a vast colored majority. And that majority is more and more emphatically pressing for its rights where they have not been achieved.

A new factor has entered the agrarian world of the West Indies: tourism. Many of the people live by the tourist trade and have evolved accordingly. They strike the visitor as likable, wide awake, and friendly to foreigners. They seem to have forgotten the sufferings of the past. Nor do they seem disadvantaged by the color of their skin. Throughout the West Indies, whether the inhabitants speak Spanish, French, Dutch, or English, the color line seems scarcely to exist. To be sure, in the British islands the prosperous white man goes to his country club and the prosperous colored person to his Nautic Club, but the clubs themselves are as alike as two peas. Thanks to their achievements in cricket and track, the two favorite sports of the islands, colored West Indians have become national heroes. In the legislatures and the unions the colored people are unquestionably dominant.

Nevertheless there is ferment in the Antilles. When, in a Jamaica railroad car, you see the chalk-scrawled slogan "Kill the white man!," this is neither a joke nor communist propaganda, but a visible sign of an invisible grudge. The time of slavery has been thrust back into the unconscious. But no one knows what goes on in the souls of innumerable slum dwellers. To this day a good many tales and legends of the bloody past go the rounds among members of spiritistic and fetishistic Negro sects who congregate at secret places to slaughter black cocks, sacrifice goats, and practice their cromanti, obeah, or voodoo magic. Christianization and civilization have not yet purged the old Africa from the hearts of these grandsons of slaves. And indeed, Papa Doc's Haiti has for some time now actually been calling itself an "African country." And the one-time slave songs, slave dances, slave massacres, and slave uprisings have everywhere left their mark upon West Indian popular legend, poetry, and art. That art has recently undergone a strong resurgence and has made a mark on both North America and Europe.

In Port of Spain, the capital of Trinidad, tourists consider it incumbent on them to take in a performance by one of the famous steel bands, listen to the calypso singers, and watch some Limbo dances. I, too, was eager to witness these folk arts and went to a smart night club whose patrons were both white-skinned and well heeled. The Negroes radiated good humor as they drummed on their oil canisters; the brown Limbo dancers went to great pains to please the audience; the calypso singers composed all sorts of flatteries for the benefit of the foreign guests. Aside from the deafening rhythms of the steel bands, we were lapped in an atmosphere of peace and harmony. The colored artists performed, the white guests looked on. The traditional Caribbean order of things prevailed in this room.

Later, I went to another night club down at the waterfront. This was not for tourists but for native colored folks. Here, too, a steel band was drumming. Here, too, Limbo dancers gyrated. Here, too, calypso songs were sung. Nevertheless this was a wholly different world. The men in the band looked through me; the dancers ignored me; and the calypso singers improvised sarcastic songs. I was the only white in the place. The colored artists and patrons did not conceal their annoyance at having me here. But instead of throwing me out, they charged me unusually high prices, three times what I had paid in the luxury night club. Here the colored folk were among themselves and the white man was isolated; here the new Caribbean order of things prevailed.

THE WEST INDIAN BIRTH RATE

This new order is marked by new problems, the greatest at the present time being not the isolation of the white minority but overpopulation. The excess of births over deaths in the Caribbean area is from five to seven times higher than in Central Europe, far higher than in any other region of the world except the Central American countries and the African Ivory Coast. The small islands can no longer absorb the population pressure. Islanders pour, in ever-mounting numbers, to the coasts of the mainland, seeking jobs as dock workers, day laborers, cabdrivers, musicians, singers, dancers, or prostitutes. Many of them stay, eking out miserable livelihoods, but their hope is to save a little money and return to their native island. Emigration is not solving the problem of overpopulation in the Caribbean area.

The black West Indians to be met with in the ports of Venezuela and Central America tend to feel superior to the frequently much lighter-skinned Latin Americans around them. They are hard-working and thrifty; they speak English, live under the British Commonwealth, can read and write, and so are inclined to swagger a bit. I was always pleased on the mainland when I was able to have a West Indian cabdriver. The West Indians were more alert than their Latin colleagues, they understood more quickly what I wanted to see, and took pleasure in showing me the slums which a patriotic Ibero-American would have preferred to hide. Dark-skinned West Indians give such Central American ports as Puerto Barrios, Puerto Limón, and Panama their characteristic appearance. Due to them, many coastal areas in Central America seem almost a little Africa. But it is plain to see that they do not feel especially at ease among the Latins. Their discomfort is understandable. For just as the North American Negro has long ago become an American, the Negro of the British West Indies has long ago become British.

In Port of Spain I saw many well-dressed Negroes who could be distinguished from the English gentlemen only by the color of their skin. In Curaçao the Negroes and mulattoes have the manners of Dutch burghers. Many of the colored people in the former French Antilles display the intellect and charm of the true Frenchman. The Cuban Negroes, on the other hand, are typical Latin Americans in all their outward characteristics. It is not color but culture that determines the personality of human beings. For that reason the Negroes of the British West Indies prefer to immigrate to Great Britain, although job opportunities there are smaller than they would be in Latin America, where a capable man can almost always make a living.

The wave of West Indian immigration which has been pouring into England for some time has already caused serious problems there. In recent years the influx of dark-skinned islanders has on several occasions caused race riots of a kind hitherto unknown in tolerant Britain. So prominent a Labour politician as Patrick Gordon Walker lost his seat in 1964 because his constituency, a working-class district, resented his campaigning for the rights of West Indian immigrants.

Similar problems have arisen in the United States. For until recently the surplus Spanish-speaking, mulatto population of Puerto Rico was pouring in ever-increasing numbers into the slums of American cities. The struggles between native and Puerto Rican youths for a time became characteristic of sociological conditions in the new immigrant sections of New York and have been amply recorded in the press, literature, the stage, and the movies.

The West Indies have thus become a prime field for demographic studies. Statesmen, sociologists, biologists, and medical men who regard population control as one of the most urgent of our contemporary problems point to these islands as dreadful examples of what an unrestricted birth rate means. The United States, faced with the threat of these multitudes pouring in from the south, long ago went beyond the stage of studies into actual practice. In Puerto Rico, with the backing of Governor Luis Muñoz Marín, successful experiments were conducted in checking the birth rate by free distribution of birth control pills under medical supervision.

Puerto Rico is a Catholic country where Spanish traditions run deep. Nor would she be particularly cordial toward suggestions from the country with which she is connected by ties of bitterness as well as allegiance. The island therefore was scarcely an ideal experimental field for consistent birth control practices. The Puerto Rican clergy, in fact, fought hard against the contraceptive pills. The clergy attacked Muñoz Marín, exploited the anti-Americanism of the Puerto Rican, and even imposed church penalties on those islanders who supported the liberal governor. But the clergy lost the struggle. The fear of further population increase was stronger in the Puerto Ricans than all their religious and traditional indoctrinations. In the last election Puerto Rico voted by a great majority for Muñoz Marín and his birth control program.

At the present time, however, Puerto Rico stands alone in this respect. In the British West Indies, no less threatened by the avalanche of births, the common folk have decisively rejected similar plans and proposals—not for religious reasons but because the colored people impute unsavory motives to the white man. Birth control—a project to kill Negroes! is the slogan in Jamaica. Distrust has suffocated rationality.

AT THE U.S.A.'S FRONT DOOR

The Caribbean islands describe a rough semicircle from the southern coast of the United States to the northern coast of South America. Strategically they are of enormous importance, as they were in the days when Spain's gold and silver fleets might expect British and French privateers in almost every island bay. If powers hostile to the

United States were to gain a foothold in the Caribbean area, the main link between the Atlantic and the Pacific, the Panama Canal, would be threatened. Moreover, the Antilles are still of considerable importance in the world economy. They produce sugar, coffee, refined petroleum, asphalt, and bauxite. Furthermore, the soil of the islands contains copper, iron, manganese, chromium, and other by and large unexploited resources. The desire of the United States to see that the political, economic, and social problems in this island world are solved in a peaceful fashion is only too understandable.

In the past, it was not very difficult for the United States to preserve the security of her front door. Most of the islands were colonies firmly in the hands of friendly powers. The independent countries were largely, though indirectly, controlled by the United States. If the political situation in any of the West Indian islands began to look dangerous, the United States would quickly intercede, and by economic pressure or military intervention see to it that any plots were stamped out. Cuba, Haiti, and the Dominican Republic were frequently so dealt with in the past several decades.

The chaotic politics of the two countries on the island of Hispaniola has never been very satisfactory to the United States. In 1915, after decades of upheaval, the whole island was plunged into anarchy. American marines thereupon occupied both countries and converted them into American protectorates. The American occupation brought a good many benefits to these colored republics. The finances were put in order, education prospered, and ambitious, power-hungry army officers were held in check. Nevertheless, these American efforts at re-education did not succeed in democratizing the Haitians and the Dominicans. On the contrary, political immaturity prepared the ground for future dictators. After the Americans at last withdrew, the peoples of both countries were so accustomed to being dominated by a strong hand that they eventually capitulated to native strong men. There were military coups in both countries, the usual juntas took power, and in the Dominican Republic Trujillo's star rose.

In Cuba, the course of things was rather similar, although the United States there did its best to avoid military intervention. Instead, Havana was induced to add the much-discussed Platt Amendment to its constitution. Orville Hitchcock Platt, the U.S. senator after whom the measure was named, had organized the American sugar companies in Cuba and therefore had special reasons to wish for stability in that island. The amendment, a rider attached to the army appropriations bill in 1901, stipulated conditions for American intervention in the affairs of the island. The Cubans disliked the agreement as much as the Haitians and Dominicans disliked the occupation of their countries by the American marines. But Cuba was dependent on American economic aid and the export of sugar to the United States. The intervention clause remained in force until 1934, when a Cuban ruler appeared whom Americans could regard as trustworthy. That ruler was Fulgencio Batista.

Today it is no longer possible to dictate such terms. The independent states are jealous of their rights. The colonies are approaching in-dependence. Interference encounters fierce resistance, for the new nationalisms are extremely touchy, as American intervention in the Dominican civil war of 1965 once again demonstrated. As the invasion attempt at the Bay of Pigs showed, from now on America must be prepared to abandon many illusions. Undoubtedly many West Indians do not like the policies of their countries and would welcome liberation from a dictator, a corrupt government, or a doctrinaire party. But they are generally averse to any sort of liberation coming from the United States. Washington, so long accustomed to simple, forthright methods for maintaining order in her own domain, is at a loss for ways to handle the new situation. Americans find their enforced in-activity in the Caribbean area a great trial of patience. Cuba has become an American trauma.

During the Second World War, America established military bases on several of the islands, leasing coastal strips from the existent governments. She maintains Chaguaramas on Trinidad, Old Harbour Bay on Jamaica, and a number of others. From the tenacity with which she clings to Guantánamo, in spite of all Castro's threats and demands, it is plain that she is not contemplating any final relinquish-ing of control in the Caribbean area.

POLITICAL HURRICANES?

The tempestuous climate of the Caribbean area seems to affect the mentality of the people. Political hurricanes whirl up as suddenly as did Hurricane Flora of October 1963, which destroyed a large part of the Cuban harvest, killed thousands of Haitians, and brought the Republic of Haiti to the brink of economic disaster. But, climate apart, population pressure, unemployment, housing shortages, rampant nationalism, and traumatic memories of slavery days are in themselves explosive enough.

In recent years Britain has attempted to improve the outlook in this region by setting up a new nation under the name of Federation of the West Indies. The federation was to include all former British colonies in the Caribbean Sea and on the mainland of Central and South America. Had the plan been realized, it would have started a political union of more than four million people on the road to freedom. Unfortunately, these great hopes were quickly dashed. The three largest territories did not adhere to the British plan. Trinidad, Jamaica, and British Guiana dropped out, the two last-named countries having chosen a radical path rather than one of gradual evolution.

THE SLUMS OF EMPIRE

The Chaguaramas region lies on the northwest tip of the island of Trinidad. In 1947 a plan was born to plant a modern capital city there, one of those Latin American supercities which are created on the drawing board, and which was to be the capital of the Federation of the West Indies. The British plan was to give the new federation a few years in which to find its footing, and then send it out into the world as one more dominion of the British Commonwealth.

There was only a single obstacle to the project of creating the new capital. The Chaguaramas area is an American enclave. During the war the United States leased Chaguaramas as a naval station for the usual interval of ninety-nine years and has since refused to evacuate the enclave on the grounds that the base serves as a vital link in the defense perimeter protecting the entire Caribbean region. Consequently, the dream of a new city came to nothing. Chaguaramas has remained an American naval base, as well as a luxury resort for American military men and their families—a kind of Honolulu in the Caribbean Sea.

As things stand, the U. S. Government feels vindicated in its stubborn refusal to evacuate Chaguaramas. For the Federation of the West Indies has not materialized. The dream was to transform the dirty back yards of empire into an attractive front garden to the Americas. The failure of the plan is most regretted in Trinidad, for on that island a great deal was expected of the political unification and economic co-ordination which would have followed.

THE ISLE OF THE CALYPSOS

Trinidad belonged to the Spanish Empire until 1797. But the Spaniards have left faint traces there. After the French Revolution, Spanish rule became purely nominal. Those natives of Trinidad whose mother tongue is not English usually speak French rather than Spanish. Royalist planters from the French Antilles, alarmed by the upheavals and slave uprisings which the French Revolution stirred even in the distant Caribbean region, fled to Trinidad in great numbers. Adventurers and fortune-seekers from all over the world joined them. Trinidad seems to have exerted an irresistible attraction for both groups, perhaps because the island was, at the time, only very thinly populated; its aboriginal inhabitants had been wiped out.

At first the Spanish were much upset by this wave of immigrants. In 1783, however, the Spanish king threw the country open to immigration by way of showing favor to the staunchly royalist French Creoles. The king's decree was like a breach in a dike. Within a few years the whole aspect of the island of Trinidad was transformed. "There is not a single spot in the universe which can boast such a remarkable mixture of inhabitants as Trinidad," a contemporary account states. "The island is full of Frenchmen, Englishmen, Scots, Irish, Spaniards, Germans, Swiss, Italians and Americans."

The chronicler should have added that the confusion of nationalities terminated in a political confusion in which every man's hand was against every other's. French royalists fought against French republicans, Spaniards fought against Frenchmen, Spaniards and Frenchmen fought jointly against Englishmen. Great Britain finally put an end to the turmoil. She occupied Trinidad and forced its Spanish governor, José María Chacón, to cede the island. The unfortunate Chacón, who had been unable to check either the torrent of immigration or the constant internecine wars or the English invasion, was given a cold reception by his king and ended his life as a beggar in the streets of Seville.

So we may read in the chronicles of the island of Trinidad. But the most important event of those times was given only marginal notice. Until the arrival of the immigrants, Trinidad had been a white island. The French Creoles, however, brought more with them than their traditions. The first ship from Martinique was packed with a thousand royalist planters and their black slaves. The name of that ship, the *Calypso*, lives to this day in the folklore of Trinidad.

Calypsos are the satiric songs which have made Trinidad famous throughout the world. The descendants of the slaves sang calypsos while they worked in the fields. They sang calypsos at their campfires at night, sang of their wretchedness, their hope, the traits of the fellow sufferers, and the cruelties of their masters. Later they sang of their liberation. They sang calypsos about their new fellow citizens, the Indian coolies who from 1845 on were also brought to Trinidad by the thousands. Today they sing calypsos about foreign tourists, about political events, about social gossip, about their future independence. When Princess Margaret arrived in Trinidad in April 1958 to attend the baptism of the planned West Indian Federation, she was greeted with calypsos. And carnival in Trinidad (which is said to be, after the Brazilian carnival, the most fascinating in the world) is unthinkable without the incessant singing of calypsos.

To tourists, the island seems a magically beautiful place with its blue mountain chains and white beaches, its famous asphalt lakes, its marshes inhabited by flamingos and herons. During my drives through Trinidad I at first saw no slums at all; only fine residential quarters, good business streets, illuminated amusement palaces, and clean, though tiny, country dwellings. Then I discovered that the slums of Trinidad are hidden behind well-painted stage sets. Back of the business and amusement quarters, only a few steps away from the usual tourist route, stretched those dreary, overpopulated native quarters that once prompted Lloyd George to remark that the British West Indian colonies were the slums of the empire. On the smaller islands, where multimillionaires have built marvelous beach dwellings, it is not much different. Here, too, one need only turn a corner to fill one's nostrils with the stench of misery. From Trinidad and Barbados come most of those West Indians who seek seasonal work in Venezuela, Colombia, Central America, and Cuba, who try their luck as jazz musicians, calypso singers, and striptease artists in the Negro quarters of American cities. The beauty of Trinidad is for the rich.

Nevertheless, the slums of the commonwealth cannot be compared with the Latin American slums. Just as London's Soho seems decidedly more prosperous than the *favelas* of Rio de Janeiro, or the *ranchitos* of Caracas, so the native quarters in the West Indies are not nearly so depressing as the corresponding district in the mainland port cities. What shocks Englishmen the Latins calmly accept as a God-given condition.

THE UNPREDICTABLE SIR ALEXANDER

Two men are to blame for the fact that the West Indian Federation came to nothing. Their names are: Sir William Alexander Bustamente and Dr. Cheddi Jagan. The former dominates Jamaica, the latter has dominated British Guiana; both are considered leftist radicals. Nor could Trinidad weld the eight remaining island groups into a more modest federation. The project was not viable without Jamaica, which, large and rich in raw materials, could have been the wheel horse of the federation, pulling much of the weight for her poorer brethren. But Alexander Bustamente was not prepared to make such sacrifices.

Of all the islands, Jamaica has an especially bloody past to look back upon. Political radicalism thrives there far better than in the swamplands of Trinidad or on the coral sands of the smaller islands. The Jamaicans still remember very well the maroons, the runaway Negro slaves of Spanish days who established themselves in the interior of the island and fought a century-long guerrilla war against the English colonizers. They still remember the mass deaths in the slave ships, which caused a British writer to declare that all of Liverpool was built on the skulls of Negroes. Nor did the liberation of the slaves bring an end to such miseries. The economy of the island, hitherto inseparably linked to Negro slavery, collapsed after emancipation. Innumerable freedmen threw down their tools and betook themselves to the wilderness. Their descendants today form the main body of rural Jamaicans.

The plantation owners attempted to rout the fugitives from their new settlements and force them to work once more. The result was a Negro revolution which shook the British West Indies. It has gone down in Caribbean history as the uprising of Port Morant. But its end was a massacre. The planter aristocracy, led by British Governor

Eyre, retaliated savagely. Rebellious blacks and innocent persons alike were indiscriminately hanged or shot; a thousand huts were burned to ashes; hundreds of men and women condemned to the lash. The planters even killed a member of the House of Commons who had come out for the rights of the Negroes. All this took place, moreover, several decades after the emancipation of the slaves. Nevertheless, the antiquated plantation economy on Jamaica could not be restored to its former glories even by such extreme measures.

Possibly President Bustamente of Jamaica no longer thinks of these old stories when he denounces the whites, or even flirts with Castro. Bustamente is a man of African, Irish, and Spanish descent who makes a remarkable impression upon foreigners. He is tall, stately, of noble bearing, and his mane of curly white hair is reminiscent of the wigs of baroque princes. The politics of the Jamaican president also seem baroque. Sir Alexander Bustamente began his rise as a union leader and founder of the Jamaican Labor Party, the JLP. He became mayor of the island's capital, Kingston, and ruled the city so highhandedly that at various times he was arrested and imprisoned by the British authorities for lawbreaking and open acts of terror. But by now Bustamente has become popular in Jamaica. He has gained his island independence from England, and that counts for a great deal in a country where, out of every hundred inhabitants, there are only four that do not have slaves among their ancestors.

Jamaica's Declaration of Independence in 1962 created something of a panic in the Caribbean region. Trinidad saw the end of its dream of becoming the heartland of the new dominion. The smaller islands foresaw that they would go on being beggars for crumbs from the tables of the rich. The newspapers prophesied that another Antilles island was on the way to Castroism. And the United States let it be known that she would not, under any circumstances, surrender her naval bases on Jamaica.

Sir Alexander is not an easy man to understand. He cannot be compared with Castro; the baroque labor leader in Jamaica is at least as remote from the fanatical revolutionary leader as an African autocrat from an Iberian anarchist. Moreover, Bustamente's brand of socialism does not come from Cuba, Mexico, or Russia, but from Sir Alexander himself. Nevertheless, an island which in spite of all its natural wealth has a great part of its labor force unemployed, whose people cannot live on Jamaica rum, coffee, and bananas alone, and whose bauxite ores are in the hands of American and Canadian companies, is an island full of tinder.

If Sir Alexander is justified in calling himself a socialist, then we must also grant the appellation to the Haitian dictator, Dr. Duvalier. The two dark-skinned potentates in the West Indies do indeed have the backing of large parts of their population, but they rule dictatorially, far more dictatorially than the government party in Mexico. The question is whether such dictatorships are not the only way to prepare underdeveloped countries haunted by vestiges of the bygone slave system for the tasks of the future. Certainly it is regrettable that Bustamente and Duvalier appeal largely to the emotions and hatreds of their subjects. But history has taught us that a pendulum does not swing only in one direction. The more violently it has swung to the right, the more may we expect it to swing to the left.

If the West helps the colored people of the Caribbean area to shake off at last their ancient slave trauma, then dynamic Sir Alexander will probably force his Jamaica to accept progress, but without endangering the West. If, on the other hand, the West leaves these places to their own devices, then Sir Alexander might possibly look around for other friends. If we want to see the consequences of a thoroughly misguided colonial policy, we need only look at another country in the same general area—Guiana.

BITTER SUGAR

The three Guianas do not really belong to the Caribbean region, but to the tropics of northern South America. Nationalistic Ibero-Americans have long inveighed against their mere existence. Both Venezuela and Brazil have periodically laid claim to these countries. But history has given such claims short shrift, for traditionally, politically, economically, and sociologically the three Guianas are closely linked to the West Indies.

British Guiana has shared the fate of the British colonies in the Caribbean Sea, just as Dutch Guiana has shared that of the Dutch possessions in the West Indies and French Guiana of the French possessions. Guiana is hot, swampy jungle country, with so little to commend it that the French used their section of it, Cayenne, for a penal colony. The Dutch in Surinam, on the other hand, devoted themselves more to studying butterflies than to economic experiments. And Venezuela and Brazil have not very seriously pressed their claims to such territories.

Cayenne today is a French overseas *département*. Since 1946 Devil's Island no longer contains any convicts; it is now peopled by free settlers of every imaginable hue. Negroes, mulattoes, Vietnamese, and Frenchmen practice a small amount of agriculture on the coast. The interior is inhabited by bush Negroes, descendants of runaway slaves, and a few Indian tribes whom nobody has bothered to exterminate or civilize. Although French Guiana is said to be rich in mineral treasures, the *département* is dependent on subsidies. It keeps taking money from the motherland and does not offer anything in particular in return. Cayenne is, as it has long been, a sleeping beauty. But a Canadian aluminum and bauxite company is preparing to rouse it from its slumber. The descendants of the French convicts pin their hopes on the Canadians and emphasize that, though Cayenne may not have much of a climate, the foreign entrepreneurs and engineers will at least find good French cuisine there.

Surinam, the Dutch part of Guiana, is the last remnant of the great Dutch commercial empire that once extended to Recife. Like the Dutch Antilles, Surinam today enjoys a degree of self-government. And like Willemstad, the capital of Curaçao, Paramaribo, the capital of Surinam, with its Flemish brick houses and its well-scrubbed streets, resembles a small Dutch town. Surinam is just as much of a Babel as Cayenne. Along the coast live Hindus, Indonesians, Negroes, Dutch, mulattoes, and mestizos. In the jungles wander the descendants of the runaway slaves and survivors of the Indian aboriginals. The colorful medley of people, however, seems to be calm and not dissatisfied with present conditions. The little country has the second largest bauxite production in the world, a flourishing agriculture, and rich resources of iron, porcelain clay, and petroleum.

Yet though all looks calm enough on the surface, the future of this country may hold a number of surprises. About half the population consists of descendants of Indian and Indonesian coolies. How much political dynamite is stowed away within such emancipated, radicalized Indians in South America has been apparent for the past decade in the neighboring country of British Guiana.

THE DENTIST AND RED JANET

The strongest party in British Guiana (or so say North Americans exacerbated by the case of Cuba) is flirting with the Eastern bloc. It bears the name People's Progressive Party, PPP for short, and a good many North American experts on Eastern affairs have already called it the "best organized Communist Party in the British West Indies." As early as 1961 the journalist Manfred George predicted: "Pretty soon the portrait of a handsome and somewhat dreamy looking Indian will be bobbing up in the newspapers beside the portrait of Fidel Castro. . . . In any case, British Guiana is a country that will give Latin America and America's Latin American policy many a tough nut to crack."

The "handsome and somewhat dreamy looking Indian" is a dentist by profession. His name is Dr. Cheddi Jagan; he is the head of the PPP, and from 1961 to 1964, with interruptions dictated by events, he served as prime minister of British Guiana. As long ago as 1953 he gave the world something of a turn when his party emerged victorious from the first free election ever held in his country. Great Britain thereupon thought it wise to dispatch a few warships to British Guiana in order to avert a communist seizure of power in the capital city of Georgetown.

Even at that time the outlines of the coming struggle for power were visible. British Guiana became one of the most troubled countries in the Commonwealth. Negroes and mulattoes, as well as members of the white upper class, cheered the sailors of the English warships, but the East Indians applauded the dentist turned politician. However, Dr. Jagan's principal support has been his white wife. While studying in the United States, Jagan met and married a young nurse named Janet Rosenberg. Red Janet, as she is generally called in Guiana, is regarded as a fanatical communist. Since her marriage to Jagan she has attended a number of Eastern-bloc congresses and has even hailed the Berlin Wall as an "antifascist defense wall."

There has been another party in British Guiana, the United Democratic Party, now the People's National Congress. The UDP has been backed by the real masters of the country, the British sugar planters. For two centuries Guiana was ruled and exploited by the sugar barons, who used the customary methods of the Latin oligarchy. Until

1938 Guiana was without political parties, unions, freedom of speech and assembly. The common people, half of them descendants of Hindu coolies, the other half Negroes and mulattoes, toiled in the sugar plantations and were as badly treated and as badly paid as the Cuban sugar workers.

The East Indians gradually bettered themselves, overcame the chief handicap of illiteracy, sent their children to the higher schools, acquired land, planted rice, or opened small shops in the cities. In 1957 the British attempted to propitiate the East Indian population by making the dentist Jagan Minister of Commerce and Industry. They must have hoped that Jagan and his Red Janet would soon cool down if they were given such impressive functions. In fact, Jagan did thereafter take a decidedly more moderate stand; and the newspapers ran articles reporting that his wife was no longer bound by party ties. This, however, was not enough for the British. After a stormy debate in the House of Commons, Jagan and other leading members of the PPP were required to solemnly swear that they were not communists, merely democratic socialists. Only then would England tolerate what was now the strongest party in Guiana.

THE SINS OF THE PAST

But when Jagan at last rose to the premiership, he quickly forgot his vows and his democratic professions. In the summer of 1963, he took the occasion of the arrival of a Cuban freighter in Georgetown with a cargo of Soviet goods to deliver an inflammatory speech which once again frightened the Western world. He hailed Fidel Castro as the "first socialist premier in our hemisphere" and announced that Guiana would take "its rightful place as the first socialist country in South America." Amid the flare of flashbulbs, he brandished his fist and shouted Castro's battle cry to the crowd, *"Patria o muerte"*— "Fatherland or death." President Kennedy, who was holding discussions with Prime Minister MacMillan, blurted out that sometimes colonialism could be more of a blessing to a country than a government elected by the people.

British Guiana had once again put the United States in a dilemma. America faced the bitter necessity of deciding which she preferred: power or democracy. For the United States has vigorously assailed colonialism since the end of the Second World War. The U.S. has pressed the European colonial powers to abandon one colony after another and to grant democratic freedoms to the people in their overseas possessions. In Latin America, however, it develops that colonies firmly in the hands of their mother countries do not threaten American security, whereas once they are freed they may easily follow the trail Fidel Castro has blazed. As we have seen, Sir Alexander Bustamente's Jamaica has already given the American State Department much cause for anxiety. A free Guiana under Dr. Cheddi Jagan would be a still greater evil to Washington. Americans were therefore in the anomalous situation of pleading with their British friends not to liberate any more colonies in the American sphere.

Thus Jagan had, by his mere existence, created tensions between America and Britain. While the Americans hoped that a mild form of colonialism sustained by vigorous injections of American dollars would in time deprive Jagan of a majority of his followers, London resented such American advice and intervention. British Guiana is a British colony, the British emphasize; and it is for Britain to say when, and under what conditions, it receives its freedom.

The Guayanos have never been very happy under the colonial regime. More than half the population is still employed on sugar plantations largely run by antiquated methods. British Guiana is therefore just as dependent on a monoculture of sugar as Cuba. Jagan could point out that the British have neglected the industrialization of the country and the exploitation of its resources, and that where they have done anything in this direction none of the benefits have accrued to the people. He himself looked about for ways to raise the economy of the country by its own bootstraps.

In 1962 Jagan sought advice from Nicholas Kaldor, an exiled Hungarian teaching economics at Cambridge, England. Kaldor, a socialist, had previously drafted economic plans for a wide variety of Eastern and Western countries: for Hungary, India, Ceylon, Mexico, and Ghana. In British Guiana, however, his proposals did not work. When Jagan, on Kaldor's advice, raised the customs duties on imports and increased taxes, the impoverished Negroes as well as the wealthy businessmen rebelled. Jagan also introduced a system of forced savings, but the black Guayanos took this in bad part. They demonstrated in Georgetown, burned down almost the entire business quarter, and tried to overthrow Jagan. This time, too, British warships had to intervene—but for Jagan and against the rebellious Negroes.

After the Kaldor fiasco, the Georgetown dentist got in touch with economic experts whose theories struck him as somewhat less utopian than those of the Cambridge professor. These experts, however, happened to be located in the Soviet Union, in Poland, in Czechoslovakia, and in East Germany. These Eastern advisers gave Dr. Jagan detailed proposals on the best ways to nationalize the bauxite and iron ore mines and to create a "people's" industry in Guiana. Like Castro, Jagan could count on credit from the Soviet bloc.

In many respects, however, Jagan seemed to have learned from the example of Cuba. He did not entirely trust the Eastern assurances and in spite of his Red tendencies has not been inclined to become a thoroughly loyal satellite of the Eastern bloc. Consequently, even while he was negotiating with Eastern countries, he asked the United States for economic aid within the framework of the Alliance for Progress. The request was made while President Kennedy was still alive. Kennedy, however, suspected that American taxpayers' money was going to be used for Bolshevistic experiments. He therefore refused support for the Jagan regime.

RACIAL STRUGGLE IN GUIANA

Is Dr. Cheddi Jagan really a Communist? Or is he only a socialist radical who has been attempting after his own fashion to repair the mistakes of a wrongheaded colonial policy? Did he, like Castro, throw in his lot with the East only because the West combated, slandered, and abandoned him? These are questions which cannot yet be answered. To all appearances Dr. Jagan has been at any rate as close to the Eastern brand of Marxism as Castro. But it troubles the Communists who stand for the socialist solidarity of all races and colors that Jagan's PPP has waged not only a fanatical class struggle, but an equally fanatical race struggle.

The PPP has always been the party of the East Indians in Guiana. Negroes in East Africa learned long ago that transplanted Indians can sometimes behave quite unpleasantly and that they are anything but racially tolerant. In Guiana similar things have happened. The Indians have gradually taken over key economic, cultural, and political positions, while the overwhelming majority of Negroes and mulattoes remained in ignorance and poverty. Under the regime of Dr. Jagan, the latter could not escape the feeling that they were exchanging British domination for Indian domination.

Consequently the masses of the Negro population have repeatedly rebeled against Jagan and his PPP. Street battles between Negroes and Indians have been almost a commonplace. The UDT, the party of the planters' aristocracy, gradually gathered into itself all the discontented elements in the Negro population. The only ones who have been able to keep out of this racial conflict are the few whites, who look on in dismay at the tangled situation, and the some twenty thousand aboriginals living in the jungles on the border of Venezuela.

Jagan and his wife have certainly been unhappy about these racial conflicts. If a man calls himself a socialist, it must strike at the heart of his ideology when the most exploited part of the population of a country attacks his socialism with strikes, stone throwing, and arson. Recently Jagan made considerable efforts to win the friendship of the Negro populace. He appointed two Negroes his deputies. These two politicians seemed to have succeeded in quelling the racial antagonisms in the country, for peace gradually returned to Guiana. Jagan also seemed to have stopped eying the East with such affection. Was this a permanent change? The future will tell.

British Guiana is an impoverished, sad little country forever visited by national catastrophes. In so far as it would only be a burden to the Communists, the West hopes that they will not be too eager to take it over. The permanent racial conflict is regarded as a sign that Dr. Jagan will in the long run not succeed in transforming that remote land of swamps and jungles into a "People's Democracy." But at present everything remains in suspension.

If Dr. Cheddi Jagan should succeed in lessening the racial antagonisms, the policies of the PPP might exert a magnetic attraction upon the discontented, politically amorphous masses of the colored people in the Caribbean area and in the northern part of South America. Cold war, too, needs its bridgeheads for an advance into enemy country. British Guiana still has some of the prerequisites for becoming a Red bridgehead in South America.

Most recent developments in Guiana are also not calculated to remove these fears. In 1964 Duncan Sandys, the Conservative British

Colonial Minister, abolished the previous system of majority representation, modeled on English practice, and replaced it by pure proportional representation. The purpose of this step was to give greater
weight to the votes of the Negro population—at the expense of the
East Indians. Forbes Burnham, the Negro leader, then succeeded in
expelling Jagan's PPP from power. Burnham, who for a time was
Jagan's deputy, became head of a coalition government composed
of his own African party, the People's National Congress, and the
somewhat rightist United Front. In spite of this electoral maneuver,
however, Jagan's PPP remained the strongest party in the Guianan
parliament.

Burnham's coalition, to all intents and purposes, represents the old
planters' party, the United Democratic Party. It is pro-British, opposed
to Jagan's extremism, and monarchistic—after independence it wants
close ties with England and continued allegiance to Queen Elizabeth
as head of state. It would also like to have the new independence defended by a British striking force stationed in Guiana.

Burnham has been able to offer the people some successes. The
racial disturbances have subsided for the present; money from abroad
is flowing into the little country; and the more prosperous citizens
are beginning once more to accumulate savings. Certainly the liberal
Negro leader commands the sympathies of the Western world to a far
greater extent than did the left-socialist East Indian leader.

Cheddi Jagan subsequently boycotted the London Conference on
the future fate of Guiana. The gulf between him and Premier Burnham has widened so much that it now seems scarcely likely to be
bridged. The PPP's attacks on London have grown increasingly shrill
in tone, in spite of the replacement of Duncan Sandys by Anthony
Greenwood, the Colonial Minister of the Labour Government. It would
seem that the militant East Indian party is even more disagreeable
when forced into the opposition than when in power.

Burnham, too, is committed to independence. The date is set for
February 24, 1966. At present [December 1965] there seems to be
no certainty that Jagan can be prevented from returning to power.
The defection of Great Britain's largest remaining colony, Rhodesia,
created a major problem for the whole world. England's attempts to
smooth the way to independence for her second-largest colony, Guiana,
may stir up another hornet's nest.

MAGIC AND HUMAN RIGHTS

Ever since François Duvalier, the ruler of the Republic of Haiti, took office in 1957, he had at his side a former teacher named Clément Barbot, who served as the president's private secretary. He commanded the palace guards, organized the secret police, and created a private army to protect "Papa Doc" against any possible insurgents. Barbot's henchmen were not much different from Fulgencio Batista's secret police. They arrested, tortured, or shot anyone regarded as a political opponent of the Duvalier regime.

Only one thing divided these two Haitians who otherwise were as thick as thieves: that was their skin color. The chief of the secret police belonged to the mulatto group of the population who in this black republic regard themselves as the oligarchy. In agriculture, in business life, and in the government bureaucracy the mulattoes, although they constitute only 5 per cent of the population, have long occupied the foremost positions. From the start of his regime Papa Doc resented their dominance. He declared war on the mulatto coffee planters, ejected the mulatto government officials, and appointed only those Haitians who could prove they were *authentiques,* that is to say, racially pure Negroes. To Duvalier's mind mulattoes were half Frenchmen, reminders of the one-time colonial French rule. Since the mulattoes also thought of themselves as half Frenchmen and shamelessly exploited their black fellow citizens in the manner of the old French Creoles, Dr. Duvalier invented a special term for them. The mulattoes, he declared, were capitalist "obstructionists."

No one can explain why Duvalier nevertheless tolerated and elevated the mulatto Barbot. Secretly, however, Papa Doc must have borne his police chief a deep grudge, for in 1960 Barbot suddenly found himself in the hands of this own henchmen and was chained in the dungeon of Fort Dimanche exactly as he had previously chained other hapless prisoners. Barbot was probably the most prominent victim in Duvalier's persecution of the mulattoes. However, a former police chief sometimes has resources denied the ordinary citizen. With the aid of friends, Barbot fled from the horrors of Fort Dimanche, obtained illicit weapons from the United States, and established a gang which conducted a protracted guerrilla warfare against Duvalier and his men. In the long run, however, the mulatto rebel was defeated by the black dictator. In July 1963 he was trapped in a field of sugar cane and cut down by the machine-gun bullets of Duvalier's Negro militia. Papa Doc promptly spread the glad tidings among the Haitian Negroes, declaring that "African" Haiti had won a great victory over "French" Haiti.

A majority of the Haiti Negroes are to this day attached to the voodoo cult. This curious mélange of ancient African religion, black magic, and perverted Christianity is so rife there that the situation has recently given rise to violent controversies between the Haitian Government and the Vatican. In spite of Duvalier's statements, the voodooists refuse to believe that Barbot had really been killed. Instead they assert that the ex-police chief has changed himself into a black dog which is still creating all sorts of mischief in Haiti and which can at any time change back into Clément Barbot.

Malicious tongues even claimed that Papa Doc himself believes this story. It is possible that the Haitian dictator has flirted a little with the voodoo cult. Nevertheless he is not, intellectually speaking, a wild bush man. He merely makes skillful use of his subjects' superstitions for his own political ends.

THE HAITIAN SCALE OF SKIN COLOR

Today the island of Haiti lies on the periphery of world history. Politically, economically, and socially it now lags behind other lands in the Caribbean area. Racist-minded Europeans and Americans customarily attribute this decline to the fact that the Republic of Haiti is inhabited largely by Negroes. The somewhat lighter Dominican Republic, the neighbor that shares the island of Hispaniola with Haiti, they point out, is not nearly so depraved and disorderly.

The argument is a curious specimen of racist illogic, for Haiti was once the most progressive country in the Caribbean area—not in spite of but because of its black population. The history of Haiti, along with that of Mexico, is the most exciting and most instructive in all Latin America. Mexico, however, has gradually climbed forth into the light out of the abysses of her past, whereas Haiti has sunk back into the morasses. Due to the evil times that have befallen Haiti since the beginning of the nineteenth century, it has by now been almost forgotten that Hispaniola was once the most precious gem in the colonial crown of two empires. For the Spaniards, Hispaniola was the springboard for subjection of the Central and South American mainland. For the French the western part of the island, which she occupied under Louis XIV, remained for a full century their richest and most valuable territory overseas.

At the time of the island's discovery, the aboriginal Indians of Haiti were scattered over the island in five independent "kingdoms" under caciques. There were about two and a half million of them and Columbus praised them in lyrical terms: "They are so charming, gentle and peaceful that I can declare there is not a better race of men nor a more beautiful country in the whole world. They love their neighbors as themselves. Their language is pleasant and full of grace; there is always a smile on their lips. . . . When their first alarm was over and they had gathered courage they gave everything they had so generously that one would have had to witness the scene one's self in order to believe it. If one asked anything of them they never said no."

These friendly Indians were rapidly enslaved. Forced labor in the plantations and in the gold mines of San Cristoforo resulted in genocide. Within fifteen years after the island's discovery, only sixty thousand of the natives were left. The Spaniards thereupon brought in tens of thousands of Carib Indians whom they had captured on the other islands, principally on the Bahamas. But these imported islanders likewise died like flies under the harsh conditions of forced labor. It was the extermination of the Indians on Haiti that prompted Bishop Bartolomé de las Casas to ask for his famous interview with Emperor Charles V. Las Casas recommended to the emperor the importation of Negro slaves. Negroes, he thought, were physically more robust than Indians and more accustomed to hard work in tropical climates. Thus the kindly bishop who could no longer bear to witness the suffering of the Caribs introduced the equally horrible pattern of Negro slavery into Spanish America.

The advice of Las Casas, however, had still other consequences. In spite of his efforts, the Indians died out; today there is only a small sprinkling of the Haitian Indians on the Dutch West Indian island of Aruba, to which they were once transplanted for more or less philosophic reasons. The importation of black slaves to Haiti, however, soon assumed such proportions that as early as 1565 the Italian historian Girolamo Barzoni exclaimed prophetically: "The African Negroes will within a short time raise themselves up to be masters of the island." Barzoni's prophecy was fulfilled—if two centuries can be considered a short time. It might indeed have been fulfilled in his lifetime. The Spaniards concentrated all of their energy on their possessions on the mainland. The West Indian islands were so neglected and lapsed into such misery that an organized rebellion of the slaves could scarcely have been opposed by the few whites who had remained behind. But the English, and then the French, arrived.

Just as the English established themselves on Jamaica and on the majority of the islands of the Lesser Antilles, the French seized the western part of Haiti. French Haiti, then called Saint Domingue, at first became a base for buccaneers and then a colony on which the French set up plantations. The importation of slaves increased. During the hundred and thirty years of French rule approximately one million Negro slaves were transplanted to Haiti. In the same period of time four hundred thousand Negroes were born on Haiti. Nevertheless, records of 1790 indicate only five hundred thousand Negroes in the French part of Haiti. This suggests that the French took as great a toll of laborers' lives as had their Spanish predecessors.

Between masters and slaves a third group gradually developed, the *gens de couleur,* as the French called them, the mulattoes. White women were scarce in the colonies and both the French and Spanish planters were not averse to taking their black slave girls to bed. The Spaniards, who had no particular race prejudices, permitted the mulattoes to rise in the world to some extent. The French, however, imposed extremely stringent racial legislation which we might almost compare with the racial laws of the nazi dictatorship. Only after their revolution did the French throw off these prejudices, but then they did so to an extent unmatched by any other European nation.

The Negro slave stood on the lowest rung of the color hierarchy in Haiti. The various Negro-mulatto mixtures, the *griffes, sacatras,* and *marabous,* were not much better off than he. Today they have been completely absorbed in the Haitian Negro population. The real mulatto, half white and half black by birth, occupied a somewhat higher social position. They were followed by the *quarterones* and the *octerones,* people of one-fourth and one-eighth white blood. The descendants of these people today form the core of the light brown Haitian oligarchy, those three hundred families who own the greatest part of the wealth of the land and against whom Duvalier has declared war. In colonial times and long afterward all these groups hated and despised one another. In the eyes of the French colonial masters, Negro blood in the veins of an ancestor ceased to be considered a social barrier only after six generations.

It is essential to know these demographic conditions in order to understand the island's further history and present situation. On the eve of the French Revolution, the total population of French Haiti stood at about 570,000. Of these 500,000, as we have said, were Negro slaves. The small remainder consisted half of free people of mixed blood and more or less brown color, and the other half of white or nearly white planters.

In the Spanish eastern part of the island, San Domingo, the population was only half as large, of which almost 60 per cent were mulattoes and 15 per cent were whites. Thus the Negro slaves there represented only a quarter of the population. In the thinly settled and economically undeveloped Spanish colony, which gradually declined to a land of shepherds and small farmers, they were far better off than their fellows on the coffee and sugar plantations of the French colony.

THE BLACK NAPOLEON

The French Revolution blew the whole Haitian slave system to bits. Negroes and mulattoes hailed the proclamations of Mirabeau, Lafayette, and Robespierre calling for abolition for slavery and the introduction of the rights of man in the colonies. The planters, however, almost all of them royalists by conviction, had no intention of implementing the ideas of the theorists back home. The result was a succession of Negro and mulatto uprisings. The mulattoes demanded complete equality with the whites; the Negroes demanded at least liberation from slavery. But there was an exceedingly tense relationship between the two rebelling groups, for the mulattoes feared for their special position if the Negroes were conceded the same rights as they were demanding for themselves.

Ultimately the French National Convention sent a number of commissioners to Haiti to investigate the situation on the restive island. The commissioners saw that the mulattoes would lend them vigorous support in their struggles against colonial royalism. But they also realized the abolition of Negro slavery would tend to undermine the Haitian economy. They therefore extended the rights of man to the free colored people but not to the black slaves. The Haitians' three-class system became a two-class system.

Soon afterward the whole island was in flames. The Negroes felt that the revolution had cheated them. They ran away from their masters, burned down plantations, and seized large sections of the interior. At the Peace of Bargal in 1795, the Spanish eastern part of Hispaniola was awarded to France, the French Republic having traded its conquests in the Spanish motherland for the remote Spanish colony. Thus the Negro rebellion spread to San Domingo. Since the Negroes at first had no political ideas and aims but were impelled only by obscure feelings of hatred and cravings for vengeance, both parts of Haiti were soon on the point of being engulfed in chaos and bloodshed.

In this situation there emerged a man who to this day is considered the greatest Negro leader of the Americas—the former slave, coachman, and plantation overseer François Dominique Toussaint, called L'Ouverture. Toussaint had acquired an amazing education by self-study in the library of his extremely liberal master. He had drawn many lessons from his reading in history and military science. Thus at the outbreak of the slave rebellion he pointed out that the decline of Rome had once been brought about by rebellious slaves. "Perhaps," he proclaimed, "the fate of Rome will in centuries to come be the fate of all Europe."

Inevitably, this highly intelligent man found himself at the head of the Haitian Revolution. Preceding leaders of the rebels, whose program began and ended with arson, had nothing to pit against him. Above all, Toussaint was distinguished by one quality which raised him far above his illiterate fellow fighters: he felt no personal animosity toward either the free mulattoes or the white masters. In this respect he was a genuine child of the French Revolution, a much more authentic revolutionary than the commissioners from Paris, who had found themselves in the same dilemma as present-day democrats, and who for reasons of expediency had decided against full democracy. Toussaint proclaimed the necessity for peaceful co-operation of people of all colors on the island. Since he was the only person who could guarantee the restoration of orderly conditions on the island, the Directory in Paris, in 1798, finally granted the Negroes complete freedom and equality. At the same time Toussaint was appointed commanding general of all the troops in Haiti. Even the white planters now had to obey him.

Thus for the first time a Negro had achieved power in a European colony. At first Toussaint used his authority most cautiously. He expressly declared his allegiance to the French motherland. This loyalty was based on sound considerations. Only honest collaboration among blacks, browns, and whites could transform the former slave colony into a healthy body politic founded upon free labor. The economy had to be sustained. The former slaves had to relearn the necessity of work after this period of breakdown.

Toussaint's system testifies to a prudence and insight very seldom found in victorious liberators of slaves. He issued a general amnesty for blacks, browns, and whites, for masters, freedmen, slaves, royalists, republicans, and rebels. He encouraged the planters to take up their old possessions once more and guaranteed them protection of person and of property. He confirmed the emancipation of all slaves but bound them to work for another five years on their former masters' plantations. For this work they were to be paid a fourth of the net profits. Thus Toussaint was attempting a smooth transition from the plantation economy to free agriculture. Moreover, he realized fully that a liberated slave had to be habituated slowly, step by step, to freedom, so that he would neither abuse his freedom nor quickly lose it again.

In the beginning, everything ran smoothly in Toussaint L'Ouverture's Haiti. The white planters reluctantly accepted the fact that this revolutionary was their best ally. Toussaint had occasional trouble only with the mulattoes, for the free gens de couleur, who had hoped to take over full dominion on the island of Haiti, could hardly stomach having a Negro above them. They instigated a multitude of small uprisings. These mulatto uprisings have ever since been a consistent feature of the history of black Haiti.

Gradually, the mulattoes and the discontented Frenchmen united in a game of intrigue that threatened to undermine the authority of the black Napoleon. White and brown Haitians saw their privileges vanishing. It especially irked them when Toussaint, with the moral fervor of a Robespierre, launched a campaign against the dens of vice, prostitution, and idleness. All this talk of virtue and work was foreign to the ears of French Creole society. And when Toussaint was drawn into a murderous civil war against a newly formed mulatto republic in the southwestern part of the island, petitions and denunciations of the "black dictator" began to heap up on Napoleon's desk in Paris.

In Latin America, the propertied classes have seldom known when they had a good ruler. Toussaint could have assured the republic long-term peaceful development, and he could have done this without seizing private property and without arousing racial feelings. He was politically far more foresighted than his enemies, the aristocratic Creoles and the mulattoes. Haiti has been a paradigm of the fate of many a Central and South American country. The oligarchs overthrew the moderate reformer because they disliked a certain few of his policies, and thus drew down upon themselves the radicalism that was to be their doom.

LIBERTY, EQUALITY, FRATERNITY

Disappointed by Napoleon, disturbed by French plans for invasion, and determined to preserve the gains he had painfully achieved in the country, Toussaint finally broke with the motherland. Amazingly modern legislation followed: decrees concerning social and working conditions, orders for the building of roads and schools, plans for the organization and administration of the new government. Moreover, Toussaint fought the voodoo cult. A true child of the Age of Enlightenment, he regarded the magic rituals, dances, and sacrifices as reactionary and seditious.

As yet there had been no real outbreak of radicalism in Haiti. Toussaint ruled his model state based on virtue and high principles with patriarchal severity and justice. His army was the biggest that had ever been seen in America up to that time, bigger even than the fighting forces during the American Revolution. He had nearly 150,000 men, Negroes, mulattoes and whites, under arms. The general staff, organized on the French model, was considered to be first rate. Discipline slackened only when the smoldering embers of old resentments flared. Mulattoes and Negroes still could not tolerate one another. Moreover, some Negro officers continued to be moved by dark memories of the slave days; they alarmed the white population by open hostility and occasional excesses. But Toussaint dealt with such cases with inexorable severity. He executed even his own nephew, among the hundreds of colored soldiers and workers condemned for crimes against the lives or property of white Haitians.

Toussaint's fate was sealed, however, when Napoleon began to think in terms of empire and therefore determined to recapture Haiti. Probably the First Consul was whipped up against the black reformer by his Creole wife, Josephine Beauharnais. Josephine came from the West Indian planter aristocracy; she could conceive of a Negro only as a slave. The result was the Napoleonic invasion of Haiti. The world saw the spectacle of West Indian Negroes singing the *Marseillaise* and hurling their own slogans of liberty, equality, fraternity at the French invaders. But it was not Napoleon's army that unseated Toussaint; it was rather a complicated series of treacheries. Countless mulatto officers deserted to the French. Negro leaders, including the later president and emperor of Haiti, Jean Jacques Dessalines, who proclaimed Haitian independence in 1804, avenged themselves for this treason by massacring every white they could lay hands on. The Napoleonic officers in turn took vengeance by mass shootings of Negroes. What Toussaint had been trying to stave off now took place: Haiti lapsed into chaos, into self-laceration. On top of the bloodshed came an epidemic of yellow fever that threatened to depopulate the island.

In order to put an end to the suffering, Toussaint concluded an armistice with Napoleon's general, Leclerc. He hoped that with the assistance of the French troops he could stop the destruction, calm the people, and establish a peaceful *modus vivendi*. Leclerc, however, violated the agreement. He kidnaped the black Napoleon and sent him to France. Imprisoned in a cold, damp cell in the fortress of Brest, Toussaint died after only a year. Thus the one man who could have established peace in Haiti was swept from the stage. Napoleon himself, however, never understood, any more than do present-day autocrats, that the elimination of liberal reformers does not bring about a restoration of former conditions, but only invites political avalanches. Eighteen years later, when Napoleon was in his turn a prisoner on St. Helena, he commented with a shrug on the case of Toussaint L'Ouverture: "How could the death of a wretched Negro have mattered to me!"

THE LONG KNIVES

The betrayal of Toussaint shook Haiti to such an extent that the country has not recovered to this day. Napoleon had made the hero of Haitian liberty a martyr of the black race. New rebellions broke out. This time they were headed not by an intelligent statesman like Toussaint L'Ouverture, but by the fanatical demagogue Jean Jacques Dessalines, who stirred up the masses with the battle cry "The last white dog must die." Dessalines applied his slogan literally. Wild with hatred, the Haitian troops defeated the invaders. In the spring of 1804 Dessalines instituted a "Night of the Long Knives." Everyone of white skin and French origin on Haiti was slaughtered. Power was now entirely in the hands of Negroes. When Napoleon had himself crowned emperor, Dessalines would take no second place. He assumed the title of Jacques I, Emperor of Haiti.

The black empire of the West Indies did not last long. Two years after his coronation, Dessalines was assassinated by mulatto opponents. The strife between Negroes and mulattoes broke out anew. Things were so chaotic that Spanish forces had no difficulty reconquering the eastern part of the island, the present Dominican Republic.

For twelve years in Haiti the troops of a mulatto republic under President Pétion fought against the troops of the Negro republic under the black King Henri Christophe. The war ended in the complete exhaustion of both parties. Haiti was then ruled by a succession of presidents, emperors, and dictators, some Negro, some mulatto. None of them were able to put an end to the political chaos. If a mulatto fought his way to the presidency, the Negroes rebelled. If a black seized power, the mulattoes revolted.

Around 1850 a black Haitian once more attempted to imitate a French exemplar. His name was Faustin Soulouque. Under the name of Emperor Faustin I, he declared economic war on England, France, and the United States, and attacked the mulatto Dominican Republic, which had meanwhile gained its independence. However the Dominicans were more than a match for the black emperor, who was finally forced to concede defeat. With that, San Domingo withdrew from the history of Haiti and returned to the history of Ibero-America.

The western part of the island, however, the Republic of Haiti,

continued to have a loose connection with the former French motherland to the extent that the inhabitants spoke an old-fashioned patois.
This Haitian patois has remained to this day the language of the
Negro republic. It is a somewhat stilted, baroque-sounding language
which makes a ludicrous impression, rather like Haitian politics.

In spite of the Negro majority on the Republic of Haiti, mulatto
families and clans managed to seize the larger part of the former
French landed property. Consequently the mulatto oligarchy came
out for a liberalization of trade, low tariffs, and low taxes on big business. Such policies naturally won them the sympathies of the overseas colonial powers. The propertyless Negroes, on the other hand,
demanded nationalization of the economy and stiff taxation of the
well-to-do.

Since the end of Emperor Faustin, the party struggles and civil
wars in Haiti have revolved around the conflicts between the liberal
Cacos and the nationalistic *Lizards*. The *Cacos,* which means parrots,
represented the mulattoes; the *Lizards,* the Negroes. Toussaint's idea
of gradually educating an underdeveloped people to the uses of
freedom has long since been smothered by cruelties, guerrilla warfare, and endless intrigues. Haiti swings continually between the
poles of dictatorship and anarchy. A great opportunity was missed on
this island, perhaps the greatest that was ever offered to a country in
the West Indies. When the United States occupied Haiti during the
First World War in order at last to establish order on the chaotic
island, she attempted to re-educate the members of the mulatto upper
class and teach them to be genuine democrats. Mulattoes have since
provided the majority of presidents and dictators—but not by any
means of the democratic sort that the Americans had in mind. Most of
the mulatto presidents of the recent past have ruled Haiti by force
and violence just as much as the black emperors of her earlier history.
The result was, in 1956, another Negro upsurge which brought Papa
Doc to power.

PAPA DOC AND THE VOODOO CULT

Papa Doc is both a nationalist and a socialist. What is more, he
regards himself not as an American but an African. This mild-looking
man with mournful eyes hidden behind thick horn-rimmed glasses
is not the least bit mild when the mulatto question is involved. He is

doing everything he can to strip the mulatto upper class of its power. In addition, he toys with all sorts of plans for socialization. Since the Communists and Castroites have not gained a foothold on Haiti, he has the majority of the black-skinned population on his side. Nevertheless, Papa Doc knows only too well that he cannot carry out his social reforms without aid from the United States. Haiti's foreign exchange comes principally from the sale of coffee, which in the main goes to the United States. A second source of income is the stream of North American tourists who periodically pour into the island. Haiti has a special lure for whites who are interested in unadulterated folklore and the fantastic practices of the voodooists. Such tourists are willing to accept the poverty of the Haitians as romantic local color.

Dr. Duvalier is quite well aware of all this. He therefore cannot afford to offend the Americans or to attempt a struggle with the powerful United Fruit Company and the other foreign fruit importers who control about one third of the Haitian plantations. For its part, the United Fruit Company tolerates Duvalier, although it would undoubtedly prefer a "liberal" mulatto president. For as long as the emotions of Haitian Negroes are directed against the propertied mulattoes and not against the secret masters of the country, the fruit companies, there need be no fear that the Haitian republic will turn into a second Cuba.

Nevertheless, Dr. Duvalier has recently fallen into disfavor with Americans and Europeans. He has quarreled with the Haitian Catholic Church, has taken the Archbishop of Haiti into temporary custody, and has officially sanctioned three voodoo sects, the Congos, Zombies, and Radars, as state religions. Toussaint, a child of the French Enlightenment, had viewed such cults as relapses into savagery, but to Dr. Duvalier they are natural, authentic features of Haitian religious life. To our minds, conditioned to the patterns of Occidental Christianity, the neo-African cults in Central and South America, which are steadily winning more followers, seem thoroughly abstruse. In fact they are manifestations of religious nationalism. Christianity left the Latin American Negroes to their own devices for hundreds of years. They underwent long periods of intense suffering under Christian masters. Voodoo is a religious and spiritual protest.

Since Papa Doc has come to power, the voodoo priests are once more permitted to drum their followers together in remote jungle temples for those magical ceremonies which have served as such good copy for innumerable travel writers. Black cocks and goats festooned with red ribbons are sacrificed on chopping-block altars. The holy serpent is venerated. The believers dance themselves into a frenzy which strongly resembles an epileptic fit.

The religious dances of voodooism have given rise to the sexual dances which have made Haiti so attractive to sensation-hungry tourists. Such dances are performed everywhere in the towns; they are deliberately intended as tourist bait. The performers do not dance in couples; each dances alone, pantomiming all the stages of the sexual act to the point of orgasm. The close connection between religion and sexuality among African tribes is well known. Voodoo ceremonies can frequently degenerate into mass orgies. The dances in the night clubs of Port-au-Prince, however, no longer have any connection with voodoo. They are concessions to a perverted white audience.

In Africa there is also a close bond between religion and malevolent magical practices. Voodoo, especially with the Zombie sect, often becomes black magic. It is said that the priests hypnotize the more susceptible members of their flocks, converting them into will-less tools of their sinister plans. Specialists maintain that hypnotized voodooists have frequently committed crimes under the influence of their priests. Moreover, the voodoo priests know how to produce states of death-like rigidity by hypnotic methods. They then bring the sham corpses back to life, thus demonstrating to their believers that they possess divine powers.

Of course such magical arts have existed in all religions throughout history. Voodooism should not be harshly condemned because of them. In general the Haitian sects merely satisfy the naïve credulity of the islanders—which Christianity, because of its league with the upper classes, has been unable to do. Papa Doc knows very well why he sanctions the voodoo sects. He considers it better for his subjects to exhaust their energies in dances and magical rites than in the bush wars that have been so prevalent in Haiti.

Voodoo and orgiastic dances, oppressive poverty and ignorance among the masses, child prostitution in the ports, a limping economy, and heart-rending misery in the countryside caused by hurricanes, floods, and other periodically recurrent natural disasters—these seem to have been the end result of the Haitian struggle for freedom. But upon close examination we will see that underneath all this surprising cultural energies are stirring in Haiti. Haitian poets are attracting more and more attention and respect. The naïve art of Haiti has stimulated a whole generation of European and American painters and sculptors. Haiti is by no means a primitive, archaic spot given over to macabre nocturnal jungle rites and all sorts of African savageries. Haiti is only an unfortunate country that has retreated into the past because its future was choked off on the threshold of freedom.

The road that Toussaint L'Ouverture had once taken was lost in the jungles. There were no successors to Toussaint, whose effort it was to clear away the underbrush. It will be the task of a future generation to put an end to the race war, to tear down the wall between poor and rich, to build schools, set up industries, and thus, after one hundred and sixty years, bring Toussaint's struggle to a victorious conclusion—the struggle for the rights of man.

GOD AND TRUJILLO

The United States tried to do in the Dominican Republic what it had so signally failed to accomplish in Haiti. Twice Americans attempted to terminate the tradition of dictators in that country and replace dictatorship by a liberal democracy. They used their influence in 1924 to elect a man named Horacio Vásquez as president. Vásquez, they hoped, would rule the country with lawbooks rather than guns. But a gun in the hands of Rafael Leonidas Trujillo destroyed Horacio Vásquez's lawbooks. In 1930, under Trujillo, the Dominican Republic returned to its customary dictatorship. A resigned Washington gave the dictator its blessing. When Trujillo was at last shot down, after thirty-one years of rule, the United States tried the same experiment again. After a turbulent period of transition, America managed to obtain the election of liberal Professor Juan Bosch as president. This second extension course in democracy ended like the first: after nine months Juan Bosch was overthrown by a military dictatorship, and the Dominican Republic found itself once more under the yoke of dictatorship.

An effort in the reverse direction—to stamp out a democratic up-rising and thus fortify the traditional military dictatorship—was undertaken by President Johnson in 1965, when American marines again occupied the Dominican Republic. Behind the rebellion that Johnson wanted to quell stood this same Juan Bosch of whom President Kennedy had approved. Bosch was then in exile in Puerto Rico, hoping for the ultimate overthrow of the dictatorship. This time American sympathies were obviously not on his side and that of his rebel leader, Caamaño, but on the side of the conservative rightist military rulers, Imbert and Wessin y Wessin. As a result of this intervention, the Dominican Republic once more became the center of a major crisis which has had profound repercussions on world politics.

The question inevitably arises: was it mere chance that America has had so little luck with its attempts at re-education? Periods of democratization have been very brief in Santo Domingo, whereas dictatorships have written virtually the whole history of the republic. Do Americans have so little trust in Caribbean democrats that they prefer to arrive at an understanding with a dictatorship rather than support a democratic regime to the hilt?

THE MULATTOES OF HISPANIOLA

After its separation from the Negro Republic of Haiti, the Dominican Republic traversed as tortuous a path as its unfortunate neighbor on the island. There, too, there were two rival castes: the oligarchy, consisting of Spanish ranchers and successful mulattoes, and the common people, composed of poor mulattoes and propertyless blacks.

At first the descendants of the former Spanish masters held the reins of government. They accorded the clergy the greater part of the power in the state, and as late as 1850 were planning reintroduction of the Inquisition. The Spanish landowner General Santana, who had defeated Emperor Faustin of Haiti, tried to create a little order in the republic and to control the pro-Inquisition members of his own class. But his conservative *Partido Azul*, the Blue Party, barely managed to hold its own in semimilitary conflicts with the liberal Red Party, the *Partido Rojo*. Santana consequently decided in 1861 in favor of reunion of the republic with Spain. Within four years Spanish misrule proved so onerous that the *Rojos* came to power. They promptly broke the ties with the motherland again. But the liberal president, Buenaventura Báez, could not begin to solve the problems of the country. He turned to the United States, requesting her to annex Santo Domingo. President Grant was willing and eager, but the Senate refused to ratify the treaty on the ground that it was disguised aggression against a small, weak country. There was, in addition, suspicion of Báez, whose corruption was notorious.

The Blues and Reds continued to skirmish. Toward the end of the nineteenth century a Haitian Negro named Ulises Heureaux took advantage of this permanent struggle to seize power. For the first time a representative of the Dominican plebeians had reached the presidency. The common people, however, gained nothing, for the Negro general ruled just as despotically as the Haitian emperor. Since that time, the Dominican Republic has forsworn all experiments with Negro rulers. The Heureaux regime left such a memory of horrors in the hearts of the Dominican mulatto population that to this day no Negro politician has much of a chance in Santo Domingo.

The mulattoes finally fought their way into the seats of power in the republic. However, they do not like to be reminded of their origins once they have attained political and economic prestige. Rafael Leonidas Trujillo, a typical Dominican mulatto, used to make a good deal of his Spanish blood, and his business friends in Europe and America readily referred to him as a "white." Even in the racist states of the American South, the Trujillo clan was not exposed to discrimination. Dangerous though it is for any mulatto to appear with a white woman south of the Mason-Dixon line, the male members of the Trujillo family could vacation pleasantly in Florida, mingling with white women of high society and the demimonde.

THE DOMINICAN LEADER CULT

The shadows of the Trujillo era will continue to darken the Dominican Republic for some time to come, just as the shadows of the Hitler era could not be effaced overnight in Germany. Dominican history came to a head in Trujillo; he was the most typical and most brutal representative of a long tradition. The Benefactor's father belonged to the mulatto lower class and lived chiefly by cattle theft. The cattle thief's son rose in the army and in 1930 came to power by the sort of coup that is customary in Latin America. Aside from an intermezzo of four years, he held that power firmly until his assassination. His success was due to his technique of gradually transforming the entire country into a private estate of the Trujillo family.

The Trujillo Trust held the monopolies for tobacco, coffee, cocoa, salt, matches, and the exploitation of mineral resources. Members of the Trujillo clan ran the national lottery and directed the transportation system. The Trujillos were also the largest cattle dealers in the state. They owned the biggest slaughterhouse and established the prices for meat and milk. The president had soldiers operate his dairy herds, then sold the milk to the government party. It was paid for by a special tax on government officials. Thus Trujillo could pose as the donor of milk to the poor, for the party was forced to deliver free milk to the needy. "God and Trujillo give you milk"—this lesson was impressed upon every inhabitant of the Dominican Republic. The dictator's milk business is but a small example of the practices whereby Trujillo simultaneously increased his reputation as a benefactor and his fortune.

Trujillo was very fond of being compared with God. Every water fountain in the capital, which had been renamed Ciudad Trujillo, bore the inscription "God and Trujillo supply you with water!" Under a shade tree the lounger might read "You owe this shade to God and Trujillo." On the main streets, neon lights proclaimed "God and Trujillo!" Occasionally Trujillo put himself first. The number plate of every automobile in the Dominican Republic bore the slogan "Long live Trujillo!" Anyone who obtained a driver's license in the republic would also find another reminder of the leader cult. All licenses were adorned with "Viva Trujillo!" No newspaper in the Dominican Republic could mention the dictator's name without also citing his official titles: "President of the Republic, Generalissimo, Benefactor of the Nation, Liberator of the Fatherland, Restorer of Financial Independence, Founder and Supreme Leader of the Dominican Party, Protector of Art and the Sciences." This Byzantinism finally reached such extravagance that some one hundred Dominican towns and villages bore the name of Trujillo and almost two thousand monuments paid tribute to his greatness.

Since the "Father of the Fatherland," as he also called himself, was a great invoker of God, he hoped the Vatican would show proper gratitude and at least confer upon him the official title of "Benefactor of the Church." But the Vatican was only too well informed on the many executions and poisonings which suggested that the Dominican dictator was a spiritual descendant of the Borgias rather than a model of the Christian prince. Rome therefore politely turned him down. He received a similar rejection when he proposed himself for the Nobel Peace Prize.

THE DICTATOR'S SALTO MORTALE

Although the United States appreciated the peace, cleanliness, orderliness, and excellent commercial climate afforded by Trujillo's republic, it did not like the dictator's refusal to tolerate an opposition party. The strong man was needed, but at least the semblance of democracy ought to be preserved. Consequently, after the end of the Second World War, Trujillo was urged to tolerate a political opposition. He did so, after his own fashion. He established several opposition parties whose programs differed in no way from his own and which zealously gave him their votes.

The real opposition had long since gone underground or into exile—like the opposition in Hitler Germany. But The Benefactor had a long arm. His political opponents were kidnaped from the United States or shot down in the streets of New York. He fought the underground by executing some five thousand Dominicans. In the course of his everlasting border disputes with neighboring Haiti, Trujillo troops killed some ten thousand Haitians.

Nevertheless, the American government was paying the Trujillo state an annual subsidy of $600,000. Only after clever journalists had ferreted out the fact that this sum did not reach the Dominican Treasury, but went into private pockets—only then did the American taxpayers begin to revolt. And Americans finally had enough when in 1960 Trujillo dispatched his agents to assassinate one of the most loyal friends of the United States, the then President of Venezuela, Rómulo Betancourt. Betancourt, one of the few genuine democrats among Latin American presidents, was an unswerving adversary of all dictatorship, both of the right and of the left. And Trujillo, from the beginning of his career, was out to liquidate such people.

Perhaps the era of Trujillo would not have come to so swift an end if the Dominican dictator had not essayed a particular kind of *salto mortale*. When Dominican-American relations began to cool perceptibly after the unsuccessful attempt to assassinate Betancourt, Trujillo tried to establish contact with Fidel Castro and the Kremlin. Whether he only wanted to pressure the United States, or whether he actually thought the Communists would take to their bosoms a supercapitalist like himself, is a moot question. In any case, on May 30, 1961, The Benefactor sank under a hail of bullets from rebel army officers.

THE UNDIGESTED PAST

The Trujillo Trust drained the Dominican Republic to the point of acute anemia. When Juan Bosch became president in the first free election that had taken place in his country in thirty-eight years, he admitted that he had literally to go begging abroad in order to raise funds for the government's budget. According to Bosch's calculations, the Trujillos had transferred some $250,000,000 abroad. For a country of only two and a half million inhabitants, that is a bloodletting of nearly fatal proportions.

The idealist Bosch probably lost Washington's good will primarily because it was not in his character to rule with a "strong hand." But his democratic experiment also failed partly because he had no money to carry out essential social reforms. For only a democracy with sufficient funds at its disposal can prevent the radicalization of the fermenting masses and simultaneously defend itself successfully against ambitious army officers.

The United States seemed to have far more sympathy for the subsequent military dictatorship headed by Brigadier General Antonio Imbert and the "strong man" in his junta, General Wessin y Wessin, than it had had for the short-lived Dominican democracy. The two military men were, to be sure, said to have participated in the assassination of Trujillo; nevertheless, they ruled the Dominican Republic in the usual manner of dictators until the spring of 1965.

The uprising of April started as a movement to restore the legally elected ex-President Bosch. The leader of the rebels, Colonel Francisco Caamaño, was popular, and was known to be a foe of all dictatorship and a proponent of free elections. His civilian adviser, the leftist liberal politician Hector Aristi, obviously desired nothing more than restoration of law and justice and replacement of the coercive junta rule by a constitutional government. President Johnson himself admitted that the rebels wanted to restore "democracy and social justice"; he stressed that he did not doubt the honest motives of Caamaño and his followers.

Nevertheless, Johnson suppressed the uprising by force of arms. Once again the shadow of the bearded Cuban fell across the Latin American stage; once again Washington's actions revealed the extent to which Cuba had become an American trauma. For Washington justified invasion on the ground that communistic and Castroistic elements had succeeded in taking over the leadership of the uprising. Johnson added (in an oblique allusion to his predecessor Kennedy's conciliatory policy) the explanation that he would not sit in a rocking chair with folded hands while a new communistic regime was being set up in the Western Hemisphere.

Assistant Secretary of State Thomas Mann seems to have played a key role in the intervention. Or, at any rate, the left wing of the Democratic Party charges that this expert in Latin American affairs has shown little understanding of the democratic reform movements in Latin America. A proclamation of the ADA demanded his resignation shortly after the intervention began. William Tapley Bennett, U. S. Ambassador in Santo Domingo, was attacked with equal vehemence. Juan Bosch maintains that Bennett has unequivocally backed the military dictator Imbert, and that he gave President Johnson false information which led to the intervention decision.

In any case, wherever the fault lay, Communist infiltration of the rebel movement was never proved, and probably scarcely existed— if only because the Dominican Republic has virtually no Communists. Could the alleged fifty-eight Dominican Communists have seriously threatened the security of the Western Hemisphere? Was it actually necessary to send in 24,000 American soldiers against barely 4000 democratic rebels and fifty-eight Communists, and thus (as Juan Bosch rightly said) "make more communists in Latin America within a week than the propaganda of the Russians, the Chinese and the Cubans succeeded in doing in five years"?

A CARIBBEAN PRECEDENT

The landing of American marines in Santo Domingo was also criticized with unusual sharpness in the West. General de Gaulle condemned the intervention, cited the principle of noninterference in the internal affairs of other countries, and called for withdrawal of the invaders. The Latin American dictators, logically enough, applauded Washington's action, but the four democracies, Mexico, Chile, Uruguay, and Peru, expressed protest and were particularly indignant that Washington had acted without informing the OAS. The Uruguayan delegate to the United Nations spoke of a "Johnson Doctrine" that not only aimed to keep communism out of Latin America, but also gave the United States the mandate to decide what communism is, when the danger of a communist uprising exists, and consequently when any intervention may take place.

At the end of May 1965 Washington finally realized that the constitutionalists under Caamaño might well be better friends and allies than the members of the junta, who behaved with increasing arrogance, constantly broke the truce, sabotaged negotiations, and appeared determined to stay in power at all costs. But by then it was too late. The Inter-American Force of 9000 American parachute troops and 2500 Brazilian and Central American soldiers and policemen, which replaced the U.S. expeditionary force, found itself confronting a political and moral rubble heap. Bosch's prediction that American intervention in the Dominican Republic would have "enormous consequences" throughout Latin America seemed on the verge of proving true.

No matter how the State Department justifies this intervention, the fact remains that it represented a glaring breach of the principle of nonintervention which the United States was pledged to by treaty. American foreign-policy makers are fond of upholding their actions on moral grounds; their moral position therefore depends on faithful observance of treaties, as they themselves never tire of repeating. The fact remains, however, that Johnson first "overreacted" and favored the junta, then declared himself neutral, then took up negotiations with the rebels, and finally tried to force the junta to resign. But this last was exactly what Bosch and Caamaño had also wanted. Any unbiased observer must therefore ask: what was the point of the whole intervention? The moral arguments have, at any rate, been completely turned inside out.

What will the future hold for this pitiable country, still so dogged by its disastrous past? In conjunction with the OAS the United States is now endeavoring to sustain a relatively acceptable interim government until free elections can be held. A variety of politicians, all of them Bosch men, were presented to the contending parties: Bosch's former minister of agriculture, Antonio Guzmán; Bosch's former foreign minister, Hector García Godoy; Bosch's economic experts, Milton Messina and Alejandro Grulo. The junta, offended by the American about-face, for a while rejected one after the other, and by periodic attacks on the rebel-held sectors kept the civil war alive.

Even if the liberal lawyer Hector García Godoy succeeds in leading the Dominican people to constitutional elections, the restiveness that has been perennial in the country will not come to an end. There is still no saying how long occupation by OAS troops will last, in view of the two bitterly hostile camps into which the country is divided. Washington's attitude, too, in spite of the moral reversal, is as yet by no means clear and unequivocal. Since Ambassador Bennett still maintains his contacts with conservative rightist circles, while former Ambassador Martin negotiates as a special envoy with the constitutionalist rebels, liberal democratic Latin Americans fear that the United States is still practicing a Janus-faced policy in the Dominican Republic.

This episode has reawakened fears that the United States will use the pretext of communistic infiltration to support conservative oligarchies and military dictatorships even against moderate democratic movements. One genuine Latin American democrat, Chilean President Eduardo Frei, commenting on the Dominican events, concluded that Latin America is threatened equally by violent Marxism-Leninism and by capitalistic oppression.

"The people of Latin America want real political and economic independence," Frei stated during his European tour in the summer of 1965. "They want a system without hegemony." In the Dominican Republic the way to such a system is still beset by all sorts of pitfalls—and by traumatic memories of Trujillo and the intervention. How many more such Caribbean crevasses will gape open in the future?

CHAPTER 3

The Banana Republics

MR. KEITH FOUNDS AN EMPIRE

We have frequently mentioned a commercial firm that has played a significant part in the destinies of the Caribbean islands: the United Fruit Company. On the Central American mainland, United Fruit long ago established its real empire.

The founding of the Banana Empire can be dated fairly precisely. In 1871 a dictator named Tomás Guardia ruled the small and then completely insignificant republic of Costa Rica. Since there was then no canal across Central America connecting the Atlantic and Pacific, it occurred to Guardia to persuade a family of American millionaires to build a railroad connecting the two seas across the narrowest part of his little country.

Guardia hoped that the Americans would undertake the project in return for various concessions. The outcome of the negotiations was that a member of the American family, a young engineer named Minor C. Keith, pitched his tents in Carare (now Puerto Limón) and hired several thousand workers to begin the railroad. But the white and mulatto workers were decimated by the yellow fever for which the place was notorious. Finally Keith imported a sizable number of Jamaican Negroes, who proved to be more resistant to the fever. The descendants of Mr. Keith's railroad workers are to this day living in the region around Puerto Limón.

The railroad journey across Central America carries the traveler through one of the most enchanting landscapes on the face of the earth. It begins on the tropical coast of the Atlantic Ocean, leads up into the mountains through forests of orchids into the grand volcanic mountains of Costa Rica to the capital of the country, San

José, and then down through gorge-pierced jungles to Puntarenas on the Pacific. No one can deny that the railroad represents a remarkable technological feat for the pioneering American engineer. However, the present-day passenger cannot escape the feeling that the rattling, uncomfortable railroad cars date back to the days of Mr. Keith.

TURNING FRUIT INTO MONEY

There are a good many versions of the story of what Mr. Keith did next. The most incisive and perhaps most unsparing is told by John Dos Passos. He portrays Mr. Keith as "a brighteyed man with a hawk-nose and a respectable bay window, and an uneasy look under the eyes. Minor C. Keith was a rich man's son, born in a family that liked the smell of money, and they could smell money half way round the globe in that family."

According to Dos Passos, Keith's founding of the United Fruit Company came about in this way:

"In 1882 there were twenty miles of railroad built and Keith was a million dollars in the hole; the railroad had nothing to haul. Keith made them plant bananas so that the railroad might have something to haul, to market the bananas he had to go into the shipping business; this was the beginning of the Caribbean fruittrade. . . . He built railroads, opened retail stores up and down the coast in Bluefields, Belize, Limón, bought and sold rubber, vanilla, tortoiseshell, sarsaparilla, anything he could buy cheap he bought, anything he could sell dear he sold. In 1898 in cooperation with the Boston Fruit Company he formed the United Fruit Company that has since become one of the most powerful industrial units of the world."

The annals of the fruit company record that Keith had foreseen the rapid development of steam shipping. In the past, bananas had not proved a practicable export item because they spoiled so quickly. But if they could be transported by steamship, they arrived in good condition and sold very well. Consequently, Keith put all his energy into the establishment of banana plantations. According to Dos Passos, the uneasy look in Minor C. Keith's eyes was due to his knowledge that the United Fruit Company's workers died like flies of whiskey, malaria, yellow fever, and dysentery, and that the firm was as deep in politics as it was in business. The United Fruit Company influ-

enced the building of the Panama Canal and the planning of a future
Nicaraguan canal. It brought more than half a dozen Latin American countries under its sway, changed the face of a whole section
of the globe, and relied on Washington to protect its interests. Only
in one case, so far, has that support failed—the case of Cuba.

Over a million acres of land in Central America, the Antilles,
Colombia, and Ecuador belong to the United Fruit Company. Another concern, the Standard Fruit & Steamship Company, provides
competition now, and likewise clears jungles, sets up plantations, and
plays politics. The boom in bananas has, however, subsided somewhat; Americans and Europeans have eaten their fill of the mealy
fruit. Moreover, the monoculture of bananas led to increased sus-
ceptibility of the trees to a number of diseases.

The two great fruit companies met these setbacks by diversification.
They have planted coffee, cocoa, sugar cane, hemp, lemons, oranges,
cotton, coconuts, oil palms. They boast of their pioneering achievements, for everywhere in their empires they have set up hospitals,
clinics, and research laboratories, have built roads and introduced
hygienically packed American foods. The schools and workers' settlements they have built are regarded by outsiders as exemplary. And if
anyone calls the banana kings colonialists and imperialists, the public
relations men for the fruit concerns quickly point out that Central
America owes all its progress and economic prosperity solely to the
genius of Minor C. Keith and his successors.

THE CENTRAL AMERICAN PATCHWORK QUILT

Looking at the map of Central America, we may wonder why
there are so many dwarf nations there. From the Mexican to the
Colombian border there is a row of six republics: Guatemala, El
Salvador, Honduras, Nicaragua, Costa Rica, and Panama. In addition,
two regions are in the hands of foreign powers: British Honduras,
which is claimed by Mexico, Guatemala, and Honduras, and the
Canal Zone, which the Panamanians would like to have returned
to them. By European standards, the Central American republics are
not so very small, with the exception of El Salvador. But, compared
to the countries of South America, they are Lilliputian and seem
scarcely viable.

Once in Central America, however, the foreigner will find that the inhabitants of each republic will constantly stress the fine nuances which distinguish one country from the other. For the natives of Central America, those differences are extremely real. Guatemala is probably half inhabited by pure-blooded Indians, among whom are the descendants of that great ancient civilization the Mayas. In El Salvador an Indian-Latin mixed population has formed, but a clan system going back to pre-Spanish days still persists in much of the country. Mestizos constitute the majority of the population in Honduras, but the influence of Negroes and mulattoes is marked. Nicaragua offers a panorama of races and racial mixtures: pure Indians, mestizos, Negroes, mulattoes, Negro-Indians, and whites. Costa Rica, except for the Negro banana port of Puerto Limón, is a white country. Panama, on the other hand, is full of Negroes.

But what has split Central America into a mosaic of countries is not ethnological diversity but the intrigues and jealousies of the *caudillos*. The Central American dictators, most of them scions of the Spanish-Creole upper class, realized that a dwarf state could be more easily dominated than a large federation. Thus the Central American land bridge became the playground for ambitious autocrats who were unwilling to give up an iota of their power. All attempts to create a Central American federation were thwarted by the cabals of one dictator or another.

When Mexico won her independence at the beginning of the nineteenth century, the Mexicans hoped to incorporate the Central American provinces into their new nation. But the lands in question, controlled by antirevolutionary governors, remained loyal to the mother country for the time being. In 1821, Spain finally lost her hold on all but two (Cuba and Puerto Rico) of her remaining colonies in the New World. In seven Central American regions, provisional governments were formed. At the time, these governments had no definite ideas about the future of their countries. For a while they vacillated, unable to decide whether to join Mexico or to put themselves under the protection of Colombia or the United States. For fifteen years these small states formed a loose federation which rather pompously called itself the United States of Central America.

The most powerful of these "United States" was Guatemala. The other countries, however, would not put up with rule by Guatemalan Creoles who aped the autocratic ways of their recent Spanish masters. Incessant partisan struggles and civil wars led to the breakup of the federation in 1839 into five independent republics. Aside from Costa Rica, these republics with their illiterate masses were so underdeveloped economically that they were always on the verge of ruin. Only the Creole oligarchy enjoyed a relatively secure life on their haciendas. Their Indian and half-Indian workers languished in a state of barely disguised serfdom.

Twelve years after the collapse of the "United States," Honduras, El Salvador, and Nicaragua once again formed a union. But without wealthier Guatemala, the new federation could not survive. The federation therefore declared war on the Guatemalan dictator, Rafael Carrera. The conservative Guatemalans inflicted bloody defeats upon the liberal federation. During the following decades Guatemala once more took the lead in Central America; the republics of Honduras, El Salvador, and Nicaragua became dependencies. Only Costa Rica kept to herself; the Costa Ricans did not like the clerical, dictatorial regime of Guatemala.

YES, WE HAVE BANANAS

Gradually, the conservative dictators were replaced by more liberal rulers. Instead of the clergy, the dollar came to dominate Central America. Guatemala remained, as in the past, the strongest power in the region. Several times Guatemalan presidents attempted, by diplomatic and military means, to force the neighboring republics into a Central American federation. But the miniature state of El Salvador bravely held out against her stronger and bigger neighbor. In 1896 another union was finally formed under the name of *República Mayor de Centro-América*. But this, too, was destined for only a brief existence. It seemed impossible to unite the five Central American countries.

In our sketchy historical survey, we have made no mention of the Republic of Panama. All this time the Isthmus of Panama belonged to the South American republic of Colombia. Panama was born only for the sake of the Panama Canal—an illegitimate child of the United States. We will come back to this story later.

Toward the end of this turbulent period of constant vacillation between federation and separatism, the United Fruit Company began staking out its banana empire. The disunity of Central America had clear advantages for the fruit company. On the other hand, bellicose dictators invading neighboring countries would have been bad for the banana business. Consequently, the United Fruit Company tried to soothe the Central American troublemakers and supported any regime, conservative or liberal, that kept the peace and gave concessions for more jungles to be turned into plantations. Aside from a brief interlude in the twenties, there have been no more strong efforts to achieve Central American unity. For some time negotiations for a customs union have been in progress, but Costa Rica at least—the permanent outsider—has been opposing such a Common Market for Central America. The unifying elements in Central America are only the twin commodities, bananas and coffee.

The United Fruit Company ships some one and a half million tons of bananas annually from its Latin American empire to North America and Europe. This is big business by any standards, and United Fruit is well aware of it. The company has always been prepared to defend its interests whenever necessary. But for the most part, there has not been violence. The last disturbance took place in the ancient country of the Mayas, the land of the sacred quetzal: the Indian republic of Guatemala.

THE QUETZAL'S RED UNDERSIDE

The quetzal is a handsome bird with emerald-green feathers, a fan-shaped tail, and a red underside. It was considered a sacred bird by the Mayas, that great civilized Indian people who created a large number of impressive city-states in Guatemala from the fourth to the tenth centuries A.D., and who later, for reasons unknown, moved into southern Mexico and established a new empire. According to Indian traditions, the quetzal played a part in the struggle against Pedro de Alvarado, the cruel conquistador. When Alvarado's mercenaries slaughtered some thirty thousand Mayans on the battlefield of Quetzaltenango, so the legend goes, countless quetzals flew down to earth from heaven and formed a deathwatch, covering the dead Indians with their green feathers. The blood of the Indians soaked the feathers of the birds, and since then, say the Guatemalan Indians, the quetzal is red on its underside.

Neither Alvarado nor his successors managed to liquidate the Indians in Guatemala. To this day some one and a half million Mayan

descendants, members of the Quiche and Cakchiquel tribes, raise
corn on the Guatemalan plateau or work on the plantations. Guatemala, like Bolivia, and far more than Mexico and Peru, has remained
an Indian country. Two-thirds of the Guatemalans are pure-blooded
Indians; even the Guatemalan mestizos, who proudly call themselves
Latins, usually have more Indian than Spanish blood. As in pre-
Columbian days, the plateau Indians still live in villages which are
both production and living communes. Such *municipios* are not rigid
units; they form and dissolve again, depending on the migrations of
the Indians, who move about in quest of a livelihood.

These descendants of the Mayas still lead a relatively free life
outside modern civilization. They scarcely speak Spanish and have
kept wholly apart from the politics of their country.

THE PRIVILEGIO SYSTEM

The situation of the many Indian families who work on plantations
and haciendas is quite different. By the custom of the country, these
Indian workers are paid very little money; their compensation comes
largely in the form of *privilegios*, which in Guatemala means corn
and other food. Since the Indians are, moreover, compelled to do most
of their buying on the plantations, and since as a rule they are ignorant of reading, writing, and arithmetic, they invariably come to
be heavily in their masters' debt. The plantation owners readily extend credit. In that way the sons must work off the debts of the
fathers, and the grandsons the debts of the sons. In view of their
permanent indebtedness, it is almost impossible for the Indians to
leave their place of work. The *privilegio* system amounts to a kind of
inherited peonage, and the Indians find it harder to buy their freedom
than did the Negro slaves of the past.

Like all methods of exploitation, the Guatemalan *privilegio* system
has had its defenders. It is admitted that the employers find it easy to
trick their workers by clever purchasing and adroit calculations. But
on the other hand, it is argued, given the mentality of the Indians,
corn means more to them than cash. The Indian, dully taking life as it
comes, unaccustomed to handling money, is relieved of all the cares
he might otherwise encounter in providing for himself. He does not
have to worry about price fluctuations. The employer assumes all such
responsibilities. In addition, every Indian family on the plantation

has its adobe hut, enjoys medical care, and is even given a free gift of a bright-colored poncho at the time of the traditional Indian festivals.

In the matter of *privilegios* the foreign companies have adjusted to the customs of the country. They wanted a permanent labor force, which would increase of its own accord, which would not quit or go on strike. Everywhere on the fruit companies' plantations clean, hygienically irreproachable shops have been set up where the Indians can buy everything their hearts desire—on credit against their wages. Since the articles sold in the companies' stores come largely from the United States and therefore (so the Americans believe) are of better quality than native products, their prices are naturally higher. Thus it is that on the banana plantations also the debts of the fathers must often be paid off down to the third and fourth generations.

The Guatemalan coffee planters adopted the same customs. In 1873 a liberal president, Justo Rufino Barrios, replaced the previous clerical-conservative dictatorships. He expropriated the property of the Church, banished the archbishop, and encouraged foreigners to come and take up land for farming. The German immigrants in particular were quick to see the opportunity for growing coffee on the slopes of the Guatemalan volcanoes. They worked like demons, as Germans abroad are wont to do. The first generation cleared the jungles with the most basic tools; the next generation had a somewhat easier task; and the third generation made fortunes. By the outbreak of the Second World War, this group, a bare eight thousand, had virtually a monopoly on coffee growing in Guatemala. They owned the most profitable coffee plantations and had even taught German coffee drinkers back home to develop a taste for Guatemalan coffee.

Thanks to the *privilegio* system, it was possible for the German coffee planters to dump their coffee on the world market at favorable prices. Coffee culture is an extremely hazardous business. More coffee is produced than is consumed on this earth. Brazil has had to burn her entire coffee crop more than once because overproduction would have depressed prices to a point far below costs. A coffee country that has a sufficient supply of cheap labor and pays its plantation workers in rations of corn rather than in hard cash can undersell the world market. Thanks to German planters and the *privilegio* system, Guatemala became the third largest coffee-producing country in the world.

But canny planters and promoters were not the only thinking people in the country. There were also discontented intellectuals who began to toy with ideas of reform. They followed the example of their fellows in Mexico: they read Marx and Lenin, watched the development of Mexican agrarian and nationalization policies, and went into the countryside to proselytize the Indios. As these left intellectuals saw it, the economic structure of the country had to be fundamentally changed. A comprehensive agrarian reform was necessary. Only if the Indians were given land could they move upward from serfdom to the relative freedom of small farmers. To the upper class, the spokesmen for such agrarian reform were, of course, communists. The dictator of Guatemala who came to power in 1931, General Jorge Ubico, made onslaughts against anyone tainted with intellectualism and reformism. In the course of his thirteen-year reign he acquired the nickname of the "Napoleon of the Tropics."

The United Fruit Company found the Napoleon of the Tropics an easy man to deal with. The German coffee planters also liked the dictator—at least until 1942. For in that year, under pressure from the United States, Ubico expropriated coffee plantations in German hands and expelled all Germans from the country. The measure was similar to that taken in other Latin American countries at war with Hitler Germany.

The expelled planters hoped that at the end of the war they would recover their holdings. In other countries they did, but in the meantime Guatemala underwent an upheaval which gravely reduced the Germans' chances for returning. A man had come to power who thought little of the sanctity of private property: former university professor Juan José Arévalo.

THE CASE OF ARBENZ

Arévalo belonged to the circle of leftist liberal intellectuals who wanted to provide the Indians with land. In order to overthrow the Napoleon of the Tropics, he had chosen a method extremely unusual for Latin American conditions: the calling of a general strike. Since the army, too, joined the action, a provisional revolutionary junta took over on July 1, 1944. Arévalo assumed the presidency the following year. He soon undertook a second venture unusual for Latin America: he proclaimed a new democratic constitution with free general elections for all, including illiterates. Guatemala seemed on the point of following the same path as Mexico. The leftist liberal president launched his agrarian reform program by installing Indians in the former German coffee plantations. Then he grew bolder. He began to lay hands on the property of the great power in Guatemala—the United Fruit Company.

The German planters, however, were far from beaten and the fruit company successfully fended off all attacks on its property. Arévalo's free elections were scheduled for 1950. The Indian masses were considered to be apathetic and without interest in politics. The coffee and banana kings hoped to influence them by concessions and bribery. In any case it is a general rule in Central America that the dominant economic powers can utilize elections to get rid of inconvenient presidents. The German planters let it be known the world over that Guatemalan coffee production had decreased by a fifth under the management of the Indians. The United Fruit Company declared that the banana production would suffer the same fate if the agrarian reform were carried out.

Nevertheless, the victor in the elections of 1950 was not a moderate politician with whom the propertied classes might have come to terms, but someone even more radical than the liberal Arévalo: the war minister of the Arévalo government, Jacobo Arbenz Guzmán.

Arbenz was the son of a Swiss immigrant. While still minister of war he had enjoyed great popularity among the Indian population. He had, for example, trained a personal guard of Indios to block possible attempts at a coup by the oligarchy. Jacobo Arbenz's Indio militia terrified the white upper class, not because it behaved with undue brutality, but because the Indians, as soon as disturbances broke out, surged through the streets of the capital brandishing machetes. Then they would post themselves at the scenes of trouble and wait calmly until the sight of their knives brought the rioters to their senses.

In order to carry out his plans, Arbenz had to accept an alliance with the Guatemalan Communists. For the Communists too had been busy agitating among the Indians and trying to persuade them of the advantages of collective economies. The Indians have long been familiar with life in communal productive enterprises; José Fortuny, the Guatemala Communist leader, could therefore be sure of a strong Indian following. From the time he came to power, Arbenz faced the same dilemma later to confront Fidel Castro. If he wanted to keep the Communists within bounds, he would have to strike a bargain with the United Fruit Company and shelve his plans for reform. If, on the other hand, he wanted to carry out his agrarian reform, he would have to work with the Communists and incur the opposition of the Western world. Since United Fruit had spent a great many dollars to block Arbenz's victory in the election and discredit his policies, Arbenz chose alliance with the radical left. The quetzal bird was slowly growing redder on the underside.

Jacobo Arbenz's economic and social measures, which soon brought him into ill repute as an arch-Communist and friend of Moscow, were actually quite moderate in the beginning. The Mexicans in Lázaro Cárdenas' day had behaved a good deal more radically. Arbenz first announced that he would maintain no relationships with Franco's Spain or any other dictatorship. Then he endeavored to pursue his predecessor's agrarian reform in a somewhat more orderly fashion. Up to this time, many of the Indians had regarded the distribution of the land as an invitation for large-scale pillaging. Arbenz did not want the Guatemalan economy to suffer any further damage and decided to put the unions in charge of nationalizing the coffee plantations. But there remained the problem of United Fruit. The fruit company owned vast areas of land which had not yet been cultivated and turned into banana groves. Arbenz expropriated this unused land and offered it to landless Indians.

The result was a bitter struggle for power between the president and the banana lords. The U. S. State Department intervened and demanded acceptable compensation for the expropriated lands. Arbenz complied—but offered only the ridiculous original prices. Thereupon revolt began stirring here and there in the country. Jacobo Arbenz found himself threatened by a succession of abortive coups. He flatly accused the United States of being behind these uprisings. Finally, he expropriated all large landholdings in Guatemala, confiscated all banana plantations, and simultaneously withdrew from the Organization of American States. Guatemala, it was now said in the West, had in effect become a Red bridgehead in Latin America.

BOMBS OVER GUATEMALA

Was Jacobo Arbenz really a Communist? He probably was as much and as little as the Mexican revolutionaries of the past had been, no more than Castro was at the beginning of his revolution. He did only what has long been overdue in Latin America: he liquidated feudalism in his country. Undoubtedly the numerically small Communist Party of Guatemala was able to occupy a great many key positions in the unions during the Arbenz period. Arbenz himself (like every social reformer who quarrels with the United States) received loud applause from the Kremlin. But the Guatemalan left socialist was sensible enough of all the implications to close his country's embassy in Moscow—for economy reasons, so he said.

Moderates, familiar with Guatemalan conditions, hoped that Arbenz would be able to follow the path of Mexico. The Indians hailed their liberator and grumbled only slightly when the union organizations insisted on regulated work. Moscow counted on Guatemala's trained Communists, who would be able to put the quarrel with the United States to their own profit. The German coffee planters bade a final sad farewell to their plantations and vigorously reviled Arbenz. American newspapers called the social reformer's government an "extremely dangerous reign of terror." The Mexicans alone watched the Guatemalan experiment with obvious sympathy, although without openly taking sides.

Then, on June 25, 1954, bombs were suddenly dropped.

The bombing planes came from the banana republic of Honduras. They were American Thunderbolt planes and could carry out their mission unopposed, for Guatemala possessed only four antiquated warplanes.

The previous week, a Guatemalan named Carlos Castillo Armas had crossed the border between Honduras and Guatemala with four hundred well-armed insurgents. Arbenz had never taken such invasions very seriously. In the past his response had been to denounce American imperialism, mobilize his Indians against the invaders, drive them back, and issue statements to the effect that an American enterprise had hired the insurgents in order to recapture their land.

But a squadron of Thunderbolts was another matter entirely. Since the bombing of a capital is considered a belligerent act all over the world, the Guatemalan president immediately appealed to the United Nations, asking for protection and assistance against the unknown aggressor. But the American UN delegate, whose turn it was to hold the presidency of the Security Council, on that day refused to consider the matter and instead placed the situation in Indo-China on the agenda. The events in Guatemala, he declared, were purely internal in nature and therefore lay outside the sphere of the world organization.

The Thunderbolts of "unknown origin" did some damage in Guatemala City, killed a number of people, and demoralized the country's
military forces. The officers were not prepared to risk a war against
the United States. If that were in the offing, it would be better to
depose this troublesome man Arbenz and make a deal with Castillo
Armas' invaders. Arbenz left the country and Castillo Armas became
president of Guatemala.

Castillo Armas did precisely what had been expected of him. He
returned expropriated lands to their former owners and tried to
whiten the quetzal bird again. In place of Jacobo Arbenz's social-
reformist slogans, he offered the rather vague shibboleth "God, Country and Liberty"—a phrase consonant with almost any political system
and one that meant very little indeed to the Guatemalan people.
What did mean something was the aid in dollars that Castillo Armas
received in gratitude for his struggle for liberty. The United States
pumped some fifteen million dollars into the country, and United
Fruit resumed its old practices of clearing jungles, planting bananas,
and paying its workers by *privilegios*.

Only the German coffee planters came away empty-handed. They
seemed to have no friends at all. For Castillo Armas had to make at
least one concession to his reform-minded countrymen. Thus in 1956,
by government decree, the former German coffee plantations were
definitively expropriated without compensation and taken over by the
state. Since then, Guatemala has dropped to sixth place among coffee-
producing countries.

Castillo Armas did not belong to the usual run of dictators. He was
a political enthusiast who vaguely dreamed of crusades against communism and against the devil. Nevertheless, he was shrewd enough
to revoke the franchise that had been given to the illiterate Indian
masses. Not that this helped him. He had no opportunity to offer
himself to the people in an election rigged or otherwise. On July
26, 1957, a member of his own bodyguard shot him. The murderer was
promptly denounced as a Communist or a follower of Arbenz. But to
this day malicious tongues in Guatemala City whisper that the secret
powers behind Castillo Armas had engineered the assassination to
get rid of a henchman who was becoming a burden.

TWO ELECTIONS—BUT NO CHOICE

Only a third of the Guatemalan people were permitted to participate in the elections that followed. The Arbenz party was banned;
so was the Communist Party. Since it was nevertheless feared that
other reform movements might win a hearing among the Indians,
representatives of the legal parties went from village to village paying ten cents for the vote of every registered Indian. The elections
finally had to be declared null and void because in the end more votes
were counted than the country had registered voters. A good many
sly Indians had sold their vote several times over. In the next election the conservative General Miguel Ydígoras Fuentes emerged as
victor. He had managed to forge a coalition among all the parties in
the country that opposed social reform.

Ydígoras Fuentes ruled in the tried-and-true manner of a Central
American dictator. Since he proclaimed himself the chief opponent
of Castroism, the United States granted him ample subsidies and
credit. But as so often in the history of the country, the dollars that
flowed into it quickly found their way into the pockets of the upper
crust. The social and political reforms that the United States Government demanded of Ydígoras Fuentes came to nothing after the first
halfhearted beginnings. The adherents of ex-Presidents Arévalo and
Arbenz once again began gaining ground. Groups of conspirators
formed in the universities, in the unions, and in the army. The Indians longed to see the golden days of agrarian reform return.

Jacobo Arbenz went into exile in Fidel Castro's Cuba. His somewhat more liberal predecessor Arévalo preferred Mexican exile, and
in 1963 secretly returned to Guatemala in order to run in the impend-
ing presidential elections. Although he had to hide from Ydígoras
Fuentes' police, he was nevertheless generally considered the candidate with the best prospects. Discontent had meanwhile become so
widespread that even well-organized purchase of votes would not
have won the presidency for another conservative politician.

Then, several months before the election, bombs once more exploded in Guatemala City. Tanks rumbled through the streets, soldiers
occupied key positions, and planes roared in the sky above the city.
A military junta took power. It suspended the constitution, postponed

the elections, and simultaneously declared its intention of maintaining the most cordial relations with all free countries in the world. Or at least, with all those well and conservatively governed.

Washington was alarmed at first, for it was not clear whether the army officers who had seized power in Guatemala might not be followers of Arbenz. It was, moreover, disturbing that President Ydígoras Fuentes promptly flew to Nicaragua and asked for political asylum. But the State Department breathed easier when Ydígoras Fuentes announced from Nicaragua that he welcomed the military coup and regarded it "as in the best interests of Guatemala and all of Central America."

Because of the provisions of the constitution, General Ydígoras Fuentes could not have run again. He had therefore prompted his army to make a coup against himself in order to prevent elections and block all possibility of the reformer Arévalo's legally returning to power. His defense minister, Enrique Peralta Azuardia, became the new president of the country. Everything was going to remain the same in Guatemala. Only the names of the cabinet ministers were shuffled.

Perhaps a liberal like Arévalo might have been the only politician who could have injected new life into Guatemala without being forced into the same balancing act as Jacobo Arbenz. "I do not like Communism and will not become a Communist," Arévalo had told a group of foreign correspondents in his Guatemalan hiding place shortly before the coup. He pointed out that during his presidency the Communists had never supported him, but on the contrary had violently attacked him. He expressed his eagerness to co-operate with the Kennedy Alliance for Progress. And since his political shading is about the same as that of Venezuela's Betancourt, there is no reason not to credit this statement.

The 1963 coup again barred the way to a democratic course in Guatemala. It made the opposition even more radical than it had been. Rather than securing the property of the United Fruit Company, it endangered those holdings the more. For a radical leftist "Revolutionary Movement of November 13" has recruited guerrillas to terrorize the country, and carries out bombings in the capital. The *Fuerzas Armadas Rebeldes,* as the guerrillas call themselves, attack military posts and incite the peasants to action against recalcitrant owners of coffee plantations and the latifundia. The populace gives aid and comfort to these elements—whether from sympathy or fear of reprisals is hard to say.

Their leader, Marco Antonio Jon Soza, is pro-Peking and is waging the guerrilla war exactly according to the doctrines of Mao Tse-tung. For this reason he has incurred the hostility of the underground Communist Party of Guatemala, which sides with Moscow. A grotesque aspect of the whole story is that Jon Soza before 1960 was trained by Americans as an anticommunist, antiguerrilla fighter. He was a lieutenant of the Guatemalan army in Fort Gulick, the special training camp set up by the Americans in the Panama Canal Zone to teach Latin Americans how to combat communist guerrilla tactics.

In the *departamentos* of Zacapa and Izabal the November 13 men are training an army under the red flag. The dictators have not been able to change the color of Guatemala. On the contrary, the underside of the quetzal bird is flushing a more and more bloody red.*

ON THE BRINK OF THE VOLCANO

My travels through Central America took me high into volcanic mountainous country. At one point I stood on the brink of a huge crater. All around stretched black sterile masses of lava. It was very cold up there in the biting mountain wind, but far down at the bottom of the crater a reddish mass heaved and bubbled. Now and then choking clouds of smoke and steam rose from the depths.

A Central American with a flair for the dramatic stepped up beside me, pointed into the boiling lava, and said: "If you fired a gun into that now, the volcano would erupt."

I did not try it. Who would willingly rouse a dangerous volcano from its slumber? Very likely the man was exaggerating for effect. But there was a profound symbolic significance to his words.

All of Central America today is one great volcano. At the bottom of the crater there is seething and hissing. We stare into the boiling lava and feel a kind of voluptuous thrill. We sense that a single shot, a tiny coup, a minor political jolt, could cause the volcano to erupt. And when Central American volcanoes erupt, the ground on which we are standing also quivers.

* *See note p. 147.*

A CRAMPED COUNTRY

One of the most volcanic countries in Central America is the dwarf state of El Salvador. Only one-fifth as large as its neighbor, Guatemala, El Salvador has a population of almost the same size. With its one hundred twenty-six persons per square kilometer it belongs among the most densely populated countries on the globe. To make matters worse, El Salvador is a purely agricultural land which earns the major part of its income from coffee growing. A certain amount of light industry has been developed, but it hardly plays a significant part in the Salvadorian economy. It is a cramped country then, and one with a curious population. Indians and Spaniards have interbred to form what is almost another race in its own right. The mestizos of El Salvador are unlike the mestizos to be met with everywhere else in South America. They are Salvadorians: a strong, hard-working breed of men, obstinate, individualistic, averse to taking orders. The passionate temperament of the Salvadorians has become proverbial in Central America. These capable, ambitious people hold the world's record in homicide and assault and battery. Perhaps one reason for this is that too many of them are crowded together on too small a patch of the earth's surface, hemmed in so closely that they suffer from a kind of national cabin fever.

El Salvador may hold still another world's record. It may have the highest percentage of unlegalized marriages and the most illegitimate births of any country in the world. Only one-fourth of the adult males are married. Seventy per cent of all the children are born to couples living together without benefit of the sacraments or a civil ceremony. The reason for this is clear enough. In El Salvador, as well as in Peru and other Latin American countries, weddings cost money. The fees that the priests alone charge are exceedingly high; in El Salvador they amount to more than a week's wages for a worker. Most Salvadorians, however, are not employed as industrial or agricultural workers. They till tiny patches of land on which they raise corn and beans. In consequence, they virtually never lay hands on any sizable amount of money. Many couples save their whole lives in order to be able to afford a legal marriage when they have become grandfathers and grandmothers.

Consequently, among the small farmers and wage laborers in El

Salvador, men and women simply live together in a form of marriage that dates back to their Indian past. It has become typical of the country. At one time the majority of the Indians lived under matriarchal conditions. The men went hunting while the women ruled the family. That has remained largely true in El Salvador to this day. The men till their cornfields or earn their bread as day laborers on the *fincas,* while the women function as heads of the families. The Salvadorians consider these marriages just as legal as those performed with the blessings of the Church.

The matriarchal system has certainly not checked the increase and multiplication of the Salvadorian people, for El Salvador has the highest birth rate in the world. Their only escape from population pressure is to do as the inhabitants of the British West Indian islands have done. They emigrate in vast numbers and try to establish themselves in the neighboring countries. In the two decades between 1930 and 1950 alone, 30 per cent of the Salvadorians left the country.

The wave of emigration is not likely to subside in the future, since the tillable land in the country can scarcely be increased. Most of the *terrenos,* the plots of Salvadorian small farmers, are less than twelve acres, and almost without exception they are situated in the rough, unfruitful mountain zone suitable only for corn and beans. Such tiny enterprises can scarcely feed the large Salvadorian families.

THE FOURTEEN FAMILIES

At the top of the social heap sit the "fourteen families" of El Salvador, which have been so often described in travel books. There are actually no longer fourteen, but rather some hundred families who own almost the entire country. They possess two-thirds of the usable land, including all the better soil, of course, and rent parts of their vast holdings to sharecroppers. In the main, however, the upper one hundred plant coffee, a mountain coffee which is called the best in the world. The claim is open to question: every Central American country boasts that its coffee is the best. Alongside the hundred Creole families are the *Turcos,* immigrants from the Levant who control the commercial life of the country.

Big concerns like the United Fruit Company are not particularly active in El Salvador. Consequently, the United States has hardly ever intervened in the country's politics. This does not mean that its political life has not been extremely turbulent; poverty, the sharp class divisions, and the population pressure have seen to that. El Salvador felt the aftertremors of the Mexican Revolution. In 1932, in fact, the Communists seized control of the government. Since then, right extremist and left extremist governments have alternated periodically like high and low tides. When the radicals of the left won power, they were hailed by the intellectuals and the small farmers. When the radicals of the right recaptured the government by a coup, the hundred families applauded.

The army of El Salvador will stage a coup for leftist as well as for rightist interests, providing the officers are paid enough. The hundred families of the oligarchy naturally can offer more than the intellectual reformers and the small farmers on their *terrenos*. Consequently, the business world seldom takes a Salvadorian leftist revolution seriously. It is assumed that by and by a few army men will be willing to tip the balance the other way in return for cold cash.

Thus there are perpetual rumblings at the bottom of El Salvador's crater. Whether in the long run the hundred families will be able to hold their position seems highly doubtful. Any genuine democratization of the dwarf republic is inconceivable as long as the cruel social demarcation persists. And yet one would expect that the hard-working Salvadorians, of all the people of Central America, are predestined to form a sound and viable middle class. However, for any such agricultural middle class to get started, the large coffee plantations would have to be broken up. The coffee oligarchy opposes all such projects on the ground that the quality of Salvadorian coffee would suffer. There can be no imperiling of the "best coffee in the world." And yet, unless fundamental social experiments are undertaken, the volcano of El Salvador will continue to seethe, and sooner or later will erupt with a vengeance.

SHORT HISTORY OF A WELFARE STATE

El Salvador's neighbor to the south, Honduras, seems even less suited for democratic experiments. The Hondurans are as rebellious a people as the Bolivians. They have gone through more than one hundred revolutions, consuming one hundred and twenty presidents in the process. Some of these presidents were easily the match for Trujillo in megalomania and cruelty—as, for example, the "Tiger of Central America," General Santos Guardiola, who ruled around the middle of the nineteenth century.

Another unlamented despot was Tiburcio Carías Andino, who seized power at the same time as Hitler in Germany but lasted three years longer, that is, until 1948. General Carías stood high on the list of the dictators whom democrats in Central America wanted to see liquidated as quickly as possible.

In spite of this unpromising past, for a while Honduras seemed about to accomplish the kind of democratization that liberal Americans hoped would ultimately be achieved throughout Central America. In fact, the Hondurans went even further than their most ambitious North American re-educators had bargained for. For six years the most turbulent country in Central America practiced full parliamentary democracy and had the most progressive labor and social laws in all of Latin America. Its population enjoyed maternity benefits and job security such as have not yet been established even in Mexico, and was headed by a president whose honesty could not be impugned even by the most malicious enemies. In short, Honduras had become a welfare state, almost comparable to the countries of Scandinavia. But the Hondurans were not Scandinavians and had not yet learned that life in a welfare state combines obligations as well as benefits for its citizens. Consequently, the machinery of the Honduran welfare state has never been very well oiled.

THE BACK YARD OF CENTRAL AMERICA

There was a time when the rays of Mayan culture reached as far as Honduras. In the jungles of northern Honduras archaeologists have laid bare what is probably the most remarkable of the Mayan cities, Copán, which ecstatic visitors will compare with Athens. But while descendants of the Mayas remain in Guatemala, in Honduras they have completely vanished. Only the wild tribes in the Honduran jungles escaped extermination by the Spanish conquerors. With little to commend Honduras for colonization, it remained relatively unpopulated except for the deserters and criminals who might take to its jungles to escape the reach of Spanish law. These elements gradually merged with the savage Indians. Aside from a few Indian tribes still living as nomads, and a rather considerable number of Negroes along the coast, the present Honduran population consists overwhelmingly of mestizos.

The mestizos of Honduras have been somewhat maligned by writers on Central America. While the industry and toughness of the Salvadorians are usually praised, the Hondurans are described as lazy and undisciplined. Even the Honduran clergy comes in for such charges. As late as the turn of the century they were still being characterized as "ignorant, uncultured and immoral." The Honduran upper class, however, consisting of some ten clans, can scarcely be distinguished from the upper classes of the neighboring countries of Central America. A constant struggle goes on among the clans for control of the government. To them, however, domination meant less political power than profitable business opportunities. Consequently, most of the Honduran presidents have called themselves "liberal." In other words, they were commercial-minded rather than clerical. When one of the clans encountered hard times, it bent all its efforts to get at the feed trough as soon as possible so it could mend its fortunes.

In 1936 the dictator Carías finally put an end to this ugly game. He stopped the restless pushing and shoving for the presidency by passing a law providing that the clans would supply presidents from among themselves one by one, in turn. At the end of his six-year term, a president would not be allowed to succeed himself, nor could any member of his clan run for the highest office. Thus the way would be left clear for the next clan, which after six years would likewise have to withdraw from the race. If the Carías system had been followed, in the course of six decades each of the clans would have had its turn at the government pork barrel.

But Carías was, as has been mentioned, one of the best-hated dictators in Central America. Consequently, his system did not last very long. During the early postwar years, as we have seen, democracy in the Caribbean area had gained ground somewhat. In Cuba, the social democrat Grau San Martín and the conservative Prío Socarrás temporarily replaced dictator Batista. In Venezuela, the social democrat Gallegos won the first free elections that had ever been held in the history of that country. In Guatemala, the social reformer Arévalo took the presidency, and in Costa Rica the socialist-liberal Figueres. To be sure, all of these men, one after the other, had soon to step off the political stage again, but around 1948 they believed in the future democratic evolution of the Caribbean and felt strong enough to declare ideological war on the ruling dictators. Along with Trujillo and Somoza, one of their main targets was Tiburcio Carías.

The political refugees from all over Central America gathered in these temporary democracies. They formed a "Caribbean Legion" and tried—more by intellectual than military means—to cause trouble for the dictators. The dictators struck back hard. In consequence, in December 1948 a regular war very nearly broke out between the heavily armed dictatorship of Nicaragua and the unarmed democracy of Costa Rica.

The United States was profoundly disturbed by this situation. Once more, Washington found itself in a dilemma. On the one hand it would have liked to promote the democratization of the Caribbean region; on the other hand, American business interests were adjusted to a regime of strong men. If America checked the zeal of the Caribbean democrats, she might appear to be a partisan of dictatorship. If she did the opposite, she lost loyal friends and in addition might be faced with military maneuvers and possible war in the vicinity of the strategically important Panama Canal.

To the relief of the United States, these matters settled themselves. The democrats were overthrown; only Costa Rica remained democratic. The "Caribbean Legionnaires" went underground or found some other asylum. Burgeoning Central American democracy was blasted. In Honduras, the Gálvez clan followed the Carías clan, and the Lozano clan followed the Gálvez clan. The next clan was already impatiently waiting for its turn. Then, in 1956, a flame suddenly leaped up from the embers of democracy.

In Honduras and in Nicaragua, revolutions broke out, guided by antidictatorship forces. Anastasio Somoza, the old dictator of Nicaragua, paid for his misdeeds with his life, and President Lozano of Honduras was abruptly deposed. Again the United States was deeply concerned. In both republics, Americans had sizable economic interests. Honduras and Nicaragua were banana colonies of the United Fruit Company.

In spite of the assassination of Somoza, the Nicaraguan revolution failed. Somoza's sons took their father's place and were able to suppress the uprising. In Honduras, however, the rebellion succeeded. A revolutionary junta seized power and held free elections which brought to the presidency a socialist-liberal doctor named José Ramón Villeda

Morales. In theory and appearance at least, however, the events in Nicaragua and in Honduras had similar results. For both the dictator Luis Somoza and the democrat Morales passed comprehensive social-welfare laws. Here was a chance for both countries to show the world what was better for Central Americans—a totalitarian welfare state or a democratic welfare state.

The Somozas' experiment in social welfare will be discussed in the next chapter. The Honduran democrats do not think very much of it; they called the Somozas brutal dictators and exploiters, hailed their own Dr. Morales, and were soon engaged in a cold war with Nicaragua which in 1960 came very close to exploding into a hot war. But Honduras became a sterling example for those Americans who firmly believe that a Caribbean republic could be transformed into a democracy on the Western pattern solely by law and without revolutionary experimentation, without agrarian reforms and similar invasions of private property.

The Honduran mestizos liked their new welfare state. For centuries they had been kept in ignorance, prevented from developing into citizens and consumers, and merely exploited for their labor power. A man who receives only the barest necessities of life for his work and who sees no chance of amounting to anything, of climbing the social ladder through any honest effort, regards work only as a necessary evil or oppressive compulsion. He will therefore use every trick at his disposal to escape wage slavery. Dr. Morales' welfare state provided the Hondurans with many opportunities for just such shifts.

Honduran workers henceforth had remarkable job security; an employer who fired a worker had to continue his wages for ten months. Honduran working girls and women were now entitled to a three-month paid vacation at pregnancy. The workers were free to strike whenever they pleased. They could even (if they were literate) read Communist and Castroite newspapers, for Dr. Morales' democracy guaranteed the rights of free press. Hondurans were even permitted to swear in public at Americans and at the United Fruit Company.

The United Fruit Company did not like this sort of thing. Honduras had always been its favorite ward. The unfortunate Castillo Armas had started his march on Guatemala City from Honduras. The airport from which the Thunderbolt fighter bombers had flown to overthrow Arbenz had been situated in Honduras. The real metropolis of Honduras is not the capital of Tegucigalpa, but the modern city of San Pedro Sula, where the banana lords rule their empire.

In the past few decades, as it happened, the United Fruit Company had somewhat lost interest in Honduras. Two epidemics of banana disease, the Sigatoka disease and the Panama disease, had destroyed about half of the Honduran banana plantations and done great damage in neighboring Nicaragua. The banana kings painted a black future; their ledgers showed that they were suffering from a permanent deficit. Under the regime of Dr. Morales, they discharged hordes of workers. Moreover, since their books no longer showed a profit, they stopped paying taxes to the welfare state. Hitherto, Honduras had lived on banana money.

With taxes from banana production no longer flowing into the treasury, Dr. Morales soon found himself without funds to continue his social experiment. The increasing unemployment put an excessive strain upon the government's budget. To be sure, United Fruit, in spite of its deficit and its gloomy view of the future, continued to transform jungle into tillable land, drain marshes, enlarge its railroad networks, and train new banana inspectors in its modern school of agriculture. Evidently it accepted Dr. Morales' new social experiment, however much it groaned about the cost of job security, maternity benefits, forty-five-hour weeks, and lavish Christmas bonuses.

The Kennedy Administration approved of Dr. Morales' progressive policy. It seemed as if American re-educators had at last found an experimental plot in the Caribbean where the seeds they wished to sell would grow without the accompaniment of all sorts of nasty weeds. At the end of 1963, Honduras was due for new elections. Washington watched the preparations with concern, hoping that liberal Dr. Morales would be succeeded by a similar democrat with perhaps a charier attitude toward social welfare.

TRAMPLED SEED DOES NOT SPROUT

Meanwhile, all sorts of rumors were going around in Honduras. The radical leftist papers tolerated by the government, it was said, were too openly carrying on propaganda for Fidel Castro. The president was, to be sure, a pro-Western statesman, but he was also a hopeless idealist. His cabinet was infiltrated by pro-communists. The way things were going, the country's model democrats might easily be replaced in the coming elections by socialistic expropriators like Arbenz or Castro. Ten days before the presidential elections, Honduras underwent the same type of sudden upheaval as Guatemala ten years previously. The welfare state was struck down. A military junta took power, dissolved the congress, banned all political activities, and thus prevented the holding of the elections. Morales fled into exile in Costa Rica. The "democratic miracle" in Central America had been only a six-year wonder. Once again the traditional masters of the country were in the saddle.

This time the United States reacted quite sourly to the new dictatorship. Though it had hailed the fall of the Arbenz regime in Guatemala, and had permitted the Somozas to do as they liked in Nicaragua, it was displeased by the liquidation of the infant democracy in Honduras. The State Department even considered the possibility of sending naval units into Central American waters to protect legality. Venezuela and Costa Rica called a meeting of the OAS in an effort to reverse the coup in Honduras. But the Honduran army men modestly and respectably declared that they had only wanted to check the danger from the left. As soon as it was safe they would permit the postponed elections to be held and let the citizens engage in political activity once more.

Such declarations are characteristic of military juntas the world over. These fine-sounding promises are hardly ever fulfilled. Dictators and military rulers can always point out that the danger from the left persists, so that the country must be kept on a tight rein for a while longer. Thus they remain in power and in the majority of cases are not replaced by freely elected governments but by the makers of other coups—military men or radicals.

These military juntas, however, are committing a fateful error. Peoples who have once tasted some of the blessings of freedom and a welfare state will, in the long run, not stand for their development's being set back by several decades. Even though Dr. Morales' social-welfare program did not work well in Honduras because the Honduran people lacked the necessary maturity, the Hondurans nevertheless made some progress under Morales and must feel bitter at the loss of their privileges. Since a liberal democratic system proved too weak to preserve these gains for them, they may very well turn to left extremists.

A CARIBBEAN FAMILY TRUST

South of the Honduran border, the volcanoes smoke even more ominously than in the northerly part of Central America. In fact, actual tremors are felt in the islands of the Great Lakes, the largest of which bears the same name as the country: Nicaragua. Nicaragua's history has two aspects: the ordinary political history, which differs little from that of its neighbors to the north; and the history of a trans-Nicaraguan canal, which gradually transformed Nicaragua into a virtual protectorate of the United States.

We need not go into the details of the early political history. Conservative cliques of a distinctly clerical cast have pitted themselves against liberal cliques whose interests were largely commercial. There were some revolutions, some dictators, and a number of guerrilla wars. There have even been frequent belligerencies with the neighboring republics, in which Nicaragua did not come out very well. In 1937 the internal upheavals ceased, for in that year the liberals at last came up with a strong man who settled accounts with conservative opposition: General Anastasio Somoza. Since then the history of Nicaragua has been the family history of the Somozas.

VANDERBILT, MORGAN, AND SOME POSTAGE STAMPS

The other, secret history of Nicaragua is the history of the American millionaire family of the Vanderbilts. The financier and railroad king Cornelius Vanderbilt was, to be sure, not the first to conceive the idea of cutting a canal through Nicaragua to link the Atlantic and Pacific oceans. As long ago as the sixteenth century, Emperor Charles V considered such plans. The San Juan River and the Great Lakes of Nicaragua were so ideally lined up that they could easily be incorporated into a trans-Nicaraguan canal. But in the end the Spanish colonial power preferred to build overland roads, the more easily to reach the supposed golden treasures of the highland Indians.

The seafaring Britons were far more familiar with the problems of water routes. As early as the colonial days, when the Spaniards were still firmly established there, Lord Nelson cast an eye on Nicaragua's interesting geography. After the country won its independence, the

British made a number of efforts to seize the Atlantic coast of Nicaragua, the so-called Mosquito Coast. On their maps, in fact, they gave British names to a number of Nicaraguan cities: Bluefields and Greytown, for example. The port of Bluefields, the largest in the country, bears that name to this day, for the Nicaraguans have become accustomed to it.

In 1848 it occurred to Cornelius Vanderbilt to steal the march on the British. Vanderbilt owned a number of river steamers and horse-drawn vehicles with which he transported adventurous countrymen by rather complicated routes across North America to the goldfields of California. By ship, Vanderbilt thought, such transportation would be easier, cheaper, and more profitable. North Americans thereupon began reaching out their hands toward Nicaragua. An American colonel named William Walker got himself "elected" president of Nicaragua in 1856 and attempted to drive the English from the Mosquito Coast. Walker grew so swell-headed that he challenged not only the British but also the neighboring republics of Honduras and Costa Rica. Eventually he was captured and shot in Honduras.

Meanwhile, disputes with Great Britain had continued. They were finally more or less settled in 1850 by the Clayton-Bulwer Treaty, which checked British expansion in Central America. Cornelius Vanderbilt was then able, as a prelude to his canal-building project, to found a shipping company which transported freight and passengers by river, the lakes, and overland from the Atlantic to the Pacific coasts of Nicaragua. The route of the canal was also mapped. In 1880 his son, William Vanderbilt, persuaded President Grant to found a company for the building of the canal, the Nicaragua Canal Construction Company. A bill was passed in Congress and the necessary sums appropriated. The Vanderbilt dream seemed on the verge of realization.

But there was another millionaire family in the United States interested in a shipping canal across Central America. This was the banking firm headed by John Pierpont Morgan. While the Vanderbilts obtained the necessary land as a gift from Nicaragua, the Morgan banking house paid forty million dollars to Ferdinand de Lesseps' international canal company for its concession.

De Lesseps, the builder of the Suez Canal, had spent decades vainly trying to cut across Central America at its narrowest point. His company, as we shall see, had gone bankrupt in one of the greatest financial scandals of all time. Morgan hoped that American engineers would do better than the French in solving the problems of building a canal across the Isthmus of Panama.

The rivalry between Great Britain and the United States was now replaced by rivalry between the houses of Vanderbilt and Morgan. Initially the Vanderbilts held the better cards. Congress, the law, and even nature were on their side. For every technician knew it would be far simpler and cheaper to build a lockless canal utilizing the inland waters of Nicaragua than to cut across mountainous Panama and go to the expense of equipping the canal with locks. Where Ferdinand de Lesseps, the great builder of the Suez Canal, had failed, the Morgans also would fail. So the Vanderbilts thought.

At this point John Pierpont Morgan performed a stroke of genius. Theodore Roosevelt, his close friend, had become President of the United States. But Roosevelt had been unable to sway an obstinate Congress, which still favored the Nicaraguan plans. Morgan therefore bought a batch of Nicaraguan postage stamps and distributed them among the members of Congress. The volcano Momotombo had just erupted in Nicaragua and the country's stamps were proudly embellished with the picture of a volcano spewing fire. Morgan accompanied the gifts of the stamps with elaborate explanations that Nicaragua was an extremely volcanic and hence dangerous country. A Nicaraguan canal, he argued, could easily be destroyed by masses of glowing lava, whereas a Panama canal would be at a safe remove from dangerous volcanoes. The stamps drove the lesson home to the legislators. The House of Morgan won out over the House of Vanderbilt, the Panama project over the Nicaragua project. The builders, safe from the erupting volcanoes of Nicaragua, now had to confront the perils of yellow fever in Panama.

THE HOPE OF ANOTHER CANAL

But the Vanderbilts did not give up hope. Nicaragua was, in any case, firmly in the hands of the United States. From 1912 on, the republic was occupied by American marines, who were there allegedly to quell the eternal conflicts between the conservatives and liberals. Successors to Cornelius Vanderbilt were just as interested in the building of a Nicaraguan canal as he himself. Sooner or later, it was obvious, the time would come when it would be necessary to supplement the Panama Canal by another Central American canal. For the time being, however, the matter slumbered. The United Fruit Company planted bananas on the Mosquito Coast. In the Bryan-Chamorro Treaty of 1914 the United States paid the Republic of Nicaragua a sum of three million dollars for a perpetual concession to build a canal. In addition, the United States leased a naval base in the Gulf of Fonseca which would guarantee its influence upon Nicaragua even after the withdrawal of the occupation troops.

The American troops were withdrawn in 1925. Less than two years later, however, they returned to stop another fracas between conservative and liberal elements. Experience had, alas, shown that only a well-drilled, well-armed army could prevent anarchy in Nicaragua. The United States now began training such an army of Nicaraguans. When Anastasio Somoza seized power, the United States could safely withdraw from the country. Thanks to American preparatory work, Somoza had the strongest and best-equipped army on the Central American mainland.

Since the time of Anastasio Somoza, the history of the country and the history of the canal have flowed together. Somoza and his sons did very little to improve their country's transportation facilities. They confidently expected that the Americans would now build the canal which would bring prosperity to Nicaragua. With keen interest, the Somozas watched the development of modern shipbuilding. The narrow Panama Canal was no longer adequate for the new giant tankers and aircraft carriers. There seemed every reason to think that, sooner or later, the United States would be forced to build that second canal through Nicaragua.

In the meantime the Somozas proceeded to transform the country into a family trust. Thanks to the strength of their army, they had little to fear from the conservative opposition. In desperation, the conservatives actually joined with the left socialists and communists in 1956 to plot and carry out the assassination of old Anastasio. But his sons, Luis and Tacho, had no great difficulty defeating this strange coalition. Luis Somoza, moreover, showed himself magnanimous toward the rightist conspirators and pardoned them after a brief imprisonment. The leftists, however, stayed behind bars for a much longer time.

Virtually everything worth owning in Nicaragua that is not already American property belongs to the Somozas. They run coffee and cotton plantations, cattle ranches, factories, trading companies, banks, shipping companies, and airlines. In addition, they have milked the foreign entrepreneurs who have invested money in Nicaragua by pocketing 50 per cent of the investments as "taxes." To be sure, the Somozas actually need all the money they can get. It is very expensive for so small a country to maintain so strong an army. The private expenditures of the family likewise consume considerable sums. As a result, the Nicaraguans are considered to be one of the poorest peoples in Central America.

THE SENSITIVE INFANT

The social misery in Nicaragua, as in the neighboring countries to the north, might someday unleash a storm which the Somozas, for all their power, will no longer be able to quell. But Luis Somoza had learned certain lessons in popularity from European dictators. He does not torture and kill the way Trujillo and Batista did. His prisons are silent places and no one knows the numbers of their inmates. He makes himself accessible to his people—every Nicaraguan may talk and shake hands with his president, or come to him with his troubles and grievances. Since 60 per cent of the Nicaraguans cannot read and write (and another 20 per cent are so-called functional illiterates), the fat, jovial-looking Somoza is regarded by many of the common people as a kindly father of his country, concerned for everyone's welfare.

Just as the nazis called themselves socialists, so Luis Somoza calls his policies "socialistic." He has generously dug into his own pocket to transform his country into a welfare state—though a very different sort of welfare state from the kind Dr. Morales tried to create in Honduras. Somoza has put through a body of laws providing employees with job security, sick pay, and regular vacations. Such measures were scarcely pleasing to his old opponents, the conservatives. He has even had some difficulty with American businessmen. Somoza, however, can point out that the costs of social welfare are borne not only by the conservative oligarchy and foreign businessmen, but also by his own family.

Does this mean that the Somozas represent happy exceptions to the usual run of dictators? No, it is only that they are somewhat shrewder than their colleagues in neighboring countries. They are willing to sacrifice a little of their vast fortunes in order to hold on to the rest. They are doing what the United Fruit Company should have done to escape debacle in Cuba. They are doing what the Creole oligarchy should have done to avoid left socialist revolutions. In 1963 the Somozas were even able to hold elections. Since the reins of power were firmly in their control, it was no surprise when a friend of the Somozas was elected the new president of Nicaragua—the former foreign minister René Schick. The constitution disbars the Somozas from running again, but they can go on ruling in the background.

The Somozas' welfare state lacks schools, hospitals, industries, and a sound middle class. The transportation facilities of the country are antediluvian. The regions stricken by the banana disease are reverting to jungle. In the villages, the people live in hovels without water, electricity, or sanitary facilities. Prices have risen so high that a cup of coffee or an orange in this coffee- and fruit-growing country costs as much as in Europe. But the Nicaraguan worker earns as much by the day as a North American worker earns by the hour.

Nevertheless, Nicaragua is tranquil. No doubt many Nicaraguans resent the Somoza Trust, but they keep their mouths shut. The army and the police, so well trained years ago by the Americans, take care that the Somozas' totalitarian welfare state is spared the fate of Honduras' democratic welfare state.

Old Anastasio Somoza once remarked that Caribbean democracy is a delicate baby which cannot be fed with too much freedom, for that would be fatal to it. The Somozas have adhered to this principle. However, they feed their baby so little freedom that it suffers from permanent undernourishment. That, too, can be fatal in the long run.

THE SWITZERLAND OF CENTRAL AMERICA

When I arrived in Costa Rica, I thought I had come to another continent. In vain I looked for the heart-rending slums and the ragged, wretched figures so characteristic of other parts of Central America. This pleasant, flourishing, clean little country looked as well ordered and as freshly washed as Switzerland. The richly green pastures in the volcanic mountains and the tinkling bells on the cows also reminded me of Switzerland, as did the bright window boxes and the fine bookshops in the capital city of San José, where Costa Ricans can obtain the best of current European and American literature.

As soon as you enter the "Lemon Port," Puerto Limón, the only Negro city in Costa Rica, you are pleasantly surprised, especially if you have known the port cities of other Caribbean countries. Puerto Limón has a steaming tropical climate and was once a hotbed of yellow fever. But it is quite without the typical smells of an Ibero-American tropical port: odor of rotting fish, human sweat, decay, drains, and DDT. Puerto Limón is a smart though perhaps rather drowsy-looking place, populated by likable, dark-skinned Costa Ricans, descendants of the West Indian Negroes brought to the country by Minor C. Keith to build his famous railroad. As if the rich tropical flora about them were not enough, the people's little wooden houses are touchingly brightened by flowers, planted, for want of anything better, even in tin cans.

Puerto Limón is the starting point of the railroad line which gave rise to the banana empire. Bananas, however, no longer grow in the low-lying tropical plains around Limón. Once the largest banana producer in the Americas, Costa Rica was hit by the same scourge which attacked the banana plantations of Nicaragua and Honduras. The cultivation of bananas is now confined to the Pacific coast of Costa Rica. On the eastern coast, cacao and Manila hemp have taken over.

Cacao plantations are a prettier sight than the monotonous stands of banana trees. They also harmonize better with the general Central American landscape. Cacao is a native plant; the Indians of pre-Columbian America used cacao beans not only as a stimulant but also as currency. This custom actually continued down to the eighteenth century. Since there was a constant shortage of money in the colonies, the Spanish government for a time made the cacao the official coin of the realm. The cacao forests of the United Fruit Company merge imperceptibly into the orchid-rich jungles that cover the mountains, while the vivid blossoms and birds which lure orchid collectors and ornithologists to Costa Rica make splashes of lovely color amid the dark green foliage of the cultivated areas.

THE FABLE OF THE RICH COAST

The Costa Ricans sometimes speak with some scorn of the "Negro port" of Puerto Limón, for Costa Rica is otherwise a white country. Remnants of the aboriginal Indian population live only in certain remote jungle areas. The Spanish conquerors practiced a policy of ruthless extermination back in the sixteenth and seventeenth centuries, so much so that they found themselves without native labor and had to pitch in and work themselves. At this, patrician interest in the country quickly faded.

The name of Costa Rica, "Rich Coast," was coined by Columbus himself when in 1502 he first set foot on the mainland of Central America in the vicinity of present-day Puerto Limón. The Indians he encountered were not only extremely hospitable, but also sported some gold ornaments. In his reports to the Spanish court, Columbus described this country as a *Castilla de Oro,* a "Golden Castile," a Dorado for every treasure hunter.

The treasure hunters who came on the strength of Columbus' exaggerated and imaginative accounts stayed only long enough to pillage and depopulate the country before moving on to fresh fields where greater profits were to be had. The only ones who stayed were those sons of Spanish peasants who were willing to labor in the sweat of their brows to earn their bread.

The Basques, always among the most hard-working inhabitants of the Spanish motherland, were especially attracted to the colony. They did not attempt to establish plantations, but only small holdings which a man and his family could till. In the lowlands, they planted vegetables and fruit; on the slopes of the volcanoes, they established small coffee plantations; and in the pastures among the mountains, they created dairy farms which remarkably resemble those of Alpine countries.

Towns were established, but a certain modesty prevailed, the citizens being artisans, small traders, technicians, and intellectuals. To this day, the capital city of San José is devoid of any palatial office buildings, any superwarehouses, any great company headquarters aside from the premises of the United Fruit Company. San José is a town of small- and medium-sized stores, workshops, and middle-class houses. It is very proud of its opera house, which is modeled on the Paris Opéra, though on a much reduced scale. In short, Costa Rica is the stronghold of the sound, ordinary, middle-class citizen.

The whole world over, the middle class is the pillar of cultural life. In Costa Rica no money is spent for soldiers or for vain display. This model country of Central America long ago abolished its army; a police force is sufficient for the protection of its peaceful citizenry. With the money thus saved, Costa Rica has built more schools per capita than any other Caribbean country. Its university is regarded as exemplary. Universal compulsory education exists in fact, not just on paper. Besides elementary and secondary schools, there are vocational, technical, and agricultural schools. Since the little republic guarantees complete religious freedom, education is in lay, not clerical, hands.

For all these reasons, Costa Rica has the smallest percentage of illiteracy in all of Central America. The 15 per cent who cannot read or write consist mainly of remnants of the Indian tribes and of the inhabitants of remote mountain valleys. At the same time, Costa Rica has also become a favorite refuge for those Latin Americans who have encountered difficulties with their own government. Conservative, liberal, and socialist exiles all sit about harmoniously and pacifically in the cafés of San José. Although the Costa Ricans regard the right of asylum as sacred, they are strict about keeping their country from becoming a headquarters for conspiracies.

A European almost feels at home there. True, the little republic has not always been so peaceful and well ordered. It too has passed through dictatorships, revolutions, civil wars, and clashes with its neighbors. But the country has conquered these childhood diseases of Latin America, even as it has come to terms with the banana monopoly of United Fruit. Many students of Latin American affairs attribute the orderly and sound development of the republic to the fact that whites rather than mestizos form the majority of the population. But if that were so, then such "white" countries as Cuba and Argentina would have attained similar political and social maturity. A better explanation might be the fact that Costa Rica was settled not by gold-hungry adventurers but by industrious small farmers.

A peaceful, orderly, middle-class country without an army inevitably has allure for heavily armed and power-hungry neighbors. The Somoza dictatorship in Nicaragua often cast a greedy eye upon Costa Rica. In December 1948 Anastasio Somoza charged that the anti-dictatorial "Caribbean Legion" in San José and other cities of Costa Rica were fomenting such plots against Nicaragua that he could no longer put up with the situation. In reality, the exiled Nicaraguans were merely sitting peacefully in the restaurants of their host country drinking good Costa Rican coffee and conducting political debates after the manner of intellectuals all over the world. Somoza, however, invaded Costa Rica with an army of some one thousand soldiers. An effective resistance would have been impossible. Costa Rica's military establishment consisted of a bare three hundred men, two-thirds of whom were merely band players. The country did not even have a defense minister. Far in advance of their times, the Costa Ricans had converted their former war ministry into a historical museum.

At the last minute, the United States was able to dissuade Somoza from continuing the invasion. This was done in spite of the fact that in the immediately preceding years Americans had had their own reasons for disliking Costa Rican policies. During the Second World War, the country had been governed by a kind of popular front composed of leftist Catholics and socialists. And when Somoza started his attack, leftist radical groups were once again coming to the fore. But the United States was well aware that the middle-class social structure in Costa Rica is the best guarantee of moderate policies. People who have property to defend may sometimes toy with social experiments, but they are not going to endanger their hard-won blessings by excessive radicalism. Should the pendulum ever swing far to the left in Costa Rica, it is certain to right itself again at the next election. The United States was therefore well advised to protect antimilitaristic Costa Rica against dictatorial Nicaragua. The Costa Ricans remain grateful to the Americans to this day.

FAIR PLAY IN COSTA RICA

In 1948, the year of Somoza's abortive attack, Costa Rica underwent a rather typical crisis. The Popular Front, which had hitherto held power, had lost the election; the new president was to be the conservative Otilio Ulate. Both the adherents of the previous government and the communists were loath to accept this situation. Teodoro Picado, the Popular Front president, challenged the results of the election and sharply attacked the rightists.

At this point José Figueres, a hitherto little-known figure, put himself at the head of an army of volunteers, staged a revolution, and deposed the obstinate Popular Front leader. Figueres, however, was a leftist liberal with socialist tendencies. He should have been on the side of the leftists, but his democratic convictions had been outraged by the annulling of the elections. Thus, a leftist politician in Costa Rica overthrew a leftist government and put in office the legally elected conservative president.

This same Figueres called upon his country to take the lead in an ideological struggle against Caribbean dictatorships. At the next election, in 1953, the people paid tribute to him as the defender of democratic procedure. The *Liberación Nacional,* the party of José Figueres, won the election. Figueres immediately began functioning as a social reformer, although there was not very much to reform in Costa Rica. He distributed town lands to the sons of small farmers and landless agricultural workers, modernized the labor laws, and during his four years in office gained the reputation of being one of the leading moderate leftists in Latin America.

The next election was once again won by a conservative, Mario Echandi, but his policies could scarcely be distinguished from those of his predecessor. All three parties in Costa Rica, the conservatives, the leftist liberals, and the adherents of the former Popular Front, are committed to more moderate policies than similar parties in other Ibero-American countries. The Costa Rican leftist parties do not look to Castro, let alone to Moscow, for it is generally realized that the country would fare worse under communism. Consequently, Costa Rica is among the most faithful allies of the democratic West in Latin America. To be sure, there are volcanoes there too, but these are geological and not political phenomena. The great seething Irazú crater, which towers high above the capital of the country and has more than once demolished the old city of Cartago, is a tourist attraction, not a grim symbol.

In Costa Rica, too, German immigrants established coffee, only to have their plantations expropriated during the Second World War. The pressure for this came from the United States, but by an odd quirk Costa Rica is still officially at war with Germany. The reason for this is purely internal. Picado, the Popular Front president, had linked the declaration of war upon Germany with a number of laws of the sort common in wartime, especially a stringent rent-control law. The period of rent control, however, was fixed only for the duration of the war. All subsequent governments were faced with a dilemma. If they liquidated the state of war, they would automatically rescind rent controls and thus offend the tenants. If they passed a new peacetime rent-control law, they would offend the landlords. Since politicians in Costa Rica do not like to antagonize any group, the country has had to remain officially at war with Germany.

Yet Costa Rica is traditionally a good friend of Germany. German concerns have long since resumed business in the country. West Germany buys approximately half of the Costa Rican coffee crop. In fact, Costa Rican coffee has gradually replaced the once esteemed Guatemalan coffee throughout much of Central Europe, proving that good coffee need not be produced by large-scale plantation methods, but can be grown by small farmers. Perhaps the taste of Costa Rican coffee is just a little better because it is not flavored with the sweat of exploited field hands, but with the industry of a competent free people.

THE CANAL SCANDAL

Panama is not a nation. Panama is a laboratory product, the offspring of artificial insemination. She has no history; she has merely figured in a number of stories. The most dramatic of these is the story of how the instant country was begotten. She came into being because a canal was to be built.

A trip through the Panama Canal is one of those classical voyages which belong in the experience of every globe-trotter. The ship does not pass by dirty ports and primitive native villages such as might be expected in the tropics. On the contrary, the landscape to either side of the narrow waterway looks carefully tended—the word *hygienic* leaps to mind. A segment of the United States only ten miles wide cuts through the Republic of Panama all along the canal. One-third of the working population of Panama earn their livelihood in the Canal Zone, for the operation of the canal requires considerable labor power.

As the ship passes slowly through the locks drawn by "mules," small electric locomotives, the passenger sees modern houses and administrative buildings so consummately North American that they seem incongruous on the soil of Central America. The traveler finds himself blessing the sight of an alligator, its jaws agape, sunning itself on the bank of the canal. For here is proof that the Caribbean wilderness cannot be wholly tamed but is always struggling to overgrow the sanitized ten-mile strip.

The alligators and other wild animals occasionally glimpsed from the ship come from the region around Gatun Lake. Gatun Lake also belongs to the Canal Zone, but it is no more a genuine lake than the

Republic of Panama is a genuine nation. It was made by the Gatun Dam, and the many large and small islands in this artificial lake are the hilltops of the drowned land. The animals trapped by the flood waters in their valleys found refuge upon these eminences. One of the islands, Barro Colorado, has become one of the most interesting nature preserves in Latin America.

Memories of the painful history of the canal are awakened when the ship passes through the ravine-like Culebra Cut. *Culebra,* as the canal workers called it, means "snake." This was the rocky section of the route where the French engineers met defeat, where Ferdinand de Lesseps, France's national hero, at last confessed himself worsted. Here, tens of thousands of human beings died of yellow fever, malaria, and other tropical diseases. The stubborn rock of Culebra Cut produced a bankruptcy which became the greatest financial scandal of the nineteenth century—the Panama Scandal.

FROM BALBOA TO DE LESSEPS

The plan for the Panama Canal is as old as the still-unrealized Nicaraguan plan. The Spanish conquistadors, as far back as Balboa and Cortez, thought of establishing a water link between the Atlantic and Pacific near the present city of Panama. At that time the region belonged to New Granada, later to become Colombia. It bore the name of Darién. The Spaniards, however, could not pursue these dreams, for Philip II vetoed the plan, on the grounds that such interference with nature was impious. Instead, the Spaniards made their way from Panama to the gold of Peru. Panama became a principal point for transshipping the riches of the Spanish colonies, and a favorite haunt for English pirates. When the river of gold from Peru dried up, Darién ceased to be important. It became a remote outpost of the Spanish Empire.

Toward the end of the eighteenth and the beginning of the nineteenth centuries, the old dream of a canal sprang up again. Such diverse thinkers and statesmen as Alexander von Humboldt, Simón Bolívar, and Johann Wolfgang von Goethe began considering both its usefulness and its feasibility. Goethe, in fact, proved an acute prophet, remarking in a conversation with his secretary Eckermann: "It would surprise me if the United States were to let slip the opportunity of undertaking such a task."

Sixty years later, however, it looked as if the United States were going to forgo the opportunity. Most Americans sympathized with the Nicaraguan plan; they had built a railroad across Panama and learned the hard facts of life in that part of the world. Yellow fever and parasitic diseases had raged so furiously among the labor force that according to a contemporary account "the body of a Chinese workman lay under every railroad tie." The French were more optimistic. They had built the Suez Canal, and they now acquired a concession from Colombia to reproduce their feat in the little appendage of Colombia.

Ferdinand de Lesseps founded a stock company and obstinately maintained that the future Panama Canal could be built without locks, exactly like the Suez Canal. His principal opponent, Gustave Eiffel, later builder of the Eiffel Tower, held that as a result of the difference in the tides between the Atlantic and the Pacific, only a lock canal would be possible. But De Lesseps, whose reputation was enormous because of the success of the Suez Canal, won the argument.

The Vanderbilts kept a close watch on these preliminaries. They had fixed upon Nicaragua, and they now launched a campaign in the press against the Panama plan, declaring that construction of a canal in mountainous, jungle-covered, fever-ridden Panama was altogether impossible. The only feasible route, they maintained, was across Nicaragua, and the concession for that was already held by others. This propaganda was so effective that De Lesseps initially had great difficulty selling his shares. He and the other leaders of the canal company thereupon resorted to means which, with all due respect to the builder of the Suez Canal, cannot be termed anything but bribery. In order to warm the public toward investment in their project, they bought banks, newspapers, and even politicians. They paid out millions of francs, but the corrupted bankers, journalists, and parliamentary deputies successfully pounded the publicity drums for them. The issue of 1880 was enormously oversubscribed.

For six years, De Lesseps used the money thus raised in the attempt to cut through the Continental Divide at Culebra. Terrible landslides endangered the construction work and killed many men. Thousands of West Indian Negroes died of epidemic diseases. De Lesseps had neglected to study the geological conditions thoroughly; he had also failed to do anything about the sanitation of the jungles and swamps in the Canal Zone. Among the day laborers who daily faced death in Panama was a young French adventurer named Paul Gauguin. Gauguin was lucky to escape safe and sound from the plague spot. At that time he had not yet done any of the painting that was to make him immortal.

Disease, engineering difficulties, and the constant shortage of money at last brought about the collapse of the whole undertaking. The company went into bankruptcy, leaving debts amounting to one and a half billion francs. Many French families lost their entire savings; there were a number of suicides among the shareholders in the Panama Canal. There was also a sensational trial: De Lesseps, some of his associates, and several politicians were charged with corruption. The builder of the Suez Canal was at last acquitted on grounds of senility and died a year later. The whole Panama project was completely discredited. France regarded the scandal as a national disgrace. With the exception of a single man, no Frenchman wanted even to think of the fever-ridden jungles of Panama.

MADAME SELLS A FLAG

Philippe Jean Bunau-Varilla, the last champion of the Panama project, was a twenty-four-year-old French engineer who had directed the work at Culebra Cut. He was now supposed to liquidate the whole enterprise but continued desperately to hope for a miracle. He refused to believe that all the sacrifices had been in vain, and so he first turned to Russia, thinking that he might raise money there for continuance of the work. The Russians, however, declined the chance. It is interesting to think of how nervous the United States would be nowadays had the Canal Zone fallen into the hands of the Russians.

J. Pierpont Morgan was a good deal more farsighted than other American financiers of the time. As has been mentioned, he bought the rights of the French company and prompted Bunau-Varilla to collect Nicaraguan postage stamps and send them to Washington. After Morgan had won out over Vanderbilt, the Americans had to face the problems of Culebra Cut.

First of all, however, they still had to overcome a minor obstacle. Colombia was not about to give the *Yanquis* a concession in the province of Panama for the same price as the French. Bogotá wanted dollars, as many as possible, and therefore posed unacceptable conditions. President Roosevelt once again began to incline toward the Vanderbilts and the Nicaraguan project. In this crisis of his hopes,

Bunau-Varilla thereupon turned from engineering to political gambling. He staged a revolution in Panama and put up a local veterinarian as president of a future Panama republic. Roosevelt quickly realized what was afoot. While Madame Bunau-Varilla sewed bed sheets into the flag of an "independent" Panama, Roosevelt sent a gunboat to support the Panamanian revolutionaries. The Colombian soldiers who were sent to put down the uprising were not even able to reach Panama by railroad, for the railroad was in American hands and the Americans demanded such high fares for transportation of the Colombian soldiers that Bogotá finally gave up and let things take their course.

Philippe Bunau-Varilla became minister plenipotentiary of the newly founded Republic of Panama. The brand-new nation ceded the Canal Zone to the United States for ten million dollars and an annual rental of two hundred and fifty thousand dollars. Since the Americans had decided that tropical fevers rather than the cliffs of Culebra were the principal enemies of the canal builders, they postponed resumption of the construction work and undertook a thorough sanitation of the Canal Zone.

It was another eight years before the American chief engineer, George Washington Goethals, had mastered the Culebra Cut. Immediately after the outbreak of the First World War, the first ship passed through the Panama Canal. The Americans had performed an enormous medicoengineering feat. They were now responsible for the future of their laboratory nation, the Republic of Panama.

GOLD AND SILVER

Some nine hundred thousand persons live in the country that Bunau-Varilla created. On the Atlantic coast they are mostly Negroes and mulattoes, descendants of the former canal workers. On the Pacific coast Colombian mestizos form the majority of the population. Some fifty thousand Indians are still living in the jungles. These diverse elements scarcely add up to an integrated nation. Yet in the last several decades Panamanian nationalism has flared with peculiar intensity—though it, too, is an artificial product.

North Americans have begotten Panamanian nationalism in the same way that they begot the Republic of Panama. They have imported some unpopular customs into the country. The Panamanians are embittered by the "gold and silver" methods of the *Yanquis*. North Americans who work in the Canal Zone are paid American wages in dollars, in "gold," as the Panamanians say. The colored Panamanians, however, receive their wages at Panamanian rates and in native currency, which they call "silver." Whites ride in "gold" compartments, colored in "silver" compartments. Whites use gold hotels, gold restaurants, and gold rest rooms; for the colored people there are only ramshackle silver hotels and silver toilets.

In order to insure the security of the canal, it has been American policy since 1914 to exclude all Panamanians from the zone. Natives are tolerated in the American territory only as laborers, not as inhabitants. In the city of Panama and along the borders of the zone, regular Negro and Panamanian ghettos have sprung up. And like all places in the world where people are crowded together in confined quarters these ghettos are potential trouble spots. While the movement grows for racial integration in the American South, the Panamanians continue to feel that they are victims of unabashed discrimination.

In recent years strikes, riots, and uprisings have won colored Panamanians the right to stay at American-run hotels, at least in their own capital. Panama, to be sure, lives by the canal—and recently by the registration fees from foreign ships which for tax reasons prefer to sail under the Panamanian flag. Yet the Panamanians consider these income sources paltry consolation prizes. Even the increased annual rental to $1,930,000 is, to their mind, no better than a bone thrown to them while the Americans take the lion's share of profit. According to their figures, the Americans earn twenty times the rental every year from the canal. The United States, however, contends that by far the greater part of the income from the canal is turned back to the Republic of Panama in the form of wages and goods. The canal itself, they say, shows a profit of only three or four million dollars per year. In the slum-ridden city of Panama, people smile at such statements. The Panamanians have eagerly watched the nationalization of the Suez Canal and wished they could do likewise. But the United States is big and powerful and Panama is Lilliputian.

Panamanian presidents therefore face a constantly recurring problem. In order to win elections, they must appeal to the anti-American resentment of the population. In order to stay in power, however, they must co-operate closely with Americans. In so doing they offend the populace and ultimately lose elections, are overthrown by revolutions, or are even assassinated. Their successors follow the same path and end in the same way. It is a vicious circle from which as yet no politician has found an escape.

SHOTS IN BALBOA

The presidents of the Republic of Panama are recruited entirely from the oligarchy of businessmen who economically dominate the country as the result of their collaboration with Americans. Nevertheless, in 1959 President Guardia looked on passively while crowds of Panamanians broke through the wire mesh fence at the border and poured into the Canal Zone, demanding higher wages. For Guardia, this demonstration was an effective way to show the Americans they were not the sole masters of the zone. He then insisted that the Panamanian flag be flown beside the Stars and Stripes on all public buildings in the zone.

Washington proved ready to make concessions on the flag question. Since Panama is not an adult nation-state, it suffers continually from inferiority complexes which are almost always linked with arrogance. Americans understand that very well. Some thirty-five thousand American citizens are stationed in the Canal Zone. Their higher wages are a constant offense to the Panamanians, who have long suffered from a veritable *Yanqui* trauma. Panamanian nationalists and communists have for years pitted their forces to try to tear down the barrier between "gold" and "silver" by means of strikes, demonstrations, and political assassinations. To yield on the flag question cost Washington nothing. It was hoped that this small concession would pacify the rising nationalistic party.

Yet, as it turned out, in January 1964 it was the flag question that led to the worst riots in the Canal Zone so far, and to a breach of diplomatic relations between Panama and the United States. American high-school students in the Canal Zone used to amuse themselves by flouting the two-flag agreement. They flew the Stars and Stripes over their schools and apparently derived a perverse teen-agers' pleasure in the ire of the Panamanians who missed their own flag on the second flagpole. This was a trivial matter, far less important than the ordinary discrimination to which Panamanians in the Canal Zone were exposed. But on January 9, 1964, another such infringement of the two-flag order led to a full-scale crisis.

In the Canal Zone town of Balboa, sixteen-year-old students had once again raised the Stars and Stripes without showing the flag of Panama. Panamanian students thereupon broke through the border fence and attempted to replace the American flag with the Panamanian flag. A teen-age brawl began which in other parts of the globe would scarcely have been taken seriously. In Balboa, however, it rapidly developed into a regular battle. Hordes of people from the slums of Panama City suddenly surged through Balboa throwing stones and dynamite, setting fire to American houses and office buildings. When American soldiers fired into the crowd, the Panamanians fired back across the border fence. The three-day battle took more than thirty lives. Almost four hundred persons, Panamanians and Americans, were wounded.

The president of the republic, Roberto Chiari, did no more to quell the riot than had his predecessor in 1959. The Americans had put themselves in the wrong on the flag question; moreover, they had spilled blood. Thus they created a situation which exacerbated already oversensitive Panamanian nationalism. Chiari made the slogans of the nationalistic and radical leftist Panamanians his own. He recalled his diplomats from Washington and sent three demands to the United States. For order to be restored there had to be:

One: Recognition of Panama's sovereignty over the Canal Zone.

Two: Revision of the Canal Zone treaty and assignment of a just share of the income from the canal to Panama.

Three: Complete equality of Panamanians and Americans in the Canal Zone—that is, doing away with the "gold" and "silver" barrier.

Panamanian leftist radicals set up a broadcasting station to incite further disturbances. They called for half of the income from the canal, which would have amounted to $100,000,000 a year instead of the previous $1,930,000. Red China utilized the Panama crisis for a major anti-American propaganda campaign. For some time after the "battle" of Balboa, all of Panama was in ferment.

Hitherto the United States had always had a tried and true method of cooling down Panamanian hotheads. The United States has only to threaten to build a Nicaraguan canal for political storms in Panama to subside quickly. President Johnson once again used this method in the present crisis. In fact, the Americans now have a choice of two more canal plans which are at present being discussed: one would cut through the Isthmus of Tehuantepec in Mexico, while a second canal would pass through northern Colombia, south of the Panamanian border. Every Panamanian knows that his country has no source of livelihood without the monopoly of the canal. Nevertheless, such threats cannot exorcise the *Yanqui* trauma of the Panamanian population. On the contrary, it is more and more turning into a *Yanqui* phobia.

Note (*cf. p. 118*). In Guatemala, the military, and the oligarchic groups behind it, suffered a severe rebuff at the beginning of March 1966, as this book was going to press. President Johnson had emphatically indicated to Dictator Peralta Azuardia of Guatemala that the United States wished to see honest elections in that "classical" dictatorial state. As a matter of fact, the ruling military junta did not permit really democratic elections, since the "great man" of Guatemala, ex-President Arévalo, was not allowed to return from his Mexican exile to run, and Gutierrez, leader of the radical left, was confined in a Guatemalan prison. The Guatemalan voters therefore had to choose between two candidates put up by the military junta and the liberal scientist Mendez Montenegro (Colonel Soza, leader of an unimportant social-revolutionary party, was never really in the running).

Professor Julio Cesar Mendez Montenegro had previously been a little known follower of Arévalo. On the whole the democratic forces in Guatemala had put him up for lack of anyone better to offer. His more prominent brother, who had made a reputation under Arévalo, had been the original candidate of the bourgeois liberals. But he was shot at the end of 1965—by the military, so his partisans assert. The alleged murder was covered up, the junta police calling it a suicide. But the nimbus of martyrdom that the family thereby acquired sufficed to win the election for Professor Mendez Montenegro.

All the democratic, progressive, and anti-dictatorial groups in Guatemala seem to have united behind this middle-class scholar. He is certainly no second Arévalo, let alone a second Arbenz; but he was elected because the Guatemalans were sick of the long military dictatorship. It remains to be seen whether he will be able to hold his own against the opposition of the ruling groups, and whether he will succeed in reintroducing democratic liberties and carrying out the urgently necessary social and agrarian reforms. But whatever the outcome, his election constitutes a rejection of the anti-democratic military junta, a rejection of the thin upper crust who have dominated Guatemalan society. Thus it represents another victory—though only in a small country—for democracy in Latin America.

Venezuela · Colombia · Ecuador

Caribbean Sea

TRINIDAD
AND TOBAGO
Port of Spain

Oil

Bonaire
(Dutch)
Aruba
Curaçao

Cacao

Caracas
Valencia
Barquisimeto

Iron

Bauxite
Gold
Diamonds

VENEZUELA

Oil

Maracaibo
Barranquilla

Cartagena

Coffee

Cúcuta
San Cristobal

Emeralds

Diamonds
Bauxite

Bananas

Coffee

Bucaramanga

Iron
Coal

COLOMBIA

Medellin
Bogotá
Manizales

Coffee

Nev. del
Huila
18,981 ft.

Tobacco

Quinine

Cali

BRAZIL

Rubber

Pasto

Pacific Ocean

Quito
▲ Cotopaxi, 19,450 ft.
Gold, Uranium

ECUADOR

PERU

Oil

Guayaquil

Cacao

VENEZUELA

COLOMBIA

ECUADOR

SOUTH
AMERICA

Pacific
Ocean

Atlantic
Ocean

CHAPTER 4

The Heritage of Simón Bolívar

FREEDOM—BUT FOR WHOM?

Every Venezuelan city has its monument to the liberator, Simón Bolívar, and a street or plaza named after him. Yet another celebrated figure from another sphere altogether is almost equally popular. This is the German naturalist Alexander von Humboldt. Humboldt monuments, Humboldt streets, Humboldt plazas, and Humboldt hotels are almost as common in Venezuela as the various tributes to Simón Bolívar.

In fact the two are closely linked in the historical legend of Venezuelans. Humboldt is considered to be one of those who inspired Simón Bolívar. Thus, he is indirectly a hero of Venezuelan freedom.

In reality Humboldt stood for ideas a world apart from those of Simón Bolívar. Humboldt was a universal thinker who attempted to unite the spirit of classical humanistic idealism and the thoughts of revolutionary France with the new knowledge acquired by the exact sciences. Bolívar, on the other hand, was a Napoleonic autocrat, a highly contradictory personality who seemed to have exploited the ideals of the times chiefly for his own ambitions. While all of Humboldt's work is permeated with a humanitarian spirit, Bolívar said of himself: "My element is war."

HUMBOLDT AND THE LIBERATOR

Yet the Venezuelan legend which represents Humboldt and Bolívar as intellectual brothers rests upon an element of fact. In 1804, when Humboldt had returned from his great exploration of the northern part of South America, he met in Paris a twenty-one-year-old student from a Venezuelan noble family who greatly admired him and talked with him on a number of occasions. Young Simón Bolívar belonged to the oligarchy, the rich Creole class of South America which Humboldt had criticized more than once in his travel notes. A typical comment was:

"This class of people lives only in notions about the past. America seems to them the property of their ancestors who conquered it. They hate what is called the light of this century and cultivate their inherited prejudices as carefully as if these were part of their ancestral estate."

Humboldt took a highly skeptical attitude toward the vaunted desire of these Creoles to win independence from Spain. In a letter to his brother Wilhelm, he wrote: "They expect from a revolution only the loss of their slaves, the end of the power of the clergy, and religious tolerance, which they feel as a threat to the purity of their present religion. . . . They hate all constitutions based on equal rights and have a particular dread of losing those titles and distinctions which they have acquired with so much effort and which are so essential to their happiness."

Humboldt knew only too well that the French Revolution had smuggled all kinds of liberal ideas into Spain. He knew also that the Spanish oligarchy in South America would defend its position with all the means at its command and was making every effort to keep liberalistic influences out of the Spanish colonies. This was why they wanted freedom from the mother country! The growing independence movement in South America was not a popular movement; it was, Humboldt thought, confined to those who "either because of inherited wealth or their long residence in the colonies, form a true local aristocracy."

Thus the rich young aristocrat Bolívar must have struck Humboldt as the last candidate to bring true freedom to South America. Nevertheless, the story goes that Humboldt held earnest conversations with Bolívar in Paris, and impressed him with the need of freeing Spanish America from the motherland. It is further said that this idea kindled the imagination of the young Venezuelan student. Then, the legend continues, Bolívar made a trip to the United States and studied the life of George Washington. Inspired by both Humboldt and Washington, he returned to South America to become the liberator of a whole continent.

No one knows what Bolívar and Humboldt really talked about.

Probably the famous scientist merely chatted a bit with the cultivated South American who looked up to him with the ardor of a youth and a Latin. No doubt Humboldt did think it desirable that South America achieve independence, but he felt freedom essential not only for the rich Creoles but for all the people. On this point the ideas of Bolívar and Humboldt were miles apart. Again and again in his writings Humboldt stressed the idea of human equality: "There are more educable and more highly educated nations, there are nations ennobled by higher culture, but there are no nobler nations. All are equally destined for freedom." Bolívar, however, did not hold with the ideal of equality. "Of all lands," he once declared, "South America is perhaps the one that is least suited for republican government because its population consists of Indians and Negroes."

Like most Creoles, the liberator of South America had some Indian and Negro blood in his veins, but he felt himself to be a white man. "As a white man," writes Salvador de Madariaga in his biography of Bolívar, "Bolívar was the heir of a tradition that took power and rule so much for granted as to be no longer conscious of itself. That the land, the cattle, the slaves, and those Indians who could be subjugated and assimilated belonged to the whites was no more doubted than the fact that day is day and night, night. Such a tradition, which is more deeply rooted than all ideas and theories, confers upon the whites in America, the 'sons of the conquerors,' their proud certainty that it is their right to rule and not to work."

Now, after three centuries of suppressing the natives, the Spanish crown had begun to accord certain human rights to the colored populations of its colonies. But in the eyes of the Creoles, the Spanish governors implementing the new policy were no longer allies but despots. The white South Americans who had hitherto plumed themselves on belonging to the Spanish motherland, looked toward the United States and began to call themselves Americans. They suddenly discovered all sorts of lacks and inconveniences in Spanish colonial rule. A ferment began in the upper classes. The determination to preserve the old traditions became curiously mixed with revolutionary sparks from France and North America, with the result that a nobleman from one of the best old Spanish families, like Simón Bolívar, could work himself up into a fury against his motherland, and expound principles which in progressive circles of Europe and North America were taken as passionate outcries against colonialism, but which were only the anti-Spanish resentments of a well-to-do Creole.

"A continent separated from Spain by infinite seas, more populous and more prosperous, has been groveling in degrading dependency for three hundred years!" ran one of the Liberator's many proclamations. "For three hundred years America has groaned under this tyranny, the harshest ever inflicted upon humanity. The savage Spaniard was spewed forth to transform the most beautiful part of the world into a vast, hated empire of greed and cruelty. Since his arrival in the New World, death and destruction have marked his path . . . and when his rage no longer encountered any living being whom he could annihilate he turned against his own sons, who had settled upon this stolen soil."

Such rhetoric might suggest that the liberators had become friends of the Indians, idealists who wanted to make restitution for historical injustice. But the opposite was the case. The Creoles wanted to go on reaping the fruits of their "stolen soil." They wanted to go on exercising control. Certainly they did not want to upset the pattern of property owners and impoverished masses. Undoubtedly Bolívar was also inspired by the ideas of the French Revolution, but his followers meant the slogan of Liberty, Equality, Fraternity to apply only to their own class and not to all the inhabitants of the continent.

THE UPRISING OF THE LLANEROS

South Americans are very sensitive concerning any criticism of their idol, Simón Bolívar. The Venezuelans are particularly sensitive. Bolívar was born in Caracas, the present capital of Venezuela. It was in Venezuela that he kindled the torch of freedom and it was there, too, that his megalomaniac dream finally foundered. His war of independence was marked not only by battles and heroic deeds, but also by excesses and murders. His personal ambition caused him to betray Francisco de Miranda, the first hero of Venezuelan freedom, whom he saw as an inconvenient rival. In his intoxication with power, he toyed with a plan for imitating Napoleon and becoming Emperor of South America. He began his struggle in 1810 with the battle cry of "freedom." Eighteen years later he had transformed freedom into absolute dictatorship. He was the first of a long succession of Latin

American dictators who for a century and a half have reduced the continent to a political bullfighting arena.

The sides in the struggle were the very opposite of what one would expect in a national liberation movement. On the side of the liberators stood the real masters of the country; on the side of the colonial power stood the oppressed masses of the population. In Venezuela, the forces pitched against Bolívar's insurgents were called *Godos*, that is "Goths." These Godos consisted for the most part of Indians, Negroes, and mestizos. Bolívar's most stubborn opponent was a man named José Tomás Rodríguez, who has gone down in Venezuelan history under the name of Boves. Boves mobilized the *llaneros*, the Venezuelan gauchos, and agricultural laborers against the insurgent nobility. Allied with Boves, the Spaniards unleashed a popular revolution in order to crush the uprising of the oligarchy. Boves' colored followers massacred the white population, and the whites in their turn slaughtered the colored adherents of the Spaniards. The war of independence gradually degenerated into a race war, as a result of which Venezuela lost a third of her population within fifteen years.

Due to the opposition of the llaneros, Bolívar at first failed in Venezuela. He had more luck in Colombia, where he took up the struggle a year later. From Colombia he undertook one of his famous campaigns into the western part of South America. Meanwhile, however, his prestige had increased significantly as a result of his victories over the Spaniards, and the llaneros in his homeland shifted to his side. As time went on, the Spaniards had to evacuate their positions everywhere in Latin America. In addition to Colombia and Venezuela, Bolívar also liberated Ecuador, Peru, and Bolivia. He was at one time or another president or dictator of each of these countries; Bolivia, in fact, took its name from him. For a while he was able to unite Venezuela, Colombia, and Ecuador into a federation called Greater Colombia. But the claims of the ruling families in the various countries of the federation imposed insuperable difficulties.

The Creoles had sown the wind and they reaped the whirlwind. Bolívar ultimately attempted to realize his Napoleonic Pan-American dreams by Napoleonic methods. He suppressed freedom of the press, banished political opponents, and made overtures to England and France with the idea of transforming his newborn republican federation into an elective monarchy. These aspirations pleased neither the Creole upper class nor the by now seething lower classes. One after another,

Bolívar's followers abandoned him. In 1830 the Liberator finally gave up the struggle for the unity of South America. He left behind him chaos, a disrupted economy, and a shattered social structure.

After Bolívar's fall, a man of Indian blood became the master of Venezuela. He was José Antonio Páez, a former llanero who had risen to the top during the turbulence of the revolution. The Creole aristocracy had meant to defend the privileges of birth and property, but its rebellion against Spain had brought about a social reshuffling which could no longer be undone. What had taken place was exactly what the Creoles had hoped to avoid. The upheaval had created a powerful class of parvenus, men whose power rested not on inherited privileges or property but on soldiers and bayonets. Páez, a cavalry leader from the *llanos,* the plains of the interior, was one of these. He was the first of the *caudillos,* those upstarts who rose up out of the depths and used military power to make themselves leaders of their nation.

The oligarchy, however, adopted the policy of swiftly incorporating these new men into their ranks. The caudillos seized stray estates whose masters had disappeared or died, acquired wealth, and, in the effort to make everyone forget their origins, behaved even more conservatively and with greater devotion to tradition than the Creole aristocracy. Some of the ideas from France, England, and the United States had affected the rich Creoles at least to the extent that nine-teenth-century economic liberalism had made its way into their consciousness. The Creoles, townsmen, and merchants formed the germinal groups of the later liberal party. The families of newly rich landowners, on the other hand, largely provided the leaders of the conservative party.

Venezuela remained a land of unrest, of anarchy, and of repeated instances of military domination. Like most South American countries, it cannot look back upon a long slow course of historical growth. Its boundaries were set by chance. Dictators installed themselves in the capital city of Caracas and held sway by virtue of their troops. In the more remote provinces, local governors established more or less arbitrary regimes. For many decades the country went through alternating revolutions and counterrevolutions. Conservative rulers, the so-called Unitarians, wanted to transform the country into a centralistic state, but the opposition finally prevailed, so that the country now is a federal union which calls itself the United States of Venezuela.

Venezuela has been dominated by clans such as that of the Monagas, who used to disband the congress by force when they were defeated in elections. Venezuela has also been dominated by strong men, a good example of whom was General Guzmán Blanco. He resorted to harsh measures in the interests of good government, for he was determined to establish order and straighten out the country's tangled finances and economy. Venezuela has also had a namesake of Fidel Castro as one of its dictators: General Cipriano Castro, who stirred up a wave of violent xenophobia among the people as a basis for expropriating foreign capitalists. Venezuela has also had a forerunner of Batista, General Juan Vicente Gómez, who earned the nickname "Tyrant of the Andes" because he invented particularly exquisite tortures for his political prisoners. Above all, the Venezuelans have had ample opportunity to study the principal vice of Latin American dictators: corruption.

As a rule, Venezuelan dictators do not come to the end of their careers by sudden death, but spend their declining years peacefully in exile. In this respect, too, they follow the precedent of Simón Bolívar. Just outside the Colombian port of Santa Marta there is a country mansion in typical Iberian colonial style. In Bolívar's lifetime it belonged to a Spaniard. There Bolívar went after he was overthrown, and died a few months later. Today a kind of national sanctuary, the white one-story house is surrounded by a vast garden, brilliant with tropical flowers. In the distance glitter the snow-covered peaks of the Sierra Nevada. The grounds are very quiet and rather solemn. There is no one in sight. The tropical heat broods over the carefully raked paths. Inside the house, a kind of chilly dustiness prevails. Sunlight and flowers have been excluded, for Latins always keep nature at a small distance from themselves. The rooms in which Bolívar spent the last months of his life have a stiff, museumlike air. There are a great many mementos of the Liberator, but none of them seem to bring Simón Bolívar any closer to us. The impersonal coldness in these rooms is not due only to the lack of sunlight; it seems to have settled in the very walls. A cool, remote attitude once enabled the Spaniards to maintain their morale and their identity in the hot climate and primitive world of South America. Simón Bolívar, heir of that tradition, ended his life in cold solitude. Bolívar is described by his biographers as a hot-blooded man ablaze with passion, but here in Santa Marta it is hard to escape the feeling that the man who came to this place to die was, whatever his outward temperament, no warm lover of humanity, and perhaps even a cold scorner of the human race.

In one of his last letters addressed to a former comrade, Bolívar summed up the bitter lessons he had extracted from his struggle. "The man who serves the revolution," he wrote, "plows the sea. . . . This country is bound to fall into the hands of an ungovernable band of petty tyrants belonging to all colors and races and almost too insignificant to be noticed. Worn out by all sorts of crimes and ennervated by impetuosity, we will be despised by the Europeans. . . . If any one part of the world could sink back into primitive chaos, South America would do that. . . . The only thing one can do in South America is emigrate."

EL DORADO

El Dorado—it was a pretty fable, a fantasy typical of the age of discovery: the dream of the golden land, an earthly paradise where men bathed in gold dust. Four hundred years ago persons in Spain and in much of the rest of Europe believed firmly in the existence of this gold country. El Dorado was even marked on the maps, expeditions were fitted out to search for it, in its probable hiding place in the jungles of the Orinoco River. The legend of El Dorado actually came from Colombia, where the rulers of the civilized Chibcha Indians would, for ritual reasons, cover themselves with salve and powder their bodies with fine gold dust. The Spaniards conquered the small city-states of the Chibchas, but the gold they found there did not content them. They kept transposing the legend of the golden paradise to other parts of the continent. As the result a remote and hitherto scarcely noted colony became the focus of their interest. This was the territory around the great Lake Maracaibo, whose Indian inhabitants lived in pile dwellings and villages built out into the water. Therefore the Spaniards called the region Little Venice—Venezuela.

This part of Venezuela, the western sector of the present-day country, had meanwhile been pledged by the Spaniards to two foreign bankers. Emperor Charles V had contracted such enormous debts with the Augsburg merchants Bartholomäus and Anton Welser that he had to assign the territory of Little Venice to them as security. The Welser brothers, too, believed in the existence of El Dorado. They sent several expeditions to Venezuela to find out how much they were likely to recover of the twelve tons of gold they had lent to Charles V.

The Spaniards already in the colony observed their operations with displeasure. A race began to the legendary land of gold. From Colombia the conquistadors Quesada and Belalcázar started out on a predatory expedition toward the southeast, for according to the Spanish view El Dorado must belong to the Spanish colony of New Granada. From Venezuela the German conquistadors Nikolaus Federmann and Philipp von Hutten started on an expedition toward the southwest, for to the Augsburg way of thinking El Dorado must lie in the area held in pawn by the Welsers. Both parties slaughtered Indians, fought one another, and lost several of their leaders—but found no gold. Thereupon the interest of the Augsburg banking house in Venezuela faded. Eighteen years later, the concessions reverted to the Spanish crown. Venezuela was enlarged eastward but remained an insignificant, underdeveloped, minor colony of the Spanish West Indies. It remained minor and underdeveloped even after the tempests of Simón Bolívar's revolution had passed. No one suspected the true wealth of the country. For Venezuela was, in truth, El Dorado—not a land of gold but a land with one of the greatest reserves of petroleum in the world.

Neither the Welsers nor the Spaniards had done very much about the exploration of Venezuela. They had only massacred the Indians and brought Negro slaves to the coast. From a mingling of Indian, European, and African elements there sprang an illiterate rural population which awakened suddenly and violently during the wars of independence and which has been filled with a variety of fierce resentments ever since.

XENOPHOBIA

Venezuela is considered one of the most xenophobic countries in South America. Again and again, political upheavals have led to excesses against foreigners. After the fall of the dictator Pérez Jiménez, the fury of the people turned not only against the dictator's followers but also against the Italian construction workers Pérez Jiménez had brought into the country. The hail of stones, rotten eggs, and tomatoes with which Venezuelans greeted Vice-President Nixon on his good-will tour through Latin America is still remembered in the United States. Foreign engineers and workers have periodically encountered the hostility of the natives, and any foreigner unlucky enough to have any dealings with the Venezuelan police will invariably find himself put in the wrong.

I myself became acquainted with this animosity toward everything foreign not among the chiefly dark-skinned population along the coast, nor in the capital of Caracas, which is a veritable Babel, but among the Venezuelan Indians. I visited many Indians in Latin America, from the jungle tribes of Brazil to the nomads of the Gran Chaco and the descendants of the Incas in Peru and Bolivia. Everywhere I was received with friendliness; everywhere I found I could, with a little patience, establish human contact. But in the Venezuelan port of Maracaibo I was attacked by Indians before I had even be-come aware of their presence. The Goajiros, who still inhabit the region of the original Little Venice, seem not to have forgotten resent-ments that go back to Spanish colonial times. If you visit their markets you are likely to be beaten up. If you drive through their villages they throw filth at your car. If you unexpectedly come across them while on a country outing, they break into savage curses and spit in your direction.

The half-Indian llaneros, who live in the plains along the Orinoco, are said to be among the most vicious knife wielders in Latin America. To this day, a journey through the llanos is not without its dangers. The Spaniards, in fact, never really conquered the llanos and not until fifteen years before the end of their colonial rule did they succeed in founding the first city in the Orinoco region—Angostura, today called Ciudad Bolívar, which in the past few decades has become the center of Venezuelan iron and steel production.

Despite this prejudice, foreign entrepreneurs became extraordinarily active in Venezuela even in the nineteenth century. The wars of independence had thinned the ranks of the oligarchy and reduced the old colonial economic structure to total chaos. Overseas firms attempted to fill the resultant vacuum and set up a new economic oligarchy. There were German companies that had control of the Venezuelan railroads. Dutch, English, French, and Italian companies divided Venezuelan trade among themselves. John D. Rockefeller, the founder of the Standard Oil Company, and Henri Deterding, the director-general of Royal Dutch Shell, also took an interest in Venezuela. The first oil wells were discovered there in 1866 in the region around Lake Maracaibo. Soon afterward Standard Oil and Shell obtained concessions in order to keep out potential competition, though oil was not yet the source of great wealth it was to become. It was still used primarily for kerosene lamps, and North American production sufficed to keep those alight.

In 1899 a particularly xenophobic dictator seized power in Caracas. He was the above-mentioned namesake of Fidel Castro who, like the present Cuban leader, declared war on the foreign capitalist. General Cipriano Castro at first attempted to expropriate the German and English enterprises. Then he reached out for Italian property. But in those days big business handled such crises by direct methods. German, British, and Italian warships blockaded the Venezuelan coast and bombarded the military harbor of Puerto Cabello until the dictator backed down.

A few years later the same little game was repeated. This time General Castro took on the French, Dutch, and Americans, and this time French, Dutch, and American warships attacked Venezuela. In 1908 Castro stepped down. The Venezuelan presidency fell to the man to whom Venezuela owes both its oil boom and its political instability: General Juan Vicente Gómez.

THE GREAT OIL BOOM

Gómez is counted among the most cruel and violent of the many dictators of South America. One of his ingenious ideas was to connect the prison of Puerto Cabello with the sea, so that every time the tide came in the political prisoners would be up to their necks in water. Sailors on ships that docked in Puerto Cabello during the twenties and thirties still recall the screams of the tormented men, which could be heard within the harbor. Nevertheless, European and American business maintained close ties with Gómez. The dictator, to be sure, was by origin a llanero and as such not very fond of foreigners, but he was still less fond of the economic experiments of his predecessor Castro.

The era of Juan Vicente Gómez lasted for twenty-seven years, that is, until 1935. The great oil companies and other foreign business concerns in Venezuela to this day refer to it as a time of unprecedented prosperity during which the Venezuelan economy expanded mightily and an incessant stream of foreign capital poured into the country. Gómez was the first Venezuelan president who had some notion of the hidden treasures of his native land. But in order to get at them, money was needed, and this money could only come from abroad. Foreign investors required political stability so that their capital might work profitably. The corpselike peace of the Gómez regime provided that stability.

As early as 1912, when the future triumph of petroleum was only faintly adumbrated, Gómez decided to sell the oil resources of his country to foreigners in return for participation in the profit. He turned first to Germany. German businessmen, however, were blind to the dawning age of oil. Gómez then began to flirt with the two largest oil companies in the world—Standard Oil and Royal Dutch Shell. They fought one another bitterly for the dictator's favors, and these struggles have continued right up to the present time.

Shell won the first round. The Deterding empire transformed the Dutch West Indian island of Curaçao, which lies off the Venezuelan coast, virtually into one vast oil refinery. In linking the fortunes of his country with oil, Gómez had started an avalanche. He had initiated the most radical, the most complete transformation that the economy of any South American nation has yet undergone. Venezuela, until then a thinly settled land of forest and plains, a country of planters, ranchers, and coffee growers, of small farmers raising corn and to-bacco, has since 1928 more and more drawn its income from oil.

Forests of derricks replaced the jungles of the Maracaibo basin and even pushed out far into the lake. Desolate fishing villages were transformed into tanker ports. Oil pipelines crawled across jungles still inhabited by savage, warlike Indian tribes. Innumerable peasants left their plantings and cattle and poured into the oil fields to find work and earn dollars. In the thirties, this flight from the land as-sumed such proportions that agriculture in Venezuela almost ceased. The Venezuelans had to import a large part of their food. The coffee production of the country, which around the turn of the century had been the third largest in the world, fell away to almost nothing.

The artificial forest of derricks which today dominates the Mara-caibo Basin has a little of the cold, bloodless, diabolic quality of a futuristic painting. The choking stench of oil hangs permanently in the air; it even wafts toward you when you sail out toward the islands in the lake. For these islands were not created by nature; they are made of concrete and support vast pumping equipment. Twelve per cent of the world's oil reserves lie in the depths of the earth in this region. One hundred and twenty to one hundred and fifty million tons of crude oil are shipped annually from the port of Maracaibo. Thus Venezuela has become one of the foremost crude-oil exporters in the world. Today not only Shell participates in the exploitation of the black gold, but—as we shall hear—some ten smaller companies and also Shell's principal rival, Standard Oil.

At some distance from the wasteland of the derricks lie the pleasant bungalow settlements of the foreign engineers and employees. In sharp contrast to these, the wretched hovels of the natives line the streets like ulcer sores. Venezuelan workers earn good money in the oil fields, but even in Maracaibo not much has yet been done about the *ranchitos,* the slum dwellings of the common people.

As soon as you strike up a conversation with the foreign businessmen, you hear that Venezuelans are unusually lazy and work-shy. For evidence, they point to the gigantic bridge meant to span the lake at its narrowest point. The plans for the bridge were drawn up by an Italian engineer. The construction itself is being carried out by a consortium of one Venezuelan company and four German companies. Over five miles long, the Maracaibo Bridge will someday be one of the most impressive in the world. It was to have been completed in 1962, but has been far behind in schedule. The German engineers maintain that the delays are caused by the fact that the project employs only a hundred Europeans as against twenty-five hundred Venezuelans.

As a result of its wealth in oil, Venezuela became a rich country with a balanced budget. However, it was also a country with a high cost of living, one of the most expensive spots in the world. Gradually a small but extremely active middle class of businessmen, technicians, brokers, and white-collar workers formed alongside the traditional South American upper class. This middle class was by no means delighted with the Gómez dictatorship, but it did not want to imperil the torrents of money pouring into the country from abroad. Consequently, Juan Vicente Gómez was able to die peacefully in his bed in December 1935.

RANCHO GRANDE

It is quite possible that the dictator himself did not really believe all would end so smoothly. A few years before his death he conceived the idea of building himself a refuge which might be useful in case of revolution. He studied the map and settled on a suitably inaccessible point on the ridge of the mountains between Lake Valencia and the Caribbean Sea, in the dense, fog-shrouded jungles of Aragua. The first thing was to build a good highway through the forested mountains. Then Gómez had a tremendous shelf hacked out of the slope, on which his fortress could perch. Building materials and labor had to be brought from Maracay and Valencia. The planning alone required a large staff of scientists and engineers. Given the site, problems abounded, particularly the dangers of landslides during the rainy season.

Finally El Rancho Grande, "The Big Ranch," was built—crazy, ugly, illogical, stark, sinister, though impressive in its own way, like some Babylonian ruin or surrealistic fantasy. Officially it was called the Government Hotel and the dictator's guesthouse. In reality, however, it was meant to serve a far more important function. The city of Maracay, where Gómez frequently stayed, was only an hour's drive to the Rancho Grande, and the fortress only another hour's drive to the coastal town of Turiamo, where a yacht could be moored, always ready to spirit a dictator to safety.

The Rancho Grande was the first gargantuan structure planned by a Venezuelan dictator—predecessor of the many gigantic buildings put up twenty years later by the second of the oil dictators, Pérez Jiménez. Gómez did not live to see the completion of his project. When the engineers and construction workers at Portachuelo Pass heard the news of the dictator's death, they immediately threw down their blueprints, pickaxes, and trowels, for they felt sure the next dictator would plan altogether different projects and would therefore not pay them a centésimo of their wages. The Rancho Grande was left uncompleted and lies so to this day.

Finished, the Rancho Grande would have been one of the weirdest structures on the face of the earth. It is an architectural nightmare, an abortion in stone, a vast collection of engineering and construction errors that mock all the laws of building. There are round, oval, semicircular, square, and triangular rooms. Some are mere cubicles which are, nevertheless, twenty feet high. The place reminded me of the Minotaur's labyrinth. This monstrosity, moreover, has been exposed to the inroads of the jungle for a quarter of the century. Vegetation has rooted itself in the crumbling walls. The perpetual drip of water from the higher altitudes has created stalagmites and stalactites as in limestone caves. Frogs, snakes, and possums have made themselves at home in the halls. Vivid birds nest in crevices and drainpipes.

The Rancho Grande did not, as it turned out, serve as a bastion for a dictator. Nevertheless, it has been put to use. After the last war, the Creole Petroleum Corporation, Venezuela's largest oil company, established a biological research station there. Under the auspices of Standard Oil, which owns most of the stock of the CPC, noted scientists came to study the flora and fauna of the Aragua jungle. The biologists, however, waged a constant and almost hopeless battle with the invading forest, the pervading moisture, and paper-eating vermin.

Climbing from the sultriness of the rancho onto its roof, I saw outstretched before me the landscape through which the Spanish and Swabian conquistadors had once marched in their search for El Dorado, from the Andes to Lake Valencia and the jungles of the south. The forest of Aragua is extremely peaceful and very thinly populated. Venezuela is as large as Texas and New Mexico combined and in spite of—or perhaps because of—its oil boom still consists for the most part of little-explored wilderness. Up at the Rancho Grande you do not smell Venezuela's too prevailing stench of petroleum. It is three hundred miles from the derricks of the Maracaibo Basin to the unfinished castle of the first oil dictator.

SKYSCRAPERS AND RANCHITOS

The hills above the Venezuelan port of La Guaira seem a curious mottle of bright colors. The first impression is droll and exotic, but as one gets nearer, one realizes that these camouflage effects are created by a vast number of *ranchitos,* adobe huts, shacks, and hovels made of flattened-out tin cans. The mulattoes along the Venezuelan coast are as fond of color as the dark-skinned inhabitants of other South American coastal towns. They have splashed bright paint all over their miserable dwellings.

But are these Venezuelan ranchitos abodes of poverty and misery? Goats grazed in front of the huts, but cars were also parked outside them. Weekdays most of the children ran about with nothing on, which in view of the infernal heat was perfectly sensible. On holidays, however, they were all dressed up in party clothes. The roofs of many of the ranchitos were topped with radio and television antennas. Inside the huts I saw a great deal of dirt and little furniture, but many contained refrigerators and record players.

The Venezuelans, a saying of the country goes, have gone with one leap from palms to Cadillacs. The workers of Venezuela do not, as in most Latin American countries, live on the bare margin of subsistence. They earn good wages, make installment payments, and have become avid consumers. On the other hand, they will go to great lengths to avoid paying for certain things. Electric bills, for instance, seem to them an imposition. They therefore tap the nearest street light—a testimony to their technical skill—and run their refrigerators and television sets for free.

There are frightful slums in Latin America: the *favelas* of Rio de Janeiro, the *callampas* of Valparaiso, the *barriadas* of Lima. But when you see the autos and television sets in the Venezuelan ranchitos, you cannot but feel that the appearance of their homes is due not so much to poverty as to the mentality of the population. The ranchitos are certainly unhygienic. For water, the people go to the nearest public well, and any rusty vessel will serve as water jug. Life is also quite dangerous in the ranchitos; for during heavy rainstorms the slopes begin to slide, and sometimes whole slum quarters are swept away. But within a short time the Venezuelans have glued more motley swallow nests to the gashed hillside.

A SOUTH AMERICAN URBAN MIRACLE

A modern four-lane highway takes you in barely twenty minutes from La Guaira to the capital, Caracas. This highway itself deserves to be included among the features which have earned Caracas the title of a South American urban miracle. The creator of modern Caracas, Pérez Jiménez, wished to connect the capital city with its port by the shortest possible route. The road is cut straight through the sixty-five-hundred-foot-high coastal cordillera, an engineering feat of no small magnitude. Multitunneled and free of curves, it is only half as long as the old mountain road with its notoriously perilous three hundred and sixty-five curves.

I had imagined Caracas as rather like some futuristic metropolis out of a movie. Since I had been powerfully affected by the bold, unconventional architecture of other Latin American artificial cities, I looked forward to similar architectural pleasures in Caracas. I certainly did not expect ranchitos.

The reality was quite different from my conception. Pérez Jiménez's Caracas is in part a vast construction site, in part a planless assemblage of cubistic skyscrapers clothed in screaming colors, in part a display of marble ostentation worthy of a Nero. It is as though a child had been playing with colored blocks and had dumped them all on a garbage heap. Some of the buildings seem impressive, some overwhelming, but they lack the lightness and grace typical of Brazilian skyscrapers. Among the impressive ones is the Centro Bolívar, a dual skyscraper thirty stories high. A maze of underground passages contain many shops, a bus station, and vast parking facilities. Caracas also boasts the Heliocoide, the "Snail House," strangest and most expensive shopping street in the world. The Heliocoide is a prime illustration of the way the builders of new Caracas dealt with natural obstacles. A huge stone hill, the Tarpeya Rock, thrusts up out of the heart of the city and could not be removed. Left with no choice, the architects incorporated the Tarpeya Rock into their conception. Some three hundred shops were cut into the rock like cells in a honeycomb. Room was even found in it for a number of cinemas and bars. A spiraling automobile road leads in ever-narrowing windings to the very top. The whole is crowned by a gigantic glass dome. From the air the Heliocoide actually looks like the shell of a monstrous snail.

The shops in the Centro Bolívar are expensive. So are those in the Heliocoide. The Humboldt Hotel, high up on the peak of the Ávila, is among the costliest hotels in the world. Great stadiums have been constructed, at great expense. Money has been poured into Caracas, wealth pumped from the oil-rich Maracaibo Basin.

But as yet Caracas is by no means a utopia, for countless ranchitos like those I saw in La Guaira are crowded in among the cubistic skyscrapers. The ranchitos cover the hills, are dotted here and there along the splendid streets, and peer out of every gap between buildings. It is almost impossible to photograph modern Caracas without getting a few outcroppings of the slums into the picture. In 1940

Caracas had only a quarter of a million inhabitants. When Pérez Jiménez had the old Spanish houses, the narrow winding streets, and the shady patios razed in order to make room for his supermetropolis, he brought vast numbers of Venezuelans into the city as construction workers. The population increased fivefold within a few years. Today every sixth Venezuelan lives in the capital.

In keeping with Venezuelan custom, the new arrivals immediately began setting up shacks here, there, and everywhere. This kind of unregulated growth did not suit Pérez Jiménez's plans. But since like every dictator he needed popular support, he had a number of modern skyscraper apartment houses assigned to the construction workers. But the workers' families did not like them. In the apartment houses they lived under close supervision and had not only rent to pay but also fees for electricity and water. Moreover, they could not keep goats and plant a few banana trees.

Pérez Jiménez was forced to recognize that the Venezuelan countryman could not be transformed overnight into a metropolitan apartment dweller. He then tried to lure the obstinate squatters into the skyscrapers by offering them the apartments rent-free, but even that proved fruitless. Many families did in fact move into the modern apartments, but only long enough to tear the doors off their hinges, take out the windows, carry off the furniture, and cart all this loot back to their ranchitos.

With unlimited power at his disposal, Dictator Pérez Jiménez now began to apply more rigorous methods. He deployed soldiers, drove the squatters from their slums, and brought in bulldozers to sweep away the shacks. But in doing that he made bitter enemies of the new inhabitants of Caracas. The very people whom he had brought in to build his great capital formed those ferocious radical mobs who supported the uprising against Pérez Jiménez and after his fall massacred the dictator's followers and the innocent Italian workers who had been recruited to help with the building.

AT THE PUBLIC TROUGH

European and American observers have regarded this mania for ranchitos on the part of the common folk of Caracas as a significant example of the ineradicable inertia of the Venezuelan people. If even a Pérez Jiménez could not pound the idea of progress into the

Venezuelans, it is argued, the present democracy will certainly not succeed. What this argument overlooks is that no nation on earth can simply leap over whole stages of development. Before the beginning of the oil boom, Venezuela was the poorhouse of South America. The country has very few splendid mansions from colonial days; even the upper-class Spanish colonists lived in quite modest dwellings.

Under Gómez, the first dictator, the Venezuelans remained poor unless they happened to work in the oil fields. Money did not flow into the hands of the people until the building boom began. But the construction workers in Caracas, whose pockets were suddenly filled with clinking bolivars, had come straight from the country. They were country people accustomed to living in huts, to the comfort of earthen floors, to the convenience of keeping small animals. For them, the leap from the rural ranchito to one of Pérez Jiménez's skyscraper apartment houses meant losing the warmth and security of natural living in favor of the impersonal termite existence of advanced civilization. The experiment was bound to fail. Evolution cannot be so accelerated.

The transition to urban life would certainly have been easier for Venezuelan rustics if, instead of skyscrapers, they had been offered colonies of simple, small houses. But in the days of Pérez Jiménez, Venezuela was so thoroughly caught up in the building boom that only the most modern of the modern would do. No one thought of so ordinary a matter as human preferences. Even today, under democracy, this intoxication with building for its own sake is not yet over. To be sure, construction proceeds rather more slowly than it did under the dictatorship, for there is less money around. But when buildings are put up in Caracas, they are big apartment houses, not one-family dwellings. For that reason, South America's urban miracle resembles a jungle consisting of towering steel and concrete trees and tangled thickets of shacks.

The influx of population into Caracas goes on. Venezuela's capital is bursting at the seams. But the people who entered the metropolis after the dictator's fall came not in order to work in Caracas, but to be unemployed there. Betancourt's government has passed a number of progressive labor and social laws creating a democratic welfare state, as opposed to Pérez Jiménez's totalitarian welfare state. Since life in the capital is more expensive than in the countryside, proportionately higher unemployment relief is paid in Caracas. In January 1962 the dole came to fifteen bolivars a day, equivalent to about three dollars and seventy-five cents. Since in the country and in small towns it takes a day's hard toil to earn fifteen bolivars, it is not surprising that more and more Venezuelans come to the capital and briefly take on any kind of work in order to quit their jobs as soon as possible and get on the unemployment rolls.

There is an acute shortage of labor in the capital. A great many projects remain unfinished because it is impossible to recruit enough workers. There is as great a shortage of domestic employees as in Europe and the United States. A wage laborer in Caracas normally earns only three or four bolivars more than his unemployment payment. Consequently he prefers to be unemployed, stay in his ranchito, surreptitiously tap the urban power line, and enjoy *dolce far niente*.

Rómulo Betancourt has taken on a difficult heritage in Venezuela. He is trying to liquidate the evils of the dictatorship and to disburse some of the benefits from the country's great oil wealth to the masses of the people. But the masses, still largely illiterate, have not yet received their diplomas from the school of democracy. They tap the resources of the state just as they do the street lights of the cities.

THE DILEMMA OF DEMOCRACY

Venezuelan democracy, which by the end of 1963 had only twice elected a president, is still very young, delicate, and vulnerable. It arose toward the end of the Gómez dictatorship out of a curious liaison between a number of Venezuelan leftist intellectuals and Standard Oil. The leftist intellectuals objected to the fact that the men at the public trough devoured so much of the petroleum wealth of the country. Standard Oil, for its part, protested that Shell was skimming the greater part of the cream. A secret revolutionary movement, the *Acción Democrática*, sprang up. It was led by two men who wielded the pen rather than the sword: the writer Rómulo Gallegos and the journalist Rómulo Betancourt.

The death of the "Tyrant of the Andes" put an end to Standard Oil's flirtation with the Venezuelan left, for the next dictator, López Contreras, was sympathetic to the Rockefeller empire. Under López Contreras, the Creole Petroleum Corporation, the Venezuelan affiliate of Standard Oil, far outstripped its Shell rival.

ESSO AGAINST SHELL

Shell men can look back upon a long grim fight with the Venezuelan partisans of Standard Oil. A general of the anti-Shell clique, Rafael Simón Urbina, not only took part in attempts to overthrow the Shell-disposed dictator, Gómez, but also launched an attack with armed bands upon the Shell island of Curaçao and occupied the enemy's refineries. Then, however, Standard Oil gained a few laps in the Venezuelan oil race; and Urbina played the part of a gray eminence during the reigns of the two dictators who followed Gómez. For ten years the Acción Democrática was left out in the cold. There seemed little chance of its making gains of its own in the struggle between Standard Oil and Shell. Nevertheless, the democrats assiduously recruited followers among the army officers. They knew that in Venezuela political success could be won only with the aid of the army. When the hour struck at last in 1945, the military leader of their revolution was a general staff officer, then no more than thirty, named Marcos Pérez Jiménez.

Having carried off the revolution, the two Rómulos cherished quite different aims from those of Pérez Jiménez and his army men. While the Acción Democrática promised free elections, drafted plans for nationalization, and toyed with the idea of expropriating the oil companies, Pérez Jiménez made his own bid for authoritarian power. For the present the young general staff officer remained aloof from both Standard Oil and Shell. He did not want to deliver Venezuela completely into the hands of the Americans, and tried instead to increase his personal power by maneuvering skillfully between the two companies.

Unfortunately, the two reformers allowed their ambitious ally to take the post of chief of the general staff. From this seat, Pérez Jiménez looked on calmly for a while as Betancourt introduced social reforms and collaborated more or less satisfactorily with Standard Oil. In 1948, however, the somewhat more radical Gallegos emerged as victor from the country's first free elections. Since Gallegos was suspected of intending to nationalize the petroleum industry, Pérez Jiménez decided that his time had come.

This was the period in which foreign companies throughout Latin America were growing increasingly uneasy and girding themselves for a campaign against the social reformers. The Acción Democrática seemed to be on the point of repudiating Standard Oil. It was accused of left-socialist machinations similar to those of Arévalo and Arbenz in Guatemala. Pérez Jiménez believed that he had both oil companies behind him, and he drove out the literary democrat.

But still the power-hungry general had not climbed the highest rung in the government hierarchy. Adherents of Royal Dutch Shell were in the majority in the military juntas that swept away Venezuelan democracy. Consequently, Pérez Jiménez did not acquire total power. A pro-Shell man, Delgado Chalbaud, forestalled him. But Urbina, the gray eminence, continued to exert power within the ranks of the Venezuelan general staff. Pérez Jiménez had to content himself with the post of war minister in the new government.

During the two years of the Chalbaud dictatorship, the struggle between the two oil companies took the form of a violent feud in the press. Since Shell was on top once more, every Venezuelan newspaper heaped praise upon the creative work of Henri Deterding. North American newspapers, on the other hand, violently denounced Venezuela and called the dictator a fascist.

In the autumn of 1950, Chalbaud was shot by an army officer. All of Venezuela knew that Urbina, the eternal troublemaker, was behind the murder. When both the assassin and his employer died in a manner still unexplained, Venezuelan gossips maintained that Pérez Jiménez had killed two birds with one stone. First he had seen to the liquidation of Shell's man and then of Standard Oil's man.

This time, too, the army did not make Pérez Jiménez president. It once again chose a Shell man, Germán Flamerich. Pérez Jiménez remained minister of war.

Flamerich, too, ruled for barely two years. In 1952, in response to American insistence, free elections were again held. Pérez Jiménez ran for the presidency, intending finally to displace the Shell regime. While the votes were still being counted, the war minister mobilized his troops, occupied all post and telegraph offices, and confiscated the ballot boxes. What was the meaning of this impetuosity? According to the conjectures of American journalists and opinion researchers, Pérez Jiménez was clearly beaten in the election. But the soldiers who counted the ballots reported an overwhelming electoral victory. Pérez Jiménez became president and dictator of Venezuela.

"TO STEAL DEMOCRACY'S BANNER"

As we have noted, the six years of Pérez Jiménez's dictatorship have been called by European and American businessmen the six most prosperous years in Venezuelan history. Pérez Jiménez imitated Dictator Gómez, with the single difference that he showed no preference for either of the two oil companies but allowed each to participate equally in the petroleum industry. He collected almost 50 per cent of the oil profits, attracted foreign capital, and guaranteed the security of foreign investments. He built his supercity, raised wages, fussed over the ranchito dwellers, had swamps drained and jungles cleared, with American backing established big mines and steel plants along the Orinoco, and thus propelled Venezuela with vigorous shoves into the modern age. In order to take the wind from the sails of his democrat opponent, he bandaged the social wounds of his country with dollar bills. He wanted, as he himself said, to steal the banner of democracy.

No one can deny that Venezuela did indeed prosper under Pérez Jiménez. And there is even a kernel of truth in the dictator's statement that the Venezuelan people were too sluggish and ignorant to make the most of their opportunities and therefore had to be forced to do what was good for them. The regime of the second oil dictator might have had more pluses to its credit if Pérez Jiménez had not had the same unfortunate tendencies as his colleagues in other Latin American countries. But he too somehow accumulated a fortune of over six hundred million dollars, and substituted for free elections plebiscites in which the people could only vote yes or no. He did a great deal to advance the economic and technological development of the country. But his totalitarian approach gave the people no opportunity to keep pace with technical developments and thus gradually learn how to cope with modernity.

Meanwhile, Rómulo Betancourt had spent ten years in exile in the United States waiting for a new chance for democracy. He studied American conditions, learned from them, dropped some of his earlier socialist ideas, and wooed the support of influential American circles. In the meanwhile, moreover, the at first highly praised dictator had been growing more and more unpopular in the United States because of his wasteful habits and his personal corruption. In exile, the once disliked social democrat steadily gained prestige.

Pérez Jiménez committed his greatest error when he challenged the Catholic Church. High churchmen in Venezuela had criticized the dictator's peculations. Thereupon Pérez Jiménez had several priests arrested. This unpopular act encouraged a new reformed "Popular Junta" to call for a general strike against the dictator. The junta had all the church bells rung to announce the general strike. Pérez Jiménez high-handedly sent out his soldiers and occupied the churches. By that act he offended nearly all the major power factors in Venezuela: the Church, the unions, the democrats, and the conservative military men. In January 1958 the navy mutinied. Pérez Jiménez put up no resistance. He fled—along with Argentine's ex-dictator Perón, who had sought refuge in his country, to the United States—taking his money with him.

The Venezuelan naval coup degenerated into a bloody popular uprising. Beneath the dictatorship's surface prosperity, the Venezuelans had stored up murderous hatred for the adherents of Jiménez, for foreign entrepreneurs, and for the Italian workers the dictator had brought into the country. For a few days anarchy reigned in the streets of Caracas. There was widespread pillaging and killing; tanks were sent rolling over the bodies of real or alleged supporters of Jiménez. When the leader of the naval rebels, Admiral Wolfgang Larrazabal, at last became master of the situation, he found himself confronting a revolutionary populace more inflamed with radicalism than at any time before in Venezuelan history.

In Latin American countries the navy as a rule stands far to the right. Naval officers are almost always sons of leading families and therefore not very receptive to socialism. Admiral Larrazabal, however, acted more radically than any previous Venezuelan chief of state. He held office for only a few months as temporary head of the government until democratic elections could be held, but during that brief time it looked as if Venezuela were on the point of following the examples of Mexico or of Guatemala under Arbenz. "Handsome Wolfgang," as Admiral Larrazabal was called in Venezuela, promised the rebellious masses everything they wanted: work and bread, agrarian reform and industrialization, a greater share in the oil wealth—in short, a better life. He himself went about in shirt sleeves visiting the ranchitos and accepting the cheers of the populace as a hero and liberator.

He governed by emergency decrees which went far beyond the one-time program of the Acción Democrática. Foreign investors were already beginning to see red. They suspected that "handsome Wolfgang" was a Communist in disguise.

But the admiral never had the chance to carry out his program of authoritarian socialism. Betancourt returned to Venezuela, won the elections, and hastily packed the dictatorial liberator safely off to an ambassadorial post in Santiago de Chile. From then on his Acción Democrática governed the course of Venezuelan politics.

Betancourt had brought back from America a catchword still new to Venezuela—evolution. He had perceived that all attempts to coerce the people into vaulting over major stages of development were bound to fail. He therefore relinquished all plans to take the modern age by storm and instead put forth a carefully balanced development program aimed at guiding the people step by step to maturity. It was, to be sure, a development program involving many compromises. Consequently it provided his opponents with many points of attack.

Betancourt completely abandoned the Acción Democrática's former plans for nationalization. He encouraged the oil companies to increase their production and used the tax on their profits to further industrialization and to expand the mines and iron foundries on the Orinoco. He permitted American companies to exploit the iron ore, bauxite, and manganese resources in the Venezuelan tropics. The revenue from these sources was to be used to solve pressing social problems.

Betancourt also abandoned the battle cry for agrarian reform. He did not want to antagonize the big landowners, but rather to persuade them to modernize their plantations and to pay their agricultural workers better. In America, Betancourt had learned that the greatest incentive in a free economy is competition. He therefore distributed fertile, fallow land to some twenty-five thousand small farmers, helped them establish themselves by providing modern equipment and generous government credit, and hoped that the rural feudal lords would soon feel their competition and begin to utilize their land better. In all such reforms, Betancourt was aiming to increase industrial and agricultural production, to cut back on expensive imports, and obtain more foreign exchange from greater exports—in short, to increase the national income in such a way that all Venezuelans would share in the prosperity.

It was a persuasive program which naturally pleased the United States Government. To Americans, Venezuela became Latin America's model democracy, and Betancourt, who staunchly opposed all dictatorships of the right and the left, the ideal Latin American government head. There is no question but that Betancourt and his successor, Leoni, have been the most honest, responsible, and democratic presidents Venezuela has ever had. Any nation, even one with a healthier and longer evolution behind it than has been vouchsafed the Venezuelan people, could well have been content with such chiefs of state.

But during the days of Pérez Jiménez, and the interregnum of Admiral Larrazabal, the Venezuelans had tasted blood. Everywhere in Latin America, the hatred of the masses, once aroused, is directed against the oligarchy, and since the real oligarchy in Venezuela is composed not of natives but of foreigners, Venezuelan hatred was directed against the foreigners. Betancourt worked amicably with Americans. Consequently the masses regarded their democratic, compromising president as a friend of the *Yanquis*, a henchman of the exploiters. It followed, further, that the average Venezuelan tried to get everything he could out of the government, and the generous welfare and unemployment laws were universally abused.

Betancourt could not afford to trim the excessively high cost of welfare payments. Had he done so, he would have driven the majority of the voters into the radical camp. The Venezuelan man on the street refuses to see why he should work when he can get along without work. Every day he can see how much money foreigners make in Venezuela. He is thoroughly convinced that the riches of his country belong to himself alone but are being stolen by foreigners. The gradual evolution that Rómulo Betancourt dreamed of met with the enthusiastic assent of Venezuelan intellectuals, but the Venezuelan proletariat has so far been cold to the idea. The people are not grateful to the government for its generous support. They take their welfare and unemployment payments as their right and argue that they would receive a great deal more if the foreigners did not carry so much of the wealth out of the country.

The most difficult task that Betancourt's successor, Leoni, has faced since 1963 is to make the people understand that it is necessary to work for a living. Moreover, the Venezuelan Government suffers from a constant shortage of revenue, in spite of the very large sums the treasury receives from the taxation of oil wells and mines. Welfare consumes vast portions of the budget, and the debts left by Pérez Jiménez are an enormous burden. The greatest handicap to Venezuelan development, however, is a constantly growing flight of capital. The Venezuelan rich trusted the dictatorship and let their money work in Venezuela. But they do not trust the democracy and are transferring their profits and their capital abroad. Pérez Jiménez had ample money at his disposal inside the country. His credit was good and he had no trouble raising the capital to build his new Venezuela. But democracies in Latin America have never enjoyed very good credit. Betancourt and his democrats have stood with empty pockets before an ever more demanding people.

The democratic president had not built futuristic skyscrapers, four-lane highways, barracks, and marble monuments. He built research institutions, hospitals, and peasant villages. But above all he built schools. More than half the people of Venezuela still cannot read and write. Literacy, Betancourt hoped, would engender in the people a sense of responsibility and a willingness to work. It is moving to see the banners that are strung everywhere in Venezuela—in parks, across the façades of buildings—urging the populace (who cannot read them) to attend the adult-education schools. With passionate earnestness, the government exhorts the people to let themselves be educated. The democrats know they are running a race against time. If they cannot raise the people to maturity quickly enough, their democratic experiment may be crushed by another dictatorship of the right or the left.

PROGRESS AND MOSQUITOES

Admiral Larrazabal, who in the election held at the end of 1963 won almost 10 per cent of the vote, continues to preach his authoritarian socialism, the outlines of which are so vague that there is no telling whether it is fascistic or leftist. The propertied classes mock at the government party, which alone can preserve their property for them, and are taking the precaution of building themselves luxurious homes abroad. Former followers of the Acción Democrática have long since gone over to the opposition; they have formed a "Republican-Democratic Union," and some of them even take part in the demonstrations of the MSR, the "Left Revolutionary Movement." These radical parties call for elimination of American influence, demand measures against the flight of capital, expropriation of the oil companies, and *rapprochement* with Cuba. The army, on the other hand, demands stronger government, an end to the coddling of the unemployed, and more building in the supercity of Caracas. Caught in this cross-fire of stern demands, the Acción Democrática has difficulty holding its own. Nevertheless, it won the election, although taking only about a third of the vote. Betancourt has remained the "strong man" behind President Leoni, but Leoni, a former union leader tends to take a course somewhat further to the left than his predecessor.

Another opponent of Venezuelan democracy has arisen as a result of the Cuban crisis. A Castroistic movement, which calls itself the Fighting Force for National Liberation, has engaged in bombing and organized sabotage. The regular Communists are also operating vigorously. Until the party was banned, one would come across its headquarters in many of the cities of Venezuela, the building identified by being painted a bright red with the inscription *Partido Comunista* in huge letters across its façade. In the past, the Communists were not very important in Venezuela. Marx, Lenin, and Stalin were after all foreigners, and we have mentioned that Venezuelans are not fond of foreigners. But ever since Cuba, a Latin American country, turned toward the East, the attitude of the Venezuelan proletarian toward communism has changed. Though not allowed to function openly, the Communist Party is flourishing, and whips up the ever-latent xenophobia wherever it can, for hatred of foreigners can easily be converted into hatred of capitalists. The party tried to sabotage the last election by terroristic methods. During the political disturbances in 1963, it made a practice of setting fire to the polling places.

In Venezuela, foreigners are not only the entrepreneurs, but also, to a large extent, the engineers, technicians, white-collar workers, and skilled workers of all kinds. By law, only one-quarter of the personnel in any given company may be of foreign origin. But since the foreigners are all more able than the natives, they quickly take the better positions and receive higher wages than their Venezuelan colleagues. The radical parties make use of this fact to persuade the common people that all foreigners come to Venezuela only to take money out of the country. The president, though dependent upon the abilities and skills of foreign labor, must constantly swallow the charge that he has sold the Acción Democrática to the gringos.

The question arises whether it is even possible to lead so under-developed a nation step by step along the road toward progress. Venezuela has lost a great deal of time in its long bouts of dictatorship. Meanwhile, there has awakened in the people an overemphatic nationalism but nothing approximating civic consciousness, upon which the survival of democracy ultimately depends.

The leftists and rightists have nothing but propaganda to oppose to the Acción Democrática's development program. So far, the govern-ment has succeeded, even during election periods, in preventing riots, attempted coups, and minor uprisings. But there are many Venezuelans who mourn for the prosperous times of Pérez Jiménez. There are still more Venezuelans who have been taken in by the conjuring trick of demagogues. To most of the rural population, democracy is not a native plant, but an imported growth from hated North America. The owners of the great plantations who originally brought all kinds of botanic specimens to Latin America always gave these plants the tenderest culture in order to adapt them to the new soil and teach them to bear fruit under the new conditions. But the question arises, do the foreigners who now are often in charge of the imported plant of democracy give it sufficient care? The oil companies, whose understanding and friendly assistance Betancourt has sought, preserve an attitude of cool reserve toward him and Venezuela's democratic government. The democrats have disavowed all nationalization projects, but they have taken possession of those oil resources for which, as yet, no concessions have been granted, so that these may be exploited by a state-owned company. According to their plans, the government will enter into fair and open competi-tion with the private firms. But the mere suggestion of this project, which is natural enough to any sovereign state, has caused the oil companies to turn increasing attention to Colombia, a country perhaps as rich as Venezuela in oil. Instead of collaborating with the Venezu-elans, the great oil companies are threatening to shut off a vital source of Venezuelan income.

Many businessmen in Venezuela have been attacking the social-minded government of Betancourt and his successor as harshly as if these Venezuelan presidents were Castroists in disguise. Time and again I heard European businessmen denounce Betancourt and Leoni as socialists or ex-communists. They besmeared the reputations of the men who were defending the principles of free enterprise, and they do not see, or refuse to see, that by such conduct they were only playing into the hands of radical Dr. Villalba of the Republican-Democratic Union, or the demagogic popular hero Larrazabal, not to speak of the Communists. The Acción Democrática represents Venezuela's only chance of escaping from the toils of the past, but hitherto the two extremes in Venezuela—the Venezuelan people, who hate the foreign business world, and foreign business, which despises the Venezuelan people—are obstinately blind to that.

"A los mosquitos!" the milling masses cried, when the United States extradited Pérez Jiménez to Venezuela. "Let the mosquitoes eat him!" One can only hope for the people's sake that the many mosquitoes buzzing around their country do not also devour their fragile democracy.

IN THE VISE OF VIOLENCIA

The traveler who went from Venezuela to Colombia a hundred years ago moved from South America's poorhouse to South America's treasury. If you take the same journey today, you jump from the twentieth century back to the eighteenth century. Colombia is still a very wealthy country, a country of emeralds, of gold and platinum mines, of wonderful coffee, and promising terrain for oil wells. To judge by its natural resources, Colombia ought to be one of the most prosperous countries in Latin America. But it is a country still living in the colonial past. As yet, everything worth owning in Colombia is in the hands of an oligarchy of Spanish descent.

Whites constitute only about 20 per cent of the population of Colombia. The rest of the Colombian population consists of mestizos, Negroes, mulattoes, zambos, and Indians. But any colored Colombian who has gotten anywhere in the world—unless he happened to be exceedingly dark-skinned—is considered a white. "White" in Colombia is not a racial but a class concept. Since, however, the core of the upper per cent is actually formed from old Iberian families, the ruling class is, on the whole, considerably lighter in pigment than the ruled class.

In Venezuela, the old order of colonial days was completely liquidated by the war of independence, the uprising of the llaneros, and the industrialization of the past several decades. In Colombia, however, it appears to be still intact in all its hierarchic rigidity, as if the century and a half since the liberation of the country had scarcely made any difference. To be sure, a good many industrial areas have been formed. The urbanization of the people is proceeding at a very rapid rate. Both in the cities and in the countryside, economically independent middle classes have developed. Only a small proportion of the Colombian coffee plantations are owned by large landowners and United Fruit; as much as 80 per cent of the country's coffee is raised by small farmers and sharecroppers, whose lands average less than fifteen acres. Nevertheless, there appears to be no other political, economic, and cultural power in Colombia aside from the light-skinned upper class.

THREE COLOMBIAN CITIES

In Venezuela the colonial past has been harshly erased. Colombia looks like one great colonial museum. The port of Cartagena, on the Caribbean Sea, is probably one of the most beautiful cities in South America. It is full of proud patrician houses, grandiose baroque palaces, ornate churches, monasteries, patios, wrought-iron balconies, and winding streets that call to mind the ancient cities of Spain. Significantly enough, the House of the Inquisition is one of the most prominent buildings in Cartagena. The huge fortress of San Felipe, towering over the port, awakens memories of the golden age of piracy. In the days of the Spaniards, Cartagena was the great port for gold and silver. From here, the rich loot from all parts of Spanish America was shipped out to the motherland. No wonder Cartagena exerted a permanent allure upon such corsairs as Drake, Morgan, and Dampier. After Francis Drake had conquered and destroyed the port, the Spaniards spent millions in gold pieces and the lives of numberless slaves in building their tremendous fortress, which from the point of view of defense technology was one of the most ingenious in the world.

The lover of historical architecture will find much satisfaction in Cartagena. His delight may, however, be somewhat diminished by the slums at the foot of the fortress, and by the many crippled, rachitic, hungering children who twist their thin limbs in dreary dances in order to coax a few centavos out of the tourists.

The flourishing port of Barranquilla, on the Río Magdalena, will also impress the foreign visitor by its architecture. Barranquilla, however, is not strong on buildings of the colonial period, but on modern commercial buildings, clubs, and private homes. Only a few decades ago Barranquilla was considered one of the most depraved ports in Latin America, a breeding place of vice and of crime. The waterfront itself still has much the same filthy, decadent atmosphere as other Latin American ports. But the new residential districts are architecturally as skillful, graceful, and charming as the modern architecture of Brazil.

However, my delight in all this was soon dampened. During my first few hours in the country, while driving through the shopping streets in the heart of the city, I saw a dark-skinned man come flying out of a doorway, a knife in his back. He fell to the pavement, bleeding heavily. In a moment the street was deserted. I flung open the door of my cab, instructing my driver to go for help. He hastily pulled me back into the cab and sped away. No Colombian dares interfere when someone is attacked or murdered. For the real ruler of Colombia is not the reigning upper class, but the *violencia*, the brute force exercised by the bandits.

The capital city of Bogotá is situated deep in the mountainous interior of the country, eighty-seven hundred feet above sea level. It has been modernized, so that in spite of a number of lovely colonial buildings, it is far less a museum town than Cartagena. Laid out like a chessboard, with perfectly straight streets dotted here and there by skyscrapers, it reminds one of a lady of old Spain on the point of putting on an Yves St. Laurent dress, and suddenly interrupted while dressing. Rows of houses have been started and left unfinished. Roads are laid out but have not been paved. From the skeletons of skyscrapers hangs the washing of squatters who have taken up residence in them. The display windows of shops which sell valuable objects are as heavily barred as the windows of a prison cell, for even here in the capital the violencia prevails.

Countless persons have died as a result of the violencia, the incessant bandit wars in Colombia. A single civil war, the so-called "war of the thousand days," cost the country a hundred thousand lives. Practically speaking, a state of unrest has existed in Colombia for the past sixty-five years—bloody fraternal warfare among the political parties, bloody banditry, bloody terrorism. Where many people die, there will always be many orphans, neglected children. Colombia is full of such *gamines,* boys and girls who live in obscure nooks and corners and creep like rats from their holes to dispute the contents of the garbage cans with stray dogs.

Repeatedly there have been regular childrens' demonstrations in Bogotá. Teen-agers gathered in swarms made an infernal din with all sorts of tin instruments and tried to collect money—money for shoe-shine kits, so that they could earn their bread honestly. The police try to send the gamines off to orphanages, but the wild youngsters regularly succeed in escaping and returning to their dens. Moreover, there are not enough orphanages in Colombia. There is insufficient social welfare of all kinds in Colombia. There are not enough charitable persons in Colombia to supply the money to equip the gamines with shoeshine kits or to provide them with other kinds of work. From these hordes of beggarly children the bandits of the violencia constantly garner new recruits.

MONTAGUES AND CAPULETS IN THE LAND OF GEMS

The history of the violencia is the real, the underground history of Colombia. On paper there are only two political parties in the country. They are the two traditional parties of Latin America: centralistic conservatives and federalistic liberals. Virtually every Colombian is born into his party as an Indian is born into his caste. Although both parties long ago splintered into a great variety of mutually hostile factions, a Colombian is either a conservative or a liberal. There are extreme and moderate conservatives; there are conservative and socialistic liberals. There are even conservatives of the right opposition who conspire with liberals of the left opposition.

Up to 1953, Colombian history consisted of an almost unceasing family quarrel between the conservatives and the liberals of the upper class. In the course of this family quarrel, both parties made use of every conceivable method of defamation, bribery, inciting to rebellion, murder, and warfare. The conservative oligarchy wanted to turn Colombia into a Unitarian (*i.e.,* centralist) clerical state under the leadership of the old Spanish families. The liberal oligarchy called for a federal union, restriction of the rights of the Church, and liberalization of trade. These programs would indicate that the conservatives are centered more in the interior of the country, which is less sensitive to the operations of the world economy, whereas most of the liberals are located along the coasts. Among the liberals are the numerous Marrani, the baptized Jews who immigrated to Colombia in the sixteenth and seventeenth centuries to escape the Spanish Inquisition and who have helped to make the province of Antioquia one of the country's most flourishing regions.

When the conservatives were in power in Bogotá, the liberal provinces rebelled and waged a kind of guerrilla warfare against the central government. When the liberals won, the conservatives went underground and in turn resorted to violencia. The last open civil war broke out in 1948. It was caused by the splintering of the liberals into a right wing and a left wing. The right wing wanted to go on ruling in the old style; the left wing proved receptive to all kinds of new ideas which had begun to flow into Latin America after the Second World War: ideas of agrarian and social reform, expropriation of the large landholdings, and similar radical measures. The struggle within the party weakened the liberals and permitted the conservatives to win power once more. The troublesome leader of the leftist liberals, Jorge Eliécer Gaitán, was probably murdered by the conservatives' violencia. This act reunited the liberals. They, likewise, turned to the tried and true method of violencia: forming *bandoleros*, bandit troops that terrorized the country for five years.

Just as the Mafia is the real ruler of Sicily, the conservative or liberal "mafias" are the real masters of the conservative or liberal provinces of Colombia. Since no political party likes to dirty its hands publicly, the bandoleros are made up of hired freebooters and adventurers. Mercenaries, however, will risk their lives only if there is rich booty in the offing. For this reason the bandoleros have not only fought opposing gangs, but have also set fire to villages, robbed banks, and attacked groups of travelers on their own account. They have confiscated food supplies to provision themselves and waylaid railroad trains and buses to get their pay. They have probably committed more murders than any other gangster organization on earth. It is because of them that Colombia to this day gives the impression of being so archaic a place.

A chief of the general staff whose ambition had been thwarted was the first Colombian to attempt to quell this disorder. The conservative government of President Gómez had made the mistake of dismissing Chief of Staff General Gustavo Rojas Pinilla. In a rapid coup in June 1953 he overthrew the conservative clique, despite the fact that he belonged to it by birth. As a conservative, Rojas Pinilla did not think much of the liberals. He therefore suppressed all political activity and set up a one-man dictatorship in place of the previous dictatorships of party cliques. The consequence was that the hostile families formed an alliance against him, united their bandoleros, and attempted to dispose of him.

Like every Latin American despot, Rojas Pinilla caught building fever. He sprinkled skyscrapers all over Bogotá, laid out highways, and started work on a new government quarter—where today the washing of the poor hangs from skeletons of buildings. But as a city planner, he was far behind Pérez Jiménez of Venezuela. Most of his buildings were left unfinished, for in May 1957 his one-man dictatorship was overthrown by the united violencia of the conservatives and liberals. This successful action had been preceded by a unique development among the leaders of the conservatives and the liberals. During their years in the political underground, they had agreed to cease their ruthless attacks upon one another and divide the power fraternally between them. A "patriotic pact" between the two parties was signed and sealed. They promised to rule by coalition for sixteen years, during which period a conservative and a liberal would alternately take the presidency.

"FROZEN DEMOCRACY"

This agreement conveniently overlooked the other political groupings in Colombia. The rightist conservatives were by no means ready to bury the hatchet. The leftist liberals, for their part, were not prepared to collaborate with the men who had killed their former leader, Gaitán. For the moment, however, the moderate forces in both parties were stronger than the extremist wings. They had included a special clause in the pact, by way of safeguarding the alliance. During the sixteen years of peace, the country was to hold elections every four years in accordance with custom. But no matter how the elections turned out, the legislative seats were to be divided equally between the conservatives and the liberals. This would effectually keep any other party or party factions out of the congress. This arrangement quickly won the name of "frozen democracy."

The patriotic pact was kept, and the world public hoped Colombia would at last experience some years of political tranquillity. The first president of the coalition government, Alberto Lleras Camargo, was put up by the Liberal Party; the second president, Guillermo León Valencia, by the Conservative Party. The agreement was honored. The government politicians withdrew their support from the bandoleros. The freebooters were called upon to surrender their weapons and uniforms, and to devote themselves henceforth to less belligerent activities. The bandoleros, however, had not the slightest inclination to return to ordinary life. Men who for decades have been free to rob, plunder, and murder, under the protection of one powerful party or another, are rendered unfit for a quiet civilian existence. The bands retained their weapons and their uniforms; they went on with their robbing, plundering, and killing for their own benefit, without the slightest political aims. The Colombian army can do very little against the bandits in their wild mountain retreats, any more than the Italian *carabinieri* can control the Sicilian Mafia. The underpaid police and soldiers are more inclined to make deals with the bandoleros than to fight them. The result is that tourists foolhardy enough to go into the interior can expect to meet half-uniformed robbers who will not only take the shirts off their backs, but in some circumstances their lives as well. And in the cities, shops are robbed, cab passengers held up, and people stabbed. Wherever the violencia erupts, the streets are suddenly deserted.

The bands' power is strongest in the central cordillera, especially in the Territorio Vásquez, not too far from Bogotá, and along the Río Magdalena, where the Texaco Company is tapping the vast reserves of petroleum. They are thus endangering one of the most important industries of the country. There are now well-organized groups of bandoleros under the influence of the pro-communist or pro-Cuban *Frente de la Liberación Nacional*. The leader of the ultraleftist guerrillas, who bears the nickname "Tirofijo," has already become a terrifying legendary figure in Colombia.

The frantic flight of bystanders who happen to witness a violencia attack is a double-barreled safety measure. The bandoleros are experienced ruffians; it is not easy to catch them. The Colombian police, however, like police the world over, like to provide a criminal for every crime. Their practice is to arrest anyone who happens to have been near the scene of the crime. While this fate may not be quite as bad as offending the violencia, anyone who has ever been in the hands of Latin American police knows it is difficult and expensive to get out of their clutches again.

Policemen, incidentally, are seldom seen. The bandoleros shoot indiscriminately at the police and soldiers. Since the government pays pensions of a mere ten dollars a month to the family of a dead policeman, and since their wages in any case amount to barely forty dollars a month, it is understandable that these minions of the law have no great urge to risk their skins. Since police protection is so sadly lacking, most civilians of any substance carry arms. Even ladies of society have learned to handle revolvers. For members of the oligarchy are more and more often being kidnaped by the bandoleros.

Two prominent Colombian millionaires have been victims of the violencia: ex-Minister Harold Eder, whose body was found shortly after his kidnaping, and landowner-industrialist Olivario Lara, who has not been found, alive or dead, despite a massive hunt by large posses of soldiers. Since these events, rich families pay the demanded ransom as quickly as possible without notifying the police, as soon as the first threatening note arrives. Martín Vargas, one of the richest men in Colombia, was thus relieved of no less than four million pesos (about one and a half million dollars) for ransom. It is said that the bandoleros take in some thirty million pesos per year from kidnaping and blackmail alone.

THE SOUTH VIETNAM OF LATIN AMERICA

The guerrillas of the Frente de la Liberación Nacional could not be defeated even by strong army units equipped with planes and modern artillery. Though reports come in of annihilating defeats of the guerrillas, or of the death of their idol Tirofijo, these accounts always turn out to be false. The East's estimate of the strength of these bandoleros, and the hopes it is placing in them, is evident from a remark made by the Cuban Communist Guevara. He prophesied that the National Liberation Front will turn Colombia into the "South Vietnam of Latin America."

I talked with a German who had lived for thirty years in Colombia.

He had founded a great variety of enterprises: a general store in the interior of the country, a small iron foundry, a hops plantation. But again and again he suffered from the violencia. His buildings were burned down and pillaged. He loved Colombia and would have liked to remain there. But after he had been wiped out six times by the bandoleros, he gave up and returned to Germany.

Colombia is one of the most beautiful countries in South America, one of the richest, and also one of the most cultured. To this day it is a place of treasure. In 1959 and 1961 new sources of emeralds were discovered, the gems finer and in greater quantity than anywhere else in the world. Steel plants are rising in the Andes. Texaco, Colombian Government Oil Company, Echo Petrol, are exploiting the petroleum reserves in the valley of the Río Magdalena. The industrial and commercial city of Cali, in western Colombia, has quintupled its population in the last ten years. The coffee grown in the Colombian highlands is considered particularly mild and aromatic; after Brazil, Colombia is the most important coffee-producing nation on earth. The Colombian coffee economy is on a far healthier footing than the Brazilian, since the many small coffee planters have united in an extremely active and politically influential *Federación Nacional de Cafeteros*.

Culturally, Colombia has all the preconditions to outstrip her neighbors. Back in the days when Simón Bolívar was constructing his Greater Colombia out of Venezuela, Colombia, and Ecuador, a popular phrase had it that the Venezuelan capital of Caracas was the country's barracks, the Ecuadorian capital, Quito, the country's monastery, and the Colombian capital, Bogotá, the country's university. Colombia has at least twenty-three universities, twenty-eight radio stations, thirty-seven daily newspapers, and three movie companies. Its upper classes are interested not only in their traditions and a comfortable life, but also in literature, science, and art. But the culture of which Colombia is so proud has not yet reached to the people. Almost half of the fifteen million Colombians cannot read and write. Attempts, to be sure, are being made to combat illiteracy by radio broadcasts, but even that presupposes the possession of a radio set, a relatively rare thing among the common folk.

The two government parties are like two oxen who, having warred all of their lives, have now been yoked by force to the same cart. One ox pulls to the right, the other to the left. Or instead of pulling, they try to gore each other, and the cart remains stuck in the mud. The liberals want agrarian reform in order to weaken the conservative landowning class. The conservatives fight it on the grounds that any such reform would destroy the agricultural base of the country. The extreme right wing of the conservatives would like to annul the Patriotic Pact, but it can do so only by collaborating with the extreme left wing of the liberals. The leftist liberals have gathered under their banner all those political forces which in other Latin American countries would be called socialistic, Castroistic, or even communistic.

Two Colombian provinces have fallen into the hands of pro-communist local politicians, and six other regions have become "independent republics." It is generally believed that the Colombian unions and organizations of agricultural workers have been infiltrated by the communists since the Patriotic Pact. I talked with Colombian businessmen who estimated that 30 per cent of the Colombian people were more or less favorable toward communism. More precise figures on the strength of the communist and other extremist movements cannot be compiled, for even a fanatical communist, or a passionate follower of Fidel Castro, will, when asked his political views, evasively reply that he is an oppositionist liberal.

Even Senator López Michelsen, half Danish, and sympathetic to Fidel Castro, does not call himself a socialist or a communist. Michelsen, whose candidates won more than a fifth of the votes in the last election, is true to Colombian convention and calls himself a liberal. His movement bears the name *Movimiento Liberal Revolucionario.*

The universities of which the country is so proud are steadily becoming redder. Many young faculty members are convinced that the violencia is still a tool of the oligarchy. The bandits plunder whole regions until the inhabitants are forced to leave, these young academics point out. By this device, they say, the feudal lords obtain the land of the small farmers cheaply.

While religious freedom exists on paper, Catholicism is in fact the state religion of Colombia. The Catholic Church—as in prerevolutionary Mexico—is the largest landholder in the country. Adherents of other religions find themselves handicapped as far as professional and social advancement is concerned. Hence an intense anticlericalism is developing among the younger faculty at the "red" universities. They inveigh against the Church, which has remained as conservative and oligarchic as it was in the days of the Spaniards. In other Andes countries, they say, the Church has shown a more progressive tendency, at least among the lower clergy.

On June 9, 1965, Colombia's "University Day," a highly significant demonstration took place. More than fifteen hundred students paraded to Bogotá's Plaza Bolívar. They carried a gigantic banner reading, "The President is a murderer," and once at the square, attempted to overturn the Washington Memorial. Fiery speeches were made hailing the pro-communist guerrilla fighter Tirofijo and the "independent republic" of Marquetalia, which he controls. The police, who rode alongside the parade in patrol cars, saw no reason to intervene.

Students will sometimes take an active part in the excesses of violencia. For example, guerrillas in the summer of 1965 attacked the village of Simacota. The band consisted of some forty members who gave themselves the bombastic title of "National Army of Liberation." It subsequently turned out that they were students at the Industrial University of Bucaramanga. Several of them had recently returned from studying at Prague, Leipzig, and other universities of the Eastern bloc.

The Patriotic Pact has not brought peace to Colombia. It has produced only a feeble government almost incapable of action. It has not banished radicalism; on the contrary, it has encouraged it by paralyzing political evolution. It has not satisfied the army; the soldiers long for a new Rojas Pinilla, and are only waiting for the right moment to strike and unyoke the two-party oxen from the Colombian cart. Above all, the pact has not succeeded in quelling the violencia; it has merely changed political freebooters into ordinary bandits.

CUBA LIBRE IN BUENAVENTURA

The chief Colombian port on the Pacific is Buenaventura. Structures built on piles extend far out into the water. The lagoon swarms with bright-sailed boats. The canals and streets are thronged with dark-skinned Colombians, peddling fruit, dickering, shining shoes, or simply out strolling. They take their siestas out on the street, stretching out in shady corners, their faces covered with newspaper. There is much about Buenaventura that reminds one of an African coastal city. Sailors consider it the most licentious and dangerous port in Latin America.

The Colombian coastal provinces along the Pacific, populated largely by Negroes, have separatist tendencies and are politically extremely unstable. In November 1963, for example, the white governor of the province of Choco was stoned by the colored populace. Political passions do not run quite so high in Buenaventura. Though the city is said to be somewhat deficient in honesty, it was in Buenaventura that I experienced the touching concern of Colombians to shield foreigners from the crimes of the violencia. Unlike the Venezuelans, the Colombians are anything *but* xenophobic. They are delighted to have foreigners visit their country and want them to carry away good impressions. Aware that foreigners may easily be exposed to unpleasant incidents, they look out for their welfare. Foreigners are repeatedly warned by people in the streets against carelessly carrying pocketbooks, cameras, or wrist watches—"for there are many bandits in Colombia." If a stranger wanders into a dubious-looking waterfront café, a Colombian is sure to come over to him, advise him to go to a more respectable place, and offer to guide him. Colombians are saddened at their country's bad reputation and endeavor to show foreigners that not every Colombian is a bandolero or pickpocket.

In the shadow of the bandoleros, ordinary crooks have flourished in the cities and ports of the country. Since the violencia has made whole provinces unsafe, the shabbiest little punk feels justified in putting his hand into the nearest pocket. There are occasional criminals everywhere in the world, but such petty lawbreakers can grow into a mighty army in a country that cannot keep its major criminals in check.

On my last night in Colombia I was sitting at a table of a sidewalk café, watching the picturesque street life of Buenaventura and drinking a Cuba libre, the mixture of rum and cola which was called Cuba libre—"free Cuba"—long before Castro's day, though in recent years the name has taken on a double meaning.

The people strolling by were ordinary citizens, most of them extremely poor, but good-humored and quick to laughter—at a child who let some eggs fall to the pavement, or at a street peddler leading an agouti, a small rodent, on a leash like a dog. No one looked askance at me, as people had in Ecuador. After a while several Colombians sitting inside the café invited me to have a drink with them. They were businessmen and real-estate brokers of the flourishing city of Cali. I was the only foreigner in the café and they seemed eager to show me some kindness. They wanted me to take back home the knowledge that honest, decent, and likable people could be found in Colombia, and indeed my hosts were as honest, decent, and likable as people can be. We talked about Colombia, about questions of irrigation and power, about platinum and emeralds, and many other matters. "What treasures, what fantastic possibilities we have here," one of the men exclaimed, "if only the government were not so weak!" When I got up at last to return to my ship, my new friends spontaneously insisted on accompanying me to the waterfront. I said that I wanted to stroll about the streets for a little while, but the Colombians would not take no for an answer. They insisted on seeing me safely on board, for at night not only the rats creep out of their holes in Colombia, but also the men of the violencia.

SHRUNKEN LAND—SHRUNKEN HEADS

Between little Ecuador and big Peru persists an ancient enmity that goes back to the days of the Inca Empire. Four and a half centuries ago the Incas conquered Ecuador and, to facilitate administration, built a second capital city there. The next-but-last Inca ruler, Huayna Capac, was an itinerant emperor. He liked to move back and forth between his two capitals, Cuzco in Peru and Tomebamba in Ecuador. The result was that he begot a son in Ecuador as well as in Peru. The Peruvian prince was named Huascar, the Ecuadorian Atahualpa.

After Huayna Capac's death, the Peruvian pretender to the throne refused to recognize his Ecuadorian half brother because he had been begotten "abroad." The two princes fought, and Atahualpa won. It was the only victory that Ecuador ever won against her domineering neighbor, Peru—and even at that it was a pyrrhic victory. For the civil war between Ecuador and Peru so weakened the Incas that they quickly fell prey to the Spanish conquistadors.

When the Spaniards took over, Ecuador was once again considered part of Peru. But the Ecuadorians would not have this, and finally were allowed to unite with the viceroyalty of New Granada, part of which was later to become Colombia. After independence, the Ecuadorians began to chafe under the hegemony of Colombia. They freed themselves—and henceforth were clamped in a vise between two larger powers. Both powers claimed the little country, and Brazil likewise displayed a hankering for Ecuadorian territory. In 1885 there was a war with Peru, five years later with Colombia. If Ecuador came out of these wars tolerably well, it was by making capital of her reputation of being the "monastery of Latin America." Under the conservative dictatorship of García Moreno she had become the most clerical country in Ibero-America, thus assuring herself the support of the Vatican and the Jesuits. In 1873 she even changed her name for a while, proudly calling herself the "Republic of the Most Sacred Heart of Jesus."

The proclerical conservatives were concentrated chiefly in the capital city of Quito, while the liberals prevailed in the rapidly growing port of Guayaquil, which quickly outstripped Quito in population. Conservative and liberal dictators alternated in Ecuador just as they did in most other Latin American countries. Almost every president was overthrown by a coup before he completed his term of office.

As time went on, Ecuador's wicked neighbors ceased respecting the "Most Sacred Heart of Jesus," especially since this elaborate appellation was abandoned for the simpler *República del Ecuador*. Peru, Colombia, and Brazil laid claim to the broad territories of Amazonian jungle that Ecuador had regarded as her own ever since the establishment of an independent state. And with the recurrent coups plunging the country ever deeper into anarchy, each of Ecuador's neighbors took occasion to carve out for itself as big a portion as possible of the Ecuadorian pie.

The Brazilians succeeded without much difficulty. They seized some seventy thousand square kilometers of jungle—about a fifth of Ecuador as it was at the time. The Colombians were less effective and got nothing. The Peruvians, in 1941, marched across the Ecuadorian border and occupied more than one hundred and eighty thousand square kilometers. This meant that Ecuador was reduced to almost half its previous extent. A conference of American foreign ministers in Rio de Janeiro, held the following year, confirmed the conquest. The Ecuadorian Amazonian territories were joined to Peru's Oriente Province. Especially painful to Ecuador was a declaration that her foreign minister was forced to sign, one clause of which was headed: "Statement on Amity, Peace and Boundaries."

These amicable feelings were a fiction of the conference, and Ecuador has never really recognized the new borders. Her stamps still show the old boundaries, along with a significant slogan: *"Ecuador—*

País Amazónico." If anyone in Ecuador unfolds a map of South America showing the new boundaries of the republic, he may come in for violent abuse, or even be beaten as a Peruvian agent. And since the U. S. State Department had a decisive influence at the Conference of Rio de Janeiro, Ecuadorians are not very friendly to foreigners. They regard every foreigner as a Yankee.

The Ecuadorians have every reason to feel intense bitterness. Their country has been cut in half. Moreover, they say, they have been robbed of the most fertile regions of their land, for many of their coffee, cacao, sugar, and cotton plantations are owned by foreigners. Another cause for ire is that one of the most distinctive exports of their country is not named after Ecuador, but Panama. The finely woven *toquillas* made in the Ecuadorian province of Manabi are called "Panama hats" all over the world only because Panama was their port of transshipment during the colonial era.

VELASCO IBARRA, THE JACK-IN-THE-BOX

Ecuador resembles the Central American republics in a number of respects. The population is composed of remnants of one-time civilized Indians, the Quitos and Caras; of Indian jungle tribes, among whom are the head-hunting Jívaros, beloved of cheap journalism, coastal Negroes, Indian-Negro mixed bloods, and mestizos. The white upper class comprises barely 8 per cent of the population. It controls Ecuador in the same way as the white oligarchies control the Central American banana republics. Along the *Costa*, the tropical coastal region, bananas are grown, just as in the Central American lowlands.

The latent discontent in Ecuador has periodically found release in radical experiments. A nation that feels itself cheated by history inevitably inclines toward extremism. Two years after the "Statement on Amity, Peace and Boundaries," the first leftist revolution broke out in Ecuador. A radical politician named José María Velasco Ibarra seized power and began hastily socializing the country. Velasco Ibarra's fate was similar to that of Arbenz in Guatemala and Villeda Morales in Honduras. After a three-year-rule, a military junta swept him aside. Five years later, however, he was elected president again. He enjoyed great popularity among the common people. Conservative Ecuadorians, however, and foreign investors do not like to recall the regime of Velasco Ibarra. To their minds, this first social reformer of the little equatorial nation was a crypto-Communist.

In actuality Velasco Ibarra was nothing of the kind. This "demagogic wizard," as he is dubbed in Ecuador, called for somewhat the same reforms that President Kennedy's Alliance for Progress recommended to Latin Americans: redistribution of the land, obligatory social insurance, raising of the general standard of living, and a war on illiteracy. In addition, he wanted to give the workers a share in the profits of native and foreign enterprises, and win back the territory annexed by Peru. But his law providing that employees were to receive 7 per cent of the profits of any business seemed so alarming that the propertied classes did all in their power to unseat him.

First the army revolted. For a short time it succeeded in restoring a conservative politician to the presidency. But Velasco Ibarra was to prove himself the jack-in-the-box of Ecuadorian politics. In 1952 he won again. He suppressed several attempted coups, but in 1956 had to give way once more to a conservative. In 1961, however, he made another comeback. Although only the literate minority can vote in Ecuador, the majority of these were obviously on the side of the social reformer.

In November 1961 tanks rumbled through the streets of Quito. The army was determined to force this obstinate benefactor of the people to give up office for good. The immediate reason for this coup was Velasco Ibarra's announcement of a higher tax on large incomes, to save the republic from its permanent financial crisis. This coup took place two years after the victory of the Cuban revolutionaries. President Kennedy had meanwhile taken office, and the United States had declared that henceforth it would refuse to recognize any Latin American government that came to power by a coup rather than free elections. The Ecuadorian air force, which had in the past taken an extremely conservative stance, saw fit to go along with the new American view. In order to keep Ecuador on good terms with Washington, it sent jet fighter planes roaring over the roofs of Quito and compelled the army to install Velasco Ibarra's vice-president, Carlos Arosemena. Thus the more dangerous man was overthrown, but the democratic system was preserved to the extent that the elected vice-president rather than a military dictator took his place.

The oligarchy in Quito and the businessmen in Guayaquil were altogether dissatisfied with this solution. As they saw it, a relatively moderate social reformer had been overthrown only to make room for a radical leftist. Arosemena was accused of the same type of extremism as the liberal-socialist presidents in Central America. People began talking about the rising danger of Castroism in Ecuador.

But to the surprise of the political prophets, Arosemena quickly shifted into a lower gear. He slowed down the inauguration of social programs, left private property untouched, and eased the pressure for heavy taxation of the rich. He knew that he could hold office only with the benevolent approval of the United States. His aims were the same as those of Velasco Ibarra, but he would try to attain them at a somewhat slower tempo, lest he also be driven from office by tanks.

The business world breathed easier; it seemed as if the dreaded wolf were turning out a nice, tame sheep. The liberals in Guayaquil applauded, for Arosemena's policies coincided with theirs. The masses grumbled that the president had been bought by the Americans. Conservatives in Quito remained warily aloof; they did not believe that the former Velascoist had undergone so great a change of heart. The army, too, watched warily, prepared to answer any relapse into the practices of the Velasco era by immediate force.

The new president did his best not to be tripped up by any of Ecuador's perennial problems. There were really only two things which he could be reproached for. In the first place he was a leftist liberal, and therefore put no curbs on any political activity. The result was that a leftist "Revolutionary Youth Union" was able to build up a great following. In the second place, he occasionally had a nip too much to drink. His leniency toward leftist organizations did not provide his opponents with a strong enough pretext for overthrowing him. But his fondness for alcohol was—to mix a metaphorical cocktail— the pitfall into which he stumbled.

THE FATEFUL TOAST

In 1964 elections were to be held in Ecuador. The Ecuadorians regarded Arosemena's administration as an interim government, and expected the Velascoists to win again. Arosemena probably expected the same. He was most circumspect in his political statements. But in July 1963 he slipped up at an official banquet. After the regular toasts, he raised his glass, turned to American Ambassador Bernbaum, and said: "The peoples of Ecuador and the United States enjoy cordial relations. But the cordiality exists only between our two peoples, not between the governments. The government of the United States exploits Latin America—and it exploits Ecuador."

The guests, businessmen, shipowners, army officers, and feudal landowners shuddered at this plain speaking. Arosemena, conscious that he had gone too far, tried to make amends. "Please don't be angry," he begged the ambassador. "I was only speaking my personal opinion. I hope you understand and privately hold the same opinion."

Perhaps Arosemena, when he offered this scarcely diplomatic toast, was thinking of the masses of children who to this day work for foreign interests on Ecuadorian plantations and in Ecuadorian ports. I saw them sitting in baking-hot sheds, sorting coffee beans—girls ranging in age from six to ten, stooped over from morning to night, breathing the fine coffee dust, cheated of their childhoods, cheated of play, idleness, schooling, and all the possibilities of self-development that are taken as the natural due of children in civilized countries. Ecuadorian children seem almost to have been born with adult expressions on their faces.

The United States is proud of the opportunities she provides for her children. But the conditions proper for American children seem not to pertain to Ecuadorian children, according to a good many coffee and banana planters. In North America and in most European countries, child labor is nowadays regarded as barbarous. But in underdeveloped countries the members of such civilized nations have no scruples about drawing on the cheap labor of small children wherever they can.

It may also be that Arosemena was thinking of the city of Montecristi, where the finest *toquillas* in the world are woven. Many thousands of women in Ecuador make these Panama hats at home. It takes some eighty hours to produce a single hat. The resulting product is so fine that the hat can be pulled through a ring or packed into a matchbox. From constantly handling the hair-thin fibers of the *toquilla* plant, many of the women suffer from eye diseases or have even gone blind. A hatmaker in Montecristi receives between ten cents to at most fifty cents for the manufacture of a Panama hat. The same hat costs about a hundred dollars in the United States. The profit is pocketed by the Ecuadorian and American middlemen.

Arosemena might also have been thinking of the Negro port of Esmeraldas, capital of the northernmost province of the country.

Esmeraldas was named after the emeralds that the Spaniards long ago seized from the Indian aboriginals. Today the province has neither emeralds nor Indians; descendants of Negro slaves work on the plantations and load freighters with bananas, coffee, tobacco, and rubber. They seem to hate present-day planters as deeply as their ancestors hated the slaveholders. Practically speaking, they hate everyone with a white skin and regard all whites as exploiters, or at least potential exploiters.

As I walked about the streets of Esmeraldas, the natives fell silent when I approached. They were a far cry from the good-natured, openhearted coastal Negroes of Brazil, Cuba, and Colombia, who are always ready to talk with foreigners. In shops, I was served with cold languor. The beggars did not meekly request alms; they rudely demanded tribute. When I gave a ragged man a cigarette, he growled something at me between his teeth, spat, and made off. Wherever I sat down, the Negroes immediately moved away. Icy rejection or venomous hatred stood between them and me like an insurmountable wall. The Ecuadorian dislike for foreigners goes so far that European ship captains who have sailed the Ecuadorian coast for years, and are fully acquainted with the psychology of the inhabitants, will nevertheless incur senseless assaults or even unjustified arrest.

GRAVE-ROBBING AND OTHER NATIONAL SPORTS

Profit has been wrung from even the savage Indians, the tribes who live in the jungles east of the Andes. The Jívaros have a fine art of shrinking the heads of enemies they have killed. The trophies are about the size of a child's fist, and because of their horribly lifelike appearance have become highly desired collector's items. Rich tourists pay several thousand dollars for a genuine tsantsa. In recent years, to be sure, head-hunting has rather gone out of fashion among the Jívaros—the government has tried to stop the practice and the Jívaros have taken to pursuing somewhat more productive occupations. But the dealers in curiosa were alarmed at the drying up of business. They have encouraged the Jívaros to transfer their skills to monkey heads and the heads of exhumed corpses. The same Indians whom American missionaries tried so hard to convert to peaceful ways were recruited for the grisly industry of removing the bones from human heads, then shrinking the boneless heads in ashes.

Ecuador has put a ban on the export of tsantsas, in order to stamp out head-hunting and grave-robbing. But the law has little force, for the Jívaros live in the Amazonian regions the Peruvians seized from Ecuador. Consequently, Peruvian tsantsas are now coming on the market. A Peruvian estate steward of German origin, who had a tsantsa in his baggage, was particularly proud that the shrunken head was genuine, that is, not made from a corpse, but from an actual victim. He had sent his Indian workers out to kill a harmless Indian woman and prepare the head for him. The operation seemed as natural to him as the shooting of an animal for its trophy value by a big-game hunter.

But these may have been only minor charges in the mind of Arosemena when he spoke up so bluntly to the American ambassador.

In his walks through the capital, Arosemena would see not only Quito's magnificent colonial palaces and her fifty-seven sumptuously ornamented churches, but also the emaciated cholos and Indios who constitute the majority of the city's population. The average wage of the Ecuadorian is barely ten dollars a month. Yet prices are not much lower than in the United States, aside from the country's native food-stuffs. Conditions are somewhat better in the thriving port of Guayaquil, where industrialization affords part of the population something approaching a livelihood. Old Spanish families, however, still retain something of that luxurious way of life which Alexander von Humboldt saw among the Ecuadorians.

Everywhere in Latin America lordly mansions and magnificent residences stand in sharp contrast to the misery of the slums. Prosperity and poverty literally exist side by side, with the shacks and sheet-metal dwellings of the underprivileged abutting the estates of the privileged. Along the coasts of Ecuador, however, even the homes of the few well-to-do look extremely modest—they are on a scale that in other countries would be considered lower middle class. Business offices and warehouses in the ports are often so shabby that the concerns appear to be on the verge of bankruptcy. Natives and foreigners alike invest as little as possible in this remote country.

Arosemena made efforts to get along as well as possible with Americans. Consequently, the Peace Corps is now working in Ecuador. These idealistic young Americans are to be commended for teaching the natives to use garbage cans and to burn their rubbish in order to improve hygienic conditions in the country. But it would be more to the point if someone would see that wages rose, that the national income was distributed more fairly, and that child labor was eliminated. Along with Paraguay, Ecuador is the poorest, economically most unstable and socially most depressed country in South America.

Arosemena's faux-pas spelled the end of his program of gradual social reform. The army deposed him for "drunkenness in office," sent him into exile in Panama, and outlawed the Revolutionary Youth Union, other left-oriented groups, and the holding of elections. When the United States protested against the military junta and threatened to break diplomatic relations, the army men quoted an epigram once coined by interim President Galo Plaza Lasso, the conservative opponent of Velasco Ibarra. It was unthinkable to forbid the Ecuadorian army to revolt, Plaza Lasso had said; in Ecuador, coups were a national sport.

Betancourt, that staunch democrat, withdrew the Venezuelan ambassador from Quito. Mexico and Bolivia took a cool view of the Ecuadorian coup. The United States, however, quickly forgot her principals and recognized the new military government. Nevertheless, on the second anniversary of the Alliance for Progress, President Kennedy averred that a peaceful revolution was in progress in Latin America, giving promise that millions of "our American brothers" would have a better life in the future.

Alas, since those fine words were spoken, there have been nine military coups in as many Latin American countries, each of which has brought down a democratic government that had been co-operating with the United States. These military uprisings are always hailed by the country's native and foreign propertied classes. Washington cannot rebuke the power-hungry army men without offending those Americans who earn good money in Latin America.

Those fifteen hundred scientists, teachers, engineers, and Peace Corps people who are maintained by American taxpayers to pave the way for a better life for Latin Americans are undoubtedly full of good intentions. Yet Edwin Martin, a State Department Latin American expert, proposed a change of course after the military revolts of recent years. The army, he suggested, could not be eliminated from political life in Latin America; therefore the only thing to do was to make some arrangement with it.

BANANAS BIG AND SMALL

Such an arrangement with the army would mean democracy's capitulation to force and the end of all the great hopes linked with the Alliance for Progress. Little Ecuador, at any rate, as has been evident ever since Arosemena was deposed, has not been pacified by military rule. The country has instead become considerably more restive. The demonstrations and revolts against the military, usually started by students and by discontented bourgeois groups in the traditionally liberal port of Guayaquil, are more and more conspicuously directed against the gringos.

As in Central America, bananas are partly the cause of the latent anti-Americanism of much of the population in Ecuador. The owners of the banana-producing coastal areas are dependent on American fruit companies and fruit exporters; United Fruit and Standard Fruit Company are their chief customers. Banana exports are vital to Ecuador; more than 61 per cent of the government income is said to be derived from them. In recent years Ecuador has lost the big Japanese market, for the Japanese now obtain their bananas principally from Taiwan and the Philippines. In addition, the Ecuadorians are dependent on the modern American refrigerator ships (aside from a few German, Israeli, and Eastern bloc vessels), most of which are owned by United Fruit.

United Fruit, however, is primarily interested in transporting its own bananas from its Central American fruit empire; it takes only the best of the Ecuadorian harvest. In its television advertising, it promotes the small bananas from Central America at the expense of the big bananas from Ecuador. Ecuadorians charge (whether rightly or wrongly) that the big fruit company drives prices down and impedes Ecuadorian exports. Whatever the truth of this charge, the greater part of the banana harvest in Ecuador goes unsold; and the penetrating stench of rotting bunches of bananas has become familiar in the whole coastal region.

As a result of these real or fancied practices, United Fruit has become even more unpopular in Ecuador than the military junta. While the people seem almost to have forgotten aging Velasco Ibarra, who in Argentine exile has become a highly respected professor of international law, Arosemena—who is certainly not especially pro-American—has risen to the status of a popular hero. There is constant agitation, chiefly in Guayaquil, to force Admiral Castro Jijón, head of the military junta, to grant new elections and general democratization. Demonstrations passionately hail Arosemena, who has returned to Ecuador, and glorify his "anti-Americanism."

When the junta finally ordered Arosemena's arrest in July 1965, a general popular uprising broke out in Guayaquil. The hated junta had to resign, and was replaced by an interim government. The new regime has now attested to its loyalty to Washington, but new elections can hardly be held off any longer. And the men who will emerge as victors from these elections will in all probability, if the experience of the past few years is any guide, be unable to shift back to a lower gear. Rather, they will attempt far more forcibly than hitherto to direct Ecuador toward the "better life" that their great neighbor to the north has proclaimed.

ECUADOR　COLOMBIA

PERU

BOLIVIA

Pacific Ocean

Atlantic Ocean

Inca Empire at the time of Pachacuti (1438-63)

Acquisitions under Pachacuti & Topa Inca (1463-71)

Acquisitions under Topa Inca (1471-93)

Chimu Empire at the time of the Inca conquest (ca.1460)

■ Ancient Inca city

● Conquistadors' settlement (1517-50)

□ Ruined cities

Pacatnamu

Chanchan

Moche

Chavín de Huantar

Pargamonga

Lima

Machu Picchu

Pachacamac

Machu Picchu

Ollantaytambo　Sacsayhuamán

Pisac

Cuzco

Pucara

Arequipa

Lake Titicaca

Tiahuanaco

La Paz

Reed boat on Lake Titicaca

BRAZIL

N

Pacific Ocean

BOLIVIA

Potosi

Uyuni Salt marsh

Quechua Indian with llama

CHILE

ARGENTINA　PARAGUAY

CHAPTER 5

On the Ruins of the Inca Empire

THE NIGHTS ARE COLD IN CUZCO

This is not a city for peaceful, leisurely strolls. It swarms with tourists from every land. Hotels, restaurants, cabdrivers, guides, souvenir shops, peddlers, and beggars make their pitches for the favor of every visitor. Cuzco, the ancient Inca metropolis in Peru, is regarded as the archaeological capital of South America. It is chock-full of the past, a breath-takingly magnificent past. And yet there is something sinister about the streets of Cuzco.

Cuzco is really very beautiful, built entirely in a consistent style that fuses Spanish and Indian elements. Architecturally, the seat of the Incas ranks with Cartagena and Bahia as among the loveliest cities in South America. The Spaniards filled it with palaces; the patrician houses have carved balconies and exceptionally delightful patios. In Cuzco they built more elegantly than in the capital city of Lima. But the buildings lack the amiable charm of Bahia's Jesuit baroque, and they have none of the delicately curved elegance of the colonial style in golden Cartagena. They are austere and not easily accessible.

One does not have to look too hard to discover that the whole center of the city is built virtually on Inca foundations. The Spanish architectural style is quite literally superimposed. The homes of the conquistadors consist of thick Inca walls made of gigantic blocks of stone so closely fitted that the joints hardly show. In spite of three centuries of colonization, Cuzco has remained an Inca city. The Spaniards did their utmost to destroy the advanced civilization of the Quechua Indians, but they succeeded only in decapitating the Inca world and placing a Spanish head on the Indian torso. The body remained sound.

The Inca walls have remained so sound that they even withstood the great earthquake of 1950. Many modern houses collapsed in Cuzco during that quake. But the cyclopean blocks of stone heaped up centuries ago by the Incas stood fast, safeguarding Spanish roofs and Spanish balconies. This, however, does not mean that the two cultures so closely intermixed in Cuzco have ever really entered into a living symbiosis. They exist side by side in a kind of petrified hostility. The longer you stay in Cuzco, the more intensely you feel that the deep-lying Indian spirit is extremely vital, far more vital than the Spanish overlay. Ultimately, the colonial buildings begin to look like stage sets which can be swept away at any time.

So far, the only part of the overlay that has been removed is a section of the church and the monastery of San Domingo. There, the earthquake of 1950 exposed the ruins of the Inca Temple of the Sun. The chronicles of the conquistadors record that in Inca times the inner walls of the temple were coated with pure gold and set with jewels. The treasures of the Inca temple vanished, but for once not into Spanish hands. The Indians removed them to a safe hiding place, where they perhaps remain to this day. The Temple of the Sun is at present being restored. The fact that this is being done at the expense of a Christian church is a novelty in Peru.

Such endeavors do not mean that Cuzco has resolved to affirm and revive its Indian past, as Mexico has done. The object is solely to offer an attraction to the tourists who overrun the city. For there are no longer any completely preserved Inca buildings in or around Cuzco. The great fortress of Sacsahuamán, which looms high above the city, is only a chaotic mass of stone blocks, empty arches, halls split in half and staircases that end in empty air. The road watchtower of Kenko is merely a circle of stone. And the baths of the Inca rulers have also been leveled to their foundations, although the water still pours out of the old conduits.

HUNGER IN THE ANDES

Yet it is not the decapitation of the greatest civilization of South America that gives one such a sense of uneasiness in Cuzco. That uneasiness arises from, as much as anything else, walks through the strangely theatrical streets at night. With every breath you inhale the harsh, biting wind of the Andes. In winter, Cuzco, situated eleven thousand feet above sea level, is so cold that the icy air seems to be cutting your lungs to shreds. Patrolling policemen wear woolen masks over their mouths and noses. The narrow streets or the wide, wind-swept plazas are almost deserted at night. Now and then a cab cruises by. The blue moonlight emphasizes the intense cold. In that light, the colonial churches and palaces look like the abandoned tombs of a necropolis. The Inca walls, however, look even more mighty and indestructible by night than by day, when the feeble winter sun glances off the crystal of the rock.

On such nights you encounter the impoverished rather than the resplendent side of Cuzco. There is a great deal of misery in the heart of the former Inca Empire. In the moonlight, women sit under the overhangs of walls, holding their children pressed firmly to their bodies to keep them warm. From under ragged blankets protrude bare feet, blue with cold. I went up to one woman who sat half dozing, her head swaying back and forth. She had two children in her arms. The younger was no more than two, the elder possibly six. She started up and stared at me in fright when I gave her a few coins. She was so startled she scarcely managed to murmur thanks. The children did not stir. I was a white, and the Indians of Cuzco are not accustomed to friendly gestures from whites.

Many of the inhabitants of Cuzco must spend the nights in the open. Homeless children wander through the streets. If I offered one of them a roll, a crowd formed instantly. The bigger children tried to wrest the roll away from the little one. Even adult Indians who passed by, or who squatted along the walls of buildings, stared with hungry longing at the food. Nowhere else in Latin America did I see a child bite into a piece of dry bread so eagerly as in Cuzco.

In the Latin American tropics, there are countless people who do not have a roof over their heads. Often, on night walks in Rio de Janeiro, I stumbled over persons lying in the street, peacefully slumbering. Such conditions shock the foreigner, but to the natives they are not intolerable. You do not shiver with cold under the tropic sky. Tropical rainstorms are violent but brief; and after they are over it is usually warmer. But in the cold Andean regions, lack of shelter can be almost equivalent to a death sentence, especially if coupled with undernourishment. Tuberculosis or pneumonia can easily develop. On the Peruvian plateau, moreover, there are no wild tropical fruits with which the hungry can fill their bellies in lieu of bread. There is no evading hunger in the Andes.

Destitution bears down heaviest on women with small children. There are often no husbands to help them feed their families. Marriage costs money—that is just as true in Peru as in El Salvador and other Latin American countries. Many of the Quechua have no money because they have no work, or because their tiny plots of land yield scarcely any cash crops. The result is that many Indian men and women simply live together. Such informal unions are about as cohesive as legal marriage. But when misery grows intolerable, when the man is seized by despair at the sight of his growing family, he may make off, leaving wife and children helpless. No one can force an Indian to maintain children conceived out of legal wedlock. The priests are forever denouncing these illegal unions, but they are in no position to perform marriages without compensation. The lower clergy in the Indian areas are just as poor as their parishioners; and the higher clergy still live in the feudal past.

I shall never forget an experience I had in the cathedral of Cuzco. I stood before the magnificent silver altar, admiring the art of the baroque silversmiths. A short distance away knelt a small Indian boy, clothed in rags and pitiably thin. He looked to be about eight, but was possibly a good deal older. These neglected children of the Peruvian highlands usually look much younger than they are. Their eyes alone give their age away: the eyes of adults, knowing and without hope, but at times filled with hatred that flashes like a warning signal.

The boy had his hands clasped and was absorbed in prayer. I had in my pocket a roll left over from breakfast. I gave it to him. In uncomprehending astonishment, his dark eyes stared at me. His "Muchas gracias, señor!" sounded like a prayer of thanksgiving. And no doubt it was that. A miracle had happened to this little boy. Perhaps he had been asking God for something to eat, and he had received it immediately. When I emerged from the church, he was standing at the door and smiled at me with sweet, heart-rending gratitude. I got into the waiting cab. Slowly, the boy moved forward, passed the cab, and once again smiled his fervent gratitude. And I had given him nothing but a roll which I would not have eaten anyhow. It is often a painful thing to belong to a privileged group.

AN INDIAN WELFARE STATE

Almost 50 per cent of the Peruvian population consists of pure-blooded Indians. More than 40 per cent are mixed-blood Indians, of whom a good many regard themselves as Indians. The Indian languages, Quechua and Aymara, are used by about half of the Peruvians. In the Andes, the majority of the population consists of the same Quechuas who were once the ruling nation of the Inca Empire.

The Peruvian Indians had a long and splendid history of civilization behind them even before the founding of the empire. Around the beginning of the Christian era the titanic Chavín culture flourished around the region of Chavín de Huantar, producing its mighty monoliths, stone portraits, and animal frescoes. A few centuries later the Mochica in northern Peru created their world-famous ceramics: richly decorated heads, statuettes of warriors, market women, beggars, and lepers, all sorts of animal figurines, charming and sometimes exceedingly realistic love scenes, and even depictions of torture and executions. Aside from the Greeks, there has scarcely been a culture as earthy, realistic, lively, and sensual as that of the Mochica.

In the southern part of the country the Nazca created equally astonishing ceramics, more austere and abstract in feeling, and far more charged and transcendental than those of the bucolic Mochica. Three hundred years before the birth of the Inca Empire, the realm of the Chimú flourished in the north. The Chimú, later the traditional enemies of the Incas, built the gigantic adobe capital of Chanchan and produced an art that in some ways resembled the Etruscan. There were many other Indian cultures before the Incas appeared on the scene: the Ica, Paracas, Pachacamac, Chancay, who established a confusing multiplicity of small states and local art styles which archaeologists are still striving to disentangle.

The most amazing aspect of these advanced Indian cultures is the fact that they should have arisen in a country like Peru, infertile and scarcely hospitable to human habitation. The Peruvian coast is a desert, the Peruvian highlands are rugged mountains. When we study the pre-Columbian cultures of Peru, we are tempted to conclude that harsh natural conditions and forbidding terrain may spur a people to maximum achievements in culture and civilization. For while the Indians in the lush tropics of South America remained on the level of Stone Age nomads and food gatherers, the Peruvian Indians had to make their deserts and mountains fruitful in order to exist. They treated every river, every tiny watercourse which flowed from the Andes westward into the Pacific, or eastward into the headwaters of the Amazon, as a kind of miniature Nile, whose waters could be used, channeled and guided onto terraced fields. The predecessors of the Incas fought an incessant battle against the encroachment of desert and the progress of erosion. They emerged victorious from that battle.

Along the coasts the Indians had to build their cities, temples, and palaces of adobe because they had no other building materials at their disposal. In the High Andes, however, they hewed stones for their mountain roads, walls, settlements, fortresses, and places of worship. When the Incas, Quechua Indians from the vicinity of Cuzco, transformed their small mountainous kingdom into a mighty empire which at its peak comprised a fourth of South America, their victory was, as it were, the triumph of stone over mud brick.

At the beginning of the Spanish conquest, some six to seven million persons inhabited the Inca Empire. Because of their highly centralized government, their remarkable irrigation system, and their ingenious terracing, which checked erosion of the topsoil, they were all well fed. The Incas and their predecessors had developed most of the cultivated plants which play so large a part in present-day agriculture: the potato, the bean, the squash, the banana, the tomato, and the pepper plant. There were still other plants which the Incas had inherited from other pre-Columbian people: corn, cotton, cacao, cucumbers, and papayas. Out of the shy guanaco, the Peruvian Indians bred a beast of burden essential for human life in the Andes: the llama. Two animals related to the llama, the alpaca and the vicuña, supplied the South American Indians with a wool which to this day is regarded as the finest in the world.

Edward Hyams, the British agriculturalist and cultural historian, maintains that the Inca tribes were the only peoples on the face of the earth who did not parasitically exploit the soil, but on the contrary, vastly increased its fertility and extent. Never before in human history, says Hyams, has there been a human society in which agricultural practices and social organization were so closely intertwined to form a splendid human environment.

In the Incas' Empire of the Sun there was no hunger, no cold, no homelessness. The community supplied such services as maternity care, child care, and provision for the aged. The Inca Empire has been called the first socialist state in world history, and indeed, many of the Inca laws may well be compared with the social legislation of modern times. The soil belonged to the community and was tilled co-operatively; anyone who did not do his share was severely punished. The Inca bureaucracy assigned all citizens their occupation and place of work. It even governed family life, ordering marriages and supervising the upbringing of the children. The socialist principle that only those citizens who served the community may derive personal benefits from the community was carried to extremes by the Incas.

To our minds, such a utopia is not altogether congenial. There are many persons in South America who contend that the Spanish colonial masters by no means repressed and enslaved the Indians, but on the contrary liberated them from the state slavery of the totalitarian Inca Empire. Today's Peruvian white upper class likes to represent the ancient Empire of the Sun as a kind of Indian forerunner of the Soviet Union, and to compare the subjects of the Incas with the ideologically enslaved inhabitants of the lands of the Eastern bloc. But such parallels take no account of the mentality of the Andean Indians and the historical facts of the region.

Indians are not Europeans. The subjects of the Spanish king at the time of the conquest were, in all probability, no less unfree than the subjects of the Inca rulers. What is more, the Incas never practiced religious suppression and mass slaughter in the style of the Spanish Inquisition. The nature of the Indian is such that he tends to lack a sense of private property even where he does not live in a tightly centralized state, but in a small hunting or agricultural community. To this day, in Peru, the village folk till the soil in common, although no one makes them do so. Anyone who has seen the sparse soil of the Andes understands that no people could thrive there without tight organization, obligatory work, and collectivization of the land. The Incas' socialistic state was a product of tradition and natural conditions. In the few hundred years of its existence, it functioned far better than any of the economic and social forms adopted in Peru during the succeeding four centuries.

A few decades after the Spanish conquest, only some five million persons were left of those who had inhabited the territory of the Inca Empire. Most of these survivors lived in conditions of grinding poverty and scarcity. In their hysterical desire to wipe out all traces of the "heathen" culture, the Spaniards had destroyed not only the magnificent architectural works of the Incas, but also much of their terracing and many of their irrigation systems. Perhaps this passion for destruction stemmed from the conquistadors' fear of an awakened Indian resistance. In any case, by ruining Indian agriculture, the Spaniards opened the way for increasingly severe erosion. The good soil the Quechua had built up on their terraces was blown or washed away; and soon not a blade of grass would grow in what had been flourishing fields of corn, potatoes, or beans.

The Peruvian Andean region has not yet recovered from that devastation. The descendants of the Incas continue to till whatever terraces remain intact. But there is not enough good land to feed the four to five million highland Indians. Thousands upon thousands of the Indians therefore poured out of the villages and into the cities, where there might be some kind of livelihood. But the cities, too, have little to offer them. Peru's wealth has been concentrated in the capital, Lima. As is the case almost everywhere in Latin America, it is in the hands of the small upper class. Among the members of that upper class there are still some who to this day consider the Indians not as Peruvian fellow citizens, but "beasts" who are hopelessly "asocial."

THE MIRACLE ON THE URUBAMBA

Impressions such as these intensified my feeling of uneasiness. From Cuzco I rode down the valley of the Urubamba toward the north where, among misty, ravine-slashed mountains, I visited the "eighth wonder of the world"—Machu Picchu, the best preserved of the Inca fortresses. These remarkable fortifications, cleverly built into the rock at the top of the mountain, were never found by the Spaniards. The Quechua kept to themselves their knowledge of the fortress. In 1911, almost four hundred years after the Spanish conquest, an Indian put Hiram Bingham, the American archaeologist, on the trail of Machu Picchu. For a while the citadel was regarded as the long-sought "lost city" of the Incas. Present-day archaeologists say that it was a border fortification which after the Spanish invasion was built up into a mammoth refuge.

Machu Picchu is an answer in stone to the eternal plaint of white-skinned Peruvians that the Indians are by nature sluggish and incapable of any important achievements. In all of Peru, there is no European-inspired structure to compare with this gigantic and architecturally brilliant complex of terraces, stairways, gates, towers, walls, and citadels. Machu Picchu is situated almost thirty-five hundred feet above the valley of the Urubamba. The Incas must have brought their building material up from the valley, probably using tree trunks as rollers, for they had no block and tackle, no wagons, no large beasts of burden. Everything was done with manpower. I consider Machu Picchu an architectural miracle equal to the monumental structures of the civilizations of the ancient Orient, and, from the technical point of view, surpassing these.

One small example shows that the glorious pre-Spanish past is still very much alive among the Quechua Indians. After the war, a tourist hotel was built near the Inca fortress. The builders were faced with the problem of bringing water up to this height. While various expensive solutions were being discussed, an Indian came to the architect and showed him an Inca water conduit hidden beneath rubble and dense underbrush. When the conduit was cleared, it functioned as well as it had four hundred years earlier. Inca conduits now supply water not only to the hotel, but to the other buildings around Machu Picchu.

The Quechua have by no means forgotten their proud past. Enslaved and oppressed, they have always regarded their misery as a temporary condition. In colonial days, Indians were driven into forced labor on the estates of the Spanish masters or in the mines. Their governmental organization and their social structures were shattered. As a people, they seemed to be crushed into hopeless submission. Consequently, the recurrent Indian uprisings took the Spaniards by surprise. As late as 1780, after the Indians had been subjugated for generations, a Quechua named José Gabriel Condorcanqui rocked all of Peru and Bolivia. He gave himself the name of Tupac Amaru, one of the greatest of the Inca rulers, and, some believe, came very close to restoring the ancient Inca Empire. The Spaniards had a hard time suppressing this Quechua rebellion.

Immediately before the war of independence, another Indian revolt broke out. Its leader this time was an Indian officer of the Spanish army named Pumacagua. This revolution also failed, but it so weakened the Spanish armies that a few years later the liberators from Argentina and Colombia managed to expel the colonial troops from Peru.

Even the Bolivian dictator Andrés Santa Cruz, whose mother was descended from the Inca nobility, dreamed of an Inca renaissance after independence. He conquered Peru, united it with Bolivia in a federation, and established his capital in Cuzco, whence he intended to create an Indian-mestizo empire. Santa Cruz was, to be sure, only a typical Latin American dictator who used the Indians for his own ambitious ends. When he mustered the mountain Indians and sent them to occupy the coast of Peru, the Quechua died by the thousands from the effects of the lowland climate. This disaster spelled the end of Santa Cruz's dream of a reborn Inca Empire.

As I walked through the streets of Cuzco and the winding lanes of Quechua villages, I noticed, among the many party slogans on the walls, an inscription which contained the name of another Inca ruler of the distant past: Tupac Yupanquin. A local Indian leader who was running for the congress had given himself the name of the emperor under whom the Inca Empire had reached its height. The Quechua in the vicinity of Cuzco are highly responsive to such names. Memories of the distant Inca times are not dead history to them, but a warming fire beneath the colonial ashes.

The small towns and villages around Cuzco have remained almost entirely Indian. It is as if the Spaniards had paid only a fleeting visit to them. This is true not only of the architecture, which is conceived wholly in the spirit of pre-Columbian times, but also of the people. They still speak Quechua. They know to this day who among them is a descendant of the Inca, that is, a member of the ancient Indian noble caste.

ARE THE INDIANS TURNING RED?

In one of these villages I spoke with the alcalde, the Indian mayor. He had heard that I was a German, and in keeping with South American custom he praised my native land. After a few polite exchanges, he set forth his political beliefs. To my surprise he did not profess adherence to the Indian leader Tupac Yupanquin, but made an ideological confession I had not expected to encounter in this remote Indian valley.

"You are a German," he said, "and I am an Inca. Germans and Incas are good people who understand one another. But Peruvians and Americans are bad people. That is why I am a communist."

I could not talk him out of his curious communist views. And I found that there were a good many Indians in the Andes who thought along the same lines. For centuries, the Quechua shed their blood in unsuccessful rebellions against the Spanish overlords. Though it may seem that they have given up the struggle, their hatred is perhaps as strong as ever. The Peruvian communists were the first political organization in Peru who, during the brief periods of licit activity, couched their propaganda in the Quechua language. The communists were also the first to take up the idea of a rebirth of an Indian Peru. They called for a union of the Indian regions of Peru and Bolivia into a Quechua and Aymara soviet republic constructed on ancient Indian lines. Consequently, many Indians believe that communism would give them what the government in Lima has hitherto withheld. These communistic leanings may be blamed entirely on the stupidity of the Peruvian oligarchy, which refuses to regard the Indian as fully human.

At one point, the train on which I rode through the Urubamba valley came to a sudden halt. A Quechua boy had rolled a large rock onto the track, to sabotage the train full of gringos. He stood watching with interest as the brakes screeched, and did not begin to run until the train had halted and it became clear that there would be no accident. A boy's prank, to be sure, but also symptomatic of the present situation in Peru. The Peruvian Indians are awakening, and are keeping close watch on the course of events in neighboring Bolivia, where the Indians have been given full rights as citizens.

In Cuzco I talked with a Peruvian teacher about Indian education. The man was of Spanish extraction; nevertheless, he proved to be a passionate advocate of Indian rights. The mountain Indians, he told me, are by no means inferior to the white Peruvians in intelligence or ability. They have a much harder time in the schools than children of Iberian descent, for Spanish is the official language of the country and consequently the sole language of instruction in Peru. For the Quechua, however, Spanish is a foreign language, the learning of which calls for considerable effort. Once they overcome this hurdle, my informant said, they frequently outstrip the whites and mestizos, largely because they are more tenacious, more persevering, and stronger in character than the often frivolous children of the Latin middle classes.

I mentioned the Indian leader Tupac Yupanquin and the communist alcalde. The teacher shook his head vigorously. "Neither local politicians nor ideas from Eastern Europe can help our mountain Indians," he said. "There is only one movement in Peru today that is honestly for the Indian. That is the APRA."

THE MAN WHO MOVES THE EARTH

He may well be the most cultured and intelligent politician in Latin America. He is certainly the most hated and hounded party leader in his native land. His name is blazoned in large letters on the walls not only of cities but of the remotest Indian villages: Víctor Raúl Haya de la Torre. A fantastic variety of personages have played a part in his life. He was a friend of Roosevelt and Clement Atlee. For a time he was in close contact with Trotsky. As a writer, he learned a good deal from Romain Rolland. As a historian, he earned the respect of Arnold Toynbee. Albert Einstein called him one of the twelve persons who had really understood the theory of relativity. Nelson Rockefeller thinks highly of him. President Kennedy hoped he would win the election. But in the Peruvian upper class, the mere mention of his name starts a ripple of uneasiness.

His party is the only political force in Peru which can lay claim to a genuine evolution, a strict organization, and a clear program. The other parties of the country are little more than bodyguards for their leaders. But in the forty years of its life, this party has been able to function publicly for only fifteen years. The rest of the time it has been banned, outlawed, persecuted, driven underground. Since his entrance into politics, there have been only intervals when Haya de la Torre has been able to move about freely in his native land. For more than fifteen years he lived in exile in Mexico and Europe. He spent six years in the asylum of foreign embassies in Lima, and eight years in the underground. Three times he stood before the raised rifles of an execution squad; twice he was saved by a last-minute pardon and once he succeeded in escaping.

All this may give the impression that Haya de la Torre's party is an exceedingly radical movement that endangers the very existence of the Peruvian Government. In reality, however, Haya de la Torre is a modern leftist liberal, a stalwart fighter against rightist and leftist extremism, a man who shares the principles of such unequivocal democrats as Betancourt in Venezuela and Figueres in Costa Rica. He ruined his reputation with the Peruvian military and moneyed aristocracy only because he violated three taboos sacred in Peruvian politics.

First, he antagonized the feudalistic landowning class by advocating agrarian reform.

Second, during a revolt his partisans executed several of the higher-ranking army officers.

Third, and above all, he holds that Peru is not a Latin American country, belonging without question to the descendants of the white conquerors, but an Indo-American country in which the Indians who constitute the majority of the population must be given the same rights as the white minority.

A COUNTRY ON CRUTCHES

In colonial days Peru was the pampered child of the Spanish motherland. The white Peruvians were by no means eager for independence. Perhaps the united effort of Simón Bolívar, from the north, and of General San Martín, from the south, would not so rapidly have pried this most glittering of jewels from the Spanish crown had Peru not been weakened beforehand by its Indian revolts.

For a while the country was governed by San Martín, the hero of Argentine liberation. Then Bolívar made himself dictator of Peru. When these alien regimes were ultimately replaced by the rule of white Peruvians, the country that had been Spain's richest colony sank into a morass of family disputes, military coups, civil wars, moral degeneration, terrible poverty, and perilous depopulation. For a while Peru became the prey of Santa Cruz, the Bolivian descendant of the Incas. Later a native half-Indian, Ramón Castilla, fought his way to the presidency. Castilla freed the slaves, abolished the poll tax on the Indians, weakened the hold of the Church, and established universal suffrage. These experiments in emancipation terrified the white oligarchy, which by far preferred the state of things under colonial rule.

Foreign capital began playing its role in Peru under Ramón Castilla. The mestizo president and his successors struck up ties with Europe for commercial reasons. The Peruvian army was organized along French lines. English businessmen exploited the guano and mineral resources of the country. But political life in Peru remained violent and unstable. A hundred years ago Peru fought a senseless war against the former Spanish motherland. Between 1879 and 1883 she lost the Saltpeter War against Chile and thereby forfeited two rich provinces. It would appear that "golden Peru" was ill equipped to look after her own best interests.

After the disaster of the Saltpeter War (which was usually called the War of the Pacific), British and later American capital began trying to straighten out Peruvian affairs. Gradually things improved for the white upper class. As in Venezuela, Peru's mestizo parvenus had won a place for themselves in the oligarchy. A new upper class formed, composed of landowners, merchants, industrialists, and mine-owners. When lead, copper, zinc, silver, bismuth, and vanadium were found in the Peruvian mountains, and oil near the coast, it began to seem as if Peru could again look forward to an era of prosperity. The old colonial social order was restored. Presidents and dictators were recruited from the upper class and the army. The downtrodden Indians lived on the fringes of society, as had been the case in Spanish days.

Among the white and almost white members of the Peruvian oligarchy, memories of the uprisings of the past one hundred and fifty years have produced a dread of the Indians stronger than in any other Latin American country. The psyches of the descendants of the Spaniards seem permanently scarred, so much so that the whites make every effort to ignore the existence of the numerically superior Indian population. They despise the Peruvian Indian, hardly speak of him, distort the pre-Columbian past, and have erected a barrier of taboos against the very word Indio. That word is seldom heard in Peru; at most it is used as an insult.

In the summer of 1962 I had a pleasant talk with a cabinet minister of the military government then in power. He was highly pleased at my interest in Peru, but when I mentioned the Indians, the minister grew cool and soon brought the conversation to an end. On the other hand, another member of the upper class listened attentively when I spoke of the Indian influx into Lima and the consequent alarming growth of the slums. At last he said, with sovereign composure, that this problem was insoluble, for unfortunately the Indians could not be mowed down with machine guns, although to do so would be in the best interests of Peru. "Perhaps that sounds inhuman," he said, "but you must consider the matter from the economic and political point of view. These people do not work. They pay no taxes. They are not consumers. They are of not the slightest use to the nation. They are only a burden."

THE BIRTH AND RISE OF THE APRA

Haya de la Torre is the son of a newspaper publisher in the provincial capital of Trujillo. This city has nothing to do with the one-time Dominican dictator. It is merely one of the jokes of history that Haya de la Torre should have been born in a town that bears the same name as one of the dictators he has most abhorred.

He became a lawyer and made a name for himself when he was still quite young by founding the first university extension courses in Peru. He went into politics after he had become acquainted with the Peruvian highlands. While serving as the secretary to a provincial government, he realized that the chief problem of Peru was the Indians. He determined to solve this problem.

"The Indians I saw," he wrote later, "were abused and beaten with riding whips. They were ignorant and lived in misery. It profoundly shocked me to see how low they had sunk since Peru was conquered by Pizarro in 1532. I could no longer look on dispassionately at such conditions. And so I became an obsessed fighter against the wrongs being inflicted upon the Indians."

Haya de la Torre's sympathy for the Indians went down so ill with ruling circles in Lima that the young lawyer had to flee to Mexico to escape arrest. There he met an altogether different type of Indian. The Mexican program of re-Indianization had already begun. Presidents Carranza and Obregón had nationalized the natural resources and divided the latifundia. They had begun to forge a new social order whose benefits would go principally to the Indians and mestizos. Like Arévalo and Arbenz in Guatemala, and like the later leaders of the Bolivian MNR and Fidel Castro, Haya de la Torre eagerly absorbed the lessons of Mexico.

It is significant that Mexico has been the model for all the vital Latin American reformist movements. Liberalism, socialism, Marxism, and other ideologies from Europe have usually been of secondary importance, compared to the Mexican example. Haya de la Torre, however, went far beyond other Ibero-American opposition parties in his political program. He was the first Latin-American politician who looked beyond national frontiers—the first Pan-American. Just as the communists called upon the workers of all countries to unite, Haya de la Torre envisaged a union of the oppressed peoples in all the countries of Central and South America. Their great bond, as he saw it, was not their common Spanish speech, but their common Indian-American origin. His key concept was: Indo-America.

In 1924 he founded in Mexico the *Alianza Popular Revolucionaria Americana*—the APRA. He called it a "socialist anti-imperialist, pro-Indian movement fighting for the unity of Indo-America," and published a book to exposit his aims. This book, *Politica Aprista*, created vast excitement in all Spanish-speaking countries.

Although Haya de la Torre called his APRA a socialist movement, it was as far from European socialism as Mexican practical politics was from the ideology of bolshevism. Like the fathers of the Mexican Revolution, Haya de la Torre had read Marx and Lenin. As a student he had met Trotsky in the Soviet Union, and later renewed the acquaintance in his Mexican exile. In Paris and Switzerland he had discovered the humanitarian philosophy of Romain Rolland; and in Italy he had studied the rise of Benito Mussolini. But the intellectual roots of his APRA can be traced to neither Marxism nor fascism nor European humanism; they are native to Latin America. They sprang from Peruvian soil and achieved their full growth in Mexico. The APRA, along with the Mexican government party, offers the most interesting and dynamic program to be conceived in Latin America in our century.

Plans for comprehensive agrarian reform inevitably form the heart of any Latin American social movement. Haya de la Torre recognized that. The Peruvian Indians had been liberated from serfdom in 1858. Most of them work as sharecroppers, as day laborers on the latifundia, and as miners. More than half of the highland Indians live in *comunidades*, communes which have preserved many of the social features of Inca times. But crops are sparse due to the infertility of the country, the ruthless destruction of the colonial period, and primitive methods of agriculture. Haya de la Torre therefore saw the need of restoring and modernizing the agrarian structure that had prevailed under the Incas. The Indians must be given enough land to restore the descendants of the Incas to economic health. For economic health, he had learned from history, is consistently followed by an intellectual and spiritual upsurge. The strength and intelligence of the Indians, he believed, was the greatest unexploited natural resource of Peru.

Haya da la Torre regarded the Latin American oligarchy as a sterile, dying class, whose corruption, luxury, and internal anarchy were leading it rapidly to suicide. To his mind, any talk of a revival of *Ibero*-America was sheer fantasy. The continent could be reinvigorated only by liberating the latent forces of the people. Latin America must be transformed into *Indo*-America. The transformation, however, could not take place all at once or by violence. Haya de la Torre had studied all the revolts and revolutions in Latin American history. Although he called his party revolutionary, he was, like his friends Betancourt and Figueres, an evolutionist.

"It is not our purpose to confiscate the wealth of the rich," he stressed in his *Politica Aprista*. For, as he reasoned, the propertyless must slowly become accustomed to acquiring and dealing with property. "We want to create wealth for those who are poor."

In other words, APRA was planning to create an Indian peasantry, an Indian middle class, an Indian cultural renaissance. Along with its pledge not to confiscate the property of the oligarchy went the warning that it did not mean to allow an unlimited amassing of wealth as had been the case in the past. All the still-untapped resources of Peru (and these are enormous in that economically mismanaged country) were henceforth to be used for the benefit of the people, which meant primarily for the benefit of the Indians.

Democratic as Haya de la Torre was, his program was viable only if he could put an end to the tax cheating, the continual flight of capital, and the medieval conditions on the Peruvian latifundia. His efforts naturally antagonized the Peruvian oligarchy. The conservative presidents and dictators of the country, and especially General Benavides, unleashed an all-out campaign against the APRA. Nevertheless, in 1936, Haya de la Torre ventured to leave his asylum in Mexico and run for the presidency. His experiment failed. He had to run for his life from the bullets of the police, and henceforth conducted his operations from hideouts in the country's interior.

Within a short time, however, he had won so many followers that APRA became the most powerful political force in Peru. Members of the white-skinned intelligentsia, professors, teachers, students, unhappy with prevailing conditions, flocked to Haya de la Torre's banner. They were particularly attracted by the APRA leader's personal simplicity. He did not engage in politics as a business, as had every previous military dictator and professional politician, but as a historical mission. Here was someone who was equally familiar with world literature and the history of his country. Someone who was the friend of Einstein, Toynbee, and Rolland, and whose book *Time and Space in History* belongs among the most discussed historical works of the present age, had far more appeal to educated minds than any of the crude profiteering presidents the country was accustomed to.

Nevertheless, Haya de la Torre's greatest following came from the group whose foremost advocate he was—the Indians. The Peruvian highlands became solid APRA territory, with the Indians prepared to contribute a tithe of their scanty incomes to help finance the *jefe supremo,* the chief of the movement. The Indians had long since ceased to regard Haya de la Torre as a white-skinned foreigner. To them he was almost the reincarnation of an Inca. The Quechua conferred on him the proud Indian title of *Pachacutí*—"The Man Who Moves the Earth."

AN UNSUCCESSFUL EXPERIMENT

It was not until 1945 that Haya de la Torre was able to undertake his first serious effort to move the Peruvian earth. From its inception, Washington had regarded the APRA with benevolent attention. Peru is one place where the Americans have not allied themselves with the sterile upper class to the extent they have done in other countries of Central and South America. President Roosevelt considered the APRA the only force in Peru that might bring prosperity to the country. In his many conversations with American politicians and statesmen, moreover, Haya de la Torre had never shown himself arrogant or xenophobic. He had solemnly assured Washington that should he become president he would settle Peruvian debts with the United States. The promise was credible—whereas Washington knew that other Peruvian presidents preferred to line their own pockets rather than meet foreign obligations.

In the meantime the APRA had formed a kind of coalition with the *Acción Democrática* in Venezuela, the *Liberación Nacional* in Costa Rica, and the leftist liberals in Argentina. These parties held a con-ference in Caracas, where they discussed their aims and took a stand against all forms of dictatorship. Their program called for free elections, democratization and liberalization of their countries, a sound social program, redistribution of the land, and close collaboration with the United States. Haya de la Torre knew that without American aid and American investments he could not carry out his programs. There was no reason for American companies to be his opponents; on the contrary, they could become his allies in the struggle against the petrified traditions of Peru which were as great hindrances for American businessmen as they were for the *Apristas*.

Washington therefore interceded and called for the legalization of the APRA. The United States wished to see the Apristas given a share in political responsibility. Threatened with the loss of American aid, the oligarchy and the army were forced to yield. In 1945 a compromise was arranged: José Luis Bustamente, a minor political figure but friendly to the APRA, took power. Haya de la Torre was given the post of minister without portfolio.

The experiment failed. The heterogenous composition of the government prevented thoroughgoing reforms. The minister without portfolio was also without power; Haya de la Torre was not able to guide the country's policies. Nevertheless, the Bustamente government set up a system of compulsory social insurance, made laws against child labor, enforced the eight-hour day, and made similar improvements in the labor conditions of the workers. The rural Indians gained nothing from such measures, for Bustamente and most of the other members of his government were more interested in making a good thing of their power than in improving the lot of the people. The Indians of the Peruvian highlands were patient, however, and firmly convinced that *Pachacutí* would win the next elections, when he could really begin to move the earth.

Nowadays the upper class of Lima invariably cites the Bustamente administration as an example of the Apristas' incapacity to govern. The accusations are corruption, suppression of the opposition, and raiding of the treasury—the very charges that could be leveled against any Peruvian administration. No one can say that the situation was any worse under the democrats. However, all the blame for the shortcomings of this first democratic government in Peru is heaped on Haya de la Torre. The reactionaries do not mention that the government was in fact an ill-assorted coalition in which Haya de la Torre was merely the fifth wheel on the wagon.

While I was in Lima, I had to listen to many denunciations of the greed and incompetence of the Bustamente democrats. But no one bothered to say that Haya de la Torre's own integrity was above question and that he could scarcely be made responsible for the fiasco of the democratic experiment.

Had elections been held, there is no doubt that the Bustamente administration would have been succeeded by an Haya de la Torre government. For Haya de la Torre was not only a politician of sound ideas; he was also a remarkable speaker who could sway the masses. It was this very power that made him an object of suspicion to the oligarchy. This passionate opponent of dictatorship was likened by the upper classes to Hitler and Mussolini. This man who kept more strictly to the rules of the democratic game than any of his opponents was vilified as a leader of semifascist and semisocialist terrorists. The upper class became uneasier year by year, as the APRA continued to grow. The condor, symbol of the APRA, swooped over Peru on its gigantic wings and seemed on the point of descending upon Lima and settling there permanently.

The Peruvian masses had awakened. Under the weak Bustamente government a large number of strikes broke out. There was also a rash of political murders, as some of the Apristas who had previously been so violently repressed settled scores with their enemies. Haya de la Torre quarreled with Bustamente and in disappointment resigned from the government. As the situation approached a crisis, the oligarchy prepared its counterstroke. The army rose up and in October 1948 deposed the democrats. General Manuel Odría became military dictator.

Odría committed all the sins which (justly or unjustly) had been laid at the door of the Bustamente government. During his eight years in office he became one of the richest men in Lima. He treated his political opponents harshly. The APRA was outlawed and had to go underground once more. Again Haya de la Torre fled from an execution squad to the asylum of the Colombian Embassy. General Odría was burning to lay his hands on the APRA leader. The Peruvian army cherishes a special hatred for Haya de la Torre.

When the Bustamente government was obviously tottering, Haya de la Torre seemed about to abandon the methods of democracy for the methods of revolution. He must have recognized that he would never be allowed to come to power by legal means, not even if four-fifths of the people were behind him. The APRA attempted to anticipate the military coup and called upon the people to revolt. There were a number of local uprisings: in the Indian areas, in some provincial cities, and in the chief Peruvian port, Callao, where the marines lined their commanders against a wall and shot the lot. But in executing military officers the APRA had committed sacrilege. From that moment on, the military conceived its deathless hatred for Haya de la Torre. Determined to catch their quarry, who had taken refuge in the Colombian Embassy, Odría exchanged an endless series of notes with Bogotá. Colombia was currently being racked by the gang wars unleashed by the assassination of the leftist liberal party leader Gaitán. No one in a responsible position was inclined to sacrifice another leftist liberal and thereby worsen the disturbances at home. The Colombian Government therefore insistently demanded a safe-conduct for Haya de la Torre in keeping with international custom. Odría repeatedly refused, in defiance of the right of asylum and safe-conduct which has obtained in all Latin American countries since 1928. Even the World Court, in The Hague, was called in to decide on the life or death of Haya de la Torre.

A POLICY OF RECONCILIATION

For almost six years the APRA leader stayed inside the Colombian Embassy. Passers-by in Lima could see him when he leaned out the window or sat on the roof, reading. At last, in April 1954, world public opinion forced Odría to let his archenemy depart for exile in Europe. Two years later the dictator condescended to hold elections. He thought that by now the APRA had disintegrated. Since other Peruvian parties had been banned, there was no one of any importance to run against the candidate of the conservative party, Manuel Prado. In any case, the majority of the Indian population, who were opposed to the government, did not have the vote. Prado was elected president.

Prado was a banker, one of the richest men in Peru, and regarded as the prototype of the solidly conservative archreactionary politician. But he enlisted the co-operation of someone who was less concerned with the interests of the oligarchy than with the country's potential for development. Pedro Beltrán, premier and minister of finance in the Prado cabinet, was again identified with conservative circles, but he happened to be one of those modern industrialist conservatives who realize that a country cannot, in the long run, stay frozen in a political and social structure dating back to past centuries. Under Prado and Beltrán, a vigorous industrialization of Peru began. Note was taken of the abundance of fish in the Humboldt Current. Fish-meal factories sprang up everywhere along the Peruvian coast. The Peruvian fisheries, which had hitherto been an insignificant branch of the economy, grew into the fifth largest in the world. Amaro, a Japanese immigrant, made the most of the boom in fishing and within a short time became a multimillionaire. Thanks to its copper mines and steel plants with the most modern equipment, Peru could once more become a great metal producer. Beltrán dreamed of a highly industrialized Peru that would help supply the world's ever-growing hunger for metals and would, at the same time, solve its own economic difficulties.

In order to promote industrialization and to exploit the vast and largely unused resources of the country's interior, the population of the mountain areas had to be stirred out of its sleep. The Spaniards and the Peruvian dictators of the past had merely skimmed the cream of Peru's mineral wealth. They had taken the lives of their Indian forced laborers as recklessly as they had taken the most accessible treasures. Beltrán, however, was a representative of the industrial age; he knew that a sound, industrial economy can thrive only on a base of skilled, well-qualified labor.

Consequently Beltrán proposed a plan for the development of the Indians which in a number of respects surprisingly paralleled the plans for APRA. The Peruvian conservatives and the reformist Apristas found themselves in agreement in their practical aim, although their reasons for desiring Indian emancipation were quite different. President Prado lifted the ban on the APRA. In August 1957 Haya de la Torre returned home from European exile. His conservative rival, Beltrán, had no special animosity toward him. Indirectly, in fact, the APRA exerted a rather considerable influence upon the government's program of emancipation and industrialization.

In the course of its development, however, the APRA has become not only an advocate of Indo-Americanism but also the rallying point for many of the discontented and the rebellious forces in Peru. Although Haya de la Torre was willing to enter into a fruitful collaboration with the more flexible wing of the conservative party, extreme Apristas condemned the alliance with Peru's captains of industry. There were also nationalistic APRA groups who were against Haya de la Torre's pro-Americanism. Various factions splintered off from the mother party. One of the most talented of the Apristas, a man who represented the strongly social reformist wing, Fernando Belaúnde Terry, finally broke with Haya de la Torre and founded the *Acción Popular,* which took a much more nationalistic and socialistic stand than the APRA. Belaúnde's defection from Haya de la Torre was so radical that the two former friends became bitter enemies.

Haya de la Torre is an intellectual idealist, Belaúnde a pragmatic politician. The Acción Popular could not offer a clear party program like the APRA; its strength came chiefly from the personality of Fernando Belaúnde. But it won the favor of a great many voters. The Indians, the fight for whose human rights lay at the heart of the APRA program, could never have helped Haya de la Torre to win an election, for the overwhelming majority of them were illiterate and therefore disenfranchised. Political decisions were made by those among the middle and lower classes who could read and write, and among them were a great many socially disadvantaged and underprivileged Peruvians of both white skins and brown. Belaúnde carried on his agitation among these groups, concentrating his fire on the working-class quarters of the cities, the industrial regions, and the slums. Since he took a far more progressivist tone than Haya de la Torre, he appealed to a great many of the discontented and won away many of the APRA's former followers.

As new elections approached once more in 1962, after six years of the conservatives' government of national reconciliation, the following situation had arisen in Peru: four men were running for the presidency—Haya de la Torre, Belaúnde, Beltrán, and ex-Dictator Odría. Beltrán had scarcely any chance, for the oligarchy and the military had long since abandoned this lukewarm conservative and gone over to the rightist totalitarian *Odristas.* Haya de la Torre was considered the favorite. By his gentleman's agreement with the conservatives, he had promoted internal peace. He knew that he had the United States behind him and he believed firmly in his popularity. Belaúnde was an unpredictable factor, since it was difficult to estimate how much enthusiasm his nationalistic, reformist program had aroused in the people. General Odría hoped to profit from the division of the APRA into two hostile parties.

The Peruvian constitution provides that a presidential candidate must win at least one-third of all the votes in order to assume the presidency. If none of these candidates receives a third of the vote, the congress chooses among the front-runners the man it prefers.

Haya de la Torre won the election of 1962, but he did not receive the requisite percentage of the vote, since his former follower and present opponent, Belaúnde, captured many of the APRA votes in cities and industrial regions. Belaúnde had the second largest number of votes, followed by ex-Dictator Odría. Immediately after the election, however, the Peruvian military made it abundantly clear that it would not accept Haya de la Torre as the appointed president. If Haya de la Torre did not withdraw, there would be a civil war. The army went so far as to demand that the APRA give its votes to its former persecutor, Odría, to prevent the reformer Belaúnde from taking power.

Haya de la Torre had to withdraw in order to forestall a military revolt. His withdrawal did not, however, help Peru achieve a democratic government. The army pulled all the stops in its efforts to crush its old enemies. First the results of the election were challenged. In fact there had been a number of irregularities, as there are in every Peruvian election, but these had not really affected the outcome. The military, however, used these as a pretext to depose and arrest President Prado. A military junta took power, composed of the chiefs of the three branches of the armed services.

AND STILL ANOTHER COUP

It was a bloodless *coup d'état* that proceeded like a well-rehearsed play. Prado had refused the military's demand to annul the election. In Lima, however, it is said that he was quite prepared for the consequences of his intransigence. Upper-class Peruvians will tell you, with a wink, that the president waited impatiently for his arrest, his bags already packed. The one thing that annoyed him, they say, is that the colonel assigned to arrest him appeared at the Presidential Palace in field uniform. "How do you dare come before your president not wearing dress uniform?" Prado is said to have snapped at him. The surprised colonel came to attention, saluted, and stammered:

"But Mr. President, your arrest is a revolutionary act, after all. For a revolution we have to wear field uniform."

Whether Prado, in spite of his former amity with the APRA, did or did not have a secret agreement with the military rebels can scarcely be determined. It may well be, for his protest against the rule of bayonets was brief and unconvincing. After a few weeks he was allowed to depart for Paris. In an interview there, Prado is said to have spoken of the new dictators as Peruvian patriots and even as his "friends."

The military revolt was hailed enthusiastically by ex-Dictator Odría. He, too, assured the military junta of his friendship and hoped they would help him come to power once more. Belaúnde and Haya de la Torre denounced the new regime in vain. A general strike called by the unions had no effect on political developments. The APRA leader asked for asylum once more—this time in the Venezuelan Embassy. The white upper class in Lima was pleased that the specter of Haya de la Torre had once more been exorcised. The populace, on the other hand, was profoundly depressed, and the Indians of the mountains became even more rebellious than they had been before.

The Peruvian military revolt of 1962 disturbed the United States greatly, and cast graver doubts on the possibility of democratizing Latin America than all the other violent uprisings of recent years on the southern continent. While the military in other countries could argue that they had only wished to prevent leftist radicals from coming to power, the action of the Peruvian military had been directed against a centrist notably friendly to the United States.

Washington reacted impulsively by breaking off relations with Peru. President Kennedy stated that the military revolt against the constitutional democratic government violated the common aims of the Alliance for Progress. The Alliance, he pointed out, obligated the governments of the Western Hemisphere both to social and economic collaboration and to the strengthening of democratic institutions. American economic aid to Peru was immediately halted.

How far Kennedy's conception of democracy was from that of the Peruvian oligarchy is dramatized by the reply of Pérez Godoy, the military dictator: "Washington evidently does not understand that we have solved the problem of preserving the democracy in our country in the Peruvian way."

Washington, in fact, did not understand. The United States recognized the Peruvian military regime on condition that the juntas would promise to hold free elections within a year. Perhaps one of the main reasons for this forgiving spirit is the fact that American businessmen have some eight hundred million dollars invested in Peru.

The military government kept its word. It took the precaution, however, to exclude its archenemy, Haya de la Torre, permanently from political life. A law was passed providing that no Peruvian who had ever been sentenced by a court might run for the presidency. Haya de la Torre had in fact been sentenced by a Peruvian court at the time the APRA was being mercilessly persecuted. The military junta hoped this would spell the end of the APRA. The result was, however, that many previous APRA voters switched to Fernando Belaúnde's *Acción Popular*.

THE CONDOR'S CLIPPED WINGS

Haya de la Torre was a man of sixty-eight in 1963, when his APRA once more entered an election campaign. He had been forced to make compromises. He had gradually acquired the air of a middle-class conservative and—at least according to the charges of his opponent Belaúnde—had allowed foreign sugar companies and industrialists to pay his campaign expenses. The long decades of persecution had worn away his revolutionary ardor. He clung steadfastly to only one principle: his belief in Indo-America, in the rebirth of the Indian spirit.

Many white voters had been deterred from supporting the APRA because of their complex about the Indians. Belaúnde, however, did not talk about the Indians so frequently. He spoke in highly general terms about the Peruvian people and thus succeeded in winning over a number of reform-minded members of the upper class. The APRA had become a condor with clipped wings and blunt claws. Belaúnde won the election of 1963, and since he had not spilled the blood of generals, or proclaimed the ideals of an Indo-America, the military did not, this time, interfere.

Belaúnde is not a fascinating personality. He does not have the charisma of Haya de la Torre. Rather, he is a typical Latin American social reformer. His Acción Popular is an illegitimate child of the APRA, somewhat more pallid, less distinctive, less intellectual than

the party from which it sprang. The words in which Belaúnde out-
lined his program when he took office strike one as extremely general
and deliberately noncommittal. Apparently Belaúnde wished not to
give offense to any element in Peru.

"I intend," the new president declared, "to provide the Peruvian
people with the bread that nourishes them, the roof that shelters
them, and the work that sustains and ennobles them." Nevertheless,
Belaúnde had imbibed enough of the APRA spirit so that he had his
government messages translated into the Indian languages, Quechua
and Aymara. He has endeavored to steal something of Haya de la
Torre's nimbus among the Indians by making frequent journeys into
the mountain territory and addressing crowds at village election ral-
lies. Like Haya de la Torre, Belaúnde has also sponsored agrarian
reform. The result of his land-reform laws, however, was the sudden
seizure of land by Indians in many parts of the country. The new
president then had some trouble convincing the Indians that even
under the aegis of the Acción Popular they could not take whatever they pleased. It is questionable whether the mountain Indians
will be satisfied with his education program, which envisages a slow
assimilation of the Indians into the Latin cultural sphere. Haya de la
Torre wanted to revive Indian culture; Belaúnde wants to integrate it.

It is gratifying that Peru at present has a democratic and social-
reformist government engaged in a large-scale development program
to combat the feudalistic pattern of the past. But the Apristas think
that Belaúnde is only circling cautiously around Peru's real problem,
that of the Indians. The Indians will not become full and equal
members of Peruvian society by assimilation into the Latin proletariat.
As long as every successful Indian or mestizo endeavors to become a
Latin as quickly as possible, the real forces of vitality in the Peruvian
highlands will never be released.

"Peru is a colony ruled by sixty or eighty families," an APRA proclamation reads. "They fear the people, they fear the masses of
the Indios. They are evading reality, evading a just decision. They
are attempting to postpone all matters that concern the Indian."

Belaúnde rules in Lima. In the Indian villages of the highlands,
however, Haya de la Torre, even as a condor with clipped wings,
remains "The Man Who Moves the Earth." Perhaps that is the greatest
tragedy of Peru: that her most important political thinker has never
been given a real chance.

THE CITY WITH THE GOLDEN MASK

One does not notice the *barriadas* at first. They are on the edges of the cities in the lowlands of the Rimac Valley, on barren hills, or in the sands of the desert. If one glances casually at them, as one drives past, they look colorful, gay, like a child's clutter of toys. It is not immediately apparent that these are slums, perhaps the saddest slums in South America.

In the days of the Spaniards, the Peruvian capital was called "Golden" Lima. The present-day visitor sees no good reason for this bombastic epithet. Perhaps the conquistadors were only thinking of the Inca gold they had annexed here. For architecturally and artistically, aside from a few churches, the palaces of some nobles, and patrician houses, the Spaniards left no special marks of grandeur upon Lima. I was struck by the old Renaissance fountain on the Plaza de Armas, by the archbishop's palace and the Rotte Tagle Palace, now quarters for the Foreign Ministry. In Cartagena and Cuzco, the architectural achievements of the Spaniards are far more impressive. But Lima seems only to have been a source of treasure; the Spaniards invested remarkably little in the capital of their richest colony.

Toward the end of the eighteenth century a few feeble efforts were made to transform Lima into a second Versailles. However, Viceroy Don Manuel Amat, who ruled Peru at the time, is remembered not so much for his political and architectural enterprises as for his famous affair with the half-Indian actress Miquita Villega. In order to please her—Perricholi, as she was popularly called—Amat laid out parks, built churches, palaces, a bullfight arena, a country retreat, and a water-lined avenue with arcades, fountains, walls, and ramps in a somewhat adulterated French style. Amat's buildings are unimportant as architecture, neither pure in style nor impressive for any special magnificence. They do not call to mind Versailles; instead they remind one of the permanent pinched economy of the Peruvian viceroys.

An architectural monstrosity, immortalizing the bad taste of several generations, assumed its present form around the turn of the century. This is the gigantic government building on the Plaza de Armas. It is flanked on one side by the archbishop's palace and on the other by a monument to the conquistador Pizarro. The front entrances are guarded by soldiers of Indian appearance, dressed in gaudy uniforms which seem to have been borrowed from a French operetta. At the back of the building the Rimac flows sluggishly in its dirty bed, and on the other side of the stream are house fronts gray with age, their stucco cracked, defaced by peeling posters with screaming election slogans.

PIZARRO AND THE SMELL OF MONEY

The cornerstone of the cathedral on the Plaza de Armas was laid by Francisco Pizarro. The cavernous church would be acceptable, though not so impressive as the cathedrals of Cuzco and Cartagena, had it not been adorned with surpassingly wretched paintings. The Spaniards do not seem to have imported talented painters and sculptors into Peru; and Lima has scarcely profited by the great gifts of native Indian artists. The most gruesome and depressing sight in the cathedral, however, is a glass coffin displaying the mortal remains of Pizarro, the most brutal of all the conquistadors. The one-time swineherd and subsequent ravager of the Inca Empire was mummified in the Indian manner and remains preserved in the flesh to this day.

The mummified Pizarro lies with teeth bared in a horrible grin. Pizarro on the monument to the left of the government office building towers up balefully in the misty air of Lima, and has remained a symbol of the white invaders' harsh rule over the brown descendants of the Incas. The monument, however, was being put to sensible use when I first saw it. Some union men had hung posters on Pizarro and his pedestal. The unionists were making a silent demonstration for the release of opposition politicians whom the then ruling military junta had arrested. Pizarro looked haughtily out above the heads of the demonstrators as if they were vermin.

In the two main shopping streets of the heart of the city, Jirón Unión and Carabaya, tourists seek and find another aspect of "Golden" Lima. Here are the jewelers' shops with their famous gold and silver jewelry. It is a rare traveler who can resist the urge to buy Peruvian jewelry, although gold and silver are not a whit cheaper in Peru than in Europe or North America. But Peruvian craftsmen have preserved some of the one-time greatness of the Indian goldsmiths' art. Necklaces, bracelets, and earrings are carved with Indian motifs: stylized llamas, miniature gods, and so on. The Indians are despised, the Indian past slandered, and pro-Indian parties crushed, but since Spanish Peruvians have proved not particularly creative, imitations of Indian craftwork are offered to the tourists.

Broad avenues and boulevards, big hotels, banks and government office buildings, European-looking cafés and supermodern department stores determine the general appearance of the city. It is a very pleasant city for shopping—if you have the money. Because of its vigorous export trade, Peru imposes no foreign-exchange restrictions. Consequently, goods from all over the world are piled up in the shopping centers and supermarkets: French cosmetics, Russian caviar, American canned goods, German sausages, Strasbourg *pâté,* Chinese delicacies, Italian shoes, Viennese woolen goods. There is nothing you cannot buy in Lima—if you have the money. And people do have money in Lima. Although the epithet "Golden" may have been rather inaccurately applied to Lima in the past, it is accurate today.

Elegant residential suburbs stretch out in all directions, so rich in greenery as to make one almost forget the kind of landscape in which the Peruvian capital is actually situated. Lima was a small oasis in the Peruvian coastal desert, watered only by the modest stream known as the Rimac. Today all of suburban Lima is a vast flowering garden. Fine country houses and luxurious mansions lie close to exclusive clubs, tennis courts, and swimming pools. These suburbs are where most of the European and American businessmen live; some of the embassies are also located there. And there the oligarchy resides—far from the hectic pace of the metropolis, in the midst of well-tended estates lavish with flowers the year round. Bougainvillaea drips and foams over the walls of Miraflores, one of the choice residential areas near the coast. Perhaps Lima has so few and such sparse public parks because every citizen of means lives inside his own park. These residential quarters literally and unashamedly smell, very sweetly indeed, of money. And if you have previously visited Cuzco, and the mountain villages, the perfume of the luxury displayed in Lima takes your breath away. I have talked with many non-Peruvians who have settled in Lima. All of them say it is an extremely pleasant place to live. And so it is. It is a delight to live in golden Lima—if you happen to belong to the class that has money. The plateau is far away.

THE BARRIADAS

One-sixth of the total population of Peru lives in the vicinity of Lima. And if you explore a bit, you discover that the social cancers of Peru are eating their way into the capital from all sides. There are the shabby tenements and streets on the other bank of the Rimac, over which stretch gigantic banners of APRA and the *Acción Popular*. And then there are the *barriadas*. The barriadas of Lima are for the most part improvised slums whose destiny is still uncertain. They may develop into regular quarters of the city or they may crumble under the assault of bulldozers.

On the eastern edge of Lima, the foothills of the Andes begin, the Cordillera Negra. An hour's car ride takes you to the mountains; in three hours you can reach the highest railroad station in the world, at an altitude of over fifteen thousand feet. The Andes east of Lima are rich in copper, but the lives of the inhabitants are none the better for it. Innumerable Indians and mestizos eke out the barest livelihoods as wretched, hungry, and futureless as their fellows in the heart of the one-time Inca Empire. In increasing numbers they trickle down into the capital and there, on bare rocks or dry desert soil, set up their tents of mats or their shacks built of odds and ends of wood. For a long time Lima has been unable to say what its population is, for the number of squatters is incalculable and their habits unpredictable.

In the course of time, some of these slums have been provided with electricity. Thus they have been legalized after a fashion, and when darkness falls and lights are turned on in the shacks, the impression from the distance is one of something approaching respectability. Other immigrants from the mountains are not so fortunate. As chance would have it, the barren rock or desert sand on which they have settled may belong to one of the powerful men of the country. Land is an important commodity in Lima. The landowner usually calls the police. Regular battles between the police and the squatters are common. The end of the story is that police clubs and bulldozers transform the slum back into barren desert. The expelled pick out a new patch of bare ground and try again.

They pour into the city every day, men from the highlands who often come vast distances, magically drawn by the golden mask of the capital. They settle down wherever there seems to be a patch of unused land. They defend themselves with stones and bare hands against the power of the government. They riot and cling to their hope of appropriating at least a faint gleam of the golden splendor. Along the highway which leads to the desert stand ragged children, begging from every passing automobile. They are collecting money for a monk who on his own initiative is looking after some of the innumerable orphans of the slums. With the aid of his protégés he has erected a few wretched barracks in which he lives with his charges, feeds them, and gives them some schooling. He is dependent upon the charity of passing motorists, for, rich as the higher clergy is in Peru, the lower clergy must beg if it wishes to help the poor.

In Lima the *barriadas* are ignored, as the misery of the mountain Indian is ignored. The riots in the squatters' settlements are attributed not to the conditions that violate the basic dignities of man, but to the seditious activity of demagogues and agitators. In the eyes of the oligarchy, it is not destitution that causes the ferment among the lower classes; the fault lies with all who criticize and wish to change such conditions. The rich in the golden quarters of Lima live their lives with fantastic thoughtlessness, never questioning their right to every luxury. Social life has a feverish note of artificial gaiety. The members of the oligarchy eat from silver dishes and close their eyes as they roll past the *barriadas* in their big imported cars.

Yet the artificial gaiety betrays the underlying anxieties of the Lima moneyed aristocracy, anxieties they will not admit even to themselves. Profits and inherited money are hastily invested abroad. Commercial enterprise and initiative are displayed chiefly by Europeans and Americans. The oligarchy, whose members consider themselves the incarnation of the true Peru, no longer believe in Peru.

After the military coup of 1962, the first reaction of the upper classes was a sigh of relief. Nevertheless, it was obvious to every prosperous Peruvian that the generals could not retain their power for very long in the face of American opposition. The next president would undoubtedly be an agrarian reformer. Consequently, all those who would be affected by land reform availed themselves of the breathing spell afforded by the military regime to take timely precautions. Large landholdings were divided up and parceled out *pro forma*. They were transferred to strong men, were even deeded to children and still-unborn family members. Every stratagem was used to make them unavailable for a future land-reform program.

As had been expected, the president who followed the military regime, Fernando Belaúnde, was indeed an agrarian reformer. He found himself balked by the mountain of bequests and legal complications, so much so that his program of speedy agrarian reform ground to a virtual halt. No Peruvian, no matter how feudal-minded, openly questioned the necessity of agrarian reform, for land conditions in Peru were a world-wide scandal. Far more politic to procrastinate, to see to it that the new land-reform laws had no teeth in them. Hasty measures, the landowners contended, could do the country the greatest harm; it was madness to turn well-managed, high-yielding land over to incompetent illiterates who would let it go to ruin. The Indio, they repeated for the thousandth time, was incompetent, dull-witted, a coca addict, drifting through life in narcotic dreams.

When, in reply to such statements, I cited the achievements of the Indians in the days of the Inca Empire, I was told that in those days the Indian had been a slave of the state and had worked only under compulsion. Freedom, the argument ran, was bad for the Indian, and exposed him as the stupid semihuman he really was. The proponents of this theory did not mention that in the days of the Spaniards also the Indians had been nothing but slaves of the state—under far more oppressive conditions than in the past. As alleged "state slaves" under the Incas, they had built a great civilization, but in the four and a half centuries since the conquest, in spite of all coercion, they had accomplished nothing of importance. Quietly and unobtrusively, they have lived in misery and died in obscurity. The brutalization of the Indios, a favorite topic of conversation in Lima, is clearly not a racial characteristic, but a consequence of colonial rule.

A DRUGGED PEOPLE

Any journey into the parched vicinity of the capital vividly reveals the vast capabilities of Peruvian Indians even in the days before the rigid Inca organization. Lima itself stands upon vast ruins from pre-Inca times. To the north and south of the capital are some of the most famous ruined cities and temples of the Peruvian coastal cultures: Cajamarquilla, Ancón, Chancay, and splendid Pachacamac, with its magnificent terraced temple. The scene is the same wherever you go in the Peruvian coastal desert. Suddenly the tan-colored wasteland is

crossed by a river valley. Above the valley, great urban ruins worn
by wind and weather become visible. Gargantuan walls and remains
of buildings tower into the sky. Crumbling adobe citadels and enormous temple enclosures occupy the highest points in the landscape.
These ruins, already reduced almost to dust, do not in themselves
disclose the creative achievements of the coastal Indians. Their finest
artifacts and the story of their lives lie under the ground.

On the margins of these crumbled adobe cities, buried beneath
rubble, are innumerable graves. Ever since the conquest, vast quantities of gold and silver ornaments have been dug up out of these graves
—usually, alas, not by scientists, but by grave robbers who melted
down the precious things they found. The mummies were wrapped
in textiles of a fineness that cannot be duplicated even by modern
looms. Along with gold and silver ornaments, the Indians buried a few
huacos, ceramics of singular artistic quality, in every grave. These
huacos are a marvelous record of the lives, culture, and government
of the Indians who inhabited this region a thousand to fifteen hundred
years ago.

Here in the coastal desert, the traveler becomes vividly aware that,
long before the founding of the Inca Empire, Peru had a highly developed civilization. The coastal Indians settled wherever the river
valleys crossed the desert. Along these rivers there was water, the
great prerequisite for agriculture, for founding cities and for forming
small states. The fruitful soil, however, was so precious that the Indians used it solely for agricultural purposes. They built their houses
only on the arid desert sands. Every river valley, from the extreme
north to the extreme south of Peru, spawned its own distinctive kind
of urban architecture, ceramics, and weaving.

THE DEMON COCAINE

But those same Indians who created high cultures almost Greek in
their emphasis on life in this present world, and Etruscan in their
veneration for the dead, now look dully out at you from mask-like
faces. They appear sad, resigned, apathetic. Sudden cold hatred
flashes in their eyes only when they think themselves unobserved. They
till the sparse soil by methods more primitive than those used in
the days of the Incas, with hoes and stone clubs which serve to break
up the clods. Wherever you see Indians, you will notice that the

muscles of their jaws are moving. They are chewing coca. The majority of them seem to have succumbed to cocaine addiction. This image of the lethargic, drugged Indio who would rather sit in a stupor than lift a hand to improve his condition is forever being evoked by the oligarchy when talk arises of Indian emancipation.

Why do whole nations become drug addicts? In Europe, too, in times of acute scarcity or depression, whole classes of the people have resorted to alcohol. When conditions are so bad that men have not the strength to picture a better future for themselves and their families, they all too easily seek refuge in intoxicants. In pre-Inca and Inca times, the leaves of the coca plant were known to be stimulants which helped the Indians perform unusual exertion in the thin air of the mountains. Coca stimulates, dulls pain, and represses feelings of hunger. To the llama drivers and construction workers in the Inca Empire, coca was no more harmful a poison than is nicotine for the European working under the nervous tensions of an industrialized society. In Inca days, the Indian did not suffer from a pronounced cocaine addiction.

The Incas were well aware of the potential dangers of coca. They designated the shrub which bears the scientific name of *Erythroxylon coca* the "plant of the gods." Like everything in the Inca Empire, coca was subject to strict regulation. The Inca priests boiled coca leaves as incense. Indian doctors used coca as an anesthetic in operations. Coca powder was employed for the healing of wounds. The state doled out the precious leaves only to those subjects of the Inca who had special tasks calling for unusual stamina, such as messengers on the mountain roads, or soothsayers who would prophesy from a trance. In pre-Columbian Peru, unauthorized persons were never allowed to grow habituated to the poison.

It is, therefore, an infamous falsification of history when white Peruvians today maintain that cocaine addiction is a hereditary vice of the Indians. For it was the Spaniards who enlarged the Inca coca plantations and distributed the poisonous plant freely among the people. They hit on the idea of paying the Indians in coca. The sacred plant of Inca days was profaned and dispensed among the masses as a cheap way to pay the Indians for their work. Spanish landowners controlled the coca crop. Thirty years after the conquest of Peru, the Spanish historian Pedro de Cieza de León could write:

"Many have become rich men by raising the coca plant and selling it in the Indian markets. Coca has another great advantage: the tithe paid from the coca crop provides the greater part of the income of the bishops, the canons, and the clergy of the cathedral of Cuzco."

In the Republic of Peru, the coca trade became a state monopoly. The undernourished and often physically abused serfs on the latifundia cannot be blamed for having fallen upon the coca in order to anesthetize their souls and the nerves of their stomachs. Even estates owned by the Church followed the practice of paying the Indian workers with hard liquor and the leaves of the narcotic plant. On many haciendas this is the custom to this day. In the course of centuries the Indians have become so used to coca that they are unwilling to work unless they receive regular rations of the plant. Or rather, to put it bluntly, they cannot work without coca because they have become addicts. If the narcotic were taken away from them overnight, they would collapse.

Cocaine is an alkaloid which has long been used in medicine. It is employed for local anesthesia. Small doses of cocaine stimulate the functioning of the brain, produce a more cheerful attitude toward life, diminish the requirements for sleep and food, and give men the feeling that they can accomplish remarkable things. Persistent use of larger doses of cocaine, however, impairs the capacity to think and produces physical and intellectual degeneration which may ultimately lead to complete loss of will, to indifference, lethargy, and insensitivity to all impressions from the outside world. Thus, cocaine can be used to produce ideal slaves. Cocaine addiction is even harder to cure than morphine addiction. Virtually nothing is done in Peru to wean the Indians away from their coca chewing. The very classes who have reduced the Indians to apathetic, will-less creatures now shrug their shoulders and aver that a people of coca chewers are good-for-nothing and cannot profit by emancipation.

Yet in spite of their coca addiction, the Indians have not entirely lost their will to act. A good many landowners have been murdered by their "apathetic" Indios. Of their own accord, Indians have attempted agrarian reform by forcibly occupying untilled fields. Belaúnde, the reformist president, has had to use all his eloquence in the *cabildos abiertos*, the open councils of the Indians, to prevent the descendants of the Incas from making a general assault upon the rich lands of the latifundia. In the sierra, the trackless mountains, the authorities have long been hunting an Indian dentist who has called for open resistance against the government. The dull-witted coca chewers have found ways to hide this rebel leader. No one can read in their faces the extent to which they are in league with him.

WHERE IS PERU GOING?

Belaúnde has conceived a variety of plans to resolve the contradictions which wrack his country. He would like to integrate the Indians into the modern social and economic order. He would like, with American aid, to open up the vast and still not wholly explored territory of Peruvian Amazonia, which Peru took from Ecuador. But since he is a democratic president who must obey the decisions of the congress, not a dictator, many of his ideas come to grief in the bureaucratic machinery. The congress is dominated by Haya de la Torre and his Apristas; and the APRA has far more radical notions about Indian emancipation. The Peruvian Senate, however, is dominated by ex-Dictator Odría; and the *Odristas* are scarcely wild about granting the president the funds he needs for his development program. The Americans, for their part, would rather work with their traditional friend Haya de la Torre. Belaúnde is not regarded as unconditionally pro-American. Standard Oil has already had a few bouts with him, for Belaúnde asserts that the American oil company owes some seventy-five million dollars in taxes. He demands that Standard Oil pay up or be expropriated.

The ruling circles in Lima are skeptical about democracy—either because they are against democracy in itself or because they recall the corrupt regime of Bustamente. Belaúnde, too, they say, makes a practice of rewarding his followers with the juiciest administrative posts. In fact, the Acción Popular has no big "angels"; it relies upon the modest contributions of friends and founding members. Of course the dictators and conservatives enriched themselves at the expense of the Peruvian state. It would not be so illogical for Belaúnde's People's Party to want to have its share in the available booty.

Dissension broke out in the Belaúnde party in September 1963, when Marshal Tito came on a visit to various Latin American countries. Belaúnde is one of the reform politicians who would like to be somewhat independent of Washington. The fact that the Peruvian president greeted the Yugoslav chief of state with the characteristic Latin American embrace caused quite a hubbub in "white" Lima.

Clerical circles in particular were highly exercised over this show of cordiality to a Marxist.

Nevertheless, the *Acción Popular* won the regional elections at the end of 1963. It is currently much stronger than the APRA and the Odría party together. That part of the Peruvian people who have the franchise have manifested their confidence in the democratic president. At the same time, however, new Indian rebellions flared in the vicinity of Cuzco—a sign that the descendants of the Incas are not as contented with Belaúnde's reform program as the white and half-white voters. Naturally, the word is that these rebellions are directed by communists. In the era of Belaúnde, too, many Peruvians still see red when the oppressed fight for their rights.

In order to make a public demonstration of the president's sincere desire for reform, the Acción staged a march to the government office buildings on Belaúnde's birthday. Belaúnde was presented with great piles of hoes and spades to be given to the poor Indios. This theatrical bit did not work quite as planned, for on the same day the APRA likewise marched through the streets of Lima to protest the slow tempo of Indian emancipation. Belaúnde had to call out the police to keep his hoe-and-spade marchers from tangling with the APRA marchers.

Sooner or later the mass misery in Peru will drive the Indios and cholos to acts of desperation. If the landless inhabitants of the Andes are not appeased by a comprehensive agrarian reform, they are bound to resort to violence one of these days. In much of the highlands the Indians have long been in more or less open rebellion. Nobody knows who is leading the Indian partisans in the valleys of the Andes. Like the Bolivian Indians in 1952, the Peruvian Indians have now awakened. Is their struggle hopeless? No one can answer this question. In Peru, as in Bolivia, the horrors the Indians have suffered since the Spanish conquest has left a heritage which weighs heavily upon all political and social relationships.

THE GATEWAY TO THE SUN

The Incas considered Cuzco the navel of the world and Lake Titicaca the womb of mankind. According to the legends handed down by the Indian chroniclers, the first Incas came from the Islands of the Sun and the Moon, in Lake Titicaca, and spreading out from there, acquired dominion over all the Andes. The present-day lake dwellers, builders of balsa-wood boats and rafts of rushes, proudly call themselves "the oldest people in the world."

It is not known whether the Uru Indians of Lake Titicaca once had a culture similar to that of the Quechua and Aymara Indians. The Urus themselves say they did. Their myths relate that long ago they founded a gigantic empire in the highlands and took up their abode in the lake only after a natural catastrophe had put an end to this empire. On the northern shores of Lake Titicaca still stand mysterious tower-like structures fifteen to thirty-five feet in height, the so-called *chulpas,* which cannot be traced to either the Quechua or the Aymara. The mysterious *chulpas* may be the remains of a long since vanished Uru culture. We simply do not know.

The Urus live on rushes and from rushes. Their rush huts stand on great islands of rushes which drift about in the water or are anchored by long taproots. They fish from boats or rafts made of rushes and kill birds with bolos, which they throw with great skill. They dry the meat of the birds and exchange this and dried fish with the Quechua and Aymara Indians for potatoes, corn, and millet.

According to the recent ethnological research, the Urus are among the first Indians to have immigrated into South America. They are said to have been established around Lake Titicaca as long as seven thousand years ago. It is unfortunate that the Urus cannot read or write and that their mythology is so vague, for these Indians have witnessed everything that took place in the past, in the whole area around Lake Titicaca: the rise of the pre-Inca cultures, the birth of the Inca Empire, the great expansion and decline of the foremost civilization of South America. Above all, the Urus would be in a position to tell us about that strange advanced culture south of Lake Titicaca which has inspired a whole history of speculation—the culture of Tiahuanaco.

SOUTH AMERICA'S MOST PUZZLING HIGH CULTURE

The Urus know nothing about Tiahuanaco, and the Aymara, whose ancestors once created that extraordinary culture, know no more. Tiahuanaco was radically erased from the memory of the peoples who lived there. Until a few decades ago it was impossible to say who had built the gigantic monoliths of Tiahuanaco or when they had been built. The Incas regarded the structures as products of their own pre-history. The Spaniards had scarcely any inkling that a Tiahuanaco culture had existed, and made only a few vague remarks about the mysterious domed buildings. The first archaeologists who dug there half a century ago thought they had found one of the oldest of human cultures. Thor Heyerdahl believed Tiahuanaco had been the source of the Polynesian megalithic cultures.

Today the Carbon 14 test and other modern methods of investigation have determined that Tiahuanaco is barely a thousand years old. However, these modern tests cannot tell us why the Aymara built this titanic temple complex on the barren plateau south of Lake Titicaca, or why it fell to ruin. Less is known about this fascinating culture than almost any other high culture in the world. Links, however, have been discovered between Tiahuanaco and the coastal cultures of Peru. Ethnologists are apt to speak of several Tiahuanaco stylistic eras which influenced art in broad areas of Peru and Bolivia before the coming of the Inca. But the ruins themselves are silent.

I visited many pre-Columbian ruins in Latin America. I explored the fortress of Sacsahuamán, climbed up and down the steps of Machu Picchu, lost myself in the labyrinths of Cajamarquilla, strolled through the temple of Pachacamac, and looked at the stone figures of gods and men of the Chibcha and the Maya. But nothing I saw stirred me so deeply, nothing seemed to me so remote from all earthly things, than those upright or fallen monoliths on the rust-colored Altiplano under the searing sun of Bolivia.

Tiahuanaco looks as though creatures from another planet had hewed gigantic blocks of stone in an alien manner and piled them one atop the other. Then, for inexplicable reasons, they set up in the midst of this chaos of stone a gate adorned with fantastic symbols—the Sun Gate. The gate leads into nothing; it simply stands there in the midst of the Altiplano, the great Bolivian plateau. The titanic images of gods and the towering calendar stones also seem to be simply standing there. Only if we study the maze of archaeological excavations which riddle the ground at Tiahuanaco does the arrangement of the mysterious stones take on meaning.

A palatial structure designed for meetings must once have stood here. This may be deduced from the many stone benches which unmistakably show a systematic arrangement. It may also be assumed that the Sun Gate was the entrance to a temple. The calendar stones are not placed at random; they are arranged precisely in a line of sight directed at a still-visible point in the distant mountain chain. All indications are that Tiahuanaco was once the greatest center of Indian worship in the Andes region.

What is most stirring about Tiahuanaco is the incredible loneliness of its situation. The rolling plateau, with its blowing yellow grass, looks altogether deserted; the cold, piercingly blue sky, high and cloudless, seems very far away. The only living beings around the ruins, aside from Bolivian, American, and German archaeologists, are a few Indian boys and llama drivers. The llama drivers pass indifferently by the ancient stones. The brown-skinned children offered me shards stolen from the excavation trenches. There are no organized tours to Tiahuanaco as there are to the Peruvian Inca ruins. There are no facilities for staying overnight in the nearby village. The railroad which runs from La Paz to the southern shore of Lake Titicaca stops very briefly at Tiahuanaco station. Up here you feel as if you are alone with the gods of the High Andes.

In recent years these gods have moved into La Paz. A mighty monolith from the ancient temple city and many statues, some of them reproductions, now adorn a large plaza in the Bolivian metropolis. Even there, in the heart of the city, the gods of Tiahuanaco affect you strangely. You must ascend a few steps to come close to them. But they preserve their distance; they tower into the blue sky as sublimely as they do in their original site on the Altiplano. It is as though the Indian inhabitants of La Paz still feel a certain timidity in their presence. Everywhere else in the Bolivian capital, Indians swarm around the plazas, monuments, the corners of houses, the markets, and walls. You find them squatting on their heels wherever there is some idle space. But here in the plaza of the old gods you scarcely see a living soul.

In Bolivia, the Indio revival has barely begun. Bolivians have not yet repossessed their Tiahuanaco past as Mexico has the past of the Toltecs and Aztecs. Bolivia, as yet, has no artist who—like the Mexican Diego Rivera—extols the Indian cultural heritage and denounces the Spanish conquerors. But then, so little is known about Tiahuanaco, compared to the vast information amassed about the Toltecs and Aztecs. The monuments themselves tell us that a thousand years ago the highlands of Bolivia were dominated by a culturally advanced people who probably subjugated the south Peruvian coastal regions, and who created an empire capable of mobilizing enough manpower for such remarkable architectural feats. But we know nothing specific whatsoever about the history of that empire.

A FRAGMENT OF ANCIENT AMERICA

The deity of Tiahuanaco is frequently depicted with tears in its eyes. The tears run down over the face in the form of serpents. The people of Bolivia have shed many tears since those monuments were first carved. The MNR revolution was not a genuine Indian revolution; it was a revolution of the cholos, the mixed breeds. But the cholos who for a while governed Bolivia awakened the heirs of Tiahuanaco from a sleep four hundred years long. The Indian in Bolivia became a completely different person from the Peruvian Indian.

La Paz is some twelve thousand feet above sea level, and is thus the highest capital city in the world. It is, without doubt, the most remarkable metropolis on our planet. It is difficult to say what the magic of La Paz is. Perhaps it is the vast number of Indians in brilliantly colored clothing who pour out of the adobe houses and stroll through their streets with their characteristic "llama gait." Perhaps it is that underneath all of the veneer of civilization something of ancient America is still alive in this mountain city.

La Paz is astonishing at first glance. At an altitude of about thirteen thousand feet you ride toward what appears to be a crack in the earth, a slash in the Altiplano made by a gigantic knife. Gradually the gorge opens up before you, the valley of the Río Choqueyapu, and you realize that it is completely covered with houses, down into depths that you can only dimly perceive. The adobe huts of the suburbs rise so naturally out of the soil that they seem to be a part of it. You see no slums—and there are no slums in La Paz. The Indians have always lived in adobe huts; adobe houses are not felt to be a sign of deprivation, but stable, natural dwellings which suit the needs of the population.

On the very rim of the gorge you look down into what seems an underground lunar landscape and are able to make out some of the details of the city below. The business center is built around the

Prado, the main street; it consists of modest skyscrapers and a few handsome old churches. Still farther down are the mansions of the well-to-do citizens. A few hundred yards' difference in altitude makes a vast difference in comfort in La Paz. Consequently, the rich have built their houses as low as possible, while the adobe huts of the cholos and Indians cling to the steep slopes. Aside from a very few business streets in the heart of the city, there is not a lane or a street in La Paz that runs level. Wherever you go, you must climb. Loving Bolivia is strenuous; every walk turns into a mountain-climbing expedition.

The business center, I was told, had a backwoods look as recently as thirty years ago. Today office buildings, shops, hotels, and restaurants line the streets. In particular, there are a great many jewelry shops with unusually beautiful gold and silver jewelry, which is much cheaper in Bolivia than in Peru. The creation of a modern business quarter is largely the work of the immigrant Jews who left Germany and other European countries during the thirties. Bolivia and Uruguay were the only South American countries that accepted Jewish exiles in unlimited number, and it is thanks to the industry and initiative of these new Jewish citizens that La Paz took its first steps into the modern age.

In spite of its vigorous commercial life, and the fine residential quarters in Obraje and other low-lying parts of the city, La Paz has none of the unpleasant gigantomania that so frequently afflicts modern metropolises. There are more Indians living in La Paz than in any other big city in South America, and the cholos in Bolivia have for the most part not become a half-white proletariat, but have remained true to Indian traditions. Cholos wear Indian dress and have developed a folklore of their own based on Indian sources. The Indian cultural influence is so strong that in the Bolivian tropics I even met Negro and mulatto women who wore the typical tribal hats and shawls of the Aymara Indian women and who, in spite of their Negroid appearance, seemed altogether Indian in their general manner.

In Peru, every white man will tell you that the Indians are hopelessly lazy and uneducable. Bolivia quickly convinces you of the contrary. At first glance, the many Indian women and cholos who sit around in the streets offering things for sale do not seem especially diligent. They wear several wide petticoats, one on top of the other, and on their heads the native hat, which looks rather like a European man's fedora and varies in color and shape with every tribe. The shawls wrapped around their shoulders are brilliantly colored and handsomely patterned; these shawls also hold either their wares or their babies. Every so often the black-haired little head of an Indian baby will pop up out of the shawl, and black cherry eyes will stare curiously at you. These Indian peddlers usually have only a little fruit, a few textile or craft articles to sell. But if you ask for something they do not have, they will stand up, walk off with slow, swaying gait, and return in a few minutes with the desired article.

These Indian women and cholos are not idle, however, as they sit about the streets. Walking, standing, or sitting, they are forever knitting or spinning. The Indian men, too, are constantly active. They carry great loads on their backs up the steep lanes; they drive herds of pack llamas through the streets of the suburbs; they make improvements on their adobe houses, work as gardeners, houseboys, and day laborers. These Indians are by no means apathetic. Their needs are few, though, and they do not see that they ought to work solely for the sake of work. But they provide the things they and their families need for a livelihood.

In Bolivia you realize how rapidly the Indian, in spite of centuries of desperation, can regain pride and joy in life. Bolivia's Indians do not confront a foreigner with dull indifference or stifled hatred as do their fellows in Peru. Their whole manner is one of natural and self-assured dignity. When I visited some Aymara villages on the Altiplano, the warnings of my Bolivian hosts were still ringing in my ears. They had told me that the Aymara, after drinking *chicha*, a drink of fermented corn, often became quite pugnacious. But I saw no sign of such pugnacity in the Aymara villages, although at the time of my visit one of the traditional Indian festivals, a succession of banquets and masked dances, was being celebrated. It may be that a foreigner who behaves badly would have trouble with the Indians. But if you meet the Aymara with ordinary courtesy and respect, they immediately respond with their innate hospitality. They permit a stranger to join in their celebrations and treat him as an equal.

Many of the new citizens of Bolivia were disgruntled about the Indian revival during the MNR period. Some of these were the extreme rightists among the German immigrants, who have played a fateful part in Bolivian history on more than one occasion.

FASCISTS ON THE ROOF OF THE ANDES

Bolivia has an old and deeply rooted fascist tradition. Even General Santa Cruz, who after the achievement of independence wanted to use Bolivia as the focal point from which to restore the Inca Empire, was less a champion of Indian culture than a fascist despot. Bolivian fascism proper throve during the period of the Chaco conflict, that is, in the decade from 1928 to 1938. In the struggle for the oil of the Chaco, the Bolivian mountaineers were decimated like their Paraguayan opponents. The consequence of this conflict, which all but bled the two nations to death, was the same on both sides: in Paraguay and in Bolivia men from the battle front came to the top, rough soldiers who used slogans in much the same way as the leaders of Europe's fascist party.

In Paraguay it was Colonel Franco, in Bolivia Colonel Toro. Involved for a time in the beginnings of Bolivian fascism was the selfsame Captain Röhm who became the leader of Hitler's Storm Troopers, and was later liquidated by the German dictator as a "traitor." In a sense, all these Bolivian and German-Bolivian men were playing with treason; they were pitted against both the ruling oligarchy and the genuine Popular Reformist movement.

The key figure in Bolivian fascism was Germán Busch, son of a German father and a Bolivian mother, a one-time soldier in the Chaco and friend of Röhm. Busch made Colonel David Toro dictator, although Toro did not really have his heart in it, and when the dictator began talking a little too much about socialism, Busch mobilized his soldiers and deposed him. Busch rose somewhat higher than his former crony Röhm, but he came to a similar end. After ruling for two years, he was assassinated. To this day, the official version in Bolivia is that Busch committed suicide for unknown reasons. In reality, the Bolivian oligarchy wanted to be rid of him, for Dictators Toro and Busch had evinced too strong an interest in "state socialism," and had ventured to attack the tin companies and Standard Oil. In addition, they were all too blatantly pro-Hitler.

Many German-Bolivians were among the most fanatical followers of Germán Busch. In La Paz at the time, the Germans talked about a "national socialist government" in the same terms as they did back home in Germany. A pamphlet of the Busch era called the fascist regime a "government of action" dedicated to serving the "people as a whole." The fascist propagandists even attempted to depict the hero for whom Bolivia was named as a forerunner of Busch and Hitler. "Bolívar," the above-mentioned pamphlet contended, "wished to embody the leader principle in his new system of government, and in the person of the chief of state create a power that would stand above the disagreements of parties."

For some time La Paz became a major field of operations for German Nazis. A local group of the National Socialist Party under District Leader Achim von Kries was formed in La Paz and received the blessing of the authorities. The murder of Ernst Röhm somewhat clouded relations between Hitler and Busch. Nevertheless, Berlin went on waging a vigorous propaganda campaign in La Paz, with the aim of transforming Bolivia into a fascist stronghold in South America.

Busch's mysterious death and Bolivia's return to the older oligarchic forms of government put an end to such dreams. The tin dictators were followed by the two MNR revolutions under Villaroel and Paz Estenssoro. At first the old followers of Busch tolerated the MNR in the belief that the revolutionary movement represented state socialistic tendencies similar to those of the dictatorships they admired. But the MNR was, in fact, leftist, opposed to the military, and in favor of the Indians, who constituted the majority of the population. Consequently shortly after the 1952 revolution, the fascists became the principal opponents of the leftist government party. The various groups of fascists united to form a party called the *Falange Socialista Boliviana*. Several times this party attempted to overthrow the pro-Indian revolutionary regime. Paz Estenssoro's worker and peasant militia dealt so firmly with the Falange's rebellions, however, that at last in 1955 the fascists abandoned their underground work. Since Bolivia was a democracy during the MNR period, the Falange party was not banned. It continues to put up candidates in every election, but with little success.

FALANGE AND DICTATORSHIP

The incorrigible admirers of "Fuehrer" Germán Busch long bemoaned the downfall of the "government of the battle front spirit." During the twelve years of MNR rule they hated the revolutionary regime of Paz Estenssoro, Siles Zoazo, and Lechín as the German National Socialists hated the true Socialists. The MNR leaders were denounced and defamed; the pro-Indian policy of the MNR was either mocked or condemned as a dangerous attempt to awaken Bolivian subhumans. The fascists nostalgically recalled the times when Indians were prohibited from entering the business center of La Paz or the better residential quarters.

Other residues from the Falangist past continued to be bandied about among certain groups of the white-skinned population. German-Bolivian ex-fascists continued to keep aloof from democrats of German extraction, and reacted with covert or overt anti-Semitism toward the Jewish immigrants. In 1962 Bolivian schoolboys from Falangist families, who attended the German school in La Paz, used the occasion of the showing of a documentary film on the nazi period to demonstrate openly against the Jews. The ambassador of the German Federal Republic called in the principal of the school and requested him to prevent any repetition of such incidents. Whereupon German-Bolivians lashed out against the ambassador—as if Hitler were still in power in Germany.

Up to the end of 1964 it appeared that such fascist remnants in Bolivia were anachronisms which could be expected to fade away of their own accord before too long. The MNR government viewed such discourtesies on the part of German and Bolivian fascists and Falangists with no particular alarm. In the elections the few "National Socialists" made scarcely any impression. The numerically small foreign colonies had ceased to be of special importance in Bolivia. Since their economic power was no longer nearly so strong as it had been before the revolution, it seemed unlikely that they would be able to wield much political influence.

But after General Barrientos' military coup, fascist, semifascist, and radical rightist elements swiftly rose to the top again. They are the ones who most loudly applaud the new ruler—and especially his ultrarightist co-president, army commander Ovando. They are the ones who incessantly describe how terrible conditions were under the government of Paz Estenssoro, and who denounce the miners' unions as "communistic gangs." Since the coup anyone who attempts to make objective and favorable statements about the MNR period will encounter alarmingly fierce hostility from the Falangists and many of the German-Bolivians. In fact, the propagandist atmosphere unpleasantly reminds the German observer of the days of Joseph Goebbels.

The Barrientos government may yet find that this revival of the ugly fascist spirit represents a serious danger to its survival. René Barrientos himself is undoubtedly no friend of the Falange or of similar groups; he sincerely means to transform the dictatorship into a "Second Republic," a government of social justice which will further develop the ideals of the MNR instead of destroying them. But the workers' militia is either smashed or in open rebellion; and real power in the country is more and more falling into antirevolutionary and, in part, extreme rightist hands.

Even among the university students, fascism has shown a surprising renaissance since the coup. In contrast to most Latin American state universities, in which the majority of the students are leftist, and in contrast also to the Bolivian university of Cochabamba and the Technical Academy in the mining city of Oruro, the majority of the student body of the big state university of La Paz has a Falangist orientation. While the students in Cochabamba and Oruro demonstrated against Barrientos because they thought him too far to the right, the students in La Paz demonstrated against him because he was still too far left for them.

The unstable Barrientos regime is therefore threatened from two sides: by the rebellious miners, who since the coup have become redder and more leftist than ever, and by the rightist Falangists and their sympathizers, who sense the dawn of a new day for themselves and are once again dreaming of "National Socialism."

SCHOOLS—ONE WAY OR ANOTHER

Bolivia's future depends in large measure on whether future governments will be able to continue the educational program of the MNR, while concurrently pursuing economic and land reforms. For if the educational plan is carried out, it will mean that political life in Bolivia will involve the Indian. That alone (whether the upper class likes it or not) will lead Bolivia along the path that Mexico has taken so successfully.

The unions today, now that they have been smashed, are charged with a tendency toward anarchy and every other possible sin. But those unions during the MNR period had dedicated themselves to the task of Indian education. They provided radio lessons in the Aymara and Quechua languages. For every fifty illiterate workers they supplied a teacher who received a bonus if his pupils attended lessons regularly. Attendance was enforced by a policy of docking the wages of those workers who cut their classes. Those who could not show certificates of attendance were made to wait until last on all official occasions, and were barred from going to the movies.

Such coercive measures were essential. They are still essential in Bolivia; and if the new government is still serious about popular education, it will have to build on the work that the unions initiated during the revolutionary years. In Europe, too, a good many children would not learn to read and write if education were not compulsory.

The MNR conducted a similar campaign against cocaine addiction. Coca leaves could still be bought in Bolivian markets, for the vice could not be outlawed overnight. But businessmen were no longer allowed to distribute coca among the people. Hand in hand with adult education, a campaign of enlightenment went on, aimed at weaning the Indian away from coca chewing.

Mexico, too, took fifty years to clear away the rubble of the past. In Bolivia there will be many another setback, and a good deal more unrest for some time, before the worst abuses left over from the past are eliminated. But even now a new generation is growing up which makes a very different impression from that of the dull, drugged, dreaming Indio of the not so distant past. You feel this most strongly when you leave the highlands of the Andes and travel into the newly opened-up Bolivian highlands.

THE FUTURE BEGINS IN THE JUNGLE

Bolivia is not just mountains; the greater part of it consists of dense tropical jungles. Within a few hours you can descend from La Paz deep into the yungas, the subtropical valleys along the eastern slope of the Andes. Such a journey is a rapid plunge from the cool roof of South America into a zone of dripping rain forests.

In colonial times Alto Peru, which subsequently became Bolivia, embraced an area many times larger than that of the present republic. Bolivia had a coastline—Chile seized it in the course of the Saltpeter War. Broad regions of the Mato Grosso belonged to

Bolivia—the Bolivian dictator Melgarejo gave them to Brazil in 1870, the story goes, in exchange for a white horse and a military decoration. The Chaco, too, used to be Bolivian territory—Argentina and Paraguay carved the best pieces out of it. Up to 1903 the Bolivians by their folly had lost more than a third of their territory.

They retained possession of vast jungles and savannahs that extend eastward from the Andes to the Río Beni and other headwaters of the Amazon. These provinces are remote indeed, cut off from the movements of world trade, peopled only by jungle Indians, Negroes, and mestizos who have drifted in from Brazil, and a few *hacendados* who are principally cattle ranchers. No Bolivian government had succeeded in joining the almost unpopulated tropical regions to the densely populated highlands. The provinces between the yungas and the Río Beni remained a haven for naturalists who discovered there a unique animal paradise, and for the makers of anthropological movies.

In the last years of the MNR regime, however, the Bolivians proceeded, with American aid, to carry out a project that may be decisive for the country's future destiny. They built three highways from La Paz to the Río Beni. These roads, which incidentally rank among the major engineering achievements in the world, are of tremendous economic importance. For they connect the barren highlands with the fertile lowlands, and thus open up new areas of settlement for the masses of highland Indians who can barely grow enough to feed themselves on the Altiplano.

Since 1962 new villages and towns have sprung up along the margins of the roads, and new plantations and new farming communities. I drove over one of these roads to the point at which it ends abruptly in the jungle. The car had to ford rivers, but bridges were in the process of being built. At times bulldozers would clear the way for me until it was absolutely evident that the road went no farther. One must make such an expedition into the tropics to appreciate properly what was being done in Bolivia in the days of the calumniated revolutionary government.

NEW LIFE IN THE YUNGAS

For hours we drove through jungles, passing small streams at which Indian women were doing their washing. These were highlanders who had begun a new life in the tropics. Along the highway, resettled Indians and cholos had cleared the wilderness. They were cultivating plants new to them: bananas, papayas, yuccas, and sweet potatoes. In front of their huts, small black pigs wallowed. Children with schoolbooks under their arms walked along the jungle paths. Here, too, in the newly opened tropical regions, the government is striving to put an end to illiteracy. By the roadsides lie piles of plantation fruits which are regularly picked up by trucks and transported into the city. The resettled Indians are not paid very much for this produce, but what they receive suffices for their modest needs. Of far more psychological importance than earning money is the fact that they at last own their own land and therefore look forward to a hopeful future.

I stayed for a few days in Caranavi, a town that did not exist a few years ago and which to this day cannot be found in any atlas. The new town even boasted a hotel bearing the proud name of Hotel Splendid. It was built of adobe and, seen from the street, looked very inviting. The rear, however, was still incomplete. The rooms looked like a pile of chicken coops; to reach them, you climbed an extremely rickety, banisterless staircase. There was electric light, but the switch had not yet been installed. I had to carefully bring together the bare ends of the two wires that dangled from the ceiling in order to complete the circuit.

The condition of the half-finished hotel was symbolic of the growing town. Adobe bricks are shaped out of clay, put to dry in the sun, and the builders then set to work. All over the town people are building houses, market places, a school, and the façade of a hotel. The town is permeated with an incredible faith in the future. People improvise; they do whatever is most urgent at the moment and push forward with the work as best they can.

Every guest who spends a night at the hotel supplies the cash that will help to finish the building. Perhaps my stay enabled the landlord to buy light switches. The next guests may enable him to replace the rickety ladder with a real stairway. Thus the work goes forward step by step, and as you watch it you feel confident that the hotel will one day be a real hotel and Caranavi a real town.

Latin American supercities like Caracas tempestuously overleaped whole stages of evolutionary development. To the Indian, however, such crash programs are altogether alien. He has plenty of time. Beginning at the lowest level here in the Bolivian jungle, a settlement developed into a village and a village into a town. Nowhere did I feel so strongly faith in a new Bolivia as I did here in the heart of the jungle, in the newborn town of Caranavi.

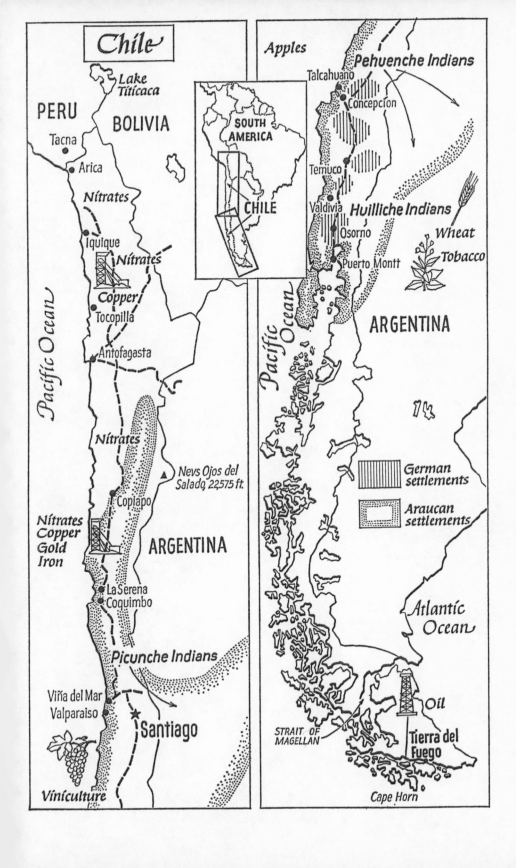

Chile

PERU

BOLIVIA

Lake Titicaca

Tacna

Arica

Nitrates

Iquique

Nitrates

Copper

Tocopilla

Antofagasta

SOUTH AMERICA

CHILE

Apples

Pehuenche Indians

Talcahuano

Concepcion

Temuco

Valdivia   Huilliche Indians

Osorno

Puerto Montt

Wheat

Tobacco

ARGENTINA

German settlements

Araucan settlements

Pacific Ocean

Nitrates

▲ Nevs Ojos del Salado, 22,575 ft.

Copiapo

Nitrates
Copper
Gold
Iron

ARGENTINA

La Serena
Coquimbo

Picunche Indians

Viña del Mar
Valparaiso

★ Santiago

Viniculture

Pacific Ocean

Atlantic Ocean

STRAIT OF MAGELLAN

Oil

Tierra del Fuego

Cape Horn

CHAPTER 6

The Undefeated Condor

A TAPEWORM NAMED CHILE

Benjamin Subercaseaux, a Chilean writer, has called the geography of his native land "somewhat crazy." That is putting it mildly, for Chile probably has the most crazy geographical shape of any country in the world. It is a tapeworm that winds along the coast of the Pacific Ocean twenty-six hundred miles long but averaging only one hundred and twenty-five miles in width. The tapeworm's head should have been dried out long ago—it is located in the hot, waterless, salt-peter desert. The tail is nicked by frost—it is washed by the waters of the Antarctic Ocean.

The Chileans, however, are proud of the peculiarity of their ribbon-like country. Chile, they are in the habit of saying, only seems to belong to the South American Continent. In reality, they maintain, it is an island, cut off from its neighbors by formidable natural barriers. The Pacific Ocean forms the western boundary. In the east rises the wall of the Andes, mountains towering to twenty thousand feet. To the north stretches the largest and most forbidding desert of South America. In the south the storms of Cape Horn rage around the glaciers and fjords of Tierra del Fuego. While all the other countries of Latin America have been squeezed into their present borders more or less by chance, the boundaries of Chile do indeed seem to have been established by nature. Or so the Chileans proudly maintain.

In this respect, national pride has been guilty of some exaggeration. At the time of the wars of independence Chile was a good deal smaller than it is today. In fact, measured by South American standards, it was extraordinarily small—one of the most insignificant of the countries that were precipitated willy-nilly into freedom. The fact that the Chilean tapeworm gradually grew longer and longer may be attributed partly to the Chileans' good fortune in war and partly to the colonizing activity of one of the most capable and vigorous peoples of Latin America.

Their vigor and competence have not earned the Chileans a good reputation among their neighbors. The Peruvians lost two of their southern provinces to Chile. The Bolivians lost their coastal outlet, along with the valuable saltpeter and copper resources of the Atacama Desert. A number of arbitration awards cost the Argentines a salt desert, several Andean plateaus, and some territory in Tierra del Fuego (according to the Chilean version, however, they were compensated by the territory around Lake Nahuel Huapí). The British finally were forced to relinquish their dream of a foothold on the Strait of Magellan. Consequently Peruvians, Bolivians, and Argentines regard the Chileans as notorious militarists and land grabbers. The British consider them as, at best, troublesome chauvinists.

MILITARY HISTORY AND WIT

And yet Chile is, curiously enough, one of the least military countries in the world. That is a fact, although the Chilean army was built up on German models. Chilean military bands play a large number of German marches. These dogged me from the farthest south to the extreme north of the country. But the Chileans only grin and tell jokes about the Prussian march music which keeps their soldiers stepping lively. Thus the story is told of a Chilean who traveled to Germany and on his return was asked about his impressions. "Germany is a great country," he replied, "a strong and rich country. There is only one thing I do not understand: how is it that so powerful a country has not developed any march music of its own? The Germans are constantly playing our Chilean marches."

But the band concerts in the plazas and the clacking boots of the soldiers are all that Chile has retained of German militarism. Chilean warships are used for ordinary passenger traffic as well as for military purposes. I sailed on a Chilean torpedo boat from the naval base of Talcahuano to one of the sea-bird islands. In order to get a better view of the birds I climbed up on the gun turret. Immediately afterward the Chilean captain climbed up beside me, greeted me courteously, and chatted with me about my travels for a quarter of an hour. Finally he casually dropped the remark that the gun turret was really a rather uncomfortable place for me to be; he suggested that I go down a deck lower where I could rest comfortably on a bench. In other words, he was telling me that civilians had no right to enter the gun turret, but he did so in the most gracious and unmilitary manner imaginable.

Since Chile has such a long coast, she has all sorts of coastal fortifications. In other countries, such fortifications are usually barred to outsiders by guards and fences; in Chile they are frequently the goal of Sunday outings. Picnics are held on the military reservations, and the *asado,* a type of barbecue, is prepared at open fires right alongside the trenches. The coast guards do not interfere, and they generally take part in the feasts.

The Chileans exercise their celebrated wit even on their grandest military exploit. It was between the years 1879 and 1883 that Chile became a nation which was taken seriously in Latin America. The then quite small republic defeated her northern neighbors, Bolivia and Peru, in the Saltpeter War. The Chilean navy overwhelmed the Peruvian fleet. Chilean soldiers ultimately marched into proud Lima. While the people of Lima still preserve the trenches which were dug as defenses against the Chileans, and show them off with determined patriotism, the Chileans would have it that the defeat of the Peruvian fleet was largely a matter of chance.

A favorite object of Chilean wit is the naval hero Arturo Prat, who sacrificed his life in the attempt to scuttle the Peruvian armored cruiser *Huascar*. As Chileans tell it, Prat never intended the exploit; after setting foot on board the enemy ship, he angrily turned toward the Chilean coast and called out: "Who pushed me?" As for Admiral Grau, who sank the Peruvian fleet, the story goes that he was dead drunk and went aboard the Peruvian flagship instead of his own, whereupon, the story goes, the Peruvians were so terrified that they all raised their hands in surrender. Consequently, the admiral had no choice but to take them prisoner and send the warship to the bottom, although he would rather have gone to bed to sleep it off.

These are only whimsical anecdotes, of course. In reality, the Chileans were extremely capable soldiers in the Saltpeter War, who honestly won their victories over their northern neighbors. But Chileans are not inclined to blow up their national history; they humanize it and make light of the deeds of the past. Chilean wit is comparable to the ready wit of the Berliner, the London Cockney, and the Parisian;

and Chilean delight in wry anecdotes somewhat resembles the humor of the Brazilian who will tell a joke as long as a good short story, with at least three distinct points. Perhaps this intellectual agility has enabled the Chileans to deal more effectively than other South Americans with the burdens and crosses of their history.

THE WILD SOUTHLAND OF SOUTH AMERICA

They are indeed a very curious people with a distinctive character who inhabit the narrow strip between the High Andes and the Pacific Ocean in the far southwestern part of Latin America—an area which in colonial times was regarded in the most literal sense of the word as the dread end of the world. In the times of the Spanish conquest, the northern and central provinces of present-day Chile belonged to the Inca Empire. The Indian tribes who dwelt there, the Atacameños, had acquired a little of Inca culture. But they had no gold and no other riches. The Spaniards therefore could not draw much profit from Chile. In addition, for the first time in their easy conquest of western South America, the Spaniards met an enemy they had to take seriously—the Araucan Indians of Chile. To this day the central Chilean provinces in the area of the Bío-Bío River and Lake Villarrica are called Frontera, the frontier. There the expansion of the Inca Empire had been checked; there too the power of the Spaniards ceased. The Araucans were the first Indian people who soundly trounced the conquistadors.

Thereafter, the Chilean colony became a borderland troubled by constant Indian wars—the wild south of South America, as it were. The colonial masters were never able to conquer the Araucans. All the land south of the Bío-Bío, which constitutes about half of the present Chilean republic, remained in the hands of the Indians. The few cities and fortifications the Spaniards built along the southern Chilean coast were in constant danger of being annihilated by Indian attacks.

Since, therefore, Chile could promise no treasures but only a life of danger and privation, it was avoided by Spanish soldiers of fortune. Colonists had to have perseverance, physical endurance, and strength of character if they hoped to survive. In the Spanish motherland Chile was considered so rough and inhospitable a frontier territory that for centuries no white woman was allowed to go there. The Spanish colonists therefore had to take wives from among the natives. In this way the Araucan population north of the Bío-Bío was wholly absorbed into the Chilean people. The Chileans today, to be sure, call themselves a white nation. With embarrassment or indignation, they deny that their forefathers mingled with Indian women, but the rural population of Chile is in reality a mixed population composed of Spanish and Araucan elements. As Chilean history has taught, the mixture is an extremely successful one, for it was a case of a Spanish elite uniting with an Indian elite.

PIONEERING SPIRIT

The resultant nation has inherited its culture and its way of life from the Spaniards, its stamina and love for liberty from the Araucans. Chileans were the first people to penetrate into the empty Atacama Desert and maintain themselves there. Chileans settled the High Andes, colonized lonely islands, and even managed to develop land in the harsh climate near the Strait of Magellan and in the subantarctic Tierra del Fuego. Chile's conflicts with her neighbors, moreover, as was the case with the Saltpeter War, fought for the Atacama Desert, generally arose from her efforts to obtain political recognition of previous peaceful conquests.

The Chilean pioneering spirit, among other things, opened up the silver mines, the Chile saltpeter (sodium nitrate) works, and the great guano deposits along the Atacama coast. The Bolivians and Peruvians, to whom the coast (which is now northern Chile) belonged, looked on with envy. Instead of imitating the Chilean example, they tried to force out the pioneers from the south by high taxation. The Chilean colonists thereupon complained to their government; and to the beat of Prussian music the excellent soldiers from Santiago marched across their borders to come to the defense of their countrymen. By these methods Chile increased the size of the country in the north by one third.

In the south (if we ignore minor quarrels with Argentina and Great Britain) there was no power to make life difficult for the Chilean pioneers. In that part of the country a new element of the population was added to the mixture—one to which Chile owes not only her military music but also a good many of her cultural and economic achievements. Under the presidencies of General Bulnes and Manuel Montt around the middle of the last century, Chile conceived the plan of encouraging German emigrants to settle the then sparsely inhabited provinces of the central south. Chile was fortunate in these immigrants, for the first immigrant families from Germany were political refugees looking for a new home after the failure of the revolution of 1848. Thus, once again an elite group came to join the old Spanish and old Indian elite. The German-Chileans bravely cleared the jungle and transformed the provinces of Llanquihue, Valdivia, and Osorno into a segment of Central Europe in South America.

In their push to the south, the Chileans were not even stopped by the drift ice of the Antarctic Ocean. They now claim a sizable sector of the Antarctic continent—those south polar regions which lie directly south of Tierra del Fuego. Among the islands, peninsulas, and mainland territory they claim are lands that have long been marked on English maps as British possessions. In England they bear such names as Graham Land, the Palmer Archipelago, the South Shetland Islands, and the Ellsworth Highland. In Chile, however, they are simply lumped together as Territorio Chileno Antártico or (in honor of the hero of the Chilean liberation) Tierra de Bernardo O'Higgins. I did not meet a single person in Chile, whether a native or an immigrant, who was not prepared to defend stoutly Chile's right to a share in Antarctica.

In order to preserve this claim the Chileans send one of their naval vessels into the antarctic every year and raise the Chilean flag there. The British, however, are not about to stand by and watch passively. They therefore also send a ship at the same time to raise the British flag. Year after year the same ceremony takes place: the ritual has now been perfected. The Chilean commander formally hands the British commander a letter of protest from his government against the English presence. The British commander thereupon hands the Chilean an English protest couched in similar language. After the formalities have thus been observed, the British produce their whisky and the Chileans their pisco; they sit down together, celebrate brotherly love and toast the future of the south polar region—the British referring to Graham Land and the Chileans to the Territorio O'Higgins.

The Chileans have even established themselves quietly and secretly in Polynesia. Easter Island, famous for its mysterious stone monuments, which have piqued the imagination of travelers and the wonder of archaeologists, was discovered by the Dutchman Roggeveen, then rediscovered by the Englishman Cook. The island then unfortunately attracted the interest of Peru, who saw in it a source of slave labor for the guano industry. Large numbers of hapless Polynesian natives were captured and worked to death by their Spanish-Peruvian kidnapers. Aside from this, no one paid any further attention to Easter Island.

In 1863, however, Chilean missionaries turned up there to convert the much reduced island population. Although Easter Island is some two thousand miles from the coast of Chile, Chile based her claims to it upon this missionary activity. In the nineteenth century the island was occupied and settled by Chileans. As a result, a Chilean-Polynesian mixed population now inhabits the island. Chilean warships continue to visit it at regular intervals.

As a visible sign that Chile actually owns a piece of real estate in the Pacific, one of the megalithic monuments has been transported from Easter Island to the Chilean coast and set up on the beach of the popular resort of Viña del Mar. Its presence there reminded me of those ancient Oriental religious statues that the Romans would seize on their campaigns of conquest and set up in the capital of their empire, where they would take the precaution of paying reverence to them.

Whatever the Chileans do, whatever political measures they take, wherever they establish a foothold, and whomever they fight—they are convinced, with an amazing and disarming naïveté, of the rightness of their actions. They are, for Latin America, a singularly patriotic people. In Chile a person is not primarily a member of the oligarchy or a foreign colonist or a member of the lower classes—he is a Chilean. In fact Chileans have such verve, and such conviction about being Chileans, that their attitude does not strike the foreign observer as nationalism, let alone chauvinism, but rather as a natural character trait. Europeans who have been settled in Chile for only a few years would advocate the cause of Chile in conversation with me with as much vigor and feeling as if they were descended from at least three generations of Chileans.

TURNING OFF THE WATER

When I was in the north Chilean city of Arica in the summer of 1962, I witnessed another episode in Chilean aggrandizement. Every Chilean was vigorously denouncing Bolivia. Europeans who had come to Chile only a short time before were likewise condemning Bolivia. At first I did not understand what the dispute was all about. I concluded that Bolivia had unjustly seized Chilean property and violated Chilean rights. Gradually, however, I found out that just the reverse was the case. The Chileans had diverted Bolivian water—prompted, to be sure, by their well-known pioneering spirit, for their intention was to irrigate several Chilean valleys. It did not matter that by doing so they were turning off the water desperately needed by the bordering Bolivian province, which in any case was already suffering from drought. Everyone in Chile was intoxicated by the plan to make the desert bloom in the region above Arica. It was incomprehensible that the Bolivians could possibly object to such a wonderful development project.

The matter at issue had a long history behind it. It was connected to that oft-mentioned Saltpeter War, which in Chile goes by the proud name of Great Pacific War. That war cost Bolivia her entire coastline, and since then she has fervently longed for a new port on the seacoast. Not even the most nationalistic Bolivian presumes to think of regaining the former Bolivian coast in the vicinity of Antofagasta and Mejillones. Consequently, the Bolivians' desires have focused upon the port of Arica, the northernmost city in the country, which in the past the Chileans took from the Peruvians.

Chile has built a highly modern and comfortable railroad from Arica to La Paz. Moreover, Bolivia has been allowed to use Arica as a free port. As a direct result of these commerical bonds, many Bolivians have settled in the northern Chilean port. Since, moreover, Arica is separated from the rest of Chile by desert-like wastelands, the city rather gives the effect of a Bolivian or Peruvian hat sitting loosely on the Chilean head.

For Chile, isolated Arica has become something of a problem. She would of course like to keep the port city, for the possession of Arica was hard-earned; the struggles, disputes, and arbitration negotiations dragged on until 1929. In order to make Arica relatively independent economically, the Chilean Government for a long time permitted the city to be a free port. The result was, however, that Chile was flooded with import goods brought into the country through Arica. The stability of the country's currency was threatened by the mounting tide of imports. Another way had to be found to provide for the district of Arica. If not, there was always the danger that the mixed Chilean-Peruvian-Bolivian population might someday seek to rejoin Peru or perhaps vote in favor of annexation by Bolivia. Hence the idea of creating a grand agricultural project in the northern province which would make Arica self-sufficient. The plan provided for irrigating the valleys east of Arica with the waters of the Lauca River, thus transforming wasteland into fertile plantations and orchards. It was a plan typical of the energy, the pioneering spirit, and the competence of the Chileans. Unfortunately, however, the Lauca River belongs to Bolivia; only a small part of it flows through Chile.

The Chileans, however, were past masters at handling the rulers of their neighboring countries. When the Lauca plan was conceived, the MNR revolution had not yet taken place in Bolivia. The Chilean Government had no great difficulty in making an arrangement with the military dictatorship in La Paz. Since the project was not quite ready yet, Santiago waited, oblivious to the upheaval which had meanwhile taken place in Bolivia, and for the present saying nothing about the treaty. Around 1960, however, the problem of Arica became so pressing that the Chileans fetched out the old agreement.

The Bolivians protested that any agreement made by former dictators was invalid. But the Chileans simply ignored the Bolivian protests. They diverted the waters of the Lauca, transformed several arid valleys of the northern province into rich rice and vegetable fields, and plumed themselves on having once again enlarged their "living space." The result was a breach of diplomatic relations between the two countries in the summer of 1962. The Chilean-Bolivian conflict over water came very close to outright hostilities. I admit I found it impossible to judge the question. The Chileans asserted that a treaty was a treaty and that there could be no legal objections to the diversion of the Lauca River. On the other hand, the Bolivians whom I later spoke to commented bitterly that the Chileans not only had based their action on an antiquated and completely unacceptable agreement, but had also violated that agreement by divert-

ing much more water than the treaty allowed. This was at the expense
of the already dry Bolivian frontier region.

Whatever the case, Chilean pride in the newly cultivated land is
in no way diminished by the Bolivians' woes. By similar methods in
the course of the past one hundred and fifty years, the Chileans
have nearly tripled the size of their country and have made a blos-
soming paradise out of the rough and inhospitable land between the
Andes and the Pacific. I must admit that, although I was sorry for
Bolivia, when I saw the lush vegetation in the newly irrigated regions
I was inclined to sympathize with the Chilean side of the story.

KING ORELIO AND THE ARAUCANS

Chile and the bordering Andean regions of Argentina contain from
two to three hundred thousand Araucans. This is a modest figure
compared with the size of the Indian population in other Andean
countries. But around 1900 only from twenty to thirty thousand
Araucans were left in Chile. Thus, the number of aboriginal inhabitants has increased tenfold in half a century. The Araucans are by
no means "a dying race decimated by disease," as travel narratives
had it at the beginning of the century. They have retained their
integrity, and in the provinces of Maule, Bío-Bío, Arauco, and Cautín
form virtually a state within a state.

Chile has no Indian problem, which means that the white upper
class has no phobias about Indian emancipation. The Araucans have
made a place for themselves in Chilean literature. Chilean intellectuals take some pride in the fact that their Indians are the only
undefeated aboriginals of the Americas. There are exceptions, of
course; those who regard a white skin as a sign of natural superiority
look down on the Araucans as backward and savage. But on the
whole, emancipated Araucans have little difficulty in entering the
mainstream of Chilean life. They work all over Chile as teachers,
doctors, scientists, and army officers without attracting any special attention.

The cholos do not deny their origin in the way of the Europeanized
half-breeds in other Latin American countries. Many among them,
in fact, are careful to stress their Araucan descent. It is not very
easy to distinguish an emancipated Araucan from a Chilean of

Iberian blood. In their physiognomy, their color, and their manner the Araucans differ considerably from other highland Indians. They might easily be taken for members of some Mediterranean people, although they are perhaps somewhat darker and have broader cheekbones than the majority of Mediterraneans.

These aboriginal inhabitants of the land, who today live peacefully as part of the Chilean people, were in former times the most defiant, the most bellicose, and the most freedom-loving Indians in the Americas. That is expressed by the very name their Spanish adversaries gave them. The word Araucan comes from the Mapuche language. *Aucaes* means simply "rebels." Their own name for themselves stressed the same quality. It was *Moluche,* which means "warriors."

They can be seen every day in the streets of Temuco, the capital of Cautín province, selling their wares in the market place. Many of them still wear traditional Indian costume. Their women mostly wear their rather stiff, straight hair in long braids, wrap themselves in colorful shawls, and favor silver jewelry. In this city, which lies within the territory of the one-time Frontera, the Araucans keep their distance from the whites, for this is the heart of the old Indian country, of the Araucan state within a state.

LAUTARO

Since the Chileans honor the Indian as well as the Hispanic past of their country, they have erected a monument in Temuco to the greatest of the Araucan leaders, Lautaro. Unfortunately there was no native artist available to do the work, and the commission was given to a North American sculptor. As a result, what we see is not an Araucan army leader in full regalia, but a half-naked Sioux Indian crowned with feathers and swinging a tomahawk. The monument is a favorite butt of Chilean wit. Some Temucons say that the American sculptor had more commissions than he could properly keep track of and by mistake shipped Sitting Bull off to Chile instead of Lautaro. Hence, they argue, there must be a monument to an Araucan standing somewhere in the United States. Other Chileans maintain—and they are probably closer to the truth—that in those days every Indian was a Sioux to a Yankee. The Araucans, however, who hold their market day around the absurd monument to Lautaro, say nothing about it at all. They simply do not recognize the naked figure on the pedestal as a member of their nation.

Lautaro, who belongs as fully to Chilean national history as the circumnavigator of the globe, Magellan, and the liberator O'Higgins, entered world literature between the years 1569 and 1590—that is, only a short time after his death. Lautaro's generalship caused such a stir in Spain, so much admiration touched with envy, that a Spanish epic poet, Alonso de Ercilla y Zúñiga, was moved to turn the story of the Araucan leader into verse. The Spanish poet took twenty-one years to compose his epic of the Indian war. Over that long span of time the wellspring of his verse ran dry, so that the three-volume work, *La Araucana,* became a mixture of chronicle, novel, and poem.

Another Spanish writer, Álvarez de Toledo, took up the same theme in his poem *Purén indómito.* Both works on the Araucans are amazingly objective. One senses that the authors were glad for the chance to deal with Indian victories in the cause of liberty, rather than with the crude heroics of the conquistadors. At great length and with considerable gusto, the poems describe how the Araucans defeated Spain's generals, and slaughtered, tortured, and roasted their Spanish prisoners over slow fires. The Araucan epics should by all rights have discouraged the Spaniards from further expeditions. But unfortunately, the conquistadors apparently were not influenced by the poets.

But those works are still read. Chilean school children to this day must wade through *La Araucana.* The Araucan deeds of glory have been treated repeatedly by Chilean writers and are a favorite subject of Chilean juvenile literature. Every Chilean child is as familiar with the tale of how eighteen-year-old Lautaro, the Araucan, defeated the conquistador Pedro de Valdivia, as every American child used to be familiar with the *Leatherstocking Tales,* and every German child with the Lay of the Nibelungs.

In 1535 the Spaniards had advanced from Peru into the region that would subsequently become Chile. Their leader, Diego de Almagro, soon returned in disappointment to Peru, declaring that the country was ghastly, the water undrinkable, and the population excessively hostile. A good place to keep away from, he said. But five years later Pedro de Valdivia tried once more. Apparently he was not so put off by the taste of Chilean water or the lack of Chilean gold, for he founded Santiago, Concepción, Valdivia, and a number of other cities. He drove the Araucan bands of warriors into the interior of the country and imported European cultivated plants in order to start an agricultural system on the Spanish pattern. Since Pedro de Valdivia was short of soldiers, he impressed a large number of Indians into his army as auxiliaries, taught them to ride and shoot, and was greatly pleased at the alacrity with which they learned European military techniques.

Among these Araucan trainees was an eighteen-year-old boy named Lautaro, who served as the Spanish general's groom. Lautaro took part in a number of campaigns against his fellow tribesmen and observed the cruelty with which the Spaniards treated the Araucans. Secretly, he organized a conspiracy among the Indian auxiliaries. One night, the conspirators stole the Spaniards' horses and guns and fled into the woods. Deep in the forests of the interior, Lautaro taught the Araucan tribes who were fighting the Spaniards how to handle horses and guns. The new Indian cavalry defeated the Spaniards in several battles, and burned down the fortresses and settlements of the conquerors. In 1554 Pedro de Valdivia himself was captured by Lautaro's warriors, and—if we may believe the old Spanish epic—tortured to death in a long and gruesome ceremonial.

The successors of Pedro de Valdivia had little better luck. They could not subdue the Araucans. Reports sent to the Spanish motherland regarding conditions in Chile were so depressing that the above-mentioned decree was issued, forbidding European women to be brought to so inhospitable and dangerous a country. Finally, in 1641, after more than a hundred years of unavailing effort to conquer Chile, the Spaniards officially recognized the Bío-Bío as the border between the Spanish colony and the free land of the Araucans. Spain had to be satisfied with only the head and part of the neck of the Chilean tapeworm. Nevertheless, the battles for this small part of Chile had cost Spain twice as many soldiers as the conquest of all the rest of her empire in the Americas.

THE INVINCIBLE SPIRIT OF REBELLION

European powers, envious of Spain's New World empire, vigorously intervened in the Indian wars. Sir Francis Drake negotiated with Indian tribes while he burned down Valparaiso. Despite the peace treaty of 1641, the Dutch repeatedly incited the Araucans to war.

Even in the Spanish colony north of the Bío-Bío, the Indians were anything but tame. In the eighteenth century, Governor José Manso attempted to settle Indians in cities and villages so as to accustom them to living pacifically side by side with the colonists. Manso's experiment ended in a great Indian uprising. In 1775 the Spaniards reluctantly had to make extensive concessions to the Diaguites and Araucans north of the Bío-Bío. In Santiago, in fact, an official Araucan ambassador was appointed to represent the rights of his nation to the crown. Every attempt by the Spaniards to cross the Bío-Bío invariably ended in a disaster.

The first European to prevail over the Araucans has also won a place in the history of Chilean independence—though not as a hero of liberation, but as the father of the liberator of Chile. This man, Ambrosio O'Higgins, was an Irishman by birth. He became governor of the Spanish colony of Chile with the title of Marquis of Osorno, and was so effective a one that most of the Araucan chieftains, at least *pro forma*, acknowledged Spanish sovereignty. The Marquis of Osorno had an illegitimate son by a Chilean woman with a trace of Indian blood. This son, whom he had educated in Europe and who was later to drive the Spaniards out of the country, was Bernardo O'Higgins.

The Spanish policy toward the Indians before the wars of independence was as unstable, as prone to earthquakes and volcanic eruptions as the land of Chile itself. Whenever the Spaniards took a harsh line and attempted to coerce the Indians into slave labor, there were native revolts, with the free Araucans south of the Bío-Bío rushing to the aid of their Hispanicized brothers. On the other hand, the Araucans on both sides of the Bío-Bío could be quite amicable when no pressure was put on them. During such periods of peace the greater part of the northern tribes, the Diaguite and the Picunche, gradually merged with the white colonists to form the Chilean nation. The Huilliche, on the island of Chiloé, went their own way. The Spaniards had built only a few forts and towns on that island, and applied themselves rather to energetic missionary work. The Indians proved willing to accept the Spanish culture, so much so that even after the wars of independence they remained loyal to the Spanish crown, at least for a while.

The first decades after independence were fairly quiet times in Chile. Bernardo O'Higgins, one of the most progressive presidents of the newly liberated country, made it the cornerstone of his policies to raise the standard of living of the poor and to liberate the rural populations from their semiserfdom on the large estates. These were aims that could appeal to the Chilean mestizos and Indians. But after the fall of O'Higgins, the white oligarchy seized control in Chile. As in the neighboring countries, conservative-feudalistic presidents alternated with liberal-mercantilistic presidents. The Chileans gradually began to penetrate the large Indian states south of the Bío-Bío. The result might have been a peaceful mingling of white and Indian Chileans had it not been for the treachery of the whites, who proceeded to rob the Araucans of their lands in much the same way as the North American Indians were dispossessed.

AN INDIAN NAPOLEON

The last great Indian war in Chile was incited by a French lawyer named Orélie Antoine Tounens, who, having had difficulties with the Chilean authorities, escaped arrest by fleeing into Araucan territory. He there won the confidence of several chiefs, and seems to have cut so impressive a figure that the Indians ultimately elected him Great Toqui, Supreme Chieftain of the Mapuches. Probably Tounens' model was his fellow countryman Napoleon III. Tounens assembled an Indian cabinet, issued legislation on the French pattern, and at last, in 1861, appointed himself hereditary monarch of the Araucans under the name of King Orelio.

King Orelio eventually declared war formally on the Republic of Chile. He traveled diligently around the Araucan territories urging the various tribes to battle against the republic. Chile, he reminded them, was an Indian name; the country must be restored to its Indian owners. His yen for travel, however, proved his undoing. A year after his coronation, while on a recruiting trip, he fell into the hands of the Chileans and was taken to Concepción. The Chileans behaved with remarkable indulgence. They had the French adventurer examined by doctors, who pronounced him insane. The French consul finally managed to have him deported back to France.

Nevertheless, the excitement Tounens had whipped up among the Araucans did not abate. The Indians quickly elected a new Great Toqui who united sizable parts of southern and central Chile under his rule. The region along the Bío-Bío became *frontera* once again—

bitterly contested frontier country. According to the Chilean version, the Araucans were defeated in two great battles in 1868 and 1869, and agreed to a treaty of peace on January 22, 1870. According to the Araucan version, the Indians were victorious and forced their Chilean opponents to make peace. The truth probably lies somewhere between the two stories.

Ex-King Orelio had meanwhile not been inactive. In France he recruited freebooters who were prepared to die for the liberty of the Indians. He also thought he could count on support from Napoleon III, since Napoleon was even then arranging the Mexican adventure of Maximilian of Hapsburg. Napoleon would surely look as favorably upon a Frenchman as King of Chile as upon Maximilian as Emperor of Mexico. Tounens returned to South America, going first to Argentina, where he recruited a number of gauchos into his band. In view of the permanent disputes between Chile and Argentina, the Argentines were not at all averse to stirring unrest in the neighboring republic.

By way of one of the southern passes of the Andes, King Orelio's forces invaded the present-day province of Maule. There Tounens reestablished his kingdom, his court, and his cabinet and repudiated the peace treaty. The Indian war went on, with shifting fortunes, until Orelio began running out of money. He therefore returned to France and asked his emperor for direct aid. But Napoleon's Mexican adventure had meanwhile failed. Nevertheless, he might have taken up Tounens' cause if Bismarck had not interfered. The outbreak of the Franco-Prussian War spelled the end of Tounens' hopes. Unable to return to Chile, he stayed on in France, founding a newspaper in which he pleaded the cause of the Araucans. But France had other things to think about. In 1887 the one-time Indian king died in the Dordogne, a poor forgotten figure.

For a while the Araucans waited patiently for the king to return. Then they agreed to a final settlement with Chile. A treaty was drawn up that could satisfy both parties. The Mapuches, the only still-intact Araucan tribes, were confirmed in the possession of their territory. No Chilean might buy land from them. Their customs and *mores* were to remain inviolate. In return, the Mapuches agreed to become part of the Chilean nation.

To this day Chile has faithfully observed the treaty with the Araucans. In the following decades, the Araucans lived in part as nomads, in part as small farmers, completely free under the Chilean flag.

Within their territory, their old tribal traditions had the force of law. All attempts at missionary work among them came to naught. They continued to worship a principal god and several subsidiary gods; they lived polygamously and paid small heed to political events in the country of which they nominally formed a part.

This peaceful coexistence led, after 1900, to a gradual merging of large parts of the Araucan population with the Chileans. The inhabitants of the Araucan heartland, around Temuco, ultimately accepted German Capuchin fathers as missionaries and were gradually converted to Christianity. They did not, however, want to renounce either polygamy or other Indian customs which were not exactly compatible with Christian doctrine. Today they are probably the only people in the world who call themselves Christian and nevertheless are allowed to practice polygamy.

The Capuchins made the best of the situation, preferring to overlook marital conditions in Araucan country. They set up almost two hundred elementary schools, several seminaries, and a preparatory school where gifted Indians were given the background they needed to attend the university. Thus Chile acquired a good many excellent citizens. Thanks to the Capuchins' tolerant educational policies, there nowadays exists a growing class of Araucan intellectuals.

IN THE LAND OF THE UNDEFEATED

When I arrived in Temuco, everyone told me it was quite impossible to visit the villages and settlements of the freedom-loving Indians. People tried to put me off by showing me Indian films or pointing out the Araucans who regularly came to market their wares in Temuco; with a little skill and good luck you could take pictures of them through your car windows. It was not that my informants were ill-disposed toward me; on the contrary. But they all agreed that even today it was extremely difficult, and not altogether safe, to penetrate the regions inhabited by the Araucans. The unassimilated Indian population kept their distance from whites, I was told, and were extremely touchy about being molested by camera-toting tourists.

To make matters worse, a short while before, an Andes expedition from East Germany had made an unsuccessful attempt to penetrate the Indian territory. Starting out from Temuco, the members of the expedition had done exactly what they had been warned against. They had barged into an Araucan village with movie cameras and tape recorders, had entered huts, and had begun taking pictures without even bothering to ask permission. When these Indians are gaped at, photographed, and filmed as if they were animals in a zoo, they react in a very healthy manner—by giving the intruders a beating and chasing them away. They had done so this time. The good socialists from the German Democratic Republic had returned to Temuco with most of their equipment smashed.

Nevertheless, I did not give up. With the aid of an estate steward's family who occasionally employed Araucan household help, and a Chilean teacher who directed a local Indian museum, I was able to make the acquaintance of some Araucans, and finally ventured a foray into Indian country. On the way, I realized some of the difficulties the Chileans must have encountered in their wars with the Araucans. The rain came down in buckets; the roads dissolved under my feet. In the rainy winter climate of central and southern Chile, lightly armed Indians familiar with the country would have a marked advantage over regular soldiers. I wore high rubber boots, waded through treacherous mud, crawled through hedges of broom and barbed-wire fences, was barked at by Indian dogs, and at last stood before the first *ruca*.

A *ruca* is a wooden hut with a firmly tramped earthen floor and a peaked roof of twigs, such as the Chilean Indians have inhabited for ages. Around a group of rucas lay the fields and meadows of the Araucan farmers. Everything looked very neat. There were grazing cattle, and I saw fields of potatoes, corn, and other crops. Araucan territory includes some of the most fertile soil in Chile. Many white landowners have already cast greedy eyes upon it. But the treaty of 1881 continues to preserve the land for the Indians.

Lautaro's descendants proved to be friendly, accessible people once their confidence had been won. But they have clear ideas of their identity. The first Araucan woman I talked to insisted that she was not a Latin-American. She was a Mapuche, she proudly informed me. When I asked an Indian mother whether her baby could talk yet, she gave me a reply characteristic of the Araucans: "He doesn't speak Spanish yet, but he speaks Chilean." To the Araucans, Chile is still their own country; they are the real Chileans and their language the real Chilean language.

Another Araucan woman had spent several years in Temuco. But she had by no means become a Chilean. She was glad to be living in a ruca again, and declared that here she was in her own country, whereas she had never really felt at home in the city. One of the last of the Araucan silversmiths, whom I watched making a traditional Indian ornament, was likewise a decided opponent of the modern age. He lamented the decline of his art in much the same terms that a European craftsman would nowadays.

"There just aren't any apprentices left," he said. "The young people won't go to the trouble of learning a decent trade. And the grownups do not have their jewelry made by an artist any more. They go to Temuco and buy factory trash in the shops."

In several of the rucas I sat with Indians, cats, dogs, and chickens around the fire hole dug into the earthen floor, the firelight only dimly illuminating the semidarkness of the hut. A kettle was suspended above the flames. From the ceiling hung ears of corn and strings of onions. At the back of the hut were piles of hides which the Araucans use for beds. The smoke made its way out through the brush of the roof and did not bother us. It was comfortably warm in these rucas. In comparison to them, the huts of the Chilean agricultural workers that I later visited were far more primitive and so filled with smoke that I had to flee after a few seconds.

Inside the rucas, or in front of them, Araucan women sat at simple looms, making those handsome rugs which are popular among white Chileans also. A single rug represents about a month of labor. From dawn to dusk, the women's fingers move the wooden shuttles from side to side. Bought from a dealer, such rugs cost about twelve dollars and fifty cents. The silversmith went about his work with equal patience. He produced his silver ornaments with the aid of a single hand bellows, melting the silver in a hardwood scoop, then skillfully hammering it into the proper form.

The silversmith became distinctly embarrassed when I asked him whether he had several wives. At first he did not want to talk about it. But the woman weaving at the back of the hut giggled and called out that he had three wives and should admit it. Grinning, the silversmith said nothing and went on with his hammering.

The Araucans do not look as if they were once the most fearsome Indians in South America. They live a happy life in their simple rucas. If they want to, they can go to any school in the country, and with their competence and capacity for hard work they succeed in all occupations. If they do not want to, they are let alone. The only recent disturbance in Araucan life came when the Pan-American Highway was built through the Indian territory. The Chilean authorities wanted to eliminate the rucas on either side of the great highway. They therefore built the Indians neat wooden houses on piles, with wooden floors and iron stoves.

It was a misguided project. The newly built houses are dreadfully cold and drafty in winter. The stoves do not warm them nearly as well as the open campfires warm the rucas. Cold seeps through the cracks in the wooden flooring. The Indians maintain that they sleep far more warmly on their earthen floors covered with hides than on the proper beds in the wooden houses. Consequently, many of them use the houses only as sheds in which to store their corn, onions, and livestock feed. They themselves continue to live in the old rucas. To my mind, they are quite sensible. On those damp, cold winter days their traditional rucas seemed to me far warmer, pleasanter, and more homelike than the drafty prefabs on piles.

NITRATE SAGA

The coasts of the Pacific Ocean are washed by the cool Humboldt Current, which teems with fish. Peruvian and Chilean fisheries depend on the billions of *anchovettas,* the sardines that swim in this cold current. So do the birds. For thousands of years cormorants, pelicans, and gannets have fed on the *anchovettas.* They nested by the millions on the Pacific coast and on the outlying islands. And as sea birds usually do, they remained faithful to their nesting places for thousands of years.

A fish-catching sea bird is a kind of small chemical factory. Its digestive apparatus manufactures the most valuable fertilizer in the world—guano. Sea birds have an extremely rapid metabolism. The nesting places on the shores of the Pacific Ocean became covered with dense layers of bird droppings. In some places masses of guano more than two hundred feet thick were deposited.

Even in pre-Inca times the Indians had recognized how valuable these bird droppings were. With the aid of *huano,* as they called it, they were able to make the desert bloom along the coast. The Incas imposed strict regulations to protect the fertilizer industry. Their laws imposed the death penalty for killing a guano-producing bird, or even for unauthorized visits to a guano island.

The Spaniards took no interest either in the birds or in the guano. The consequence was that large areas of once fertile land along the coast reverted to desert. It remained for Alexander von Humboldt to recognize the potential wealth on the cliffs and islands inhabited by the birds. Even so, some forty years passed before the Peruvians began using the guano as the Indians had done. Circumstances forced them to. The Peruvian treasury was empty; the government had to obtain capital from abroad. British financiers had long since realized that the bird droppings represented a valuable commodity. They lent money to the Peruvians, and in return were given concessions to mine the guano.

GUANO AND THE PIONEERING SPIRIT

Henceforth, the British and Peruvians co-operated in the guano trade. For a while thereafter, almost every ship that sailed from Peru reeked of ammonia. A lingering stench of ammonia should have been noticeable in the Peruvian treasury department as well. For during the fifties of the nineteenth century, the taxes on guano constituted three-fourths of the income of the Peruvian Government. The bird droppings conjured up railroads, highways, public buildings, whole sections of cities. Enraptured with this wonderful source of riches, the Peruvians overshot the mark, with the result that the country again went heavily into debt. But this time the British were no longer willing to advance money; the finances of Peru had become altogether too shaky. In 1868 Peruvian President Balta was finally forced to obtain credits from the Dreyfus Bank in Paris at very high interest rates. As security, he pledged the state's share in the profits from the guano industry.

The Balta era saw the death of millions of sea birds, for the guano cliffs were stripped so ruthlessly that the pelicans, cormorants and gannets scarcely had a chance to nest. This was the period in which the Peruvians transported the peaceful population of Easter Island to the guano areas for forced labor. The interest the French bank demanded finally led to bankruptcy of the state. Balta was overthrown by a revolution and killed.

Just as the Peruvian guano industry was gradually beginning to recover, a new specter appeared on the horizon. South of the borders of Peru, a rival threatened to displace guano in the world economy. This was the Chile saltpeter, or sodium nitrate, of the Atacama Desert. The coastal strips and deserts of Atacama, which now constitute the northern third of Chile, then belonged to Bolivia. As long ago as the eighteenth century, a German named Thaddäus Hanke had discovered that the region was rich in Chile saltpeter. The Spaniards used the mineral chiefly to manufacture gunpowder for fireworks, with which they frightened rebellious Indians. Exploitation of the Chile saltpeter stopped after the end of the colonial period. It was revived by the intrepid instinct of the Chilean pioneers to seek and find a living even in the most inhospitable regions.

The Chileans are among the most active emigrants in Latin America. Partly this is due to the poverty of the Chilean rural population, which leads them to seek their luck in other countries; partly it is due to the mixture of Spanish and Araucan blood, which has made large numbers of Chileans adventurous nomads. When gold was found in California, some thirty thousand Chileans rushed to the gold fields. Another five thousand sought their luck in the Australian gold fields. More than twenty thousand Chileans went to Peru to work in the guano deposits and on the building of railroads. Chilean pioneers established themselves in the subantarctic, caught seals and whales along the coasts of Tierra del Fuego, and mined coal and other minerals near the Strait of Magellan.

It was inevitable, therefore, that the hardy Chileans would pour in increasing numbers into the vacuum to the north—the saltpeter deserts. Neither the Bolivians nor the Peruvians had paid much attention to the territory of Atacama. But in 1866 two Chileans, José Santo Ossa and Francisco Puelma, found tremendous deposits of Chile saltpeter in the vicinity of the present city of Antofagasta. Chilean immigrants began busily mining the saltpeter. And since they had no capital to attack the newly discovered riches on a large scale, they turned to the same European power which two decades before had drawn their attention to the bird droppings on their coast—England.

Chilean pioneering spirit and British capital created factories, roads, and towns in the desert. The production of Chile saltpeter rose within the first five years from 15,000 to 285,000 tons per year. Bolivian President Mariano Melgarejo (the one who allegedly traded a third of his country to Brazil for a white horse and a decoration) at first looked on benevolently. For Mejillones, the only port on the Atacama coast, belonged to Bolivia. Melgarejo signed two treaties agreeing not to tax the Chilean-British saltpeter production for a period of twenty-five years. All he wanted was a 50-per-cent share in the shipping fees in Mejillones.

The Chilean immigrants promptly reacted by building, with English aid, a new port on a hitherto uninhabited part of the coast—Antofagasta. Melgarejo was furious, but his anger was directed not so much against the Chileans as against Great Britain, for he regarded that country (and not so mistakenly) as the prime force behind the Chilean saltpeter producers. Feeling ran high, and there were anti-British demonstrations and excesses in Bolivia. These resulted in that historic moment which has entered the world's treasury of anecdotes: Queen Victoria wanted to protect her subjects in La Paz by dispatching some units of the navy, but learned from her ministers that La Paz could not be reached by ships. Whereupon she angrily expunged the Republic of Bolivia from her maps.

Antofagasta flourished; within a short time it had become the greatest Chile saltpeter port in the world. As usual, the Chileans had outwitted the Bolivians. They had to acknowledge Bolivia's sovereignty over Antofagasta, but the port was their creation. Since they were not shipping the saltpeter by way of Mejillones, they did not have to pay the transit fee to Bolivia. The world made all its gunpowder with Chile saltpeter. What is more, the same saltpeter was a much cheaper fertilizer than guano. Consequently, the Peruvians found the markets for the guano dwindling, and once again faced bankruptcy.

Peru was left with no choice but to intervene in the Chilean-British-Bolivian intrigues. The Peruvian Government concluded a secret treaty with Bolivia providing that Bolivia was to stop the exploitation of saltpeter in the Atacama Desert, in return for which she would receive a share in the profits from Peruvian guano.

About a million tons of guano were already piled up in Peruvian ports, permeating the environs with their stench. There were few buyers. But if Chile saltpeter shipments were stopped, Peru and Bolivia realized, the world would be forced to resort to the bird droppings again.

In Bolivia, President Hilarión Daza had meanwhile replaced Melgarejo. He annulled the contracts with the Chilean-British saltpeter company, imposed an excessively high tax on saltpeter from the Atacama Desert, and sent troops to occupy the whole area and collect the tax. Thus Bolivia was well on her way to keeping her agreement with Peru.

THE GREAT PACIFIC WAR

Chilean President Aníbal Pinto retaliated. He announced that Chile was compelled to defend her industrious saltpeter miners in the desert against Hilarión Daza's arbitrary actions, and would do so with all the means in her power. Just as Chile is now insisting on her Lauca Treaty, she then insisted on the saltpeter agreement. In 1876 Chilean troops drove the Bolivians out of the Antofagasta region. The Bolivian relief army, composed chiefly of mountain Indians, wandered around for weeks in the trackless desert without encountering the enemy. At last they withdrew to the mountains. From then on, Peru could continue the war.

In the course of this war, Chile became a real nation for the first time, as well as the terror of her neighbors. On January 17, 1881, five years after the outbreak of the war, the Chileans took the Peruvian capital of Lima. They had demonstrated that the warlike talents of the Araucans were happily conjoined in them with the military skill of the old-time Spanish elite troops who had settled the country.

The quarrels over the conquered territories dragged on for a considerable time. In 1884 Chile at last concluded a treaty with unfortunate Bolivia, the real victim of the war. Bolivia had to cede her entire coastline and the adjacent deserts behind it to Chile. Since then, Bolivia has been a landlocked country. In November 1902 the Chileans also collected some additional desert areas that had hitherto been contested between Bolivia and Argentina. The Argentines, for their part, did not quite dare to dispute the issue with Chile. They had profited by the lesson of the Saltpeter War.

The Chileans did not have quite so easy a time of it with Peru. In 1883 Peru had to cede to Chile her southern province of Tarapacá, including the harbor of Iquique. But the Lima government was unwilling to part with two other provinces, Tacna and Arica. These two provinces had nothing to do with the actual cause of the war, the dispute over saltpeter. But the Chileans insisted that they had honestly conquered Tacna and Arica and therefore intended to hold on to their gains. Both countries finally agreed that after ten years a plebiscite would be held in Arica and Tacna. The population of the two provinces was to decide whether to remain true to Peru, to give Bolivia a strip of coast, or to be integrated into expanding Chile.

The Saltpeter War simmered down in the Tacna-Arica farce. It was played with rapidly shifting sets and actors. The first uninvited participant, who had nothing to do with the script, was Washington. The United States had watched the expansion of Anglophile and Germanophile Chile's power with extreme distrust. Washington wanted no further enlargement of Chilean territory, and therefore voiced her doctrine that no country in the Americas must aggrandize herself by acts of violence and wars. The United States first promulgated this thesis after the Mexican War, in which she had reduced Mexico to nearly half her former size.

American pressure led to a permanent postponement of the plebiscite promised in the treaty. The three countries involved were not really averse to this, for none of them could be sure of emerging as victor in the popular vote. Bolivia reluctantly resigned her hopes of recovering a seaport, and Chile profited by the delay to build up the harbor of Arica, which had gravely deteriorated. Thenceforth Peru and Chile stood like two gladiators awaiting the signal to begin battle. Peru organized her troops on the French model; Chile obtained German military advisers. For a while it looked as if the Franco-Prussian War of 1870–71 was to be refought in South America.

Thanks to her newly acquired territory, Chile abruptly became one of the richest countries in Latin America. The Chile saltpeter boom can only be compared to the gold rushes in California and Alaska. Chile saltpeter made the ports of Antofagasta, Taltal, Tocopilla, and Iquique thriving metropolises visited by the world's fastest ships. Great shipyards, trading firms, and munitions factories in Europe and America owed their rise to the Chile saltpeter trade. Saltpeter also transformed the bleak landscape around the desert city of Antofagasta into a blooming oasis of flourishing tropical flora.

Lots of money was being made in Antofagasta, and her citizens therefore wanted to do something with the city set so drearily in the desert. The British, who had stood godfather to Antofagasta, set up a small model of Big Ben on a plaza in the center of the city. In addition, the city fathers made it a rule that every foreign vessel docking in the port was to bring a sack of earth from its homeland. Thus countless sacks of humus from all parts of the world were unloaded in Antofagasta. The flowering shrubs and palms in the saltpeter city grow in truly international soil.

THE CHILEAN ECONOMIC MIRACLE

Along with Chile saltpeter, copper became a dominant factor in the life of Chile. At the end of the last century, the uncrowned copper king of the world was the American Daniel Guggenheim. He already controlled most of the copper resources in the United States and Mexico, and began casting an eye on Chile, where the Spaniards had at one time mined considerable copper. His interests were eventually acquired by Anaconda Copper, which to this day runs the biggest copper works in the world in El Teniente, near Rancagua and in Chuquicamata, east of Antofagasta.

Copper and Chile saltpeter not only filled the Chilean treasury; they gave rise to a wave of avarice and luxury on a scale hitherto unknown in the country. Rich Chileans became stockbrokers. In 1890 a liberal president held office in Santiago de Chile. Month after month President José Manuel Balmaceda watched the expansion of the Chilean economic miracle with growing uneasiness. He determined to tame the flood of wealth and channelize it, so that it would benefit not only the old rich and the new rich, but would also fructify the whole country. In other words, he wanted to transform the by now chaotic free economy of Chile into an orderly planned economy.

Balmaceda's principal idea was to use the money from Chile saltpeter and copper to build railroads, schools, and public buildings. Some of the wealth also went into hiring German army officers and buying German weapons. As Balmaceda saw it, a vigorous Chilean army trained along Prussian lines was the best assurance that the Tacna-Arica question would be settled as Chile desired.

The Balmaceda era ended in 1891 with a bloody civil war. This war was a curious phenomenon, highly typical of Chilean mentality, for it not only plunged the country into chaos, but also gave birth to Chilean democracy. Balmaceda was without doubt a sensitive economic planner with a highly modern outlook. The only trouble with his plans was that the Chilean congress would not agree to them. The Conservatives were against Balmaceda because he fought clericalism, introduced civil marriage, and separated church and state. Many of the Liberals were incensed when the president raised taxes in order to provide funds for his reforms. Only a minority of the Liberals remained loyal to Balmaceda. Since his day the great Liberal Party, which had hitherto been the strongest party in Chile, has been split into right and left factions bitterly hostile to each other.

Because of congressional resistance, Balmaceda could carry out his reforms only by dictatorial methods. In his concern for the future development of the country, he attempted to do so. But Chileans had meanwhile tasted economic and individual freedom; they were allergic to all kinds of dictatorship, even one prompted by benevolent and rational motives. The congressional majority deposed the president. And since Balmaceda refused to withdraw voluntarily, executive troops and legislative troops fought for power for nine months. Foreign countries also took sides in the civil war. The United States sympathized with Balmaceda because it counted on him to expel European capital from Chile. The European powers, England, France, and Germany, supported the congressional forces in the hope that this party would let them continue participating in the Chilean economic miracle.

What was at stake in this civil war, the only serious one in Chile's history, was not the hegemony of a particular clique or any radical social change, but preservation of democratic institutions. For Latin America, that was a novelty. It is significant that Chile was decades in advance of other Latin American countries in its respect for parliamentary democracy. Nowadays historians argue that the civil war was in truth a struggle for power between the United States and Europe for economic hegemony in Chile, the struggle being fought at the expense of the Chilean people. There is some justification for this view. Nevertheless, the fact remains that the civil war was also a test of Chilean democracy. The elected representatives of the people were able to enforce their will upon an outstandingly capable president.

Balmaceda lost the civil war because the conservative navy went over to the side of the congress. With the revolutionaries controlling the ports, they were able to buy foreign arms and land on any spot along the Chilean coast. The fighting cost Chile ten thousand lives. Balmaceda ultimately committed suicide. His successor, Jorge Montt, the leader of the rebels, discovered soon enough that Balmaceda had been right after all. Montt introduced his own brand of planned economy, which was not so different from Balmaceda's but was more acceptable to the democratic majority.

Chile's economic boom continued. During the First World War she exported Chile saltpeter to the tune of three million tons annually. Her position was so secure that she could declare herself a neutral. Bolivia and Peru, however, joined the Allies, hoping that in return the United States and the Western powers would help them recover the old bones of contention, Tacna and Arica, from Chile.

When the time came for peace negotiations, Chile's pro-German "neutrality" stood her in ill stead. The Allies were redistributing territory at Versailles and Saint Germain, and Peru and Bolivia clamored for a new and anti-Chilean order in South America. Peru wanted Tacna, Bolivia wanted Arica. Chile hastily entered the League of Nations, where, however, her delegates were received icily. There seemed every likelihood that Chile would have to give up Tacna-Arica as Germany was yielding Alsace-Lorraine.

In the course of these negotiations, the Chileans proved that they were not only good fighters and militant democrats, but also adroit diplomats. Peru and Bolivia claimed that the restoration of Tacna and Arica was essential to preserve international law, that the treaties of 1883–84 had been imposed under duress and represented a historical injustice for which Chile must make amends. The Chileans skillfully countered this argument by pointing out that by this reasoning the treaties of Versailles and Saint Germain would also have to be revised as historical injustices. Not wishing to create a precedent, the League of Nations hastily dropped the Tacna-Arica question.

In 1920 the Chilean elections were won by the *Alianza Liberal,* a party that evoked the memory of Balmaceda and found its principal support in the industrialized north. Its leader, a lawyer named Arturo Alessandri, endeavored to settle the Tacna-Arica question peaceably. He asked the President of the United States to arbitrate. The Chilean army objected to North American intervention and overthrew Alessandri. Meanwhile, however, the United States had acquired great influence in Bolivia. Washington was anxious to prevent unrest along the Pacific coast of South America. So much American capital was invested in all three of the embroiled republics that any new collision among them would have been very costly to Americans.

The then Senator Kellogg drafted a plan aimed at definitively separating the two gladiators, Chile and Peru, and thereby ensuring peace and quiet for American copper, tin, and steel interests. Tacna and Arica were to be ceded to Bolivia but demilitarized. Bolivia would pay Peru and Chile compensation for the region. Kellogg furthermore planned to internationalize the Morro, the fortified mountain which dominates the harbor of Arica, garrisoning it with a mixed body of troops under North American command. Should disputes break out, the United States would be in a position to intervene immediately.

The Bolivian mineowners' government was enthusiastic. Peru and Chile, however, had different views about sovereignty. The U.S.A. already dominated Cuba, Puerto Rico, Nicaragua, and Panama; given a foothold in Arica, she would be able to dominate the three Andean republics also. Behind the back of the United States, Peruvian Dictator Leguía and Chilean Dictator Ibáñez, who had overthrown Alessandri, came to their own agreement in 1929. Tacna was restored to Peru, Arica remained with Chile, and Bolivia received nothing. The United States approved the settlement grudgingly, while American newspapers published editorials on the unreliability of Latin American military dictators.

The nationalistic population of Chile, however, regarded the settlement as a defeat—the first defeat in the history of their country. Ibáñez was overthrown and the social reformer Alessandri recalled. There were, to be sure, other reasons for the fall of Ibáñez. After fifty years of prosperity, Chile had been plunged into the worst sort of depression. Her great source of wealth had been her nitrates. Just as the economy of other Latin American countries was entirely bound up with coffee, sugar, tin, and oil, so the economic life of Chile was utterly dependent on the sale of Chile saltpeter.

In 1912, German chemists began developing a process for manufacturing nitrates from air, which is four-fifths nitrogen. At first the product of the German laboratories went only to the armaments industry. In the twenties, however, artificial nitrates gradually began conquering the field. They were cheaper than imported Chilean nitrates. Munitions and fertilizer factories more and more turned to the synthetic product.

The result was an abrupt collapse of Chile's economy. North Chile, which had been won by such bitter struggles, faced ruin. It would probably have reverted to desert again had it not been for the

Guggenheim mining interests, which tried to meet the crisis by increasing copper production. The Guggenheims even invested American capital in Chilean nitrate works between 1927 and 1929 in the effort to revive them. They acquired a major share of the now unprofitable nitrate fields, and during the Ibáñez era controlled the cartel of Chilean saltpeter companies. The Chileans were furious with Ibáñez for having allowed the Americans to take over Chilean nitrates, as they had taken over Chilean copper.

The Guggenheim investments could not halt the rapid decline of the saltpeter trade. Before 1920, Chile had furnished 90 per cent of the world's supply of nitrate fertilizer. By 1930 the percentage was reduced to only 8, and has not risen since. President Alessandri, concerned over the growing influence of foreign finance capital in Chile, once again tried to save the day in 1934. He declared nitrates a state monopoly. But the Guggenheim concern scarcely reacted; by then Chilean saltpeter had become such a drug on the world market that it was not worth quarreling over.

Instead, the Guggenheim company pushed copper production in northern Chile, where it had a monopoly no one at the time was prepared to contest. Chile became the greatest copper-producing country in the world. More than one-third of the world's reserves of copper are to be found in the deposits of Antofagasta. The Chilean people, however, did not profit from the copper boom to nearly the extent they had profited from the now defunct Chile saltpeter boom. Foreign concerns largely controlled the copper wealth of Chile. Anaconda Copper, which had acquired the Guggenheim holdings, and several smaller companies were joined, after the Bolivian revolution, by the Hochschild company in Mantos Blancos, which had hitherto been one of the three major producers of Bolivian tin.

THE LIVING DESERT

A journey through the desert regions to the east and north of Antofagasta provides a dramatic picture of the downfall of the nitrate industry and the rise of copper. After the sudden end of the Chile saltpeter boom, most of the desert settlements in the interior of the country were abandoned. The saltpeter workers had made good money, which led to a mushrooming of boom towns in the desert where they could spend their wages on drink, gambling, and women.

With the collapse of the saltpeter industry there was a mass exodus to the ports or the copper mines. Although the Chilean saltpeter industry has revived somewhat in recent times, only a few of the old nitrate plants are in operation. Most of the buildings have long since fallen prey to wind and sand.

I drove through one ghost town after the other. Bleached remnants of walls of houses thrust from the sand. Blue sky showed through blank window openings. Faded signs commemorated barbershops, drugstores, groceries, and hotels. Looking into one of these empty places, I could still read the surly warning "No credit given." Another ruin could be identified as a bordello, where girls of many races had sold their services at sinfully high prices.

Everything still stood, the factories, houses, shops, brothels, and taverns from the days of the saltpeter boom. The roofs and window frames were missing, the former inhabitants having carted away whatever was worth the cost of transportation. The wind filled the ruins with sand. Now and then a sagging building collapses. The yellow desert is punctuated with whitish places, where the earth seems coated with some sort of mold. These are the crusts of saltpeter which fifty years ago represented untold wealth. Today, people no longer even turn to glance twice at the stuff.

Hour after hour, you drive through the desert. Blue sky, yellow sand, here and there a small wooden cross. Sometimes a tin can holding a bunch of flowers will be standing in front of the cross. It is an unwritten law that passers-by give the flowers fresh water. Who can tell but that just such a wooden cross may someday be erected for him? The desert is hostile to man and has already claimed many victims.

After the ghost towns, the solitude, the miles and miles of desert, it is something of a shock to come upon a highly modern copper mine, which all at once brings you back into our loud and bustling twentieth century. Huge power shovels eat away the sides of entire mountains. Trucks incessantly transport the lumps of greenish ore to a mill where they are ground to powder. Gigantic tubs are filled with blue copper solutions. There are belt conveyors, glowing furnaces— the mines are largely automated. There is something uncanny about such mechanization in the midst of the lifeless desert. The greenish chunks of rock that are poured into the grinding mill are transformed as if by magic, from station to station, into pure, tawny, identical bars of shining copper.

Large parts of Chile have changed from agricultural regions to mining and industrial areas. In addition to the great copper deposits, in north and central Chile, the country is rich in iron, manganese and coal. Oil is being extracted in the far south, in Tierra del Fuego. The Bethlehem Steel Company rules over the iron and steel industry of Chile as Anaconda does over the copper. After the difficult birth-pangs of the nitrate era, northern Chile has become an industrialized region.

The cliffs outside Antofagasta still swarm with guano-yielding sea birds, with which the nitrate story began. Now and then you still encounter small plants in the desert that are obtaining nitrate fertilizers from the *caliche,* the surface coating of the sand. But the ships that dock in Antofagasta today rarely take on nitrates. They are loaded instead with ore and the tawny copper bars. As far as anyone can predict, the Chileans will be living for a long time to come on the copper wealth of the north. How they acquired this section of their country is a story in itself.

GERMANS WITH PONCHOS

They came to a country that at the time of their immigration was universally described as a wilderness, gloomy and impenetrable, hostile to man, and fatal for civilized Europeans. They made their way into the interior, to a great lake scarcely anyone had ever seen, the subject of terrifying legends. Lake Llanquihue, it was said, had tides like a sea, was constantly lashed by storms, and was the home of terrible head-hunters. But they pushed on, in spite of all warnings, and found that the lake had no real terrors and that the soil in the surrounding jungles was good and fruitful.

They were democrats, partisans of the revolution of 1848, and had left their fatherland so that they could remain faithful to their democratic ideals in another continent. But when they set about clearing the jungles around Lake Llanquihue, they discovered that democracy is not so easy in practice, not even in the wilderness. They had to battle the Araucan tribes of the Pehuenche and Huilliche. They had to expel, enslave, or kill the Indians. The Chilean Government had given them the land, but they had to fight to take possession of it; and they did so without making much fuss about it. To this day their descendants do not like to talk about those harsh, ruthless, undemocratic days. Their Araucan wars are not recorded as glorious pages in Chilean history. When the Indians were gone, they spread the poncho of silence over the bloody beginnings of their colonization and gradually transformed the south Chilean wilderness into agricultural provinces that look amazingly like replicas of their German homeland.

The person who conceived the idea of settling German immigrants in Chile was a seaman and traveler from Berlin named Bernhard Philippi. From 1830 to 1832 Philippi had taken part in a voyage around the globe. He liked what he saw in Chile, and since he was intensely interested in the flora and fauna of the country, the Prussian Government assigned him to explore the Chilean interior. On one expedition Philippi reached Lake Llanquihue and the Osorno volcano. He mapped the regions which were later to become the center of German colonization, and discovered that the vicinity of Lake Llanquihue had something of the climate of Central Europe. That was what inspired him to bring German settlers to this wilderness.

CONQUEST OF THE SOUTH

If we compare Philippi's descriptions with the present appearance of the provinces of Llanquihue, Osorno, and Valdivia, we can appreciate the vast labor done in the course of a century. The ground was so swampy that it was like a water-soaked sponge. Every step in these morasses was an effort. Under the gigantic jungle trees, lush undergrowth barred movement. A man could go through the jungle only by cutting a path with his machete. The air was thick with gnats and mosquitoes. The only large living creatures Philippi encountered were wild pigs and pumas. In the few places where vegetation was somewhat scantier, Philippi and his companions had to climb over slabs of lava from the volcanoes.

Today this area is like one great park, a succession of well-tilled fields, fat pastures, pruned and tended forests, and farmyards that might have been plucked straight from Central Europe. In clearing the land, the German settlers at first used the same methods as the

Iberian settlers in other parts of Chile. They burned down the forests and enriched their fields with the ashes. But while the devastation of the forests in central Chile was carried so far as to suggest that the Chileans were a nation of pyromaniacs, the Germans followed up the initial clearing by intensive reforestation. German colonists could not have lived in a land without trees. To the German farmer, a forest for his Sunday strolls was as essential a part of existence as tillable land and meadows. And this timely reforestation proved to be one of the vital achievements of the Germans in southern Chile. As you go through this region, you do not have the depressing feeling, as you do elsewhere, that this is a land parched and exhausted by man. The three southern provinces are not bothered by erosion, which is spreading in central Chile as inexorably as a cancer. In general, one may say that Germanic and Slavic peoples are lovers of forest, whereas the Latins have no special feeling for it. South American Latins frequently behave as if they were actually afraid of the forest; they push back the woods wherever they can. The result has been that the larger part of the original jungle areas of Chile have been transformed into sad, monotonous, overcultivated plains.

Before the arrival of the Germans, the Spaniards and Chileans had been able to hold their own only in a few places in central Chile. Cities such as Valdivia and Osorno had, to be sure, been founded in colonial days, but at times they had to be abandoned—partly because of the Araucans, partly because of earthquakes. The hinterland, the Chilean Switzerland of today with its azure and emerald lakes, its glowing volcanic cones and fresh green mountain forests, was terra incognita. The rainy and cold climate of these parts deterred the Iberians from exploring more closely what is probably the most beautiful landscape in the southern part of the continent. Here, too, however, the Pehuenche and Huilliche, the southern Araucans, had not formed tightly organized communities. They wandered nomadically through the forests, hunted and fished, and perhaps envied their northern fellow tribesmen, whom they met only now and then when an Araucan general would once more call upon his people to battle the white invaders.

Even the characteristic animal of the southern Andes, the guemal, was so little known to the Chileans that they represented it in their national coat of arms as a grotesque monster. The condor and the guemal are the two heraldic animals of Chile. The condor, the great vulture of the Andes, is depicted in all its majestic reality, but the guemal, the legendary Andean stag, is represented as a cross between a horse and a llama. The guemal suffered the same fate as the Pehuenche and Huilliche Indians. It is almost extinct today.

Under the presidency of General Bulnes, Philippi's suggestion that German settlers be lured to southern Chile met a response. Real immigration, however, did not begin until after the leader of the progressive right, pro-German Manuel Montt, took over the government in 1851. Philippi became one of the new president's closest associates. He had meanwhile become a nationalized Chilean, had risen in the military and political hierarchy, and later held office as governor of the southernmost province of Magallanes. His descendants have played important parts in Chilean politics and science.

President Montt had certain clear ideas when he drew up his immigration policy. He was not interested in flooding southern Chile with people of dubious reputation that Europe would be glad to get rid of; he wanted genuine democrats and idealists. The first group of immigrants, in fact, made a pledge to democracy which on the whole they have fulfilled. They promised their new country that they would become honest and industrious Chileans and would defend the republic as staunchly as the most patriotic native Chilean.

Such oaths of allegiance are easy to make and sometimes difficult to keep. There were cultural, historical, and sociological gulfs between the Central European immigrants and the Ibero-Indian populace of Chile which to some extent have not been bridged to this day. Germans often find it hard to throw off their heritage and become easily and completely assimilated into a new country. The result has often been that disagreeable, jingoistic type of hyphenated German who unconditionally adores everything German and waxes lachrymose at his fate in a foreign land. That, however, has not been the case in Chile. Most of the members of old German-Chilean families I spoke to were loyal Chileans.

The first ship with German settlers arrived in Chile on February 12, 1853. A few years later Chileans and Germans together founded Puerto Montt, today one of the principal ports in southern Chile. From Puerto Montt and the already existing cities of Valdivia and Osorno, the settlers advanced into the region of jungle and lakes. They cleared paths through the jungle with axes and machetes. Several families took possession of territories the size of European principalities. The pioneers of German extraction were gradually followed by Chilean pioneers. To this day, however, the region around Lake Llanquihue has remained a patch of Germany in Chile, praised by the Chileans, but sometimes regarded with a touch of suspicion.

ASSIMILATION—BUT HOW?

This Chilean suspicion flares up whenever the Chileans of German extraction make much of their exclusiveness. The Germans marry among themselves. They have preserved the culture and habits of their forefathers almost without adulteration. They speak a German that may not always be stylistically pure but is without accent. They devote themselves to German literature, music and art—and sometimes, unfortunately, to German politics. The German schools are exemplary. They read German newspapers and even maintain several journals that try to comment objectively on the rapidly changing political events within Germany.

The Chileans, however, are a people who believe passionately in assimilation. They would like to transform every immigrant into a Chilean as speedily as possible. Although the German-Chileans manifest a proper degree of Chilean nationalism, they have often been criticized for remaining aliens within the country, in spite of their having been there for a century. Shrill, clumsy demonstrations of sympathy for the land of their ancestors on the part of German-Chileans during two world wars have contributed to this feeling. It seems that German hearts periodically begin to pound nationalistically under the poncho, much to the ire of 100-per-cent Chileans.

Many German-Chileans with whom I spoke honestly admitted that their feelings had been with Wilhelm II in his time, and with Hitler in his. They also honestly admitted that they had been wrong in both cases. Events in Germany had looked very different from a distance. But all the German-Chileans who visited Germany during the nazi era had returned to their democratic Chile with their enthusiasm considerably dampened. It is true that you can still hear nazi and anti-Semitic sentiments in Chile (and almost everywhere else in South America). But after the end of the war, when the full extent of the horrors of the Hitler regime were revealed, the German-Chileans were far more courageous about coming to terms with the past than the Germans themselves.

Chile can easily digest her approximately fifty thousand citizens of German extraction, the majority of whom are farmers, scientists, teachers, engineers, and manufacturers. After the First World War, however, plans were afoot for settling some half million Germans in Chile. The authors of the plans pointed out that the Germans were the only people who had achieved lasting success in clearing and tilling new land. Chilean intellectuals, however, were alarmed at the prospect and strongly opposed any such German invasion. A Chilean writer, Joaquin Edwards Bello, expressed their feelings somewhat drastically when he wrote: "For us Chileans to invite half a million Germans to our country, would be as if the anchovettas in the ocean asked for five hundred thousand sharks." The cleverness and efficiency of the Germans, it was feared, would swiftly transform Chile into a New World Germania. Consequently, nothing ever came of the planned mass immigration.

Nevertheless, Chileans do not resent the Germans' ability, so long as there are not too many of them. And anyone familiar with conditions in Chile can scarcely blame the Germans for their aloofness—which, aside from occasional political escapades, has persisted. Complete assimilation would be equivalent to total adoption of Latin culture, Latin customs. Immigrant Germans are by no means incapable of assimilation; those who immigrate to the United States become unadulterated Americans by the second generation. But the situation is far more difficult in Latin America. For when Germans come there, two worlds collide—worlds almost incompatible because of entirely different historical development.

The Chileans, in spite of their Europeanization and democratization, still live wholly within the old Latin-Catholic traditions—traditions that have long since been overcome in Central Europe during a slow evolutionary process. The South American Latin rules his family in a patriarchal fashion. Latin American wives are consigned a place at the stove and the cradle. As is customary in Latin countries, a husband is entitled to keep one or several mistresses who lead a semilegal life on the fringes of society. Although Latin American girls and women have the same educational and vocational opportunities as their European sisters, they do not fully utilize these opportunities. In addition, there are archaic social conventions and archaic marriage and divorce laws.

Besides all this, there is a sharp cultural disparity between Central Europe and Latin America. To be sure, science, literature, and the arts have been flourishing in many Latin American countries for decades, but the practitioners and consumers of culture are numerically very few at the present time. The Latin American masses are still outside cultural developments for lack of education.

The German settlers in Chile were mostly liberal democrats and Protestants to whom the Latin conventions of their new country inevitably seemed alien and medieval. For the German-Chileans, adoption of Chilean culture would have meant a relapse into the discarded past. Assimilation, moreover, entails intermarriage. A German-Chilean girl who marries an Iberian-Chilean risks throwing away a hundred years of feminine emancipation—without which a Central European woman can no longer conceive marriage and family life. A German-Chilean man who marries a Chilean woman must reckon with the possibility that he is not acquiring a comrade and companion for life, but merely a docile mother for his children. Although the Chileans are extremely tolerant in matters of religion, most German-Chileans who marry Iberians give up their traditional Protestantism. The customs of the country force them into that typical Latin American form of Catholicism which has been separated from Central European Catholicism by whole centuries and is still deeply rooted in the Middle Ages.

All these factors have led the German-Chileans to live in isolated settlements, to set up their own schools and churches, and to form a "state within a state" similar to that of the Araucans. Probably assimilation into the liberal, open-minded middle class in Chile, especially in the large cities, would not have been difficult for the German immigrants. But in the countryside, at any rate, the old German-Chilean families to this day have a horror of a liaison between any child of theirs and an Iberian-Chilean. Indeed, a century of intermarriage among German-Chileans has already led to a degree of inbreeding that is beginning to be dangerous. After the end of the last war, when refugees from the countries of the Eastern bloc, especially Hungary and Yugoslavia, found new homes in Chile, they became highly desirable marital partners among the Germans. This seems strong proof that Chileans of German extraction are not set on marrying only Germans. They want husbands and wives whose social and intellectual development is approximately at the same stage as their own.

On top of all this, there is one unpleasant trait which is shared by descendants of other European stocks: the race complex. There is fear of taking Indian blood into the family. Despite the loud claims of the Chileans that they are as white as any European people, Chilean intellectuals well realize that more than two-thirds of the people have Indian blood in their veins. As a matter of fact, the mixture has proved an excellent one, and Chilean intellectuals are waging a passionate campaign for the *raza chilena*, for affirmation of the splendid qualities of Araucan blood and culture. Nevertheless, German-Chilean parents find it hard to accept the idea that their grandchildren may be stiff-haired, cherry-eyed mestizos.

THE PRUSSIANS OF SOUTH AMERICA

The race complex is fading. The unpleasant habit of some German-Chileans of calling Chilean agricultural workers and fellow citizens "blacks" is likewise fading, at least among the younger generation. The Chilean people are breaking the fetters of medieval social traditions; in this respect they are several steps ahead of other Latin American countries. In the last forty years Chile has made every effort to overtake Europe's century-and-a-half head start in social evolution. As soon as Chile reaches the same sociological and cultural plane as Central Europe, there will no longer be any obstacles to complete assimilation of the German-Chileans.

German military music, German army discipline, and Prussian bureaucracy in Chile have resulted in the Chileans' being called, half in compliment and half in condemnation, the "Prussians of Latin America." Prussianism was introduced into Chile by the same President Balmaceda around whom the democratic civil war of 1891 had revolved. Balmaceda dressed his soldiers in the handsome uniform of the Prussian Guards. In addition to bringing German officers to Chile to reorganize his army, he was the first head of state anywhere in the world to introduce the repeating rifle with automatic bolt invented by the German engineer Ferdinand von Mannlicher. The novel Mannlicher rifle was partly to blame for bringing the Balmaceda regime to such a precipitate end. A majority of the troops officered by Germans under the command of General Körner took the side of the congressionals. In the battle of Viña del Mar, the rifles proved their worth for the first time. Since the days of General Körner and his "secret weapon," no South American doubts that Chile has the best-drilled and most effective army in Latin America.

One Sunday morning I was wading through the muddy streets of Puerto Aysén, capital of that remote province in the deep south of Chile which was opened to the world only a few decades ago. As I stepped gingerly on the plank walks that formed bridges over the worst morasses, I suddenly heard the loud blare of German march music. For a moment I actually started in alarm. Then I saw that the *carabineros,* the border guards of Aysén, were giving their Sunday band concert on the plaza. Prussian guards could not have marched more crisply or looked more keen and disciplined than these carabineros. But in their barracks these same troops had a remarkably lax and civilian air. Their casino was more like an existentialist club than a Prussian officers' mess. Here, among the carabineros of Aysén, I was given a taste of the cordial, spontaneous quality of Chilean hospitality. To please me, the carabineros were ready to throw their whole schedule of duties to the winds. In spite of General Körner and the Prussian uniforms, the Chilean people have remained a heart-warmingly unmilitaristic nation.

THE MAN-EATING SHEEP

Punta Arenas is the southernmost city on earth. It is true that Ushuaia, capital of the Argentine part of Tierra del Fuego, lies somewhat more to the south than the Chilean port on the Strait of Magellan. But by no stretch of the imagination can Ushuaia be called anything more than a subantarctic foothold in the wilderness. Punta Arenas, on the other hand, is a real city with paved streets, a number of stone houses, traffic lights, hotels, restaurants, and sailors' dives. Above all, Punta Arenas, in spite of its unprepossessing wooden mole extending far out into the Strait of Magellan, is an important harbor.

The Patagonian-Tierra del Fuegan region of Chile has become a land of sheep. Wool is shipped from Punta Arenas all over the world. On the other shore of the Strait of Magellan lies the town of Porvenir, which optimistic Chileans already regard as a kind of little Maracaibo. The campfires of the Indians, which gave the great southern island its name, no longer flicker in Tierra del Fuego, but the great flames from oil wells light up the night sky. The petroleum deposits of Magallanes Province were discovered as recently as December 1945. Apparently the usually keen scent of Shell, Standard Oil, and the other big oil companies did not function in the South American subantarctic. The Chilean Government, at that time a Popular Front administration with Communists included, promptly took hold of the newly discovered oil domes. They are now operated by a state-owned company.

Taking my first stroll through Punta Arenas, I was struck by how oddly familiar this southernmost city in the world seemed to me. I walked down the long wooden mole on which were piled barrels, iron pipes, and bales of wool. I passed workmen squatting by the edge of the mole, their belongings in packs beside them, transients who came here only for the summer season. I looked at the many wooden houses of the city, the heavy-garmented people in the streets, the somewhat old-fashioned offices of the merchants, the fishing boats along the beach, the dirty snow on the hills, the glaciated mountains off on the horizon. I was here for the first time, and yet it seemed to me that I had seen all this before.

After tramping through Punta Arenas for several hours I realized what the city on the Strait of Magellan reminded me of. It was the spit and image of a port in northern Norway transplanted to the Southern Hemisphere. It looked like something described by Knut Hamsun, or as if the Chileans had constructed a replica of Hamsun's town of Segelfoss. Even the smell of fish, blubber, and hides was the same as you would find in a thriving yet remote port on the Arctic Circle.

Recollections of Knut Hamsun vanished when I looked more closely at the inhabitants of Punta Arenas. A veritable Babel of peoples has collected there: Chileans, Argentines, Yugoslavs, Englishmen, and Germans; traders, sailors, petroleum engineers, adventurers, and descendants of convicts; brown-skinned seasonal workers from Chiloé, poncho-wearing gauchos from Patagonia. Among them were a number of persons of small stature with rather Mongolian features and stiff black hair—evidence that the pioneers at the Strait of Magellan once mingled with the aboriginal inhabitants of Tierra del Fuego.

FROM MAGELLAN TO O'HIGGINS

Three monuments symbolize the key points in the story of Patagonia and Tierra del Fuego. The great monument to Magellan, who discovered the strait and thus also the bay of Punta Arenas, also reminds us that this voyager proved, for the first time in man's history, that the earth is really round. At the feet of the bearded navigator crouch two bronze Indians—a Tehuelche from Patagonia and an Alacalufe from Tierra del Fuego. They are involuntary symbols of the cruel triumph of the conquerors and colonizers over the native races. Ferdinand Magellan stands with foot outstretched, presumably to impress upon the Indians their lowly status. Anyone who kisses this foot, it is said in Punta Arenas, will always return to the city. The foot, it must be said, shows few signs of being worn down by excessive affection. As I walked past the gray, dusty-looking houses, I too felt little inclination to kiss Magellan's foot. Later, after I had become acquainted with the melancholy beauty of the Patagonian pampas, I somewhat regretted that I had not performed the rite of the kiss.

The second monument represents the liberator of Chile, Bernardo O'Higgins. He symbolizes the battle of the Republic of Chile to establish a foothold in this southernmost part of the New World and thus possess herself of the vital passage between Atlantic and Pacific desired by so many sea powers. All attempts of the Spanish to secure the Strait of Magellan failed. A fort built by Philip II in the vicinity of Punta Arenas is to this day called Hunger Harbor, for every man of the Spanish garrison died there of starvation.

Toward the end of the eighteenth and the beginning of the nineteenth centuries British research ships, Portuguese corsairs, and Argentine adventurers haunted the southern tip of South America. Around the middle of the century Chilean President Bulnes recalled the old Hunger Harbor. Alongside the former Spanish structure he built a Chilean fort, Fuerte Bulnes. The Argentines immediately protested loudly. While Great Britain continued to hope that the no-man's-land around the Strait of Magellan would someday fall to her, Argentina and Chile began contending for the territory in an extremely curious way.

The chief sources of manpower in both countries were their criminals. Both the Argentines and the Chileans hastily began deporting their convicts to the far south. The principal center for the Argentine exiles was little Ushuaia, on Tierra del Fuego; the Chilean convict colony was established on that sandy spit of land that Magellan had once steered toward: Punta Arenas. Apparently the Chileans had a larger supply of convicts, for Punta Arenas grew to a town of more than a thousand inhabitants. The Chileans, who already regarded themselves as in possession of the entire region, had their troubles with their criminal pioneers. Convict uprisings made southern Patagonia and Tierra del Fuego an extremely unsafe region. At one time an exile of Czech nationality managed to make himself briefly King of Tierra del Fuego.

In 1881 Argentina decided to seize the Strait of Magellan by force. Under General Roca, the Argentines had conquered the greater part of Patagonia, almost exterminating its Indians. Now Argentina wanted to occupy southern Patagonia and Tierra del Fuego as well. Chile resisted, and war between the two countries was barely averted. At the last moment British mediators, who obviously sympathized with Chile, were able to persuade the rivals to sign a treaty making "the highest peaks of the cordillera, at the parting of the waters," the boundary between the two republics.

The struggle passed into a quiet phase: Chileans and Argentines reciprocally accused one another of dishonest surveys and mis-measurements of mountains. Moreover, the treaty of 1881 was ambiguous. For the highest peaks of the Andes were by no means the divide whence the waters flowed either into the Atlantic or the Pacific. The disputes dragged on to the end of the century. Apparently Chile's surveyors were more skilled than their Argentine colleagues, for in the end Chile owned not only the entire shore of the Strait of Magellan, but also the sharply contested southern Patagonian region of Última Esperanza and more than two-thirds of the main island of Tierra del Fuego, including the land that now yields coal and oil in abundance. Nevertheless, many Chileans to this day maintain that their country was shamefully cheated in this surveyors' dispute, because Chile did not get everything.

DARWIN AND THE TIERRA DEL FUEGANS

The third monument in Punta Arenas is the most attactive. It is located at the northern end of the city, on Avenida Bulnes, which leads out to the pampas; and it represents not a conqueror or a statesman, but a Patagonian shepherd with pack horse, dog, and sheep. The people of Punta Arenas showed tact and restraint in representing the great economic change in southern Patagonia and Tierra del Fuego not by a statue of one of the first wool kings, but of a humble shepherd. The anonymous man on the pedestal is peacefully going about his business. Had a monument been raised to Señores Nogueria, Menendez, or Campos, truth would have required a heap of murdered Indians under the feet of the wool king.

For once the pampas and the bush of the region had been signed over to the sheep, there began a campaign of genocide that continued into the twenties of the present century. When the British research vessel *Beagle* investigated the waters around the Tierra del Fuego archipelago in 1834, the garrison had some trouble with the aboriginals. But young Charles Darwin, whose part in the expedition was to make both him and the *Beagle* famous, was able to regard the primitive Indians of Tierra del Fuego with the eyes of a scientist. The original thought occurred to him that mankind has not always been as it was now, but must have passed through a gradual evolution. In those days the Tierra del Fuegans were still unmolested and were living their ancient folkways. Darwin noted in his travel journal that the natives were apparently holding their own numerically, which must mean that their life was satisfactory to them, despite the harsh climate. Things became a good deal harder for them when convicts and adventurers began pouring into the region. But around 1890 there were still between eight and fifteen thousand aboriginals, divided into the distinct tribes of Onas, Yahgans, and Alacalufes. Their great enemy turned out to be the sheep, who advanced in armies of millions.

Sarah Braun, an immigrant Lithuanian, could never have imagined how fraught with consequences would be the idea that came to her at the sight of the pampas. Sarah Braun's second husband was a Portuguese adventurer and whaler named Nogueria, who held concessions for sizable areas of land on the Strait of Magellan. In those days, the second half of the nineteenth century, a fortune hunter with a little business sense could carve out huge portions of the no-man's-land of Tierra del Fuego at small expense. Nogueria had no idea what to do with his vast holdings. Sarah Braun recommended that he follow the customs of her native land, raise sheep and deal in wool.

The experiment succeeded. Within a short time Nogueria and his wife became rich. The Compañía Sarah Braun has remained to this day the most powerful concern in Punta Arenas. Its success lured Argentines and Scots to Tierra del Fuego. Ten years after the company had been established, a million sheep were grazing in southern Patagonia and on the main island of Tierra del Fuego. Meat-freezing plants were built; wool merchants settled in Patagonia. Within a few decades a large part of the pampas along the Strait of Magellan belonged to a few clans, with the family firms of Braun, Menendez, and Campos still the leaders.

In order to protect the sheep from the nomadic Indians, the ranchers fenced their land with barbed wire. But the Tierra del Fuegans had no conception of European livestock and European ideas of property. They lived as fishermen and hunters in a primitive world and regarded the sheep as a new and easily hunted animal. For a while their bliss knew no bounds. Soon, however, their happy days were over. The sheep raisers put a price on their heads. They poisoned with strychnine the beached whales the Indians were accustomed to eat. They even employed professional Indian hunters who shot down these Stone Age people like rabbits. The Argentine wool king Menendez, whose descendants are still among the richest people in Patagonia, was particularly notorious for this sort of thing. It occurred to no one to attempt to make peaceful arrangements with the aboriginals. The sheep raisers, on the contrary, were actually proud of the number of Indians they had killed in a season. Hunting clubs actually made a "sport" of shooting Indians from passenger liners.

The captain of a German freighter shipping Patagonian wool to Europe has left an account of a meeting with a Scottish sheep raiser which took place in 1903. The Scot, who lived at Useless Bay, triumphantly displayed a rifle with innumerable notches on the butt. Every notch, he boasted, meant a native he had killed. "To judge by the notches," the captain wrote in his memoirs, "the man must have sent some fifteen hundred of the Fuegans to the other world. I upbraided him for this human butchery. He replied unmoved that the Indians had killed a thousand sheep out of his herd. He had therefore sworn not to rest until he had freed the camp of the last Indian. When I saw him again a few years later, he was a prosperous man."

By 1920 these sheep-breeding mass murderers had reduced the number of Indians to some three or four thousand. Civilization had entered Tierra del Fuego, and with a vengeance. The Indians who escaped annihilation were infected by their contact with the whites with all sorts of diseases. Epidemics of smallpox and tuberculosis swept away whole tribes. Many settlers amused themselves by intro- ducing the Indians to alcohol. They were entertained by the drunken dances of the aboriginals, who quickly became addicted. Alcoholism transformed the sturdy Stone Age people into miserable human wreckage. The remnants of the Tierra del Fuegans were finished off by poisoning their wells.

Today the Ona are completely extinct. Of the Yahgan, only a single man is said to be left; he is on display as a tourist attraction in Puerto Williams. I myself had the opportunity to see what was left of the Alacalufes, who were the fishing and boating people among the Indians. Aside from a few nomadic families, concerning whom there are only vague reports, the last Alacalufes have been settled in Puerto Eden by mandate of the Chilean Government. Puerto Eden is a small military base on Eyre Bay, in the archipelago of southwestern Chile. I learned that there are exactly forty-two members of this tribe in Puerto Eden, only a third of whom are women. The last Alacalufes are inexorably dying out. The protection at last granted them by the Chilean Government has come far too late.

VISIT TO THE STONE AGE MEN

In the morning light I saw the first Indian boats approaching our ship from Puerto Eden. I was on board a ship that regularly plied the straits among the islands, and the Indians call on all the ships that anchor outside Puerto Eden. My first look at these Stone Age people somewhat disappointed me. They looked like very down-at-heel beachcombers. None of them wore the traditional, weather-wise garb of seal and otter skin. Men, women, and children were swathed in worn-out European clothing given them by the sailors of passing ships. Inside this international assortment of clothing styles were small, stocky men with brown, leathery faces, broad cheekbones, slanting eyes, and boldly jutting noses.

Agilely, they climbed up a rope ladder let down to them from the deck. They warmed up on hot coffee, shamefacedly asked for cigarettes, and swapped sacks of shellfish and bundles of sealskins for clothing and goods. In many travel books the Alacalufes are described as an extremely primitive and nowadays degenerate people. I did not have that impression. Dressed neatly in clean clothing, they would merge into the populace in, let us say, working-class districts of Santiago de Chile.

It is not quite clear what the Chilean Government intends to do with this diminishing remnant of a tribe. As a people, the Alacalufes can no longer be saved. The few female inhabitants of Puerto Eden are eager to take up with any passing sailor or itinerant worker. Evidently they no longer feel content in their artificial Indian settlement. To this day the Alacalufes live in huts of wood and hides as did their ancestors. They share the dwellings with their dogs, sleep on skins, cook on open fires, and go hunting as men did in prehistoric times. But the conditions for such a life no longer exist in Chile.

On the ship's deck these people, who are regarded as culturally among the lowest on earth, moved about with an amazing grace and naturalness. They were rather shy, but managed to make themselves understood in broken Spanish, and smiled charmingly in conversation. They offered the strongest proof of Humboldt's thesis of the unity of the human race. They have been shot and poisoned like animals, but the survivors prove that in every human being, no matter where he lives, what race he belongs to, or what his cultural level, the basic elements of humanity are exactly the same as among us, the often so arrogant members of the white race.

Punta Arenas has grown big as a result of sheep raising and the annihilation of the Indians. Today the city holds more than fifty thousand inhabitants. The last native Tierra del Fuegans will soon have vanished from the globe, and their traces will have to be sought in a small museum in the Salesian monastery in Punta Arenas, where some mementos of the life, customs, and art of the Indians have been collected. It can only be hoped that a serious scientist will someday be called in to reorganize this museum. At present it houses a muddle of ethnological curiosa, stuffed animals, incongruous cases of tropical butterflies, corny pictorial reconstructions, and trashy devotional items, so that it is almost impossible to concentrate on what is of value.

About forty years ago a Salesian monk, Pater Alberto de Agostini, began studying Tierra del Fuego. He is still considered the foremost cartographer of and specialist on the Magallanes territory. The monks he brought with him did all they could to champion the cause of the Indians. They went about their enterprise, however, with at times unfortunate side effects. For instance, they might be blamed for the deaths from smallpox of several hundred Ona. The monks had collected clothing for the Indians and had failed to disinfect the gifts thoroughly.

In the course of their missionary and rescue work, the padres collected all sorts of tools, carvings, weapons, tents, boats, and ornaments in the Indian settlements. Their cluttered little museum contains veritable treasures from the world of the aboriginals.

A short distance from the museum is the famous home of Sarah Braun, which has now been converted into a clubhouse. From that house the victorious advance of the "man-eating" sheep began. A few streets farther on there is a dreary, battered old bar which bears the name of "Beagle"—a reminder that Darwin received the first glimmerings of his theory of evolution at the sight of the aboriginals of Tierra del Fuego.

BETWEEN *RICOS* AND *ROTOS*

The southwestern corner of Chile crumbles into innumerable islands and archipelagos. A voyage among these silent, deserted islands reminds one of the ancient myth of Scylla and Charybdis. The captain and helmsmen must draw upon all their seamanship not to wreck their ships on the hidden reefs, the precipitous walls of rock that rise up from the narrow straits, and the drifting ice floes.

The development of Chilean democracy and social policies was, similarly, a voyage through perilous waters. Today there are two dangerous reefs that the Chilean ship of state must continually skirt. The many attractive traits of the Chilean people sometimes obscure the fact that this droll, long and skinny country in the southwestern part of South America suffers from the same dichotomies besetting most Latin American lands. Chile's political, diplomatic, and economic competence is often admirable. Her charm and hospitality warm the heart of the foreign visitor.

But in this climate of cordiality and affection, it is all too easy to overlook the agrarian problems, the social tensions, and the slums that disfigure other Latin American countries which are less superficially pleasing. The Chilean Scylla is the class of *ricos*. The Chilean Charybdis is the class of *rotos*.

AGRARIAN KINGS AND LUMPENPROLETARIANS

Ricos is the name given the rich landowners who held half of the tillable land in colonial days and who today own not much less. The Chilean landed oligarchy, like that in other Latin American countries, is extremely small, extremely conservative, and marked by a striking degree of social incomprehension. Precisely because Chile is a democracy whose political life is vigorous rather than frozen, this incomprehension on the part of the ricos strikes the observer as the more shocking. One begins to feel that the glaring social injustices in rural areas are less an outcome of disparities of wealth than a heritage of Spanish colonial rule. For in the part of Chile settled by Central Europeans things look altogether different.

The landowners of German extraction have naturally taken on some of the manners of the ricos. Until very recently they lived in the traditional rico style. Nevertheless, they are unconsciously influenced by social developments in their former homeland. They are seriously concerned about existing conditions. Many of their sons and daughters take an active part in shaping social policies. Nowadays they take it for granted that they must provide neat, decent cottages for their hired hands. Wretched, poverty-stricken day laborers are seldom found in the southern part of the country. The housing for agricultural workers in central Chile, on the other hand, often looks worse than the most primitive cattle barns. And the misery of the rural population in that part of the country constitutes a major and dangerous problem to the government.

Rotos, "ragged ones," is the Chilean name for agricultural workers. After the industrial boom began, the term was extended to factory workers and miners. The majority of the Chilean country population consists of rotos. More than two-thirds of the rotos are mestizos, although they consider themselves white Chileans. Thus the greater part of the Chilean people are proletarians—in fact what Marxists would call lumpenproletarians. Small farmers, rotos who have somewhat bettered themselves, till only 1 per cent of the land. Hence the agrarian question is just as burning, just as explosive as it is in the plantation countries of Latin America.

The tasks this situation imposes upon Chile were as apparent to Bernardo O'Higgins as they are to every modern social thinker. But the liberator did not succeed in dealing effectively with these problems, and his successors have done no better to this day. The reformer Eduardo Frei must struggle with the ricos today in his efforts to carry out his "revolution in freedom."

In Chile as in other Latin American colonies, the rich landowners were the leaders in the attempt to throw off the yoke of Spanish government. But, again as elsewhere, the Spaniards found support not only among the clergy and the army, but also among the common people. Both the rotos and the emancipated Indians realized that the ricos were suddenly so keen for independence only because they wanted to retain all their privileges.

The Chilean war of independence made this paradox especially plain. The rotos regarded the Spaniards as the lesser evil compared to their native ricos. Thus the Iberian masters were so popular, especially among the fishermen and small farmers of Indian blood who inhabited the island of Chiloé, that even after the end of colonialism the Chilotans dreamed for decades of a return of the Spaniards. When the *Beagle* dropped anchor at Chiloé in 1834, Darwin and his fellow voyagers were wildly hailed by the Chilotans—the natives thinking they were Spaniards who had come to take the island back into the possession of the motherland.

Similar feelings characterized many of the *huasos*, the Chilean gauchos, sharecroppers, and smallholders of the countryside. And the *inquilinos*, the agricultural workers who lived as indentured servants or serfs on the estates, and who were often treated not much better than slaves. Since the ricos consisted of only a few dozen families and had no support among the people, the Spaniards easily inflicted a smashing defeat on the revolutionaries at Rancagua. The military leaders of the ill-fated independence movement were forced to seek refuge in Argentina.

Chile was not wrested out of Spanish hands until the colonial regime collapsed in Argentina. San Martín, the hero of Argentine liberation, regarded the tightly organized military colony west of the Andes as a menace. He crossed the mountains with five thousand men, imagining that Chile would fall into his lap like an overripe apple. But San Martín, who had hitherto worn the aura of invincibility, suffered his first bitter defeats in Chile. It turned out that the Spanish elite troops, who had been stationed there because of the constant Araucan threat, had benefited from their experience in Indian warfare. And it also turned out that the masses of the Chilean common people responded indifferently to the slogans of the Argentine liberators. All in all, it was two years before San Martín defeated the Spaniards.

The British naval hero Thomas Cochrane had a good deal to do with the victory of the independence movement. Cochrane had placed himself at the disposal of the new republic and used his fleet to cut the Spaniards off from their supplies. Although a monument to Bernardo O'Higgins stands in every Chilean city, the real heroes of Chile's fight for freedom were two foreigners: the Argentine San Martín and the Englishman Cochrane. These two men had only a lukewarm interest in creating a Chilean nation. San Martín merely wanted to seize the small Chilean colony as a bridgehead in order to advance on Peru. When after the conquest of Peru he was unable to agree with Bolívar on the future of South America, he resignedly betook himself to France, leaving Chile to her fate.

The British adventurer Cochrane was even less interested in the country itself than the Argentine general. Cochrane had distinguished himself as a naval commander in the wars against Napoleon. But he had been charged in Parliament with various illegal manipulations and speculation on the stock exchange. After serving a prison sentence of a year and a half, he immigrated to South America. The Chilean revolutionaries made him an admiral, but this honor did not cause him to strike roots in his new home. He turned his back on Chile and successively commanded the Brazilian and then the Greek navies. After his rehabilitation in Great Britain, this expert in revolutions climbed the ranks of the naval hierarchy and ended his career as a rear admiral.

THE LIBERATOR AND THE WIGMAKERS

Chile fell into the hands of a forceful personality who had taken part in all the turbulent upheavals. Bernardo O'Higgins, the illegitimate son of the Marquis of Osorno, ought, by origins and education, to have been on the side of the Spaniards. His father had been

Governor of Chile and Viceroy of Peru. While studying in London, however, O'Higgins had absorbed enough of the spirit of British democracy to realize that the future of Chile did not lie with either the Spanish colonial masters or the insurgent ricos. He united in his own person the blood of three nations: the Irish, the Spanish, and the Araucans. Irish and Araucan rebelliousness drove him into the ranks of the fighters for freedom. As a general under San Martín, he made a decisive contribution to the victories of the revolutionaries at Chacabuco and Maipú. Since the ricos considered him one of their own, they turned the government over to him after San Martín's withdrawal.

The oligarchy discovered that it had been gravely mistaken in its choice of O'Higgins. The rebel by temperament had no Napoleonic ambitions, such as motivated Simón Bolívar, but he also did not incline toward a strictly conservative class government, like San Martín. He was perhaps the one important revolutionary in South America who consistently and persistently attempted to translate the ideals of the French Revolution into reality on American soil. Instead of sanctimoniously denouncing the Spaniards, he voiced ideals that abruptly opened the eyes of the ricos to his real intentions: equality of all Chileans without social or racial distinctions; education for the masses; opportunity for the capable. The rotos, too, O'Higgins announced, were to be free to rise to the highest positions in the government, after appropriate education.

As soon as he had become head of state, O'Higgins set to work to solve the country's major problem. The answer was the same then as it is today: development of a sound rural middle class. O'Higgins knew the members of his own class, the oligarchy, only too well. If the new republic were to prosper, it must not be left to the tender mercies of the ricos. The inquilinos must be freed from their serfdom. A comprehensive agrarian reform must give sufficient land to the people to permit the formation of a new class of economically viable small farmers.

The second crying problem was the poverty of the innumerable rotos. O'Higgins hoped to cure it by a number of extremely progressive social laws for improving the standard of living among the lower classes. To carry out these measures, however, he needed a great deal of money. He obtained it by vigorously taxing the oligarchy. It is remarkable that this first president of the Chilean Republic had the same fundamental conception of social legislation as the most radical Popular Front governments of the nineteen forties and as President Frei today. In the hundred and thirty years since O'Higgins, the central problems of Chile have scarcely changed.

Although O'Higgins' program was defeated by the opposition of the ricos, it was fortunate for Chile that a consistent social reformer thus stood at the cradle of Chilean independence: a man now venerated alike by members of all parties. Early in the nineteenth century, there was small prospect for Latin American social reformers to carry out their programs by persuasion, while preserving democratic procedures. The ricos were too powerful and the rotos too degraded. In most Latin American countries, this is still the case. O'Higgins therefore set up a dictatorship rather than a democratic regime. Only in this way could he collect the taxes which were essential if he were to keep the ricos within bounds and propel the masses ahead. But the government of O'Higgins was a progressive dictatorship, in contrast to the reactionary dictatorships which took control in most Latin American countries after independence was won.

Progressive dictatorships, however, must also employ coercion and cannot long avoid staining their benevolent intentions with blood. The ricos put up a grim fight against the popular hero and liberator of their country. Before the tale was told, O'Higgins was compelled to execute his one-time companion in arms, the conservative General Carrera, and his two brothers. He also abolished all titles and privileges and forbade the ricos to strut around in operetta-like uniforms. But the conservatives proved too much for him. In addition, he incurred the hostility of the clergy because of his emphatic sympathy for Freemasonry. After four years in office, O'Higgins was overthrown by a rico coup; he went into exile in Peru and died in Lima in 1842, an embittered man.

The conservative presidents who followed O'Higgins quickly reversed the reform measures. They were far less concerned with the plight of the rotos and inquilinos than with enlarging their still modest-sized country. But the populace had tasted blood during the O'Higgins era. Various army officers, angered by the bad pay the republic offered them, rose in revolt in imitation of O'Higgins. Chile, like neighboring Peru, became the scene of constant coups, uprisings, and guerrilla wars. The unpaid soldiers remunerated themselves by attacking and pillaging whole cities. For a while Chile knew conditions similar to the *violencia* in the worst periods of Colombian history.

During this epoch, Santiago, the capital, became synonymous with lawlessness. It boasted more homicides per capita than any other city in the world. The roto gangs of Chile made people in Peru and Argentina shudder with horror. European explorers and travelers came back from Chile telling stories that closely resembled tales later to be told about North America's Wild West.

Gradually the ricos, supported by the Church, won control. Since these conservatives obstinately clung to all old customs and would tolerate no innovations, the liberals ironically called them *pelucones*, "wigmakers." Conservatives fired back by dubbing the liberals who followed the traditions of O'Higgins *pipiolos*, "visionaries," for the ricos regarded such ideas of reform as pipe dreams which were bound to lead to economic disaster. To this day the Conservatives in Chile are "wigmakers," and to this day the Liberals seem somewhat visionary.

THE OTHER SIDE OF PROSPERITY

The spirit of Bernardo O'Higgins remained alive in Chile. In the course of time it even penetrated gradually into the governing Conservative Party. The Chilean treasury grew pleasantly full with the discovery of the rich silver mines of Chañarcillo. The small republic began flexing its muscles. It soon intervened in the politics of its neighbors by issuing an ultimatum forbidding Peru, Bolivia, and Ecuador from ever uniting to form a federation.

Among the rico presidents there was no "Tyrant of the Andes" and no "Napoleon of the Tropics," but there were a number of clever men who had a sense of the special situation of their country and its opportunities. Chilean agriculture was thriving at the time gold was found in California. Since there was then no Panama Canal and the overland route across the United States was terribly toilsome, Chile undertook to supply food to the new settlers in California. Valparaiso developed into the biggest port on the western coast of Latin America, and has remained that to this day.

The programs of the progressive Conservatives were in some respects as strikingly modern as those of Bernardo O'Higgins. The most important representative of this group, Manuel Montt, actually broke away from the ricos around the middle of the century, and together with his cabinet minister Antonio Varas formed a new national Chilean party whose followers were called *Monttvaristas*. Montt, as we have seen, brought German settlers to southern Chile to open up the forests around Lake Llanquihue. He coined slogans astonishingly like the "prosperity for all" and the "no experiments" of the recent postwar years in Germany. With the defection of the Monttvaristas, the hold of the conservative oligarchy was broken, with the result that in 1861 the government fell into the hands of businesslike liberals who thought in terms of the world's economy.

Within a short time the liberals had refashioned the country along European lines. The climate helped, for in large parts of Chile it is quite European. The level of popular education was raised; with 20 per cent illiteracy, Chile today stands in fifth place educationally in Latin America. Unlike her neighbors, Chile did not model herself on Spain or the United States, but on Great Britain and Germany. Even in the nineteenth century Chileans were generally considered highly receptive to outside influences. No other South American country passed so rapidly out of the chaotic early stages of its history.

But the liberals could not bridge the terrible gulf between ricos and rotos. No liberal president, aside from Balmaceda, dared to attack the oligarchy as forcefully as O'Higgins had intended. On the contrary, the liberals made it possible for a new class of extremely wealthy urban ricos to arise. The Saltpeter War, copper mining, and expanding trade only made the rich richer. Few crumbs of this new wealth fell to the rotos, except for those brave souls who ventured into the Chile saltpeter desert as pioneers, or went to Magellanes Province.

In the industrial regions, the rotos have long since changed from inquilinos, day laborers without any rights at all, to modern factory workers. But the big manufacturing, copper, and steel companies wish to amortize their Chilean investments as quickly as possible. In order to do so, they try their best to skimp on wages. The same principle is followed by the ricos in the rural areas, who exploit the labor power of the rotos without offering a just equivalent. Thus, to the traditional tensions between rural ricos and rotos have now been added the far more explosive tensions between industrial ricos and industrial rotos.

For some time, however, the rotos in industry have not been as badly at the mercy of their masters as the rural rotos. The industrial workers early began founding unions and taking a strong interest in politics, as fences and walls in every working-class district testify. Since the 1920s, the overwhelming majority of Chilean industrial workers have tended to the far left. They form the traditional voters for the *Frente Popular*, the Popular Front, in which reformist socialists, apostate leftist liberals, and communists usually support joint candidates. The ricos maintain their power over the industrial rotos only because there is such a vast labor pool of the unskilled in Chile, who will work for extremely low pay. The result is an abysmal wage scale, with the day's pay of an unskilled industrial worker in Chile less than what a comparable unskilled American worker would receive for an hour.

The real and secret tragedy of the rotos, which O'Higgins could not possibly have foreseen, is the fact that they are far too numerous, both in the country and in the cities. Although Chile is many times larger than the nations of the Caribbean and Central America, she suffers from the same population pressure. On a casual tour of the country you do not see much of this soaring birth rate. On the contrary, you have the impression that there are still many thinly populated areas in Chile which could be beneficially settled. But these seemingly deserted regions are mostly latifundia owned by ricos. Even leftist governments in which the communists participated have not been able to effect a redistribution of the land. They have not even succeeded in perceptibly raising the living standards of the rotos.

In the rural districts, until late in the 1920s, not the slightest attempt was made to moderate social tensions. The ricos reigned as they had done in colonial times. Legally, the inquilinos were regarded as free laborers, but in practice they virtually never had the chance to move from a low-paid job to a better-paid one. Should an inquilino family leave the estate on which it had always lived, it would be black-balled on any other *fundo*. The ricos formed a cartel of sorts and made sure that wages were held down and freedom of movement restricted.

Everywhere in the world, misery seeks escape into some form of intoxication. Just as the Peruvian and Bolivian Indians became addicted to coca, the rotos resorted to the heavy red wine of Chile, which is cheap in the rural areas. Undernourished people succumb to alcohol more quickly than the well fed. If you drive about the Chilean countryside on a payday, you might think that half the country people are arrant drunkards. *Huasos* in their traditional dress droop drunkenly on their horses or sprawl in the ditches while their horses patiently graze by the roadside. There is a high accident rate among drunken inquilinos who go to sleep on highways or railroad ties. According to the ricos, this widespread vice only proves the laziness and depravity of the rotos. But as every sociologist knows, drunkenness as a mass phenomenon is a sure sign that something is rotten in the social order.

"SHOOTING UP LIKE MUSHROOMS"

I visited many inquilino huts. They were so dreary, so pitiable, so swarming with children that I could well imagine why the father of the family did not go home on payday, but instead headed straight for the nearest wineshop. The social-reformist governments of the past several decades have passed minimum-wage bills which also apply to unskilled rural workers. But the rotos' rate of increase is so high that there are always enough men around who are prepared to work at cut-rate prices. Many estates pay illegally low wages. A day's pay of around ten cents is quite customary. If an inquilino receives an extra allowance of about seven dollars a month, he can be quite content. The tiny patch of land that every inquilino family is allowed to till for itself will support a few chickens or a pig. But aside from native farm products, the cost of living is just as high in Chile as in Europe.

The winter months in Chile are cool and rainy. Ragged inquilinos need warm clothing and good shoes. Since their wages scarcely suffice to feed them, they make sandals out of old automobile tires, or go barefoot. They wear their clothes until the rags are almost falling off their bodies. Since life offers them so little, their sole amusements consist in getting drunk on red wine and begetting a child every year. Families of agricultural workers with between sixteen and twenty children are no rarity in Chile. But Chilean husbands are Spanish enough to feel it as a slur upon their honor for their wives and daughters to go to work. And so the growing daughters of inquilinos sit around the huts doing nothing. Their illegitimate children add to the swarming families. What estate owner could resist hiring laborers at next to nothing from among all these excess human beings?

Chile would be an ideal area for such experiments in state-directed birth control as are being attempted in the islands of the West Indies. But the Catholic Church at present opposes any such step with particular obstinacy. Contraceptives, including pills, are freely sold everywhere in Chile, but the lower classes are too ignorant to use them, and have no money to buy them. Yet if Chile does not succeed in checking the new avalanche of births in the inquilino huts, the country may well die of its own fertility someday. No redistribution of the land, no matter how generous, can assure decent lives to these hordes who multiply so rapidly. And no government, no matter how radical, can improve the Chilean economy so much that all the rotos and their offspring can possibly have work and bread, unless the torrent of births is checked.

The new social-reformist government of President Frei, which has been in office since the end of 1964, has recognized this central problem more clearly than any previous regime. Eduardo Frei is a quick-thinking and modern-minded man, and he has ventured one of the boldest and most desirable programs in Chilean history: active promotion of birth control. Amazingly enough, this step, which inevitably outraged the clergy, was proposed not by Popular Frontists and not by the Liberals (who in Chile traditionally sympathize with the Freemasons), but by a Christian Democratic chief of state. For that very reason he may be successful. For the Church in Chile cannot afford to break with Eduardo Frei's Christian Democrats; to do so would be to advance the cause of the Popular Front.

In August 1965 President Frei had Dr. Francisco Mardones Restat, his director-general of the National Health Office, explain the revolutionary decision. Mardones Restat stressed the "explosive increase in the population of Latin America," and pointed out that it is precisely the poor families which have so many children that the government cannot possibly "give their sons and daughters a suitable education and proper food." In other words, the success of Frei's work for reform was dependent on population control.

The Christian Democratic government does not intend to make birth control obligatory, but the state will vigorously further it—by education, by supplying contraceptives gratis, and by such practices as have already proved successful in Europe and Puerto Rico. So far, the clerical opposition has not commented on these measures—the first that an independent Latin American country with an overwhelmingly

Catholic population has ever undertaken in the matter of birth control.

What will happen to these masses of rotos if political propaganda succeeds in "radicalizing" them? For centuries the Chilean agricultural workers accepted their wretched conditions as God-given. Their weekly binge was likewise God-given, they felt. And so was the appalling number of their children. But today village teachers are awakening the masses; the majority of Chilean teachers, students, and university professors are for thoroughgoing social reforms, even if they are not politically far to the left. In addition, the two great labor union organizations, and especially the CUT, the socialist union, are steadily gaining adherents among the inquilinos. And the communist propaganda in the rural areas, although it may strike sophisticated Europeans and Americans as quite uninspired and barren of ideas, strongly affects the rotos because of its very simplicity. Without considering actual economic conditions, the communists demand more thoroughgoing agrarian reforms than any of the other Chilean reformist parties. And the slogan "agrarian reform" garners more inquilino votes than any other political propositions.

Innumerable rotos have poured into the cities and industrial regions in the course of the past half century. As we have mentioned, they receive considerably higher wages in industry than on the land. The ricos in industry seldom venture to undercut the minimum pay scale. But only in the copper and petroleum industries are the workers paid more than the minimum needed for bare existence.

On the edges of Chilean cities, on the hills above Valparaiso on the Pacific Ocean, and even on the mud flats of the Bío-Bío at Concepción, stretch the same kind of slums found in other countries of South America. In Chile they are called *callampas*, "mushrooms," because they shoot out of the ground overnight as mushrooms do after a warm rain. There are callampas adjacent to the most lordly mansions. Throughout Central and South America I saw countless wretched huts and whole slum districts, but I had to come to the otherwise clean, pretty, and well-tended metropolis of Santiago de Chile to see with my own eyes how little the ricos are embarrassed by the misery around them.

One of the richest men in Santiago, who lives in a veritable palace, permits a roto to live in a hideous, tumble-down sheet-metal shack on his grounds. Why? He wanted to save the expense of a gatekeeper and therefore permitted one of the "ragged ones" to put up the shack next to his palatial home. In return for permission to use the land, the roto is obligated to guard the master's house day and night without pay. It never occurred to the rich man that he might at least have built a decent porter's lodge. Keeping a roto was cheaper than keeping a dog, which he would have had to provide with food.

REFORM, FASCISM, POPULAR FRONT

In 1920, about thirty years after the debacle of the social reformer Balmaceda, a new president came forth who strengthened parliamentary democracy in Chile and once more attempted reform on a generous scale. President Arturo Alessandri was a lawyer who belonged to the left wing of the Liberal Party. He began precisely where O'Higgins and Balmaceda had had to stop. He, too, considered that Chile's great problem was to establish a balance of power between the ricos and the rotos. The wide variety of laws which he put through has remained to this day the foundation of Chilean social legislation. He fostered schools and other educational institutions. He tried to assure the rural as well as the industrial workers a decent livelihood. But on the whole he failed to carry out his reforms, just as O'Higgins had failed.

Alessandri had to contend not only with the parties of the right, but also with the socialists, who in the 1920s had grown into a powerful party and who were not going to let Alessandri take the wind from their sails. Assailed by ricos and by rotos, Alessandri had to stop at a halfway point in his reforms. In the eyes of the rich, he was too leftist, in the eyes of the poor, too rightist. That is the fate awaiting virtually every Chilean reformer. At the present time Eduardo Frei is meeting the same problem.

Arturo Alessandri's first administration came to an end in an atmosphere of crisis. We have already mentioned that Alessandri's willingness to compromise the Tacna-Arica conflict led to a military coup—one of Chile's few coups. This was in 1927. General Carlos Ibáñez was brought to power. Ibáñez also had to deal with the problem of the rotos, and did so after his own fashion. He was a forerunner of Perón, Pérez Jiménez, and Somoza, one of those modern Ibero-American dictators who hoped to build their power on the favor of the populace as well as on bayonets. Ibáñez waged vigorous propaganda among the lower classes. The process that in Germany later expanded into a tragedy for the entire world took a farcical turn in Chile. The discontented, largely radicalized masses went over to Ibáñez. Chile temporarily went fascist. Like Hitler and Mussolini, Ibáñez promised the lumpenproletarians everything they wanted, and conjointly stirred up popular jingoism. But while in Europe the world-wide depression fostered fascism, in Chile it spelled an end to the fascist experiment. Ibáñez could not keep his promises, for Chile was struck harder by the economic collapse of 1929–30 than her neighbors. The dictator was unable to cope with the simultaneous inflation and increasing unemployment. When in 1931 he finally turned the foundering nitrate industry over to the Guggenheim interests, the congress and the military united to overthrow him. The Chileans recalled Arturo Alessandri.

Meanwhile, the leftist parties had gathered strength during the depression and the dictatorship. Both the Socialist Party and the Communist Party of Chile rank among the best-organized Marxist parties in the Americas. They now tried to take power, categorically refusing to support the old liberal president. Alessandri thereupon made one of those about-faces typical of modern Chilean politics. He became a rightist liberal, adopted the traditions of the *Montt-varistas* of the past, and hoped he would be able to carry out his plans with the support of the right.

Arturo Alessandri is generally considered the outstanding Chilean statesman of the twentieth century. The country owes fundamental social reforms and progressive social legislation to him. He was the first president to attack foreign finance capital. He fortified the separation of church and state, which makes Chile considerably more liberal than her neighbors in religious matters. But he could not destroy the secret cartel of the ricos. Most of his laws and executive orders remained paper reforms.

The consequence was that in 1938 the *Frente Popular* emerged victorious from the elections, deriving most of its support from the growing class of Chilean industrial workers. Thus the Chileans were the second nation in Latin America (after the Salvadorians) to allow the Communists to share the responsibilities of government. The rotos had to all appearances won a decisive victory over the ricos. The Popular Front, a coalition of Socialists, radical Liberals, and Communists, also won the two succeeding elections. Chile went her own way, watched with suspicion and anxiety by the rest of the world. Her policies were probably the most independent in all of Latin America.

During this period, Chile's primary goal was freedom from North American influence. The Popular Front insisted on government participation in the copper mines of the Guggenheim interests. It nationalized the merchant marine. It even stayed out of the democratic world's war against the fascist Axis. Although the socialistic government parties in Chile should have had every reason to declare war on Hitler and Mussolini on ideological grounds, the Popular Front government withstood all the pressures from the United States. Aside from breaking diplomatic relations with the Axis Powers, it remained neutral in Europe, though declaring war on Japan in April 1945. During this period the social policies of Arturo Alessandri were continued, although under socialist direction and with the enthusiastic assent of the Communists.

The Popular Front governed Chile for thirteen years. It too passed progressive legislation, though most of its laws again remained paper achievements. During the war the Popular Frontists did not dare to carry out any such radical land reform as O'Higgins had envisioned. The economy was too delicate a mechanism to be tampered with at that time. After the war, when it set about solving the agrarian question, a new problem arose which ultimately put an end to the "red" coalition. That was the Communists' radical demand for power.

The Communists were not satisfied with the Popular Front's plans for evolutionary reforms. They campaigned strongly in the rural districts, winning ever greater influence in the unions and periodically calling strikes in the mines. The Socialists and radical Liberals found their Communist ally an increasing embarrassment. When at last the Communists openly rebelled against the government of which they were members, Popular Front President González Videla had to employ his military forces. Thus the left in Chile made an about-face similar to that of the earlier liberal president, Arturo Alessandri. In 1947 the government expelled the Communists from all administrative posts, pronounced them enemies of the state, and broke diplomatic relations with the Soviet Union. Chilean democracy had proved its survival qualities under the banner of the Popular Front also.

Unfortunately, the social regeneration of Chile that the leftist parties had dreamed of was buried under the rubble of political fragmentation. Communist troublemaking proved far from beneficial to the rotos. The Communists in Chile, as everywhere in the world, were more concerned with strengthening the power of their party than with the people's welfare. Since 1952 the *Frente Popular* has been in the opposition again. Excluding the Communists from its ranks amounted to an act of renunciation, for the Popular Front thereby lost a fourth of its voters.

Once more the discontented, politically relentless rotos went over to former dictator Ibáñez, who had founded a "Peasants Workers Party." Ibáñez, this time a democratically elected president, followed up the thirteen years of socialist rule with six years of social-fascist experimentation. He drew heavily on the popularity of his Argentine friend and colleague, Juan Perón. But again the Ibáñez regime increased rather than alleviated the internal unrest and social tensions of the country. After Ibáñez had immortalized himself in characteristic dictator's fashion by building houses, streets, and bridges and introducing a hitherto unknown degree of corruption into Chile, the ricos once again returned to office in Santiago. In 1958 Jorge Alessandri, son of the liberal reformer, was elected president.

"REVOLUTION IN FREEDOM"

Honest and conscientious, but colorless and not especially popular, Jorge Alessandri also did not succeed in solving the social problems of his country. During his administration the left seemed to be growing stronger than ever. Socialists and Communists had united with the National Democrats to form a new Popular Front, the FRAP, which was headed by the Socialist Party leader, Dr. Salvador Allende. A well-to-do physician and skilled demagogue, Allende was beaten by Alessandri in the 1958 elections by only a few thousand votes. The FRAP dominated the unions. They called for open struggle against the government, for general strikes, for expropriation of the latifundia and of foreign enterprises.

Neither the conservative-rightist-liberal government coalition nor the politically unstable radical Liberals, who wavered between the two camps, were able to offer a real alternative to the Popular Front. The majority of Chilean voters, on whom the future fate of Chile depended, were agreed on one point: something decisive had to be done to ease the frightening social pressure.

Since 1960 the Western world had been looking on with concern at the prospect of an electoral victory by the *Frente Popular*. There was already talk in Europe and the United States—talk characterized by deplorable simplifications—of a threatening Communist seizure of power in Chile. FRAP leader Allende is no Communist, and the FRAP is not a Communist organization; the Communists in the Popular Front are a minority and have no impressive personality with whom to oppose the experienced Socialist leader. Moreover, the earlier Popular Front experiments in Chile have proved that the Socialists and leftist Liberals in the partnership are not inclined to submit to Communist domination. But the West, as a consequence of the Cuban trauma, took alarm all too easily and saw a potential Popular Front president as a Chilean Castro.

Before 1964, the ricos and the middle class stared at Allende's Popular Front like a rabbit at a snake. The propertied classes had, to be sure, long had a way of escaping the unpleasant possibility of FRAP rule, but this alternative seemed to the ricos (for a while, at least) almost as intolerable as a victory by Dr. Allende. A rather grotesque situation had arisen in Chile as a result of widespread radicalization and the ever-louder cry for significant social reforms. Even bourgeois movements were behaving in a more and more leftist, more and more radical manner, in order to steal the slogans of the Socialists and Communists. Allende's social and political demands already went far beyond those of the Communists. And from 1961 on, a Christian Democratic Party leader from a conservative background began to steal Allende's thunder. He proposed a massive social, financial, and administrative operation to transform Chile from a reactionary feudal country into a modern welfare state. This party leader, whose forefathers came from Switzerland, was named Eduardo Frei.

Frei offered himself to the Chileans as the only possible alternative to the Popular Front. But he was opposed both by the ricos and the traditional parties. Word went around that he was even redder than the FRAP, probably a potential ally of the Communists. He was accused unjustly of being quite ready to go along with the Communists if the left satisfied his ambition and accepted him as head of state. He was accused also—justly—of intending to replace Chilean parliamentary government, with its creaking, slow-running, and badly oiled party and administrative machinery, by another and superior apparatus. It was charged that he intended to introduce direct appeals to the people, plebiscite and referendum, into Chilean democracy.

Far apart though the traditional parties of the right and left were, ricos and rotos suddenly found themselves in agreement on one thing: Eduardo Frei was a danger to the existing system, a danger to party rule, a new and uncertain factor in Chilean politics. Consequently, the conservative right fought him because it feared his welfare state, and denounced him as a left extremist. The liberals and radicals fought him and compared his legislative innovations to the fascistic tricks of Hitler and Mussolini. The left, finally, attacked him on the ground that his reform program really meant "a new era of reaction," a "modernization of the traditional system of exploitation." Thus Eduardo Frei had all the political forces in Chile against him.

Who was this man, who is perhaps the most interesting reformist politician of recent times in Latin America? And what did he really want? As a young conservative, Frei had broken with the right over the social question. He called the party he founded Christian Democratic because he looked for support for his reform program not—like Allende—to the freethinking and Marxist group among the intellectuals and workers, but to progressive Catholics. He might be called today a "left Catholic"—although that term, too, is far from entirely satisfactory. His Christian Democrats are not nearly so emphatically religious in their views as the Christian Democrats in Germany and Italy, or as the French Popular Republicans.

Frei himself once defined his political position and that of his party this way: he is "far to the left of the German Christian Democratic Party, but also to the left of the German Social Democratic Party." That is a definition easily understood by Europeans. While the German Christian Democrats regard planned economy and the welfare state as terrible heresies, and while the German Social Democrats have long ago become advocates of a liberal, solid middle-class private economy, Frei's economic and social programs have distinct features of socialistic ideology.

In 1961 Frei's Christian Democrats first won seats in the Chilean congress. They at once became the third largest party, after the Popular Front and the Radical Liberals, with 23 of 147 congressmen and 3 of 45 senators. This minority sharply opposed Alessandri's conservative-liberal government, and all the other parties besides. It waged a constant campaign for reform of both the congress and the executive.

The administrative apparatus in Chile had actually become intolerably swollen. The machinery of the congress limped creakingly. A bill voted down by the congress could not, according to the constitution, be presented for another year. This provision spelled death to much legislation that concerned the vital interests of the people. Measure after measure was tabled in order not to offend one or another party, or in order to preserve the coalition, and was never seen again. Frei's insistence on constitutional reform, so that in such cases the legislation could be submitted to a popular referendum, was therefore wholly justified.

Since the hostile congress gave short shrift to the proposals of the Christian Democrats, Frei again and again turned to the people, trying, with long speeches at meetings and on the radio, to win the masses to his cause. He called for modernization of the feudalistic agriculture of Chile, for comprehensive land reform, for radical reorganization of the apparatus of government, for higher taxation of the wealthy, for introduction of a tax on capital—with which he intended to finance a 38.5-per-cent increase in the shockingly low salaries of government employees. Many of his demands were already on the program of the Popular Front in one form or another. Frei even had designs against sacrosanct Chilean copper. He did not intend expropriation of the big American copper companies, but he wanted the Chilean Government to obtain a large enough share of them to become a partner and thus help bring about social peace in the industrial regions of Chile.

Just shortly before the 1964 elections it dawned on the ricos and the middle class that if they continued to reject Frei they would undoubtedly reap a victory of the FRAP for their pains. One of the elements that helped bring them to this insight was the strong support and sympathy Frei had won in Western Europe, especially in France and Germany. Traditional German-Chilean relations led to increasingly close ties between the German and the Chilean Christian Democrats. The (rightist-oriented) German CDU vigorously backed Frei's (leftist-oriented) party in the elections. And since fear of Allende and the red FRAP had been skillfully stirred up, Frei finally won the votes of both the ricos and the masses, and emerged as victor in the elections. Thus Chile started on her revolution in freedom.

DYNAMITE IN THE LAND OF NITRATES

During his first months in office, Frei was unable to launch his high-flying plans, for he had the congress against him. But the congressional elections of March 7, 1965, gave his young party an absolute majority: 80 of 147 congressional seats. The FRAP, hitherto the strongest opponent of the Christian Democrats, had already discovered in the presidential elections that an alliance with the Communists can boomerang. That alliance now began to dissolve.

During the campaign Frei had blamed his rival Allende for all the misdeeds of the Eastern bloc, from the crushing of the Hungarian revolt to the Berlin Wall. For since the FRAP and the Christian Democrats advocated virtually the same social and political line, Frei had to pitch his campaign on questions of foreign policy, and particularly attack Allende's alliance with the Communists. He did so very demagogically and very skillfully—with the result that in the next congressional elections the left put up a Popular Front joint list in only twelve electoral districts. Everywhere else, the Socialists, National Democrats, and Communists once more split up and ran separate lists of candidates. Dr. Allende was not again going to risk having thrown at him the Berlin Wall and other Communist crimes for which he bore no responsibility.

Eduardo Frei is very serious about his reforms. He has undertaken redistribution of land far more vigorously than any other Chilean politician in the past. His cabinet is considered competent; his program meets the needs of Chile decidedly better than the plans of his predecessors. In practice, his social reforms coincide with almost all the aims of the Popular Front. If he is successful—and it may be hoped for his and Chile's sake that he will be—he will be proving by persuasive example that the leap over a whole century, which Latin America so urgently requires, can be taken without revolution, without violent upheavals and drastic revaluations.

It testifies to Frei's prudence and skillful tactics that he will not hear of the total expropriation of American companies, such as Allende has demanded. Such a program could not be carried out without violence. And violence would mean the loss of American friendship and development aid, hence isolation and economic disaster for Chile. Chile is not Bolivia, and copper is not tin. The Bolivians in the MNR period could do many things safely that the Chileans cannot afford without risking the gravest consequences. For the Republic of Chile, with its immense coastline and many ports, is far more dependent on world trade and the good will of the Western world than the land-locked mountain republic of Bolivia. Frei's plan to become a share-holder in the copper companies instead of nationalizing them is there-fore—in spite of Dr. Allende's dialectical arguments—the only feasible recourse for a social reformer in Chile.

How this matter is worked out will show whether Frei can actually find his "third road between Marxism and capitalism." For if the cop-per companies for selfish reasons refuse the offered association with the Chilean Government, the radical left will immediately be strength-ened. Allende could then justifiably proclaim that Frei's welfare state is a fiction and can never be achieved while the rotos are impotent and the ricos so powerful.

The oligarchy, too, may thwart Frei's plans. Any journey through the Chilean countryside, any glance at the walls smeared with party slogans, provides evidence that Chile must still solve her primary problem: bridging the gulf between ricos and rotos. It is reassuring to the Western world that Chile, in contrast to most Ibero-American countries, has a healthy, democratic foundation and an intelligent, vigorous, social-reformist president. But it is disturbing that even Chilean democracy, which has so far dealt so skillfully with radical attacks from right and left, is still—in the days of Eduardo Frei—faced with the same social tasks that confronted the liberator, Bernardo O'Higgins. As in the times of O'Higgins, the ricos of Chile today are still highly feudalistic, highly conservative, utterly lacking in social understanding. They have, it is true, thrown in their lot with Frei, in order to prevent a victory for the Reds, but they are a long way from favoring Frei's program. And as in the days of O'Higgins, the rotos today are extremely poor, extremely numerous, and extremely re-bellious. They have placed their hopes in Frei's agrarian reform, in his promised welfare state, and in the vision of a "revolution in free-dom." But if the reactionary right frustrates the announced reforms, or if it attempts to undermine them by amendments, the roto masses will undoubtedly turn back with noisy enthusiasm to the Popular Front, and might vote it into power tomorrow.

The oligarchy would like to hang on to its privileges. It resists, openly to some extent, surreptitiously to some extent, the program of agrarian reform. It resists modernization of methods of tillage and cattle raising. It opposes closing the loopholes in the system of taxation, which greatly favors the ricos. It is against referendums, against participation of the workers in the direction of industry, and against many other vital points in Frei's program. Is Eduardo Frei tough and resolute enough to put across that program against the opposition of the ricos? He has the support of the democratic West. Although he is no friend of Washington's Latin American policies, the United States is backing him. But the success of his policies and thus the possibility of a "third road" will not be decided abroad. The decision will be made in Chile itself.

Since Frei's constitutional and administrative reform, the sand has been removed from the machinery of democracy in the Land of Nitrates, but a great deal of dynamite has been left. The whole of democratic Latin America is looking toward Chile—toward that traditionally democratic country which today has the great opportunity to carry out a peaceful revolution by democratic methods. Whether that opportunity is taken will depend far more on the ricos than the rotos. True success for Eduardo Frei might well be of far-reaching and possibly fateful importance for the whole of South America.

BOLIVIA

PARAGUAY

Lead
Oil

GRAN CHACO

Cotton
Cotton
Cotton

Asunción

Maté
Corn
Rice

CHILE

Sugar
S. Miguel de Tucumán

Resistencia

Santiago del Estero

Corrientes

Catamarca

ARGENTINA

BRAZIL

Córdoba

Santa Fe

Coal
Copper

Irrigation
Mendoza

Paraná

Rosario

Wheat
Cattle
Sheep

Pergamino

Santiago
Oil

Viniculture

Buenos Aires

Montevideo

URUGUAY

PAMPAS

Cattle
Wheat
Corn

Oil
Neuquén

Mar del Plata

Bahía Blanca

Sheep

PATAGONIA

Agriculture

Cattle raising

Barren areas

Oil

Atlantic
Ocean

Sheep

Coal

FALKLAND
ISLANDS
(British)

Sheep

TIERRA DEL
FUEGO

PARAGUAY

ARGENTINA

URUGUAY

CHAPTER 7

Lightning on the La Plata

SOCIALISM UNDER THE CROSS

The land was somewhat mountainous, very wild, and wondrously virginal. No man might have been here before me. I rode through sparse forests overtowered by haughty palms and wreathed with peerlessly beautiful orchids. Not a living soul in sight. From the treetops I could hear the chattering of monkeys and the screeching of parrots.

Suddenly I came upon a small town. It lies there today just as it was built three hundred years ago—an oasis amid the greenery of a primeval forest. There are no signs that bloody wars, cruel mass expulsions, and an almost unique extermination of a people have swept over the country of Paraguay since the town was built. The town has forgotten time and has been forgotten by time. Only on its edges a few modern cottages have covertly established themselves.

In the middle of a broad, sunny plaza stands a handsomely proportioned church, not too large and not too small, genuine Jesuit baroque without any fake ornamentation, possessing an artistic clarity and purity of style comparatively rare in Latin America. At a glance you can see that not the command of a conquistador or mania for ostentation built this church, but naïve piety. It served as a point of assembly for the Indians whom the Jesuits intended to educate. In the most literal sense it formed the center of the small community that was built here, dominating everything from its central position, at once dignified and modest.

Around the plaza, in an accurate square, lie the former dwellings of the Jesuits, the former schools, hospitals, and administration buildings. They too are marked by functional beauty. They too radiate the quiet harmony of early baroque, which had no traffic with superfluous accessories. Thick walls keep out the heat; windows are small, so that the sun cannot send its searing rays into the interior. The vigorous colors of the paint can still be distinguished; in the flood of glaring light their effect is muted and pleasant.

Seated in a twentieth-century automobile, I felt something of a noisy intruder in that plaza. Its solemn siesta mood passed into me. I studied the church and the houses, saw that in this spot the distant past still retained an astonishing vitality. Here the past did not scurry through the present as a disturbing phantom, as in the capital of Asunción. It has remained the present because it was in every respect good and right. We of the twentieth century have nothing to add to it.

In many regions of Latin America the existence of a colonial past full of blood and tears produces an oppressive sense of pervasive injustice. There were blood and tears here too, though these were not the doing of the Jesuits but of their Spanish and Portuguese opponents. Yet the place does not arouse that sense of oppression. Rather, it calls forth something akin to gratitude toward that devoted band who once accomplished exemplary and nearly perfect cultural and educational work in Ibero-America.

To this day pupils still sit on the old benches in the schools once set up by the Jesuits. Here, in this solitary and remote town, you no longer remember the blood baths two centuries ago, in which the Jesuit state was drowned. For the spirit of the "Holy Experiment" still lives on in such isolated communities as this. Every arch, every cool block of stone, testifies to it.

An old woman crossed the square, an earthenware pitcher on her head, her hair hidden beneath a black shawl. So might she have looked three hundred years ago. Perhaps she is living today in the same cool house as her great-grandmother; certainly she eats the same manioc porridge. When the brutal violence of the colonial powers destroyed the Jesuit state, time stood still in the small communities which had once been Jesuit settlements. Those who survived the cataclysm stopped counting time in 1768—and have not yet begun again.

MONTAIGNE AND THE CONQUISTA

Most of the churches and "reductions," as the Jesuit settlements were called, have been reclaimed by the jungle or the vegetation of the plains. There are only a few left in Paraguay and in the Argentine province of Misiones, places that escaped the onslaught of the Portuguese-Brazilian *bandeirantes* and the Spanish soldiery. In history books the present-day Republic of Paraguay is frequently character-ized as a major field for Jesuit social experimentation. In reality, however, the reductions in Paraguay were only last, desperate refuges for the padres and their Indian protégés.

Originally the Jesuits set up their socialized state along the Paraná, in what is now southern Brazil. Constantly harassed by the ban-deirantes, they had to retreat from the vicinity of São Paulo farther and farther to the south and southwest. The way-stations were the Rio Grande do Sul, Misiones, and finally the valley of the Río Paraguay. The Spanish and Portuguese decree of 1768 which finally expelled the Jesuit Order from Latin America ended forever the "Holy Ex-periment."

The history of the Jesuit state along the Paraná and Paraguay rivers is a bitter refutation of everything defenders of Iberian coloniza-tion of America have urged in justification of the *conquista*. Many writers and historians to this day praise the Spanish and Portuguese conquest of America as a grand Christian mission, a sincere although not always successful effort to confer the blessings of Christendom and Occidental civilization upon pagan Indians. But what really hap-pened in the Ibero-American colonies was long ago described clearly, in words that are still valid, by a contemporary of the conquest, the French philosopher Montaigne:

"We have used the ignorance and inexperience of the Indians to mislead them, by our example, into treachery, unchastity, greed and every kind of inhumanity and cruelty. Are trade and the profits of trade really worth all that? So many cities have been destroyed, so many peoples have been exterminated, so many souls have been put to the sword; and the richest and most beautiful part of the world has been devastated in order that we might traffic in pearls and pepper. Never before have the ambitions and hatreds of nations to-ward one another driven men to such horrible acts of violence and engendered such great misfortunes."

Montaigne not only exposed the spuriousness of the colonial "mis-sion"; he also referred in the plainest words to the other possible way, the peaceful path of genuine missionary work to which the Jesuits devoted themselves for several decades. "The Indians," Montaigne wrote, "possessed devoutness and loyalty to law, kindness, generosity, honesty and candor. . . . They have been destroyed because of their very virtues. What satisfaction it would have been, what an improvement for the progress of the universe, if our example and conduct had summoned these tribes to admiration and imitation of virtue and had created between them and us fraternal harmony! How easy it would have been to live in prosperous community with people who so thirsted for knowledge and who for the most part had already made such fine beginnings of their own accord!"

The pious Jesuits and Montaigne, the atheistic philosopher, had the same view of the *conquista,* of the mentality of the Indians, and of the ways that ought to be taken to "improve the progress of the universe" by peaceful assimilation of the two cultures to one another. In 1608 Captain-General Hernando Arias de Saavedra brought the first Jesuits to Paraguay. At that time the territory of the Spanish captain-generalcy of Paraguay was more than twice the size of the present republic. It included parts of northern Argentina and extensive tracts in what are now the southern states of Brazil. The Jesuits entered a country demoralized by ghastly Indian massacres, repeated uprisings of the natives, and a bloodsucking *encomienda,* or tributory-labor, system. There could be no talk of the blessings of Christianity and Western civilization in Paraguay. The Guaraní Indians were on the verge of liquidation by the harsh Spanish regime.

Before the conquest the Guaraní tribes in the La Plata region and the closely related Tupí tribes in nearby southern and central Brazil had lived in large and small communities almost socialistic in character. Like most of the Indian peoples they had no concept of private property, performed all necessary work collectively, and were culturally far superior to the Indians of the forests and plains. To this day the Guaraní language is the common language of the lower classes in Paraguay and in the Argentine province of Misiones. The encomienda system, which the Spaniards forced on the Guaraní, outraged their ethnic character and their traditions; it beheaded their culture just as the corresponding system of forced labor in the conquered Inca Empire did to the glorious Andean civilization.

Encomienda means "mission," a bombastic term for an ugly reality. For the mission the Spaniards carried out in the conquered territory did not involve the education and civilization of the Indians, but their total enslavement. The free Guaraní were forcibly distributed among the *repartimientos* of the Spanish conquistadors and settlers—much as the conquered loot of gold and jewelry was divided among the invaders.

A HOLY EXPERIMENT

The Jesuits whom Saavedra brought to Paraguay had already had a hard time of it in Portugal's Brazilian colony. From Bahia to São Paulo they had tried to convert the Indians peacefully and to protect them from mistreatment by the colonists. They had exerted their excellent connections in Lisbon to force through a law forbidding Indian slavery and the buying and selling of Indians. But the interior of Brazil, and especially the territory of the future State of São Paulo, was held by tough white adventurers who kept harems of Indian and mestizo women and raised up their own mestizo militia for purposes of conquest. The Brazilian *bandeirantes* succeeded in driving the troublesome Jesuits farther and farther to the south.

The gigantic clan descended from a man named João Ramalho gradually developed into the chief adversary of the peaceful padres. This Portuguese soldier of fortune is said, according to semilegendary traditions, to have kept several hundred Indian women in his harem. He is considered the begetter, literally, of the core of the *Paulistas,* who comprise the exceedingly idiosyncratic and expansionist rural population of the present State of São Paulo. The Indians called his half-breed children *mamaruca,* "people of mixed descent." But the Jesuits, horrified by the crimes of Ramalho and his *mamaruca* and remembering similar atrocities once committed by the Mohammedans in the Mediterranean countries, referred to the *Paulista* bands by the ethnologically dubious but psychologically accurate term of "Mamelukes."

Constantly molested by the Portuguese Mamelukes, the Jesuit Order decided to move into the adjacent Spanish colonies. There the wretched Guaraní at first viewed the Jesuits with suspicion, for the Indians had lost all faith in the good will of whites. But within a few decades the Spanish, Portuguese, and German padres amazingly succeeded in converting some two hundred thousand Indians and in persuading them to settle voluntarily in their reductions. The secret of the Jesuits' success in Paraguay was due above all to their interfering as little as possible with the Indian social structure. Aside from a small field which every family could till and harvest as it pleased, there was no private property in the reductions. The greater part of the land remained *abambaé,* community property, which the Jesuits called God's property. Following ancient tribal custom, the Indians worked four days a week for their family and two days for the community. Like modern economic planners, the Jesuits watched that all went well in the fields, the stables, and the workshops of the villages. A trading organization, the *Candelaria*, sold the surplus of the communities, thereby providing the reductions with money for raw materials and implements.

The most extraordinary feature of the Jesuits' "Holy Experiment" was the fact that not a single Indian had to be coerced into working for the reductions. The Jesuits' government so commended itself to the Guaraní that they voluntarily joined in the building of churches, schools, hospitals, and factories. The Guaraní language became both the language of ordinary communication and of writing in the missions. The word of God was preached and the children were taught their ABC's in Guaraní. With no special difficulty, the Jesuits succeeded in reconciling the native piety of the Indians with Christian doctrine. The Indian goddess of water and fertility was transformed into the Virgin Mary; the Indian Bringer of Light became Jesus Christ. Whereas elsewhere in the world, mission work among the natives proved tantamount to stamping out the pre-Christian religions, the Jesuits contrived, by adroitness and a great deal of tact, to raise the Indian nature religion into a kind of primitive Christianity.

Perhaps the baroque churches in the early reductions strike the European observer as so moving because they have not been imposed by force upon a violently Christianized country. Instead, they were created by the Indians themselves out of a genuine, naturally evolving religious feeling. The churches and the ruins of churches are full of Indian religious symbols. In contrast to the rest of Latin America, where every missionary charged like a crusading warrior against the last remnants of pagan symbolism, the Jesuits in Paraguay showed tolerance. They knew that only a healthy symbiosis of both cultural elements could lead to a genuine Christianization of the Guaraní. None of the representations of the Madonna in South America moved me so deeply as the wooden Madonna Guaraní, her Indian features transfigured by suffering, that a pious Guaraní artist carved three hundred years ago.

Countless books have been written about the Jesuits' theocratic state, and innumerable contradictory interpretations have been offered. Some historians describe it as a patriarchal, authoritarian regime, others as a socialistic or primitively communistic state. There is truth to both definitions. The Jesuits in Paraguay did not actually form a real state; their reductions were scattered over a vast area, from the central Paraná to the pampas of the Gran Chaco. Formally, they were subject to the authority of the King of Spain. In practice, however, they skillfully fended off all Spanish influence.

Experience had taught them that the greatest enemies of their project were Spaniards or other Europeans. Mestizos, mulattoes, and Negroes were also dangerous. Their strategy, then, was to preserve the isolation of their wards, the Christianized Guaraní. In the Spanish law which established the legal position of the reductions, there was the significant statement "Example has shown that the whites or mestizos who temporarily or permanently settle in the reductions are restless persons of bad character, thieves, gamblers, vicious and decadent people whose excesses might cause the Indians to flee or abandon the reductions."

Thus the Jesuits hoped to keep away from their settlements the very people who held power in the rest of Latin America. Moreover, they wanted under all circumstances to prevent a mingling of whites and Indians, not on racist grounds, but in order to protect the offspring of the Indians from the uprooting and debasement that were taking place elsewhere in Latin America. In order to strengthen the morale of their Christianized Indians, the padres gradually introduced self-government into their reductions. These Indian administrations were more democratic than any that came after them in Paraguay. The Guaraní elected their community heads and officials from their own ranks. The padres assisted the Indian *alcaldes, regidores,* and *mayordomos* only as advisers.

In the early eighteenth century the Paraguayan Jesuit state was the most prosperous and most peaceful unit of government in Latin America. If the Iberian conquerors of the time had really had any desire for humanitarian missionary work, they would have smiled upon the Jesuit missions and learned from their example. But the opposite was the case. Operating from Brazil, the *Paulistas* launched an endless succession of predatory expeditions into the territories of the missions. They carried away thousands of Christianized Indians and crowded them into forced labor camps—the world's first concentration camps. The Jesuits were forced to arm their peaceful Indians and to make soldiers out of their protégés. Gradually, they had to abandon their last settlements on Portuguese territory. Their Indian converts fled to the forests and were lost again to Christianity and civilization.

In the Spanish colonies of the Río de la Plata region, the Jesuits were able to hold their own for a few decades longer. But there, too, the Spanish settlers resented the reductions as a permanent threat to their privileges and property. The Guaraní knew that they could lead a peaceful, secure, and happy life under the protection of the Jesuits. Consequently, every enslaved Indian longed to escape from the whip of his Spanish master and flee to the padres. Rumors were circulated among the Spaniards that the Jesuits had accumulated vast quantities of gold and gems in their reductions; and since all such treasures belonged to the King of Spain and his satellites, the Jesuits were periodically charged with illegally hoarding treasure. The charges ultimately were aired in the Vatican. Although the Jesuits had always dutifully sent their tithes to Rome, the Spanish and Portuguese intriguers implanted the suspicion in the Pope that the padres might be using the riches they had purportedly collected more for their own coffers than for the ends of the Church.

THE END OF THE JESUIT STATE

Historians consider Pope Benedict XIV one of the most tolerant and enlightened of supreme pontiffs. Even freethinkers like Voltaire and Frederick the Great thought well of him. But this pope who was so liberal in theological questions was in political matters a supporter of absolutism, and consequently complaisant toward Spain's imperialistic aims. He was among the popes who were not well disposed toward the Jesuits. Consequently the Spanish and Portuguese colonial masters could count on meeting no serious opposition from the Vatican if they gathered their forces for a decisive blow against the Jesuit state in Paraguay.

Spaniards and Portuguese, who hitherto had never been especially friends of each other in South America, now joined in an elaborate game of intrigue. In 1750 João V of Portugal and Ferdinand VI of Spain concluded a treaty to correct the boundaries of their lands in

South America. Portugal ceded to Spain the territory of Sacramento in the present Republic of Uruguay. In compensation, the regions in which the Jesuit projects were operating were transferred from Spain to Portugal. Evidently the Spaniards did not care to destroy the reductions themselves. They preferred leaving this bloody business to the savage Mamelukes from São Paulo. The Jesuits answered this bald threat with a virtual declaration of war upon Spain and Portugal.

Until 1758 their Indian militia fought desperately against the united Spanish-Portuguese armies. It was a hopeless struggle. The Jesuits were defeated, and in 1768 they were abruptly seized in one fell swoop throughout all the Spanish American colonies and were deported. More than one hundred thousand Guaraní fell into the hands of the victors. When the Jesuit state had been annihilated and its population forced under the yoke of colonialism, Spain and Portugal divided the booty. The reductions on the Paraná and the Rio Grande do Sul were handed over to the Portuguese, those in the vicinity of the Río Paraguay to the Spaniards.

Few peoples in the world have had the cultural achievements of a whole century wrenched from them as absolutely as the Guaraní. Those Indians who escaped the Iberian soldiers fled the reductions and returned to the nomadic life of their ancestors. In the settlements, the Spaniards found no treasures of gold and gems. The Jesuits had not heaped up riches of any kind. As a concession to the primordial feminine craving for ornament, they had permitted the Indian women of the settlements to wear a few modest gold chains and gold combs. The victorious marauders had no eyes for the artistic treasures in the churches, nor for the well-tilled fields, the excellent schools, and the exemplary administrative apparatus of the Society of Jesus.

Paraguay went downhill so rapidly that within a few years it was transformed from the most thriving to the most wretched region in the Iberian colonial empire. Five years after the expulsion of the Jesuits there were only fifteen thousand Guaraní living in remote reductions. The destruction of the Jesuit state was comparable to the destruction of the Inca Empire. In both cases lust for power and greed for gold took precedence over religious conversion and the dictates of humanity. In both cases the "progress of the universe" which Montaigne had dreamed of was negated. History's clock was turned back several generations. Time has since stood still in those lands.

LAND OF WOMEN

Paraguay today still seems haunted by the shade of an old man to whom the Guaraní once referred in reverent whispers as *El Difunto*, The Deceased. Dr. José Gaspar Rodríguez Francia, the founder of the nation, has been dead since 1840, but Paraguayan legend has made him into a South American Barbarossa who will someday rise from his tomb to complete the liberation of the Guaraní.

Since the days of Dr. Francia, the Paraguayan people have lain in torpor. Asunción is not a dead city; it is an exhausted, a sleeping city which cannot summon up the courage to awaken. One hundred and fifty years ago, in the days of Dr. Francia, Asunción looked, on the whole, much as it does today. One-story houses in colonial style, painted many colors but chiefly that gentle pink which looks so well in the glaring sunlight of the city, alternate with baroque churches, villas set in parks of rich vegetation, and antiquated-looking palaces which in part are merely enlarged colonial houses and in part are imitations of French pomp. The picks and bulldozers have not yet invaded Asunción. Paraguay's capital is two centuries away from the skyscraper cities of other Latin American countries. It has still the air of a sleepy little viceroy's residence.

The past haunts the streets, the buildings, and the souls of the people. Among the most imposing palaces in Asunción is the one Dictator Francisco Solano López had built by Indian children a hundred years ago. The sight of the López palace made me feel that the tears of the mothers, who saw their children keeling over under the inhuman strain, have not yet dried, and that the very stones are still wet with the blood of the little slave laborers killed by drudgery.

Nowhere in Latin America is the past so heart-rendingly present and alive as it is in Paraguay. The stern Guaraní faces of the people are marked by it. The bowed backs of the Paraguayans seem unable to straighten. The Guaraní have been fearfully reduced in numbers, the Guaraní men in particular. For the past hundred years Paraguay has not been an Indian country ethnologically, but a country of mixed breeds. Nevertheless, the Guaraní seem to have triumphed in the end. For Paraguay does not give the impression of a former

Iberian colony shaped by the Spanish spirit. At the core of its being, Paraguay has remained a Guaraní country which has swallowed the Spaniards and spewed them out again undigested.

In the second half of the eighteenth century, shortly after the expulsion of the Jesuits, a muleteer and his family emigrated from the Brazilian province of São Paulo to Paraguay. His name was França and he was a *caboclo,* that is, a man with some Indian blood. It may be that this França first came to the former Jesuit state in the train of the "Mameluke" marauders. Exact details are unknown, for his son, the creator of the Republic of Paraguay, shrouded his origins in mystery. His feeling for family was certainly extraordinarily feeble. Even after he had made himself supreme dictator, he ignored his indigent parents and gave no thought to his illegitimate daughter, who earned her living as a *peineta de oro,* what we today might euphemistically call a "hostess." He was, to be sure, equally little concerned about his personal welfare. In fact, he was the most ascetic, spare-living ruler that Latin America has ever had. Possessing absolute power, he died penniless.

This Gaspar Rodríguez, the muleteer's son, studied first theology and then jurisprudence. When the war of independence broke out in the countries bordering on the Río de la Plata, he was already a man of fifty and a respected lawyer whose incorruptibility had given him a legendary reputation in Asunción. Out of respect for the French Revolution, and in particular for the man he most admired, Robespierre, he had long since changed his name to Doctor Francia. This was no empty gesture. The spirit of Robespierre seemed to have been reincarnated in its most extreme form in this Paraguayan mestizo.

Paraguay was so remote, so cut off logistically from the Spaniards, that she won her independence without much bloodshed. In spite of the massacres and the deportations following the expulsion of the Jesuits, the overwhelming majority of the population still consisted of Guaraní Indians. The Spanish oligarchy made several attempts to seize the reins of governmental power, but the ideas of Simón Bolívar kindled far less enthusiasm in Asunción than the ideals of the French Revolution. Francia, the honest lawyer, first served as secretary of the revolutionary junta. From this key post, he rapidly climbed the political ladder. The government was organized on a model of the French Republic. Francia became elected consul, then consul for life, and finally dictator.

For a quarter of a century this remarkable man governed the new Indian state of Paraguay. He governed it on Robespierrean principles: with virtue, justice, incorruptibility, and patriarchal severity. As Robespierre in Paris kept the guillotine busy eliminating the enemies of the state who stood in the way of the establishment of paradise on earth, Dr. Francia in Paraguay kept his execution squads busy annihilating the enemies of the new republic, in order to create a South American paradise.

His principal enemies were the members of the Spanish upper class and the Catholic clergy. Francia secularized all the monasteries in Paraguay, nationalized all church property, and issued severe and eccentric-sounding marriage ordinances compelling pure-blooded Spaniards to marry Guaraní Indians. Those old Spanish families who refused to give their sons and daughters in marriage to Paraguayans of Indian blood had to obey a special law even more outrageous to Spanish minds: the dictator commanded them to mingle their blood with that of Negro slaves "since Guaraní blood is not good enough for them." In this way, Francia thought, the Spaniards would be absorbed by the colored population and Paraguay would become a Guaraní country without a foreign white element in it. This was the first attempt at re-Indianization in newly independent Latin America.

Francia had learned from the example of the Jesuits that the Guaraní had to be protected from alien influences if the people were to remain intact. Hence Francia turned his Paraguay into one great reduction. He forbade all immigration and emigration, all private trade with foreign countries, and all contact with neighboring countries. He insisted on a state of autarchy more complete than anything ever since attempted anywhere in the world. His planned economy even prescribed what the owners of land should plant. He was the first Latin American dictator to mobilize the forces of industry.

At the heart of the Paraguayan economy was a plant whose sale, both within and without the country, filled the national treasury. This was *Ilex paraguayensis*, from which the national beverage of the Guaraní, yerba maté, was prepared. Even the Jesuits had recognized its importance and arranged for its cultivation in their settlements. They had also contrived to keep the secret of how the ilex seeds are made to germinate. Francia imitated their example. Since *Ilex paraguayensis* grows only in the forests of Paraguay, he strictly banned the export of maté seeds and thus obtained a complete monopoly. One of the most prominent naturalists of the time ran into difficulties because of the laws regarding maté. He was the French botanist Aimé Bonpland, an erstwhile traveling companion of Alexander von Humboldt.

Bonpland had become a passionate maté drinker in Paraguay. With the dictator's permission, he settled in the country, established a maté plantation, and published scientific reports on the Indian plant. One such report proposed that "maté tea be planted in other countries also, for it is preferable to Chinese tea, coffee, cocoa or any other beverage." This suggestion rebounded against its author. Francia called it a crime for a European to suggest that any country but Paraguay should grow the plant. He arrested the French botanist and kept him in chains for nearly ten years.

The imprisonment of Aimé Bonpland has been a major stain upon the reputation of Paraguay's patriarchal ruler. Francia was no crueler and no more absolutist than any other Latin American ruler of the age. His country was in many respects more progressive than the other young republics that had shaken off Spanish dominion. Francia was the only South American liberator who clearly aligned himself with the interests of the Indians. To be sure, he ruled them as a strict, pedantic father rules his children. In his last decade, when the economy and governmental apparatus of Paraguay were functioning smoothly and the old Spanish opposition had been stripped of most of its power, El Supremo, the absolutist ruler, became a thoroughly benevolent dictator, a kindly and forbearing father of his country. But the civilized world never forgave Dr. Francia his highhanded treatment of Bonpland.

EL DIFUNTO AND THE LÓPEZ DYNASTY

A fact the world overlooked was that the victim himself took the incident in surprisingly good part. When the dictator began loosening the rigidity of his rule, he released Bonpland and offered to let him return to Europe. Bonpland remained in the country, however, worked as a physician and planter, and seemed to have so thoroughly fallen in love with Paraguay that Europe held no attractions for him.

After the death of the "barbarous cazique," as Bolívar had called Dr. Francia, Bonpland went to Uruguay, where he helped develop the famous breed of Merino sheep which were to become so important to the Uruguayan economy. Bonpland died as a small trader and village doctor in Estancia Santa Ana on the Paraguayan-Argentine border. This was shortly before the outbreak of the murderous war which took such a toll of the people of Paraguay.

At the ripe age of seventy-four El Supremo exchanged the governmental palace, which he had built in the style of the Louvre, for a modest Indian grave. In the hearts of the Guaraní he then became El Difunto, the immortal spirit the Indians venerated like a god in spite of his sternness—although it must be granted that much of the veneration came after his death. He was succeeded by Carlos Antonio López, also a mestizo, who rapidly changed the Robespierrean atmosphere of Paraguay into a Napoleonic climate. López did not have himself crowned emperor, like his French model, but he converted the republican authoritarian regime into a regime of the López dynasty. He and his relatives became virtually the "royal family." The period of his government was probably the most prosperous and hopeful era in the history of Paraguay, in spite of the domination of the López clan and considerable political oppression.

López had keenly analyzed the principles of his uncle's government, and meant to eliminate whatever aspects of it he thought mistaken. He did away with autarchy, with curbs on commerce, with bans on immigration and emigration. He opened the country to foreign merchants, liberalized the entire customs procedure, and thus turned Paraguay from a hermetically sealed "reduction" to a busy mart of free trade. During the period of his rule the first railroads and factories on Latin American soil were built in Paraguay. Paraguay was able to defend herself successfully against her neighbors' annexationist ambitions. She became the most dynamic and progressive country in South America, a country with an astonishingly modern legal and educational system, blessed with several million gold pesos in her treasury and no debts.

The greatest achievement of Carlos Antonio López was his educational legislation. He established more than four hundred schools, was the first Latin American president to institute free compulsory education for all, and had the children of the poor clothed, sheltered, and fed by the state. Paraguayan pupils in the López area were not thrown on the streets or sent back to their parents after their schooling was finished. Following the Jesuit model, they were given free instruction in all sorts of trades, weaving, tailoring, shoemaking, and carpentry. López wanted to create a healthy Indian class of artisans—the sound lower-middle class which to this day is lacking in most Latin American countries.

The frightful disaster which was to destroy the Guaraní people began in 1862. Before the death of Carlos Antonio López, Paraguay had had some one and a half million inhabitants—a great many less than during the most prosperous time of the Jesuit state. Eight years after his death only 220,000 persons were living in Paraguay, only 28,000 of whom were men—about one ninth. Paraguay had become a land of women.

Francisco Solano López, the son and successor of Carlos Antonio, modeled himself not after Robespierre or Napoleon I but after Napoleon III. As a diplomat and his country's military attaché, he had learned in Europe French manners, Prussian military drill, and the florid splendor of the third Napoleon's court. He had also brought back the Irishwoman Eliza Lynch, Paraguay's future Pompadour, who lashed his ambition and was probably partly to blame for his power mania, his overestimation of himself, and his aggression against his bigger neighbors in South America.

EXTERMINATION OF A PEOPLE

When Francisco Solano assumed his father's mantle in 1862, he spent the revenue accumulated by his father's thrift in buying weapons and making the Paraguayan army the largest and strongest fighting force in Latin America. With these forces he intended to annex the Republic of Uruguay, then regarded as Paraguay's sphere of influence and natural outlet to the sea.

He was even able to secure the support of the Uruguayan Government party, the *Blancos*, for voluntary union. The opposition party, the *Colorados*, under Venacio Flores, was against the plan and appealed for help to Brazil and Argentina. Paraguay's relations with these two big powers had long been tense. The borders were by no means settled. Many Guaraní Indians lived under the authority of Argentina or Brazil. López regarded himself as the standard-bearer of *Indianismo;* he wanted to free these Indian regions and annex them to Paraguay. Moreover, he entertained the illusion that a declaration of war upon Argentina would at least persuade the separatistic Argentine provinces of Entre Ríos and Corrientes to come over to Paraguay's side.

The younger López's dream of creating a Guaraní empire in South America is reminiscent of Santa Cruz's visionary plan to restore the Inca Empire. Both men overestimated themselves and the potentialities of their countries; both suffered from megalomania. López may claim a degree of sympathy, for his Brazilian and Argentine opponents were anything but Indianophile. Paraguayan liberation of the Indians in the Río de la Plata region was in itself a humane, desirable goal. But López, obsessed by power, was not the person to bring it about, and the little Republic of Paraguay was not strong enough to force through such a re-Indianization.

López made a good many perilous political miscalculations. In Uruguay, Flores and his *Colorados* won power, and that country then supported Brazil. The rebellious northern provinces of Argentina put aside their separatist ambitions and backed Argentine President Mitre. Not a single neighboring region showed any disposition to accept the rule of López. Brazil, Argentina, and Uruguay concluded a Triple Alliance, aimed at deposing the Paraguayan troublemaker, demilitarizing the Paraguayan people, and humbling the ambitious Republic of Paraguay. López responded by marching his armies into Argentina.

For six years he waged a desperate struggle against the united great powers of South America—a war that gradually degenerated into a ghastly hunt on the part of the Brazilians, who rounded up the Guaraní like wild beasts. López was defeated, forced to flee from Asunción, and continued to wage bitter guerrilla warfare in the interior of Paraguay. Before he left, however, he had little children —since all the men were in the army—build that resplendent palace which stands today as the last symbol of his regime and as terrible evidence of his heartless and ferocious dictatorship.

Toward the end of the war, López seems to have succumbed to the sort of madness of which Adolf Hitler provides a modern parallel. He decimated his own followers and members of his clan by mass executions, slaughtered thousands of prisoners of war, and ruthlessly incited the sad remnants of the unfortunate Guaraní to resist to the last the assaults of the Brazilian Negro regiments. Historians record with amazement and near incredulity the fact that the Paraguayan Indians remained loyal to the crazy dictator until his last breath. But the Guaraní knew only too well that the Triple Alliance had converted their fight against the tyrant into a planned campaign of extermination directed at the whole Paraguayan nation. They laid down their lives for López very nearly to the last man, until on April 1, 1870, the slash of a Brazilian Negro cavalryman's sword ended the dictator's life.

In northeastern Paraguay this destroyer of the Guaraní people is still venerated like a saint. In Asunción, too, the second López is idolized by the descendants of the Guaraní as a second father of his country. One of the pompous buildings erected by the elder López looks like a copy of the Dôme des Invalides in Paris. There, in the oratory on the Plaza de los Héroes, López *fils* rests in his sarcophagus, like Pizarro, that butcher of Indians, in the cathedral in Lima. On the anniversary of his death tremendous crowds of people of Indian blood pour into the oratory and pile cascades of flowers upon the final resting place of the man to whose ambition a whole nation was sacrificed.

THE SOUTH AMERICAN POORHOUSE

For biological reasons alone Paraguay became a country of mestizos in the course of the following decades. The manless Guaraní women drew to themselves male foreigners from all over the world. Within fifteen years after the end of the war, Paraguay swarmed with Argentines, Brazilians, Italians, Frenchmen, Spaniards, Germans, mulattoes, and Negroes. If the narratives of the day may be believed, every ship that sailed upriver to Asunción was virtually attacked by man-hungry women. From all sides, boats and canoes raced toward the ships. The Paraguayan women clambered up on deck, threw themselves into the arms of the sailors, and dragged them over the gangways to their huts. All male visitors to Paraguay were beset by Guaraní women who begged them to stay at least long enough to give them a child.

The consequence was that since the López war most of the nations and races of the world have left their mark upon the Guaraní people. I saw innumerable mulattoes who spoke Guaraní. I saw Guaraní with the flaxen hair and deep blue eyes of Scandinavians; I saw Guaraní with Mongolian features. In spite of this indiscriminate mingling during the maleless decades, the Indian element has gradually won out again. In the capital and the small villages the prevailing face has the high cheekbones, stiff black hair, and somber brown eyes of the Guaraní. And the agony still persists, the harvest of genocidal war.

You see them sitting on the sidewalk, wherever there is room—old women with furrowed faces, knotted hands, bony legs, and sunken breasts. They offer fruit or some worthless trinkets for sale, everything heavily covered with dust. On gaunt donkeys and mules, the leather-faced men and defiant-looking young fellows ride through the streets, the starved mounts laden with baskets of fish or manioc roots. Everywhere, little, pitiably thin children with lifeless old men's eyes hold out their hands, mutely begging for a crust of bread or a few coins. In front of the government buildings and barracks mestizo guards stand with shouldered rifles, so spindly they look like retarded adolescents. Their faces are grayish green, their hungry eyes fasten upon every passer-by, and they look as if any moment they will collapse under the weight of their weapons.

Paraguay has become South America's poorhouse. And Paraguay is still a country with an acute shortage of men. Today the republic again has approximately one and a half million inhabitants—the same number as at the beginning of the López war. Barely 40 per cent are males. For the Chaco War with Bolivia from 1932 to 1935 again thinned the ranks of Paraguayan men. And the bitter civil war in 1947, in the course of which the *Colorados*, the Liberals, overthrew the previous authoritarian regime, resulted in further bloodletting.

For these reasons, unformalized marriages and illegitimacy flourish in Paraguay. The authorities tolerate extramarital alliances, partly from tradition, partly in order to repopulate the country. Even in Jesuit times it was no disgrace for a Guaraní girl to bear an illegitimate child; the disgrace, rather, was to remain childless. The Jesuits had discovered that the Paraguayan system of concubinage could not be eliminated, and in their reductions had simply looked the other way when Indians lived together without marriage.

A further consequence of the shortage of men is employment of women to a degree unknown elsewhere in Latin America. Most of the professors and teachers in Paraguay are women, as are most salespeople and textile workers. There are even female masons, machinists, and road builders. Women occupy a correspondingly high position in Paraguayan society. This is partly the heritage of ancient Indian matriarchy, which has come down from the descendants of the Guaraní to the rest of the population.

Paraguay is a fertile country, a country full of unexplored natural resources and unexploited potentialities. But the past lies so heavily, so crushingly, upon the country that there has scarcely been any effort to make use of these potentialities. During the decades after the López war, a rapidly developing oligarchy seized the greater part of the cultivated land. One and one half per cent of the agricultural enterprises in the country contain 54 per cent of the arable land. On the other hand, almost half of the peasant plots are smaller than twelve acres. As in the early Indian times, the *ocupantes*, transient agricultural workers, still drift from region to region. They burn down jungles, clear and till the land, reap, and wander on to burn down new jungles. Scarcely anything is left of the industries Dr. Francia and the elder López once established—aside from slaughterhouses and leather factories.

As a result of the shortage of men and her unexploited potentialities, Paraguay has periodically received influxes of European immigrants. During colonial times, only some ten thousand Spaniards entered the country. These, moreover, mingled so thoroughly with the Guaraní during the era of Dr. Francia that there is not much trace of a Spanish element in the Paraguayan population. The number of German and Italian immigrants long ago exceeded the number of Iberian Paraguayans. In Asunción and in the cultivated heartland of Paraguay there are today some forty thousand Paraguayans of German extraction.

Emigration from Paraguay has long been far larger than immigration into the country. Almost as many Paraguayans live outside the borders as inside the country itself. Distress and economic disaster forced three-quarters of a million Paraguayans to immigrate into the adjacent Argentine provinces. Half a million found new homes in southern Brazil. During the last hundred years twenty times as many persons have left Paraguay as have immigrated.

These mass migrations have depopulated vast regions of the country. Other regions, especially in the north and northwest, have remained thinly populated. There are no economic centers, no markets, no communications. Nevertheless, the remote northern part of Paraguay has repeatedly attracted idealists and utopians.

UTOPIANS AND MENNONITES IN THE CHACO

Among those visionaries was Bernhard Förster, the philosopher Nietzsche's anti-Semitic brother-in-law. After the First World War, Förster established a settlement in the Paraguayan wilderness. Called Nueva Germania, it was supposed to bring to fruition its founder's vague ideas about Germanism and race. The colony still exists, although without any racist philosophy. But it is so remote, so cut off from all communications, that it can barely survive, let alone thrive. Similar failure awaited other experiments by European, North American, and Japanese colonizers who were willing to go into the Chaco. The country that had the best communications in South America during the days of Carlos Antonio López is today—aside from the region around Asunción—so poor in roads and railroads that most settlers in the vast area west of the Río Paraguay have no way of sending their products to market.

The only immigrants who succeeded in attaining a modest degree of prosperity in the Paraguayan Chaco were Canadian, German, and Russian Mennonites. In the short or long run the Mennonite sect has encountered difficulties with the authorities in every country in which it has settled and spread. For the Mennonites reject worldly power as an institution alien to the Kingdom of Christ. They reject legal oaths, war, and military service. Therefore they repeatedly antagonize the governments under which they dwell. The upshot is that the Mennonites, who feel themselves subject to religious persecution, are always immigrating to remote regions of the globe, where governmental authority can scarcely reach them. In southeastern Paraguay, Canadian Mennonites have engaged in intensive fruit growing. In the Chaco, Russian and German Mennonites from the Ukraine established a variety of agricultural settlements after the war with Bolivia. Since they are completely unmolested in Paraguay, they have gradually brought some fifty thousand acres under the plow.

The Mennonites, however, pay for their tranquillity in Paraguay by renouncing all the achievements of civilization. Their settlements, too, are autarchic reductions. Many Mennonite families, as far as their dwellings and way of life are concerned, have sunk to the level of the Indians. Until the Republic of Paraguay is linked to the wider world by new roads, the only colonists who can survive in such remote places are those whose religious zeal is stronger than any desire to rise socially and to live like civilized men of the twentieth century.

After the last war, irresponsible agents once again organized extensive Central European immigration into the wilds of Paraguay. The colonization was to proceed along the lines of the notorious sharecropping system which has earned such obloquy in the history of Brazilian colonization. Financiers bought great tracts of land and supplied the colonists with the funds for transportation and support during their first few months. In return, the immigrants contracted to work for the financier until the advances, together with interest, had been paid off. The profits from the settled lands were divided; the supplier of capital received one half, the colonist the other half—out of which, however, he had first to pay off his debts. But climatic and transportation difficulties usually do not allow the tenants to pay off their debts for many years. As a result, they work for decades, or in the worst cases all their lives, for the financier.

Brazil used this system after the abolition of slavery to maintain coffee growing in the state of São Paulo. But even before the middle of the last century the Prussian Government, along with the governments of most Central European countries, banned the soliciting of immigrants under such conditions. The ban was known as the Von-der-Heydt Rescript.

The Von-der-Heydt Rescript had long been forgotten by the time the practice was resumed after the Second World War. Likewise forgotten were the nineteenth-century outcries in Germany and Switzerland condemning the sharecropping system as "importation of white slaves." Large European companies lured many eager emigrants from refugee-crowded Europe to the Paraguayan wilderness under conditions that did not differ greatly from the old, discredited sharecropping system. The settlers died, were reduced to the level of the Indians, or fled to Brazil to escape their creditors. The failure of these attempts has once more shown that Central Europeans (unless they are Mennonites or members of similar sects) cannot wrest a livelihood for themselves under the conditions now prevailing in Paraguay. However capable and hard-working they may be, they are worsted by the utter remoteness of the interior of the Chaco.

"IMPOSSIBLE TO CIVILIZE"

The vast and thinly populated Chaco begins right across the Río Paraguay, which runs outside the capital and extends to the jungles of Bolivia and Brazil. A few hours' journey into the interior brings the traveler into contact with the first savage Indians. These Chaco tribes were scarcely touched by the Jesuit missions, by the era of Dr. Francia, the López war and subsequent political events. For the most part they are still regarded as impossible to civilize or convert.

Before I crossed the river, I had to stop at a military post where I was asked to leave my full address. When I asked why, the guard on duty answered indifferently that he would need my address to inform my family in case I did not return. Paraguayans are wary of visiting the Indian areas. No inhabitant of Asunción will enter the Chaco unless he has some compelling reason. When the Chaco Indians appear in the capital to sell their dusters made of nandu feathers, the citizens hastily close their windows and doors, as people used to do in Europe when gypsies turned up. And yet 90 per cent of the population in Asunción has Guaraní blood. I had some difficulty in persuading my Paraguayan host to accompany me on a trip into the Chaco.

Time has stood still in the Chaco, too, but it is a time several centuries earlier than in the rest of Paraguay. The Mataco and Macá tribes on the west bank of the Río Paraguay live as if there had never been a white man in South America. Their villages are surrounded by palisades. The huts have three walls of adobe and one open side which serves for door and windows. I passed small, weedy fields of cotton, tobacco, corn, and manioc. Old men swung primitive hoes, straightened, looked me over expressionlessly, with no curiosity in their wrinkled, broad-boned faces, then indifferently resumed their work. The huts swarmed with babies, cats, dogs, chickens, and pigs. Over the fireplaces steamed pots of manioc, the food of the poor in Paraguay.

Gradually, the village street came to life. A few men passed by, walking stiffly erect, odd-looking scythes over their shoulders, highly polished blades sparkling in the sunlight. Women strolled toward us, naked except for a loincloth, babies in their arms and a swarm of children around them. Silently, the Indians gathered to scrutinize the visitors. Some held out woven belts and blankets of brilliant colors. A number of men, women, and even small children were marked with those ornamental scars that travel writers have made much of, but the majority were without them.

Within the first hour it became evident that the women are dominant in these Chaco villages. The men treated them with respect and took orders from them. When the Indians, with somewhat embarrassed expressions, improvised a war dance, the two girls who joined in received the lion's share of the money I distributed in return for the privilege of seeing the dance.

These Chaco Indians are still profoundly primitive. Nevertheless, or perhaps for that very reason, they give the impression of being far healthier and more contented than the Guaraní mestizos in Asunción and the villages of Paraguay. The children are well nourished, the men strong and tall, the women amazingly pretty in spite of their sometimes excessive plumpness. The *conquista* left the Chaco Indians virtually untouched. However, the chances are that they will soon be wrenched forcibly out of their primitive paradise, for the Chaco is rich in raw materials and is being looked to as a land of the future.

AN EX-DICTATOR'S GAMBITS

Granted, not even the present has yet begun in Paraguay, let alone the future. After the López war, the republic was for a time dependent on her neighbors, who had taken a third of her territory. Weak liberal governments were continually being overthrown by ambitious army officers. Foreign capital for the most part gave a wide berth to restless Paraguay.

After the Chaco war, fascist army men seized power, as they did in Bolivia. The fascist era of Dictators Franco and Morínigo terminated in a general uprising of the people, a civil war which in 1947 brought the liberal *Colorados* to the top again. But the *Colorados* in Paraguay have little in common with the liberal parties of other South American countries. From the ranks of the *Colorados* military dictators periodically emerge, suspend the constitution, and institute a rule quite as authoritarian as that of El Supremo and the two Lópezes. During the six years from 1948 to 1954 Paraguay underwent ten coups. The last of them brought to power Alfredo Stroessner, a general of German descent.

Stroessner was a Peronist at the time, and basically has remained a Peronist to this day. He staked his hopes on Perón, in the faith that in the shadow of the Argentine dictator he would be able to revive his country. Paraguay has no coastline and must export her products downstream into the La Plata basin, through Argentine territory. This bothersome and expensive mode of transportation is Paraguay's major handicap when it comes to having to compete. Perón and Stroessner therefore planned an Argentine-Paraguayan economic union which would certainly have proved advantageous for Paraguay's development. To be sure, the Argentine dictator probably also had in mind gradual absorption and eventual annexation of Paraguay.

Perón's fall put an end to all of Alfredo Stroessner's plans. The anti-Peronist governments of Argentina, which succeeded the dictator, boycotted Paraguay. As early as 1956 it was expected that Argentine economic pressure or outright intervention would bring about the overthrow of Alfredo Stroessner. But in spite of several rebellions, Stroessner managed to hold office. The Paraguayan people hate him, blaming him for the country's inflation and the precipitate rise in the cost of living. So far, however, no political force in Asunción has proved strong enough to push the dictator from his pedestal.

The economic policies of anti-Peronist Argentina, especially the freight monopoly the Argentines have established in the Plata region, compelled Alfredo Stroessner to take a peculiar economic and political risk. In 1960 this last Peronist in control of a Latin American government turned to Brazil, then governed by leftist liberals and socialists, in order to escape the Argentine vise. The Brazilians granted the Paraguayans free ports in Santos and Paranaguá; and the extension of the railroad and highway system in southern Brazil, which will shortly link up with the Paraguayan communications network, will presumably make it easier for the Paraguayans to transport their products in the near future. What has kept Alfredo Stroessner in power is primarily his skillful bargaining with Brazil.

In spite of all her agricultural and industrial potentialities, Paraguay is still sound asleep. This country, the first in Latin America to grant the Indians civil rights, to educate the lower classes, and to introduce a planned economy, now has the lowest educational, economic, and social level in all of South America. From 40 to 60 per cent of the Paraguayans are illiterate. There is scarcely any social welfare at all. Nowhere else in Latin America did I find hotel personnel sleeping on the bare floor in the hall at night. It did not even occur to the owner of the hotel to provide his employees with a decent bed. If the mestizo bellboys or chambermaids were to demand a bed, or better food than the everlasting manioc porridge, they would be accused of impudence or even suspected of communism.

The well-to-do in Paraguay have no Indian trauma, unlike their counterparts in Peru. Nor do they use the word *Indio* as a term of abuse. On the contrary, they employ the Guaraní language when dealing with the common people, since most Paraguayans did not speak Spanish well. These prosperous citizens do not hate the lower classes, nor do they feel it would be dangerous to make too many concessions to them. Rather, they simply do not think about the common people at all. On the whole, the Paraguayan oligarchy is just as lethargic as the Paraguayan plebs.

In the port of Montevideo I was able to see the attitude of other Latin Americans toward the once brave and now so pitiable Paraguayans. Even the most ragged dockworker looks down on the people of the "Land of Women." Two men had fallen to quarreling and were hurling the ugliest, most obscene curses at one another. They began with a simple *"Pederaste!"* and gradually raised the pitch of their insults to *"Analfabeto!"* and then *"Americano!"* Finally one of the men put an end to the war of words with *"Paraguayano!"* There was no surpassing this last insult.

THE OCTOPUS

Neither a rebel nor a general was the hero of Argentine independence, but the Chamber of Commerce of Buenos Aires. Six years before Bolívar called for revolution, a British squadron forced its way into the Río de la Plata, blockaded the coasts, and landed troops to occupy Buenos Aires. Spain at that time had already become a dependency of Napoleonic France, and the British wanted to crown Nelson's victory at Trafalgar by occupying the Spanish possessions on the Plata.

When Sir Home Popham appeared with his fleet in the port of Buenos Aires, he did not at once reveal his aims. Instead, he announced that he had come as a liberator, and called upon the Argentines to free themselves from the yoke of Spain. The merchants of Buenos Aires wavered for a time. Free trade, which the English promised them, tempted them greatly. But the gauchos of the surrounding pampas and the lower class of the population in the city regarded the British as what they really were, foreign invaders, and drove them away. The British fleet, however, continued to blockade the coast, conquered Montevideo, and stopped all trade, so that Buenos Aires was soon on the verge of economic ruin. The ships that had hitherto carried away Argentine hides and other leather products, and returned with imports urgently needed by the people who dwelt along the Plata, lay at anchor in the river. The colonial government in Argentina, most of whose revenues came from the customs of the port, suddenly found itself without funds. The rich cattle raisers in the interior, whose gauchos had expelled Sir Home Popham, could not sell their products, and swiftly realized that their premature patriotism had affected their pocketbooks.

Back in the Spanish motherland the troops of the legal king, Ferdinand VII, were waging a guerrilla war against the troops of the king by-the-grace-of-France, Joseph Bonaparte. The Spanish viceroys who rapidly succeeded one another in Buenos Aires had no means whatsoever for shaking off the strangling English blockade.

Finally the *Junta General de Comercio,* the Chamber of Commerce of Buenos Aires, came to the decision to negotiate with the British, prepare for independence step by step, and in return request freedom to import and export—in other words, a lifting of the blockade. The British consented. There was a minor misunderstanding when foreign ships wanted to bring some twenty thousand pairs of boots to Buenos Aires. Leather goods, the Chamber of Commerce insisted, must be excepted from the gentleman's agreement on free trade, in order to protect the native tanneries and shoe factories. When the matter of the boots was settled, Argentina found herself confronted with independence, which she had not really wanted and did not know what to do with.

SAN MARTÍN

The Spanish colonial territory along the Río de la Plata was at that time an extremely heterogeneous region. It was the most sensitive area in the whole Spanish Empire. Barely three quarters of a million persons were then living in the region comprising the present republics of Argentina and Uruguay. Of these, only ten thousand were white-skinned, of Spanish or Spanish-Creole descent. A sixth of the population consisted of Negro slaves. Some two hundred thousand inhabitants were pure-blooded Indians; about four hundred thousand Argentines were mestizos. In other words Argentina, today the "whitest" country in South America after Uruguay, was one of the most "colored" countries on the continent a century and a half ago.

Buenos Aires, the governor's seat, was regarded even into the middle of the eighteenth century as one of the dreariest and most wretched cities in the Spanish colonial empire. Every traveler who visited the Plata two hundred years ago complained of the filth lying around the muddy streets, of the tumble-down adobe huts, and the unhygienic conditions which were to blame for the recurrent epidemics of malaria, cholera, and bubonic plague. The only attraction of Buenos Aires was a plaza sporting a total of four bars and a bullfight arena. This uninspiring port had a population of a few tens of thousands who needed wooden palisades to protect themselves from the attacks of the plains Indians.

Three decades before the end of the colonial period, things began looking up for Buenos Aires. In 1776 the Spaniards separated their Río de la Plata provinces from the viceroyalty of Peru and appointed a viceroy, Pedro de Cevallos, for the colonies on the Plata. Cevallos realized that because these colonies lacked proper communications with the other colonies in Latin America they could not survive unless they participated in world trade. Though Spanish colonial policy was opposed to allowing its colonies to trade with other countries, an exception was made of the Río de la Plata viceroyalty. Buenos Aires became an overseas port, exporting hides to Europe and North America. The *Porteños,* the inhabitants of Buenos Aires, made a good living out of this export trade. A local merchant oligarchy grew up, which, once having tasted the joys of trade, did not want to let them go again. Even before the Buenos Aires Chamber of Commerce opted for independence, the Porteños were looking overseas rather than toward the interior of the country.

In the interior, on the other hand, the spirit was reactionary, as was the case everywhere among the holders of latifundia in Latin America. The cattle raisers ruled their *estancias* like petty kings. Every landowner had equipped himself with an army of mestizo gauchos, with whose aid he annihilated the Indians, occasionally made war on his neighbors, and sometimes relieved merchant caravans of their goods.

On May 21, 1810, a *cabildo abierto,* a revolutionary council, proclaimed independence in the town hall of Buenos Aires, following the time-honored procedures of Spanish councils. But the Porteños had not a single man and not a single rifle to defend their new independence against their former Spanish masters. They were dependent on the wild gauchos of the *estancieros.* In practice, the capital of the new country thus relied on the good will of the cattle raisers and cowboys in the pampas.

While the *llaneros* in Venezuela took the part of the Spaniards, the gauchos in Argentina sided with the young republic. The Argentine cattle raisers were clever enough to realize where their advantage lay. But the gauchos were not strong enough to expel the Spanish armies. Their traditional method of riding down their enemy, effective enough in the Indian wars, did not work when they encountered well-trained troops from Peru. The ranchers were unwilling to sacrifice their gauchos to fill the pockets of the Porteños; they waged the war of independence with little enthusiasm. And when for propagandist reasons the Buenos Aires junta ordered the execution of the former Spanish viceroy, who had voluntarily stepped down, almost all the provinces abandoned the capital and formed anarchic separatist governments.

Then, on March 9, 1812, a man arrived in Buenos Aires aboard the British warship *George Canning*—the man whom both Argentines and Chileans now hail as the liberator and father of their countries. José San Martín, a Spaniard born in Argentina, had been serving the motherland as an officer in King Ferdinand's army. Discharged and disaffected, he returned to the land of his birth and offered his services to the revolutionary junta. The Porteños received him with open arms. Probably the main reason for their warm reception was that he belonged to the same lodge of Freemasons as the ruling families of Buenos Aires.

The merchant oligarchy of Buenos Aires had been anything but united in the confusion that followed upon the proclamation of independence. There were pro-Spanish, conservative, Anglophile, and determinedly Argentine-nationalist families; there were clericals and anticlericals, revolutionaries and evolutionaries, centralists and federalists. The only united and politically effective group in the port had gathered around a lodge of Freemasons which, interestingly enough, bore the name of the old Araucan fighter for liberty, Lautaro, and which soon afterward was to play a great part in the South American struggle for independence, for most of the prominent fighters for freedom belonged to it or joined it. The brothers of this lodge were key figures in the revolutionary junta and entrusted to their friend San Martín command of the Argentine northern army.

San Martín, the experienced professional soldier who had already distinguished himself in the struggle against Napoleon, transformed the undisciplined horde of gauchos into an effective fighting force. With it, he succeeded in wresting the Argentine and Chilean provinces from the Spaniards and delivering the deathblow to Spanish colonial rule in its chief bulwark, Peru. Like Simón Bolívar in the northern part of South America, San Martín became the military liberator in the south and west. On July 26, 1822, the two *libertadores* met in the Ecuadorian port of Guayaquil to confer on the future of South America.

The fate of the continent depended on two men of very different character. Bolívar, ambitious, obsessed with power, a military amateur, was riding high on the waves of the movement for independence, and already saw himself autocrat of South America. San Martín, the sober professional soldier, had no political ambitions and exercised no political functions; he regarded the struggle for liberation merely as a military task. Undoubtedly the Argentines would have made San Martín chief of state if he had been able to follow up his military victories with success in his negotiations with Bolívar. But he failed.

Bolívar sensed that San Martín was a dangerous rival. He demanded strict subordination of the Argentine army of liberation under his command. Although San Martín in Chile and Peru had done at least as much for the independence of South America as Bolívar in Colombia and Venezuela, he agreed, after some hesitation, to accord Bolívar the precedence. But that was not enough for the autocratic Venezuelan. The exact course of the fateful conference of Guayaquil is unknown; historians have been able to offer only a fragmentary reconstruction. But it seems clear that Bolívar demanded that the southern general retire to Argentina and turn over his army to him.

San Martín realized that the only logical answer to this affront was open warfare. But at the same time he knew that a clash between the two victorious armies of liberation would set loose inconceivable

chaos. Tired of the political intriguing, he gave no answer, and returned to Argentina. There chaos had already broken out. The centralistic Porteños were at odds with the separatistic inhabitants of
the cattle-raising provinces. Both parties stubbornly fought one another; the result was an incessant change of governments and progressive dissolution of the new republic. San Martín, disgusted by
these egotistic struggles for power, turned his back on South America
and never again set foot on his native continent. In 1850 he died,
lonely and forgotten, in the French port of Boulogne sur Mer.

BLUE AGAINST RED

Ever since those days, Argentina has been a battleground between
the *Pulpo*, the capital, extending out in all directions like an octopus,
and the pampas, the provinces of the gauchos and ranchers. While
Paraguay, under Dr. Francia and the elder López, was developing
into a politically and economically integrated country, the Republic of
Argentina broke up like a rotten raft in a high sea. Uruguay, Corrientes, Santa Fe, and Entre Ríos seceded from Buenos Aires. When
a unitarian Porteño occupied the presidency, the capital was isolated
because the rest of the country opposed all its policies. As soon as a
Federalist from the pampas acquired dictatorial powers, things went
ill for the Porteños. For although the Federalist promptly transformed
himself into a unitarian, he did so in a way not to the liking of the
Porteños: he transferred the seat of government to the interior. Under
Federalist governments the unimportant city of Paraná in the province
of Entre Ríos became the capital, and remained so for decades.

The party flag of the Federalist plainsmen was at that time red,
while the flag of the Porteños was blue. The gauchos so detested the
storekeepers and merchants of Buenos Aires that no one in the interior
dared to wear a blue article of clothing. In the middle years of the
last century, a harmless Porteño or foreign traveler who happened to
appear in the pampas with a blue shirt or blue tie ran the risk of
being beaten or even lynched. The first liberal president of Argentina,
Sarmiento, denounced this hostility between red and blue as the "struggle between barbarism and civilization."

The tensions between Buenos Aires and the provinces were far
more serious than the usual bad blood between a bustling mercantile
metropolis and its agrarian, semifeudal hinterland. After indepen-

dence, Buenos Aires had opened its doors wide and received vast numbers of European immigrants. In some years more than two hundred thousand Europeans came to Argentina. The majority remained in Buenos Aires. Within half a century the port on the Río de la Plata multiplied its population more than tenfold. Around 1890 the half-million mark was passed. Buenos Aires rapidly developed into the biggest city in Latin America, and has remained that to this day. In 1962 the city numbered five million inhabitants. If we include the unincorporated suburbs, which are actually integral parts of the city, the South American Babylon has nearly eight million inhabitants today. The rest of Argentina has a total of only about thirteen million. The octopus on the "Silver River" holds more than one third of the whole population of Argentina.

As a result, Argentina became a country of whites. The Italians, Germans, Frenchmen, and other Europeans who became Porteños absorbed the native Creoles, mestizos, and Indians as a giant squid swallows its prey. Even the Negroes and mulattoes, who at the beginning of the last century constituted a sixth of the Argentine population, mingled so thoroughly with the other elements of the population that the marks of origin in their descendants are barely detectable today.

The Indians and mestizos, who at the time of the declaration of independence constituted 80 per cent of the inhabitants, have been more radically assimilated than anywhere else in Latin America, except for Uruguay. Among the gauchos in the interior and among the *descamisados*, the "shirtless" peons and urban proletarians, there are still a good many persons with the brown skin, broad cheekbones, and stiff Indian hair, but the present-day visitor to Argentina has the impression of being in an altogether white country inhabited by the descendants of Europeans.

Nevertheless, *Indianismo* in Argentina was not destroyed by racial assimilation alone, but also by the deliberate policy of federalistic dictators. When a gaucho chief pushed his way to the top in the Argentine Confederation, he stopped the immigration of Europeans in order to prevent "denationalization" of the Argentine population. Nevertheless he would also declare war on the pampas Indians in order to extend the territory of the confederation to the south and to secure new latifundia for the *estancieros*.

The first Federalist tyrant, Juan Manuel de Rosas, acquired a grim kind of fame after he worked his way up to absolute dictator. Rosas forbade all immigration and all contact with Europe. He organized the notorious *Mazorca*, a gang of bandits who were supposed to purge Argentina of Unitarians. He decimated his enemies and the pampas Indians, and his own followers as well. During his twenty-three years of rule he acquired tremendous personal wealth in land, cattle, and peons.

An even more brutal butcher of the Indians was Julio Roca, the conqueror of Patagonia, likewise a Federalist who in 1880 blockaded the city of Buenos Aires to bring the hated Porteños under his yoke. Today monuments to Julio Roca grace the towns of Patagonia. The Argentines have many objections to his regime, but they celebrate him because in the course of several campaigns he liquidated the Indian aboriginals of Patagonia. After Roca's campaigns, southern Argentina underwent a complete economic change. The Patagonian pampas became sheep pastures and wheat fields.

The gaucho chieftains in the presidency thought entirely in terms of their own interests. They drove Argentina into national bankruptcy. There was, however, a pleasant intermezzo from 1868 to 1874. The moderate Federalist Domingo Faustino Sarmiento changed his spots, became a Unitarian, and tried to break the hold of the gauchos. Sarmiento, also a member of the Lautaro Lodge, like San Martín and O'Higgins, was a liberal intellectual who as a young man had belonged to the circle of Alexander von Humboldt's friends. He passed a series of the most tolerant religious laws in South America of the time, separated church and state, and revived immigration.

Although he was a Latin himself, he did not think much of immigrants from Latin countries, and instead advocated Germanic immigration. "At the moment," he contended, "our country lacks labor power and all comforts. Agriculture can develop only if it is pursued intelligently by industrious families. Today all the wealth with which nature has blessed our country is being squandered by the indifference, ignorance and laziness of its inhabitants, whereas it could be well exploited by capable settlers."

Sarmiento had learned to appreciate the proficiency of the Germans as settlers. German colonists, he thought, could gradually transform Argentina into the South American counterpart of the United States. "Once the German emigration movement has started," one of his proclamations reads, "the settlements will soon advance up the rivers into the heart of South America and bring civilization, agriculture, and industry to lands that are still covered by wilderness and jungle. South America will then be able to compete with North America in power and wealth."

Sarmiento inaugurated a mass emigration of Germans from Germany and Russia which has not ceased to this day. Every political upheaval in Central Europe has washed a new wave of German immigrants on the coasts of Argentina. At present a quarter of a million persons of German descent live in Argentina, more than in all the other Spanish-speaking countries of South America taken together. Since both the Hitler dictatorship and the collapse of nazi rule brought emigrants from Germany to the Río de la Plata, the politically active German-Argentines are split into two hostile camps—an antifascist and a fascist camp, in whose publications a permanent feud is waged.

During Sarmiento's presidency, Argentina undertook her first serious efforts to raise the level of popular education. But his successors of the Roca clan were used to dealing as they pleased with illiterate peons; they ruled the people as a whole much as they did their own farm workers. Sarmiento's emancipation program remained largely an unrealized project.

Meanwhile, Buenos Aires continued to swell and bulge. The Europeanized, commercialized metropolis had had enough of the brutalities of gaucho chieftains. A middle-class party formed, the *Unión Cívica Radical,* which henceforth became the most important element in the country's political life. But it was not until 1916 that the Radicals were able to take over the reins of government. Their first president, Hipólito Irigoyen, a lawyer of Basque descent, became the creator of Argentine liberalism and is regarded by Argentine democrats today as the country's greatest statesman. Irigoyen established universal suffrage, introduced the first social-reform legislation, and opposed the economic imperialism of the United States. During his two periods in the presidency, from 1916 to 1922 and from 1928 to 1930, Argentina prospered greatly and developed into the economically and politically leading country of Latin America.

The unity of the powerful middle-class party was destroyed, however, in disputes over the policies of Irigoyen. Some of the Radicals had hoped that he would grant democratic freedoms such as were customary in Europe, and when this did not happen withdrew their allegiance from him. Ever since, the *Unión Cívica Radical*, the greatest political force in Argentina, has been split into two factions, Personalists and Antipersonalists—or, as they call themselves today, Popular Radicals and Intransigent Radicals. One of the Intransigents in the presidency was Arturo Frondizi, who between 1958 and 1962 attempted vainly to banish the ghosts of the Peronist past. Arturo Illía, who became president in 1963, is a Popular Radical who also has to fight renascent Peronism.

In 1930 Irigoyen, the great liberal, was forced by a military coup to resign. Thus the first shadows of the fascist era in Argentine history began to appear.

THE SAINT OF THE SHIRTLESS ONES

Today Argentina is again a politically unstable country with shattered finances, a weakened economy, and a limping democratic system—a country one-third of whose population abstained or cast blank ballots in recent elections. But during the era of liberalism, when the *Unión Cívica Radical* held power, Argentina was economically the steadiest, politically most enlightened, and intellectually most independent country in South America.

The megalopolis of Buenos Aires, thanks to its European immigrants, is partly reminiscent of a large Italian city, partly of a German residential suburb, but above all of many parts of Paris. Shopping streets, bookshops, and art galleries, restaurants and antique shops à la Paris, have shaped the aspect of the city's heart. The Palermo quarter, with its fine boulevards, parks, ponds, islands, groves, and lawns partly resembles the Bois de Boulogne, partly Hyde Park, and partly the Berlin Tiergarten. During the 1920s the low, flat-roofed houses gradually vanished. Wide diagonal avenues were created. Buenos Aires developed into a city of palatial banks, stock exchanges, trading companies, and shipping agencies, as well as into a cultural center of the first rank, with many museums, libraries, academies, theaters, and scientific institutes. The city felt itself to be the head and heart of South America.

World trade and flourishing agriculture created an economic boom in Argentina similar to that stimulated by nitrates in Chile. Cattle, sheep, and wheat conquered the country. With cattle raising as a major industry, mechanized packing plants sprang up, as well as modern *frigoríficos* (refrigerating plants) and factories that made clever use of the by-products. These included leather, margarine, stearine, glycerine, soap, and bone meal. In *saladeros* dried and salted meat was prepared; other plants produced canned meat and meat extract. Grain silos and huge flour mills rose on the banks of the Plata and the Paraná. The wool and dairy industries throve in the pampas.

THE GREAT ABATTOIR

Argentina owed her remarkable economic upsurge to the French engineer Charles Tellier, inventor of the first refrigeration ship. Before 1876 the Argentines would ship their meat surplus overseas preserved in salt. But Argentine salt beef did not please European palates. Some two hundred patents were registered for transporting refrigerated meat to Europe, but most of these experiments failed. In 1876, however, Tellier successfully shipped thirty-five tons of refrigerated meat from Argentina to France aboard his steamer *La Frigorifique*. The feat had been accomplished—and the next shipment of frozen meat to Europe was actually approved by the Queen of England and the Prince of Wales.

Since England was particularly interested in obtaining a supply of meat from Argentina, the Argentines prepared their product to suit British tastes. The amity that swiftly developed between the two nations proved an irritation to the United States. Argentine meat was cheaper than American meat. Americans started rumors that Argentina was plagued by hoof-and-mouth disease, which could be transmitted by the frozen meat. Finally, the United States Government instituted a ban on the importation of Argentine meat products. In 1928, during the presidency of Hipólito Irigoyen, the controversy over Argentine frozen meat became the central issue of the Pan-American Conference.

The Argentine economic boom smoothed over—at least to the outward eye—the antagonisms between the Federalist, reactionary, xenophobic provinces and the Unitarian, liberal, cosmopolitan Porteños. In the upper classes of both groups, the traditional tensions yielded to the desire to share as quickly and as amply as possible in the new wealth. The opulence of Argentine meat, wool, and wheat millionaires became proverbial in Europe. Rich Argentines, who loved to spend their vacations in Europe, filled the passenger liners with resplendent uniforms, expensive dresses, and sparkling jewelry. They were so pampered and extravagant that some of them actually took live cows with them on their vacation trips. For even in Europe, the children of Argentine millionaires had to have fresh Argentine milk to drink.

The extreme wealth of a small upper class in Argentina was purchased by increasing proletarianization and impoverishment of the masses of the people. Buenos Aires and other Argentine cities spawned the same type of dirty, noisome slums that may be seen in almost all Latin American metropolises. *Conventillos*, "tenement houses," is the name given to these slums in Argentina; colloquially they are accurately called *villas miserias*. Here live the *desamparados*, the "abandoned ones"—day laborers and occasional workers, migrants from the countryside, outcasts. Here homicide and other crimes run rampant. And here are the yeast cells of political fermentation.

In 1930, at the time of the world-wide depression which led to the overthrow of Irigoyen's liberal government, the proletarianization of the Argentine people accelerated. Ever larger numbers of gauchos and peons poured into the cities and settled in the villas miserias. The military governments of the following years, which were constantly threatened by new coups, only worsened the economic crisis and led to an increase of mass misery. The Argentine boom proved to have been a sham in which only a very small percentage of the population had participated.

Argentina's lower class is lumpenproletarian to an even greater extent than the roto class of Chile. Socialistic ideas from Europe had scarcely found their way into the villas miserias. Italian and Spanish immigrants did, it is true, import syndicalist ideas; they spurred the founding of unions and laid the cornerstone for a modest and moderate socialism. But the overwhelming majority of the desamparados and descamisados consisted of peons and the offspring of politically unenlightened agricultural workers. The ideologies of class struggle were foreign to the peons; they could not think beyond the problems of bare subsistence or conceive of any goal greater than winning some minor improvement in their living conditions. The *Confederación General del Trabajo*, the Argentine labor organization, fought largely for economic rather than political goals. For these reasons the fascists rather than the socialists succeeded in gaining control of the CGT.

IN HITLER'S FOOTSTEPS

Argentine fascism is a stepchild of European fascism. It took root in the minds of young army officers who, in contrast to the leading military men, came from the middle class rather than the oligarchy, and drew their ideas from Hitler's Germany and Benito Mussolini's Italy. But Argentine fascism was given its peculiar tone by an unusual woman who at heart was an extreme leftist socialist. The liaison between the radical-rightist Juan Perón, who sympathized with Hitler and Mussolini, and the social-revolutionary labor-union agitator María Eva Duarte constitutes one of the strangest political marriages in history. That marriage turned the ragged Argentine masses into fanatical Peronists.

Juan Perón came out of the world of the estancieros. He was born in 1895 in the provincial town of Lobos, but his family was not part of the landed oligarchy. One of his great grandfathers was an Italian, one of his grandmothers an Indian. Perón became a professional soldier and founded the *Grupo de Oficiales Unidos,* an association of discontented young officers who were toying with fascistic and nationalistic ideas. Under the military governments and the military-influenced conservative presidents of the 1930s, these fascist officers attained enough influence to become alarming. To disabuse itself of the troublesome leader, the government dispatched Perón to Chile and later to Europe in the role of military attaché.

This proved a fatal mistake. While Perón's young comrades gradually climbed the military hierarchy, and some even moved into key posts, Juan Perón spent years as military attaché in Berlin. During the years before the outbreak of the Second World War he formed a friendship with Hitler and studied with keen interest the methods by which a single man succeeded in hypnotizing and mobilizing the masses in Germany. Already, Perón could envision himself as chief of state in Argentina.

He began formulating his program. "As in Germany," he wrote, "our future government will be an inflexible dictatorship, although at the beginning it may be necessary to make certain concessions in order to establish ourselves firmly in the saddle. We must hammer into the masses an ideology that will enable them to march on the avenues of heroism." All this was sheer bombast with nothing behind it. At that time Perón had no goals, no ideology—he simply wanted power.

When he returned to Argentina, he recognized that Hitler and Mussolini had made some mistakes. "Mussolini," he declared in 1945, "was the greatest man of our century. But he committed certain disastrous errors. I, who have the advantage of possessing these forerunners, will walk in his footsteps but avoid his errors."

Perón entered the political stage in 1943, when another military coup took place in Argentina. The coup was directed against the conservative government of Ramón Castillo, which had been supported mainly by reactionary generals and rich cattle raisers, and would have entered the war on the side of the Allies. The rebellious members of the Grupo de Oficiales Unidos wanted to keep Argentina out of the war. They expected the Axis to win, and hoped to glean benefits for Argentina from such a victory. But the course of the war soon put an end to these hopes. Three weak, politically vague military dictatorships followed hard upon one another. Argentina did not want to come away empty-handed in the distribution of the war booty, and shortly before the end of the fighting finally declared war on the Axis powers. By that time pro-Hitler Perón had long since become the key figure in Argentine Government.

Under Dictators Rawson, Ramírez, and Farrell, Perón held a variety of posts from 1943 to 1945. But he consistently retained the post of Secretariat of State for Labor and Social Welfare, even though this job gave him a great deal of trouble at the beginning. For the proletarians were the real sufferers from the military coups. Dictator Ramírez had banned all democratic activities and dissolved all leftist labor organizations. The government in which Perón functioned as minister of labor and social welfare was anything but a welfare state.

At a benefit in Buenos Aires' amusement park, the reactionary minister had a fateful encounter. He met a young actress who should, by all rights, have been one of his bitterest opponents. María Eva Duarte was the daughter of an agricultural worker from the provincial town of Los Toldos. She was working as an announcer at the Belgrano radio station and was one of the few women in Argentina who had joined the CGT. Her vigorous agitation for unionism and for improvement of the lot of the poor earned her the nickname of "Señorita Belgrano" among the Porteños. (This was fame indeed—as if an American radio announcer were to be called "Miss CBS.") Perón struck up a friendship with the radical young lady, made Eva Duarte his mistress, and installed her in a leading position in the CGT.

In those days Eva's political ideals differed fundamentally from those of Juan Perón. If at the time Argentina had had a functioning socialist movement, Eva, with her passionate championing of the rights of the proletariat, would probably have landed in the ranks of the left socialists. But since there were no such opportunities, she used Juan Perón to bring her ideas to fruition. With the aid of the descamisados, she suggested to Perón, he could overturn the existing system and become the creator of a new Argentina.

Perón had met Eva Duarte at a critical stage in his own career, when the end of the short-lived military dictatorships and thus his own political demise seemed in the offing. The Axis had lost the war. Perón's idols, Hitler and Mussolini, were dead. A first wave of democratization flooded through Latin America; in many countries democratic and social-revolutionary governments replaced authoritarian regimes. In Argentina, too, the *Unión Cívica Radical* and the conservative oligarchy were seeking to eliminate military rule. In the early autumn of 1945 four hundred thousand persons demonstrated against Farrell and Perón in the streets of Buenos Aires. It was the greatest mass demonstration in Argentine history.

Perón answered it with totalitarian measures such as Argentina had not known for decades. He ordered the arrest of opposition politicians, union leaders, and liberal journalists, as well as many of the demonstrators. He staged merciless manhunts even in the workers' districts, and filled the prisons with his victims. No one knows what Eva Duarte, the workers' friend, said about these methods. The Argentine army, at any rate, considered such violent measures fruitless. It revolted and on October 9, 1945, deposed Farrell, the puppet dictator, and his strong man, Perón.

A week later Eva Duarte proved to Juan Perón that power could be based on the descamisados. She won over Cipriano Reyes, the union leader, by promising that Perón would transform Argentina into a labor-union state. Together with Reyes, she called upon the masses in the villas miserias for a general strike and a march on the government district of Buenos Aires. A horde of ragged peons and laborers, inflamed by Eva Duarte's incendiary speeches, surged through the streets of Buenos Aires. The army had never seen such a spectacle; paralyzed, it watched passively as the descamisados hailed Juan Perón.

AN UNEQUAL MARRIAGE

October 17, 1945, the day of the Shirtless Ones' march through Buenos Aires, was celebrated by the Argentines during the following ten years in the same spirit as celebrations of the October Revolution by the Russians, the March on Rome by the Italian Fascists, the seizure of power by the German Nazis. It was the great day of Eva Duarte. Farrell and Perón, who had contributed nothing to this victory of the streets, returned to the government palace. Perón promised the CGT the pro-labor, syndicalist policy it demanded. Four days after the march through Buenos Aires, Argentina's strong man married the "saint of the descamisados."

After Perón's fall, a great many contradictory stories went the rounds concerning this marriage. Conservative Argentine circles maintain that Perón had been a henpecked husband whom Eva forced into marriage and afterward treated like a foolish boy. One of the many mistresses whom Perón kept after Eva's death subsequently published what purported to be a tape recording of Perón's, in which he said: "I hate that woman; I never loved her. But in the game of politics I could not free myself from her, and that was my misfortune." By that time Perón may well have forgotten that he would have been thrown out of the political game had it not been for Eva Duarte. After October 17, Eva's ideology won out over Juan's shopworn political notions.

In the eyes of Buenos Aires' society, the marriage was a startling breach of custom and tradition. Perón had done something that a successful South American cannot do without destroying his social standing: he had married his mistress. The institution of mistresses is semilegal in Argentina; no one objects if an unmarried or married Argentine has an official mistress. But it is unthinkable that such a mistress be promoted to the rank of wife. Moreover, Eva Duarte had come up out of the proletariat. Even when Perón was at the height of his power, the ladies of society demurred at receiving the dictator's wife in their salons. Argentine society gossip still retails the perhaps apocryphal story that Eva Perón once dared to enter one of the exclusive ladies' cafés, but the ladies promptly drove her out with slaps. This assault on La Presidenta, the tale goes, had no consequences because even Perón could not protect his wife against the power of Latin convention.

But if Eva Perón was hated by the upper class, she was loved by the common people. She saw to it that the descamisados helped Juan Perón win the elections of February 24, 1946. She became minister of social welfare and chairman of the CGT, traveled about the country incessantly, and delivered fiery speeches in which she portrayed herself as the "mother of all the poor, weak, and needy, the comrade of all workers, and elder sister of all the women of Argentina." Moreover, she proved to the descamisados that these were not empty words. As Perón's grip on the country strengthened, she was able to keep most of the promises she had made to the Shirtless Ones.

The Peronist dictatorship was a curious phenomenon, resembling the fascist dictatorships of Europe in some respects, but in social policy basically different from them. In his foreign policy Perón behaved much like other Latin American autocrats. He concluded treaties of friendship with Franco's Spain and with Dictators Salazar, Peréz Jiménez, Ibáñez, Stroessner, and Trujillo. He tried to make Argentina the dominant power in Latin America. He attacked Wall Street and foreign investors. He took in a number of Nazi leaders for whom the soil of Europe had grown too hot. He even toyed with the idea of making Argentina an independent atomic power, and for this purpose provided a Professor Richter with a research center in the Andes resort of San Carlos de Bariloche, in which he sank about a half billion dollars.

In his domestic policies also, Perón scarcely differed from the dictators in Spain, Venezuela, and the Dominican Republic. He suppressed all opposition. Among his victims was the old union leader Cipriano Reyes, who had helped him win power on October 17, 1945. Although Reyes had the same political aims as Eva Perón, in 1948 he was arrested and tortured. Many members of the former Grupo de Oficiales Unidos likewise found themselves imprisoned. The principle behind this suppression was a simple one, which Perón once phrased as follows: "Peronism is popular in its essence. All special agitation is unpopular and therefore not Peronist." Anyone who engaged in such "special agitation" was accordingly locked up.

In spite of this highhandedness, however, Peronism had distinctly feminine features. And that was something entirely new in Latin America. Latin American countries belong to the men. Politically

active women are great rarities in all Latin countries. But Eva Perón
was the real motive force behind Peronist social policies. She identified
herself more and more with her part as idol of the masses. The Latin
cult of the Madonna helped a good deal. Peronist propaganda compared her variously with Catherine the Great, Queen Elizabeth of
England, Isabella of Castile, and Joan of Arc. Finally, Perón capped
this Eva cult with a most remarkable military order. He appointed
the Argentine national saint, Nuestra Señora de Luján, Generalissima
of the Army—as a kind of symbol for La Presidenta. According to
the legend, this saint once protected the city of Buenos Aires from the
British fleet under Sir Home Popham. Nuestra Señora de Luján actually received the salary of a generalissimo; the money was turned over
to the Church every month.

This was only one of many gestures by which the Peróns tried to
conciliate the Catholic Church. The clergy had lost much influence
in Argentina during the periods of liberalization. Perón knew he
would have to rely on an active Catholic Church as well as the
descamisados if he wished to fortify his power. He therefore went
further than symbolic gestures; he also annulled all the laic laws that
had been passed since the days of the reformer Sarmiento. Civil
marriage and divorce were done away with. Religious instruction in
the schools, under the control of the Church, was reinstituted. During
the first seven years of Juan Perón's rule, the Catholic Church regained
almost all the privileges it had lost. The consequence was that Perón
was re-elected by a huge majority in 1951, receiving three and three
quarter million votes. Only two million Argentines voted against
Peronism.

Eva Perón provided for a further bulwark to Perón's power. She introduced women's suffrage, proclaimed the equality of women in
the social and labor fields, created a social-welfare organization that
really functioned, and issued decrees establishing minimum wages and
protecting the unpropertied. In her hatred for the propertied classes
who snubbed her socially, she disregarded the needs of the economy
and the country's productive capacity. If the unions asked for a 50-
per-cent wage increase, Evita, as the descamisados called her, granted
an increase of 75 per cent. She ignored the question of profitability of
business. In her incessant propaganda speeches, she lashed out against
Argentine landowners, businessmen, and bankers, as well as against
foreign capital. She promised to set up national industries to provide

the descamisados with good wages. The railroads, radio broadcasting system, and the banks were nationalized. Perón seized the Argentine oil regions. It was, of course, Eva Perón's policies of nationalization and social welfare that more and more outraged foreign countries and generated increasing hostility toward the Argentine dictator abroad.

Foreign observers could rightly point out that La Presidenta's wage policies were leading to a collapse of the Argentine currency and economy. In a land once famous for its enormous meat surpluses, people had to queue up for hours to buy a bit of beef. Because the Peronist system suffered from a shortage of foreign exchange, the export of meat was increased to the maximum at the expense of home consumers. Inside the country, the prices of consumer goods rose precipitately. This in turn brought new wage demands by the CGT. The magnanimity of the president's wife had created a vicious circle. The descamisados had meanwhile been stirred up to such an extent that Eva Perón was compelled to grant them extensive concessions in order to hold them in line.

TRIUMPH OF FEMINISM

Eva Perón was no coolheaded thinker, and she knew nothing about political economy. She was a passionate woman guided by her emotions. Her social policies were not based on any carefully thought-out system like those of the Marxists. Perón defined his and Eva's policy in the most simplistic terms: "In the capitalist world, the yield of production is regarded as the product of capital and therefore belongs to the capitalists. In the communist world the yield of production belongs to the state as the all-embracing owner of capital and labor. To us Justicialists, however, the yield of production is a product of labor and therefore belongs to the workers." This muddled mixture of fascism and Marxism wrought havoc with the economy of Argentina.

The shibboleth "justicialism" first arose in 1949, when Perón extended his own powers by the device of introducing a new constitution. Hitherto his party had availed itself of the venerable name *Unión Cívica Radical*, to which it added a few flourishes, calling itself *Partido Laborista y Junta Reorganizadora de la Unión Cívica Radical*. The new *Movimiento Justicialista* that Perón formed out of this party contained only a few of Juan Perón's own ideas. It distinctly bore the feminine features of La Presidenta. Today, many years after Perón's fall, this is even clearer than it was while he still reigned as dictator.

The Peronist doctrine of "justice" propounded many of the principles of the democratic, social-reform movements in other Latin American countries which Perón had previously denounced: national prosperity, narrowing of the gap between poor and rich, the country's economic and political self-sufficiency. One typically Peronist element was the call for close co-operation between the conservative army and the revolutionary masses. From fascist ideology Perón had borrowed the slogan that the rights of the individual must be subordinated to the rights of the community. The upshot of this muddle was that Peronist social policy periodically conflicted with Peronist authoritarian politics. Perón tried to escape this dilemma by assuring the unions they would receive everything they asked for. In return the unions had to promise unconditional political obedience.

The success of this program with the Argentine masses was due primarily to the personality of Eva Perón, secondarily to the fact that no socialist or social-reform forces existed in Argentina as possible alternatives to Peronism. The dictator was anything but popular in Argentina. But the common people forgave him much for Evita's sake. Eva Perón, on the other hand, knew only too well that she could not carry out her political program without her husband. "I was no more than a sparrow," she once said. "Juan Perón was and is the mighty condor who flies high and secure above the peaks, close to God." Another time she went so far in her concession to Latin masculine dominion as to say: "The history books will record no more about me than this: At Perón's side there was a woman of whom we know no more than that the people tenderly called her Evita."

In reality, however, Eva was fully conscious of her worth. When it became apparent that she would soon be dying of cancer, the dictator began construction of an Eva Perón mausoleum. The sick woman for whom the tomb was intended herself delivered the dedication address. "This century," she declared, "will go down in history not as the century of atomic energy, but as the century of feminism triumphant. Long after my physical decease I shall live on through this monument as a force dominating our country."

Evita was right. Today Juan Perón remains an exile in Spain, and most adherents of Peronism do not really want him back, despite their noisy assurances that they do. But Evita lives on in the souls of the descamisados. All the accumulated resentments, all the social injustices which in other countries of Central and South America drive the people into the arms of social-revolutionary and radical leftist parties, combine to make at least a third of the people of Argentina cultivate the Evita legend to this day.

In her last year of life Evita was immortalized in Argentina in a manner reminiscent of the personality cult of Trujillo, the Dominican dictator. Libraries, scientific institutes, schools, streets, villages, and towns were rebaptized in her name, including the important provincial town of La Plata. When Argentine astronomers discovered a new star, they hastily named it "Eva Perón," and it retains that name still. Monuments showed Evita as an angel showering blessings. Paintings of the Madonna bore the features of La Presidenta under the aureole. Toward the end, Juan Perón actually wanted to appoint his wife vice-president. Thus Evita would have become chief of state and commander-in-chief of the armed forces in the event of his death. But that was too much for the military. They protested, and Perón had to drop the plan.

After Perón's fall, a Porteño once remarked bitterly to me that Evita had taught the people how to hate. He was quite right about that, but he was wrong in seeing this only as the most negative and dangerous side of Eva Perón's work. Every social-revolutionary ideology necessarily opens the people's eyes. And hatred inevitably arises out of such consciousness, hatred of the dispossessed for the possessors. It was the same in Mexico and Bolivia. Hatred makes the underprivileged realize their situation fully; and only the negative emotion of hatred can give rise to the positive will to act, to change circumstances, to advance into a better future.

Since the years of Evita's dominance, no Argentine government has been able to make the descamisados forget what she taught them. The amorphous, politically passive masses were tranformed into latent rebels with whom henceforth every political power in Argentina must reckon. The hatred that Evita kindled aroused the slumbering forces of the Shirtless Ones. No one in the villas miserias takes much interest nowadays in Perón's vague justicialist doctrines. But the Argentine peons and laborers cling fanatically to the social goals that Evita promised to achieve. They stand today where Evita always should have stood, by virtue of her origins and her ideology—on the left wing of the political parties.

THE EVITA LEGEND

In July, 1952, Evita died of cancer. Her social policy died with her. After Evita's death the Peronist dictatorship returned to standard dictatorial behavior. It became clear that without his wife Perón was a nonentity, a pallid, pedestrian imitator of European fascists. Economic conditions deteriorated so rapidly that he swiftly lost prestige among the people. The opposition of conservative, feudalistic circles to Evita's labor-union policies forced him to found an employers' association whose task was to apply brakes to the wage demands of the descamisados. Gradually, Perón also rescinded his nationalization measures. He persuaded Standard Oil and other foreign companies to finance his economic plans; he made up with Wall Street, which he had formerly so violently attacked. From now on the principal task of the unions was to be the prevention of strikes. In short, he developed into an Argentine Trujillo.

He also abruptly broke his pact with the Catholic clergy, which had assured him a majority in every election. The reasons for this reversal are not quite clear. After Evita's death Perón had apparently expected the Vatican to canonize La Presidenta. When sainthood was not forthcoming for Evita, he attacked the Argentine clergy and thus antagonized the Catholic Church in his country. Perón may have felt the Vatican's disobliging attitude as a psychological defeat. The descamisados, at any rate, were disappointed that Evita was not canonized, and blamed the dictator. It is, however, probable that the increasing strain between Perón and the Church was due primarily to the change in his mode of life. As a widower, Perón espoused the pleasures of the flesh much like his fellow dictators in the Caribbean. He began changing his mistresses as often as his shirt. His escapades led to indictments, after his overthrow, for rape and seduction of minors, so that today he does not dare set foot on Argentine territory for fear of being haled into court on morals charges. For his successors, these charges have been a handy method for reducing him to political silence. In the Argentine clergy, however, his conduct aroused widespread indignation even while he still held power. The descamisados, for their part, regarded Juan Perón's loose living as a posthumous betrayal and insult to their Evita.

Infuriated by the opposition of the Church, Perón recklessly struck back. He abolished the privileges of the clergy, gave sanction to divorce and prostitution, arrested clerical critics, and finally reintroduced absolute separation of church and state. In other words, he took the very path that soon afterward led to the fall of Pérez Jiménez, the Venezuelan oil dictator. When Perón's mobile squads began attacking churchgoers, setting fire to churches and robbing poor boxes, the Pope, in June 1955, excommunicated him. That put him beyond the pale as president of a Catholic country.

But Evita was once more victorious even beyond her death, if only for a few months. The army rebelled against Perón and tried to force him to change his course. It demanded that he stop his anticlerical campaign, countenance opposition parties, and strip the unions of their excessive powers. While Perón was still vacillating, the descamisados once more marched through the streets, called a general strike, and bombarded the soldiers with Evita's old slogans. The reprieve was only temporary. In October 1955 Perón came to the end of his road. A second, better-prepared coup repressed the descamisados by force of arms. Perón fled the country, going first to his colleague Pérez Jiménez, then to Trujillo, and finally to Franco's Spain. The Evita legend, however, remained a force in the country.

No Argentine government has yet learned how to deal with this Evita legend. After the overthrow of Perón, the conservative military circles under Lieutenant General Pedro Eugenio Aramburu ruled the country until 1958. Aramburu tried to turn the clock back one hundred years, annulling the constitutional reforms of an entire century and restoring the old and long-outmoded constitution of 1853. He seemed bent on erasing from Argentine history not only the Peronist era, but also the great liberal epochs of the past. He had Evita's mausoleum leveled and her coffin buried on a remote island. But by that act all he did was to strengthen the halo of Evita.

In 1958 semidemocratic elections, from which Peronists were banned, brought to the presidency the leader of the Intransigent Radicals, Arturo Frondizi. For a while Frondizi, who was willing to make compromises, entertained the idea of having Evita's coffin brought back to Buenos Aires. He allowed requiems to be held for Evita, offered greater concessions to the Peronist masses, and permitted the Peronist party, the Unión Popular, to participate in provincial and parliamentary elections, which it promptly won.

Frondizi tripped over his own good-will policy. But the military men who overthrew him were equally at a loss when it came to coping with the heritage of Evita. Peronist riots and revolts shook the army-supported Guido regime until the elections of July 1963. The unexpected victor in these elections, the liberal physician Dr. Arturo Illía, enjoys the confidence of the world public because of his integrity. He is a man of the same spirit as Hipólito Irigoyen. But it may well trouble Illía that he did not come to power by true democratic procedure. The masses of the Peronists cast blank ballots, and continue to practice passive resistance toward the government.

The past with which Argentina has not yet come to terms, as the Germans have been unable to come to terms with nazism, bears the name of Evita Perón.

GORILLAS, MIDDLE CLASS, AND PROLETARIANS

Since Perón's overthrow, Argentine democracy has faced an insoluble dilemma. The powerful CGT, the alliance of labor unions, has two and one half million members, of whom the overwhelming majority are still Peronists. Thus a third of the Argentine people sympathize today with the Movimiento Justicialista. Another 25 per cent are attached to ex-President Frondizi and other "conciliators" who would like to deal gently with the Peronists. The number of Argentine Communists and Castroites is unknown, but it seems clear that the leftist radicals will necessarily sympathize with the justicialist movement, at least for tactical reasons.

The anti-Peronists, on the other hand, except for Illía's Popular Radicals, do not form a coherent front. They are unorganized. Hardly a single political party in Argentina ventures open criticism of Peronism, for fear of losing followers. On the contrary, every party and faction employs Peronist slogans and makes promises to the people similar to those identified with Evita. At the same time every party faction blames all the country's political and economic ills on the Perón era. Almost a decade after his fall, Juan Perón remains the whipping boy of Argentine politics. Such is the schizophrenic nature of political life in Argentina.

On the whole, the descamisados see through the Evita masquerade adopted by party leaders of every conceivable faction. As soon as a CGT leader speaks of the coming revolution, they look up and listen.

But they wait. The Argentines are not an especially revolutionary-minded people; they lack the deep-seated rebelliousness of their Chilean neighbors. In politics, the descamisados tend to believe nobody and to stick to their views with mulelike obstinacy.

FOUR POLITICAL EXPERIMENTS

Since Perón's fall, four attempts have been made to deal with the shade of Evita. Lieutenant General Aramburu believed it possible to restore the old conservative traditions. He tried to crush Peronism by banning all political activity and penalizing every public mention of the name of Perón. His transitional government was basically nothing but one of the usual military dictatorships such as Argentina had experienced in the thirties, a police state poisoned by suspicion, which only earned the scorn and dogged resistance of the masses. Aramburu has since apparently found a political model in Charles de Gaulle. He has founded a "Union of the Argentine People," which aims to absorb Peronism in much the way that De Gaulle has absorbed political radicalism in France. But Aramburu lost the 1963 elections. Conservativism of his brand, it appeared, only led to *rapprochement* between the Peronists and the radicals of the left.

Arturo Frondizi tried the opposite direction. He had suffered persecution under the Perón government. Nevertheless, during his presidency he made a pact with the moderate wing of the Peronists in the hope of bringing the dangerous mass movement under democratic control. Frondizi fully realized that so large a force in Argentine politics could not be permanently excluded from participation in public life. If its venom were drawn, he hoped, and if it were to put up moderate candidates, the danger of spreading radicalism among the masses could be averted.

Among the moderate Peronists was Dr. Raúl Matera, secretary-general of the Movimiento Justicialista and also an internationally respected neurologist and brain surgeon. But he refused to play President Frondizi's dangerous game. Because of his independent attitude he has long since been expelled from the ranks of the justicialists, allegedly as an anti-Peronist. The more radical, politically leftist Peronists under the leadership of Andrés Framini, the labor-union leader, rose to positions of power under Frondizi. Nevertheless, Frondizi went ahead with his experiment. In the elections of 1962 he permitted the Peronist Unión Popular to put up a slate of candidates. A third of the seats in the congress and two-thirds of the governorships were at stake in these elections.

Frondizi's conciliatory step was a test both of the strength of the Peronists and the strength of Argentine democracy. The results were dismaying to all Argentines who had hoped that Peronism was on the wane. Andrés Framini and his Unión Popular won forty-four of eighty-six congressional seats and nine out of twelve governorships. More than half of the Argentines entitled to vote (illiterates who are not allowed the ballot amount to about 15 per cent of the populace of voting age) voted for Peronism, seven years after Perón's overthrow.

The third attempt to eliminate the Peronist danger was just as dismaying to Argentine democrats. It was undertaken by the "Gorillas." In Argentina this is the name given to the ultraconservative military men who hold that no Peronist party ought to be allowed to function, and that Peronism must be fought by dictatorial methods.

Ever since the army overthrew Juan Perón, the erstwhile alliance between the military and Peronism has turned into a kind of feud. The high-ranking military officers might have tolerated an extreme-rightist Peronist movement, or at least not persecuted it with such hatred as they now display toward the Unión Popular, had it not been for the heritage of feminism in Peronism. They resent above all the ideas of Evita, the justicialist social policies and the syndicalism preached by Andrés Framini. The mass movement has long since slid to the left, they maintain; and they now see communism hiding behind Peronism.

Frondizi had to give way to the Gorillas. The top military men denounced the president as a criminal for having allowed a Peronist party to participate in the elections. He was deposed and deported to an island in the Río de la Plata. Guido, the president of the Senate, became the new president, or rather dictator, by grace of the military.

The year of Gorilla rule was the blackest year in Argentina since Perón's overthrow. The economy declined steadily; inflation grew to ever more menacing proportions; and the restiveness among the common people mounted. For economic reasons, Guido had to invite into his government the minister of economics in the deposed Frondizi cabinet. Domestic unrest, as well as pressure from the United States, forced him to assure free elections for 1963. The Gorillas staged a series of rebellions, and for a while formed a short-lived military junta. But the Argentine masses, for their part, were forever staging militant demonstrations, during which they hurled stones and slogans at the Gorillas. The troubles of the Black Year cost the Argentine budget some five billion pesos, about the same sum that Argentina received during this period from the International Monetary Fund for the support of her economy.

Under pressure from the world public, the Gorillas had to capitulate and consent to the holding of elections. These elections of July 7, 1963, were the fourth attempt to neutralize Peronism. Ten presidential candidates and twenty-three party lists wooed the Peronist masses. Up to the appointed day it was doubtful whether the election would take place at all. The Gorillas roared through the streets in their armored cars. The minister of justice of the Guido government resigned a few days before election day, sooner than bear the responsibility for an electoral maneuver he considered thoroughly illegal.

The intrigues, the secret pacts and arrangements reached a climax when the Peronists concluded a temporary alliance with Frondizi's Intransigent Radicals, with one of the conservative splinter parties, and with four other tiny factions. Their candidate for president was an opponent of Perón who had gone into exile in Uruguay during the fascist dictatorship: Vicente Solano Lima, a lawyer. The *Frente Popular y Nacional,* as the temporary alliance called itself, could count on about 55 per cent of the votes. Thus a return of the Peronists to the government, or at least a coalition including Peronists, seemed assured. That, undoubtedly, would have evoked a new coup by the Gorillas.

At the last moment, the alliance exploded. The government refused to accept the candidacy of Dr. Lima on the ground that Peronists were not eligible and that, consequently, a man serving as a front for Peronists was likewise not eligible. The Frente Popular y Nacional was stricken from the ballot. In return, both the Peronists and Frondizi's followers decided to cast blank ballots. Those among the Intransigent Radicals who would not follow Frondizi's course put up a candidate of their own, Dr. Oscar Alende.

Dispiriting though this farce was, and explosive though the situation seemed, the outcome proved a relief to Argentina and to all of democratic Latin America. The semileftist Popular Radicals of Arturo Illía, lineal descendants of the great traditional party, the Unión

Cívica Radical, unexpectedly won the election. Second place was taken by the other traditional party, Alende's Intransigent Radicals. The conservative "Union of the Argentine People," under the leadership of General Aramburu, had been backed by the Gorillas, and had generally been considered the favorite, because of the strong-arm methods that preceded and accompanied the election. But it was decisively trounced. After the turbulent events of the past three decades, Argentina seemed to wish to return penitently to the womb of liberalism.

A DOCTOR AT THE ARGENTINE SICKBED

Illía dramatized his taking office with a symbolic gesture. By Argentine custom, on the day of his inauguration the president receives a rod of office and a sash. Illía had a new rod and a new sash made because, as he declared, his twenty-eight predecessors had completely worn out these symbols. That act was a small sign of his determination really to begin anew. Since 1930 Argentina had not had a president who could have been called modest, undemanding, and a man of personal integrity. Illía's inauguration address, in which he maintained that the constitution and the law would again be respected in Argentina, struck a new tone after the harsh jangle of slogans and counterslogans during the decades of dictatorship.

As the legitimate intellectual successor of Hipólito Irigoyen, Illía has striven for civil peace among the parties and reconciliation with the many electors who had cast blank ballots. He has also returned to the economic policies of the twenties.

Irigoyen had declared war on foreign capital and had converted sizable branches of the Argentine economy into state monopolies. Illía has continued along these lines. He has announced the intention of creating a planned economy and has begun nationalization of the natural resources and basic industries. During the last years of the Perón dictatorship and the presidency of Arturo Frondizi, Argentine petroleum drifted into the hands of American oil companies. Illía has once again brought it under the control of the YPF, the Argentine state oil company, although in so doing he antagonized American financiers. He has established ties with Peruvian President Belaúnde, who is also undertaking gradual nationalization of key industries and expropriation of the oil companies.

Illía has tried to take the wind from the Peronists' sails by inviting a number of labor leaders to join his staff of advisers. But he has had small success, as the constant Peronist bombings, marches, demonstrations, and street battles indicate. Nevertheless, Peronist activity is no longer quite so popular as it was in the past. I constantly heard it remarked in Argentina that the descamisados and desamparados were sick and tired of rebellions, demonstrations, and agitation, that the man on the street wanted to be let alone for a change and enjoy decent wages.

Unlike the Peronistas, the Gorillas have for the present remained pacific. For the first time in thirty-three years it seems as if the Argentine military clique has pulled out of the political arena. Shortly after taking over the government, Illía declared that his prime task should be to eliminate the influence of the military clubs from politics. That is, in fact, the most important task for a liberal president. The new Argentine democracy will stand or fall on his success with this.

Ever since the officers overthrew Illía's model, Irigoyen, in 1930, they have played first fiddle in Argentina. Their jack boots trampled on all the democratic forces stirring in the country; their bayonets thrust back all efforts at social betterment. For three decades they regarded themselves as the prime power in the state. They set up or controlled all the governments of the period; only Evita Perón and Arturo Frondizi were able to maintain themselves in opposition to the Gorillas for a while.

The military men naturally nurse deep-rooted suspicions of Illía. The president added to these suspicions in the fall of 1963, when he proposed a sharp cut in the military budget. The possibility of a military coup in Argentina is ever present. But Illía is an extremely skillful tactician who is doing his best not to provide the pretext for a coup. So far, the Gorillas have played a waiting game.

Meanwhile, another woman has emerged from the ranks of the one-time followers of Evita to become leader of the radical Justicialists. While some of the Peronists more or less openly support Castro and the Eastern bloc, Delia Parodia has revived justicialism as a revolutionary movement. Delia Parodia, however, lacks the charisma which was Evita's. It is questionable whether she has a sizable body of followers among the Argentine people.

A political sensation seemed in the offing in the autumn of 1964, when Perón attempted a sudden return to Argentina. His plan was foiled at the last moment. But did the Peronists seriously intend to let the old man become their chief once more? Or was Perón's abortive comeback only a bit of histrionics? The Peronists today are split into three violently antagonistic parties. The largest group of them forms the Unión Popular, which represents the uncompromising, revolutionary "hard" line. What could a Perón do for it? As its program indicates, it has long ago become a party of socialistic class struggle.

The Unión Popular's demands are: general political amnesty, abandonment of the "outmoded liberal system," abrogation of the military agreement with the United States, establishment of an "Economic and National Council for Reconstruction," nationalization of the banks, and stringent control of all foreign investments. On this program it entered the congressional elections of March 1965 and won more votes than any other party: 3,200,000 against only 2,600,000 for the government party. Only the complicated Argentine electoral system prevented it from winning most of the seats in the Chamber of Deputies. Illía's Popular Radicals now have 75 of 192 representatives; the Peronists 54.

Illía's attempt to win over a sizable portion of the Peronist voters has so far failed. To the Peronists, that is a further encouragement to try to seize power in Argentina. The president habitually pleads with his fellow countrymen: "Once again we at last have a government—guard it!" The slogan is justified. For after all the many governments that came to power in Argentina by coups or electoral frauds, Illía's administration has been duly and honestly elected. And even the most spiteful of its enemies cannot claim that it is corrupt, that it has dictatorial leanings, or that it depends on the favor of the Gorillas or other military groups. But the question is: are the descamisados now really interested in guarding this decent, respectable, rather slow-moving, and awkward government?

In most Latin American countries foreign visitors are accustomed to courteous, deferential service from workmen, elevator operators, cabdrivers, waiters, and so on. In Argentina, however, it is necessary to jolly along the common man or he will get his back up. Neither the people nor the upper classes have forgotten the days when the descamisados ruled the streets. The common man in Argentina, in spite of all the errors and failures of the Peronist era, has a sense of his own worth. Politicians have to reckon with him. The statesmen of the rest of the world, too, must henceforth reckon with an awakened, politically mature Argentine people.

AN EMBATTLED MODEL COUNTRY

It was only due to a succession of accidents that Uruguay became a Spanish-speaking country. And it was due to foreign interests that Uruguay has remained a viable buffer state between the big powers of Argentina and Brazil. It was due, furthermore, to competent immigrants from Europe that Uruguay developed into a model nation and a welfare state that has no match on the continent of South America.

Barely 5 per cent of the Uruguayans are illiterate, and these are mostly older rural folk who carry little weight politically. Within a few years Uruguay will be a wholly literate country. She already has the highest level of education in Latin America. The school system in the little La Plata republic is exemplary. Uruguay long ago carried out the type of school reform which is still under discussion in Central Europe. After attending elementary school, young Uruguayans are passed on to compulsory intermediate or vocational schools; the more intelligent may attend free state universities, agricultural, architectural, or engineering schools. In this small country of barely three million inhabitants more than twenty daily newspapers are published, the largest with a circulation of 150,000. Its movie, radio broadcasting, and television companies compete successfully with their counterparts in the larger neighboring countries.

In Argentina religious tolerance exists only on paper; in Uruguay it is one of the pillars of the country's democracy. State and church are truly separate. Although the people of Uruguay, like those of all Ibero-American countries, are overwhelmingly Catholics, Baptists, Methodists, Waldensians, and other Protestant sects carry on active missionary work under government protection. The numerous Jewish and Moslem immigrants enjoy exactly the same religious rights as Catholics. All vestiges of medieval Catholicism, which has put its stamp on the traditions and social life of other Latin American countries, have vanished from Uruguay.

The Uruguayans are well off—more so than any other inhabitants of the continent. Uruguayans consume some two hundred twenty pounds of meat per capita annually—the highest meat consumption in the world. Every seventh Uruguayan drives a car—a higher percentage than in any other South American country. Uruguayans have the highest average income in Latin America. In addition, they have the most progressive social legislation in the Western Hemisphere.

As early as the beginning of the twentieth century, Uruguay laid the cornerstone for her present enlightened social policies. Referendums held in 1934 and 1952 led to two fundamental changes in the constitution which transformed the small republic into a federal democracy on the Swiss model and at the same time into a mildly socialistic welfare state. The forty-four-hour week was made a reality in Uruguay when it was still only a timid item in the programs of the labor unions in Europe. The Uruguayans enjoyed free medical care years before the Labour Party in England succeeded in writing medical care into law. Uruguayan families received extra allowances for children before such grants were even thought of in Germany. At the age of sixty every Uruguayan becomes entitled to a pension amounting to as much as 75 per cent of his previous income; even the professions, as in Sweden, are not excluded from this rule.

Legal minimum wages are actually paid in Uruguay—first, because the country is by and large law-abiding, and secondly, because Uruguay must cope with the same shortage of labor and domestic help as the highly industrialized countries of Europe. Unemployment relief, care of invalids, maternity benefits, and various sorts of youth legislation have been normal components of social life in Uruguay for decades.

Naturally enough, you look in vain for slums in Uruguay. The Uruguayans do not even have a term to describe slums. The workers live in clean, orderly developments. The only dirty quarter of the city of Montevideo lies at the foot of the Cerro, the mountain from which the city once took its name. But the dirt and stench of the Villa de Cerro are not the product of misery; they come from the great slaughterhouses of the district.

No president, dictator, or strong man heads the Uruguayan Government. The constitutional reform of March 1952 abolished the office of president. Its place has been taken by a National Council on the Swiss model, consisting of nine members elected by popular vote every four years. The two traditional parties, the liberal *Colorados* and the conservative *Blancos*, are constantly represented in the National Council. Thus the opposition always shares in the responsibility of government, since the National Councilors take turns as chairmen. The stronger party can outvote the weaker, since it is bound to have the majority in both the Senate and Chamber of Deputies. On the other hand, the weaker party is able to keep a close watch on the governing party and prevent any relapse into authoritarian practices.

Exemplary Uruguay contrasts so sharply with the reactionary dictatorships, the unstable democracies, and the dangerous political experiments in most of the other countries of Latin America that the question promptly arises: how was it possible for this smallest of the South American republics to become the most progressive of them all?

THE BUFFER

Uruguay was once a country of gauchos, just like the provinces of Argentina. She was, in fact, an Argentina province, no different from the self-willed La Plata provinces of Santa Fe, Entre Ríos, and Corrientes, which for so long conferred turbulent times and cruel dictators on Argentina. And Uruguay would probably have gone the same way as provincial Argentina if she had not always played the part of the apple of discord between Portuguese and Spanish South America. The Hispano-Portuguese disputes over the eastern bank of the Río de la Plata basin caused much suffering and confusion in Uruguay deep into the nineteenth century.

The basis for those recurrent quarrels was laid before a single Portuguese had yet seen the Western Hemisphere. In 1494, two years after the discovery of America, the Treaty of Tordesillas, following the papal bull of 1493 of Pope Alexander VI, divided the world between his two favorite children, Spain and Portugal. The treaty's intent was to give Portugal the rights to lands still to be discovered in Asia and Africa, while Spain received the as yet unknown lands in the New World. With a ruler, the Pope drew a longitudinal line across the map of the Atlantic Ocean, whose true shape was only conjectured. The Spaniards were to possess all territory lying 360 *léguas* west of the Canary Islands, the Portuguese all territory to the east of the line.

The papal boundary corresponded approximately to the fiftieth degree of longitude. No one knew at the time that a sizable portion of South America lay to the east of this line. When the Portuguese by chance discovered the coast of Brazil six years later, they realized that the Pope had presented them with extensive areas of the New World. All of eastern Brazil, with the heartlands around São Paulo,

Rio de Janeiro, Bahia, and Pernambuco, is east of the demarcation line, as is part of the Brazilian hinterland as far as the first tributaries of the Amazon.

In the course of the three following decades, the Portuguese contrived to almost double the size of their South American possessions. Portuguese colonists and *bandeirantes* from São Paulo paid little attention to the *Raya de Tordesillas*, the papal line of demarcation. They wandered up the Amazon, advanced into the Mato Grosso, attacked the Jesuit reductions on the Paraná and the Rio Grande do Sul, begot —with Indian women and black slave girls—an excessively land-hungry mestizo and mulatto population, and pushed the Spaniards out of virtually the entire central basin of South America. In the Treaty of Madrid, in 1750, the Spanish kingdom grudgingly accepted the enormous Portuguese "border rectifications."

Still the expansionist urge of the Portuguese and Brazilians was not yet satisfied. They felt they should have a foothold on the eastern bank of the Plata. As early as 1680 the Portuguese had established Fort Colonia de Sacramento there. In response, the Spaniards built the city of Montevideo forty-four years later. The two powers of the Iberian Peninsula confronted one another in Sacramento and Montevideo. Uruguay, then called the Banda Oriental, the "East Bank of the Río de la Plata," became a prime bone of contention between the two Latin empires.

Portugal lost the first round. After the expulsion of the Jesuits, she exchanged her colony of Sacramento for the conquered Jesuit reductions along the Paraná and the Rio Grande do Sul. Uruguay became a province of the viceroyalty of La Plata. The Brazilians, however, never really gave up the country. Their smugglers operated continually in Uruguay. Illegal trade in the province reached such proportions that it threatened the Spanish economy in the La Plata colony. After Argentina's declaration of independence and a temporary occupation of Montevideo by the British, Portuguese-Brazilian troops advanced into Uruguay (1817) and annexed the Banda Oriental.

This was during the period after the fall of Napoleon, when Portugal was *de facto* controlled by England. The British therefore approved the annexation of Uruguay by Brazil. It appeared that the language of Uruguay would henceforth be Portuguese. Argentina, then feeble and almost breaking apart, did not seem in any position to put up significant resistance to the Portuguese.

Soon afterward, however, the political winds shifted. In 1822 Brazil had parted company with the liberalized motherland, now a satellite of England. Her new sovereign, the Portuguese crown prince who was crowned Emperor of Brazil as Pedro I, was married to a Hapsburg and was regarded as Germanophile. The British no longer had any interest in contributing to the expansion of Brazil. Nor were they anxious to strengthen the unreliable Argentine Republic. Consequently, they supported the gaucho chief José Gervasio Artigas, who had been engaged in a guerrilla war with Argentina and Brazil since 1811.

Artigas was a changeling among the gaucho leaders of the time. Although he belonged to the group of fanatical federalists who kept Argentina in upheaval for nearly a century, he was no tyrant, no *caudillo*. Rather, he was a genuine popular hero and lover of freedom. He was determined to save his country from its wicked neighbors. This Uruguayan who could scarcely read and write drafted one of the most progressive constitutions in the history of South America. This was the foundation stone for Uruguay's distinctive democracy.

As Artigas conceived it, Uruguay was to be divided into a number of departments which would enjoy a great deal of independence of the central government. The estancieros, gauchos, and peons in the then very thinly populated country were to choose regional leaders who would meet periodically in the capital to shape policy for the country as a whole. The rough outlines of the present Uruguayan system of council government was already limned in the Artigas constitution.

But the democratic gaucho became a casualty of the great-power struggle. A century was to pass before Uruguay matured sufficiently for real democracy. First a war over Uruguay broke out between Brazil and Argentina. The British intervened, separated the contenders, and imposed their own solution. In 1828 Uruguay became nominally independent, although in reality she was a protectorate of Great Britain.

BLANCOS AND COLORADOS

The English, experienced colonizers and merchants that they were, had recognized at the beginning of the nineteenth century that the country on the eastern bank of the Río de la Plata had a promising economic future. The Uruguayan pampas could become Great Brit-

ain's storehouse of meat. British textile mills could obtain their wool
from Uruguay. At the same time, Uruguay was an ideal economic
bridgehead in South America. Consequently, while the young republic was still undergoing its birth pangs, the British gained a hold
on Uruguayan trade and a considerable portion of Uruguayan land.
To this day, Urugray is a favorite refuge of British capital, and the
capital of Montevideo still betrays English influence in its banking
and commercial districts.

Unfortunately for Uruguayan democracy, the British protectors
paid very little attention to the domestic politics of the republic. The
creator of the constitution, Artigas, had to yield to opposition gaucho
chiefs, and died in Paraguayan exile. Up to the end of the nineteenth
century Uruguayan politics were basically a struggle between two
rival groups of gauchos, the Blancos and the Colorados, which alternately collaborated with Argentina, Paraguay, and Brazil, unleashed
civil wars, and tried to murder their opponents. When matters became
too hectic, the British intervened to protect their economic interests.
But most of the time they watched the rivalry of Blancos and
Colorados with cool composure, or at most with slight dismay.

Uruguay's anarchy became almost proverbial. Her eventual development into a socially minded democracy was the work of her
numerous European immigrants. In colonial times, the pampas on the
eastern shore of the Plata were almost deserted. The Spaniards had
assiduously reduced the numbers of the Charrua and other Indian
tribes. Hernando Arias de Saavedra, the conquistador who brought
the Jesuits into the Plata region, turned a small number of cattle
loose on the grassy plains in 1580. These grew into vast herds. At that
time Uruguay was practically one huge pasture. The cattle were periodically hunted. The colonial power, bent on preserving this state
of affairs, allowed no settlers to take over any of this region.

However, all sorts of adventurers and shady characters moved into
the cattle country. They mingled with the remnants of the Indians,
shot bulls and cows, and led a free life—celebrated by a host of
romantic songs still popular in Uruguay. The real old inhabitants of
Uruguay are descended from those free gauchos. After some contact
with civilization, the more businesslike among them developed into
estancieros. They kept Merino sheep, which had been introduced by
the Spaniards—we will recall that the French botanist Bonpland contributed to the development of the breed. Uruguay proved the truth

of the proverb that "the hoof of the sheep brings gold." Her sheep grew such thick coats that according to a contemporary account "only the light-colored nose, the tips of the ears, and the legs from the pastern-joint down protrude from the fleece."

For all her wealth of cattle and sheep, Uruguay was a country of less than one hundred thousand inhabitants at the time of the struggles for independence. In the century between 1826 and 1926, however, some seven hundred thousand people immigrated into the country, chiefly Spaniards and Italians, but also Frenchmen, Portuguese, Brazilians, Argentines, Englishmen, and Germans. To these were added during the 1930s numerous Jewish immigrants; also Syrians, Lebanese, and others from the Near East. The new citizens soon exceeded the number of native Uruguayans. They increasingly influenced economic and social life, and they conferred an altogether different aspect on the traditional political parties.

The party of the Blancos gradually developed into the native Uruguayan party. It took a conservative and distinctly nationalistic stand and fought the introduction of alien manners by the new arrivals. Consequently, it opposed the extensive economic influence of foreign countries in Uruguay. The Colorados, on the other hand, became the party of the new citizens. Since the immigrants from Europe had brought with them all sorts of liberal and socialistic ideas, the *Colorados* gradually changed from a liberal democratic to a moderate socialist party. The outnumbering of the natives by the immigrants resulted in a great shift in the balance of power. By the last decades of the nineteenth century, the Colorados commanded enough votes to win elections. Thereafter they remained the government party up to 1961, and were able to carry out their social programs step by step, without serious interference from the Blanco opposition.

THE LAND OF SOCIAL REFORMS

The birth of the Uruguayan welfare state was preceded by an economic boom which at first enriched only the large landowners, the merchants, and the meat, wool, and banking firms, which were mostly in foreign hands. By 1885 there were approximately one hundred head of cattle to each person in Uruguay. Enormous herds of animals that had run wild ranged over the country. There were some six million cattle, seventeen million sheep, and a million horses.

Montevideo built its first big *saladeros,* meat and preserving factories, in which two hundred thousand head of cattle were processed annually. In Fray Bentos a German engineer named Giebert built the first meat-extract factory, which converted 350,000 head of cattle annually to bouillon cubes. Uruguayan wool production outstripped that of Spain, the homeland of the Merinos. Yet in the following half century it increased thrice over. Along with the *saladeros, frigoríficos,* and meat-extract plants, vast wool sheds sprang up all over the country, where the fleeces were washed and sorted.

In 1903 José Batlle y Ordóñez, a Colorado, was elected president of the republic. A park in the capital still bears his name. The Uruguayans are particularly proud of the monuments in that park, for they represent idyllic scenes from Uruguayan history rather than generals or statesmen. There is one showing the *carreta,* the old two-wheeled oxcart used in the peaceful conquest of the pampas. There is another of a friendly mail coach with rearing horses, the coach that formerly provided the only connection between Montevideo and the hinterland. There are statues of the prototypal schoolteacher and other nameless pioneers.

The administration of Batlle y Ordóñez was as sensible as the monuments in his park. He was the first Latin American president to recognize what was then a novelty, although it has long been an accepted doctrine in Europe and North America: that the economy of a country can thrive only if the masses of the people share in prosperity. To increase Uruguay's national production, Batlle wanted industrial and agricultural workers to become vigorous consumers. But since the lower classes, in line with Latin American custom, were virtually without rights and had no social security whatsoever, Batlle first had to introduce guaranteed wages and protection of the rights of labor. The economic and social legislation he initiated in his two administrations (1903–07, 1911–15) laid the foundation for that moderate state socialism which still characterizes Uruguayan domestic policy.

Further Spanish and Italian waves of immigration after the First World War exerted pressure on José Batlle's successors to accelerate this tendency. They had a good deal of trouble with oppositionist estancieros, who realized that the rule of the landed oligarchy in Uruguay was irrevocably coming to an end. The number of latifundia diminished from decade to decade, partly as the great landholdings were parceled out among heirs, partly by enforced sales to pay taxes, and chiefly because of a comprehensive program of agrarian reform. The Colorado administrations left a number of large, economically sound cattle and sheep ranches intact, since they did not want to impair their country's principal economic resource. But they stripped the majority of ranchers of their power. Uruguay is still predominantly an agricultural country. Yet for the past forty years the large land-owners have exerted nothing like the fateful influence on public life that is characteristic in most countries of Ibero-America.

Almost unnoticed by the world public, Uruguay has socialized to an extent that can be matched in Europe only by the welfare state of Sweden. The railroads, the apparatus of distribution, the insurance companies, and most of the banks have been nationalized. The state controls oil, the construction industry, medicine, fuel production, and even the manufacture of brandy. With state aid, shipbuilding, paper, rubber, and oil industries have been set up to supplement the existing wool and meat industries. Thus Uruguay not only supplies her own needs, but also exports to other Latin American countries.

As a result of all this state control, it is no longer so easy to become a millionaire in Uruguay. It is possible, in this model state, to attain a fair-sized fortune by industry and initiative, but taxes are as high as they are in European welfare states. In Uruguay, moreover, the taxes are actually collected, whereas almost everywhere else in Ibero-America tax evasion is a favorite sport of the upper class. The Uruguayan tax collectors are far more obstinate than their colleagues across the borders. The state needs its income largely for social expenditures, and has no intention of whittling these expenditures.

For all these reasons, Uruguay is generally presented by Latin social reformers as a model to be followed, whereas European and American capitalists regard the country with distaste. Uruguay, the latter maintain, will soon have no farmers left, with the masses pouring into the cities in ever-increasing numbers, where more money can be earned in industry. There is no doubt that Uruguay is the most urbanized country of Latin America. More than a third of the inhabitants live in the capital, less than half in the countryside. Thus, Uruguay is passing through an evolution similar to that of the booming industrial countries of Europe. And as in Europe, Uruguay is plagued by periodic strikes for higher wages. Uruguayan workers also take advantage of sick leave now and then, as American and European workers will.

In Uruguay the same wage-price spiral exists as in the EEC countries. In short, economically and socially, Uruguay shows all the earmarks of a European welfare state.

Such conditions are, as we have seen, unusual in Latin America. Industrialists, merchants, financiers, and even journalists still regard Latin America as an underdeveloped economic colony, and are often in high dudgeon at the state of affairs in Uruguay, where workers dare to go on strike, despite their forty-four-hour week, where members of the lower classes enjoy paid vacations and drive their own cars to the beaches. In Europe even the most ferociously old-fashioned capitalist would no longer dare to question the rights of workers to make wage demands, go on strike, and share in the general wealth. But Uruguayan workers who behave so much like their fellows in Europe evoke angry criticism from foreigners. They are Latin Americans, and who ever heard of Latin American workers being treated as well as European or American workers?

Only members of the intellectual professions are discontented in Uruguay. Their situation resembles to some extent that of the rotos in Chile: there are too many of them. An excessive supply of labor always and everywhere leads to bad pay. Uruguayan youth is passionately devoted to education, and since the universities are free, even the less well-to-do qualify themselves for academic careers. The joke goes that in Uruguay there are more teachers than pupils, more doctors than patients, more lawyers than clients, and more architects than builders. Of course that is not true. But members of the academic professions are relatively poorly paid, often worse than skilled industrial workers. In this, too, the situation resembles that of the highly industrialized countries of Europe.

University professors, teachers, doctors, writers, and other members of the intellectual professions must often resort to "moonlighting" in order to maintain their standard of living. The students are considered extremely radical in politics. When statesmen of the Western Hemisphere met in the Uruguayan bathing resort of Punta del Este to confer on hemispheric policy toward Cuba, leftist students in Montevideo demonstrated for Castro. Their action was dictated not by any desire to introduce Castroistic measures into Uruguay, but by the determination to steer clear of any North American movements against Cuba. Similarly, they demonstrated vigorously against Washington's intervention in the Dominican Republic.

Along with Mexico, Bolivia, Brazil, and Chile, Uruguay belongs among the five Latin American countries that have opposed the barring of Cuba from the Organization of American States. Uruguay has given asylum to politicians of leftist leanings banished from their homelands by dictators, as, for example, ex-President Goulart of Brazil. Dictators, on the other hand, such as Brazil's present ruler, Castelo Branco, are extremely unpopular in Uruguay.

DANGEROUS CAUDILLISM

Gratifying as are conditions in Uruguay, there is nevertheless a major threat to the *status quo*. It is not the oft-decried danger from the left, but a danger from the right, a heritage of the old days of the gauchos. The gauchos were an idiosyncratic, headstrong people. The immigrant Italo-Spanish majority of the population seems to have taken over some aspects of the gaucho mentality. People adhere not so much to a party, a program, or a political line as to caudillos—chieftains—the leaders of political factions. The Blancos and Colorados are not homogeneous parties; they have splintered into many factions, each governed by its boss and directed like a troop of gauchos.

The absence of party discipline, the independence of the deputies and senators, and the multiplicity of views within the government parties are certainly proof of a robust degree of democracy. But as a result the Colorados, the creators of the welfare state, lost their majority in the National Council and in both houses of the congress in 1961.

The *Batllistas* form the core of the Colorados. Their avowed policy is to continue the present liberal-socialist program on a moderate basis. But the factions to the left of the Batllistas refused to follow them, and called for a somewhat more radical course. Their views coincided with those of the extreme right wing of the Blancos—with whom, curiously enough, the Communists also have many points of agreement.

These "Herreristas" correspond approximately to the strongly nationalistic parties of other countries. They have waged passionate campaigns against North American finance capital and North American trade, for after the last war, Americans replaced the English in the economic role the latter had traditionally played in Uruguay. The *Herreristas* were all for autarchy; they fought the liberal trade and foreign-exchange policies of the Colorados, and preached the kind of economic chauvinism favored by the most extreme rightist governments in Latin America.

Leftist socialists and communists can no longer win votes in Uruguay by demanding social improvements. Practically everything that can be done in the way of social welfare has already been done. Nationalistic arguments, however, touch a responsive chord in the common people. Uruguayan nationalism has several times checked the flood of immigration. Today Uruguay has the strictest immigration quotas in Latin America. And the appeal to chauvinistic resentments ultimately brought the Blancos to power again.

The Blancos are so thoroughly checked and balanced by the present Colorado opposition in the National Council that they can scarcely effect decisive changes in the political course determined during the past fifty years. But their economic policies have already caused a tremendous weakening in the Uruguayan peso, hitherto the hardest currency in the Americas. The Blancos are more and more insistently demanding abolition of the democratic council system and its replacement by a "strong" president. Such a constitutional change would threaten all the democratic liberties the Uruguayans have won since 1903. It is equally disturbing to observe that in foreign policy the Blancos have been most unwilling to follow the good-will course inaugurated by the United States during the presidency of Kennedy. Uruguay's state-socialist government has always been loyal to the West; until 1961 Western policy was able to count on the little republic's political stability. But since the nationalists have come to power, an element of uncertainty has entered the picture. Moreover, opposition to the conservative Blancos is driving the Uruguayan youth, especially the students, more and more into the arms of the radical leftists.

The situation in Uruguay is in one respect similar to that of other overseas countries in which European and American firms want to earn good profits; the business circles are always glad to see the defeat of progressive social-welfare governments and the rise of authoritarian nationalists. They find it hard to realize that the latter represent the greater danger to their own interests. To keep their place in the sun, the Uruguayans must renounce their tendency toward caudillism and unequivocally support their hitherto successful social democracy.

Brazil

COLOMBIA

VENEZUELA

ERU

PERU

Jaguar

BRITISH GUIANA
★ Georgetown

SURINAM

Paramaribo

FRENCH GUIANA

Cayenne

Manaus

Cayman

AMAZON

Vanilla

La Paz ★

BOLIVIA

Rubber
Brazil nuts
Cacao
Rice

Belém

Manganese

São Luis

Fortaleza

Kayapo Indian

★ Brasília

Goiânia

Diamonds

Cattle
Sugar
Cotton
Coffee

Recife

PARAGUAY

Asunción
★

Salvador

Chromium
Manganese
Iron
Nickel
Bauxite
Cobalt

Gaucho

Belo Horizonte

RGENTINA
ARGENTINA

Curitiba

São Paulo

Sheep
Copper

Blumenau

Rio de Janeiro

Vitória

RUGUAY
URUGUAY

Pôrto Alegre

Coffee
Bananas

Coal

Montevideo

N

Atlantic
Ocean

BRAZIL

CHAPTER 8

Brazil—A World in Itself

MANOR HOUSE AND SLAVE HUT

The city of Recife, in the state of Pernambuco in northern Brazil, has been regarded as a center of intellectual life for two hundred years. Out of Recife come revolutionaries, political firebrands, nonconformist journalists, and avant-garde writers. Out of Recife has also come Gilberto Freyre, the university professor, congressional deputy, and sociologist who was the first to make a comprehensive analysis of his native country in all its peculiarities and variety. Freyre gave his book the significant title of *Casa grande e senzala*—"Manor House and Slave Hut," published in the United States as *The Masters and the Slaves*. The title is applicable in many respects to Brazil's present as well as her past.

As we have seen, Brazil became Portuguese as a result of the arbitrary *Raya de Tordesillas* and the chance discovery of Pedro Álvares Cabral. Since the Portuguese were the most active slave hunters and slave traders in the age of the conquistadors, Brazil became a country of slaves. The number of Africans transported in Portuguese slave ships to the Brazilian coast has never been precisely determined. Estimates range between two and a half and fifteen million. Perhaps a third of these unfortunates died during the crossings.

Although Brazil had fallen into the lap of the Portuguese by a whim of fate, the lucky possessors at first did not know what to do with the country. In Lisbon men dreamed of a second India, of noble metals and other treasures such as the Spaniards had found in such profusion in their spheres of interest in America. But Brazil was jungle, a lush "green hell." The way to its potential wealth had been pointed to by Pedro Vaz de Caminha, the country's first chronicler.

Caminha, one of the company of the discoverer Cabral, had written: "So far we have been unable to discover whether there is gold, silver or iron here. But the country has very good air, fresh and moderate. There are countless streams. Nature is so amiable and rich that in these regions, thanks to the abundance of water, everything ought to thrive."

The Portuguese would have had to become planters—"an occupation which at first did not suit them," as Gilberto Freyre writes. The small nation of sailors and explorers on the Iberian Peninsula had become, because of its possessions in Africa and Asia, one vast merchant company, at whose head was the king—boss of the enterprise, so to speak. The Portuguese did not want to go overseas to work, but to trade and increase their fortunes.

THE SUGARLOAF AND THE MORENOS

In the early days Brazil was used largely as a place of banishment. Mutineers and criminals, Jews and victims of the Inquisition were brought to the *Terra do Brasil*. These unwilling inhabitants were soon joined by adventurers, pirates, slave hunters, and shipwrecked mariners whom chance had spilled upon the eastern coast of South America. This variegated assortment of humanity showed little taste for hard pioneering work. The early Brazilians hunted Indians and parrots, collected dyewoods, and lived from hand to mouth until the first captain-general of the colony, Martim Affonso de Sousa, energetically set about importing sugar cane from Madeira and Negroes from Africa. The labor of slaves transformed Brazil into a land of sugar.

One testimony to the former dominance of sugar in Brazil is the conical rock which has become the symbol of Rio de Janeiro—the *Pão de Açúcar*, or Sugarloaf. The name is reminiscent of that time of slaves and plantations, already almost legendary, when Brazil was still the principal sugar-producing country in the world. In those days sugar was transported from Brazil to Europe in the form of loaves.

By the time of the abolition of slavery, the dominance of sugar was ended. Certainly sugar plantations ceased to be profitable after the planters had to pay wages to their workers. But some time passed before that stage was reached. Brazil was for many years the largest slave-holding country in the world, and the very last to free its black slaves.

The Portuguese had considerable trouble with other colonial powers that likewise wanted to obtain a foothold on the eastern coast of South America. For a quarter of a century the region around Pernambuco was in Dutch hands. The Dutch harassed the Portuguese traders, waylaying slave ships and seizing the living freight. The French, for their part, had an eye on Rio de Janeiro. Twice in its history the "most beautiful city in the world" fell briefly under French influence. In the sixteenth century Huguenots under Admiral Villegaignon wanted to found an "Antarctic France" on Guanabara Bay. In the eighteenth century Louis XIV had his navy capture the city; the booty was 600,000 gold pieces, one hundred sacks of sugar, and two hundred eggs.

The Lusitanian colonists managed to hold their own despite all this. They fought off the troops of foreign powers, imported more armies of slaves, enlarged their plantations, and worked their way into the interior of the country, where they at last came upon gold and gems in what is today Minas Gerais. Since there was always a shortage of women in Brazil, and since the settlers were anything but monogamous, Brazil swiftly became a land of mixed races. The adventurers, prospectors, and soldiers of fortune provided themselves with harems of Indian women. This Portuguese-Indian mingling produced the *caboclo,* the Brazilian rustic of the present day. It was the constant reprehensions of the Jesuits against Portuguese polygamy that prompted the bandeirantes, the "standard-bearers," as they grandiloquently called themselves, to make their raids against the Jesuit reductions. When the bandeirantes discovered the rich gold resources of Minas Gerais, the King of Portugal actually gave his blessing to their polygamous practices as well as their predatory expeditions. For the court of Lisbon was entitled to a fifth of any loot.

The settled sugar planters also contributed vigorously to making Brazil a land of colored people. There was by no means an unbridgeable gulf between the manor house and the slave hut. On the contrary, at the time of feudalistic rule most planters favored the semilegal institution of the *mulher da cama,* the black "bed woman," with whom the white planter cheerfully begot children.

Of all the European peoples, the Portuguese mingled most readily with other races. Thus Brazil became a country in which every imaginable skin shading is represented. Everywhere in Brazil one sees working people of mixed blood and diverse origins. The muscular dockworkers, who look like Iberians; the gigantic stonecutters, who might come from Angola; and the slant-eyed caboclos, who would fit well into any Indian movie, are in fact almost all *morenos*. Practically every member of the Brazilian working class has at least a few drops of some alien blood.

Racist Europeans and North Americans have to restrain their anti-Negro feeling in Brazil, for the Brazilian racial laws are among the most progressive in the world. Nevertheless, if you sit in one of the air-conditioned clubs reserved for foreigners, you will hear much whispering about the drawbacks of racial mixing. Pure-blooded Negroes represent only a small percentage of the Brazilian population today—aside from the northeast. Consequently, mutterings of this sort are directed more against mulattoes than against Negroes. And there are so many colored skins in Brazil that the whites must often falter in their conviction of supremacy.

The whites created the racial mixtures. Now, in Brazil's great melting pot, the people of mixed blood have proved that skin color need not be a barrier between people. Brazil demonstrates to the Euro-American that the day is coming when he will have to step down from his pedestal and sit together with people of all shades of skin, in modesty and without enjoying any special privileges—just as the white workmen and traders today sit with their colored counterparts in the restaurants and streetcars of the Brazilian cities.

It repeatedly happens in Brazil that white-skinned parents will have a dark-skinned child. Perhaps they are not very happy about this unexpected demonstration of the laws of heredity, for even in Brazil people like to conceal their colored ancestry under their own white skins. But the dark child is there, grows up, and becomes as good a Brazilian citizen as his lighter-skinned fellows. The mingling of black, white, and red is gradually producing that *raça brasileira* once proclaimed by President Getulio Vargas—to which the majority of Brazilian congressmen, writers, artists, and scientists already belong.

In curious contrast to the country's enlightened laws, which ban all racial discrimination, Brazilian population statistics are madly confused. All the statistical summaries contradict one another. One survey gives the proportion of colored and semicolored persons in the Brazilian population as 37 per cent, another as 52 per cent. Unofficial estimates maintain that some colored blood flows in the veins of three quarters of the Brazilian population. Brazil has a popular saying:

"Quem escapa de negro, branco é." Freely translated: "Whoever is not entirely black, is white." The statisticians have worked by this definition. And a racial fanatic who does not recognize colored persons as his equal may take solace in the thought that at least on paper Brazil is more white than black.

More interesting than tabulations of skin color are the studies of Brazilian sociologists, which indicate that shades of color, in spite of all equal-rights laws, remain a class matter in Brazil. In the big cities, with the exception of those in the "white" south, approximately four-fifths of the businessmen are white, only one-fifth colored. Among the workers, nine-tenths are colored, only one-tenth white. The emancipation of the colored people, which began seventy-five years ago, is still far from complete. Brazil, too, has her race problem. But its manifestations are entirely different from those in the rest of the world. We shall return to this subject.

"INDEPENDENCE OR DEATH!"

Brazil made her way toward independence without the co-operation of her colored population. Portugal's rule was so oppressive that as early as 1787 a dentist named Joaquim José Xavier da Silva put himself at the head of an independence movement. The rebellion failed; its leader was executed by the Portuguese. But he is regarded today as the real forerunner of Brazilian freedom. A reminder of him remains in the Praça Tiradentes, the "Tooth Puller's Square," in Rio de Janeiro—which, however, has for a long time represented another kind of freedom. For it forms the entrance to Rio's modest but untrammeled amusement area.

It was Napoleon—who also accelerated the declarations of independence in the Spanish-American colonies—who supplied the decisive impetus to Brazilian independence. Prince Regent João of Portugal escaped the Napoleonic troops, was welcomed in Brazil, and had himself crowned king there. The everlasting rebels of the Pernambuco district suspected, quite rightly, that as soon as Napoleon was out of the way, King João VI would forthwith return to Lisbon, leaving Brazil to continue in the dreary condition of a colony. Consequently, in 1817 they staged a revolution which the king barely managed to repress. As the Pernambucans had predicted, in 1821 he moved back to Lisbon with his court, accepting the protection of the British. He left his son Pedro behind in Brazil as regent.

Pedro quickly realized that new rebellions would flare up all over Brazil unless he actively anticipated the freedom-hungry planters and city dwellers. He therefore broke with his father and his fatherland. On September 7, 1822, in the present Praça do Monumento in São Paulo, he summoned the people to "independence or death!" and declared himself Emperor of Brazil. King João could not bring his disobedient son to reason, for the Portuguese troops in Brazil promptly deserted to Emperor Pedro I. In this way Brazil won her freedom without bloodshed.

The government of the first Brazilian emperor was not especially popular. Pedro I was blamed for the unfortunate outcome of the war with Argentina and for the loss of Uruguay. He was criticized for interfering too much in the disputes over the Portuguese throne, which in the Brazilian view should no longer have concerned him. The Brazilians disliked the Austrian court camarilla which his wife, the Hapsburg Archduchess Leopoldine, had brought from Europe. Brazilian counts and barons took offense at having Austrian and German counts and barons ranked above them. The consequence of all this discontent was the outbreak of a new rebellion in 1831. Pedro abdicated in favor of his minor son, and also saw to it that his elder daughter Gloria was crowned queen in Lisbon.

After some nine years of confusion the young Pedro II assumed full powers. He proved to be the real creator of Brazil, one of the most interesting and remarkable rulers of the nineteenth century. The Brazilians cherish their history and have a penchant for historical relics. Thus, the emperor's summer residence of Petrópolis in the mountains above Rio de Janeiro, with its baroque summer palace and its remarkable collection of coaches, has remained a favorite spot of Brazilian and foreign tourists. Petrópolis was founded by German settlers and looks like a rather sleepy Central European spa. The palace's splendid halls and the showcases full of costumes, weapons, and jewelry are less extraordinary than Dom Pedro's study. The modest furnishings, the multitude of books, the telescope, and other scientific apparatus are scarcely what one expects in an emperor's private chamber, and they indicate that Pedro II must have been an extremely unusual monarch.

A Venezuelan president once called Pedro's empire the only democracy in Latin America. The statement is somewhat rash, but there are facts that argue in its favor. In his youth Pedro studied the Constitution of the United States, seeking to learn from it what would suit his own country and to avoid his father's mistakes. Pedro was also on friendly terms with liberal European writers and scholars. He attracted many artists, scientists, and literati to Brazil, corresponded with men like Victor Hugo, Alexander Graham Bell, and Louis Pasteur, translated Shakespeare and Longfellow into Portuguese, wrote sonnets, studied astronomy and archaeology, and transformed the backward semicolony of Brazil into a civilized country.

Mementos of the second and last Pedro strike the tourist as soon as he sets foot in Rio. There is the Ginásio Pedro Segundo, which the emperor founded and where he himself taught the elite of Brazilian youth geography, history, and German literature. It was a bold project from various points of view: what other emperor has chosen to take the part of a secondary-school teacher? But, more important, here was an institution of higher learning that was not run by a Catholic order.

The emperor may also be seen on a number of monuments, though never presented as a majestic equestrian figure, as is the usual thing for rulers. He looks down from his pedestal like a quiet scholar, a book in hand or a telescope at his side—a serious, introspective man, not at all regal, and very human.

In the end, Pedro's dedication to humane principles resulted in his deposition. His crime was to tear down the last bulwark of feudalism in Brazil—slavery. To this day there are members of the Brazilian oligarchy who speak of the emperor's reign with contempt, if not hatred. To this day Brazilian history books contain highly contradictory estimates of the reign of Pedro II, the liberator of the slaves.

THE LAST REDOUBT OF SLAVERY

In 1841, when the sixteen-year-old Pedro took the throne, Brazil was a state dominated by cliques, weakened by revolutions, and threatened by chaos and separatism. One after another, the provinces of São Paulo, Minas Gerais, and Rio Grande do Sul tried to make themselves independent. Pará and the Amazon regions also sought separation from the empire. The permanent disputes between unitarian monarchists and Federalist republicans had made Brazil a powder keg with a glowing fuse. The army mutinied; in many places the slaves and lower classes staged uprisings.

Thirty years later, Pedro and his advisers had shaped this crumbling mosaic of provinces into a peaceful, prospering, and consolidated empire. Of course Brazil at this time was not a developed nation in the European sense. It lived on the yield from its plantations. The big *fazendeiros* managed the economy. The country's work was performed by people whose forefathers had for centuries been transported from Africa as living chattels. Brazil was the only sizable country in the world that had not yet abolished slavery.

Brazilians today like to romanticize the slave days. They represent slavery as a special kind of patriarchal social order in which the feudal lord played the part of a kindly father and the slave that of an obedient child. They pretend that Portuguese America knew none of the horrors of slavery typical of Spanish-America and Anglo-America.

The reality was far grimmer. There are many unimpeachable witnesses to that. One of them is Charles Darwin, who in his *Voyage of the Beagle* condemned in the strongest terms the treatment and auctioning of slaves in Brazil. Portuguese planters, too, at various times denounced the excesses of certain slaveholders, though primarily because they regarded the slave as an investment, an object of value, so that it violated elementary economic rationality to damage him.

Portuguese and African agents either hunted down their Negro slaves directly or bought them from their tribes in exchange for mirrors, baubles, or whisky. The captives were crowded into the holds of the slave ships, chained, and suffered the most unbearable conditions. Many simply suffocated in the course of the voyage. Those who came down with some serious illness were dumped into the sea, like spoiled goods.

Once on the sugar plantations, the Negroes were kept with fetters on their feet almost all their lives. The tiny steps of the samba, the old slave dance which has become fashionable nowadays, originated as a result of this fettering. When the master of the house chose a *mulher da cama* from among his slave girls, a jealous lady of the house might have her killed, without ever being called to account.

The average life span of a slave in the mining areas was about seven years, on the *fazendas* little more than ten years. The separation of families, the selling off of slave children, was so much taken for granted that no words were wasted on the matter.

The result of these atrocities was that innumerable slaves escaped from their masters. Many of the runaways founded *quilombos* deep in the jungles, settlements of their own, one of which, on the Rio Mundaú, in northern Brazil, was able to survive for half a century as the République dos Palmares, until it was finally destroyed by a bandeirante from São Paulo. In the nineteenth century Negro slaves, led by Mohammedan Hausa, tried to establish their own state in Bahia. The majority of the black revolutionaries ended their lives on the gallows; the rest were hastily shipped back to Africa by the frightened slaveholders. Every runaway slave who was recaptured by the *capitães do mato*, the dreaded rural gendarmes, was subject to whipping and other brutal punishments.

Due to the high mortality, natural reproduction could not meet the demand for labor, not even when the master and his sons, true to Brazilian custom, diligently participated in the breeding of additional slaves. Consequently, the shipments of human freight went on arriving in greater and greater numbers until the middle of the nineteenth century, in spite of rising costs. They probably attained record figures between 1840 and 1850—at a time, that is, when most other civilized countries had long since abolished slavery or at least banned the slave trade.

In reply to these facts, Brazilian historians claim that every Negro captured in Africa welcomed the news that he was being shipped to Brazil. That seems to have been the case. Despite the hardships that awaited an African in Brazil, the slave in that country had a real chance of advancing into the class of freedmen.

Many planters, plagued by a shortage of labor, began buying the freedom of slaves on condition that they work on the plantations. They did this not out of humanitarianism, but because they realized that a freedman worked harder than a slave; thus the invested capital yielded higher profits. Moreover, the governors of several Brazilian provinces had, for reasons of provincial particularism, imposed bans on the export of slaves out of their provinces. Thus it became difficult or impossible to buy slaves in the traditionally "black" regions of the country. But no law prevented the buying of a slave's freedom. Naturally, the more skilled Negroes benefited most from this custom. Even in the eighteenth century there were a number of black craftsmen in Brazil, especially watchmakers and mechanics, who gradually acquired full independence.

Most of the freedmen, however, were not really free in the sense that they could choose their occupations and their place of residence. Most of them had to obey the *caudilho,* a white leader who functioned as a plantation overseer or steward and made sure that they did not leave their places of work. The freedmen often received a patch of land and a few chickens from their caudilhos or fazendeiros, and were paid meager wages. In practice, however, their fate differed only slightly from that of actual slaves. They lived in fear that they would be reduced to slavery again if they tried to set up on their own. Therefore they preferred to remain on the fazendas, selling the yield of their tiny fields to the fazendeiro. Gradually, in return for their pitiable wages, they transformed Brazil into the greatest coffee-producing nation in the world, and São Paulo into the richest city in South America. Nevertheless, they were proud that at least on paper they were free citizens and not slaves like their fettered fellows.

Emperor Pedro II was an enlightened spirit who regarded slavery as an abomination. But he knew only too well that the slave problem could not be solved by a stroke of the pen. Emancipation would incur a revolt by the planters and economic collapse of the country. Pedro therefore attempted to carry out emancipation step by step— a policy that later caused historians to call him hesitant and indecisive. First the further importation of slaves from Africa was prohibited. Then the fortunes of smugglers who broke the law were rigorously confiscated. Finally, the Visconde de Rio Branco, the Prime Minister of Brazil, proclaimed on September 18, 1871, the *Lei do Ventre Livre,* the "Law of Free Birth." All children born into slavery after that day were to be free. Thus, Pedro thought, slavery would gradually die out.

The consequence of the law, however, was to split Brazil's free inhabitants into two parties: the *Abolicionistas,* who wanted to free adult slaves as well, and the *Escravocratas,* who sabotaged the new law. Planters falsified the birth dates of their slaves. The coffee producers in the south obtained new slaves from the remote northeast, where the government was hard put to enforce its decrees. Beatings for runaway slaves once more became fashionable. The oligarchy began applying thumbscrews to the liberal government. Once again Brazil stood on the verge of a serious crisis.

THE GOLDEN LAW

The emperor openly sympathized with the Abolicionistas. He permitted them to found associations in all the provinces of the country. The Abolitionist clubs gave aid and comfort to runaway slaves, checked attempts at smuggling, reported physical chastisement, and took care that the regulation that slaves over the age of sixty should be emancipated was not too openly flouted. They also exercised enough moral influence to persuade large landowners of their own accord to free more than one hundred thousand Negroes, and obtained the complete abolition of slavery in three provinces, Ceará, Amazonas, and Rio Grande do Sul. Journalists and other writers began a systematic campaign to wear down the resistance of the planters. The army refused to capture runaway slaves. All signs seemed to point to the probability that within a few years gradual reform would emancipate the last black worker on the land.

But at this point Brazil's new and major economic force—coffee—interfered. Brazilian coffee first appears in world economic statistics in 1818. In the following half century, thanks to the fertile volcanic *terra roxa* on the plateaus of São Paulo and thanks to the vast army of Negro slaves and ill-paid freedmen, it soon conquered all the markets in the world. Brazilian coffee could outstrip all rivals as long as the prevailing labor system was unchanged. It was the same for coffee as for sugar. But Brazilian coffee had gradually become far more important than sugar. Brazil became just as dependent on her coffee as, later, the Central American republics on bananas, Chile on nitrates, and Bolivia on tin.

When coffee raising was introduced into Brazil, more than half of the Brazilian population consisted of slaves. The capital, Rio de Janeiro, was a Negro city, aside from the luxury districts. Within a few decades Pedro's reforms reduced the number of slave laborers to one and a half million, that is, about 10 per cent of the population. European immigrants, who worked on the fazendas under a sharecropping system that often bordered on slavery, did not adequately replace the freed Negroes, who poured into the port cities. Costs of production rose and the value of the currency fell. The majority of fazendeiros refused to train and pay reasonable wages to a class of free, hard-working agricultural workers. The planters more and more insistently pointed out that abolition was ruining coffee production and that this meant total ruin for Brazil.

The planters demanded compensation for the capital they had invested in their slaves. Emperor Pedro could not grant compensation for two reasons: the idealistic reason that he did not want to pay men who had committed injustices; and the financial reason that the Brazilian government did not have the funds, what with the flagrant tax evasion of the oligarchy and foreign entrepreneurs. He also did not dare to issue a final act of emancipation because that would have meant civil war. Consequently, he remained between two stools. The Escravocratas turned away from him because of his reforms, the Abolicionistas because of his half measures. In the traditionally rebellious provinces of Pernambuco and Rio Grande do Sul, people of both parties were already openly calling for a republic.

In May 1888, while traveling in Italy, the emperor fell ill with pneumonia. For a short time he had to hand over the reins of government to his daughter Isabel, who was not well liked by the common people or the intellectuals—the latter mistrustful of her excessive clericalism. As regent, Isabel attempted to win popularity by yielding to the Abolicionistas. She issued the *Lei Áurea*, the "Golden Law," which stated flatly: "Slavery in Brazil is hereby declared defunct."

That was an overhasty action fraught with great consequences. For Isabel had put an end to a system four hundred years old without considering what was to become of the freed slaves. She started an upheaval that has not yet ceased.

The liberals, who had reached their goal, cheered the princess. The radical Abolitionists pointed out the absence of sensible enforcement provisions in the "Golden Law," and warned that the masses of slaves would be reduced to misery. The former slaveowners called for open defiance. They united with the republicans, carried on agitation in the army, and won over a number of discontented officers.

A year and a half later, on November 15, 1889, Emperor Pedro was overthrown by a military coup and banished from the country. The victorious revolutionaries were composed of heterogeneous elements: conservative fazendeiros, shrewd coffee speculators, ambitious general-staff officers, and social-reformist republicans. One group wanted to abrogate the *Lei Áurea*. Another hoped that the overthrow of the monarchy would undermine the value of the currency and enable them to make quick speculative profits. A third group desired a republic on the French pattern. The struggle for power among these cliques henceforth determined the character of Brazilian politics.

Pedro's abdication once more brought Brazil to the brink of ruin. The milreis lost two-thirds of its value. The hordes of Negroes who fled from the fazendas went into the forests, died on the highways, or collected in swarms in the big cities. Annually, hundreds of thousands of European immigrant laborers poured into the country to replace the former slaves. The apparent surplus of money, which had arisen from the inflation, tempted the planters to expand their plantations with the aid of these immigrants. After the abolition of slavery, coffee production by no means declined. On the contrary, Brazil was soon producing more coffee than the world could consume.

Forty years after the liberation of the slaves, after Brazil had experienced a number of military dictatorships, a variety of rebellions, and only a few stable governments, the currency and the economy faced total collapse. Between Rio de Janeiro and Santos, caustic yellow clouds of smoke rose into the sky. The planters were burning millions of tons of excess coffee. In those days the leader of the Liberal Alliance came to power by a *coup d'état*: Getulio Vargas of Rio Grande do Sul, journalist and lawyer, who attempted to complete the social reform and the emancipation of the colored people, and who ultimately (like Emperor Pedro II), after two turbulent administrations, was attacked and defeated by a coalition composed of the most heterogeneous elements.

The old *casa grande*, the manor house of colonial times, has long since been replaced by the millionaire's mansion, and the old *senzala*, the slave huts, by the shacks in the urban slums. The slums of Brazil are called *favelas*. They arose when the Negroes fled to the cities after emancipation, to escape the hated work on the plantations. A large percentage of the Brazilian people still live in the favelas. In Rio de Janeiro alone there are between three and four hundred thousand such slum dwellers.

LIVING IS FORBIDDEN

Rio de Janeiro is the destination of most lovers of South America, and the dream of many tourists touched by the call of remote places. Her own inhabitants call her *Cidade de Luz,* "City of Light." Travel books rhapsodize over the *cidade maravilhosa* or "the most beautiful city in the world." Her reputation is something of a stumbling block for the visitor who is searching for the real Rio. When a city has been proclaimed the most beautiful city in the world, it becomes difficult for anyone to free himself from insipid postcard clichés and see for himself.

Rio is really very beautiful; it takes a few days before you stop going through these beauties as if leafing through an album of pretty pictures, and instead penetrate to the real city. The famous beaches along the Atlantic are magnificent—Copacabana, Ipanema, and Leblon with their curved frontage of skyscrapers, the *praias.* This is the Rio of the movies, elegant, scintillating Rio, international and almost un-Brazilian. Certainly the three mountains which tower up as symbols of the city are beautiful: the often-described Sugarloaf; humped Corcovado with its colossal Christ, hands extended in blessing, at the summit; and square-shouldered Gávea beyond the jungle of Tijuca, the lush yet carefully tended park above the city, with its age-old giant trees, resplendent flowers, impressive esplanades, foaming water-falls, and dusky grottoes. Certainly the Avenida Niemeyer is beauti-ful, climbing in steep spirals up from the Atlantic shore. And there is a special beauty about the great bay around which the city curves, the Bay of Guanabara, across which great frigate birds sail, from whose waters dolphins leap, and whose islands are reminiscent of South Sea islands or fantastic strands from the Arabian Nights.

The waterfronts of Botafogo and Flamengo are, as people say in Rio, the pearl necklaces of the city. At night, when the lights go on, they do indeed look like gigantic garlands of light. Behind them rises a city of three million, framed by the high wall of the forested Organ Mountains. Here is a city in which nature and architecture have united perhaps more harmoniously than anywhere else in the world. Old promenade and business streets, spanned by bronze arches and lined by baroque houses, remain as reminders of colonial times: the

Rua do Ouvidor, the Rua do Rosário, and the Rua Gonçalves Dias. The Rio of the nineteenth-century economic boom is represented by the Avenida Rio Branco, the street of banks and trading companies, which smell of hard-working, serious-minded businessmen, but also of insecticides and the coffee drunk in innumerable tiny cups, *cafézinho*.

As in Paris, people sit outside the restaurants, right on the sidewalks, but the pedestrians are an even more colorful and variegated lot than those on the Boulevard Saint Michel. White girls with elaborate hairdos stroll past. Small brown shopgirls trip along on their spike heels. Fat Negroes in blue linen suits puff and wipe the sweat from their faces. A barefooted old woman in tattered skirt totters past the tables, a cardboard box under her arm. A Don Juan slams the door of his honey-colored automobile and casts a challenging look around. Well-nourished gentlemen in Panama hats, smoking black cigars, dignifiedly bear the weight of their paunches. Lean clerks transport swollen briefcases from office to office, and a dark-skinned youth raises his arms into the air and in complete self-absorption takes a few samba steps.

TOMORROW IS ANOTHER DAY

The romantic Old Town districts and the old-fashioned office buildings are gradually giving way to those breathtakingly bold glass and concrete skyscrapers which have won Brazil the reputation of having the world's best architects. The middle of the twentieth century is embodied in the three-hundred-foot-wide Avenida Presidente Vargas. Armies of automobiles, *lotacões,* and *camiões* roar six abreast along it, in only seeming anarchy. There are still gaps between the skyscrapers. Heaps of rubble lie beside one-story colonial buildings. The Brazilians set out to build the finest avenue in the world, but periodically their money has run out. But that grieves no one; tomorrow is another day.

The Avenida Presidente Vargas, like the futuristic new capital of Brasilia, is proof of the proverbial boldness of Brazilians. Here is a people which dispenses with calculation and launches gigantic projects without troubling its head about the consequences or the difficulties.

Where the almost frighteningly wide *avenida* runs straight through the city for over three miles from the Candelaria Church to the Praça de Bandeira, there used to be a notorious vice quarter, a joy to sensational writers and a grief to its inhabitants. During the presidency of Vargas, the prostitutes were expelled, the bulldozers came roaring in, and the rubble of a slum was covered with an asphalt pavement which would do honor to an airport. Skyscrapers with marble staircases and shady arcades were built as long as funds lasted. Later, someone will come along and continue building. In Brazil, boldness is complemented by patience.

When Cabral found the Brazilian coast, so the self-mocking legend in Brazil runs, a loud voice called to him from the jungle: *"Amanhã!"* The echo of the voice replied: *"Paciência!"* These two words express the essence of *brasilidade,* the Brazilian style of life. *Amanhã* is the same as the Spanish *mañana*—tomorrow. But that tomorrow can also mean the day after tomorrow, or sometimes not at all. *Paciência* is, of course, patience—which the Brazilians display in all situations of life. To summarize the Brazilian spirit still better, the legend should have included: *"Vamos dar um jeito!"*—"We'll turn the trick somehow!"

A good deal of invidious commentary has been written about the Brazilian habit of finding a *jeito* on all possible occasions. Someone who causes an automobile accident first makes his getaway, then settles the matter by a jeito. But a jeito is by no means always a dishonest act. It means every bright idea, every skillful dodge, every trick used to master the difficulties of everyday life without bluntly offending one's fellow men or falling prey to the long arm of the law. Brazil is a country of live and let live. And the Cariocas, the natives of Rio de Janeiro, are in this respect perfect Brazilians.

Rio is really lovely, full of charm and grace. It is pleasant on a sultry summer evening to sit on the roof garden of a restaurant at the beach, where the houses are fewer, the waves of the sea heavier, the cliffs more bizarre, the hills greener, and the mountains less cultivated. Cars skim by on the road below. Groups of palms guard the shore like stiff sentinels. Torn leaves of banana trees crackle with a papery sound. A pear-shaped moon hangs in the sky, its copper hue reflected in the foam of the surf. Neon lights reach up at the drifting clouds—but as usual they are somewhat out of order, and stammer their advertisements uncertainly into the night. The windows of other restaurants on the Sugarloaf glow as yellow as egg yolk. From a dark veranda sounds shrill music, a lashing rhythm that breaks off abruptly. The *morros,* the hills that rise above the massed houses, twinkle as if covered by swarms of lightning bugs. Rio is really very beautiful.

You come upon the other Rio, the rotten reverse side of this beauty, when you leave the ship in the harbor. The dock is full of garbage and assorted stenches. Light- and dark-skinned workers squat on the loading platforms, eating their supper. Then they sleep in a corner or lying squarely across the walks. They do not go home because they want to be on the spot any time there is a call for work. At every step, green coffee beans crunch underfoot. Some persons have special licenses to gather them up and sell them.

Leave the luxury districts and you will see ragged, barefooted people everywhere. There are a great many children, who often continue at their wretched little jobs until long after midnight. With shrill cries, small boys in amusing uniforms run about the busy streets selling newspapers. Other boys besiege the patrons of cafés and use a great deal of spit and little wax to polish the shoes of those who cannot fend them off. Children push two-wheeled carts around, stopping at every street corner to sell ice-cold maté or pineapple juice in paper cups. They must keep a sharp eye out for the police, because the city ordinances provide that they may push the carts but not station them anywhere, thus transforming themselves from itinerant to stationary peddlers. And so they tramp their eternal rounds from street to street, with but short interruptions. These newsboys, shoeshine boys, and peddlers are very thin children with wrinkled, old men's skins and much too big eyes. Deep into the night, when customers are few and far between, a few boys still rush around with metal pails in which a charcoal fire burns, offering homemade sweets for sale.

One night I heard the small newsboys chanting one sentence again and again into the noisy nocturnal crowds of Rio—a slogan full of dynamic import. "*É proibido viver!*" they cried. "Living is forbidden!" That was not the ideological prelude to a revolution; it was merely the heading of an editorial. For on that day food prices had again taken a sharp rise, although the government was still discussing an increase in minimum wages. *É proibido viver*—that headline expresses life on the morros, which twinkled so romantically that evening. The slogan stands, invisibly written, above the *favelas* of Rio.

ON THE MORROS OF RIO

No one who stays in Rio even for a few days fails to see the favelas. They are repeatedly denounced as the disgraceful blemishes of the *cidade maravilhosa*. Photographers cannot resist the drama implicit in a shot of elegant mansions cheek by jowl with rattletrap shacks built of flattened gasoline cans. In reality, however, the favelas are not so much blemishes as symptoms of the Brazilian economic and social order. Members of the upper class are allergic to the mere mention of the favelas. The Brazilian oligarchy is oversensitive about any kind of social criticism. More than once, neoveristic movies which showed the frightful slums of Rio have been ruthlessly cut by the censors.

Only part of the favelas are on the morros in the heart of the city. They are easily seen there, built of scraps of ancient lumber, sheathed with cardboard or tar paper, with openings for windows and doors and a roof of corrugated sheet metal or the flattened tin cans that let in the rain and soak up the heat of the sun. There is no water on the morros. Now and then peddlers come around selling water from rusty drums. The overpopulated city of Rio de Janeiro has been suffering from an increasingly grave shortage of water for decades. The favelados are even worse off than the rest of the population. In times of serious drought there is literally not a drop of water for them. The situation became appalling during the drought of 1963. The women of the favelas massed in front of the hospitals with sick, water-starved, apathetic children. Two hundred children died of thirst.

If you ask Cariocas about the origin of the favelados, you are almost always told that they are work-shy, asocial elements who live on the hills because they are trying to escape governmental supervision. But that is no longer true, if it ever was. In the favelas workers live side by side with ne'er-do-wells, seamstresses and washerwomen with prostitutes, honest porters and cabdrivers with pickpockets. The favelas are inhabited by all those whose incomes do not permit them to pay the fantastic rents in crowded Rio de Janeiro.

Many favelados have come from the famine regions of the northeastern states. The housing projects which were built during the administrations of Presidents Vargas, Kubitschek, Quadros, and Goulart are far from big enough to house the masses of the proletariat. The lower classes must therefore live on the morros, in filth and destitution, and thereby discredit themselves still further with the fortunate possessors of villas and luxury apartments. Possibly they also have low esteem for themselves, since they find it impossible to escape the favelas, however hard they try.

Tourists are warned against visiting the favelas. Every successful Carioca would like to repress his knowledge of the existence of these slums. And he may very well have his briefcase snatched if he ventures into one. Stabbings and other acts of violence also occur on the morros now and then. For the Brazilian slums have about the same number of desperadoes as do the slums of other metropolises. In general, however, the favelados manifest the same friendly *brasilidade* as their more fortunate fellow countrymen. Tiny, naked Negro children sit among the prickly cacti, playing with battered tin cans. Mulatto women carry pitchers on their heads, walking along with the grace and gait of duchesses, for all their rags. Broad-shouldered men with gleaming brown torsos light cigarettes with histrionic nonchalance and smile good-naturedly at the foreign intruder. They have strong fists, these favelados, and I rather wondered that they did not use them, but simply kept them in their pockets.

It is also said in Rio that the lower classes enjoy their favela existence and want nothing better. But the favelados themselves tell another story. I heard of cleaning women who stayed away from work for days, giving up the wages they could ill spare, in order to get their children registered in schools. Attendance at school is the first step on the road that leads out of the favelas to a better life. During the past several decades an amazing number of schools have been built in Brazil, but there are still far too few of them. Brazil, the largest and politically and economically the most important country in Latin America, remains debilitated by the illiteracy of her proletariat. Because of the shortage of schools, parents in many districts must stand in line to register their children.

There are, however, parents who do the exact opposite. One couple on a morro forbade their daughter to continue attending school. They did not want the child to be educated sufficiently to become discontented; they did not want her to suffer from spiritual conflicts. These parents were by no means especially reactionary; they had, perhaps, too great an appreciation of the virtue of *paciência*.

Virginia Leone Bicudo, the Brazilian sociologist, has found that a majority of the colored school children from the favelas become neurotic as soon as they come into contact with white teachers and the children of the middle class. The little favelados are thrown, she writes, "into circumstances which provide intense and violent stimuli to the development of emotions of hatred and fear." The favelas produce profound environmental shocks in the children, which come to the surface when they learn that a different and better life exists.

Recently, the favelas have been described from within in the heart-rending *Diary of Poverty*, written by the colored favelada Carolina Maria de Jesus of São Paulo—a book that has been translated into many languages. Carolina's cry, "The worst thing in the world is hunger!" is the leitmotif of the whole book. She has experienced and described the hatred of the well fed for the hungry: "The neighbors in their solid houses look upon the inhabitants of the favela with repugnance. I see the hatred in their eyes, because they would prefer not to have a favela here. . . . They are disgusted by poverty.

"One who lives in the favela has no childhood, no youth, no maturity," Carolina writes. He also loses the naïve Brazilian piety: "I think of our sad life and of the words of Father Luis, who tells us we must be humble. I think: If Father Luis were married and had children and earned the minimum wage, I should like to see whether Father Luis would be humble. . . . If he saw his children eating garbage, that otherwise only vultures and mice eat, he would also rebel; for the rebellion is born of bitterness."

Carolina Maria is not a conscious revolutionary, but she often asks herself: "Does God know that there are favelas and that the people of the favelas suffer hunger?" Her political ideas are summed up in a few sentences: "Every four years the politicians change, but they never solve the question of hunger, which is established in the favelas. . . . Brazil ought to be ruled by someone who has suffered from hunger!" But official Brazil ignores the favelas, as a respectable citizen ignores scabies when he has caught it, and would prefer to deny its existence. For that reason the favelados live and die anonymously, as Carolina describes the life and death of the handsome young Negro Zinho: "He was buried as an unknown. No one went to the trouble of finding out his name. Those who live on the margin of existence have no names."

Great, beautiful, proud Brazil is sick. It has ulcers—the favelas.

And these ulcers do not vanish when people close their eyes and react with irritation to all social criticism. On the contrary, they grow in number every day. "It is said," Carolina Maria de Jesus writes in her diary, "that Brazil has been a good country. But I was not born in the age of the good Brazil. . . . This is no world in which a poor man can live."

The favelas on the morros are beginning to disappear. Rio needs new shoreline roads in order to provide for the increasing automobile traffic. Consequently, the hills are gradually being hewed away so that their soil may be dumped into Guanabara Bay. But the inhabitants cannot all be resettled in housing projects. They move somewhere else, into slums sometimes drearier than those set amid the tropical greenery of the morros.

VULTURES OVER THE FAVELAS

The Baixada Fluminense, on the northern edge of the city, which only seventy-five years ago was one of the most thriving agricultural regions of Brazil, is degenerating more and more into a vast favela. I drove through Fluminense one evening after dark. Tiny lights flickered in the low huts, from carbide and kerosene lamps which cast long shadows upon the crooked, cracked walls. Through the unglassed window openings I saw men sitting on vegetable crates, women moving about and setting bowls of food on boards that served for tables. On the walls hung ragged clothes, and in a corner a man dressed only in a pair of athletic shorts slept on a bed of newspaper. Fat Negro women with swarms of children around them stood in doorways. They gave no greeting; they merely stared silently at passers-by. Whole families stood leaning against banana trees, singing. Young men in bright shorts walked among the huts with swaying hips, whistling a samba.

Perhaps at that very moment, in one of those favelas, a samba was being created which would enrapture all of Brazil a few weeks later. The samba is not only a highly rhythmic and extraordinarily artistic dance; it is also an expression of despair and rebellion. It is a legitimate child of the favelas, of the pestilential darkness, the rickety shacks. It is an outcry, a dream, and an expression of hope all in one. Most of the great samba composers, authors, and dancers of Brazil come from the slums, just as the creators of the Negro songs and dances of the colonial period came out of the *senzalas,* the slave huts.

In Fluminense I saw the largest accumulation of vultures I had ever observed in Brazil. The mucky swamp on which the favelas stand, all of them leaning crazily and some on piles, emanates evil-smelling gases composed of the smells of human garbage, rotting meat, and evaporating urine. Great dark swarms of *urubus,* the black vultures, circle over this swampy terrain. They perch by the dozens on the roofs of the huts. They descend instantly on a cadaver. They run around the favelas like chickens and no one molests them, for the vultures are the only hygienic institution in the favelas. Without them, the favelados would stifle in their own offal.

Favelas are not only a feature of Rio. They are found in all Brazilian cities from Belém and Recife to the farthest south. In the coffee port of Santos, the poor have settled directly opposite the pilgrimage church on the peak of Monte Serrat. The church itself is enough to make one shudder. It has a chamber of horrors in which hang the grotesque testimonies to miraculous cures: crutches, all sorts of horrifying votive images, wax replicas of limbs, photographs of repellent diseases, even naïvely realistic representations of syphilis and bubonic plague.

But your shudders are far worse on Morro Fontana, the hill opposite, where the favelas are established. When I first came to Santos, large parts of Morro Fontana had suffered landslides, due to heavy rains. From the rubble, the remains of crushed huts still protruded. Farther down stood whole groups of flimsy dwellings that had been spared by the catastrophe, but were still dangerously threatened by slides. Several hundred persons had been killed here. If it rained so hard again this year, I was told, the slopes of the morro would undoubtedly slide down into the valley again.

A few weeks later I visited Santos once more. In the meantime the dreaded new disaster had actually taken place. Once again hundreds of persons were killed. A great many families who had managed to save themselves had lost their dwellings. The mud from the morro, which the rain had washed into the city, lay a foot thick in the streets. On the slope there still clung some half-crushed favelas. The sight of them was truly horrifying, for people were still living in them. In front of crushed huts I saw children playing while the sand slid away under their feet. I saw women hanging wash and shifting their weight from one foot to the other as they did so, because the mountain was flowing away beneath them. But daily life went on. These women cooked their meals and did their washing; perhaps they even sang now and then.

People with whom I talked told me: "All over Brazil, collections have been made for the homeless. Practically speaking, those who are staying on the mountain are as good as done for. But where else can they go?"

POVERTY, WEALTH, AND CRIMINALITY

Statistics indicate that the number of favelados corresponds very closely with the number of registered illiterates in the big cities. Barely 5 per cent of these are whites, as American Jim Crow laws used to define whites. Among the inhabitants of the city of Rio who do not live in favelas, the birth rate exceeds the death rate by 17 per cent. Among the favelados, the death rate is 18 per cent higher than the birth rate. Almost half of the favelados are less than twenty years old; barely 3 per cent reach an age above sixty. If a favelado ever begins to think beyond the daily struggle to consider his whole life span, he knows it will last only half as long as that of his privileged fellow citizen.

It is generally assumed that the land on which the favelas stand belongs more or less to no one. In most Latin American countries, that is the case. In Brazil, too, there is ownerless land where the poor settle because there is no rent to pay. But in Rio many favela plots belong to well-to-do private owners. For every tiny parcel holding a shack made of orange crates and marmalade pails, the builder must pay a land rent which is just as high per square foot as that for real estate in the fancy residential quarters of the city.

If the city were to take over these sections, the rentals would enable it, within the foreseeable future, to replace all the favelas by decent housing projects. But nothing of the sort is done. Although (aside from a short interlude) Brazil had social-reformist governments from 1930 to 1964, private property has remained sacred and inviolable. The landowners live so well on the centavos of the destitute that they fiercely fight any move to make them sell out to the municipality.

The favelas are the reason that Rio does not enjoy a very good reputation. The *cidade maravilhosa* reputedly has a terrifyingly high crime rate. Most writers describe the favelados as dishonest, moody, uncontrollable, and quarrelsome. And since the favelas are supposed to be so bad, the whole city of Rio bears the taint.

Since I had found the favelados to be patient, peaceful, good-natured people, I was interested in obtaining some facts about criminality in the city of Rio. Several nights I heard shots that sounded as if they came from the direction of the waterfront. Next morning I read in the newspapers that dockworkers had attempted to steal a few sacks of coffee but had been stopped by the police. Such crimes occur in every port. And if jealous men in Copacabana go at one another with knives, or prostitutes use razor blades on the face of stingy "tricks," these are, after all, trifles which are accorded no more than three lines in newspapers everywhere in the world. In all red-light districts, knife fights take place; in all red-light districts respectable citizens shed some of their respectability and consequently run the danger of being rolled.

The supposed criminality of the slums is on a similar scale. Every day the newspapers carry an array of stories like the following: a workman surprises a burglar in his home and chases him with an ax, wounding him three times in the leg. An estimable lady falls to quarreling with her neighbor and beats her with a stout stick, so that the doctor has to be called. A bar proprietor is haled into court because he shot his waiter in the shoulder for getting too friendly with his wife. A prostitute created a public nuisance on a busy street in the city. A baker is caught with a twelve-year-old girl. Such varieties of misconduct among the common people can be found on every police blotter from Liverpool and Hamburg to Boston and Pittsburgh.

But there are other types of crime to be found in the Brazilian newspapers. A company has cheated its workers of a million cruzeiros in social-insurance contributions. A camarilla of speculators has managed to sabotage the food-supply plans of the state government of Guanabara. The Ministry of Foreign Trade calls on "all honorable businessmen to put an end to illegal operations—at last." I read that the prices for food and consumer goods had risen 100 per cent within two months. I read that an Italian tailor had discovered a mountain rich in gems in Minas Gerais, only to be set on by his neighbors and robbed of all his hoard except for a few tourmalines. I read that a multimillionaire was countering all newspaper criticism of his business practices and his private life by buying the newspapers involved.

I read about a Brazilian playboy who squandered millions every year out of sheer boredom, while the workers in his company, because of the artificial inflation, could scarcely earn the necessities of life. There were also numerous shootings and killings that did not take place among the faveleros. A millionaire real estate speculator had tried to cheat his likewise millionaire broker, and had been repaid on the shore road of Copacabana by five pistol shots. Guns are drawn readily even in the Senate at the new capital of Brasilia. When debate between political opponents becomes too passionate, they may draw their revolvers and attempt to silence one another permanently.

The longer I stayed in Brazil, the more clearly I realized that the really dangerous people of the country did not live in the favelas.

COFFEE, BLESSING AND CURSE

The drive from Rio de Janeiro to São Paulo on the modern, well-built highway, reveals much of the damage done to Brazil by its coffee. If you turn off the highway, you also see something of the industrialization on which the country's best statesmen and economists pin their hopes. First you pass by luxury housing and favelas, factories and meager fazendas, the fragrance of flowers alternating with the stench of decay. Fields of corn rustle in the torrid breeze; banana groves provide a little coolness. Small children play in the filth. Before you cross the boundary between the states of Guanabara and São Paulo, you pass, to the right of the highway, situated in the valley of the upper Paraíba, a great complex of buildings that many Brazilians already regard as the symbol of Brazil's future: the steel plant and mines of Volta Redonda.

In Volta Redonda the ore of Itabira Mountain is mined and converted to steel. Itabira Mountain is in the state of Minas Gerais, and is said to hold one quarter of the iron-ore reserves of this planet. Until 1940, the jealousies of the great mining countries prevented the Brazilians from exploiting Itabira and creating her own steel industry. It was Hitler who involuntarily provided the impetus for the establishment of Volta Redonda.

A FUTURE INDUSTRIAL POWER

A year after the outbreak of the Second World War, the United
States feared that Hitler might attempt a *rapprochement* with Brazil
in order to gain a foothold on the South American Continent. The
country was then governed by Getulio Vargas, the dictatorial social
reformer. Hitherto, Americans had scarcely relished his anticapitalist
attitude. But now the Allies began paying court to him. Vargas was
no friend of Hitler, although in his early days he had learned from
Mussolini. He was less interested in compliments than in some
tangible reward for his allegiance to the Allied cause. He therefore
asked for American dollars so that he could build the largest steel
works in South America on the upper Paraíba. It was to be connected
by railroad with the ore of Minas Gerais and with the coal mines of
Santa Catarina. What Vargas had in mind was a Brazilian Ruhr. The
war was giving him the opportunity to launch the industrialization of
his country.

Washington placed a credit of forty-five million dollars at the disposal of Brazil, and Vargas entered the war on the side of the Allies.
While Brazilian soldiers fought and died on the battlefields of Europe
—the only Latin Americans to do so—Brazilian workers built railroads, blast furnaces, rolling mills, and coking plants in the Paraíba
Valley. A year after the end of the war, Volta Redonda began competing with the other large steel companies of the world.

Today, the sleepy little place has become a modern industrial city
with neat workmen's housing, clubs, hospitals, movies, an airport,
and even an exclusive cadet school. Progressive Brazilians are immensely proud of the gigantic works. Volta Redonda's steel, they hope,
will soon enable Brazil to take its place among the great industrial and
mining powers. It will be the basis for a modern armament industry
and thus transform a country of plantations into a leading industrial
nation.

There was only one difficulty. For many years the Americans, who
had provided the capital, also exercised considerable control over
Volta Redonda. The governments of Quadros and Goulart struggled
tenaciously to force the Americans out. After some tugging back and
forth, Volta Redonda has passed into the hands of the governmental
Companhia Siderúrgica Nacional. The works will shortly produce

upward of three million tons of steel annually. In the past decade a number of other major steel plants have been built: in Minas Gerais, in the vicinity of Santos, in the valley of the Rio Doce. These are partly government-owned, partly joint enterprises by Brazilian, Japanese, German, and Belgian concerns. According to the latest plans, Brazil will raise her steel production to eight million tons by the year 1970.

THE TERMITES TAKE OVER THE PLANTATIONS

I drove across the border which separates the state of Guanabara from the state of São Paulo—riding from Brazil's future to Brazil's past. The region between Rio de Janeiro and São Paulo was once the richest coffee-producing territory in the world. But I saw no coffee. Up and down the highway we went, through gently rolling hills so similar that they were almost soporific. The tops of the hills were barren; the naked stone glinted in the glaring light. Shaggy shrubs that seemed to be arranged in lines grew on some slopes. It was as though a giant rake had combed the hills.

Over all this area, decades ago, vast coffee plantations stretched in all directions, the shrubs laid out in perfectly straight lines. The coffee shrubs consumed the soil, leaching out its nutrients until there was nothing left. The coffee plants died, to be succeeded by less demanding shrubs like hardhack. But this vegetation too began to vanish. Coffee had transformed the one-time garden of Brazil into a lunar landscape.

Here was scorched earth that could not be reawakened to life. Now and then we saw beside the highway a few wretched *caboclo* huts surrounded by parched fields of corn. The cornfields would be punctuated with the charred stumps of burned trees, thanks to whose ashes the caboclos would reap a few scanty harvests. Beside the huts loomed monstrous and curiously barren mounds of clay, yards high. There were termitaria.

Hour after hour I drove through these seared, termite-ridden plains. The scene was almost always the same. Once tremendous jungles had covered this land. Then men had planted their coffee, made a great deal of money, and, when the coffee shrubs were no longer productive, had migrated to other jungles, to burn these down and plant coffee in the ashes. The coffee tree is a demanding plant. If it is not fertilized and tended, it sucks the last nutriments out of the soil within a few decades. Moreover, coffee is a mountain plant which thrives in the mountainous regions of Africa, Central America, and Colombia, but usually does not live long in tropical lowlands and on subtropical plateaus.

Scarcely anywhere on earth has the whole landscape changed so tremendously within a century as it has on the *planalto,* the plateau of São Paulo. You may see that not only on the drive from Rio de Janeiro to São Paulo; it is evident virtually anywhere you go in the great coffee state. The subtropical forest that once covered the planalto was dense jungle, with trees seventy-five to a hundred feet in height, with a rich assortment of orchids, bromelias, and ferns. The layer of red humus in these forests was thick and fertile. When the first settlers burned over the forest, they imagined that the fertility of the humus was inexhaustible. Agronomic institutes in Brazil long ago discovered that just the opposite was the case. The Brazilian jungle is, by geological standards, a very young forest growing on an extremely thin layer of good soil. Underneath that soil lies lifeless primeval rock. That is also true of the Amazonian rain forests, which certain utopians regard as a fine place to settle the overflowing population of our planet.

Brazilian geologists and agronomists emphasize that no lasting agriculture can be established on burned-over jungle. The idea that the interior of Brazil contains limitless quantities of tillable land and may someday become one of the great granaries of the human race is merely a lovely delusion. When plantings are made along the Amazon, in the virgin soil of the rain forests, they must as a rule be abandoned after anywhere from two to ten years because of the complete exhaustion of organic substances. Subtropical forest soil has a somewhat longer span; coffee trees will go on bearing for between twenty and forty years. But after this period erosion has progressed so far that the land becomes barren plain overrun by termites.

The history of Brazilian coffee ought to have been a solemn lesson to the human race. Hardly anywhere on earth has the soil been so intensively mined; and hardly anywhere else has the reckless exploitation of the soil had such profound and conspicuous consequences. Unfortunately, there is a rather blasphemous saying popular in Brazil: "God is great, but Brazil is greater." Agronomic institutions and schools of forestry have prepared vivid pictorial exhibitions in their effort to persuade Brazilians that newly cultivated jungle soil needs particularly careful and delicate treatment if it is not to relapse into wasteland. But the minds of the Brazilian upper classes, many intellectuals, and even of European and American economic experts, are still possessed by the myth that the Brazilian jungle is inexhaustible.

What is more, the coffee fazendeiro simply has a different mentality from that of the European farmer. He feels not the slightest tie to his land. He wants to get profit out of his plantings as quickly as possible, and refuses to spend good cruzeiros on fertilizers, on leaving strips of untouched forest to improve climatic conditions, or on any of the other recommendations of the scientists. He did not burn down the forest in order to establish a farm for his children and children's children, but to make what he can out of the soil. If it fails him, he abandons it and moves farther on into the forest.

The result is the conversion of vast areas to parched wasteland, an alarming decrease of the stands of forest in southern Brazil, destruction of the layer of humus, and such deterioration of the climate that nowadays scarcely any rain falls on the planalto from April to October. Irrigation is now mandatory to make continued cultivation of coffee possible. The state of São Paulo has an area of approximately ninety-five thousand square miles; some 70 per cent of this area has already been converted to wasteland or almost worthless pastures. In other words, coffee has devastated an area as large as Austria and Hungary put together. The plant that once so generously provided foreign exchange has become the demon that is killing Brazil.

If you talk with fazendeiros about the deforestation of the planalto, they frequently point to sparse, shadeless little groves consisting of thin, pole-like trees. Reforestation is going on everywhere, they say. No reason for pessimism. Those trees come from Australia; they are various kinds of eucalyptus, strangers to Brazilian soil. Yet the true reason the eucalyptus has been planted is not concern for the soil and climate, but greed for profits. The eucalyptus is a tree that grows very rapidly in poor soil; within four to seven years it can provide wood for paper and cellulose factories. This immigrant from Australia will grow even in exhausted soil. It obtains water by sending its roots far in all directions, and very deep into the ground.

There are paper factories in São Paulo that own vast plantations of many millions of eucalyptus trees. These "forests" do not have a long life. The trees are not allowed to grow; they are cut as soon as they are useful. Where eucalyptus is planted, the ground-water level drops and the wells dry out; not a drop of water remains for other plants. Whatever damage went undone by the coffee bushes, this tree from the Australian barrens is accomplishing. The eucalyptus is the last element in the annihilation of the soil. After it comes what geologists call karst, the lunar landscape.

Not all areas in the state of São Paulo have been converted to desert in so terrifying a fashion. Some regions were once open green fields and have remained so. At times a small factory complex will appear in the wasteland, new and modern, surrounded by primitive workers' dwellings. Occasionally you come across growing industrial and chemical centers. There is reason to wonder whether the eroded land may not be destined to become a single vast industrial region, as was the dream of the eccentric president Jánio Quadros.

THE LOCOMOTIVE OF BRAZIL

The nearness of the great metropolis of São Paulo is announced by a sudden restlessness in the landscape. Huge billboards line the road, advertising automobile tires, ventilators, and beverages. Huts are more numerous, industrial complexes succeed one another with greater frequency. Imperceptibly, the dusty barrens that belong to the termites pass into dusty suburban streets. On the horizon appear narrow skyscrapers with projecting top stories. Closely ranked, they reach into the sky—a kind of silhouette you might expect to see only in North America.

Your first impression of this Brazilian metropolis is not very encouraging. You pass gray, faceless row houses, depressing workers' districts, dreary residential areas. The tropics seem to have vanished, crushed by the stone masses of an active, ambitious urban life. But this city, with its nearly four million inhabitants, is a fascinating monster, a stone Moloch with an unmistakable character. It is hard to imagine a greater contrast than that between charming Rio de Janeiro, where people live and let live, and hectic São Paulo, where they work and make others work.

The traffic in the business district is even heavier, if that is possible, than in the heart of overpopulated, burgeoning Rio. The efforts to deal with it surpass in boldness anything that Rio has attempted. A huge avenue, with a great many overpasses for cars and pedestrians.

cuts through the center of the city. This is the Parque Anhangabahú, the city's main artery. It is also the street from which the city sprang. For here, four hundred years ago, the Jesuit fathers Manoel da Nóbrega and José de Anchieta stood on the banks of the marshy brook Anhangabahú and laid the cornerstones for a settlement which they never dreamed would develop into the third-largest city of South America. Only a few decades previously the valley of the Anhangabahú had been a dreary morass that periodically flooded the scattered dwellings on its fringes. The swamp vanished only after São Paulo became a great metropolis. It was first developed into a park and then became a broad, many-laned avenue which is crossed by another great traffic artery, the Viaduto do Chá, on massive pillars.

São Paulo is said to have the fastest rate of growth of any city in either of the Americas. From 1940 to 1950 the city gained a million inhabitants; another million were added by 1960. The increase is said to be six times that of New York, on a percentage basis. The building of houses and skyscrapers proceeds at a similar pace. Five new houses are completed every day in São Paulo; every week whole blocks are razed to make room for skyscrapers. Everywhere you see the scaffoldings of big buildings; everywhere blocked streets and torn-up pavement.

The *Paulistas* are a different breed of people from the gay Cariocas of Rio. They are wide-awake descendants of the old-time bandeirantes who thought of their city and their state as the "locomotive of Brazil." Paulistas have not brooded over the problem of the favelas; they have faced up to the problem of assimilating, as rapidly and with as little friction as possible, the vast numbers of Italian, German, Spanish, Jewish, Polish, and Syrian immigrants who have poured into the city.

São Paulo is also beautiful, although its beauty is of a quality quite different from that of Rio. Here the skyscrapers have attained an ultimate perfection. Many of them are sheeted with marble; because of the coolness it emanates, this material is especially suitable to Brazil. São Paulo produces an impression of grandeur. In Rio, you feel that the skyscrapers are natural cones of rock that intensify the charm of the landscape; but in São Paulo man has triumphed over nature. Here the ranks on ranks of skyscrapers no longer resemble natural landscape at all; everything is calculated planning. The city is entirely the work of man.

There is, however, something troubling about the beauty of São

Paulo: an engineering precision that unfolds like a new process of robot creation. You look in vain for old colonial houses. A one-story house does not yield much rent; how much better to tear it down and use the land, which in the heart of the business district is worth a fortune, to build a tower of Babel. The owner of land has no great difficulty financing such a project. Even before he starts, the builder sells the projected apartments to eager buyers. If he goes about the matter skillfully, and co-ordinates his sales with the progress of the building, so that inflation does not upset his calculations, he will have covered all his expenses from the first, and pocketed a neat profit in addition. Anyone who owns a building lot in the right parts of São Paulo is set for life.

The result is a real estate boom that can be compared with the California gold rush and the Chilean nitrate boom. Although Brazil has suffered from acute inflation for years, and is confronting some thorny economic problems, the real estate boom rolls on. No land-owner can escape it, even if he is not a born speculator. A dire end to the rapid development of São Paulo has often been predicted. Prophets of doom have pointed to the unhealthy price rises, the sinking currency, and to the fact that innumerable *apartamentos* now stand empty for lack of buyers who can pay for them. But the prophets of boom are still in the ascendancy; the building and speculation continue. Outlines of the crisis are apparent to anyone willing to look. The Paulistas, however, shut their eyes and go on building their five costly houses a day and a new gigantic apartment house every week.

The Paulistas have retained their distinctive character. Although most of the European immigrants to Brazil live in the state of São Paulo, and consequently might be expected to have swamped the native population, the Paulista character has continued to assert itself and has infected the new arrivals. The feudalistic descendants of the bandeirantes and "Mamelukes" have played a part in Brazilian history rather similar to that of the *Junkers* and the patrician merchant families in German history. Of course, such analogies must be taken with reservations. For although the Paulista is always concerned with increasing his possessions and his power, he can also be revolutionary. He is invariably revolutionary when the administration attempts to infringe upon his privileges.

The Paulistas have in fact staged most of the revolutions in Brazilian history. They drove out the Portuguese, overthrew the emperor, price-fixed and burned coffee, revolutionized the economy, and fought all social reformers from Getulio Vargas to João Goulart. Consequently, the Paulistas are regarded in Brazil not as conservative, but as particularly progressive and freedom-loving. Something of the antic temper of the Paulistas was illustrated during the city's municipal elections. The inhabitants thought all the regular candidates so dreary and undistinguished that, at the suggestion of a jokester, they voted into office the popular rhinoceros of the São Paulo zoo. The incident tells something about the keen wit of the Paulistas, as well as their traditional contempt for democracy.

DEADLY BLESSING

The rise of the state of São Paulo began when the coffee trees struck roots into the *planalto* by the millions. Coffee made São Paulo a metropolis, and transformed the notorious yellow-fever hole of Santos into a great port. But the first warning of trouble to come appeared as early as 1906. A record harvest of twenty million sacks piled up that year. The planters, exporters, and middlemen, the government officials and bankers could not take pleasure in this harvest. They were beginning to foresee that coffee could carry their country and themselves to destruction. Phrases like "deadly blessing" and "problem of the surplus" began appearing in Brazilian newspapers and journals that year.

In 1906 Brazil supplied some 97 per cent of the world's demand for coffee. A billion coffee trees were growing in the state of São Paulo alone. Brazil had created the largest and most dangerous monoculture that has ever existed on this globe. An oversupply of coffee, every economist realized, would inevitably depress the world market price so low that a coffee tree would become as worthless as a bundle of twigs.

Overseas coffee importers took action, for fear of being caught in a collapse of the Brazilian coffee economy. They formed syndicates whose purpose was to keep the surplus of coffee off the market. That would have ruined the Brazilian planters, of course, but would have saved the day for several thousand European coffee dealers. Other European financiers, who had invested their money in Brazilian loans or securities, did not like the prospect. They suggested instead granting large credits to the Brazilian Government so that it could buy the coffee itself and either release it or hold it back according to the marketing situation. These manipulations were the beginning of the fateful policy of "coffee valorization" in Brazil.

Brazil received the credits. Henceforth, Brazilian governments used the money to buy a large part of the coffee crop from the planters. The sacks were sent under seal to warehouses in European and North American ports. A strict ban on new plantings was imposed on the fazendeiros. By 1913 the situation seemed to be in hand once more. But after 1913 the policy of valorization no longer served to check coffee planting; instead, it led to a further increase. Since the government was supporting the price of coffee, it was to the advantage of the fazendeiros to evade the law and extend their plantings. If an occasional tough administration tried to keep too close a check on the planters, there were always enough willing politicians to send troublesome presidents and their cabinet ministers into the political deserts.

Thus, after the First World War, the great forests once more began being burned over in the remote interior of the country, beyond the reach of the central government. Coffee planting was shifted from the eroded planalto to inaccessible regions in the states of Minas Gerais and Mato Grosso. The planters even ventured into the inclement highland regions of Paraná, where the crop is blasted by frost every few years. Even small businessmen and craftsmen who had never planted anything in their lives now expected the state to take any quantity of coffee off their hands. They borrowed money, bought up parcels of forest, burned clearings, and set out coffee seedlings in the red earth. Already the outlines of a new and graver crisis could be seen—a crisis that was to change fundamentally the economic structure of Brazil.

The fazendeiros and exporters had learned nothing at all from the disaster of 1906. During the 1920s the Brazilians rejoiced in the effects of Prohibition in the United States, for parched Americans drank more coffee. Then, in 1924, came another gigantic crop which even thirsty North America could not consume. The Brazilian Government intervened and made the fazendeiros store their coffee in *reguladores,* special warehouses in the interior. They had to keep it stored until release was permitted by the State Institute for the Defense of Coffee. But the government had to reach deep into its

pocket and advance money to the fazendeiros to persuade them not
to sell their coffee.

This new system of valorization collapsed in the fatal year 1929,
when the world-wide depression began. Brazilian currency took a
terrible plunge. The government no longer had money to support
the fazendeiros. At the time of Wall Street's Black Friday, some
twenty million sacks of coffee were stored in the reguladores, while
the new crop was estimated at an additional twenty-eight million
sacks. According to the experts, world demand could at most total
twelve to fifteen million sacks of coffee a year. Thus Brazil was
burdened with a stock of coffee that amounted to four times the
world's annual consumption. And because of the world depression,
these buyers could no longer pay, and did not lift a finger to help
the Brazilian coffee kings. The whole economy of Brazil was im-
periled, for her annual income from coffee came to four times her
income from all other exports.

Brazil thereupon hit on a way out that has ever since served as
a symbol of insane capitalist economic policies. The government imposed an export tax on every sack of coffee shipped abroad, and
used the ensuing revenue to buy up the surplus coffee and destroy
it. In the vicinity of Santos, a million tons of coffee were burned.
Millions of sacks of coffee were thrown into the sea; after each of
these operations, innumerable fish, dead of caffeine poisoning, drifted
to the beaches. Coffee was used to fuel locomotives; attempts were
made to manufacture plastics, paints, fats, cattle feeds, fertilizers,
and illuminating gas from coffee beans. Between four and five million
tons of coffee are said to have been destroyed in the course of this
program.

With their destruction of coffee, the Paulistas, hitherto the leading
force in Brazil, seemed to have destroyed themselves. In 1930 a
revolution broke out that was a novelty in the empire of coffee. For
the leaders of this revolution did not come from the coffee-producing
state. They came instead from the intellectual north and from the
cattle-raising province of Rio Grande do Sul. The revolution was
sparked by the assassination of a respected liberal politician from
the north, João Pessôa, after whom the capital of the state of Paraíba
is now named. Pessôa had been one of the most active leaders of
the *Aliança Liberal,* a political movement which called for struggle
against the reactionary coffee kings and the economic monopoly of

the Brazilian oligarchy. Behind Pessôa's assassination undoubtedly stood the ultraconservative millionaire cliques. His death was the signal for revolutionaries from Pernambuco and Rio Grande do Sul to set out on a march to Rio de Janeiro and São Paulo.

The revolution was won within a few weeks. Its leader, Getulio Vargas, became president and dictator of Brazil. Vargas came from a family of cattle raisers in Rio Grande do Sul; that is, he was, as the Brazilians say, a *gaúcho*. At the time no one guessed that this man would dominate Brazilian history for a quarter of a century. Vargas propelled Brazil from her plantation past into the modern age. We shall have more to say about the Vargas era in another connection.

COFFEE, FOREIGN EXCHANGE, AND INFLATION

When Vargas took power, his financial expert, Osvaldo Aranha, later to become better known as Brazil's foreign minister, declared: "We have no foreign exchange and are confronted with overdue or nearly due obligations. The financial situation of Brazil is completely hopeless. It is impossible to determine what sums the federal government, the various states and the municipalities owe one another. Our coffee economy is threatened thrice over by the fall in prices, overproduction, and the increasing stocks in the warehouses. Our industry is moribund. In addition, we are also suffering from acute unemployment."

That was the net result of a century of unrestricted coffee growing. Vargas needed seven years to consolidate the economy to some extent. First he too had to burn the coffee surplus. He did so in order to clear the decks. At the same time, however, he supported all efforts aimed at making Brazil independent of coffee. The number of industrial plants, airports, and small farms multiplied enormously during his first administration.

The Paulistas responded with revolts financed by the coffee kings. Vargas had dictatorial powers and used them to combat the dominance of coffee. In 1937 he at last risked the great step that the fazendeiros had dreaded and coffee drinkers throughout the world had hoped for. He eliminated price-fixing and left coffee to the free play of supply and demand. Coffee prices plunged precipitously. Vargas showed no concern. Possibly he was pleased to see his bitterest enemies lose their money.

Vargas was well aware that the Brazilian coffee economy could not be placed on a sound footing unless something were done about runaway overproduction. He issued a decree that fazendeiros must eliminate an old coffee tree for each new one they planted. In addition, he converted coffee plantations into cotton fields, and coffee districts into industrial regions. Under the Vargas dictatorship, the problems arising from coffee in Brazil ceased to be quite so turbulent. In 1945, however, when so many of the South American dictators fell, even the popular Vargas had to yield to an elected president. But five years later he returned to the presidency once more, victor in the elections. In the meanwhile another coffee boom had broken out, to satisfy the long-pent-up European demand.

Once more, the regulations against new plantings were violated. Once more the planters began cultivating vast new fields of coffee so as to profit by the boom. And once more overproduction, collapse of the price structure, and a new cycle of coffee burning threatened. Vargas saw where the situation was tending. But this time he did not declare war on coffee. As a democratically elected president, he was the prisoner of his own government, restricted in his actions by his partners in a coalition administration. Instead, he too began speculating in coffee—not because he had suddenly become a friend of the coffee kings, but because he needed foreign exchange to build up heavy industry and to develop the oil resources of his country, which would free Brazil from her dependence on coffee. It was a risky speculation. Vargas did what had been done during the period of valorization: he established minimum prices high above the international market price; the government bought whole crops in the hope that world market prices would by and by reach the height of his fixed prices. But that meant deliberately unleashing inflation—the Brazilian inflation which has not yet ceased.

World market prices refused to do Vargas the favor of adjusting to his minimum prices. A buyers' strike in the United States led to a severe cutback in Brazilian coffee exports. The price of coffee dropped, instead of rising, and, to make matters worse, living costs in Brazil increased. Vargas' desperate gamble destroyed him politically. He left to his successors exemplary social legislation and a historical legend in which to this day he figures as the "father of the poor"; he also left them a vicious economic circle.

None of the three presidents who succeeded Getulio Vargas has managed to solve the problem of coffee. The coffee kings came out of the disaster relatively unscathed. By clever monetary maneuvers, they continued to take in vast profits. Foreign currency earned abroad is received by the government Banco do Brasil, and the equivalent value in cruzeiros is credited to the exporters. This system is complicated because the government guarantees the planters a minimum income. Thus the coffee economy continues to be underwritten by the state, at great expense to the total budget.

The guaranteed minimum is some 200 per cent higher than the cost of production. Since Brazil is a land of *jeitos*, of dodges and illegal agreements, clever exporters have little difficulty in making special agreements with their foreign buyers. For example, two invoices may be written out, one showing a low price and intended for the Banco do Brasil, and one showing the real price, for the firm's use. The coffee kings then arrange that the difference is paid into a foreign account in dollars. Thus they have tax-free foreign exchange at their disposal, while inside the country they pay their wages and expenses in devalued cruzeiros. This method is employed not only by the Brazilian coffee exporters; it has spread to many other branches of the country's economy. A good many Brazilians have become millionaires thereby.

Every Brazilian government since Vargas has toyed with projects for a radical currency reform which would prevent this everlasting fraudulence. But no government has yet dared to undertake any such measures. Independent President Quadros was pushed from office solely because he came out strongly against the flight of capital, corruption, and tax evasion. Hence, prices continue to rise and the value of the cruzeiro sinks ever lower; wages lag behind the cost of living, and trickery on the part of the moneyed oligarchy continues to make Brazil one of the financially most unstable countries in the world.

HOW TO MAKE MONEY IN SÃO PAULO

In the course of these turbulent years, the shrewd Paulistas have adjusted splendidly to the new times. Formerly, they dominated the Brazilian economy as planters of sugar, coffee, and cotton, employing armies of black slaves and light-skinned sharecroppers. Today they produce hardware and frozen meat, lemonade and preserves, textiles and chemicals—and so still control the economy. They no longer have slaves at their disposal, but they do have hordes of proletarians, who since the Vargas era have been pressing more and more insistently for social justice. Vargas and his minister of labor, João Goulart, worked out a body of social legislation that looks very good on paper: minimum wages, fixed pay scales, regular vacations, job security, medical and social insurance. These laws were further extended by the later leftist government of Goulart, and the present dictatorship has been unable to abolish them.

But the moneyed oligarchy has skillfully contrived to evade the social legislation just as it did the coffee-planting quotas. For instance, there is a law providing that an employee who has worked for the same firm for ten years enjoys a kind of "tenure"; he can no longer be fired. Consequently, workers are fired shortly before this period expires. Legal minimum wages mean nothing when prices are constantly rising. The wage-price spiral in Brazil is a race always won by prices. Persistent frustration has produced an increasing radicalization of the masses. This, in turn, so frightened the oligarchy that it wanted to cut short the succession of democratic, social-reform governments, and called more and more audibly for a strong man—whom the military coup of March 31, 1964, seemed at last to have installed.

Coffee taught Brazilians how to make money. Many immigrants also learned from the coffee millionaires. A considerable part of the present-day Brazilian moneyed oligarchy has come from the class of clever immigrants who saw how to profit by the boom. The big warehouses and docks of Santos, the largest in Brazil, belong not to the government or to various companies, but to a single family, the Italo-Brazilian Guinlés. They take a profit on every sack of coffee, every bunch of bananas, every bale of cotton that passes through the port. Their company, Docas de Santos, has a turnover of billions of cruzeiros. The Guinlé family also owns real estate, banks, and factories in many of Brazil's cities. Among its properties is the Copacabana Palace Hotel, the most luxurious hotel in Rio de Janeiro.

The heads of the Companhia Francisco Matarazzo in São Paulo are even wealthier. Its founder arrived in the coffee metropolis from Genoa toward the end of the last century. After a spell as a dockworker, he peddled lard, and after a few years had saved enough capital to open a small lard factory. The factory grew at the same pace as São Paulo. He opened retail shops, sold groceries, textiles,

real estate, canned goods, and many other things. Today the Matarazzos are among the richest people in the world. They manufacture
virtually everything that can be made in São Paulo, from textiles
and nylon to paper and machines. They run virtually every enterprise
that can function in Brazil, from plantations and slaughterhouses to
oil wells and mines. They import and export, own banks and finance
companies, mills, and a sizable fleet of ships. The son of the former
lard peddler acquired an Italian count's title, in spite of his Brazilian
citizenship.

At the same time, the Matarazzos are a favorite target of the press,
which claims they are niggardly to their employees. But the power
of these Brazilian multimillionaires is so great that such attacks do
not touch them. Aside from the oil sheiks of the Near East, there is
probably not another moneyed aristocracy in the world that rules so
absolutistically and bends public opinion so completely as the one or
two dozen multimillionaires of São Paulo.

From 1939, coffee's blackest year, to 1964, the Brazilian oligarchy
was unable to install a president and a cabinet that would obey its
behests. Year after year, the number of illiterates diminished; year
after year the percentage of eligible voters among the lower classes
increased. But the oligarchy did everything in its power to discredit
all the administrations of the past thirty-five years in the eyes of the
world public, or else to bring about their fall. At last it succeeded.
The man who headed this campaign, and who helped the present dictatorship to take power, has the fates of three presidents on his con-
science. He is Carlos Lacerda, journalist and governor of the state of
Guanabara.

CARLOS THE TERRIBLE

Carlos Lacerda was involved when the Vargas era ended like a detec-
tive story whose solution still remains sealed. Lacerda's journalistic
and political attacks sounded like dissonant, shrill background music
throughout the Kubitschek era, during which the new federal capital of
Brasilia was created. Lacerda was the party whip responsible for the
electoral victory of Jánio Quadros, and was likewise responsible for
the surprising resignation of Quadros. Then Lacerda became the fierc-
est opponent of President João Goulart. Today he is one of the most

ardent defenders of the military coup that overthrew Goulart. In the next elections this intrepid president slayer may possibly run for the presidency himself.

Who is Carlos Lacerda, whom all Brazil has been talking about for fifteen years, and before whom all Brazilian politicians tremble? He is the incarnate symbol of the dubious power wielded by the Brazilian press. The press in Brazil enjoys a degree of independence rare on this globe. It is so independent that it can be bought and subsequently lash out at the buyer. It is so independent that it can be corrupted and at the same time launch a campaign against corruption. It is so independent that it unabashedly accepts subsidies from dictators it intends to overthrow.

Carlos Lacerda comes from a family of politicians, and in his youth was close to the socialists. A man who wants to succeed politically in Brazil must—as in France—be either a lawyer or a journalist. Lacerda chose the profession of journalism. He became editorial writer for one of the largest Brazilian dailies, the *Correio da Manha,* which belonged to Assis de Chateaubriand, the multimillionaire and uncrowned newspaper king of Brazil. The newspaper business provided Lacerda with an ideal field for studying the principal vice of Brazilian economic life —illegal financial dealings.

Brazilian journalists who make the most of their opportunities can quickly acquire sizable fortunes. Many journalists belong to the boards of directors of large banks and corporations. In part, this is because they are paid generously by the moneyed oligarchy if they prove well disposed toward millionaires; in part it is due to the intricacies of Brazilian financial regulations.

The Brazilian Government accords newspaper publishers sizable benefits of various kinds. There are a large number of foreign-exchange categories. Publishers receive the foreign exchange they need for their outlays abroad at the lowest exchange rate; ordinary mortals, dealing in the most favored category of goods, must pay four times as much, while in the least favored categories it is twenty times as much. Virtually every publisher avails himself of this privilege, importing printing presses, office equipment, cameras, and similar goods with the foreign exchange he obtains so cheaply from the Banco do Brasil, and reselling the goods at high profits. No wonder Brazilian newspaper publishers own chemical factories, oil refineries, radio and television stations. And no wonder that any moderately competent journalist seizes the first opportunity to start his own newspaper and thus acquire wealth by semilegal foreign-exchange manipulations.

Writing in Assis de Chateaubriand's newspaper, Carlos Lacerda furiously assailed corruption, foreign-exchange swindles, and the well-nigh criminal methods of obtaining credit which were commonplace in Brazilian business at the time. He acquired the aura of a noble fighter for honesty in business and government. But when he threw too glaring a light on the financial manipulations of a Brazilian oil company, Assis de Chateaubriand promptly fired him. He did what every popular newspaperman does in such cases: he started his own newspaper, the *Tribuna da Imprensa*.

As publisher and editor in chief of the *Tribuna da Imprensa*, Lacerda enjoyed the same privileges as the circles he had hitherto attacked—and continued to attack. He, too, drew heavily on the Banco do Brasil. He, too, accepted a shower of credits and foreign exchange from the bank. Thus Carlos Lacerda profited from an economic system that he had declared war on; he enriched himself from the funds of a government which he constantly flayed in a succession of wildly aggressive editorials, whose members he denounced as a "corrupt gang of murderers." This fanatical opponent of Getulio Vargas, whom he ultimately destroyed, was at the same time making his own little pile from the policies of Vargas.

A SMILING DICTATORSHIP

Getulio Vargas, builder of the new Brazil, was a politician altogether out of the usual run. He cannot be measured by the standards we apply to other Latin American dictators. The Brazilians called his first administration "the smiling dictatorship." Vargas could strike hard if anyone attempted to block his political ideas, but he was also generous in forgiving and forgetting.

In the eyes of the communists, he was a "hireling of the capitalists." But in 1932 the powerful coffee, finance, commercial, and industrial groups financed a revolt against him, which he put down swiftly and with little fuss. The moneyed oligarchy called Getulio Vargas an anti-capitalist and socialist.

All the same, in 1934 the communists and left socialists instigated a rebellion against him, which he repressed with similar briskness and severity. He banned the Communist Party and imprisoned its leader, the still-popular veteran Communist Luis Carlos Prestes, for ten years. Because of this conduct, the fascist countries of Europe for some time regarded Vargas as their friend. But in 1938 he almost singlehandedly fought off a coup by the Integralists, the Brazilian fascists, who were attempting to storm the Presidential Palace. Thereafter he outlawed the fascist Greenshirts. Gradually it became clear that Vargas was neither capitalist nor socialist nor fascist. He was a wholehearted Riograndian.

Before the Vargas era, it had been customary for the country's two economically most powerful states to provide the president alternately. The chief of state was either a Paulista from the coffee empire or a Mineiro from Minas Gerais, the great mining state. Vargas, however, came from the cattle-raising state of Rio Grande do Sul, whose ties with the rest of Brazil have always been rather loose. Since he had no connection with Brazilian coffee planting and few contacts with old Brazilian traditions, he was able to turn the country inside out during the fifteen years of his first administration, with splendid unconcern for existing interlocking interests.

In oligarchic circles, Vargas remains to this day the great bugbear who is blamed for all the errors and omissions of Brazilian policy during the past thirty-five years. But the common people have spun a legend around the "father of the poor," similar to the Argentine legend of Evita Perón. As it happens, the Vargas legend has a far greater validity than the Evita legend. For his social legislation became the model for social-welfare laws in other Latin American countries. Vargas fought for racial equality and propagated his theory of the *raça brasileira*, the merging of all three color groups in Brazil. He worked for the assimilation of the heterogeneous elements in the population, and made sure that stubborn immigrants from Italy and Germany, who had hitherto shut themselves off from the rest of the people, learned to speak Portuguese. He drained swamps, disinfected ports plagued by yellow fever, built low-cost housing and innumerable schools. He did everything that social reformers in other Latin American countries had done or intended. Since there had been no significant reformist movement in Brazil, no vigorous socialist or socialist-liberal party, the rich *gaúcho* from Rio Grande do Sul became the symbol and the architect of social reconstruction for a quarter of a century. Only the favelas resisted Vargas' efforts at reform.

Lacerda first appeared on the scene during Vargas' second adminis-

tration. In 1945, as we have mentioned, the powerful opposition forced
the dictator to abdicate. The oligarchy's candidate in the elections
that followed was an air force general named Eduardo Gomes, but
the presidency was won by Gaspar Dutra, the war minister in the
Vargas cabinet, who had once put down the Paulista rebellion against
Vargas. The Dutra administration dedicated itself successfully to the
task of converting the previous dictatorship into a parliamentary
democracy. Yet the most popular senator in the new democratic
Brazil, the man who had garnered the majority of the votes of the
common people, was the former dictator, Getulio Vargas.

Since the Aliança Liberal, with which Vargas had originally marched
to victory in his revolution, had long since broken up, the ex-dictator
had to found a new party for a political base. He called it the *Partido
Trabalhista Brasileiro*, the "Brazilian Workers' Party." In 1950, when
Vargas ran for president, it was the smallest party in the country.
But Vargas' social legislation had made so deep an impression on the
Brazilian people that this small party defeated all its rivals. The
outcome of the election was a political sensation. Vargas was anything
but persona grata with North American businessmen; his anticapital-
ism and his battle against foreign companies had prompted American
concerns to pump millions of dollars into the anti-Vargas parties. But
neither the National Democratic Union under General Gomes nor the
middle-class party of Cristiano Machado, which called itself Partido
Socialdemocrata, were a match for Vargas. Two decades after his
victorious revolution and five years after his overthrow, the man who
since 1930 had been the personification of Brazilian politics moved
back into the Palace in Rio de Janeiro, this time as a democratically
elected president. He was one of the very few former dictators who
had kept the favor of the populace.

POLITICS AND CORRUPTION

In that year, 1950, Carlos Lacerda for the first time raised his
voice in sharpest protest against Getulio Vargas. He could not find
any irregularities in the election procedures, which had been perfectly
on the up and up. He therefore commented mockingly: "The Brazilian
people have legally voted for the wrong candidate."

Lacerda had gradually changed his plumage, transforming himself from a socialist to a conservative. He made his *Tribuna da Imprensa* more and more the mouthpiece of the National Democratic Union, of which he is now the president. The Brazilian National Democrats, once an emphatically Catholic clerical party, then a party of the millionaires, have in time developed into nationalistic rightist oppositionists who mask their struggle against all kinds of social reform behind the slogan of anticommunism. Like many an ex-socialist who has veered to the side of the extreme right, Lacerda became a rabid Red-baiter.

The second Vargas regime provided him with a variety of pretexts for attacks in his newspaper and in the congress. Vargas himself, however, was acknowledged even by his bitterest enemies to be absolutely honest; not even Lacerda was able to charge him with corruption or unsavory intrigues. On the other hand, an assortment of unscrupulous persons had collected in the "old man's" shadow and were adroitly making money out of the Brazilian economic situation and their understanding of the Brazilian mentality. Various cases of corruption were uncovered, and Lacerda gloatingly made the most of them. The conservative press blamed these affairs on the government. Politicians who worked with Vargas also had a hand in equivocal dealings. One of them was destined to play a dark part in Brazilian politics later on. He was Adhemar de Barros, the Governor of São Paulo.

De Barros, representative of an influential group of enterpreneurs in São Paulo, used to campaign with the slogan: "I steal, but I get things done!" He had founded a new party which he called the "Party for Social Progress." What Adhemar de Barros meant by "social progress" was demonstrated by the rapid growth of his personal fortune, estimated by now as between two and three hundred million dollars. Officially, he claimed his net worth at only twenty-three million dollars, probably for reasons of taxation. The basis for his wealth was an illegal form of gambling known as *bicho*. He ran this racket on a vast scale, controlling most of the bicho banks, maintaining his own radio and warning system, and enjoying a weekly turnover of many millions of cruzeiros.

One of Getulio Vargas' gravest errors was his association with the bicho king, on whom he relied to win him new supporters among the recalcitrant Paulistas. Adhemar de Barros was not interested in Vargas' social policies. He went along only because he had discovered that politics was even more profitable than gambling. The method of corruption he invented was simple but absolutely reliable. Anyone who had business dealings with the state of São Paulo, or who wanted any sort of concession, had to desposit a sum of money in a *caixinha*, an account that was at Adhemar's personal disposal. Thus manufacturers, merchants, government suppliers, night-club owners, and brothel proprietors paid tribute to Adhemar de Barros. The governor spent part of the fund for public buildings, but large sums—how large cannot be determined—found their way into his own pocket.

"With us, there is the closest link between corruption and competence in office," a São Paulo newspaper once wrote, commenting on the governor. "The one cannot exist without the other." The Brazilian state prosecutor's office took a different view. It launched a number of indictments and suits against Adhemar de Barros for fraud, embezzlement, and theft. Vargas was once forced to arrest this champion of social progress and ultimately to break with him completely. But De Barros was never convicted.

This case would only have been one among many, rating no more than a marginal note in a history of Brazilian politics, if Carlos Lacerda had not repeatedly fetched up this scandal. Lacerda whipped the servant and meant the master—he denounced the corrupt Governor of São Paulo in order to discredit Getulio Vargas' social policies.

Since the slogan of "corruption" was to play a great part in subsequent events, it is necessary for us to describe the peculiar climate of the Vargas era. Before Vargas, Brazil had been dominated by the descendants of the former colonial masters: a sated feudal class, concerned only with its own well-being, regarding the land and the people as a mere source of profit. The "Father of the Poor" then imported into Brazil the *caudillo* tradition heretofore only indigenous in the Spanish countries of the Americas. Along with him, a whole new class of politicians came to power, to whom the heritage of the feudal slave and plantation era was alien.

In order not to be displaced entirely, the old feudal class had to join the new elite, and did so wherever it was given the opportunity. The consequence was nepotism of unprecedented proportions. Irresponsibility, waste, bribery, tax dodging, debasement of government morality, and other symptoms of decay sprang up with the luxuriance of jungle growth behind the back of the "grand old man." When politicians like Lacerda, Quadros, and Castelo Branco tried to cut a few clearings in that undergrowth, they were acting quite rightly.

The difficulty was that Lacerda, apparently, was not really so exercised over the corruption of the Vargas regime. His attacks on it seem to have been a hypocritical screen; in reality he was exercised over the president's social and economic measures, which the oligarchy did not like at all. The oligarchy was no less corrupt than the adherents of Vargas whom Lacerda denounced; and the bellicose journalist knew that perfectly well. He finally went so far—in the spring of 1964—as to join forces with the man who was known throughout Brazil as the "king of corruption"—Adhemar de Barros. Together with the ex-governor and gambling king, he made a decisive contribution to the overthrow of the Goulart administration. The nimbus of a brave fighter against corruption and for clean government scarcely sits well on Lacerda.

Lacerda is a brilliant stylist and a gifted polemicist. The Brazilian people are highly susceptible to political editorials that are written with verve. Rhetoric and stylistic brilliance count for more with them than facts and logical argument. In the long run, Lacerda's journalistic barrages against the social legislation, the foreign-exchange rules, and the corruption of the Vargas administration had their effect. Moreover, Vargas had the typical gaúcho's loyalty to his friends, even when they had committed grave missteps. Some of the members of the Vargas government, including the president of the Banco do Brasil, had demonstrably enriched themselves out of government funds. Vargas did not drop them. Instead, he sacrificed to the anger of the people his labor minister, João Goulart, who had decisively contributed to the drafting of Brazil's social legislation, and whom the oligarchy particularly hated.

Corruption has always been a fact of life in Brazil. Undoubtedly the intricate foreign-exchange regulations of the Vargas period, with their many loopholes and opportunities for manipulation, were an inducement to fraud for many businessmen and statesmen. Even though no one believed that Vargas himself was implicated in these dealings, the scandals Lacerda played up in his articles and editorials ultimately produced a governmental crisis which erupted into ugly violence.

THE END OF THE FATHER OF THE POOR

On August 5, 1954, there was an assassination attempt against the troublemaking journalist. Lacerda was only wounded in the foot, but his companion, an air force major, lost his life. Lacerda promptly sat down at the typewriter and bluntly accused the president and his clique of being behind the plot. The air force was also up in arms, since one of its men had been the victim.

When investigations showed that a Negro named Gregorio, a member of the president's bodyguard, had in fact instigated the attempted assassination out of loyalty to his employer and anger at the journalist, the air force staged a coup and occupied the Presidential Palace. It has never been proved that Vargas personally had anything to do with the attempted assassination. But the rightist journalist skillfully contrived to wrap himself in the mantle of a martyr. And the generals of the air force, which had all along sympathized with the conservative groups, now saw their time had come to at last get rid of the hated socialistic government.

The subsequent events unfolded like the scenes of a Greek tragedy. Vargas knew that success of the air force coup would bring his political enemies to power. He saw his life's work threatened. Therefore he decided to snatch the martyr's crown from Carlos Lacerda and place it on himself. If he were not overthrown, but voluntarily took his own life, the vice-president would have to succeed him, according to the Brazilian Constitution, and new elections would be held. The people could then use the ballot to block the reactionaries. To preserve his life's work, on August 24, 1954, Getulio Vargas put an end to his own life. His last hour was his greatest.

Vargas left a testament that belongs among the most impressive documents in Brazilian history. Carlos Lacerda immediately branded it a forgery. But there is no evidence for his assertion. The testament exerted such power on the Brazilian people that it gave rise, immediately after its publication, to that Vargas legend which still dominates Brazilian politics. Sworn enemies of the late president told me in 1956 that of all Getulio Vargas' infamies his testament had been the worst; that by it he had fixed Brazilian policy along his lines for many years to come. There is no doubt that the testament has represented a sacred trust for Brazilian social reformers; it at last brought together Getulio Vargas' workers' party and the party of the middle-class social democrats.

"After decades of domination and exploitation of Brazil by international business and financial groups," the testament reads, "I have led a revolution to victory and established a regime of social freedom. But the international companies were soon joined by national groups that rebelled against the regime of freedom. The foreign companies made profits of up to five hundred per cent. They demonstrably deprived the state of more than a hundred million dollars by false evaluations of import goods. . . .

"My opponents cannot accuse me of any wrongdoing; they can only insult me. They are not waging an open struggle against me; they take refuge in slanders. Hate campaigns were launched against me because I had demanded an increase in minimum wages. Month after month, day after day, hour after hour, I fought, stood up to the endless attacks, suffered in silence, forgetting myself, denying myself, only in order to defend the people—the people who are now left unprotected. I can give you no more than my blood. I sacrifice this blood not to the vultures who want to go on savagely rending the people, but to all of you. I choose this road in order to be with you always. . . .

"When hunger knocks at your doors, you will feel in your hearts the strength to continue my struggle for yourselves and your children. . . . My sacrifice will unite you. To those who think they have overcome me, I oppose my victory. I depart from life to enter history."

The Latin pathos in this farewell letter affected even the insurgent air force generals so greatly that the coup came to nothing. A vast crowd surged through the streets of Rio when the president's body was brought to the airport to be returned home to Rio Grande do Sul. Only the Catholic Church held aloof. Vargas, in his own words, had always regarded the Church merely "as a fact one must reckon with in politics."

THE KUBITSCHEK ERA

A year later, Brazil elected her new president. The workers' party and the social democrats had united behind Juscelino Kubitschek, the social democratic governor of Minas Gerais. Kubitschek had pledged himself to carry out the commands of the Vargas testament. The people elected as Kubitschek's vice-president the then leader of the workers' party, João Goulart, the controversial labor minister of the Vargas government.

The opposition had little to oppose to the Vargas legend, on which Kubitschek and Goulart founded their campaign. Lacerda beat the propaganda drums for Juarez Távora, the conservative general. The Paulistas tried to promote Adhemar de Barros, who had meanwhile lost his governorship in São Paulo to a rank outsider named Jánio Quadros. The fascistic Integralists also felt their hour may have struck, and placed their leader, Plinio Salgado, on the ballot. But the alliance between the two socialistic parties held. Kubitschek received more than a quarter of the votes; and since, moreover, many opposition deputies regarded him with tolerance, he had a parliamentary majority to work with.

Lacerda, however, published the rumor that Kubitschek had won the election only by virtue of communist votes. He started a press campaign against the new president which yielded nothing in virulence to his former attacks on Vargas. Since the charge of corruption had proved to be a highly effective one, the *Tribuna da Imprensa* accused the social-democratic president of all sorts of illegal affairs and financial manipulations. A coup against Kubitschek was averted at the last moment by Marshal Henrique Texeira Lott, the minister of war, who was also commander-in-chief of the army.

The Kubitschek era was marked by a vigorous upsurge in industrial and power production, a doubling of the highway network, and a great participation of foreign investors in the Brazilian economy —those investors whom Vargas had castigated as urubus ("vultures") and foreign-exchange swindlers. Kubitschek, half European himself, did not have the xenophobic nationalistic pride of the typical Riograndian. He wanted to invigorate the Brazilian economy by priming it with foreign money. But above all, the Kubitschek era has entered history in the form of a gigantic monument: the building of a new capital, "erected by the will of one man and the hope of a nation," as André Malraux put it. The Czech-Austrian-Portuguese Brazilian Juscelino Kubitschek, together with Lucio Costa, a Brazilian born in France, and Oscar Niemeyer, a Brazilian of German-mulatto extraction, created in the interior of the state of Goiás the wonderful metropolis of Brasilia, architecturally the most grandiose city in the world.

We shall have occasion in a later section to talk about Brazil's architecture, Brasilia, and the resultant new wave of inflation. Kubitschek made a number of new enemies, first, because his building program overstrained the budget, and, secondly, because he forced his ministers and congressmen to move from charming, luxurious Rio to incomplete, neoclassic Brasilia. Moreover, Kubitschek too did not succeed in controlling the demon of coffee. The president was a Mineiro from the industrial state of Minas Gerais, and was as antagonistic to the monoculture of coffee as the gaúcho Vargas. In 1960 thirty-four million sacks of unsalable coffee were once more heaped up in the warehouses. The support purchases placed an almost intolerable strain on government finances. The money Kubitschek needed to transform the fourth-largest country in the world into a supermodern industrial nation was instead continuing to flow into the pockets of the coffee planters. The cost of living doubled; inflation kept the printing presses running without pause, turning out new bank notes.

Nevertheless, the Vargas legend has been enriched by a Kubitschek chapter. Kubitschek continued the social policies of Getulio Vargas, although he, too, could not put to flight the misery of the favelados. Even more than Vargas, he stimulated industrialization and the conquest of the vast interior, in order to liberate Brazil from the curse of coffee. Continued building of schools steadily diminished the vast army of illiterates and increased the army of voters—chiefly voters who presumably favored both leftist parties.

The Labor Party and the Social Democrats, the two leftist government parties, seemed to have so many followers among the people that in October 1960 they confidently counted on victory and therefore on being able to continue the Vargas-Kubitschek policies. As in most Latin American countries, a Brazilian president cannot run in the next elections: at least one administration must intervene before he is entitled to run again. Therefore the Labor Party and the Social Democrats put up Marshal Texeira Lott, the war minister and commander-in-chief of the army who had suppressed the coup against Kubitschek. Marshal Lott was considered to be fairly leftist, and hence a man with appeal to the masses. But since he held the highest military rank in Brazil, the leftist parties thought he would also be acceptable to conservative circles.

By this time, Carlos Lacerda had made himself somewhat ridiculous with his demagogic efforts to discredit the Kubitschek regime.

Lacerda's prospects, and those of his political friends and sponsors, of replacing the social-welfare administration by a conservative regime appeared virtually nil in 1960. The people, it was fairly certain, would no longer put up with an air force general like Eduardo Gomes or a multimillionaire like Adhemar de Barros. Search as they might, the opponents of the Vargas and Kubitschek groups could not find in their ranks any suitable person of prominence whom they could put forth as a candidate.

THE MAN WITH THE IRON BROOM

At this point Lacerda hit on one of his cleverest ideas. The state of São Paulo, as we have mentioned, had had a political landslide a few years before. The bicho king, Adhemar de Barros, had lost the governorship to the former schoolmaster Jánio Quadros. The slogans by which he had won the election curiously resembled the slogans Lacerda had devised for his fight against Vargas and Kubitschek. Whenever he delivered a campaign speech, Quadros had displayed a twenty-five-foot iron broom as the symbol of his determination to sweep away corruption and misrule.

At first the Paulistas did not take this political amateur seriously. But Quadros proved to all that his campaign against corruption was more than just a selling point; he really meant to carry out his program. His predecessor, Adhemar de Barros, fled hastily to Paraguay. Orders went out that the new administration would countenance no waste or profiteering on the part of the coffee and industrial interests. Things were made hot for tax evaders. Quadros won the respect of the industrial socialists in the federal cabinet by transforming the Cubatão region between São Paulo and Santos into a modern, completely automated industrial center, supplied with power in part by atomic energy.

Quadros had demonstrated that a competent, idealistic outsider can sometimes achieve more than a hard-boiled professional politician. That he succeeded in São Paulo, of all states, bordered on the miraculous. He would certainly have been a suitable candidate for the two government parties, with whose aims he on the whole agreed, had he not lacked the proper party card. Quadros had once been close to the *Partido Trabalhista Brasileiro*, but parted company with it in indignation over corruption in the second Vargas administration.

Lacerda proposed to Quadros, the leftist, that he run for the presidency as the candidate of the right. Quadros, extremely ambitious and seeing no other chance for winning the highest office in the federal government, acceded. In addition, Quadros and Lacerda felt as close as Siamese twins in their struggle against corruption. The corrosive *Tribuna da Imprensa* was a suitable forum for Quadros, who had already demonstrated that he took his "iron broom" seriously. It is also probable that this nervous, oversensitive man needed the kind of vigorous, outspoken support the extremist Lacerda could give him.

Lacerda now drew upon all his talents as a publicist to create a president. The campaign of 1960 was a demonstration of the genius of this journalist. That election proved to be one of the greatest political sensations in contemporary Latin American history. Quadros the outsider brought innumerable leftist voters into his camp, in addition to the rightists who had put him up as their candidate. Under the symbol of his huge iron broom, he won the election with the largest majority in Brazilian history.

Anyone who knew Jánio Quadros and the nature of the rightist parties in Brazil could have predicted what happened next. Quadros had no intention of turning the rudder to the right. He continued the social-welfare policies of the leftists even more consistently and firmly than Vargas and Kubitschek. What the Labor Party and the Social Democrats had never dared to do, for fear of forfeiting the friendship of the United States, Quadros did with staggering self-assurance. The Communist Party was legalized once more. Ernesto Guevara, the representative of Fidel Castro, was awarded the Cross of the South, the highest Brazilian decoration. The eccentric president issued sweeping agrarian reform laws. He also initiated trade relations with the countries of the Eastern bloc and declared bluntly that henceforth Brazil would stand in the neutralist camp.

His backers might at a pinch have accepted these escapades in foreign policy if Quadros had not made matters worse by wielding his iron broom. He issued new tax regulations to close the many loopholes beloved to tax evaders. He fired corrupt officials and professional politicians. He insisted on extreme economy throughout the administration. He slowed the tempo of inflation, from which the oligarchy had hitherto profited heavily. He did not tap the treasury for bold building projects and "distressed" coffee millionaires, but used government funds to eliminate favelas, raise the standard of living of the lower classes, and other such social goals.

Quadros' austerity program was something completely new on the continent of Latin America, where no one had ever been troubled by the wasteful use of others' money. It was a feasible way for Brazil to work her way out of her foreign indebtedness and her economic and financial woes.

Lacerda, the inveterate enemy of corruption, did not exactly applaud when Quadros cleaned out the Augean stables of Brazil. On the contrary, he dropped his protégé like an adder whom he had mistakenly nourished at his bosom. His *Tribuna da Imprensa* unleashed the same sort of hate-drenched attacks upon Quadros previously directed against Vargas and Kubitschek. The rightist circles behind Lacerda were horrified that the man they had supported in the election was inexorably turning off the taps from which their money flowed. Lacerda could not, of course, denounce Jánio Quadros for using his iron broom; that would have been self-betraying. Instead he seized upon the simplest argument nowadays at the disposal of anyone, anywhere, when he dislikes a political figure. He accused Jánio Quadros of communism. (On the communist side, there is just as simple and handy an insult, for which there are a number of names: revisionism, militarism, class enemy.)

For economic reasons, and for the sake of reconciling the internal contentions within his country, Quadros was an advocate of compromise between West and East. In this his views coincided in many respects with those of President Kennedy. At the same time he was unequivocally anticommunist. Those of his actions which North Americans took in bad part sprang from considerations of political utility, not from sympathy with the East. Economic necessity, not anti-Americanism, compelled him to keep a sharp eye on the North American companies in Brazil. His gesture toward Guevara was not an anti-American act, but a demonstration of solidarity with every Latin American country, no matter what its political coloration. As early as 1961 Quadros fully realized that ultimate ejection of Cuba from the Organization of American States would not improve the global political situation, but only intensify the conflicts.

Lacerda, who had meanwhile become Governor of Guanabara, urged Brazilians to stage a revolution against Quadros. The rightist majority in the congress abandoned the president. The leftist opposition had no interest in supporting the man it had fiercely opposed during the election campaign. Quadros stood virtually alone; all the political forces in Brazil were pitted against him. Since he wanted to avoid a coup or a civil war, he resigned his office. But the masses whom Lacerda had called into the streets surged through Rio carrying placards reading: *"Jánio sim, Lacerda não!"*—"Jánio yes, Lacerda no!" The resigning president called out consolingly to them: "They are sending me away, but I shall return!"

GOULART AND THE END OF DEMOCRACY

Such was the birth of the Quadros legend, which has attached itself, almost seamlessly, to the Vargas and Kubitschek legends. Quadros, after the attacks by Lacerda which led to his downfall, had become even more popular than he was during his presidency. It is a strange phenomenon that every Brazilian president whom Lacerda deposes acquires a halo. Even Adhemar de Barros, the corrupt Governor of São Paulo, seemed to have benefited by Lacerda's former enmity. After a number of years in exile—time enough for the grass to grow over his misdeeds—he returned to the campaign trail and won the governorship again.

In bringing down Jánio Quadros, Lacerda had played an extremely risky game, which boomeranged. In Brazil, the president and vice-president are elected separately. It can therefore happen that the president may be a rightist, the vice-president a leftist. Such was the case this time. The vice-president in Quadros' administration, and therefore his legal successor, was Getulio Vargas' former labor minister and Kubitschek's one-time deputy, João Goulart, who also headed the Labor Party. And Goulart was in fact many degrees more radical than Quadros. He represented the left and socialistic wing of his party. Lacerda and the entire right did everything in their power to prevent Goulart's succeeding to the presidency. Riots and uprisings, which Quadros had wanted to avoid, broke out nevertheless. But Marshal Texeira Lott, the defender of legality, once again saw to the preservation of the constitution. Under protection of the army, Goulart assumed the presidency of Brazil.

There was a brief interlude of powerlessness for Goulart; the right attempted to interpose a strong premier, after the European model, between the president and the direct exercise of his power. But

Goulart regained his full executive powers after winning a referendum. Following the congressional elections of 1962, the leftist parties once more won a majority in the congress. Under the aegis of Goulart, the iron broom was less in evidence. Brazilian foreign policy slipped as far to the left as was possible under the circumstances, with due consideration for the feelings of North American creditors. The president's brother-in-law, Leonel Brizola, Governor of Rio Grande do Sul, was already being denounced by the excessively nervous press as a Brazilian Fidel Castro because he has set about nationalizing the power plants and telephone companies of the gaúcho state and introducing agrarian reform.

The enforced departure of Jânio Quadros has not given the Brazilian oligarchy any peace, nor has it put an end to the Brazilian Government's flirtation with the East. Thanks to Lacerda's demagoguery, Brazil was to turn redder than she had ever been during the Goulart era. At the same time, the vast country grew economically more unstable and politically a good deal more susceptible to sedition than during the administrations of the three presidents whom Lacerda so viciously attacked.

The Goulart regime has been called a "dictatorship of fatuous irresponsibility, careless spending, immoderate demagoguery and unrestrained corruption." And Lacerda was, as may be imagined, one of Goulart's most vociferous critics. He hammered away at the frightening inflation, inveighed against the absence of an iron broom, against the continual social unrest, against the "demoralization of the people," and against Brazil's declining international credit rating. He pilloried the leftist tendencies of the president and painted in the most glaring colors the rising danger of communism. The former fighter against corruption became a crusader against communism, by which Lacerda means any kind of reformist policy other than his own. He made much of the fact that the president did not participate in the moral condemnation of Castro, to him a sure sign of Goulart's being soft on communism. To be sure, while President Kennedy was alive, Goulart had hailed the Alliance for Progress in emphatically pro-American terms, but he had also continued Jânio Quadros' policy of reconciliation and neutrality. "Brazil believes," Goulart once explained, "that not hostility but contact between our democratic world and the socialistic world of the East, contact which leads to an exchange of experiences on both sides, can prove useful to the nations of the world."

Certainly the democratic social-reformist era of this last President of Brazil was less satisfactory to the West than those of his predecessors Vargas, Kubitschek, and Quadros. But there were no grounds for the charge that he led Brazil toward communism by giant steps. Goulart's downfall came when he planned two measures that infuriated the oligarchy and the ultrarightists even more than all previous acts. First, he wanted to grant the suffrage to illiterates. His purpose was, no doubt, to assure the left a majority for the foreseeable future, but it was a progressive measure nonetheless. Secondly, he wanted to put a check on the rampant land speculation following from the expansion of communications throughout the country, and from the vigorous road-building program. This was a body blow to the speculators, who were frenetically driving up prices for unknown parcels of jungle in the interior.

The campaign against the president reached a climax at this point. Only a small pretext was needed to set off all the well-prepared tinder with explosive violence. The pretext came when a naval unit mutinied. Though the mutiny was suppressed, the president was not sufficiently severe with the sailors who had rebelled against their officers; they were soon pardoned and released from prison. The proud officers regarded such clemency as a slap in the face for them. They started a coup which spread in a chain reaction from the navy and air force to the army and then to the densely populated, influential states of Guanabara, São Paulo, and Minas Gerais.

Unlike Getulio Vargas, Goulart did not have the makings of a hero. For a few days he tried to hold out in his native state of Rio Grande do Sul, which had remained loyal to him, then he fled across the border to Uruguay. His regime collapsed almost as soon as the fighting began. The government might possibly have been able to stand against the two rightist governors, Lacerda in Guanabara and Adhemar de Barros in São Paulo, and their military and civilian following. But the bourgeois Social Democrats had also long ago become discontented with Goulart's leftist leanings and with the incompetence of the government. Social Democratic politicians, such as, for example, the Governor of Minas Gerais, took the side of the rebels. Even Kubitschek remained at least neutral. And the attitude of the army then proved crucial. Unlike the navy and the air force, the

Brazilian army habitually has stood strictly on the side of legality. The recent history of Brazil has seen a whole series of disturbances verging on civil war, in which the navy or air force rebelled against the government. But in all these episodes the army had defended the constitution and the president. In contrast to the castes, camarillas, cliques, clans, and juntas in the Spanish American countries, the Brazilian army officers and generals come from the middle class rather than from the feudal sector of the population. They have manifested no urgent desire to win political power. Prominent and influential army men like Marshal Texeira Lott have, on the contrary, faithfully served the government party and the administration. Consequently, there have been no army dictators in the recent history of Brazil, up to 1964.

This time, however, the army—aside from Marshal Texeira Lott and a few loyal units—emphatically threw its weight on the side of the rightist rebels. Generals took power. It is possible that they did so in the hope of avoiding worse disasters. "Worse disasters" would have meant letting the ultras around Lacerda take power and thus handing Brazil over to fascism or some similar extreme militant rightist dictatorship.

General Humberto Castelo Branco became the new head of state. Thus democracy was liquidated in the largest and most populous country of Latin America—a much maligned but quite successful, typically Brazilian form of democracy. In its place came dictatorship —but also a typically Brazilian form of dictatorship.

A COUP IS NO REVOLUTION

The *coup d'état* of March 31, 1964, is often called a "revolution" and equated with progressive popular revolutions that in the past have overthrown tyrannies. But a military coup is not a revolution. President Goulart may have failed, but he was certainly no tyrant. And the people took only a passive part in the Brazilian upheaval.

General Castelo Branco stubbornly continues to refer to his regime as a "revolutionary government"; he bases this claim on his strenuous efforts to reform Brazil and free the country of her worst national vices. In this respect he is basically trying only to follow in the footsteps of the overthrown and defamed Jánio Quadros. His program too is: honesty, thrift, austerity.

His government has ventured to collect, actually collect, the taxes imposed by law. It is trying to place Brazil's finances on a sound footing, and to make all classes of the population, rich and poor alike, grasp the bitter truth that prosperity does not come from printing presses interminably producing more currency, but only from the gross national product. It is demanding of its citizens things that have been highly uncommon in Brazil: meeting of obligations, personal sacrifices, honesty, modesty. Castelo Branco is acting like a physician who at the bedside of a drug addict prescribes a radical "cold turkey" cure. The patient, Brazil, does not like it; with each passing week the doctor becomes more unpopular.

Europe and the United States have placed great hopes in the general and conferred unusual laurels upon him. He enjoys the approval of the West not only because of his plan to straighten out Brazil's finances, but also, and chiefly, because he has smashed the leftist parties. In addition, Castelo Branco (unlike other recent Latin American rulers) has been following strictly American prescriptions for tightening the economy of his country and replacing the previous galloping inflation by a deflation. The military government has abolished subsidies for wheat and fuel and increased general government income, thereby reducing the deficit—at least according to semiofficial statistics—by 60 per cent. It is permitting prices to rise and at the same time freezing wages, with the aim of reducing purchasing power.

This forced deflation is taking place, of course, chiefly at the expense of the already wretched common man. The poor no longer have money for the barest necessities. Unemployment is growing by leaps and bounds. Whole branches of industry have been plunged into a frightening depression. In 1965 the government had to spend more than one and a half billion dollars to stimulate the economy, in violation of its own principles. It has long since become one of the most unpopular governments in the history of Brazil. Even among the groups that initially hailed it, enthusiasm has sunk to the zero point.

Thus the military regime by no means deserves those laurels. It has forfeited the favor of the people and lost the support of the oligarchy as well. Until Castelo Branco took over, manufacturers and traders counted on 100, 200, or even higher percentages of profits. Now they must be satisfied with much lower incomes, and in addition actually pay their taxes. A black and gray market in exchange transactions has led to a number of financial scandals involving even such respected companies as the Brazilian affiliate of the German Mannesmann Works. After the scandal was uncovered, Mannesmann Director Jorge Serpa Filho was arrested. The story is that Lacerda's dreaded political police in Rio de Janeiro forced him by torture to "confess" that his embezzlements had been made in order to finance a counterrevolution by Goulart.

Even more shocking were the measures that Castelo Branco's regime took against his political opponents soon after his seizing power. Most politicians fled, abandoning their jobs and posts. Political mandates were quashed in large numbers; former congressmen, senators, cabinet ministers, and governors were sent to prison or had to flee abroad. The two former presidents, Kubitschek and Quadros, were stripped of their right to vote and to run for office. Such massive attacks on political freedom were painfully reminiscent of Hitler's seizure of power. Still, Castelo Branco was at least generous enough to allow Kubitschek to depart for Europe, and Quadros to continue practicing law in São Paulo. And most of the politicians who were arrested in 1964, in the initial fervor of the overturn, have since been released.

If we put all these factors together, we see that the dictatorship of General Castelo Branco is a curious phenomenon. It has its reactionary aspects, but it is also directed against the rich. It has reformed the economy, but it has been careful not to touch the regulated coffee industry. It has arrested alleged and actual practitioners of corruption, but it has permitted the chief of them all, Adhemar de Barros, to remain in office as Governor of São Paulo. It imprisons democrats of the most varied hues, but it does not dare to ban, censor, or punish a single newspaper. It permitted elections in the townships and the states in 1965, even though it is by no means firmly seated in the saddle.

That was demonstrated with particular clarity by the local elections in the state of São Paulo in the spring of 1965. There, in the second largest city of the Americas, the opposition candidate, Faria Lima, won by an enormous margin and moved into the town hall as Mayor of São Paulo. The elections were tranquil, free, and unobstructed; every political party with the exception of the Communists was permitted to run candidates and campaign as freely as under the democracy. Within Brazil the victory of Faria Lima was regarded as a vote for democracy and against the Castelo Branco regime. But it was more than that: it was a clear manifestation of attachment to a popular ex-president. For Faria Lima was one of Jánio Quadros' men. In his campaign he openly inscribed the name of the man with the iron broom on his banners. One might say that the election was actually won by Quadros, whom the dictatorship had barred from political life.

QUO VADIS BRASILIA?

In spite of his arbitrary measures, Castelo Branco still seems too moderate to that eternal troublemaker Lacerda and the other rightist fanatics. The ultras are not pleased that the opposition is again allowed to agitate, that the press is not muzzled, and that elections are being held. The general has made it quite clear that he regards his regime as only transitional, and that he seriously means to permit new elections for the congress and the presidency in 1966. But what will happen then?

The ultras are trying to force the government in a fascist direction. Lacerda's sympathies for European fellow rightists, as for instance the French extremists, are so strong and so outspoken that General de Gaulle took affront and deliberately cut the militant Governor of Guanabara during his visit to South America in 1964. Lacerda responded with violent attacks on the French chief of state. General Castelo Branco was grieved at such treatment of a guest, but in many cases he cannot successfully oppose the ultras and semifascists.

The army regime has done virtually nothing to solve Brazil's burning social problems. The terrible misery in the poorest states of the northeast has grown even more acute since the deflation and the suppression of radical peasant movements. Many of those who know the country prophesy a bloody uprising of the *Nordistas* in coming years. Unquestionably, the army has not fulfilled the hopes of the masses in Brazil. In the long run President Johnson will probably find it by no means a gain for his Latin American policy that the Brazilian military men have leaned so closely on Washington.

"Carlos the Terrible" is a master at toppling presidents. But he fails when he makes a president—for, like Quadros, Castelo Branco seems to be the wrong man for him. At present, he is not trying to overthrow still another president, and thus perhaps add to the existing Vargas, Kubitschek, Quadros, and Goulart legends a Castelo Branco legend.

This time his purpose is to pave the way for a new president whom Carlos Lacerda considers absolutely trustworthy. This new candidate for the presidency is named Carlos Lacerda.

THE WHITE SOUTH

In area and population, Brazil is as large as all the other South American countries taken together. Brazil is a world in itself, a subcontinent, each of whose regions has its own distinctive character. Between the gaúchos in the deep south, the *Nordistas, Cearenses,* and *Garimpeiros* in the poor northeast, the Paulistas and Mineiros in the prosperous agricultural and industrial states, the Cariocas and Bahians on the coast, and the *caboclos* and Sertanejos in the remote interior, there are contrasts sometimes even sharper than those between Cubans, Mexicans, Chileans, Argentines, Peruvians, and Venezuelans. The common bonds are language and history.

In all the discussions centering around the hopeful vision of a future United States of Europe, much is made of a common history, an interdependency in politics, economics, and culture, but much is also made of the problem of reducing to a common denominator the varying characters of different nations. In Brazil this diversity in character in the various states of the federal union is no less considerable. If we set aside the common language and common history, we can scarcely imagine greater contrasts than those between a native of the boundless plains of Rio Grande do Sul and the small planter or jungle dweller in the north, between the entrepreneur or industrial worker in the central south and the Negro in a working-class suburb of Bahia, who still lives in terms of African cults. The national and linguistic differences of Europe are small compared to the regional, anthropological, and social differences in Brazil.

A MULTINATIONAL COUNTRY—AND STILL A NATION

Nevertheless, in spite of the idiosyncrasies and the separatist aspirations of many regions, the Brazilians have succeeded, without any great stir, in creating the United States of Brazil. It is a federal union in which the descendants of Portuguese colonists live together with the descendants of African slaves and Indian aboriginals, with people of mixed blood and all shades of skin, and with millions of Italian, Iberian, German, Slavic, Oriental, and Far Eastern immigrants. Brazil is a multinational country, and still a nation. In spite of some tensions and dissonances, the many peoples of Brazil are gradually merging, as Brazilian statesmen and intellectuals have long hoped, into a Brazilian people and a Brazilian race.

Aside from Venezuela, South America's largest country is the only federation on the continent. And the fact that Venezuela rather bombastically calls herself "*Estados Unidos*" is due less to geographical, historical, and ethnological necessity than to the exaggerated separatism of the Venezuelan provinces. Argentina once manifested similar tendencies, before Hipólito Irigoyen put an end to the federalistic nuisance. The federal structure of Brazil, however, is completely justified—even more justified than that of the United States of America. Each of the twenty states has its own constitution, its own executive and legislature elected by the people. In addition to the twenty states there are five federal territories which are destined to develop into states, and which enjoy a conditional autonomy. As in Anglo-Saxon federations, Brazil also has a federal district with a federal capital. At present this *Distrito Federal* consists of the vast building site of Brasilia and the surrounding savannas.

A journey through the entire Brazilian subcontinent is almost as varied ethnologically, sociologically, climatologically, and visually as a journey across the great Afro-Eurasian land mass. There are big cities, as for example Curitiba, the capital of the state of Paraná, which would not look odd if they were situated in Europe—except for that special quality known as *brasilidade*. There are peasant districts in which Slavic settlers still ride around in old Russian troikas, and rural small towns which look like tropical variants of German market towns or Italian communes—except for *brasilidade*. There are skyscraper metropolises like São Paulo or Belo Horizonte whose scale and tempo, both of traffic and work, are reminiscent of North American supercities—except for *brasilidade*.

In the vicinity of Santos you ride past tea plantations and residential areas so Japanese in appearance that you almost forget what continent this is. On the coast of Bahia, with its palm-leaf-roofed huts, its glaring white beaches, and naked black men who ride the surf on *jangadas,* a kind of raftlike surfboard, you feel transported back to an African way of life that scarcely exists any longer in Africa. When the gaúchos of Rio Grande do Sul sit under their national tree, the enormous, swollen, spongy *umbú,* preparing their *churrasco,* celebrating their weddings, baptisms, and funerals, you may think you are on the Argentine pampas or a Chilean *fundo.* And when you take a boat along a jungle river and see peering out of the *sertão* the lush fringing forest, the painted, ornamentally scarred, and pierced-lipped faces of an Indian hunting tribe—then it is as if you have returned to the Stone Age.

But everywhere, on the Afro-Brazilian coast, in the Indio-Brazilian jungle, and even in the Chinese or Japanese villages, where scarcely a word of Portuguese is spoken, some elements of brasilidade, of the typically Brazilian character, have entered.

POLITICS ON HORSEBACK

There was no deep-seated reason why the three states of the deep south—the plains country of Rio Grande do Sul, the former jungle of Santa Catarina, and the magnificent panorama of mountains and forests which is Paraná—should have found their way into the Portuguese colonial empire and later into the United States of Brazil. They did so partly because of the expansion tendencies of the bandeirantes, partly because Brazil so ardently fostered European immigration, and chiefly because of the distinct character of the Brazilian gaúcho.

Unlike his Argentine counterpart, the Brazilian gaúcho has an accent on the *u;* and that is not just a matter of spelling, but of character and mentality. The Riograndians practiced politics on horseback. They have always been fiery rebels, fighters for freedom, and warriors for justice. They did not particularly oppress the pampas Indians, but mingled and mixed with them with little friction. The chaos in the states of the La Plata region was alien to them, they liked it no more than they did the lethargic hothouse atmosphere of the Brazilian Empire. Consequently, they fought on all sides in order to obtain free air for breathing—as much independence as there was to gain.

As early as the middle of the nineteenth century Pedro II had to deal with the Farrapen Revolution, an uprising of the gaúchos of the southern states in which that intrepid Italian hero Garibaldi participated. At that time Rio Grande do Sul and Santa Catarina came within a hairsbreadth of independence, for the gaúchos could scarcely be vanquished by military methods.

Emperor Pedro, however, understood the mentality of the gaúchos. When he embraced the rebels and granted them high military ranks, instead of hanging them on the nearest tree, he won the hearts of the Riograndians. The gaúchos realized that they would be more independent within the Brazilian federation than under any other regime in the world. Born politicians that they were, they saw that henceforth they could marry their regional considerations to the politics of the country as a whole—and proceeded to do so with burning passion and striking success. In addition to Presidents Vargas and Goulart, Osvaldo Aranha, the long-time foreign minister, and many other political greats of Brazil came from Rio Grande do Sul—as well as large numbers of writers and other intellectuals who shared a single philosophy: nonconformism.

Because of its moderate climate and the unlimited potentialities of its endless plains, Rio Grande do Sul exerted a magical attraction upon European immigrants. Whole regions in the state seem to be German or Italian enclaves in Brazil. But the new arrivals, whether they came from Central or Southern Europe, swiftly transformed themselves into Riograndians. The gaúcho spirit was stronger than all the peculiarities and traditions of the immigrants. A German-Brazilian from Rio Grande do Sul may go on murdering his mother tongue, which has become a kind of pidgin German, and reading his German-language newspaper, but he is primarily neither a German nor a Brazilian; he is a Riograndian. The Negroes and mulattoes in the state capital of Pôrto Alegre and along the banks of the Lagoa dos Patos, the great inland lagoon, have assumed the temperate dignity and the intransigence of the gaúchos—that heritage of the old-time Charrua, the Pampas Indians.

IMMIGRANT HABITS, GOOD AND BAD

The states of Santa Catarina and Paraná were even more heavily flooded by immigrants than Rio Grande do Sul. But in these states there was no distinctive population to assimilate the new citizens. In colonial times, the Portuguese were settled only along the coasts, where they founded a number of picturesque, sleepy, and now somewhat decrepit but uncommonly charming ports: Florianópolis, Itajaí, Paranaguá. The populations of these colorful towns, whose market places are full of bright, varied goods and all sorts of indefinable odors, were enriched by immigrants from Madeira and the Azores, who in their new homes persistently went on making the same kind of lace and using the same techniques of fishing as in their native islands.

The interior of Santa Catarina and Paraná was opened up by Europeans, some of whom to this day do not really feel themselves to be Brazilians. The Germans in Santa Catarina still constitute the majority of the population in the small state. They began clearing the jungles a hundred years ago. In the remote valleys, they became eccentrics. They constantly had trouble with the savage Indians, and cruelly reduced their numbers. The Catarinans still seem to feel in their bones the Indian wars of the past. Most Brazilian Indian reservations make an excellent impression, thanks to Brazil's highly humane aboriginal legislation. In most of the interior of Brazil there is a virtual cult connected with the primitive Indians. But the Botokuden Reservation in Santa Catarina, with its fortress-like administration buildings, looked to me like a cross between a zoo and a concentration camp.

In other aspects of their lives and conduct, the Catarinan Germans have remained eccentrics. Brasilidade involves letting everyone seek salvation in his own way. Therefore the Germans in Santa Catarina, quite unlike the readily assimilated Germans in Rio Grande do Sul, cultivated and cherished their less amiable as well as their better qualities. There were families settled in the country for a hundred years who still spoke not a word of Portuguese. In the nazi period, swastika flags were raised in Santa Catarina and the Hitler salute came into use. Those who did not go along were boycotted. The Catarinans still revile Getulio Vargas for sending in a few Negro regiments and putting an end to such goings-on.

Nevertheless, Santa Catarina has many likable aspects. The Germans have succeeded in leaving the forested landscape relatively unharmed. The little southern state must be classed among the most beautiful in the Brazilian federation, and in addition has a model administration. The same cannot be said for its neighboring state to the north, Paraná. Curitiba, a city of five hundred thousand, grew to its present size within a few decades—and throughout that period was an arena of speculative building and corruption. The handsome, boldly planned government building remains unfinished because Paraná overstrained her resources. From the empty window openings in administration buildings I saw the washing of the poor fluttering in the breeze

—squatters had settled in the skeletal structures. A magnificent avenue ended abruptly in a huge, muddy pit. In front of the governor's palace poisonous green snakes slithered through the reeds. Plump toads sat in potholes of the unfinished residential quarter.

But its incompleteness and air of improvisation make Curitiba quite attractive. Nobody seems to mind that a project is set aside for a while, and the jungle once more takes possession of an ambitious new district. Somebody, someday, will continue the building—*paciência, amanhã!* And if there is no other way out of the dilemma, somebody will always find a *jeito*. I became fonder of Curitiba, with all its touching inadequacies, than of perfected, robotlike São Paulo. It was in this capital of Paraná that I felt most distinctly the charm of brasilidade.

Virtually every ethnic, linguistic, and color group in Brazil has settled in Paraná. This state, with its mild, mountainous climate and rich stands of forest, became promising coffee country as the erosion of São Paulo worsened. At present Paraná is gaining in population more rapidly than any other state in Brazil. Deep in the interior, some thirty-five years ago, Englishmen slashed a gigantic square out of the jungle and established a coffee center to which they gave the name of Londrina, which already has more than three hundred thousand inhabitants. German exiles who had escaped from Hitler, including a number of politicians of the Weimar Republic, followed the example of the English and created their own coffee domain, Rolandia. But Paraná coffee was not the only attraction; trade, manufacturing, and other forms of agriculture in this flourishing state constantly tempted immigrants from the Old World. The influence of Slavs in Paraná is so great that you meet Poles, Russians, and Ukrainians everywhere. Many of these Slavs do not communicate with one another in their mother tongues, nor in the language of their new country. Their lingua franca is German, which they wield in much the same way as the Slavs in the former Austro-Hungarian provinces of the Balkans.

The largest contingent of immigrants consists of Italians, who have spread out from São Paulo over all the southern states. The multimillionaire Matarazzo alone was responsible for settling a hundred thousand of his former countrymen in Brazil. Many Italians have been able to make a rapid climb up the economic and social ladder. Their clan and business connections led to further immigration by their fellow countrymen. Thus there has gradually formed in Paraná, São

Paulo, and other economically promising states an Italo-Brazilian hierarchy, crowned by Italian multimillionaires and sustained by a faithful Italian following.

The German immigrants are not alone in clinging fast to many of the customs and vices of the old country. The numerous Levantines, who are engaged chiefly in trade and the amusement industry, tend to operate by methods typical of the disreputable quarters of Port Said, Beirut, or Tangier. The prefect of Paranaguá told me that his predecessor had been shot in the street by the owners of Syrian gambling dens that he was trying to close. Normally, even a conscientious prefect in Brazil thinks twice about raiding a gambling den, for a man of power and political influence may stand behind the gamblers. But the Syrians had opened their den right next to the prefecture, literally under the eyes of the law, and the prefect had felt that he could not tolerate that and preserve his reputation. He did no direct harm to the Syrians, but circulated a petition whose signatories were demanding the closing of the gambling place. That in itself was enough to provoke the Syrians to liquidate him. My informant, the present prefect, was giving the matter a wide berth. There were no clues to the murderers, he told me, and he would be careful not to find any clues.

The endless forests of Paraná have already been plundered. The Brazilian araucaria, which is akin to the Chilean national tree, has been so devastated that there is now a law providing that ten new trees must be planted for each one felled. But Paraná is big and the capital is far away. Paraná is so big that a few years ago a hitherto unknown Indian tribe was discovered there. The charms of landscape in this state of lumber and coffee are most striking where it borders on Argentina and Paraguay. Near where the three lands meet, the Iguassú Falls thunder over cliffs more than a mile and a half in width. Their beauty is heightened by the luxuriant surrounding jungles, full of magnificent flowers and wildlife, which has happily been declared a nature preserve.

THE MINING STATE

The states of the central South are: São Paulo, with its industry, its coffee, its cattle pastures, and its money; Guanabara, with the most beautiful city in the world and the resorts in the Organ Mountains, to which Cariocas flee when they can no longer bear the laundry-room climate of Rio de Janeiro; Espírito Santo, with its capital city of Vitória, which looks like a miniature edition of Rio set in rampant tropics—something akin to what the "City of Light" must once have been before it could be called, even with the best will in the world, *cidade maravilhosa*. The most important of these states, aside from São Paulo, is the industrial and mining state of Minas Gerais, the one-time goal of gold-hungry bandeirantes and the present El Dorado of the mining industry. The inhabitants of this state also have their particular and unmistakable character. Brazilian popular humor has dubbed them the Scots of South America.

Anecdotes about the proverbial stinginess of the Mineiros alternate with anecdotes about the likewise proverbial simplicity of the rural population in Minas Gerais. The Cariocas and Paulistas mock the Mineiros with a joke classic the world over at the expense of the "hick from the sticks." Anybody, the story goes, can sell the municipal streetcar line to a Mineiro; he sees the streetcars constantly taking in money, and the lure of profit is always too much for him. Such spiteful tales no doubt have their basis in the enormous tenacity and competence of the Mineiros, in their devotion to property, and their ability to use it wisely.

Like São Paulo, Minas Gerais is a state of superlatives. Nine-tenths of Brazilian iron ore is mined there, in what is recognized as the largest coherent iron-ore region on earth. In some places the ore is shoveled directly from its mine into the furnaces. On the pitch-black highways the automobiles are riding virtually over polished iron. This region could supply the whole world with iron for hundreds of years. Minas Gerais is also said to contain nine times as much manganese as the present annual world production. In colonial days, the first gold rush began here, and at various times it has been the focus for diamond and gem fevers. The birthplace of Juscelino Kubitschek bears the name of Diamantina in memory of former riches; it used to be one of the foremost cities of Minas Gerais, but has now declined to a wretched small town. Minas Gerais also has the largest bauxite, uranium, and thorium resources of Brazil, most of the baths and medicinal springs, and some of the most important ore-refining plants. Finally, the province also contains a full eighth of the Brazilian population. It is thus, after São Paulo, the most heavily populated state in the country.

The Mineiros are regarded as reserved, suspicious, and closefisted, but also as honest, scrupulous, and reliable. Innumerable administrative officials, judges, and politicians have come from among them, chief of all being ex-President Kubitschek. His rise from an impoverished student working his way through medical school to prefect of the state capital of Belo Horizonte, then to Governor of Minas Gerais and finally to President of the United States of Brazil is regarded by the Mineiros—who remained still passionately attached to him even after his fall from power and his immigration to Paris—as the symbol of their state's future. Its wealth has not begun to be exploited, and they believe that ultimately the treasure of Minas Gerais will make Brazil one of the leading economic powers in the world.

Like the Riograndians, the Mineiros are cross-grained rebels. The first revolts against the Portuguese motherland broke out in Minas Gerais because the crown demanded a fifth of the yield of gold as its share. Minas Gerais gave rise to Xavier da Silva, the rebel dentist whose martyr's death sparked the Brazilian independence movement. The place is also famed for the Negro Chico Rei, who, back in slave times, bought the freedom of countless black slaves by his work in the gold mines, and who temporarily established a black kingdom in the mountains. Another who worked, carved, and chiseled in Minas Gerais in the eighteenth century was one of the most gifted and strange artists Brazil has produced—Aleijadinho.

BAROQUE AND FUTURISM

Aleijadinho is a nickname; it means "Little Cripple." Antonio Francisco Lisbôa, the sculptor on whom this name was conferred, was a small, stocky man who in the later years of his life suffered from curious swellings of the limbs. Ultimately his toes and fingers began rotting off, so that he was forced to produce his works with the aid of artificial limbs. Whether his disease was leprosy or syphilis is unknown. But in spite of his handicaps, he created some of the most beautiful art works in the old state capital of Ouro Preto.

He was a mulatto, and legend represents him as a semi-illiterate misanthrope who taught himself his art. Local patriotism even claims that he invented the first flying machine. In reality Aleijadinho was the son of the city architect of Ouro Preto and a Negro slave girl. He was given a thorough artistic training and was anything but a troglodytic primitive. Certain peculiar aspects of his personality are due to his addiction to alcohol and various narcotics. Given this terrible disease, it is not surprising that he became a drug addict. But even those who would like to deny the colored races any artistic talent at all cannot contest the fact that he is Brazil's greatest sculptor.

Ouro Preto, where Aleijadinho worked, is a small baroque town of barely ten thousand inhabitants, one of the few Brazilian towns officially set aside as national monuments, like Carcassonne and Rothenburg ob der Tauber in Europe. As a rule, Brazilians are less interested in their past than their future. Ouro Preto, however, is an exception. Rui Barbosa of Bahia, a leading Brazilian writer and politician, has called the town "the heart of the country, the nursery of our culture, the Athens and Olympia of Brazil." The eyes of every cultivated Brazilian light up when the conversation turns to Ouro Preto. For at the bottom of his heart every Brazilian would really like to preserve something of the past. And in this town he has a past, a baroque, picturesque past, built on the hunt for gold and gems, artistically shaped by a crippled genius who plays much the same part in Brazil that the warlike figures of sagas play in other countries.

Minas Gerais long ago chose another capital instead of the old baroque town. It was the first capital created on the drawing boards, long before anyone in Brazil ventured to dream of the supermetropolis of Brasilia. In 1897 only a tiny village stood where now the city of Belo Horizonte is growing at a pace equal to that of São Paulo. The long-winded name of this village—Nossa Senhora da Bôa Viagem do Curral del Rey—would hardly do for a future metropolis. The planners drew diagrams of a star-shaped city and with confidence in the region's radiant future it was given the name "Beautiful Horizon." By 1940 Belo Horizonte was already a flourishing middle-sized city. But to the regret of the then prefect of the city, all the stylistic atrocities of traditional Brazilian architecture seemed to have found a home there. Since Brazil's architects had currently fallen under the influence of Le Corbusier, and undergone a veritable revolution which had already yielded promising results, the prefect brought a young pupil of the great Le Corbusier to Belo Horizonte. The young man was grandson of one of the city architects of Rio de Janeiro, who had done such remarkable work in the modern vein.

This young colored architect was entrusted by the prefect with the modernization of Belo Horizonte, and with the building of a satellite town named Pampulha. The two men became close friends and formed an excellent team. The architect later wrote of the prefect: "He was the ideal employer; he told me what he wanted and gave me complete artistic freedom to achieve it."

As a result of this artistic freedom, Belo Horizonte became architecturally the most modern and exciting city in the world. The architect created one of the most extravagant churches in the world, Pampulha's St. Francis chapel. It had so bold and venturesome an air that Brazilian poets wrote poems about it. The horrified clergy at first refused to consecrate the vast vault, "God's hangar," as the atheistic architect called his creation. To counter probable clerical attacks, the prefect hastily declared the building a national monument. But the faithful were so enthusiastic about the new church that the bishop at last bowed to public opinion.

The prefect who had launched the whole project was named Juscelino Kubitschek. And the architect who had this first opportunity to follow his own biddings bore the German name of Oscar Niemeyer. The great experiment that Brasilia is was tested two decades ago in Belo Horizonte—with the same two principal stars. The friendship Kubitschek then formed with Niemeyer has been largely responsible for Brazil's becoming the world's leading nation in architecture.

A profound gulf separates the rich south, with its overwhelmingly white population, from the poor northeast, with its colored majority. Between the seven flourishing southern states and the eight indigent northern states, however, lies the state that is perhaps the most Brazilian of them all—Bahia.

THE BLACK NORTH

The state of Bahia represents Black Brazil. You sense that as soon as you reach the seacoast, even before you enter the capital of Salvador-Bahia de Todos os Santos with its Negro folklore, its Afro-Brazilian church, and its black magic.

I rode through the quivering heat of the coastal landscape, past huge fleshy cacti thrusting up from the gritty yellow sand. I saw groups of tall, slender coconut palms, with their fruits the size of a child's head, and tiny huts of sun-baked clay thatched with banana leaves. In front of the huts, naked brown children tumbled in the sand. Over the beaches walked bronze-colored women with pitchers or big, silvery-scaled fish on their heads. A raft danced in the Atlantic surf, manned by dark, curly-haired, almost naked men. It was like a scene from the heart of Africa.

The Negro villages, built in long straggling rows, almost run into each other. Primitive and natural, they are nowhere near as depressing as the favelas in the capitals. They belong to the landscape just as much as the palms, the cacti and the blue-green sea. What you see along this coast is not contemporary Brazil with her mansions and slave huts. It is African Brazil, the Brazil of freed Negro slaves who in their daily life have taken up the threads dropped by their forcibly transported ancestors.

The people along this Bahia coast do not seem like white proletarians, the serfs of white civilization, but like free Africans. Nevertheless they are Brazilians; their character, too, is marked by brasilidade. Africans can conquer an alien continent just as well as Europeans; they can place their mark on it and change it exactly as whites do. The countryside around the Bay of All Saints (Todos os Santos) has been more lastingly changed by the Negroes than by the Portuguese colonizers. Negroes have given it its vital rhythm, its color, its soul.

The city of Salvador-Bahia is like an African fruit growing inside a European rind. Salvador was once the capital of the Portuguese colonial empire in America, and you can still see the imprint of the past in old Bahia. Nowhere else in Latin America does the baroque spirit present itself in such lush, overflowing tropical exuberance. Old houses in the colonial style, with narrow, pocket-handkerchief façades, stand row on row, embellished with balconies, wrought-iron gates, and allegorical stone figures, painted in the brightest colors and showing the wear and tear of the centuries. Bahia is said to have three hundred and sixty-five churches (one for every day in the year, people say). I do not know whether anyone has taken the trouble to check this figure, but wherever you look in the city you do notice several dozen churches. Among them are such impressive structures as the Monastary of São Francisco, and some fantastically ornate buildings that seem crushed by their riot of gilt ornamentation.

THE WASHING OF A CHURCH

The oddest and probably the most typical church in Bahia is Nosso Senhor do Bomfim. It is a church for the colored people, and is the center of a cult which is a remarkable synthesis of Christian and ancient African rites. Here, under Christian disguise, as it were, you encounter the magic word that crops up wherever the old Africa breaks through the crust of Afro-Brazil. In Rio de Janeiro the word is *macumba,* in Recife *xangô,* and in Bahia *candomblé.* Whatever the name, it refers to those magical, fetishistic practices of the Brazilian Negroes which bear a close resemblance to the voodoo and cromanti cults of the Caribbean Negroes, and which have made a troubling resurgence in recent decades. In Bahia, 30 per cent of the colored population are supposed to be followers of candomblé. There are even a few whites who profess faith in these rites of old Africa, and their number is said to be growing. I talked with a German-Brazilian who admitted to me that he was the secretary of a *pai do santo,* a "father of the saints"—in other words, a candomblé priest.

The Catholic Church attempts to suppress candomblé by both gentle and rigorous methods. In this religious struggle, both parties have been forced to make considerable concessions. The clergy has to shut its eyes to a good many things in order not to totally alienate the faithful. On the other hand, candomblé followers have had to give their African deities the camouflage of Christian names so as not to offend the clergy. The African goddess of the sea and fertility, Yêmanja, became the Virgin Mary. The thunder god Xangô was renamed St. Anthony. The sky god Olorun was transformed into God the Father, and Ogun, the good god of light, into Jesus Christ. Finally, the wicked demon Exú donned the mask of the Christian devil.

In Nosso Senhor do Bomfim, Christianized candomblé has been virtually legalized. Colored believers come there to pray for health, happiness, and improvement of their material conditions. They also try to bargain with their god for miracles: let their small sins go undiscovered; let unwanted conceptions not take place; let marital infidelity have no consequences; let evil befall their wicked neighbor. Old African black magic is undergoing a surprising resurrection under a cloak of Christianity. The prayers in this church are very human, very naïve, and very pagan. Equally pagan and naïve are the gruesomely realistic votive offerings, the plaster babies, flaming hearts, photographs of operation scars, X-ray pictures of dental abscesses.

A Bahian guild of artists painted thanksgiving pictures in oil specially for Nosso Senhor do Bomfim. Construction workers who fell from skyscrapers offer thanks for being miraculously saved. Criminals praise Nosso Senhor do Bomfim for helping them escape the police. Similar pictures can be seen in other Latin churches, to be sure, but scarcely such guileless ones.

The church of Nosso Senhor do Bomfim is also a colorful African bazaar. Peddlers and beggars swarm in front of and inside the building. They hold out their hands, sell amulets, candles, and plaster casts. The noisy commercial activity reaches its peak when the festival of the cleaning of the church begins. That is the grandest, most splendid and ecstatic religious festival in Bahia. On the day of the washing of Nosso Senhor do Bomfim, fireworks are set off everywhere in the province. Processions come from far away on foot or by boat. Drums throb, there is dancing in the streets, and thousands of colored people carry jugs and tubs of water into the church to clean it as their ancestors cleaned African temples of evil spirits.

Every year, on the occasion of this festival, there are deaths from heat prostration or accidents. I was shown one place in the Bay of All Saints where thirty ecstatic Negroes from Itapagipe drowned when their boat overturned during one festival. You have only to witness the frenzy with which the people rush into the church, and, while scrubbing the stones, shriek, pray, dance, and fall into trances, to understand that such disasters are almost inevitable. The festival of Nosso Senhor do Bomfim is basically a single grand candomblé. This is true of the other church festivals in Bahia. There are water processions in which the fishermen, amid shouts and drumming, venture far out into the ocean on their jangadas. Easter Saturday is an occasion for incessant din: bells clang, automobiles toot their horns, sirens wail, and tin cans clatter. On Palm Sunday the young people deck themselves in palm leaves and dance through the streets.

CARNIVAL AND CANDOMBLÉ

White society in Bahia keep aloof from such celebrations, and in fact would prefer not to know they exist. But the whites cannot hold aloof from the carnival. And the carnival in Bahia is not only the most famous carnival in the world; it is also an African carnival, a kind of profane candomblé. The Bahia carnival is a festival of the colored people, of tomtoms, *batuquadas* and *abataques*, African drums, rattles, and iron bells. It is a festival of African dances and ceremonies, of African laughter and African joy in bright colors.

During the carnival period, it is impossible to get any sleep in Bahia day or night. There are hours in which the city is filled with a premonitory quiet, or dominated by pompous, rather stiffly ceremonial carnival processions for the white upper class. But then, from somewhere, the first Negro drums suddenly start up, in a monotonous, breath-taking, electrifying rhythm. Instantly, among all the colored people, limbs twitch, bodies quiver; their ordinary uncertain, hesitant gait becomes a vibrant prancing, a prelude to the *bataque*. Arms fly up, bodies bend forward, the crowd dances, dances, dances as if under hypnosis. The whites, too, are caught up by it; they sway along in the current, their faces damp with sweat; they dance the samba, the bataque—the old slave dance. They dance as do their black fellow citizens at the fetishistic candomblés.

For a full five days black Bahia dances through the streets without ceasing. The inhabitants of the working-class quarters of Brotas and Eugenho Velo conquer the city, and the wooden pulse of their drums never stops. People do not sleep, scarcely eat; they only dance, and now and then spray themselves from bottles of ether. Afro-Brazilians do not get drunk on alcohol; the vapor of ether suffices to throw them into ecstasies. I saw dancers going through their motions with such perfection that they could have starred in any variety show in the world. I saw children disguised as *exús*, devils, which play a considerable part in candomblé. Some Negroes had decked themselves out as savage Indians with feathers and nose rings. Roaring with laughter, they blocked my way, pointed their spears at me, and carried me along into their dance.

The black Bahians are among the gayest and most charming people in Latin America. Brasilidade seems to have wiped away all the suffering of slave days. Brazil is tolerant; consequently no one takes it amiss, except for a few arrogant new immigrants, that the Negroes and mulattoes cultivate their African heritage in Bahia. Again and again I noticed a Bahian make the time-honored lightning-swift gesture to divert the evil eye. The number *five* is not spoken for superstitious reasons. Bahian country people burn magic powders or sacrifice black cocks, coins, cigars, and bean soup at secret places. Almost everybody in the Negro quarters has *figos* dangling on his back. These are hands carved out of hard wood, ivory, horn, or semiprecious stones, of all sizes, the thumbs thrust through the clenched fingers. They protect the wearer from the evil eye, malignant curses, and from all misfortunes that may come from behind. But along with the heathen figos these people will also wear Christian amulets hanging from thin chains, or medals of saints. Both sets of symbols serve the same purpose.

When tourists in Rio de Janeiro are taken to a macumba, or to a candomblé in Bahia, they see—in most cases—just an arranged spectacle calculated to satisfy the white Western craving for sensation. A genuine macumba of candomblé is no dance festival, and above all no Afro-Brazilian striptease. It is a legitimate act of religious worship. Bahia was the greatest slave mart in the Americas in colonial times. The imported Africans were hastily baptized, but that hardly made them Christians. How could they have been, when everything made it plain that the god of their white masters was not particularly well disposed toward them. They took refuge in their African secret cults, which gave them the strength to endure and to resist. Emancipation did not end the four-hundred-year-old tradition of a secret religion. With freedom, the old religion developed into a form of worship more suited to still primitive natures than the rigid, conventionalized Christianity of the Brazilian upper classes.

Candomblés take place in *terreiros,* barnlike halls usually located in working-class districts. The walls are adorned with candles and pictures of the Virgin Mary; the believers sacrifice bread, money, and crushed cigarettes on the altar. Incense is burned. The *achôguns,* assistants of the candomblé priests, act like dutiful altar boys in a Catholic church. The *babalaô,* the high priest, might be a dark-skinned Christian preacher.

What gives the candomblé its African character is the assemblage of drums, gourds, flutes, and iron bells that summon the congregation to song and dance. The ritual language of the candomblé has to this day remained Nago in many congregations. That is the language of the old African Yoruba culture, which has vanished from Africa but is still alive, at least in liturgy, in Brazil.

As the drums thump away, the believers slowly begin a stamping dance. They clap their hands, lean forward and back. Suddenly a saint or a deity manifests himself in one of the participants; with dragging feet, the medium goes through the room, head bowed low, uttering a soft singsong. He is sprinkled with water, answers questions put to him by the babalaô. After a while he comes out of the trance and takes his place once more in the ranks of the congregation.

This goes on for hours. The drummers pound their abataques. Deities are invoked and manifest themselves in some member of the congregation. The rest twitch, writhe, dance to exhaustion. Now and then the babalaô goes into an adjoining room and dispenses counsel. He gives his followers advice on health, family and financial problems, and relieves them of their difficult decisions. There is also "black" candomblé, which traffics in baleful magic. One hears tell of grave excesses of this sort. But genuine candomblé shuns such sectarian activity much as the Christian churches fend off heretics.

There have so far been few descriptions and studies of the Afro-Brazilian cults, although the peculiarities of Brazilian Negro culture can scarcely be understood without this element's being taken into account. In order to understand what is going on in Brazil, the culture must be compared to the Negro culture in the United States. Nowhere in the States do Negroes speak an African language, wear African costume, practice African rituals, eat African foods or pray to African gods. The North American Negro has preserved a few African elements in his music and dances, but in all respects he long ago became a dark-skinned Occidental. In northern Brazil, on the other hand, Western culture has been overlaid only as a thin veneer upon the African nature of the colored population. The Afro-Brazilian has taken over brasilidade from the Portuguese (or could it be that essential elements of brasilidade come from Africa?), but he has not become a Latin. A parallel to this phenomenon may be found in the revival of Aztec culture now taking place in Mexico. In Mexico, however, the government propagates re-Indianization, whereas the government in northern Brazil takes no interest, in a positive or negative sense, in re-Africanization. Nevertheless, in Bahia the pounding of the drums drowns out the noise of technology. The carnival has become an African festival. And the number of candomblé followers is increasing from year to year.

Brazilian sociologists have frequently wondered how the African cults among the lower classes of black Latin Americans can serve them in mastering the problems of our modern age. It is not important whether a colored Bahian goes to a babalaô for advice or sacrifices a black cock to the sea goddess Yêmanja. What is important is whether such acts strengthen his self-confidence, help him climb the social ladder and make an essential contribution to the development of his people.

At present the Afro-Brazilian stands at a crossroads. His attachment to the old cults has undoubtedly helped him bring his psyche safely through the ordeals of the past. The question now is whether these cults may not have become such an obstacle to his further progress that he is incapable of assuming his proper place in Brazilian society. That is the real problem of much-maligned and needlessly clandestine candomblé.

TOBACCO IN THE RECÔNCAVO

The state of Bahia is twice as large as the states of São Paulo and Guanabara taken together. But while in Guanabara and São Paulo the population density is some fifty persons per square kilometer, Bahia has only nine persons per square kilometer. In São Paulo only every eighth inhabitant is colored; in Bahia every eighth citizen is white. The racial situation in Bahia has frequently been compared to a pyramid which corresponds exactly with the social structure. The white upper class forms the peak; the café-au-lait middle class is the center of the pyramid; and the black lower class constitutes the base. In Bahia that is felt to be the natural order of things, so firmly established that hitherto it has not yet led to racial tensions.

In Bahia, too, Portuguese adventurers like the bandeirantes once went out into the forests. Here they were called jagunços. But they did not rise to become mighty conquistadors in the jungles along the Rio São Francisco. On the contrary, they sank to the level of the semibarbaric natives. Most of them were swallowed up by the wilderness. They did not Europeanize their Indian and African wives and their mestizo and mulatto offspring. Instead, they themselves were partly Indianized, partly Africanized. To be sure, the state of Bahia also had its sugar aristocracy and its diamond rush. European immigrants established cacao plantations tended by Negro slaves. German immigrants settled in the vicinity of Ilhéus and went into the business of shipping cacao. But in the end, the colored element won through almost everywhere.

The result was the formation in Bahia of a very special type of settler, a type not to be found in the southern states of Brazil. This is the independent, capable Negro and mulatto small farmer. Around the Bay of All Saints spreads one of the most fruitful lowlands in South America—the Recôncavo. After the abolition of slavery, countless Bahian Negroes settled there. They acquired small patches of land, usually no more than an acre. Since they had an understandable distaste for the cultivation of sugar, they planted crops which did not so exhaust the land: rice and corn, cotton and oranges, but above all cacao and tobacco. Today a part of the Bahian cacao crop and virtually the entire tobacco crop is produced by these Negro small farmers. On their work stands and falls the economy of the state of Bahia.

Cacao is also grown on a more ambitious scale on large plantations. These are more profitable and supply most of the cacao for export. Consequently, the owners of cacao plantations are prominent folk in Bahia. Aside from them, however, you will meet scarcely any fazendeiros in the Commercial Club and in the business houses of Salvador-Bahia. The very rich of the town are not great landowners, but exporters and above all the wholesalers who periodically travel about the Recôncavo buying up the products of the Negro farmers.

Since most of the small farmers are wretchedly poor, the buyers give them advances on their crops. Thus the Negroes in the Recôncavo are heavily in debt. They live from hand to mouth. In the big families, everyone from grandfather to the smallest child works in the tobacco fields, snipping off the flower buds, eliminating insect pests, picking the ripened leaves, stringing them in bunches, hanging them in the drying sheds, and carefully sorting them after the drying. Almost everything is done without tools, with the bare hands. They sow and hoe, stoop thousands of times, and convincingly refute the slanders about the laziness of the black race.

The small tobacco farmer in the Recôncavo does not have the capital to keep his crop off the market for a time and thus influence prices. No one in this state thinks of price-fixing, such as was instituted to help the Paulistas with their surplus coffee. If the farmers of northern Brazil had the tools, they would be able to work more land, and if they could divert to themselves a fraction of the support that coffee has always enjoyed in Brazil, there would be no "northern problem." Those small farms which barely keep their owners alive require a tremendous output of labor power and diligence. This energy, rightly applied, could easily revive the economy of the poverty-stricken north.

THE CITY OF LITERATI

The really poor north begins north of Bahia, where eight small states form Brazil's poorhouse: Sergipe, Alagoas, Pernambuco, Paraíba, Rio Grande do Norte, Ceará, Piauí, and Maranhão. They are a heritage of the old administrative districts of colonial times, none of which wanted to surrender its sovereignty. Each insisted on becoming a state in its own right. A ninth unit is formed by the island of Fernando de Noronha, formerly Brazil's convict colony. The barely eight hundred inhabitants of this island enjoy the privilege of living in an autonomous territory.

The only city in this whole area that looks prosperous is the old gateway to Brazil: Recife. Capital of the state of Pernambuco, and Brazil's second-largest port, Recife is in population the third-largest city in the entire country. It has very nearly reached the million mark.

Recife owes its good fortune to the tremendous wall of coral reefs from which it takes its name. The sound between the reefs and the mainland beach is an ideal natural roadstead for transatlantic vessels. These bring commerce to Pernambuco. The relative nearness to the continent of Europe has also led to the building of a large airport. Textile factories sprang up in Recife to make use of the cotton crops of the northern states. Most of the sugar and the larger part of the Brazilian banana crop are shipped from here; and since what moneyed folk there are in northern Brazil come here for their shopping, the city is growing almost as rapidly as São Paulo and Belo Horizonte.

In Recife you hardly feel the all-enveloping poverty of the north. This metropolis, eight degrees of latitude south of the equator, with its milliners and jewelers, its canals and warehouses, the old forts of Dutch days and the impressive dock installations, is no São Paulo of the north, no bustling trading center. It is a city of strollers, street peddlers, and pleasant seafood restaurants. But above all it is a city of science, scholarship, and literature. A popular saying has it that every cultivated Pernambucan has published a book at least once in his life. Most of these books, as might be expected in a city of revolutionary intellectuals, are likely to contain sharp social criticism. Recife's *Diário de Pernambuco* is the oldest newspaper in South America. The *Jornal do Comércio* is the leading business journal of Brazil. A *Fôlha do Povo*, the "Newspaper of the Poor," is an oddity. It advocates communistic ideas, in spite of the ban on the Communist Party. Nevertheless, the newspaper cannot be touched; the revolutionary mentality of the intellectual Pernambucans would never tolerate any interference with it.

The intellectuals of Pernambuco are not coffeehouse literati. They are prepared at any time to mount the barricades in defense of their convictions—and have proved so many times over. They first did so when the Dutch, under Prince Maurice of Nassau and Orange, founded a South American colonial empire in Pernambuco. On November 9, 1645, the Portuguese, with the active support of the Pernambucans, drove out the Dutch occupying forces. The anniversary of that battle is still celebrated in Recife as the day that saw the creation of the Brazilian "race." For of the three generals who commanded the campaign against the Dutch, one was a white Portuguese, João Fernandes Vieira; the second, a Negro, André Vidal de Negreiros; and the third, Philippe Camarão, a pure-blooded Indian chief.

REBELLION OF THE AFFLICTED

The countryside in northern Brazil is no less revolutionary than the city of Recife. But Recife is affluent, while the rural areas in the north are destitute. Nature itself is niggardly here. The coast is drought-stricken, the inhabitants constantly threatened by natural disasters. Life is dependent more than anywhere else in the country on the arrival of the rains at the proper time. Should the rain fail, famine and unrest almost invariably follow. The coastline consists of coral reefs, sand dunes, mangrove forests, and palm groves. There is little good, fruitful soil. One of the most severely afflicted states is Ceará, more and more of whose population has had no choice but to migrate to the south.

If it rains too much, on the other hand, the lagoon country is threatened by high water. In May 1949 Maceió, capital of the state of Alagoas, a city of a hundred thousand, suffered floods like a second Deluge. Gigantic landslips of whole mountains and hills took place.

A working-class district was buried under a thick layer of mud. The world public took scarcely any notice of the 1949 flood in Maceió or the 1953 drought in Ceará. But in northern Brazil people still talk about these two disasters, although in the meantime many similar droughts and floods have visited the northeast.

Conditions are not much better in the interior. The forests are thin; dry, scrubby plains called the *catingas* cover the greater part of the area. Vast stretches of this country scarcely offer pasture for cattle. The large estates are therefore located only where *vazantes*, reservoirs of ground water, have been discovered. A number of plans for irrigation have been drawn up, but what has actually been done so far literally amounts only to a drop in the bucket. Even the rich finds of oil recently made in the area have so far done little to alter the wretched lot of the Nordistas.

The large landowners manage to get along, unless a too severe drought dries up their vazantes. The starving and thirsting inhabitants of the catingas, however, either migrate to other states or turn to a revolutionary philosophy which is becoming ever more radical. The *Ligas Camponesas*, associations of country people which include small farmers, sharecroppers, and landless agricultural workers, grew in recent years into a political movement that radiated far beyond the northeastern states and took hold throughout Brazil. Since the military coup of 1964 the movement has been banned by the police, but it continues to exist as a powerful underground force.

The Camponesa movement can be correctly understood and evaluated only if it is considered in connection with the special character of the Nordistas. It is by no means the first revolutionary movement to start in the northeast. Brazil has frequently been shaken violently by movements that originated here. The earlier reform movements, however, were usually of a religious nature. The frequency of natural disasters and the poverty of the Nordistas have repeatedly given rise to religious and political fanaticisms.

During the first half of the nineteenth century a mestizo named João Ferreira appeared as a messiah in the state of Pernambuco. He won followers among the rural workers by telling them that through him all blacks would become "white-skinned, rich, powerful, and immortal." Ferreira reintroduced pagan human sacrifice, and finally had himself sacrificed by his disciples, in order to partake of eternal bliss. The sect gradually dissolved because its members could no longer endure the stench of decay in their place of worship.

In 1890 a man from Ceará named Antônio Vicente Mendes Maciel proclaimed the coming end of the world. The existing Brazilian government was the Antichrist, he declared. Conferring on himself the impressive title of *Bom Jesus Conselheiro*—Jesus the Good Adviser— he founded a new state of Canudos. It took four years and three campaigns before the young Brazilian Republic was able to suppress this secession.

Around the turn of the century a Catholic priest named Father Cicero caused disturbances in the state of Ceará. He performed miraculous cures and led an insurrection against the governor of the state to obtain better conditions for colored smallholders. Until his death in 1934 he was venerated like an idol by the Cearans. Two years later, a small boy came forward calling himself João Cicero and alleging that he was a reincarnation of the priest. He gathered so many followers that they had to be suppressed by force. To this day there are many among the *caboclos* and *cafusos*—the people of mixed blood—in Ceará who firmly believe in João Cicero's messianic nature.

João Pessôa, whose martyr's death unleashed the revolution of Getulio Vargas, came from the northeastern state of Paraíba. The neighboring states of Paraíba and Pernambuco were the first to adhere to the Aliança Liberal of the rebel from Rio Grande do Sul. Nordistas, side by side with the gaúchos of the southern state, formed the main contingent of Vargas revolutionaries who participated in the march on Rio. Two years after the victory of the revolution, however, when it became apparent that Vargas was favoring the economic development of the south, these same Nordistas turned against the dictator's regime. In a "Revolution of the North" they attempted to make Recife the capital of the north.

Today the Nordistas are led by a lawyer named Francisco Julião. He has succeeded in welding the destitute population of the northeast into an effective political unit. At the heart of his program are the *flagelados*, the "scourged" or "afflicted," namely, the Nordistas who have been driven from their lands by the disastrous droughts. The flagelados have meanwhile been scattered over all of Brazil. They stand on street corners in big cities, peddling fruit. The majority of them live in the favelas and can rightly call themselves "exiles." Francisco Julião, who has by now become acquainted with the prisons of the military government, calls for a comprehensive agrarian reform that will help them find new lives.

Francisco Julião's Camponesa movement has been called communistic, like the other agrarian reform movements in Latin America. And in fact Julião does flirt with Peking. But the impoverished Nordistas are for the most part not interested in Marxist ideologies. They want a portion of irrigated land; they would like to build up new lives unimperiled by hunger, thirst, and natural disasters. The innumerable sharecroppers among them also desire an end at last to the extortionist *parceria,* the sharecropping system. They want to own the land they have for so long fertilized with their toil.

Several hundred thousand rustics are said to have joined the Camponesa movement. It is by now far from limited to the northeast. All over Brazil the underground movement is a political factor far more potent than the likewise banned Communist Party.

RED AMAZONIA

The *Interior* of Brazil comprises some two-thirds of the territory of the country. The interior is the vast Amazon basin whose development and settlement attract the minds of numberless political economists all over the world. The Amazon with its tributaries forms the largest river basin on earth, and includes regions that extend far to the south. Geographically speaking, the Rio Tocantins and the Rio Araguaia belong to this same basin; these are the two first tributaries of the Amazon, which are not too distant from the federal capital of Brasilia.

The state watered by the Tocantins, the state in which Brasilia lies, is called Goiás, which is one of the larger states in the federal union, but the smallest Amazonian state. The three other states of Amazonia, Mato Grosso, Pará, and Amazonas, are the largest in area and among the smallest in population in the federal union. Four autonomous territories complete the Amazonian part of Brazil: Amapá and Rio Branco in the far north, on the Guianan borders; Acre and Guaporé in the far west—territories taken by Brazil from the republics of Bolivia and Ecuador.

To this day the "Green Hell" along the Amazon and in the Mato Grosso is regarded as a mysterious, frightening region. Here many an adventurer has vanished forever. Here Indians armed with blowpipes have wiped out parties of innocent travelers with their curare-tipped arrows. Here, along the Rio dos Mortes, the "River of the Dead," lives the tribe of the Chavante. To enter their territory, it is said, is to sign one's life away. A journey into the Amazon jungles is still regarded as one of the great tests of courage possible in our age.

Alas, in this era of fact as against fancy, the legend of the Amazon has become a bit ridiculous. Some of this was true enough around the turn of the century—but not because the aboriginals of the Amazon were especially fierce or the Amazon jungles so terribly dangerous. Rather, the pursuit of rubber had literally transformed the Amazon basin into a hell, not only for the intruders of various colors, but chiefly for the peoples who were then nominally masters of the land, the Indians of the forests and plains.

THE GREEN HELL OF THE RUBBER FORESTS

The first scientist who entered these jungles was Charles Marie de la Condamine, a French mathematician. From 1735 to 1743 he explored the South American continent from Educador to the mouth of the Amazon. In the course of his travels he found orchids, parrots, and the Indians' curare poison, which is now so important in modern medicine. He also heard about a resin which the Indians called *cahuchu* and which Condamine rendered in French as *caoutchouc*.

"As long as this caoutchouc is fresh," he wrote in his travel journal, "it can be given any desired form. . . . The Indians make bottles out of it which are unbreakable; they also make spheres and hollow balls which flatten out entirely when pressed, but regain their shape as soon as they are released."

This "India rubber" which the natives extracted from the tree named *Hevea brasiliensis* became a matter of interest to the world economy only after Charles Goodyear discovered the vulcanization of rubber and Charles Mackintosh found that cloth impregnated with a solution of the substance became waterproof. In 1888 an Irish veterinarian named John Boyd Dunlop obtained a patent on his pneumatic tire. That was the beginning of the great run on the *Hevea* forests along the Amazon.

Amazon rubber was not planted like sugar, cotton, or coffee. The trees grew wild in the vast jungles, whose extent at that time could not be even approximately estimated. Nor could hired workers be depended on to harvest this crop, since even the most miserable day laborer in Brazil had no desire to die in the jungles. Consequently, the rubber agencies in Pará, Santarém, and Manaus hired heavily armed bands who rounded up a number of impoverished caboclos and partly by force, partly by extravagant promises, persuaded them to gather the sap of the rubber tree. Some half million persons were driven into the jungles in this way. The majority of them never returned. Still, the supply of labor did not suffice. Consequently, the bands began capturing savage Indians on a large scale. Whole tribes were sent into the jungle for forced labor. The more obdurate were killed.

The fate of the Nordistas and caboclos in the rubber country was described, around the turn of the century, by an American consul in Rio de Janeiro: "Were it not for the terrible famine that prevails in Ceará, Pará rubber could never be obtained. For only people at the utter end of their rope can be willing to undertake this terrible work."

The enslaved Indians or the settlers who had fled their drought-stricken plantations received advances in money and provisions from the agents. They then set out into the tangled, pathless jungle, armed only with their machetes and a lump of clay, at every step subject to attack by the Urucú and Juriti tribes, for the Indians had been aroused to fierce resistance. When he found a rubber tree, he noted the place, hacked open the bark, and shaped the clay into a vessel for catching the latex. It took some time for the pot to fill. The collector therefore moved on, searching for the next rubber tree—which might take him several hours to find. For the spheres of dark crude rubber which he brought back to the receiving camp after many days in the jungle, he obtained half-spoiled provisions at prices ten times higher than those on the coast. Thus the *seringueiro*, the rubber collector, remained eternally in the debt of his boss, the *patrão*. Most seringueiros died of fever, dysentery, exanthema, or worm infections. Others took their place, starving or shanghaied men doomed to the same fate.

The rubber boom resulted in mass extermination of the Indians. The Indian tribes which to this day are not very friendly toward visitors, such as the Chavante, suffered gruesomely from the whole enterprise. They withdrew farther and farther into the interior, to regions still exempted from the rubber trade.

In 1905 Brazil had an unchallenged monopoly of rubber. She dictated its price on the world market much as she dictated the price of coffee. More than 99 per cent of the world rubber crop was gathered by Indians or debt-ridden seringueiros. The rubber cities in Brazil grew with the speed of tropical plants. Pará, the port on the mouth of the Amazon—today called Belém—became the principal transfer point for crude rubber. In 1850 Pará had about 12,000 inhabitants; by 1907 the population had leaped to some 200,000. Even more fantastic was the development of the remote trading post of Manaus in the heart of the jungle, near the confluence of the Amazon and the Rio Negro. In 1800 the town did not exist; by 1900 it had become a great rubber metropolis with 100,000 inhabitants, paved streets, churches, palaces and hospitals, waterworks, telephone and electric light, a streetcar system, and a modern opera house. This last, with its five balconies and twelve thousand seats, was the largest theater in the world. Among the international stars to appear on its stage were Caruso and Sarah Bernhardt. No one in Manaus was fearful of the future. Amazonia produced seven times as much rubber as all the rest of the world taken together.

But Brazilian rubber suffered the same fate as Chilean nitrates. Almost overnight, the rubber economy collapsed. The man responsible for the reverse was Henry Wickham, a British botanist. Brazil had strictly forbidden export of the seeds of the *Hevea*. But Wickham contrived to smuggle seed across the border inside a stuffed crocodile. In the hothouses of the Botanic Garden at Kew, the largest conservatory in Great Britain, *Hevea* seedlings were successfully raised, then shipped to Ceylon. By 1905 the British had planted nearly a million acres of rubber trees in their Far Eastern possessions. Plantation rubber was easier to harvest and could be sold more cheaply than Amazonian wild rubber. Within ten years it was competing so severely with Amazonian wild rubber that the rubber lords of Brazil and Peru decided upon an even more ruthless labor policy, which has gone down in history as the "Rubber Atrocity."

One of the members of the commission investigating the Rubber Atrocity summed up the matter as follows: "The insatiable greed to obtain the highest possible production with the minimum of equipment was the main reason for the atrocities. The Indians who did not do enough were tortured and killed without mercy, while the stronger ones were forced with machetes and rifles to meet their quotas. The crimes stood in a proportional relationship to the yield. The greater the number of killings, the greater the production. That meant that rubber was extracted by trampling over corpses."

Not even these Draconian measures could save the Amazonian rubber economy. From Pará to Manaus, one rubber trading company after another went bankrupt. The rubber kings, agents, and dealers were mostly Europeans, not South Americans. To be sure, the brutality was in many cases administered by South American overseers, but behind them stood the directors and concessionaires from civilized European countries who had settled in Manaus and Pará and drawn ever-increasing salaries, royalties, and commissions.

By 1922 Amazonia, the former empire of rubber, had virtually vanished from the statistics of world trade. The harvest of Amazonian wild rubber amounted to only 1 per cent of the world rubber production. At various times since then, American concerns have invested vast amounts of capital in attempts to establish rubber plantations on the Amazon, and to revive decaying Manaus, whose unfinished mansions and palatial buildings were already being swallowed by the jungle. Thus in 1927 Henry Ford tried to establish a plantation on a five-million-acre territory along the Rio Tapajós, importing his workers from Japan. Ford's project had to be abandoned, however, like all similar projects. Amazonia is hostile to plantations. The virgin jungle soil fights against every kind of monoculture.

This is the overwhelming lesson of the Amazon region and one which to this day is ignored by visionary economists. Again and again we may read in serious publications that Amazonia could feed a billion human beings; that all fears of the population explosion are therefore needless. The experts who make these statements seem not to have heard that southern Amazonia is as prone to erosion as the state of São Paulo. Agronomic institutes and the specialists of international agricultural organizations agree that only the flood plains in the immediate vicinity of the great rivers can be fruitful for an indefinite period. But it is precisely here that the fringing forests are essential to prevent the flooding rivers from carrying away the soil. If the forest is cut down on the higher elevations between the river valleys, the tropical sun dries the earth to powder. The violent rainstorms then wash away the soil, down to the naked sandstone. For this reason, any intensive settlement of these regions has always failed.

The jungle is vitally necessary to Amazonia. In the shadow of the great forests settlers can carve out a secure livelihood. But only a limited number of colonists can establish themselves permanently in the jungle. Speculations about settlement of our planet's excess population in Amazonia are idle dreams, and may be dangerously misleading ones.

Far more significant for the opening up of Amazonia than the bloody *conquista* of the rubber regions was a series of peaceful and humane research expeditions which were originally concerned with communications and ultimately led to the pacification and protection of the Amazonian Indians. The organizer and leader of these expeditions was Cándido Mariano da Silva Rondon. In honor of Colonel, later Marshal, Rondon, the autonomous territory of Guaporé was recently renamed Rondônia.

Rondon did not devote himself so much to Amazonia proper, the land of rubber. He explored chiefly the great southern state, Mato Grosso, the second-largest state in Brazil. In 1892, when the Indians were still being hunted and driven into the rubber receiving camps, Rondon began building a telegraph line from Goiás to Cuiabá, the capital of Mato Grosso. During the subsequent years and decades he worked almost uninterruptedly at extending the network of telegraph lines. This pioneering technical achievement was, as Theodore Roosevelt once said, on a par with the building of the Panama Canal.

The change that Rondon introduced in the treatment of the Indians was even more important. He himself was a nearly pure-blooded Indian. Probably for that reason he had a special feeling for the persecuted aboriginals of the country. He succeeded in pacifying most of the Indian tribes of Mato Grosso, Goiás, and Guaporé without bloodshed. The slogan he chose for the SPI, the government organization for the protection of the Indians, which he created, was: "Die if necessary, but never kill!" He abided by that principle all his life, and his associates and successors followed his example.

In 1916 Roquette Pinto, one of Rondon's associates, published a book entitled *Rondônia*, which told the story of Rondon's great pacification expeditions. It remains to this day the classic work on the great jungles, worth far more than the thousands of sensational accounts of the perils of the Amazonian forests.

Rondônia describes the life of most of the Indian tribes of Mato Grosso. Here is material into which ethnologists can delve for years and years to come. Many of the Indian tribes that Rondon pacified have gradually become acquainted with white culture as a result of the slow penetration of civilization into the Amazonian jungles. Other tribes, by Rondon's decision, still live according to the pattern of their ancestors; roaming their vast reservations, they are protected from the contagion of civilization and the intrusion of unauthorized adventurers by specially trained Indian guards. The Serviço de Proteção aos Indios, Rondon's Indian Service, is considered a model agency for the protection of aboriginals the world over.

Rondon encountered a good deal of criticism for his humane treatment of the Indians. His strict injunction of nonviolence now and then led to the deaths of unarmed scientists in the Indian territories. Usually such incidents took place after the Indians had been disturbed by helicopter flights on the part of sensation-hungry reporters. In general, however, Rondon's watchword, "Be peaceful toward the Indians and they will be peaceful toward you," has proved its worth. Even the much-maligned Chavante conduct themselves peaceably within their reservations.

The change in attitude that Rondon introduced has led to a veritable glorification of the Indian, rather similar to the change of heart toward the Indian in the United States. This Indian cult reached its height in the 1950s, when an official of the SPI fell in love with a chief's daughter and married her. The white-and-red wedding was celebrated in Rio de Janeiro and degenerated into a turbulent carnival. The name of Diacui, the wild princess of the jungle, was blazoned on posters all over the city. Dresses, cosmetics, culinary specialties, and even a samba were named after Diacui. When the Indian girl subsequently died in childbed, all of Brazil mourned her. European correspondents made fun of all this fuss. But in reality the Diacui cult was a true expression of brasilidade, a passionate shift in sentiment which was greatly to the good of the aboriginals of Amazonia.

THE HEART BEGINS TO BEAT

Northern Amazonia still lies in the slumber into which it relapsed after the ruin of the rubber industry. In some places rock crystal, wolframite, and bauxite are being mined. The region is also said to have supplies of manganese, iron, tin, and petroleum, but natural obstacles still hinder systematic exploration. In spite of all optimistic forecasts, it would be rash to make any definite statements about the economic potentialities of this enormous region. Some latex is still tapped, some sugar and cacao planted; Pará nuts are picked and fine woods cut. A plant called guarana yields a beverage popular throughout Brazil. But the region's population, on the whole, still lives as mankind must have lived at the dawn of history.

In 1956 I encountered a situation that is typical in that remote region. A revolt had broken out in Santarém on the Amazon, in the state of Pará. For unexplained reasons an army officer and several soldiers had seized the town's airport and thus cut off virtually all communication between the coast and the hinterland. The newspapers reported this absurd incident as if it were the outbreak of the Third World War. Every day headlines announced the massive measures being taken to deal with a handful of rebels. Communiqués were issued, as well as resounding appeals to the patriotism of the Amazonians. Actually, a few men in this area can paralyze the whole administrative and transportation apparatus—but only until the government forces reach the unruly area. That, however, can take a while.

Mato Grosso and Goiás are much more closely connected with the navel cord of Brazil. Mato Grosso means "Great Forest"—a misnomer, for the state consists largely of savannas. These great plains were long ago occupied by fazendeiros who, like the estancieros in Rio Grande do Sul, raise cattle on a large scale. Coffee, too, has been planted in Mato Grosso. Many of the Indians have become caboclos. Caboclo—"copper-colored"—was a name formerly reserved for Indians. Later the term was transferred to persons of mixed European and Indian descent. Today every small farmer in Brazil, whether his color is brown, white, or black, is called a caboclo. New recruits constantly pour out of the Indian reservations to add to the numbers of caboclos. Brazilian sociologists hold that these reservations are no longer gigantic open-air museums for the preservation of tribes threatened by extinction, but breeding grounds for a new race who may be better equipped for the conquest of Amazonia then all previous colonizers.

The eastern state of Goiás occupies a very special place within the group of Amazonian states. Goiás was always regarded as the "heart of Brazil," not only because the state is shaped like a heart, but also because it contains, Brazilians hope, even greater mineral wealth and industrial potentialities than the mining state of Minas Gerais. Goiás experienced a period of gold rush. The state contains the fourth-largest nickel supply in the world, as well as diamonds, rock crystal, iron, and manganese. Because of its rapid industrialization, Goiás has the greatest density of population and the largest number of cities in Amazonia. For many decades all the projects for building a new federal capital in the interior of the country have centered around the mountainous plains of Goiás.

For a while the old state capital of Goiás was the favorite of the planners. But this modest country town struck the guild of modern architects as too unpretentious to represent with dignity the United States of Brazil—not even thorough renovation could lift it by its bootstraps. Consequently, they did for the state of Goiás what had already been done in the state of Minas Gerais: leading Brazilian architects created a new state capital from the ground up, and called it Goiânia. By 1950 there was a good deal of sentiment for developing Goiânia into the new federal capital.

In 1955, when Kubitschek was making campaign speeches in Goiás, and was going around American-style, shaking innumerable hands, the people asked him again and again when the government was going to carry out its plan to transfer the head of Brazil to the heart of Brazil. At that time Goiânia had barely fifty thousand inhabitants, and the fazendeiros, cattle drivers, oxcarts, and rustic markets had proved stronger than modern civilization. The laboratory city had become an idyllic small town. Moreover, as Kubitschek discovered, Goiânia was too far from the supplies of ore which would have to be the center of the state's future industrial region.

Kubitschek therefore revived the ancient Brazilian dream of creating the new metropolis out of uncultivated wilderness. He decided upon an area northeast of Goiânia which had already been noted as particularly suitable by a number of expeditions and airplane surveys back in the days of Getulio Vargas. The chosen area lay far from settled regions—though not in the geographical center of Brazil, as earlier visionary plans had conceived it, nor in the jungle, as is so often falsely stated, but at least in the state Brazilians themselves call the heart of their country.

The building of the new federal metropolis in the heart of Brazil has brought the hitherto little-known state of Goiás to the attention of the world. Whatever the future of Brasilia may be, Kubitschek's and Niemeyer's dream city will undoubtedly change the whole aspect of the *Interior*.

THE SILKEN CURTAIN

Brazil is a land of racial equality. It has, as we have mentioned, the most progressive racial laws in the world, laws that impose harsh prison sentences on any discrimination against a colored fellow citizen. In restaurants, offices, and public vehicles, white, brown, and black sit peacefully together; in the streets, *praças*, and *praias*, light and dark walk arm in arm, use the same benches, lie side by side in the sun. It is typically Brazilian that a young man will give his sweetheart, even if she belongs to the white race, pet names somewhat reminiscent of the *mulher da cama*, calling her *morena* or *negrinha*. No one in Brazil takes it amiss if a coffee-colored young man flirts with or marries a light-skinned girl.

The Brazilian intelligentsia is inconceivable without its colored members. Oscar Niemeyer, probably the greatest living architect in the world, is a mulatto. Marshal Rondon, the advocate of the rights of the aboriginals, was an Indian. Machado de Assis, one of the most important Brazilian novelists, justly famous for his accounts of the life of the common people, was colored. The lyric poet Antônio Gonçalves Dias, who wrote the country's national anthem and whose verse repeatedly called on Brazilians to take pride in their descent from three races, was also a mulatto. In Brazil's academies of poets, musicians, and painters, in her medical and legal associations, in her guild of architects, and in all the other intellectual circles of the country, colored Brazilians stand side by side with light-skinned Brazilians and are their full equals.

Everyone who describes Brazil points out the country's racial tolerance. Every white Brazilian or new Brazilian, even if he belongs to the oligarchy of millionaires or to an especially tradition-conscious clan, declares spontaneously as soon as the race question comes up that he has no race prejudices and welcomes the fact that the colored people in Brazil enjoy absolutely equal rights. Even the most exclusive clubs have colored members—although always only a sprinkling.

Brazil does, in fact, form a refreshing exception among countries that have a race problem—countries, that is, which count many Negroes and mulattoes in their citizenry. But if we look a little deeper, we will begin to wonder. Can it be that the colored members of the exclusive clubs serve the ends of "tokenism"? That their presence is a gesture of compliance with the law? As for the hasty professions on racial equality by members of the white oligarchy, these sound more than a little forced. It is hard to avoid the conclusion that here again people are anxious to stay on the right side of the law.

Still and all, it is a measure of progress that a white upper class, which in other countries insists on its exclusiveness and shuns any contact with colored persons, does fear the law in Brazil and at least outwardly lays stress on tolerance. In this respect, Brazil is miles ahead of the North American South. Nevertheless, it is worth while investigating how the law against racial discrimination came to be passed, what the colored people themselves think about it, and whether racial conflicts may not be smoldering behind the amiable façade of equality.

A GERM IS INTRODUCED

For Brazil has a race problem too. It is, as everywhere in Latin America, actually a class problem. As long as the old order dating back to the times of the *casa grande* and the *senzala* dominated Brazilian social life, this problem was not acute. The light-skinned Brazilians formed the upper class; those of somewhat darker pigmentation became a middle class; and the darkest group of all represented the proletariat. But the more this old order was weakened by the modern industrial and social-welfare state, the more resentments, tensions, and sudden outbursts came to the fore.

In slave times there were no race prejudices; a man was either a light-skinned master or a dark-skinned slave. While the liberation of the slaves in North America involved a bloody civil war and created lasting resentments, emancipation was bloodless in Brazil, in spite of the overthrow of the monarchy. After the Lei Áurea had abolished the slave system by a stroke of the pen, the constitution provided equality before the law for all races. Brazil's intellectuals, always in the van of the struggle for the rights of the colored, did everything in their power to bring about a degree of racial integration such as the world had never seen. It was in any case simpler in Brazil than in North America because there was no sharp line between white and black; there was an infinity of shades of color in between, from the coal-black *preto retinto* to the whitest of whites.

The result was that after emancipation the colored people did not form a special caste in Brazil. The overwhelming majority of them did belong to the lowest social class, but the intoxication with equality after the abolition of slavery gave the more intelligent among them every opportunity to rise into the upper classes. All attempts to discriminate against colored Brazilians were vigorously fought by writers, newspapermen, sociologists, and men of the law.

During the following decades it became more and more the rule that a successful colored man was not going to be separated by any barriers of prejudice from successful white men. Colored citizens sat in the congress, on the judicial bench, and in university chairs. They enjoyed the favor of the Brazilian public, and down to the twenties and thirties of the present century they had no cause to complain of discrimination or suppression.

The masses of the colored people, the proletarians, were sufficiently backward culturally and socially so that they did not suffer particularly from their status as members of the lowest class. The majority could not read and write. Lacking technical training, they were unable to rise to higher posts, and remained ordinary unskilled workers. The dark-skinned proletarians accepted the apparent inevitability of their situation, and felt no urge to rise up in rebellion against the traditional order of things. They were content, as simple people are, with the gratification of their physical needs. The *café-au-lait* colored middle classes and the light-skinned upper classes were likewise content because the social structure of Brazil seemed firmly, unshakably established.

Nevertheless, even then there existed a kind of silken curtain between people of different color, a barrier that ran through all ranks of society, scarcely visible, but for that very reason all the more inviolable. It existed above all in São Paulo and the other southern states where white immigrants formed the majority and relatively few colored persons lived. It existed because even in Brazil there were whites, mostly new citizens from Europe, who in principle considered the colored people stupid, unstable, unclean, and lecherous. Europeans and North Americans carried the germ of racial prejudice into Brazil. For a while it seemed as if that germ would infect the whole of Brazil as it has other countries. We must honor the Brazilians for fighting the dangerous plague of racism in the same way that they fought malaria, yellow fever, and other tropical diseases.

The new business and financial oligarchy that began to develop during Brazil's first period of economic prosperity—the coffee boom —was particularly susceptible to the germ. The colored people provided the mass of the workers; and just as European mercantilism in the eighteenth and nineteenth centuries upheld the theory that workers must be paid low wages in order not to spoil them, Brazilian mercantilism in our century maintained that higher wages and the opportunity to rise socially would only make colored workers lazy and undermine their morale.

This growing prejudice was not confined to the oligarchy. It was, if possible, even stronger among the white *petit-bourgeois* class, and struck deep roots among the naturalized immigrants who still thought in colonial terms. There were petit-bourgeois housewives who refused to have Negro household help and maintained that the colored people as a whole were dishonest, work-shy, slatternly, and undisciplined. There were white workers who went on strike if a colored worker was hired or a colored foreman put over them. There were white storekeepers who refused to employ colored salesgirls on the ground that they must consider the feelings of their customers. Thus in the southern states (aside from Rio Grande do Sul) initial tolerance gradually yielded to a stubborn drive on the part of the whites to assert and maintain social exclusiveness.

Curiously enough, this development began about the same time that samba music, created by the colored people, started its conquest of the world, and just when Negro players were at last winning international contests for Brazilian soccer teams. Their musical and athletic prowess gave the colored proletarians the self-confidence they needed to oppose the growth of intolerance. The situation in Brazilian soccer was initially similar to that in the Brazilian labor market. The Negroes had to play an especially clean and fair game and avoid any rough blocking of a white, or there was sure to be a brawl. At work the colored people were under similar handicaps. Any show of superiority toward a white fellow worker might cost them dearly. They had to pretend to be especially submissive, jovial, and humorous and to carefully hide their real feelings. Around 1930 Negro workers in Brazil behaved not very differently from Negro workers in the North American Southern states.

But the intellectual leaders of the Brazilian colored people launched a counter campaign. In 1930 the *Frenta Negra Brasileira* was founded. At a succession of congresses thereafter it aired the problem of racial prejudice in Brazil. One of the principal demands of this Negro organization was legal sanctions upon all types of racial discrimination. The demonstrations of the FNB had the effect of an icy shower on the Brazilian upper classes, which had hitherto congratulated themselves on practicing the most tolerant racial attitudes in the world.

The revelations of the FNB made Brazilian politicians aware that a burning social problem had imperceptibly arisen. The need for a solution grew more and more acute. In spite of the equal rights guaranteed by the constitution, no one could force businessmen, industrialists, and bank directors to employ colored persons. Even unskilled whites could find jobs more easily than skilled Negroes. The consequence was that in São Paulo 80 per cent of the Negroes and mulattoes had no hope of rising occupationally. The overwhelming majority of the Brazilian colored people had to earn a scanty living as bootblacks, part-time workers, porters, servants, and petty clerks.

Meanwhile, a social problem had also developed. Luxury hotels refused to take colored guests, allegedly out of consideration for their foreign patrons. In many shops, Negroes were refused service. In the Negro newspaper *O Novo Horizonte*, a Negro described a typical experience in a barbershop: "They paid no attention to me, although some of the barbers were standing idle. All sorts of excuses were given—that it was noon, that other customers had appointments, and so on. I realized that I was not being given service because I was a Negro." Another Negro wrote in the same newspaper: "Go to a big hotel in São Paulo some time and ask for a room! You'll be turned down quicker than a wink. Demand the rights you have on paper. We won't be responsible for the consequences."

Even the intellectuals in São Paulo had long since ceased to be as pro-Negro as intellectuals in the rest of Brazil. A questionnaire circulated among the students of the University of São Paulo showed that 40 per cent would reject a colored person as a friend and 90 per cent a Negro woman as a wife. More than one hundred students stated that they would welcome expulsion of the colored from Brazil. Colored sociologists subsequently determined, in the course of thorough investigations, why these attitudes were particularly strong in São Paulo.

"The foreigners who came here as poor devils succeeded in enriching themselves," a Negro journalist wrote. "Since then, they permit no one—except their relatives and fellow-countrymen—to use the opportunities that have arisen as a result of the economic development of São Paulo."

This sounds like mere grudge, but the impartial observer also cannot avoid the impression that the tense racial situation arose primarily as a result of the ever-increasing influx of immigrants from overseas.

"SURE, IF I WERE YOUR COLOR . . ."

In 1951 a scandal erupted that led the Brazilian Government to act with firmness and dispatch. A well-known North American Negro dancer was ejected from a São Paulo hotel for no other reason than that she was a Negro. Thus the mistreatment of Negroes was now being extended to colored foreigners. Liberal politicians and intellectuals realized that the situation had become inadmissible.

The Brazilian public reacted rapidly and healthily to this scandal— with vigorous press campaigns against the management of the hotel, with reassessment of the bans on racial discrimination, and with sociological studies that denounced the *status quo*. The Vargas administration was charged with having on the one hand made the "Day of the Race" a national holiday, and on the other hand having kept Negroes and mulattoes from higher posts in the navy, air force, government, and diplomatic service. Vargas pleaded guilty to the charges of his critics, and was prepared to proclaim a new Lei Áurea.

In São Paulo, too, there were prominent personages who wanted to abolish racial inequalities. A Paulista named Plinio Barreto prepared a study on various legal provisions to combat race prejudice. On the basis of this study, Afonso Arinos, a congressman from Minas Gerais, drafted a bill which the congress passed by a great majority. The new law made it a serious offense to decline to serve colored customers, to turn away colored persons from hotels, to discriminate against colored persons in institutions of learning, places of amusement, public offices, or military posts, or refuse to hire anyone on grounds of color. The passing of the bill was celebrated throughout Brazil; it was repeatedly mentioned in the same breath with the "Golden Law," which had abolished slavery in the nineteenth century.

The Afonso Arinos bill today forms the legal basis for Brazilian racial tolerance. The only question is whether a law suffices to make a fundamental change in the mentality of a certain white-skinned

minority that has occupied key economic and social positions in the
life of the country. The matter was acutely put in Plinio Barreto's
preliminary study: "As long as the white holds economic hegemony,
which he has inherited from the former slaveholders, and as long as the
Negroes, for lack of resources, belong to the poorer classes, the
prejudices will linger on. Under such conditions there is no law that
can abolish them. At no time have laws been able to shake deeply
rooted feelings or change the attitudes of a people."

Barreto repeatedly reminded the legislators that all measures against
racial discrimination would fall short of their purpose unless the Lei
Áurea was followed by a "Golden Social Law." The Negro organization takes the same view. "Poor Negroes," a publication of the FNB
states, "remain economically and morally cast back upon themselves,
without the means that could help them rise from their extremely
low standard of living. The authorities do not permit the Negro to
obtain the education he needs to take advantage of the law."

Its benefits, therefore, accrue only to a colored minority. The culturally and economically advanced Negroes and mulattoes henceforth
could walk into any luxury hotel, could apply for admission to exclusive
clubs, and could even keep white chauffeurs, servants, and household
help. But the colored proletarians in practice won only one point:
henceforth, if they were not served, not admitted, or not employed,
those concerned carefully avoided referring to their color.

The Negro organization holds that progress will be made only when
the government grants the colored proletarians tangible economic and
social support, and above all when all enterprises in the country are
compelled to hire a definite quota of capable Negroes, corresponding
to the racial proportion of the population. This is the only way the
Negro people as a whole can rise occupationally. In spite of the
apparent harmony of the races in Brazil, many business organizations
are still all white.

In Rio de Janeiro I met a highly intelligent truck driver who
seemed to possess remarkable technical skills. When I asked him
whether he did not want to become a skilled mechanic or engineer,
he merely laid his dark arm alongside my light one and said: "Sure,
if I were your color." Brazilian Negroes and mulattoes, almost all of
whom seem to have innate technical ability, might make a tremendous
contribution to the industrialization of the country. But so far Brazilian
industry has come nowhere near drawing upon their talents.

The Afonso Arinos law has granted Brazilian colored people more rights, more freedoms, and greater protection against discrimination than the majority of the colored who live under white rule in the rest of the Western Hemisphere. Nevertheless, the silken curtain still exists. The law is not criticized publicly, but it is cleverly evaded. The whites carry on whispering campaigns to the effect that such legislation only tempts the colored people into improper behavior. Vargas and Afonso Arinos ignored social differences, they say, and misled Negroes into practicing a "false equality." Anyhow, people told me confidentially in São Paulo, there are a number of places where even Negroes who can pay the high prices are not welcome. The police, these gentry hinted, instead of protecting black proletarians would do better to see that the unsavory elements among the colored people were put behind bars.

NOSTALGIA FOR IDEALISTIC COMMUNISM

It is scarcely surprising, therefore, that the Brazilian communists make capital of the inadequacies of the law. Their propaganda plays on the theme of racial discrimination, the severity of which they greatly exaggerate. Hitherto, however, the Communists have not found many followers among the colored population. The Communist Party of Brazil was, before it was banned, a party of intellectuals. It drew primarily on the prestige of its chairman, the political veteran Luis Carlos Prestes. During his imprisonment under the Vargas regime, Prestes won the sympathy of a great many noncommunist Brazilians. Nowadays, however, his personal prestige has been considerably diminished by the ideological power struggle between Moscow and Peking.

The danger of a communist takeover in Brazil was much discussed abroad before 1964. The agrarian reform movement of the Camponesas was also denounced as a red specter. Foreigners confounded the left wing of the Labor Party under Leonel Brizola with the Communists. In reality, however, the Communists long ago ceased to be a strong party. Before Vargas drove them underground, they counted some two hundred thousand members and wielded considerable influence. Today, illegal Brazilian communism is split into two camps which squabble like cats and dogs.

Before the latest ban, the pro-Russian group under Prestes behaved moderately, repeatedly expressed its faith in peaceful coexistence, and tried to influence Brazilian politics by democratic, parliamentary tactics. Behind Prestes, however, there were only some forty thousand card-carrying members, chiefly professors, teachers, students, and members of the lower-middle class. The Communist leaders João Grabois, Mauricio Amazonas, and Pedro Pomar split with Prestes over the differences between Moscow and Peking. They organized a rebel group which espoused Mao's thesis: that only a violent revolutionary upheaval can free the masses. The Grabois-Amazonas group is likewise illegal; the number of its members therefore cannot be determined. The ideological struggle between the Prestes wing and the Grabois wing had, however, under the Goulart regime already assumed such proportions that the communist movement in Brazil was virtually paralyzed.

The great majority of the colored proletarians have not the slightest understanding of such ideological disputes. On the other hand, Brazilian communism has drawn the leading intellectuals into its orbit to a surprising extent. Jorge Amado, whose novels have been translated into many languages; Florestan Fernandes, the prominent sociologist, Indianologist, and UNESCO associate; Oscar Niemeyer, the creator of Brasilia—all are regarded as communists. But they are just as much and just as little communists as Pablo Picasso. Their pro-communist views spring from that strong sense of social justice that made so many European intellectuals parlor pinks in the 1930s. Florestan Fernandes, who has intensively studied Brazilian race prejudice, once explained his position: "Only a total upheaval of the present Brazilian social structure, along the lines of social democracy, can assure all people human rights and so bring about the disappearance of color prejudice and the simultaneous transformation of the mentality of the whites."

Niemeyer probably thinks along the same lines. When the Communist Party was banned and could not engage in political activity, Niemeyer went out on the streets and personally offered passers-by the Communist newspaper *Tribuna Popular*. Like Fernandes, he has on many occasions sharply denounced the prevailing social order in Brazil, and assured Luis Carlos Prestes—who, to be sure, is one of the most honest Communist leaders in the world—of his sympathy.

In the United States during the McCarthy witch hunt, such statements went down the wrong way. When the United Nations building in New York was dedicated—Niemeyer had been one of its designers

—that "Communist" was not allowed to take part in the ceremony. This needless insult to the greatest—or at least most-discussed—architect in the world offended all of Brazil.

The rich men of the West pay astronomical sums to acquire paintings by Picasso. No democratic Western country would refuse the Spanish painter a visa because of his politics. The tolerance displayed toward the political extravagances of a great European artist should likewise be granted a great South American artist. The pro-communism of Brazilian intellectuals should not be exaggerated beyond its real significance.

Latin America has to satisfy its nostalgia for nationalism and socialism; Latin American intellectuals also have to satisfy a certain nostalgia for idealistic communism. That is a stage of development through which the majority of European and North American artists have passed without harm. The probable course of their intellectual evolution is likely to be the same. In Brazil, especially, brasilidade will insure that the leading minds of the country will preserve their intellectual independence, rather than fall prey to a foreign ideology.

RAISING THE ROOFTREE OF THE FUTURE

According to the calculations of demographers, Brazil will have more than 150,000,000 inhabitants in the year 2000. According to the hopeful prognoses of Brazilian political economists, Brazil in the year 2000 will be among the leading industrial powers in the world. The Brazilians themselves are convinced that by that year their country, the fourth largest on the globe, will have also risen to the position of a fourth great power. But the Brazilians do not merely give themselves to optimistic dreams. They have already begun building the world of the day after tomorrow, and have even celebrated the raising of the first rooftree.

The rapid evolution of Brazilian architecture, which has reached its temporary climax in the building of the new federal capital, is more than just a technological and artistic phenomenon. It is a portent for the future development of the country and people and Brazil, and of Brazil's status in the world. Nowhere else in Latin America has any nation taken such ambitious steps toward the future. Brazil's architects, her achievements in building, her magnificent cities have given her a self-confidence that has manifested itself, in the train of the building boom, in many other realms.

The Brazilian enthusiasm for building sometimes causes mirth in Europe and North America. But those who call the Brazilians mad for throwing away money on marvelous buildings, while their economy is tottering, miss a vital point in the equation. Brazil is bursting with optimism, and this spirit enables the people to deal much more easily with the troublesome problems of the present day than their neighbors. The Brazilians believe in the future, look toward the future, and live in the future.

A COUNTRY OF ARCHITECTS

Since the suicide of Getulio Vargas, Brazil has been rife with political legends. The story of Brazilian architecture may someday become another such. That legend will have to begin with Visconde Gomes Freire de Andrada e Bobadela, a statesman and builder of cities in Portuguese colonial days. The viscount shaped colonial Rio and built aqueducts in the old Roman style to bring spring water from Morro Santa Teresa to the residential districts. The legend must then continue with a doctor named Osvaldo Cruz, who was determined to overcome yellow fever and therefore persuaded Mayor Pereira Passo to tear down part of colonial Rio and build a new, hygienic city in its place. The campaign of sanitation and modernization, which Dr. Cruz also carried on in other Brazilian ports, was continued uninterruptedly for fifty years and is still not complete. Thus it was the struggle against epidemics that led to Brazil's modernization. Suddenly Brazilians became interested in architecture and the profession of architect.

After the turn of the century the handsome colonial baroque style gave way to the ugly urban monstrosities that also afflicted European cities. The style continued to prevail until 1930, before a general reaction set in. A young architect born in Toulon, the son of Brazilian parents, was the first to condemn it publicly. Brazil's guild of architects had distinguished themselves by stupidity and lack of realism, he declared. They had imitated European structures without considering the special climatic conditions in Brazil. This young man, Lucio Costa, became head of the State Academy of Art. His first act was to throw all existing textbooks and curricula into the wastebasket. He himself trained a band of young architects, and in 1936 brought Le Corbusier to Rio de Janeiro to show Brazilians what architecture of the twentieth century must be.

Together with Costa, Le Corbusier designed a new Ministry of Education. Among his associates was one young man whose great-grandfather and grandfather had already served as city architects of Rio de Janeiro. This was Oscar Niemeyer, a recent graduate from Costa's academy. Le Corbusier was struck by the young man's imaginativeness and sensitivity to the special architectural conditions of Brazil. Niemeyer dreamed up buildings as a poet does poems.

The now world-famous honeycomb-like building which looks like a gigantic matchbox bears the unmistakable signature of Le Corbusier. But the parts of the building designed by Niemeyer were so interesting and unusual that they caught the attention of Juscelino Kubitschek, then Mayor of Belo Horizonte. We have already spoken of the close relationship between Kubitschek and Niemeyer, which thus began early, when Niemeyer was still an assistant to Le Corbusier.

Anywhere else in the world of the 1930s, Le Corbusier's building would have seemed a wildly audacious undertaking which would have caused a good deal of public and private grumbling. But no one in Rio complained when the building was dedicated; on the contrary, the applause was thunderous. As a result of this public acceptance, Lucio Costa and his young disciples began building in the new, free style all over the country. Costa erected a series of modern apartment houses. Rino Levi, Lucio Meire, Carmen Portinho, and the Roberto brothers found marvelously simple solutions for the most complicated architectural problems and were soon being imitated in other countries. Niemeyer built the satellite city of Belo Horizonte and the Brazilian pavilion at the New York World's Fair. He created a suburb of Havana, collaborated on the UN headquarters, and won swift recognition as the star of the Costa group.

A novel reinforced-concrete method of building was developed, and the architects began replacing the windows of buildings with cooling *brise-soleils*. Brazil proved that a modern skyscraper city could exhibit not only great expanses of glass, but curved lines, air and freshness, wit and charm. Such was the national enthusiasm for building that in a number of cities the population co-ordinated matters by electing architects as mayors.

One danger lurked behind this building fever. Brazil began to appear a nation of real estate speculators. Lots that might serve for skyscrapers rose in price to three, four, and even five million dollars. Contrary to the intentions of the architects, who stood for the principle of artistic harmony, at the height of the building boom almost every available tract of land in the business and amusement districts of cities had a skyscraper planted on it. A notorious example is the wall of skyscrapers in Copacabana. Its curvilinear shape is esthetically intriguing. But behind the closed wall there is scarcely air enough to breathe. The builders did not consider the hordes of people who would have to live behind the brilliant but airless façade.

It is not surprising, therefore, that Niemeyer, Costa, and their colleagues began insisting more and more emphatically that the country's architecture could reach its apotheosis only if the architects themselves were allowed to call the tune, without regard for profit and speculative gains. Niemeyer was given that kind of freedom when he built his Pampulha, on assignment from Kubitschek. Lucio Costa and Niemeyer enjoyed a freedom almost inconceivable to the ordinary city planner and architect when they were commissioned to build the new federal capital.

DREAMS AND SPECULATIONS

The plan to create a metropolis in the interior of the country is not new. It was born the year Brazil won her independence. Even then, wise Brazilians foresaw the peril of massing tremendous hordes of human beings in the ports and along the thin Brazilian coastal strip. Moreover, the empire and later the young republic feared the possibility of war, and envisaged the danger of their capital's being bombarded by enemy fleets. Finally—and this was the decisive factor— as long as one hundred forty years ago Brazilians realized that the vast, unpopulated interior with all its natural wealth could be opened up only if the seat of government were transferred to one of the states of the interior.

The two Brazilian emperors preferred the easy, luxurious life of Rio de Janeiro and Petrópolis to moving into the wilderness. But after the emancipation of the slaves and the fall of Pedro II, when the masses of the colored people poured into the coastal cities, where their favelas began covering every available patch of ground, the old project of an interior capital was revived. The Brazilian Constitution of 1891 expressly stated the intention of creating a federal district, after the example of the United States, in the interior, and there erecting a Brazilian Washington. Some visionaries even called for the new capital to be established exactly in the geographical center of Brazil—in a district at the intersection of the states of Mato Grosso, Amazonas, and Pará, which was then completely unexplored.

The realists, who had their eye on the state of Goiás, won out. But even before the site for the future federal capital was chosen, Brazilians vehemently argued over its name. Was it to be called Santa Cruz or Brasilia? But nothing happened beyond talk until Getulio Vargas, two years after taking office, seriously launched the project. Vargas, as a Riograndian, had no emotional commitment to either Rio de Janeiro or São Paulo. He sent geologists, physicists, meteorologists, and engineers to Goiás by land and air. Twenty years of research went into choosing those five thousand square kilometers on the Goiás plateau where today stand some of the most daring buildings in the world.

Vargas did not live to see the building begin. But his successor, Kubitschek, was an even greater enthusiast for modern architecture and champion of a new capital. Since, however, Kubitschek had already had some experience with real estate speculators, he wanted to avoid the speculative excesses that were already an all too familiar phenomenon in Brazilian cities. He had approximately a thousand square kilometers of the federal district, what was to be the heart of the future capital, bought up by a state corporation. This corporation, Novacap, sold parcels on condition that the buyers abide strictly by Niemeyer's and Costa's architectural plans. Since his countrymen's speculative fever could not be entirely suppressed, Kubitschek cleverly used it to finance the new capital.

Countless rich Brazilians were eager to obtain land in the federal district around the new capital. They had to buy the land from Novacap, which used the funds to construct some of the government buildings. Shrewd speculators could still make fortunes by reselling the land they purchased from Novacap. For within a few years real estate prices in the federal district rose by 100,000, and in some cases by more than 1,000,000, per cent!

BRASILIA—SYMBOL AND OMEN

The creation of the city began when Lucio Costa drew a cross on a sheet of paper. From this cross he sketched a city whose outlines looked like an airplane. The fuselage of the plane was to contain, from front to back, the government buildings, radio stations, commercial and amusement quarters, banks, warehouses, and railroad station. In the two wings the shopping centers and schools were to be placed. Around them Costa grouped the residential areas and parks. Great freeways were to connect each district with the others. Supersized individual buildings were to be surrounded by generous open space, so that nowhere would be felt any sense of confinement, such as is characteristic of Rio de Janeiro and São Paulo.

Niemeyer transformed these grand plans into reality. He broke with all architectural traditions, put his buildings on stilts, erected a cathedral that irreverent Brazilians liken to a gigantic corset, built the presidential palace of glass with a chapel that looks like a snail's shell, and housed the Senate and the House of Representatives in shell-shaped structures, one of which arches upward, while the other seems to be standing on its head. These much-described and much-filmed buildings are so attuned to the Brazilian landscape and the Brazilian climate that they do not look like the eccentric sports of an architect's imagination, but like creations of nature, sprung from the very soil of the tropics.

Niemeyer's great achievement has been the merging of architecture and nature. "Until the building of Brasilia," he once declared, "architecture was to my mind something that must be regarded as and practiced as a sport. Now I live for Brasilia. Here my work has entered an entirely new phase; it has become more geometric, simpler, more monumental." The structures in concrete that look like sails, garlands, bowls, and paper cutouts have already come to be regarded by Brazilians as symbols of their country and their future.

The building of Brasilia went forward very rapidly. Too rapidly. Kubitschek realized that he had only five years in which to create his metropolis. If he did not get the new capital on its feet within that time, his successor might slow the tempo to such an extent that the city would never be completed. Attached though the Brazilians are to their dream of a capital in the interior, government officials, poli-

future as Kubitschek believed in the miraculous powers that would emanate from his new capital. And just as Kubitschek frantically pushed the pace of construction, in order not to lose a day, the Brazilians are frantically trying to jump straight from the present into the future, hoping in so doing to overleap the lush tropical thickets of past problems.

It has always been Brazilian custom to put off to tomorrow the solution of the problems facing the nation. The result has been an inordinate, intolerable increase of economic, social, and political tensions—which are today greater in Brazil than in a number of other Latin American countries. But of them all, Brazil, because of her natural resources and her human population, has the best prospects for rising into the ranks of the great powers. The Brazilians dream of that happy day. But in order to reach it, they must start to master their many difficulties with the same boldness, resolution, and passion that they have applied to the building of their capital.

For the jungle may still overwhelm the future. The pestilential air of the favelas, the stench of social injustices, economic egotism, and financial disasters still hang over the country as the red dust of Goiás hangs over the buildings of Brasilia. Brazil has taken only her first steps into the future. The land of modern architecture now faces the task of going beyond mere construction to rebuild the tumbledown, unsanitary structure of economic and social life—to fulfill the promise that for a hundred and forty years has been proclaimed on the Brazilian national insignia: "Order and Progress."

A CONTINENT AT THE CROSSROADS

What applies to Brazil applies fundamentally to the entire continent of Latin America. These fast developing lands are in greater need of a radical economic and social reordering than any other region on earth. If North America and the other Western countries protest that it is not for them to play the part of wet nurse or governess, they are right. Development aid can help a region out of its economic plight. Attempts at re-education can eliminate political abuses. But experience teaches that neither aid nor re-education leads to a real new order. The Latin American peoples must forge that for themselves.

They can do so, however, only if they are given a real chance. And

ticians, and businessmen are reluctant to leave the cosmopo
of Rio. It is astounding that Costa and Niemeyer, in the five
Kubitschek's administration, completed at least the entire go
quarter around the Square of the Three Powers.

Once that quarter was dedicated, the president, cabi
congress had to move into the new capital willy-nilly. Ev
Quadros, who disliked the whole Brasilia idea, was obliged to
presidential palace in Rio for the glass palace in Brasilia. Qu
said to have felt miserably unhappy there. His successors,
and Castelo Branco, introduced the custom of spending at 1
weekends in Rio, to recover from the psychological strain of
Brasilia.

A critic of contemporary Brazil, the journalist Gertrud
writes: "There are serious and certainly not unpatriotic peopl
who say that Brasilia is thirty years behind the times; that it is-
kibbutz, orthodox socialism, machines for living and other pro
cerebral idealism of the early twentieth century—an abstra
lectuals' dream of world reform, an attempt to translate d
board ideas of the perfect city into reality, without considering
itself, or asking people. . . . Most people would prefer, if they
choice, the architectural ugliness, the noise, the dirt, the overcr
and the chaos of Rio to the planned order of Brasilia."

But Brasilia exists; it is growing, consolidating itself, mai
itself against criticism, mockery, and political crises; and gradu
learning to hold its own against the red dust of the Goiás plate
the wind sends swirling through the streets. An artificial city, a
in stone, a futuristic creation—whatever epithets may be app
Brasilia, the new capital is gradually being transformed from a
ment to Niemeyer's and Costa's talent into a living, dynamic
with enormous potentialities for growth. It may be that Brasi
belong among those New World artificial cities that—as Claud
Strauss has put it—"in spite of their eternal youthfulness will
achieve full health." But—Brasilia lives.

For many years to come Brasilia will continue to be one va
struction site. It will take a long time before the dusty red e
Goiás is finally covered over by buildings, cement roofs, and
lawns. But in a figurative sense all of Brazil is today a vast b
site. The Brazilians are building their future recklessly, eccent
and too fast, as Niemeyer has built Brasilia. They believe i

the Western world today, faced with the increasing radicalization of Latin America, must seriously ask whether the Latin Americans have been given such a chance. The West must ask itself where it has failed, where the deeper roots of gringo hatred and resurgent nationalism are to be found, and why Fidel Castro, the revolutionary on a little island in the Caribbean, has suddenly become the idol of whole classes throughout Ibero-America. The Western world cannot act the part of nursemaid at the crib of Latin American democracy and social reform, but it must undertake to liquidate economic colonialism along with political colonialism. There is no other way to allow Latin America to develop freely and independently.

THE HIPPOPOTAMUS AND SMALLER BEASTS

Gil Blas Tejeira, a Panamanian writer and diplomat, has written a bitter satire in which the United States is represented as a hippopotamus. This hippopotamus sits down amiably in a room with many smaller animals. The room is Latin America, the smaller animals the Latin American nations. Unfortunately, the hippopotamus has a weak bladder; it must trudge out of the room every few minutes to relieve itself. Every time it does so, it tramples on the feet of its small neighbors. And because it is so large and ponderous, it inflicts considerable damage. But the hippopotamus is well bred; it always apologizes politely with a "So sorry."

What Tejeira is suggesting can be summed up in a few words. North American (and European) business circles operating in Latin America have not done much for establishment of good "interpersonal" relations. Their foremost concern is to preserve their monopolistic positions. They do not even notice when they step on the toes of sensitive Latin Americans. The result is that the Latin American masses frequently feel like pariahs in their own countries. Dollar diplomacy has too long been linked with the policy of the big stick. Dictators and strong men have too often been installed to protect foreign economic interests. North American and European business has shown no understanding for the needs of the common people of Latin America. And Latin Americans have reacted accordingly.

In the era of Franklin D. Roosevelt, in the brief administration of John F. Kennedy, much good will toward Latin America was certainly displayed by the United States. There were many sincere plans and beginnings which might have improved the Latin American climate. But such efforts were always countered by the group egotism of the companies and financiers active in Latin America. Administrators sent down from Washington also frequently undermined the good-will policy in favor of a "more realistic" and therefore harder line. Thomas Mann, President Johnson's present Latin American specialist, is said to be a member of the "hard" school.

Roosevelt's policy of reconciliation with Mexico showed how much could be accomplished by good will. The policy of John Foster Dulles toward Cuba is an example of the hard line. The Western world is now facing a fateful choice—whether to bend every effort, even at the sacrifice of some selfish interests, to promote the creation of a new deal in Latin America, or to continue to regard the South American continent as a great field for profits, with no thought for the masses of the people from whom that profit is wrung.

BETWEEN DICTATORSHIP AND ANARCHY

If the first course is chosen, the Latin American peoples must be allowed to make a clean sweep of their antiquated economic and social systems. They must depose their feudalistic oligarchies, conquer the inhuman mass misery, and stamp out the latent tendency toward dictatorship. This means putting through vital agrarian and social reforms. Basic to the welfare of these countries is a healthy middle class and an honest, because adequately paid, civil service.

At present, in most Latin American countries, even middle and higher government officials have to practice an additional profession in order to support their families. Consequently, they spend as little time as possible in their offices and are anything but immune to corruption. This unfortunate situation is due to the chronic financial straits of the governments. And those financial straits are directly connected with the high and mighty ways of the oligarchy, its conspicuous consumption, its tax evasion, and its practice of sending its money abroad for safety. The Latin American countries are subject to a continual economic and financial bloodletting.

Wherever a handful of native families and foreign concerns own nearly all the plantations, mineral resources, industries, banks, and commercial companies, dire explosions are inevitable in this age of mass emancipation. Wherever a tiny social class squanders the greater part of a country's wealth in self-indulgence, while the majority of the population huddles in adobe huts or slums, the seed of radicalism inevitably sprouts. And if the Western world continues to accept as unalterable this alarming disparity between rich and poor, if it continues to stand more on the side of the native and foreign oligarchy than on the side of the common people, Latin American radicalism will inevitably assume an anti-Western tendency.

In this case, Red China may emerge as the victor in the Cold War of ideologies in Latin America. Mao's propaganda has long been beamed toward the landless and propertyless Ibero-Americans. Chinese agents seem to have had their fingers in most of the recent disturbances on the continent. The struggle for power between Moscow and Peking is being waged with particular ferocity in Latin America. Chinese agrarian-reform practices seem to make a stronger impression there than Soviet party doctrines. And since Red China has also donned the mask of champion of the rights of the colored world, she is winning ever-growing numbers of followers among the colored proletarians of Ibero-America.

Probably Fidel Castro would long ago have swung to the side of Peking had he not been tied to Moscow by his dependence on Russian economic aid. Ideologically, the Cuban revolutionary government has been moving toward the Chinese. Practically, however, since Guevara's departure Castro has joined the camp of the opponents of Peking. Consequently, the pro-Chinese Communists of Latin America are beginning to denounce him as a "traitor." But that does not alter the fact that ideas imported from Peking have significantly influenced Cuban politicians and economists. Moreover, other agrarian and social reformers, who are neither party-line Communists nor Marxists, tend to veer toward the Peking line whenever they see no other way to carry out their programs.

Only a few Latin American countries stand on relatively firm ground, unmenaced by dictatorship and anarchy. But they, too, have their troubles. Mexico must push on strongly with her program of education and emancipation in order to forestall radicalization of the masses. Little Costa Rica is looking toward her neighbors to the north, for her model democracy is highly vulnerable as long as the other Central American states are militant dictatorships. Uruguay, since the middle-class Blancos have come to power, has been in the throes of an economic and financial crisis. Argentina has still not managed to deal with the heritage of Peronism.

In Venezuela a sound middle course has been found between the traditional system of military juntas and the anarchistic tendencies of radical leftist revolutionaries, but this pro-Western democracy remains to be consolidated. It can easily be blighted by imprudent behavior on the part of the West, as American intervention in the Dominican Republic showed. Washington's ill-will toward Juan Bosch was viewed with indignation in Caracas. Venezuela, today the most faithful friend of the United States in South America, reacts favorably toward tolerance and progressiveness, but is highly allergic to the "big stick" policy.

Chile today is the great hope of the liberal democratic West. But the West must realize that the Chilean Government can also deal out blows toward the right. It will force the large landowners to submit to agrarian reform, and probably wrest the copper monopoly from the American companies. On the other hand, it must outtrump the opponents of the Popular Front by a superior social-welfare program. Chile is a test case of whether it is possible to avoid bloody revolutions by instituting timely and courageous reforms.

Thanks to her human vitality, Ibero-America could become a continent of the future, making vital new contributions to the rest of the world. But it rests with the Western world as well as with the Latin Americans themselves what the future development of this quarter of the globe will be. Profound upheavals are already in the making. Will the coming new deal take place under Western auspices, with Western tolerance and aid? Or will it be carried out by movements like Fidel Castro's, by violence, in a manner abhorrent to the West?

The future fate of our world may depend upon the answer to that question.

Index

Latin America Today

CUBA

HAITI

DOMINICAN REP.

HONDURAS JAMAICA

PUERTO
RICO (U.S.A.)

NICARAGUA

LESSER ANTILLES

COSTA RICA

Panama

TRINIDAD AND TOBAGO

★ Caracas

PANAMA

VENEZUELA

SURINAM

Georgetown

Paramaribo

★ Bogotá

Cayenne

COLOMBIA

BRIT. GUIANA

FRENCH GUIANA

★ Quito

ECUADOR

PERU

BRAZIL

★ Lima

★ La Paz

BOLIVIA

Pacific

Ocean

PARAGUAY

Rio de Janeiro ★

★ Asuncion

CHILE

ARGENTINA

Santiago ★

★ Montevideo

Buenos Aires ★

URUGUAY

Atlantic

Ocean

FALKLAND ISLANDS
(British)